7. Promote you and your work to editors, publishers, and producers. This can result in unexpected opportunities such as a contract to write a book to a publisher's specs or a ghostwriting deal.

8. Serve as your representative to and liaison with the publishing (or film, television, etc.) industry.

9. Receive money and offers on your behalf, then bring them to you.

10. Offer professional advice.

11. Put you in touch with other people who can be helpful.

In contrast, a lazy, overworked, or underskilled agent can seriously harm your career by sending your work to the wrong people, reading and negotiating contracts haphazardly, or, worst of all, letting your work languish, unsubmitted, on his or her own desk.

1996
Guide to
Literary Agents

1996
Guide to Literary Agents

Edited by Kirsten C. Holm

WRITER'S DIGEST BOOKS
Cincinnati, Ohio

Distributed in Canada by McGraw-Hill Ryerson,
300 Water Street, Whitby Ontario L1N 9B6.
Distributed in Australia by Kirby Books, Private Bag No.
19, P.O. Alexandria NSW2015.

Managing Editor, Market Books Department:
Constance J. Achabal;
Supervisory Editor: Mark Garvey;
Production Editor: Richard D. Muskopf.

International Standard Serial Number
ISSN 1078-6945
International Standard Book Number
0-89879-715-2

Cover design: Lamson Design
Cover illustration: Chris O'Leary

Endleaves excerpt from: The Writer's Book of
Checklists, *by Scott Edelstein, published by Writer's Digest Books. Reprinted by permission of the
publisher.*

Attention Booksellers: This is an annual directory of F&W Publications.
Return deadline for this edition is April 30, 1997.

Contents

Literary Agents

Script Agents

From the Editor

Each edition of the *Guide to Literary Agents* starts fresh. At the planning stage, we sit down and study what worked and what didn't in the previous edition. With the site cleared, construction starts on the new book. There is a basic foundation, in which some topics are covered every year for the benefit of those who are purchasing their first *Guide*. The external framework offers new information for those who may be buying their third or fourth copy of the book. The interior design aims for a balance of material for writers at various stages in their career.

As with most good design, a harmonious theme (hopefully) emerges. This year, the idea of agents actively taking part in the process of building a writer has taken shape. There have been more than the usual share of coincidences. I happened to call Don Maass just as he was putting the finishing touches on his book about career planning. I spoke with Jeff Ordway and found he had been mulling over the ways he works with his clients to build their careers and was interested in sharing his thoughts.

With the 1996 edition an effort has been made to more clearly address the variable levels of experience of our readers. Even the endleaves have been commandeered for this purpose. We open with "How An Agent Can Help Your Career" and close with "How To Fire Your Agent Gracefully."

Literary agents

The articles fill you in on what lies between an auspicious beginning and an awkward end. For beginning writers, Mary Cox's interview with Jason Poston, editor at Donald I. Fine/Dutton, explores the basic reasons an editor prefers to work with represented authors. Anita Diamant's diary entries for one day illuminate the myriad responsibilities and decisions she typically encounters.

Moving a little farther down the career path, Ethan Ellenberg's article explaining basic contract negotiation points will help expand the knowledge and allay the fears of writers facing their first publishing agreement. In How Things Work: Foreign Rights, Lisa Erbach Vance explains in detail the technical aspects of what can be an extremely important part of that contract. Donald Maass, an experienced writer himself, discusses "career planning for novelists," or how agents and writers can work together from the very start to plan a long career.

Once a career is underway there are inevitable bumps in the road. One of the most jarring, as Rosalyn Alsobrook discovered, was the need to change agents. Drawing from her experience and those of other authors in a similar position, she offers insights into which indicators signal a need for a change, as well as a brief checklist to aid in making the next move—evaluating and choosing a new agent.

The Insider Reports offer a peek into career building as well. David Smith helped Beth Fowler, who had already had some success with her book, to achieve a much wider distribution—and a contract for another book. Arielle Eckstut worked with Martha Manning to create a book from an article. Alan Kellock helped develop a single idea into a multi-volume series with many different formats. Meredith Bernstein pushed a writer of romance fiction in a new direction, to collaborate with a dynamic subject that resulted in a hotly contested book sale. In these cases, and in many others throughout publishing, an agent helped a writer find what to write about, and often developed ways for the client to continue to write.

Script agents

The script agent articles are structured to follow this path as well. Beginners will find Gary Salt's introductory piece explains the basic information of finding and working with script agents. Kerry Cox, editor of *Hollywood Scriptwriter*, discusses the top ten most frequently asked questions about agents—and provides the answers.

For scriptwriters that may be a little farther along in their careers, Jeff Ordway discusses how he and his clients work together to achieve career goals with a steady upward progress. Janice Pieroni, a former executive with Universal Studios, explains some of the major deal points a newer writer and agent will encounter in contracts for movies and television.

For those writers already on their way, J. Michael Straczynski's article, A Roadmap to a Career, shows the various steps he went through, working up to the creation and realization of his own original television series on the air.

In an Insider Report, Marcie Wright, of the Wright Concept, explains how the hit movie *The Cure* "burst" onto the script market—after a ten year association between Wright and author Robert Kuhn and a solid writing career.

Things new and different

The changes and enhancements instituted last year have proven popular. This year's Insider Reports include reproductions of the book jackets. A new index groups agencies according to their level of openness to working with new clients. An interesting addition this year occurs in the bulleted editorial comments: Agents were asked what employment they held in the publishing world before they opened or joined their agency. The number of recent sales listed for each agency is substantially increased as well. Forty-four new nonfee-charging listings, fourteen new fee-charging, and nineteen new script agents appear in this edition, more opportunities than any previous year's *Guide*.

One big change will occur with the 1997 *Guide to Literary Agents*. Don Prues will be taking over as editor, and I will be moving to editor of *Writer's Market*. I have enjoyed working on the past three editions of this book, and have welcomed the opportunity to speak with so many of you, solving problems, gaining information, and happily, enjoying your successes. It has been a rewarding experience and I thank you for including me in your writing life.

Wishing you the best of luck and a successful year,

Kirsten Campbell Holm

How to Use Your *Guide to Literary Agents*

This book is exclusively for writers ready to work with a professional to find outlets for their work, whether that's a hardcover coffee table book, mass market paperback, half-hour sitcom or blockbuster movie. Your *Guide* is specifically designed to provide you with the information you need to find the most appropriate representative for your work and your career as a writer.

What's in the book

The book is divided into literary agents and script agents. Each section contains feature articles and listings. The temptation may be to go directly to the listings and start sending out your query letters. But if you've spent time writing and polishing your work until it's just right, you owe it to yourself to take the time to find the best agent.

Feature articles, written by agents and other industry professionals, provide perspectives on the author/agent relationship, as well as demystify just exactly what an agent does. The agents, editors and writers we've invited to write are all successful at what they do. Their insights come from years of experience and offer information you'll need to be successful.

Each section opens with a brief introduction, with tips on approaching literary or script agents, and an explanation of the ranking system we use to designate openness to submissions. Next are the listings, full of specific information from the agencies themselves on what they are interested in seeing and how to present it for their best consideration. "Insider Reports" are step-by-step examinations of how an agent made a specific deal happen.

Literary agents

Nonfee-charging literary agents earn income from commissions made on the sale of manuscripts. Their focus is selling books, and they do not edit manuscripts or promote books that have already been published. These agents tend to be more selective, often preferring to work with established writers and experts in specific fields. While most will accept queries from new writers, a few of them are not looking for new clients. Be sure to check the listing carefully to determine an agent's current needs.

Fee-charging literary agents charge writers for various services (e.g., reading, critiquing, editing, evaluation, consultation, marketing, etc.), in addition to a commission on sales. Since they are being compensated for additional services, they are generally more receptive to handling the work of new writers. Some agents charge a reading or handling fee only to cover the additional costs of this openness. Other agents offer services designed to improve your manuscript or script. However, in some cases reading and other fees can be extremely high, and payment rarely ensures that an agent will agree to take you on as a client.

Your best bet is to develop your novel, nonfiction book or script to the point at which it is saleable enough to attract an agent who makes all or most of her income through commissions. If you do approach a fee-charging agent, be sure to understand completely what the fee will cover. If you choose to pay for a critique or edit, request references and sample critiques. As with any financial transaction, make sure you know what you'll be getting before any money changes hands.

Script agents

Script agents are grouped in one section; those that charge fees are clearly indicated with an open box (□) symbol. Most agents listed are signatories to the Writers Guild of America's Artists' Manager Basic Agreement (copies of which are available from the WGA for $4). The WGA prohibits its signatories from charging reading fees to WGA members, but they are allowed to do so for nonmembers. Most signatories do not charge reading fees as an across-the-board policy. They are also allowed to charge for various other services, such as critiquing, editing or marketing a script.

Many agents who handle books also deal to some degree in scripts, and vice versa. Those agents handling at least 10-15% in another area, and in the case of fee-charging agents either report a sale or are a signatory of the WGA, have a cross-reference in the secondary section in addition to their full listing in their primary area of representation. Those agents handling less than 10 to 15 percent in the secondary area are listed in the Additional Agents at the end of each section.

Getting the most from the book

Once you've decided what type of agent to pursue, you can further narrow your search for the right agent in one of two ways: reading through the listings or using the Subject Index at the back of the book.

Reading through the listings gives a more comprehensive idea of who is out there and what they are looking for. It can give you an idea of relative practices from one agency to another. And if you're writing on a narrower area, that's the way to find your agent.

Another way to work is through the Subject Index. The index is divided into separate sections for nonfee-charging and fee-charging literary agents and script agents. Literary agents are further divided by fiction and nonfiction subject categories, i.e., horror fiction or military nonfiction. Subjects for scripts, such as biography or romantic comedy, are listed alphabetically.

Several special indexes in the back of the book will expedite your search. A Geographic Index is for writers who would prefer dealing with an agent located in their own vicinity. The Format Index for Script Agents will help in determining agencies interested in handling scripts for particular types of TV programs or movies. An Agents Index helps you locate individual agents who may be employed by large agencies. A new index, Client Acceptance Policies, lists agencies according to their policies of working with new writers or only with previously published writers.

Target submissions to make your queries count

With a list of the agents who handle the kind of work you create, read the listings to find the agencies that will be most interested in representing your work.

Check the number code after each listing to determine how receptive the agency is to submissions. Other areas to check are the types of work the agency handles; terms, including commission and contract information; and preferred method of submission, found under the "Handles" subhead.

Writing is not "one size fits all" when it comes to representation. Most agents are not likely to consider subjects outside their specific interests or needs, and can resent the time it takes to wade through inappropriate submissions. Consider only those agents whose interests correspond with your type of work. Study the terms to determine whether the commission and contract policies are acceptable to you. Recent sales information is extremely helpful, as it provides important clues to the caliber of publishing contacts an agent has developed. Ask for a list of sales, then check *Books in Print* for the titles. *Literary Market Place* contains thumbnail descriptions of publishers; look up some of the publishers who have bought manuscripts from the prospective agent to get a better idea of who the agent knows.

In evaluating an agent, it can also be helpful to know a little about her background. To that end we asked what employment an agent had before joining or opening their agency. The answers are included in the bulleted editorial comments within a listing.

Different readers, different methods

One reader devised her own successful scheme to find an agent. First, she went through the book carefully, particularly studying the categories of information given: subjects they were interested in; percentage of unpublished writers, sales, etc. She drew up a list of agents who dealt largely in nonfiction, which she was writing. She then made a chart and ranked those agents from a low of 1 to a high of 5. Agents who only took a small percentage of new writers received a 1, those who had been in business for a certain length of time received a 5, an agent that placed her type of nonfiction received a 5, and so on. When she was finished she totaled the points and ranked the agents accordingly. She queried them in that order, and signed with the sixth agent on her list.

Another reader adopted what he calls a "siege mentality" in his quest for representation. He made up two mailing lists for his manuscript, an "A list" of established agencies with "big" reputations, and a "B list" of mainly newer agents whom he felt were hungry for a good manuscript. At any one time he had ten query packages out with prospective agents. An A list rejection generated a query to the next A list name. Twenty-seven consecutive rejections later, he received four requests for his manuscript: one A list and three B list. He went on to sign with what he describes as "the cream of the crop." His book, *Nathan's Run*, published in February 1996 by HarperCollins, has been sold in 13 foreign countries with movie rights going to Warner Brothers.

When you are confident you have targeted the best agent for your work, submit it according to the procedures outlined in the listing. For more specific information on approaching agents, see How to Find (and Keep) The Right Agent in Literary Agents and The Ins and Outs of Working with Script Agents, as well as the introduction for each chapter.

Key to Symbols and Abbreviations

‡ *A listing new to this edition*
* *Agents who charge fees to previously unpublished writers only*
☐ *Script agents who charge reading or other fees*
● *Comment from the editor of* Guide to Literary Agents
ms—manuscript; mss—manuscripts
SASE—self-addressed, stamped envelope
SAE—self-addressed envelope
IRC—International Reply Coupon, for use on reply mail in countries other than your own.
The Glossary contains definitions of words and expressions used throughout the book.
The Table of Acronyms translates acronyms of organizations connected with agenting or writing.

Listing Policy and Complaint Procedure

Listings in Guide to Literary Agents *are compiled from detailed questionnaires, phone interviews and information provided by agents. The industry is volatile and agencies change addresses, needs and policies frequently. We rely on our readers for information on their dealings with agents and changes in policies or fees that differ from what has been reported to the editor. Write to us if you have new information, questions about agents or if you have any problems dealing with the agencies listed or suggestions on how to improve our listings.*

Listings are published free of charge and are not *advertisements. Although the information is as accurate as possible, the listings are* not *endorsed or guaranteed by the editor or publisher of* Guide to Literary Agents. *If you feel you have not been treated fairly by an agent or representative listed in* Guide to Literary Agents *we advise you to take the following steps:*

● *First try to contact the listing. Sometimes one phone call or a letter can quickly clear up the matter.*

● *Document all your correspondence with the listing. When you write to us with a complaint, provide the name of your manuscript, the date of your first contact with the agency and the nature of your subsequent correspondence.*

● *We will write to the agency and ask them to resolve the problem. We will then enter your letter into our files.*

● *The number, frequency and severity of complaints will be considered in our decision whether or not to delete the listing from our upcoming edition.*

Guide to Literary Agents *reserves the right to exclude any listing for any reason.*

Literary Agents

Why Work with an Agent? One Editor's View

by Mary Cox

Jason Poston is busy. As editor at Donald I. Fine Books/Dutton, he's got 12 titles on the production schedule, but his relaxed manner belies the number of projects he's juggling at the moment. During phone conversations, he handles interruptions with grace, wielding the hold button with aplomb. He returns to a conversation without missing a beat, picking up his thought at the precise point he left off, as relaxed and poised as ever. After three years in publishing, Poston has adjusted to the pace. "After a few months in this business you stop saying 'I'm so busy' because you begin to sound like an idiot," says Poston. "You learn to tone it down because everyone else is just as busy as you are."

In the best of all possible editorial worlds, editors could devote several hours a day just to reading submissions from writers. But for Poston and his boss, Don Fine, the legendary New York editor and publisher famed for his gift for developing unknown authors into bestsellers, that would be a luxury. Every hour of the day from nine to six is crammed with the incessant details of shepherding books to print. Like the rest of his friends in publishing, Poston routinely brings work home, spending his nights and weekends reading promising manuscripts. But he's not complaining. "We do this for *love*," he laughs. And though he pronounces the word "love" broadly for effect, it's clear he's only half-kidding. Yet if that best of possible worlds was possible, Poston concedes he would still opt to read only those manuscripts sent to him by literary agents. The non-elasticity of time is the number one consideration, he says, but there are other factors that make agents a valuable part of the equation.

Some publishers employ readers to separate the wheat from the chaff in their slush piles. Increasingly, publishers like Donald I. Fine return unsolicited manuscripts to authors and rely solely on agents' recommendations. It is a practical decision, pure and simple, says Poston, and it is not meant to discourage writers. "Editors are always looking for material. We love it when we see something that is going to work for us." It's just that editors want to make sure the manuscripts they *do* invest time reading will be the type of book they publish.

The problem with unsolicited manuscripts, says Poston, is that most of them are inappropriate. Out of 100 manuscripts, only one or two are likely to be the type of work Donald I. Fine publishes. The day's mail will include children's books, coffee table books, text books, dungeon and dragon time travel stories and genre romance novels—the types of books Donald I. Fine does not publish. Such "rejections" do

Mary Cox *is an editor at Writer's Digest Books.*

not reflect the quality of an author's writing style, says Poston. They demonstrate the complexities of the publishing industry and how difficult it is for even experienced writers to differentiate the needs of various imprints.

Even though Donald I. Fine Books (DIF) spells out preferences for nonfiction (history, biography, cookbook, self-help, current events) and fiction (adventure, ethnic, historical, horror, literary, mystery, suspense) in *Writer's Market*, it's impossible to understand what makes a DIF book a DIF book, unless you take the next step and read some titles—a step few writers are savvy enough to take. Therefore Poston feels neither guilt nor remorse when he returns manuscripts unread. He's confident any writer worth his or her salt who has written a good manuscript will take the time to, among other things, do the necessary research to find a good agent.

Agents work as a team with writers and publishers to make sure the best books are published in the most efficient, timely manner, and that each author's book gets the attention it deserves. It's an agent's job to understand each publisher's needs, says Poston. They know the intricacies of each imprint of each major publisher. Which imprints are looking for mystery novels? Which take only literary fiction? Which publish children's books? Which would be most likely to publish a nonfiction religious title? Good agents are even aware of individual editor's tastes and preferences. The best agents are already on friendly terms with dozens of editors and network daily to find out who's looking for what, who offers the best advances and the best publicity. And they know which publishers treat writers fairly.

"When an agent offers us a manuscript it doesn't take a lot of phone calls back and forth and blah blah blah to make sure it moves forward," says Poston. Editors appreciate agents who get down to business quickly when discussing projects. That's one reason editors often prefer doing business with agents they have worked with before. A sort of shorthand between editor and agent develops over time, so each can cut to the chase in transactions. "I have just the thing for you . . ." spoken by a trusted agent, carries a lot of weight.

Agents keep up with the changes in the industry. When the press reported DIF was acquired by Penguin USA on September 7, 1995, becoming a sister imprint of Dutton, astute agents had the change posted to their Rolodexes by September 8th. The best agents know each publisher's reputation, so they can confidently hook a writer up with a publisher based on that publisher's reputation. If a publisher has a good reputation there are certain expectations. "Agents know a manuscript that comes to us is in good hands," says Poston.

Much more than a letterhead

Poston warns against choosing an agent at random, or just settling for the first agent who seems interested. A good agent is so much more than a middleman (or woman). His purpose is not just to supply a cover letter on agent's letterhead so editors will look twice at your manuscript. Choose the wrong agent in haste, and you might repent later at your leisure. Many writers end up changing agents when a first relationship doesn't work out. "It's not a very happy time," says Poston, "But luckily I don't have to get involved. It's the agent's and author's job to work through the change."

Just as there are differences in the expertise, interests and quality of various publishers, there are differences between agents, says Poston. There are those who are truly interested in their authors and in building each author's career book by book, and there are those who just want to sell a particular title. Good agents work to place an author with a good publisher and develop a relationship.

Surprisingly, though publishers try to cut the best deal they can, they don't balk when agents fight for good advances for their authors. "As publisher of a book, we have an option on the next title. We understand when agents attempt to get their authors a higher advance for the next book. It's part of the business. We like to work with agents who care the most about their writers because we are hoping to establish a long-term relationship with an author who is going to produce many books for us in the long run. When an agent has faith in an author, it gives us confidence the writer will be around for a long time, that the writer has serious career plans."

Another reason agents make editors' jobs easier is because the agent can explain the argot of the publishing industry. "With first time authors particularly, the process of signing a contract and having a work published can be mysterious," says Poston. Agents speak the same language as editors. They know the lingo and can explain the business to authors so editors don't have to take the time to walk new authors through the process every time.

The classic role of the agent

Publishers often rely on agents to help them find authors for editor-initiated projects. "The classic role of an agent is to hook up an author with an editor," says Poston. When an editor has an idea for a book, he calls an agent, presents the idea, and asks if the agent knows an author who could write the book. If the agent isn't handling any appropriate authors who are free to write the book, she will do some scouting around. Often, she'll end up approaching authors who have written magazine articles or books on similar subjects. When Don Fine had the idea to publish a River Phoenix biography, he called an agent who recommended a biographer who was equal to the job. Fine used the same process years ago when he wanted to publish biographies of Warren Buffett and Colin Powell. In the case of the Colin Powell book, Fine called an agent who found Howard Means, a writer for *Washingtonian* magazine. *Colin Powell: Soldier/ Statesman—Statesman/Soldier* turned into a first book for Means.

Publishers and editors can be very good at perceiving a need for a certain book, says Poston. They have an instinct for recognizing when the ground is ripe for a certain book at a certain time. Agents know which authors are adept at certain subject matters and certain styles of writing and they regularly scout magazines to find good writers. It's not unusual for an agent to call a writer out of the blue to write a book on a certain subject. When an agent knows a publisher is on the lookout for an author for a hot subject, she begins to scout around. But just because you have been contacted by an agent doesn't mean the book is sold, warns Poston. Promising projects sometimes fall through. When a project falls through, a lesser caliber agent might lose interest in an author who is no longer useful. A good agent will continue to care about your career and look for other opportunities for you.

The secret to finding a good agent

Poston revealed a few tricks for finding agents who are truly dedicated to their authors. "Read the acknowledgements pages in books you admire. A lot of authors have the good sense and grace to thank their agents on the acknowledgements page." Find books by authors you enjoy who write things similar to your own work. Read what they say about their agent. "I want to thank my agent who believed in me and really pushed for my idea," coming directly from an author tells you a lot about the agent's style and level of dedication. When you read interviews in *Publishers Weekly* or *Writer's Digest* pay attention when a writer gives high praise to an agent. When you send your manuscript to an agent, mention in your cover letter you chose her because you admired her efforts on behalf of another author. This approach shows agents you care about your work and who you entrust it to.

The last thing you want to do is one of those impersonal mailings to hundreds of agents, thinking you're bound to hook one out of the hundred, says Poston. "You can't just fan things out and pray," although beginning writers often try. "It just doesn't work that way. You have to have a *reason* why you are approaching a certain agent."

Quite naturally, editors enjoy working with agents they've worked with before and with whom they've had a pleasant working relationship. "Even though we're open to working with agents we don't know, there's a certain level of confidence involved when we already know the agent and how he or she works," says Poston. If you dream of working with a certain house, take the initiative and do a little detective work to determine which agents already have good working relationships with the publisher. A publisher's catalog will provide valuable clues. Past DIF catalogs, for example, have included a list of the agents who handle each book's author. Check the list for books that are similar in tone and content to yours and notice who agented them. If you have written a cookbook, note the name of the agent who handles the cookbook in the catalog. If you have written a novel, note the agents who handled fiction titles. Research those agents further by reading about them in *Guide to Literary Agents* and other publications.

"There are some damn good agents who do great work, who really care about their authors—not all of whom are with huge agencies. That's the kind of agent you want to hook up with. You don't necessarily want the agent who's in the paper all the time or the one who is reputed to be 'high powered.' The idea is to find an agent who will appreciate the kind of work you do," says Poston. "Find somebody who is going to really care about your work and your career." Now if you'll excuse him, he's got to take another call.

How to Find (and Keep) the Right Agent

by Kirsten Holm

Writers create manuscripts. Agents sell them. Publishers create books. Readers buy them. It's the "literary food chain." To survive, you either have to be a very big fish yourself, or have someone you trust who knows her way around the pond and can tell you who not to swim with and what not to swallow. That someone is your agent.

But even attracting an agent's attention can, at best, be difficult. At worst, it can leave you disillusioned, having spent more money than you can afford on services that won't help. For a new, previously unpublished writer, in particular, there can be more questions than answers. This article addresses the novice writer with basic information on how to approach an agent, preparing and presenting your work and what to expect in working with an agent.

Are you ready for an agent?

Before you start looking for an agent you must have a clear idea of what you want and expect from this relationship. Too many writers jump into the pool, uninformed and unwary. Taking the time to educate yourself *before* you get involved will make you feel less like a fish out of water. To have a successful relationship with an agent, you must be realistic about your writing and what an agent can do.

First, take a long look at your work. Is it appropriate for an agent to handle this material, or would it be more effective to market it yourself? Agents do not represent poetry, magazine articles or short stories. Most do not handle material suitable for academic or small presses. The commission earned could not justify the time spent submitting these works. Those who do take on such material generally represent authors on larger projects first, and will take on these smaller items only as a favor to their clients.

Do not look for an agent with only a good idea in your head or even a first draft in your hand. You are ready to look for an agent when you have a completed manuscript—edited, revised and rewritten—that you believe has a readily identifiable, accessible market of readers.

What is an agent?

An agent is your business representative, whose primary job is to sell a work to the publisher pledging to handle it most effectively. An agent should know which publishing houses handle particular subjects or types of work well, as well as individual editor's tastes and enthusiasms. An agent must keep up with the trends in an industry that has experienced seismic changes in the past few years.

That knowledge translates into access. An agent can get a quicker read for a manuscript because editors know each submission is backed by the agent's reputation, just as the recommendation of a friend who knows your interests will attract your attention over the praise of a stranger, however fulsome that stranger's praise may be.

However, agents are not magicians. An agent cannot sell an unsaleable property. He cannot solve your personal problems. He will not be your banker, CPA, social secretary or therapist. It is primarily a business relationship, dependent on your producing manuscripts he can sell. This is not to say that a personal friendship doesn't develop, it can and often does. But the agent is not doing you a favor, working with you out of charity. He expects to be paid from the profits of your complementary efforts.

Before you begin your search you need confidence in yourself as well as your work. You will, in all probability, encounter a lot of rejection before you meet with success. You must be able to take rejection without a word of explanation and keep writing.

In the same way, you must be ready to analyze encouragement and resist jumping at the first agent to respond favorably. It is all too common for a new writer, overwhelmed by the blandishments of a persuasive agent, to pay out hundreds, if not thousands of dollars, elated that someone has recognized at last the value of her book.

Take your writing seriously; it is the biggest factor in finding a representative. Spend the time you need to make your writing singular and appealing and it won't matter if you are writing your first work or your two hundred and first. Believe in it and yourself without going overboard. Touting yourself as "better than Grisham" or "bigger than Waller" sounds empty and boastful, and will turn an agent off before you get any further. Be prepared to work at finding the right agent, not just the first one. If you're willing to do all this, you're ready to look for an agent.

Learn before you look

Finding an agent can be as difficult as finding a publisher, if not more so. Start by reading all you can about agents and authors. The articles in this book, as well as in previous editions, illuminate different areas of the author/agent relationship. Organizations such as the Association of Authors' Representatives (AAR), the National Writers Union, and Poets & Writers Inc. all have informative materials on this topic, and are listed in the Resources section at the back of the book. *Publishers Weekly* covers publishing news affecting agents and others in the publishing industry in general, and discusses specific events in the "Hot Deals," "Rights" and "Behind the Bestsellers" columns.

There are a number of paths to take in finding an agent. Most agents find clients either through referrals or direct contact. Referrals can come from current clients or editors, recommending a writer to an agent's attention. If you have friends who have already secured agents, ask if they will refer you. Don't be offended if someone will not share the name of his agent. Some will, some won't without ascertaining that your work is appropriate for that agent, and some won't, period.

Many agents report that, surprisingly, their hobbies include reading for pleasure. Agents read numerous literary and consumer magazines and often directly contact a writer whose work they enjoy. Particularly if you are writing fiction, publication of your shorter work in the larger literary or genre-specific periodicals can attract the attention of an agent whose interests match yours.

Direct contact is often made through a query letter or proposal package. Agents agree to be listed in directories such as the *Guide to Literary Agents* so writers can learn what an agent wants to see, and how she wants to see it. By checking the Subject Index at the back of the book and studying the listings carefully, you can target those agents who specifically handle your type of work, saving yourself time and money by making each submission count.

You can also make contact in person. Agents often attend writers' conferences and seminars, looking to meet prospective clients. Usually time is set aside at the end of the conference for brief one-on-one discussions, which may result in an invitation to submit your work. We have included information on what conferences an agent attends under the heading "Writers' Conferences" in the agency listings. Even if you are not seeking representation at that time, the more you know about how agents work the easier your search will be when you are ready.

Another good way to find agents is through your own reading. If there is a published book similar to your own work, check the introduction. Writers often thank their agents (which also bodes well for a pleasant working relationship!). Another tack is to call the contracts department of the publisher and ask who the agent of record is for that title. They will have this information at hand since advances and royalties, almost without exception, go straight to the agent, who deducts her expenses and commission and sends the balance to the writer.

Making contact

Almost all agents are interested in new writers. Writers die, stop writing or leave one agent for another. In order to keep up, an agent must be on the lookout for new talent. An agent does not, however, want to be buried by complete manuscripts on topics they would not ever dream of handling. They can get very testy about this, I assure you.

Spend time learning what an agent is interested in handling. While many agents say what they basically look for is good writing, most have particular areas they enjoy. Pay attention to what they say they handle. If you've written a home improvement how-to, look for an agent who has handled this type of material before, one who has her network of editors and publishers interested in this subject already mapped out.

While some very reputable agents do not belong to any professional organizations, those who do are required to maintain certain professional and ethical standards. Members of the AAR and the Writers Guild of America (WGA) have agreed to abide by a code of ethics. We have noted these affiliations in the listings. AAR's Canon of Ethics accompanies a list of its members and an explanatory pamphlet on literary agents, and is available for $5 and SAE with 52¢ postage. The WGA's Artists' Manager Basic Agreement is available for $4. Addresses for both organizations are in the Resources section at the back of the book.

Reading and critique fees

In deciding which agents to approach, the new writer will come face to face with the issue of reading and criticism fees. This issue is as controversial among agents as it is among writers.

Reading fees are intended to cover the additional costs of extra readers who report on manuscripts to the agent. This can save the agent time and open the agency to a larger number of submissions. Reading fees vary from $25 up to $450. Often the fee is nonrefundable, although some agents will refund the fee if they decide to take you on as a client. Others will refund the fee if they sell the work. Some agents include a brief critique or report for the fee.

The AAR and the WGA differ somewhat in their guidelines on reading fees.

Effective January 1, 1996, all AAR members are prohibited from directly or indirectly charging a reading fee. Prior to that date, members who charged reading fees before the October 1991 merger of the Society of Authors Representatives and the Independent Literary Agents Association were allowed to continue, provided they comply with a number of requirements designed to protect the client.

The WGA's Artists' Manager Basic Agreement enjoins a WGA signatory agency from charging a reading fee *to WGA members*. If you are not a member, a signatory agency may charge you a reading fee. Many signatory agencies do not, as an across-the-board policy.

Criticism or editorial services are offered by a number of agents. Rarely does the

Reading fee policy change

While AAR does not accept new members who charge reading fees, it permitted those members who charged fees prior to the October 1991 merger of SAR and ILAA to continue to do so until December 31, 1995. Effective January 1, 1996, all AAR members are prohibited from directly or indirectly charging such fees or receiving any financial benefit from the charging of such fees by any other party.

payment of a critique fee ensure representation. It is up to you to determine the value of these services. The fees vary widely for these services, as do the quality and extent of the critiques. One important thing to keep in mind is that an agent who devotes a significant portion of his time to editing and critiquing manuscripts will have that much less time for actively marketing a work.

Sometimes an agent will say that a manuscript is interesting but needs work. While the agent does not offer editorial services herself, she can recommend a freelance editor or "book doctor" to you. Recently a number of literary agencies have been recommending specific editorial companies. While it is not illegal to make a referral, or receive a fee for doing so, it is an approach you should be aware of. The WGA has issued a rule that their signatories cannot do this. The WGA believes that, while an agent may have good intentions, it would be too difficult to differentiate those who are trying to help from those who may have a financial or professional interest in the editing relationship that develops at their suggestion. Again, you must investigate any potential editor's qualifications before you contract for his services.

Give them what they want

Once you've narrowed down who to send your work to, you'll need to put together your submission. Check an agent's guidelines and stick to them. Most agents accept unsolicited query letters. Many request a two- to five-page outline or chapter summary. Never send a complete manuscript until you are invited to do so. Send no more and no less than what an agent asks for. Anything else, no matter how politely introduced, will irritate the reader and delay any response you hope to receive.

If an agent asks for your manuscript, make sure it looks attractive and is easy to read. It should be crisp and clean, not dog-eared or smudged. The pages should be typed, double-spaced on one side of 8½×11 paper and relatively free of typos and corrections. Make sure the type is dark and clear; computer printouts should be produced on at least a near-letter-quality printer.

Every submission should be accompanied by a self-addressed, stamped envelope (SASE). Some writers save money by sending a disposable copy of their outline or manuscript along with a self-addressed stamped postcard with various responses to be checked off. If you are submitting work to a script agent, a postcard can be used to acknowledge receipt of the work, but a SASE should also be sent since many script agents request a release form with complete manuscripts and will send you one if they are interested in seeing more.

Your query letter is extremely important. It must convey your abilities as a writer. It also must be short. It may be difficult to summarize a work you've become so close to, but you will lose your audience if you cannot hit the highlights and leave the agent wanting more.

A query letter should be a brief, one-page introduction to you and your work. Begin with stating your purpose—you have a manuscript and would like the agent to consider representing you. Include what type of manuscript it is—romance, psychology, computer how-to. Answer the agent's question: "What is it you want?"

In the next paragraph, tell why you are querying her. If you met the agent at a conference and were invited to submit your work, remind her. If you were referred by a client, say so. If you know of another author's work she represents that is similar to your own or that you particularly admired, mention it. Show that you've done a little research and know something about her interests. Answer the question: "Why *me*?"

Next, introduce the work. Tell the agent what she needs to know about your manuscript in one or two paragraphs. You *must* be able to boil it down to a bite-size summary that is informative, interesting and leaves her intrigued. Answer the question: "What have you written?"

Then, introduce yourself. Include personal information only if it pertains to your work. If you are the chef at a private supper club and have written a cookbook, or are a sex therapist who has developed a new approach that has revolutionized your patients' lives, announce those qualifications up front. Mention any previous publishing credits if you have them. If you haven't any, don't mention it. Don't apologize for the fact that you're a new writer. If the manuscript is good, it won't matter. If you haven't worked on it enough, the agent will know. Answer the questions: "Why did you write this? Why should I read what you've written?"

Close with an offer to send an outline and sample chapters or the complete manuscript. Some agents ask for a summary along with the query; some only want the query initially and will tell you what to send if they are interested.

Once your manuscript has been requested, give the agent enough time to read it. It will, in most cases, not be read immediately, but be placed at the bottom of a tall stack to be read in the evenings and weekends after the agent has taken care of business for her existing clients. Sometimes assistants are given the task of weeding out the "possibles" from the "nevers" and passing them on to the agent. It may seem unfair not to have the agent's full attention, but you will appreciate her focus on her clients once she is your representative.

If you have not heard back on your manuscript from an agent in six to eight weeks (check each agent's reporting time to be sure), a polite call asking when you can expect to hear is not out of order. Do not pre-suppose an antagonistic relationship and do not take it personally if your work has not been read yet. Agents are people, too. They have families, celebrate holidays, fall ill or have emergencies, just like you. Give it time. More than two to three months, however, and you should reevaluate whether this agent has the time to represent you adequately.

Evaluate an agent before you sign on

Once you've received an offer of representation, you must determine whether this is the right agent for you. There are no rules or regulations governing agents, no licensing or accreditation agencies. When it comes down to it, anyone with a phone and mail drop-off can call himself an agent. Before you agree to anything, determine if the agent is legitimate and has the experience, ability and contacts to sell your work. While you and your agent may not become intimate, a pleasant working relationship is important.

Remember you are entering into a business relationship: You are employing the agent. You have the right to ask for information to convince you she knows what she's doing. Ask for references or other information that will help you determine this. Most agents are happy to provide recent sales or editorial references. Call the contracts department of the publisher to ascertain that a sale actually was made by the agent claiming it. Call the editor and *briefly* state that you are considering this agent as your representative, and ask how the editor would characterize the agent's submissions.

Another factor to weigh in evaluating an agent is her level of experience. Agencies that have been in business for awhile have a large number of contacts, but newer agencies may be hungrier, as well as more open to previously unpublished writers. What an agent did *before* she was an agent could influence your decision as well. Information about an agent's publishing employment or experience before joining or opening the agency is included in the bulleted editorial comments.

Do not be won over by an impressive brochure or bullied by a dismissive attitude. Most agents are proud of their achievements and want to share them. Some agents feel this information is confidential, but may be willing to share it with writers they are offering representation to. You have the right to ask reasonable questions that will help you make a decision. Asking for recent sales is okay; asking for the average size of clients' advances is not. If you are polite in your requests for information and an agent responds with anger or contempt, that tells you something you need to know about how working together would be.

Talk to other writers about their experiences with agents. Computer services such as America Online often have writers' clubs, where you can post a request for any information about a particular agent. Writers' organizations such as the National Writers Association and National Writers Union maintain files on agents their members have dealt with, and can share this by written request or through their membership newsletters.

One reader of the *Guide* believes that clues to an agent's personality can often show in articles written by that agent. She makes an effort to find this material, or asks if the agent has written anything she could read. An agent might even be flattered to know that you would like read *her* work. To help you with this, we've included notes in the listings directing you to articles written by an agent in both current and previous editions of this book.

Understand any contract *before* you sign

Some agents offer written contracts, while others do not. If your prospective agent does not, ask for at least a "memorandum of understanding" that details the basic arrangements of expenses and commissions. If your agent does offer a contract, be sure to read it carefully, and *keep a copy to refer to.*

The National Writers Union has drafted a Preferred Literary Agent Agreement and a pamphlet, *Understanding the Author-Agent Relationship*, which is available to members. (Membership is $75 and open to all writers actively pursuing a writing career. See the Resources section.) They suggest clauses that delineate such issues as:

● the scope of representation (One work? One work with the right of refusal on the next? All work completed in the coming year? All work completed until the agreement is terminated?);
● the extension of authority to the agent to negotiate on behalf of the author;
● compensation for the agent, and any subagent, if used;
● manner and time frame for forwarding monies received by the agent on behalf of the client;
● termination of the agreement;
● the effect of termination on concluded agreements as well as ongoing negotiations;
● arbitration in the event of a dispute between agent and client.

What to expect when you're represented

Once you have become a client, you may have questions on what to expect. Your agent should be interested in your future as a writer. She will probably offer general editorial advice, but not all agents do. She will protect your business interests. She should keep in touch regarding the progress in selling your work. This doesn't mean notifying you of each rejection, but she should let you know on a regular basis where your manuscript has been and who has seen it.

When your agent receives a bid that's in the ballpark, she'll contact you and explain the offer. Ask her to explain anything you don't understand. She's your representative; working in synch will make everybody's role easier.

The publisher will send your advance and any subsequent royalty checks directly to the agent. Your agent will deduct her commission, usually 10 to 15 percent. Most agents charge a higher commission when using a subagent for foreign, dramatic or other specialized rights.

Your agent may also deduct some expenses, which may include postage, photocopying, long-distance calls and faxes and express mail or messenger services. You should discuss what expenses will be deducted before signing with an agency. Ask to be notified in advance of any large or unusual expenses.

An agent's job is not done when a sale is made. You can also call on your agent to handle disputes or problems that arise with your editor or publisher. Safeguarding an author's rights can be a very important part of the job. For example, agent Berenice Hoffman joined her client Judith Applebaum in a recent suit against HarperCollins over accounting and payment of subsidiary rights royalties that led the publisher to reform their subrights payment system.

When the party's over

Once you have an agent you may find she is not the right agent, for a variety of reasons. How do you get out of a bad relationship? First, check your written agreement to see if there are any specific procedures spelled out. If not, write a brief, businesslike letter, stating that you no longer think the relationship is advantageous and you wish to terminate it. Instruct the agent not to make any new submissions and give her a 30 or 60 day limit to continue as representative on submissions already under consideration. You can ask for a list of all publishers or production companies who have rejected any of your unsold work, as well as a list of those currently looking at your work. If the agent has made sales for you, she will continue to receive those monies from the publisher, deduct her commission and remit the balance to you. A statement and your share of the money should be sent to you within 30 days. You can also ask that all manuscripts in her possession be returned to you.

Additional information

For more information on working with agents, see the articles written by agents and other writing professionals in the Literary Agents section. The introduction to each section contains information pertaining to the agencies listed in that section and will help you understand more about the entries.

At the back of the book we've included a number of indexes. For literary agents, the Subject Index is broken down between nonfee-charging and fee-charging agents; script agents are grouped together. Subjects are listed for nonfiction and fiction categories for literary agents; for script agents the subjects are listed alphabetically. Agencies who have specified an interest in handling particular types of material are listed within each subject section.

We've also included an Agents Index, which will be helpful if you have heard about a good agent, but do not know the agency she works for. We asked the agencies to list their staff members, and then listed these names alphabetically with their agency affiliation in parentheses. The page number for the agency's listing is in the Listing Index.

Many agents are located in New York for books and Los Angeles for scripts. With computers, faxes and special phone services this is becoming less important. There is a Geographic Index for those who would prefer to work with an agent closer to home.

We've asked each agent to rank themselves from I-V, based on their openness to new, previously unpublished authors. (The key to this system is explained in the introduction to each section.) This year we've added a Client Acceptance Policies index at the back of the book based on these rankings.

To broaden the opportunities for your work, we've cross-referenced agents handling both books and scripts. Script agencies handling more than 10 to 15 percent book manuscripts also appear among the literary agents, and literary agents handling 10 to 15 percent scripts also appear among the script agents. The cross-reference contains contact information, breakdown of work currently handled and a note to check the full listing in the appropriate section. Fee-charging literary agents must report a sale or be a signatory of the WGA to be cross-referenced. Those agencies handling less than 10 to 15 percent in a secondary field continue to be listed in the Additional Agents at the end of each section.

Swimming in the deep end

Your relationship with your agent comes down to trust. In representing you, your agent trusts you are a professional, serious about your writing and able to fulfill the commitments you make. You must have confidence in her representation, in her advice, and in her handling of your book-related financial responsibilities for your relationship to be successful.

AAR Checklist for Authors

Authors don't always know what questions to ask (or are too timid to ask) about the policies, practices, and services of agents. The Association of Authors' Representatives has developed a checklist of topics which can be used by authors seeking to enter into a professional relationship with an agent. It is the hope of the AAR that this will help to create a more comfortable relationship among authors and agents, demystify agent activities, and reduce misunderstandings.

1. Is your agency a sole proprietorship?
2. Are you a member of the Association of Authors' Representatives?
3. How long have you been in business as an agent?
4. How many people does your agency employ?
5. Of the total number of employees, how many are agents, as opposed to clerical workers?
6. Do you have specialists at your agency who handle movie and television rights? Foreign rights? Do you have sub-agents or corresponding agents overseas and in Hollywood?
7. Do you represent other authors in my area of interest?
8. Who in your agency will actually be handling my work? Will the other staff members be familiar with my work and the status of my business at your agency? Will you oversee or at least keep me apprised of the work that your agency is doing on my behalf?
9. Do you issue an agent-author contract? May I review a specimen copy? And may I review the language of the agency clause that appears in contracts you negotiate for your clients?
10. What is your approach to providing editorial input and career guidance for your clients or for me specifically?
11. How do you keep your clients informed of your activities on their behalf? Do you regularly send them copies of publishers' rejection letters? Do you provide them with submission lists and rejection letters on request? Do you regularly, or upon request, send out updated activity reports?
12. Do you consult with your clients on any and all offers?
13. Some agencies sign subsidiary contracts on behalf of their clients to expedite processing. Do you?
14. What are your commissions for: (1) basic sales to U.S. publishers; (2) sales of movie and television rights; (3) audio and multimedia rights; (4) British and foreign translation rights?
15. What are your procedures and time-frames for processing and disbursing client funds? Do you keep separate bank accounts segregating author funds from agency revenue?
16. What are your policies about charging clients for expenses incurred by your agency? Will you list such expenses for me? Do you advance money for such expenses? Do you consult with your clients before advancing certain expenditures? Is there a ceiling on such expenses above which you feel you must consult with your clients?

17. How do you handle legal, accounting, public relations, or similar professional services that fall outside the normal range of a literary agency's functions?
18. Do you issue 1099 tax forms at the end of each year? Do you also furnish clients upon request with a detailed account of their financial activity, such as gross income, commissions and other deductions, and net income, for the past year?
19. In the event of your death or disability, or the death or disability of the principal person running the agency, what provisions exist for continuing operation of my account, for the processing of money due to me, and for the handling of my books and editorial needs?
20. If we should part company, what is your policy about handling any unsold subsidiary rights to my work that were reserved to me under the original publishing contracts?
21. What are your expectations of me as your client?
22. Do you have a list of Do's and Don'ts for your clients that will enable me to help you do your job better?

Reprinted by permission of the Association of Authors' Representatives.

A Monday in the Life of an Agent

by Anita Diamant

My Monday as a working literary agent begins at 8:23 when I board the Metro North train from Westport, Connecticut, to New York City. This is not an hour wasted, since my time is well spent rereading my notes on the manuscripts I took home to read over the weekend.

9:30 I enter my office and find my assistants already on the telephone, answering calls that came in over the weekend. As usual, my desk is piled high with notes referring to telephone calls after I left on Friday. I determine which calls I can answer immediately, and which calls from the West Coast I'll have to wait two to three hours to return.

I dial a client who I know is waiting anxiously. I had left a message for him indicating I had a call from an editor interested in his first novel. He is so ecstatic, he forgets to ask about the advance, the terms of the contract, etc. And it is a satisfying moment for me too. I never cease to enjoy selling a first novel!

10:00 I start telephoning editors to inquire about the fate of manuscripts I've submitted. The easiest people to reach are the romance editors—they are extraordinarily well-organized and answer at once. This is particularly easy for me since we can meet often—we are both on 42nd Street! One of my best romance writers, and a favorite at the house, has submitted a manuscript, the last of a three-book contract. The editor is delighted with the manuscript and is putting through a payment request. She is already talking about a new contract. I tell her I've had offers from other publishers, but this is one writer who appreciates the support she is receiving from her publisher and is not anxious to make a change. However, we must be assured of signficant advances, as she depends on her writing for her livelihood.

10:20 I next telephone a writer who has had some problems with her editor. She is a newspaperwoman and feels she has a better grasp of the market needs than her editor. A mistake! It is all right to discuss any problems with treatment, plot, etc., but editors in large houses have a good idea of what they can sell and what doesn't work for their line. The writer cannot have the same objectivity. I advise my client to talk to her editor and agree to some of the changes in order to get out on the market. We discuss the problems all writers have today and finally the writer agrees to be more conciliatory.

10:40 At last the mail has arrived—and since this is Monday, the number of query letters is enormous. We answer all letters if there is a stamped, self-addressed envelope included. Sometimes we will answer without the SASE if the query is particularly interesting. I take a pile of letters (there must be 30 or 40) and my assistant takes the rest, including all packages. I am appalled at the fact that so many writers are planning to write books duplicating in theme many books already on the market. After all, how

Anita Diamant *heads up a six-person New York City agency that represents over 125 writers. Her agency handles book-length adult and young adult fiction and nonfiction, as well as film, dramatic, TV and foreign rights in all markets. She is a member of the Association of Authors' Representatives and is listed in* Who's Who in America.

many *Bridges of Madison County* do we need? I read through all the letters and mark those requiring a rejection and those which are interesting and from which I will want to read a full outline and a few chapters.

11:30 I now must make a call to my London agent to discuss a possible sale abroad. I have recently returned from London where I make a yearly visit to meet and talk to British editors who are buying the rights to our books. This is a very helpful call, since I am also able to update my representative about the U.S. success of some of our books. In addition, one of the books I gave him has been scheduled for a film with top stars. This will help assure a British sale and perhaps sales on the Continent as well, and of course bring a better advance.

12:00 Now I can telephone two of my clients on the West Coast. My first call will be to California, where one of my most successful writers lives. I have finished reading his new manuscript and have sent it over to his editor, assuring her of my delight with the way in which the manuscript turned out. He tells me that he has begun to work on the next book of the series and will have an outline within a week. We discuss the terms we will demand for a new contract. Since these paperbacks sell in the millions worldwide, we agree that a new three-book contract which will be in the seven figures must give us a better percentage of British sales. I am going to insist on an auction even though this publisher has a British subsidiary. This will help increase book sales in Britain.

12:20 I now telephone my client in Oregon. We discuss the possibility of writing for one publisher, instead of the several publishers she now works with. Would it be better to put all her eggs in one basket, so to speak, or is it better for her to continue to work with several editors—all of whom are supportive. This is always a difficult decision and I suggest we get offers from each house and then determine the best way to proceed.

12:35 I have to clear my desk and leave for my luncheon date with a publisher. She has been anxious to meet with me personally after meeting two of my clients.

1:00 I walk to the restaurant. This is our first meeting and I find out that the publisher lives in Connecticut very near me. This immediately gives us rapport. She is interested in one of my writers, who has been working for another publishing house. They met at a writer's conference and the publisher liked the author and her work. I tell her it would take at least a fair six-figure advance to get this writer, and a three-book contract. The publisher agrees to discuss this at her house and let me know the result. I inform her that I could not give her film or TV rights, since this author has had a couple of films already produced and feels she can sell rights to future books as well. The publisher tells me of some new lines they are doing and asks me to think about submitting more books to them for these markets.

3:00 Back at my office, I find that a new series of calls has come in. One writer was recommended to me by an editor at a large publishing house. I return this call at once. This writer has sold two books but has had problems since she was represented by an entertainment attorney and not an agent. The attorney did not feel on sure ground in dealing with book publishers. The writer's editor felt I could help explain some of the practices of the book publishing business, as well as advise her about contract terms being offered. I debate at first whether I want to get into this, and I ask the writer to send me one of her published books so that I can ascertain just what her abilities are and what I can offer her.

3:30 My assistant has several proposals she wants me to read, since she has read them and thought they were interesting. This is the first moment I have had to look at any manuscripts. As I start to read, my Los Angeles agent calls. He has had an offer for one of our books from a large film company and the producer has a star lined up who would be interested in playing the lead. This is exciting and I suggest to my agent that he try to up the option money and make certain that all book rights are protected. We are not certain whether this will prove to be a TV series or a feature film. I get the details so that I can inform my client, who will of course be thrilled to hear the news.

3:45 A messenger delivers a jacket for a new book. This is an important book and jacket approval is in the contract. The sketch is all wrong—the colors and the design make it seem like a young adult book. I call the editor, who partially agrees with me, although she likes the basic idea. I insist on changes and she promises to call the art department and ask for a new sketch, changing the colors. I also ask for a larger typeface for the author's name. In this case, the author's name will help sell the book.

3:55 Money is owing to one of my clients from a paperback sale I made for the publisher, and I know this money has already been paid out. This is my third call and now I really insist we receive the money within the week, as my client is threatening suit. Promises, promises. The publisher will send the check!

4:10 I now continue my reading of manuscripts which I have requested. One is a mystery with a female protagonist, humor and some very good writing. I begin thinking of the right editors and start making a list of potential houses. I know that fewer mysteries are being published and several mystery editors have been discharged. However, I recall that at one of my luncheons, an editor told me she was looking for a clever mystery with a female detective. I dictate a note to my assistant, and ask her to messenger the manuscript over. I reach the writer who is pleased that I like her work. I tell her I'll do my very best to sell this, and I feel there is potential for a film sale as well. I'll call our film representative and discuss it with him.

4:30 A call has come in from the articles editor of one of the leading women's magazines. At my suggestion, a client submitted an article and the editor wants to buy it. Although we don't ordinarily sell magazine material (aside from magazine rights to books), I am pleased to know that the article is saleable. The money offered is more than fair and I accept for my client. The writer is pleased, as this opens a new market for her, in addition to the book she is writing.

4:40 My assistant announces a call from an editor considering a first novel I had submitted. He informs me that he needs an outline—he doesn't like to read any manuscripts unless he has an outline in hand. This is getting as bad as the film people who want to know in 25 words or less what a book is about! I promise to get in touch with the writer and obtain an outline.

4:45 I meet with a writer who is looking to change agents. He is very unhappy with his agent and the contract with his publisher. I discover that he has already had three agents, and has not had a good relationship with editors in different houses where he has been published. I ask him to leave his new manuscript and I'd decide how I could be of help to him. After he leaves, I call an editor to whom he has made an acknowledgement in one of his books. She advises me strongly not to become involved. He has not fulfilled his obligations to the house and has tried to borrow money from the editor. This is unfortunate, for this man is a very talented writer, but with over 100 other clients in our agency, I do not want to take on anyone with a serious problem. I decide to write a nice note, telling the writer I feel he would do better with a smaller agency who would be able to give him more attention.

5:15 I gather all the loose material on my desk, make notes as to what must be handled the next day, and with the manuscript of a new novel in my briefcase, I leave to make my train back to Connecticut.

It has been a busy Monday, and although I am tired, there is an exhiliration in this work. Somehow I feel I have achieved something and hopefully have been of help to the people I represent.

Career Planning for Novelists

by Donald Maass

Why plan?

For many writers the idea of planning a novel-writing career is weird. For them a novel is a story that unfolds organically. To "plan" a novel, let alone a lifetime's worth of them, seems to such writers a pointless and possibly dangerous exercise.

If you are that type of author—if your novels just happen, each one a calling—then for you a career plan may not be a good idea. Indeed, to attempt any novel that does not flow from a wellspring deep inside can prove a waste of time or worse.

However, if you are an outline-handy novelist, a genre writer or the author of commercial mainstream novels then you may be a bit more comfortable with the idea of a career plan. In fact, you may already have one. If so, you know that it can give you a sense of control in an uncertain industry. It can also give you a yardstick with which to measure your progress. It can even be a vaccine against common publishing ailments.

Book publishing in the Nineties is a cold, unforgiving, numbers-driven business. Small errors can be fatal these days. I know. Every week my agency gets panicky calls from novelists whose careers have crashed. Stung by low advances, lousy covers, little support, editors who left, high returns, books that went out of print too soon, or any of a host of other frequently-seen publishing disasters, these distressed authors have suddenly realized that their careers are in jeopardy.

The tragic part is that many of their problems can be prevented. All it takes is a bit of foresight, some planning for the challenges ahead. It also helps to orient oneself to what is fundamental in this business. Too many authors focus on obtaining contracts. That is important to be sure, but it is far from the final transaction. The ultimate publishing transaction is between author and reader. It is the support of readers that finally makes the difference between success and failure.

Think of it this way: Publishing a first novel is like opening a store. In that store, the proprietor sells certain goods. Customers come in. They like what they find. They come back. They become, in other words, repeat customers, the ones who will keep the owner in business and become the foundation of his future growth.

Changing the product mix in the store, moving the store to a different location or closing the store for long periods of time will result in customers shopping elsewhere. It is the same with readers: Authors who jump genres, switch from one section of the bookstore to another, or who take years off to write The Great American Novel are risking an erosion of their audience.

Now, don't get me wrong: I have nothing against growing as a writer. Sometimes radical changes in one's style or story type are healthy, even necessary. But such changes have consequences. It's prudent to be aware of them, perhaps even to get ready for them. That's planning—and what is wrong with that?

Donald Maass is president of the Donald Maass Literary Agency in New York City. He is the author of 14 pseudonymous novels and of the book The Career Novelist, *published by Heinemann in June 1996. He travels widely to writers' conferences, where he conducts seminars for new and mid-career authors called "Breaking In" and "Breaking Out."*

Planning a career can be done right from the beginning. The very choice of what to write first is, in a way, a step in a plan. Marketing decisions also form a sort of plan. Granted, many writers' plans are somewhat random but most authors have at least a general idea of where their novels belong.

Let's examine some aspects of early career-planning.

Breaking in

If you have completed only one manuscript, then your first decision may be simple: Your first submissions will be of your first novel. But hold on: Ask yourself whether this manuscript is really the one with which to launch your career.

Be honest. Is this novel as good as it can be? I am not asking whether it is good enough to get a contract. It may be. Rather, is it good enough to compete with the novels of the leading authors in your category or sub-category? Remember, once you sell your book to a publisher comes the day-by-day struggle for an audience. Given how little support first novels get, do you feel that yours can sell itself? If so, it may be the one with which to begin. If not, you may want to revise it or set it aside in favor of your next project.

If you have more than one manuscript in the drawer, take inventory. Which will be the most popular? Which might open a bread-and-butter business that draws readers back time after time? That may be the one with which to begin. Should you let the others sit? Perhaps not, but realize that the buckshot approach—fire everything and see what hits—is not a plan, it is gambling. Circulating many flawed novels will not magically make them all more saleable. If you know that some of yours have problems, why not wait until they are in shape?

Next, who is your audience? Most authors don't think much about their readers while they write. They write for themselves. There is nothing wrong with that, but sooner or later a choice of categories must be made. A true pro recognizes that his goal is to reach the readers who will become his repeat customers. To do that he must be accurately labeled and shelved in the appropriate section of the bookstores.

To identify your audience, try to place your novel in one of these broad categories:
- Romance;
- Mystery/Suspense;
- Science Fiction/Fantasy;
- Horror;
- Frontier;
- Gay/Lesbian;
- Literary;
- Mainstream.

Hard choice? Those categories correspond to those you will find in most stores. Your marketing plan begins with a decision about which section of the bookstore is the one for your work.

Don't get me wrong: I am not suggesting that authors change what they write just to fit into a category. I am recommending, though, that they select one section of the store in which to open their business. Which section? That choice is not always obvious. The one to choose is the one in which *most* of their appreciative readers will be found. Not all, just most.

Now, within your category try to identify the writer whose work most closely resembles your own in setting, style, story type, cast of characters and so on. That author is your competition. You may not like to draw comparisons, but again, if you don't do it yourself someone else will do it for you.

In identifying what makes your fiction different, even unique, you may also be putting your finger on those aspects of your work that will hook your readers. In a way, these are your business secrets, and possibly the core of your pitch to agents and publishers.

Early career planning questions

Here are some other early-career planning questions: Whom will you approach first, agents or publishers? Do you want to sell a single title, or seek a multiple-book deal? Which is the best format? Hardcover? Trade paperback? Original mass-market paperback? While waiting for a sale, which book should you work on next? When do you plan to go full time?

Interesting questions. Let's take them one at a time. Regarding publishers, many only accept manuscripts submitted by agents. That limits your pool of choices. A logical step is to first contact agents, but a good agent can be as hard to get as a publisher; perhaps even harder. You may want to try your luck, or you may decide to improve your odds by first making some short story sales, or perhaps by seeking a referral from an established author. When you have decided how to go, you have put into place another piece of your plan to break in.

Sell one book or three? New authors may not imagine they will be offered this choice but it happens more often that you would think, especially when series are involved. In fact, in the case of a series a multiple-book deal may not be a bad idea. It locks you into your publisher's schedule, and provides continuity while you wait for evidence that your series is selling. The case may be different for stand-alone novels and large-scale commercial fiction. Here it may be better to wait. If your first book hits big, you might want to cash in quickly.

Format? Hardcover first is not always the best idea. In a crowded category, it can be tough to get reviews and to push an expensive edition on the public. For some, an original paper edition may be smart. Prestige is lost, but the lower price may perhaps overcome consumer resistance. Which format is best for you? Figure that out and you have another step in your plan.

What should you write next while you are marketing your first manuscript? Here is a career planning principle in which I firmly believe: If an author has three novels that he could write next, one of those is going to be a more logical step toward his goals than the other two. It is only a matter of analysis.

Where does your next-planned novel fit into your career plan? Is it the continuation of a series? Does it move you into a different genre? Is it a step up in scope and scale, or does it explore anew a theme that is a passionate interest of yours?

In planning a sequence of novels to write, I suggest not planning too far ahead. A couple of novels down the road is far enough. As you mature, and as your craft improves, you'll find that your story interests will change too.

Lastly, how long before you can go full time? Brace yourself: It is not unusual for "breakout"—that sudden surge in sales that brings industry-wide attention—to come after ten or even twenty books. Patrick O'Brian is a case in point. So is Martin Cruz Smith. These authors served long apprenticeships. Others never make it to "breakout" at all.

You may not have to wait that long until your royalty earnings are supporting you, but nevertheless it is wise to recognize that novel writing is a slow motion business. Zen Buddhism is probably not a bad religion to embrace as one waits for success, but I also have two other outlooks to recommend.

First, try thinking of writing as an end in itself. That can be comforting in a business in which disappointment can be both likely and of long duration. Second, consider regarding the "markets" not as goals in themselves but as means to an end: readers.

Readers are the ultimate customers, after all. Everyone else in the industry is there only to aid you in reaching them

Mid-career damage control

Sometimes even the best-planned beginnings can lead to disaster. Is there any way an author can predict that she is going to get zapped? There *are* warning signs. Here is a checklist of indicators that may signal looming danger for a mid-career author:

- A low advance;
- A high advance unjustified by prior royalty earnings:
- A bad cover;
- Bad reviews;
- Low "ship in," i.e., few books available in stores;
- High returns/low "sellthrough";
- A genre switch or radically new style;
- One's latest work is a "crossover novel," i.e., one that mixes genres;
- Being "orphaned" by an editor who departs his job;
- Frequent switching of publishers;
- A contract with a low end house;
- Poor distribution;
- A backlist that is out of print;
- Having an option book turned down;
- One's agent proving ineffective;
- One's agent not returning one's calls.

None of these factors by themselves will necessarily spell disaster, but if too many items on that list are checked off, there is a likelihood of problems in the near future.

As always, the best cure for weighty publishing problems is an ounce of prevention. One pitfall can appear when a new writer is in a hurry to receive validation for all his work. If that author signs up with an inferior agent, or sells to a career-killing publisher just to obtain a quick contract, he is taking chances.

Another mistake is being passive during the publication process. Authors who care little about contract negotiations, cover design, cover copy, list position and the like are just asking for trouble. Those who sit around at home and refuse to promote themselves unless their publisher pays the bill are also short-sighted. Try to get involved. After all, it is *your career.*

One powerful medicine—easy to prescribe, hard to swallow—is to write novels that readers cannot resist. That may seem obvious advice, but you would be amazed at how many published writers refuse to revise their work. Perhaps they feel complacent, or desperate for acceptance checks, or just plain lazy. I don't know. Whatever their reasons, they are being short-sighted.

So here are some steps to take to prevent mid-career crises:

1. Take time when choosing an agent or a publisher;
2. Be active in the publication process, and in promotion;
3. Craft the best stories you can, and when done, revise them well.

Sometimes even a ton of prevention is not enough. The ax falls anyway, oftentimes through no noticeable fault of the author's. What can be done in these situations? Herewith, some ideas:

Being "orphaned" may present you with a choice: Stay with the publisher or follow your editor to his new home. Which is right for you? One crucial factor is your backlist. Leaving too much of it behind can leave you without a platform to make new leaps to higher levels of sales.

If you decide to stay, consider the situation a major crisis. Decisive action is needed.

I like to go in and pitch my clients' projects to their new editors as hard as if I were pitching them for the first time. Winning support is crucial. Sitting passively by is a recipe for disaster.

More difficult to grapple with are problems like underprinting, or overprinting and overshipping with its consequent high returns. Being remaindered too soon is another pitfall. The only strategy to pursue in anticipation of these problems is to clearly communicate career plans to your publisher in advance.

If communication does not work, changing publishers is sometimes possible. In fact, it is sometimes the *only* option. (If you have been stung by lousy numbers, though, finding a new home can prove difficult.) Switching formats can also help get unstuck. Hardcover for a paperback author, or vice versa, can throw a positive new element into the publishing equation.

Above all, plan. Meeting a crisis with passive despair is fatal. The only way through is action; that, and keeping a sense of perspective.

Suppose that in spite of all your caution, forethought, planning and hard work, things nevertheless go drastically wrong. Can anything be done to help writers who are marked to perish? There are a few realistic options.

1. Switch genres.
2. Adopt a pseudonym and try again.
3. Go away and wait. The sting of bad numbers will fade in a few years.

Humiliating options, I agree. Still, one of them may be worth choosing. After all, the most crushing plan of all is to accept defeat.

Strategies for breaking out

That term "breakout book" is bandied around a lot in publishing, but what does it really mean? Generally it refers to any book that moves an author a giant step upward in sales or name recognition. If a novel leaps onto the bestseller lists without warning, you can be sure everyone will be calling it a "breakout."

What are the circumstances that foretell a breakout? Can they be planned?

One sign of a possible breakout is a leap in an author's writing. A move out of genre fiction into mainstream, a plot newly large in scope and scale, a deeper than usual theme—any of those elements may elevate an author's newest novel into breakout candidacy. Planning such a move is possible, of course, but some over-anxious authors attempt to force their writing into molds for which it is not yet ready. That will not work.

Of course, certain breakouts are simply the result of accumulated good writing and long-term word-of-mouth. Can word-of-mouth be planned? I think it can. Authors who do years of signings, interviews and convention appearances are, in fact, cultivating word-of-mouth. They are connecting with readers, winning converts and getting the bookstores behind them.

Other circumstances that may attend a breakout are a change of format—paperback to hardcover, or vice versa—or perhaps a new "up-market" cover look. Of course, new formats and improved packaging are not by themselves enough to make a book break out. The book must "be there," as insiders say, which in plain English means that the breakout book must be damn good.

Still, planning is involved. With luck one's agent, publisher, publicist and sales force all recognize the breakout book when it arrives, and shift into high gear. A better advance, nicer packaging, blurbs, bound galleys, ads, publicity . . . any or all of those may come into play. Notice, though that none of that is accidental. It requires people working with a purpose.

Probably the biggest challenge faced by authors who are climbing to the top is that of writing good novels. It is so easy to slip. One temptation is to recycle old material. That can be fun, but it can also ensnare one in stories that are lesser in scale and weaker in substance than one's current fiction.

It is also tempting to enjoy the many distractions that are available to successful authors. Writers' conferences, guest faculty spots, ABA, leadership positions in unions and authors' organizations, TV appearances, literary feuds with other novelists . . . any of those will eat up mountains of time if one lets them. Sadly, some authors make a second career out of distractions. (Norman Mailer and Truman Capote come to mind.)

Writing quality can suffer. Again, though, the answer is to have a sensible plan. If an author is getting bored with a series, for example, time for developing new work can be added to the schedule—provided that does not mean shutting up the flagship store. Working under realistic deadlines can also help prevent burnout, that feeling of exhaustion that causes authors to revolt.

In fact, the whole trick to a healthy, profitable and fulfilling fiction writing career is managing one's time, resources and talent wisely. Doing that takes knowledge. It also takes foresight, and the ability to prepare in advance for both disaster and success. What is all that but a fancy definition of "career planning?"

When you think about it, the idea doesn't seem weird at all.

Understanding Your Book Contract

by Ethan Ellenberg

This article is for the inexperienced author whose agent is negotiating his publishing agreement. You may have thought, "Hey, I don't need to know or do anything, that's why I have an agent," but that is far from the truth. There are a number of reasons why you should understand what is going on when your book contract is being negotiated.

First and foremost, your agent will not be signing your publishing agreement, you will. It's a binding legal document that may govern an important part of your life for years to come. Another reason is that, as with just about everything in life, there are trade-offs to be made. Your agent may propose choices to you, such as a higher advance versus a larger royalty. Publishing agreements can be intimidating. The more you know about some of the issues involved, the easier your agent's job is, and the less anxious you will feel.

Publishing is a complex business. The agreement you're going to sign covers a host of issues and comprises numerous pages. The greater part of the contents are standard clauses, what are known as "boilerplate" that vary little from one contract to another. Though the boilerplate covers smaller issues common to most publishing agreements, there are important variations between publishers. Your agent will know what to do about these and may have standard changes already on file with your publisher. The issues that are really up for discussion are called "deal points" and are covered in the "deal memo." While the actual contract may take weeks if not months to materialize, your agent and the publisher will hammer out the deal memo pretty quickly. Perhaps the most important issues for the first timer are advance, royalty, rights and time of publication.

Advance

Most authors tend to focus on the advance. After all, that's the actual cash they will see from signing their publishing agreement and delivery of the book. The advance is very important. It represents a commitment from the publisher and perhaps some of the first real earnings you've seen from your labors. In many cases, it may be the only money an author ever sees from his book. Big advances are impressive, but most authors begin their careers with more modest amounts.

The size of the advance is influenced by a number of factors. There are some basic rules of thumb that your agent can explain in more detail, but generally the price of the book, the projected first printing and royalty rate are used to calculate the size of the advance. Multiply the price by the royalty percentage, and multiply that by the number of copies to be sold. This will give you a ballpark figure a publisher may reasonably be expected to pay—but don't be surprised if it's below that.

Ethan Ellenberg *has led his own New York-based literary agency for more than a decade. The agency has more than 70 clients and specializes in commercial fiction, especially romance and thrillers; nonfiction books on health/spirituality; and children's books of all types.*

Royalty

Once you've explored the question of the advance, you move on to a topic that ultimately may prove more important, the royalty.

Large advances are wonderful, I negotiate them all the time. But for the first-time author it's unlikely that the underlying economics of the deal are going to provide one. Certainly, the bigger the better, but over the long haul the royalty is more important. The advance is, technically, "the advance against royalties," the money the publisher pays to secure rights to your book. The royalty is the amount of money you earn per book sold. Your publisher's accounting department will keep track of all the royalty income your book earns and subtract it from the amount of your advance. Only when your royalty income exceeds your advance amount do you start seeing royalty checks.

Royalties are the truly great thing about book publishing. Even the most modest book can generate thousands of dollars in income if the royalty percentages are high enough. The difference between a 10 percent royalty or a 15 percent royalty is enormous if your book sells year after year. Negotiating the royalty is, in my opinion, the most important part of a first timer's deal.

The first thing your agent needs to nail down is what the royalty is based upon: "list" or "net." The list or cover price of the book means the publisher pays you a percentage of the price charged to the public. Let's say the book sells for $9.95 and the royalty is 10 percent. You'd get 99½ cents per book. Structurally this is the best royalty you can get.

The other basis for a royalty is "net" or publisher's receipts. Here you are getting a royalty based on the amount the publisher receives when the books is sold. Let's say the publisher sells your book with a 50 percent discount to a large bookstore chain. With a cover price of $9.95 the publisher is only getting $4.48 per book. Your 10 percent is calculated on that, so your royalty is only 45 cents.

As you can see, the cover price royalty is a better deal and preferable. If your royalty will be based on the amount received, your agent should negotiate a higher percentage for the royalty rate.

Many contracts also specify royalty "escalators." Escalation means the more copies you sell, the higher your royalty goes. Though you may receive a 10 percent royalty on the first 5,000 copies, you will get 12½ percent on the next 5,000, and 15 percent on all copies thereafter.

Rights

Subsidiary rights are another important area of book publishing. Your book may be a springboard for the material to appear in any number of different media that can generate income. I'm sure you're familiar with big name authors and the different formats their books end up in. Movie rights, audio rights, book club rights, foreign rights are all negotiated in the subsidiary rights section of your contract. There are industry standards which are observed for the most part. For instance, the publisher almost always has book club rights, and it's very rare for the publisher to get movie rights, but ultimately everything is negotiable and this is where your agent will really earn his commission.

In almost all cases, your agent will want to keep as many rights as possible. If your agent sells the rights the publisher does not get a percentage. The income for these rights won't be counted against your advance, which means you keep more of the pie and it gets to your plate quicker. In cases where rights are retained by the publisher your agent can negotiate the split of income. Foreign rights are often divided 75 percent to the author and 25 percent to the publisher, but a number of publishers will try to divide it 60/40 or even 50/50. Thousands of dollars may be at stake here and working out the percentages is an important part of your agent's job.

Timely publication

The fourth important area for a new author is timely publication. You want to get into the marketplace. You don't want to be scheduled years away. Publication of your first book is the most important thing you can do to advance your career. Before you accept any offer, find out when you will be published and get some sort of guarantee. Most contracts offer a time period of 12 to 18 months after acceptance of the finished manuscript. If the publisher fails to bring the book out within the time frame noted in the contract, these rights should return to you, without any further obligation to that publisher.

You not only want to be published, you want your book to be *successfully* published. Although plans will not be very firm when a book is bought, issues worth discussing include the size of the first printing, marketing plans, ideas for the cover, author participation in publicity such as book tours or media interviews. If a book doesn't sell, the royalty and rights situation is meaningless.

Outside of the deal

Your publishing contract will cover a host of other clauses related to you and your performance. Warranty and indemnity clauses, delivery clauses, non-competition clauses are all very important issues your agent needs to help you understand. But if you do your homework and work with your agent, you'll both make it through the legal maze.

How Things Work: Foreign Rights

by Don Prues

Our world is contracting, coming together like loose paper clips gravitating toward a magnet. More than ever, countries from around the world are taking an interest in cultures outside their own. And American culture is at the top of most lists. Many foreign countries are so interested in "Americana" that they're eating our Big Macs, viewing our *Die Hard*s, and buying our books by the millions. James Redfield's *The Celestine Prophecy*, for example, has been at the top of many foreign bestseller lists, earning lots of money along the way. I'm sure you wouldn't mind if your book followed a similar course. That's why you—and your agent—must possess a strong knowledge of foreign rights.

Understanding foreign rights

If you sell your manuscript to a U.S. publisher, you typically give that publisher exclusive rights to distribute an English-language edition of your book in the U.S. and its territories, the Philippines, and Canada. That's it. All other rights are yours, including "secondary" or "ancillary" rights, which consist of British Commonwealth rights, first serial rights, merchandising rights, performance rights, and, yes, foreign rights.

So what are foreign rights? "With foreign rights you are taking a book that was or will be originally published in English in the U.S. and selling it to publishers in foreign countries, which means you sell the right for a foreign publisher to translate your work and distribute it abroad," says Lisa Erbach Vance of the Aaron M. Priest Literary Agency. So when you sell a book to a foreign publisher you sell the translation rights, and, in most cases, you also give them world rights in that language. "For example, if you sell French rights to a French publisher, you give that publisher permission to publish that book in French anywhere in the world. They could even distribute the French translation of the book in the United States."

If many countries share the same language, do translation and world rights still go hand in hand? "Not necessarily," says Erbach Vance. "Sometimes, as in the case of Spanish rights, you might not sell the world rights to anyone. Instead, you might sell Latin American rights separately from continental Spanish rights. And for foreign English language publishers, as in England, you usually sell them U.K.-B.C. (British Commonwealth) rights, in which case they could distribute their edition in Australia, India, and many other countries and territories where they have jurisdiction. Of course, they couldn't sell it in the United States and its territories."

Ways to sell them

You can do one of three things with your book's foreign rights. First, you can sell them to your publisher. While most publishers pay an advance for the foreign rights, they also take at least 25-50 percent of the royalties. Moreover, they often apply your

Don Prues *is an editor at* Writer's Digest Books *and will be the editor of the 1997* Guide to Literary Agents *as well as assistant editor of the 1997* Writer's Market.

share of foreign rights proceeds to your original advance. This creates a problem if your U.S. royalties don't match your advance, because the publisher will retain your foreign rights money until your original advance is earned out. So there's a chance you wouldn't see a penny of the money when selling foreign rights to your publisher. As you can tell, it is usually unwise to just flat-out sell foreign rights to a publisher, unless you think your book won't sell in foreign markets. Then you might want to take the publisher's offer.

A second option is to let your agent try to sell the rights to a foreign publisher. While having your agent do it alone can earn you a large percentage of royalties from foreign sales—because agents only take 10 to 15 percent, thus leaving you with 85 to 90 percent—most agents prefer not to work this way. It's not that they're lazy or incompetent, it's just difficult because geographical distances create communication problems. Foreign publishers like to work person to person; they like to know who they're working with. That's why many agents most often go through a foreign subagent to sell foreign rights.

Working with a foreign subagent is a common and sensible approach when selling foreign rights. "We almost always use foreign subagents," says Erbach Vance. "It's a very effective way to do business abroad. We keep foreign subagents informed of what we have coming up, even before we have material to show them, so that they know what's in the works. And then when we have the material to show them, which is usually a complete manuscript, we get it to them as soon as possible. We then send galleys and review copies. After foreign rights are purchased, we keep the subagent updated with press material, reviews, and the book's overall status."

Another advantage of using a foreign subagent is that your book doesn't have to earn out its advance before you can begin receiving the foreign rights money. As Erbach Vance says, "The author receives the money through us right away. We take 10 percent of the sale and the subagent takes 10 percent. The writer gets the rest." Sounds great, doesn't it? It might also give you the idea that it's *never* wise to sell foreign rights to your publisher. Wrong.

When to sell them

How do you know when to keep foreign rights and when to sell them to your publisher? If your book has international appeal, don't sell the foreign rights to your publisher—unless you're offered a really big foreign rights advance. And how do you know if your book has international appeal? There are no guarantees, but we'll give you some idea.

"We've been successful abroad with big, international-type thrillers," says Erbach Vance. "Also, books that do extremely well in the U.S. and have universal appeal do well internationally. For example, *The Bridges of Madison County* has been enormously successful overseas because it is a touching, romantic, very human story—those qualities translate well in any language."

Although romantic, *Bridges* is considered mainstream fiction, not genre romance. But that doesn't mean there isn't international demand for genre romance. There is. In fact, genre fiction in general can be lucrative in other countries, because there's a general appeal in these books. In Japan, for instance, thrillers and science fiction do exceptionally well. Mystery, of course, does well in England and all of Europe, as does science fiction. And romances thrive in Australia. On the other hand, romances, especially erotic, rarely sell well in places like Italy, Spain and South America, which have strong Catholic histories. You can bet westerns don't fare so well beyond our borders, and neither do nonfiction books with subjects that are primarily popular in America, such as the American Revolution, the Civil War, and our obsessions with health, wealth and self-help. Your agent will have a good idea what you should do with your book's foreign rights. If he or she doesn't, find one who does.

In determining what to do with your book's foreign rights, it comes down to a bit of a gamble. Some books do terribly in the States but are great sellers overseas. So, yes, sometimes foreign rights pay more than domestic rights. Says Erbach Vance, "If we think that we can make more on foreign rights than what a publisher offers, then of course we'll keep those rights. If, on the other hand, a domestic publisher offers more than what we think we could make, we'll sell the foreign rights to the publisher and let them take care of it. It really depends on the book. For our agency, though, in most cases we keep the foreign rights. That's because we take foreign sales very seriously."

So should you.

Are You Ready for a Change?

by Rosalyn Alsobrook

How does a writer know when it is time to change agents? Tricky question. Because every situation is different, there are no pat answers, no preset rules to follow.

Every author-agent relationship is unique in some way, yet all are based on the same need for the writer to have someone trustworthy, who knows the publishing business as well or better than she does, to handle the marketing end of her work to the best of that person's ability.

If that need is not being met, then you, the author, have every right to look elsewhere. Having the wrong agent is like being in a bad marriage, only this bad marriage affects more than just your peace of mind; it affects the very success of your writing career.

But how can you be sure changing agents is the right move, and how do you go about making such a switch once the decision is made? Tough questions. The answers vary according to the situation.

Points to consider:

First, know that agents are busy people and different agents have different business practices in such areas as reporting on the progress of a manuscript, itemized statements of expenses and the like. Supposedly, you asked your agent what those practices were before agreeing to do business together. If not, that was *your* mistake, not the agent's, though the agent should have made those practices clear from the start.

Some reasons are unjustified

To get a better perspective of what makes a legitimate reason for change, let's start by looking at a few complaints that are *not* suitable causes for change.

- *"Somebody else's agent does such and such."* Again, every agent has his or her own set business practices. While a friend's agent may call her just to see how she's doing, or sends flowers and balloons after a hefty contract has been signed, not all agents do this, just as not all agents go to the publisher's place of business and walk a deal through, though some might. If your agent is performing the job you've assigned him or her to do, which is market your work for the best deal possible, then not receiving flowers or chatty phone calls isn't important.
- *"I've called three times this week and left a message on my agent's answering machine each time, but she has yet to return those calls."* Good agents are busy people. They have other clients besides you. It's possible that clients with more pressing needs are taking up his time just now. Or, it could be the agent is ill. Contrary to rumor, agents are human, too. Like the rest of us, they catch colds, break legs, and have car accidents. If that's the case, you will eventually learn about the problem. Give it a week or two, then try writing a polite letter asking if there's a problem.
- *"My agent never lets me know exactly where my work is."* Have you ever really asked the agent to provide this information? What was the response if you asked? Did your agent agree, or were reasons given that this sometimes might not be possible? If your agent explained at the beginning that there may be times when he is too swamped to call about

With 26 novels, **Rosalyn Alsobrook** *writes for Pinnacle, Zebra Books, Harlequin American, and is the co-creator of the Seascape series coming out in 1996 from St. Martin's Press.*

every little change, you really have no gripe. But if that agent told you to expect a regular, detailed account and you aren't getting that, then you have to wonder what other promises aren't being kept.

Legitimate concerns

I know why I recently changed agents, but to get a better perspective on what other writers think, I polled authors in the "Romance and Women's Fiction Writer's Exchange" and the "Science Fiction and Fantasy Roundtable" on GEnie Information Services. Here are several of the responses:

● It is *definitely a reason* to consider a change if in a casual conversation with an editor you find out a manuscript you thought he or she has been sitting on for the past eight months was returned to your agent five months ago. *What?* And your agent didn't bother to tell you? Definitely time to reconsider that agent. If you then learn the agent has kept that same manuscript since its return, which is why you never heard anything, find yourself a new agent—*and quick.*

● It's time for a change if the reason you went with your agent in the first place is no longer applicable. Your needs will change as your career grows. If you are moving in new directions with your career and your agent feels uncomfortable representing the new work, you have the wrong person working for you.

● You need someone else if your career has stalled and your agent does little to get it moving again. Sometimes all that is needed is a fresh approach. You'll do both yourself and the agent a great favor by moving on. Remember, unless your agent is clearly striving to propel your writing career to the next level, it's time to find one who will.

● If your agent is no longer excited about your work, find an agent who is. If the enthusiasm is gone, or at least is not evident until *after* the manuscript has sold, it's impossible for the agent to work up an editor's excitement toward your work.

● When your agent seems determined to pigeonhole your work, you're in trouble. An agent shouldn't discourage you from trying something different. Just because your historical romances are doing extremely well with Publisher A doesn't mean you shouldn't be allowed to stretch your wings and try a murder mystery with Publisher B.

● Another reason to shop around is if the receptionist knows more about your work than does the agent. Not a good sign. You should also look elsewhere if your option material sits on your agent's desk, unopened, for six weeks.

● Don't hang around if your agent lies or deceives you. Dishonesty is the unpardonable sin.

● You have the wrong agent if yours made unreasonable demands against your wishes and, as a result, lost a promising contract. Any time an agent purposely violates your instructions, it's time to find someone new.

● If you discover your agent doesn't read your material and keeps sending it to the same publisher and accepting whatever is offered without negotiating a new contract, why bother with that agent? This you could do yourself.

● Don't hang around if you find your agent likes to take month-long vacations without leaving anyone behind to tend to problems that might arise in the interim.

● When a personality clash develops that affects your writing, either work out your differences or move on.

● When a mega-bucks worth of contracts sit on your agent's desk for three months, not moving even after you have called several times to inquire about them, there's a problem.

● Don't stay with an agent whose check bounces or arrives two months late. Leave if you've telephoned the publisher and find out a check was mailed to the agent months ago, but when you call the agent no one can find a record of it.

● You certainly don't need an agent who curses at you for having the audacity to telephone and voice a few reasonable concerns.

● If your agent has lost his or her taste for the business, realize that agents can burn out too. When that happens, you're doing both of you a favor by finding someone else.

What to do once the decision is made

After you have decided you need a new agent, how do you go about finding the right representative?

(Again, not an easy question to answer.)

First, consider the old or present agent. What proposals do you have out under his name? Will this agent agree the partnership isn't working and be willing to relinquish those submissions to a new agent? If not, you'll want to wait until all submitted copies have been returned to you and are no longer under consideration by anyone before pulling them and taking them to a new agent. If, by chance, one of the submissions still out is approved, the old agent should be the agent to handle the sale.

If you have a written contract with the old agent that in any way includes a particular title, then you'll need a written release, or no matter who sells the book, the old agent can still claim his percentage. It's legal and it's fair.

But suppose you are already free and clear of the old agent? Then what?

If you're like me, the first thing you need to do is clear the butterflies out of your stomach. Although this is an important step in your career, there is nothing to fear (sure, easy for me to say–I'm not the one preparing to make all those telephone calls). In truth, agents are more bark than bite.

Second, ask around about agents at conferences, writer's meetings and on electronic bulletin boards. Find out who likes what agents for what reasons. If those reasons make sense to you, if you find qualities you would like to have in your agent, then write down that agent's name. Compile a list of at least four names that interest you.

Next, make sure you have the current address and telephone number for each agent. Because I advise calling over writing a letter, if for no other reason than it moves the process along more quickly, set aside enough time to talk to them all on the same day should you be lucky enough to catch them in their offices.

Making contact with prospective agents

Simply call and ask to speak to the agent. If someone else answers and asks who is calling, give your name and state that you are calling to ask questions about the agency. Don't give this other person your whole spiel. That is not necessary and this person does not care. Save it for the agent. This goes for an answering machine as well. State who you are and your business but do not go into depth on the machine.

When you speak with the agent, sound confident but not overbearing. State again who you are, that you are seeking representation and assessing agents, and you want to know how she does business.

Have your questions ready, but don't interrogate the agent. Work your questions into the conversation as it progresses. The conversation will take a life of its own, allowing you to find out just how compatible you and this agent might be. Conversational drift can be just as informative, if not more so, than the items you have on the paper in front of you.

After discussing how that agent does business, collecting the information you need to make a viable decision while also getting references, it is time to talk about you. Have another list of what you've written, what's been published, awards you've won, what you are working on, what you plan to work on next, and which editors are holding your submissions at the moment. If you are in the transition stage of leaving an old agent, mention that, too.

Afterward, if the agent is still interested and hasn't indicated a desire to end the conversation, just chat for a few minutes. Find out the agent's likes and dislikes. Get to know each other. Promise to send some of your work if asked, and talk about how you might work together should an agreement be reached, but don't commit during the first conversation. Even if you really like talking to this person and like what has been said, don't commit during that first telephone call. There is still a chance the next agent might impress you more.

As soon as you hang up with the agent, make notes about the call. In my case, I came up with what I call my "points list." It helped me gauge my reaction and record my initial impressions. It also helped me recall what had been discussed and what issues had been skirted.

Reaching a decision

After talking to all the agents, look over your score sheets and decide which agent impressed you the most. Send that person whatever he or she asked to see, but don't ignore the others you called. As soon as you've reached an agreement with an agent, write the others pleasant, business-like letters explaining how nice it was to talk with them but that you won't be sending them anything after all. Never leave anyone hanging. It's unprofessional.

If you really can't decide between two agents, and they haven't made an issue of "exclusive submissions only," then send your work to both. But be clear that you are multiple submitting. Always play fair.

Having had the presence of mind to ask the agent how long it will take her to get to your submission, wait several days past that time before making a follow up call. Give the agent some leeway. Who knew the agent was destined to come down with the flu, or that someone was about to plow into her car when you were promised a call back that next Friday? If the agent said Friday, give her at least until the middle of the following week.

If, after reading your submission, the agent decides maybe you weren't meant for each other after all, be gracious. Thank the agent for the time spent, then look at your points list and see who scored second highest. Suddenly, that person looks even better to you. Send that agent your work and continue from there.

Agent Comparison Points List
by Rosalyn Alsobrook

[This is a means of helping gauge which of the agents contacted is best for you. This list is just a starting point. Your priorities may differ from mine in which case you'd adjust your point spread acordingly.]

FEES & MONEY:

10%	5 points	_____
15% with low breakpoint	3 points	_____
15% with high breakpoint	2 points	_____
Flat 15%	1 point	_____
Over 15%	-4 points	_____
Charges office costs	-2 points	_____

PERSONALITY:

Interested to talk to me	2 points	_____
Sounded friendly	1-4 points	_____
Sounded enthusiastic	1-6 points	_____
Asked ME lots of questions	2 points	_____
Laughed at least once	1 point	_____
Sounded depressing	-2 points	_____

PAYOUT:

Same day turnaround	6 points	_____
Next day turnaround	4 points	_____
5 day turnaround	2 points	_____
10 day turnaround	1 points	_____
Won't be specific	-5 points	_____

MISCELLANEOUS:

One bonus point each:

Talked about career growth immediately	_____
Mentioned works well with houses I like	_____
Offered references without asking	_____

Two bonus points each:

Forwards copies of correspondence if asked	_____
Informs about all telephone calls	_____
Prefers a verbal agreement over contract	_____
Glowing reports from those references checked	_____
Attends conferences	_____

MOST IMPORTANT:

10 points:

Has personal contacts for foreign rights	_____

20 points each:

Has escrow account for royalties if needed	_____
Will provides keeping my $ out of estate	_____

Literary Agents:
Nonfee-charging

Agents listed in this section generate from 98 to 100 percent of their income from commission on sales. They do not charge for reading, critiquing, editing, marketing or other services. They make their living solely from their contacts and experience, with time their most limited commodity.

For you as a writer looking for an agent, this can cut two ways. On one hand, it will cost you no more than postage to have your work considered by an agent with an imperative to find saleable manuscripts: Her income depends on her clients' incomes. Her job is to know the market, who is buying what and when. Effective agents generally know a large number of editors who specialize in a variety of work, and know how to present a work to producers and studios interested in TV and movie rights. They capitalize on that knowledge and devote their time to selling.

On the other hand, these agents must be more selective, offering representation to writers whose work is outstanding and requires minimal shaping and editing. They often prefer to work with established authors, celebrities or those with professional credentials in a particular field. These agents simply don't have the time to nurture a beginning writer through many stages of development before a work is saleable.

Standard operating procedures

Most agents open to submissions prefer to receive initially a query letter that briefly describes your work. Some agents (particularly those dealing largely in fiction) ask for an outline and a number of sample chapters, but you should send these only if you are requested to do so in an agent's listing. It takes time for the agents to answer the detailed questionnaires we use to compile the listings. If an agent specifies what to send her, follow it to the letter. She is telling you exactly what she needs to judge your abilities and extend an offer of representation.

Always send a self-addressed stamped envelope (SASE) or postcard for reply. If you have not heard back from an agent within the approximate reporting time given (allowing for holidays and summer vacations) a quick, polite call to ask when it will be reviewed would be in order. Never fax or e-mail a query letter, outline or sample chapters to an agent without permission to do so. Due to the volume of material they receive, it may take a long time to receive a reply, so you may want to query several agents at a time. It is best, however, to have the complete manuscript considered by only one agent at a time.

Commissions range from 10 to 15 percent for domestic sales and usually are higher for foreign or dramatic sales, often 20 to 25 percent. The difference goes to the subagent who places the work.

Many agents in this section charge for ordinary business expenses in addition to the commission. Expenses can include foreign postage, fax charges, long distance phone calls, messenger and express mail services and photocopying. Some charge only for what they consider "extraordinary" expenses. Make sure you have a clear understanding of what these are before signing an agency agreement. Most agents will agree to discuss these expenses as they arise.

While most agents deduct expenses from the advance or royalties before passing them on to the author, a few agents included here charge a low ($100 or less) one-time only expense fee upfront. Sometimes these are called "marketing" or "handling" fees. Agents charging more than $100 in marketing fees are included in the Literary Agents: Fee-charging section.

Effective January 1, 1996, all members of the Association of Authors' Representatives (AAR) are prohibited from charging reading or evaluation fees.

Special indexes and additional help

To help you with your search, we've included a number of special indexes in the back of the book. The Subject Index is divided into sections for nonfee-charging and fee-charging literary agents and script agents. Each of thse sections in the index is then divided by nonfiction and fiction subject categories. Some agencies indicated that they were open to all nonfiction or fiction topics. These have been grouped in the subject heading "open" in each section. This year we have added a number of new topics, including education, how-to, humor and popular culture in nonfiction, and horror in fiction. Many agents have indicated additional areas of interest in their listings this year.

We've included an Agent Index as well. Often you will read about an agent who is an employee of a larger agency and may not be able to locate her business phone or address. We asked agencies to list the agents on staff, then listed the names in alphabetical order along with the name of the agency they work for. Find the name of the person you would like to contact and then check the agency listing. You will find the page number for the agency's listing in the Listings Index.

A Geographic Index lists agents state by state for those who are looking for an agent close to home. A Client Acceptance Policies index lists agencies according to their openness to new clients.

Many literary agents are also interested in scripts; many script agents will also consider book manuscripts. Nonfee-charging script agents who primarily sell scripts but also handle at least 10 to 15 percent book manuscripts appear among the listings in this section, with the contact information, breakdown of work currently handled and a note to check the full listing in the script section. Those nonfee-charging script agencies that sell scripts and less than 10 to 15 percent book manuscripts appear in "Additional Nonfee-charging Agents" at the end of this section. Complete listings for these agents appear in the Script Agent section.

Before contacting any agency, check the listing to make sure it is open to new clients. Those designated (**V**) are currently not interested in expanding their rosters.

For more information on approaching agents and the specifics of the listings, read How to Use Your Guide to Literary Agents and How to Find (and Keep) The Right Agent. Also see the various articles at the beginning of the book for explorations of different aspects of the author/agent relationship.

We've ranked the agencies listed in this section according to their openness to submissions. Below is our ranking system:

I Newer agency actively seeking clients.

II Agency seeking both new and established writers.

III Agency prefers to work with established writers, mostly obtains new clients through referrals.

IV Agency handling only certain types of work or work by writers under certain circumstances.

V Agency not currently seeking new clients. We have included mention of agencies rated **V** to let you know they are currently not open to new clients. In addition to those ranked **V**, we have included a few well-known agencies' names who have declined the opportunity to receive full listings at this time. *Unless you have a strong recommendation from someone well respected in the field, our advice is to approach only those agents ranked I-IV.*

‡**DOMINICK ABEL LITERARY AGENCY, INC., (II, III)**, 146 W. 82nd St., #1B, New York NY 10024. Estab. 1975. Member of AAR. Represents 100 clients. 1% of clients are new/previously unpublished writers.
Handles: Nonfiction books, novels. Considers these fiction areas: detective/police/crime; mystery/suspense. Query.
Recent Sales: *Shares*, by A.W. Gray (Simon & Schuster); *Zolar's Book of Reincarnation*, by Zolar (Fireside/Simon & Schuster); *Lieberman's Law*, by Stuart Kaminsky (Holt); *Lightning*, by John Lutz (author of *Single White Female*) (Holt).
Terms: Agent receives 10% commission on domestic sales; 20% on foreign sales. No written contract. 100% of business is derived from commissions on ms sales.

‡**ACT I, (II)**, 1523 Washington Ave., Miami Beach FL 33139. (305)674-1113. Fax: (305)672-8705. Contact: Peggi McKinley, Arnold Soloway. Estab. 1993. Signatory of WGA. Represents 15 clients. 35% of clients are new/previously unpublished writers. Currently handles: 5% nonfiction books; 10% novels; 30% movie scripts; 30% TV scripts; 5% stage plays; 10% syndicated material; 10% other.
• See the expanded listing for this agency in Script Agents.

ACTON, LEONE, HANSON & JAFFE, INC., (II), 928 Broadway, Suite #303, New York NY 10010. (212)254-5800. Fax: (212)254-6140. Contact: M. Perkins. Estab. 1976. Member of AAR. Represents 200 clients. 30% of clients are new/previously unpublished writers. Specializes in commercial nonfiction and fiction; some category fiction; some literary fiction. Currently handles: 50% nonfiction books; 50% novels.
Handles: Nonfiction books, novels. Considers these nonfiction areas: animals; biography/autobiography; business; child guidance/parenting; current affairs; ethnic/cultural interests; gay/lesbian issues; government/politics/law; history; humor; military/war; money/finance/economics; music/dance/theater/film; nature/environment; New Age/metaphysics; popular culture; psychology; religious/inspirational; science/technology; self-help/personal improvement; sports; true crime/investigative; women's issues/women's studies. Considers these fiction areas: action/adventure; contemporary issues; detective/police/crime; erotica; ethnic; family saga; feminist; glitz; historical; literary; mainstream; mystery/suspense; romance; sports; thriller/espionage. Query. Reports in 2 weeks on queries; 1 month on fiction mss and 3 weeks on nonfiction mss.
Recent Sales: *I Was Right On Time*, by Buck O'Neil with Steve Wulf (Simon & Schuster); *Stephanie Winston's Best Organizing Tips*, by Stephanie Winston (Fireside/Simon & Schuster); *Mindhunter*, by John Douglas & Mark Olshaker (Scribner); nonfiction by Phil Simms (William Morrow).
Terms: Agent receives 15% commission on domestic sales; 19% on foreign sales. Offers written contract. Charges for photocopying and express mail.
Tips: Obtains new clients through recommendations from others. Requires SASE for response.

ADLER & ROBIN BOOKS INC., (II), 3409 29th St., Suite 3, Washington DC 20008. (202)363-7410. Fax: (202)686-1804. E-mail: adlerbks@clark.net. Contact: Lisa M. Swayne. Estab. 1986. Represents 30 clients. 20% of clients are new/previously unpublished writers. Currently handles: 98% nonfiction books; 2% juvenile books. Member agents: Bill Adler, Jr. (commercial nonfiction, biographies, pop culture books); Lisa M. Swayne (fiction, particularly mysteries and first novels; women's health, pop culture books, computer books).
Handles: Nonfiction books. Considers these nonfiction areas: biography/autobiography; business; child guidance/parenting; computers/electronics; cooking/food/nutrition; current affairs; ethnic/cultural interests; gay/lesbian issues; government/politics/law; health/medicine; history; how-to; money/finance/economics; nature/environment; popular culture; true crime/investigative; women's issues/

 The double dagger before a listing indicates the listing is new in this edition.

women's studies. Considers these fiction areas: contemporary issues; detective/police/crime; literary; mainstream; mystery/suspense; romance (contemporary, gothic, historical, regency); science fiction; thriller/espionage. Query with outline/proposal. Reports in 2 months on queries.
Recent Sales: *Movie Business,* by Laurence Snelling (Kingston/HarperCollins); *The African-American Resource Guide to the Internet,* by Stafford Battle and Rey Harris (McGraw Hill); *Off Wall Street: The Theory of the Firm Unplugged,* by Barry J. Gibbons (Irwin).
Terms: Agent receives 15% commission on domestic and foreign sales. Offers written contract.
Writers' Conferences: ABA (Chicago, June); Mid-Atlantic Book Fair (Baltimore).
Tips: Obtains new clients through recommendations.

AGENCY CHICAGO, (II), 601 S. LaSalle St. #600A, Chicago IL 60605. Contact: Ernest Santucci. Estab. 1990. 50% of clients are new/previously unpublished writers. Specializes in corporate histories, stories, biographies. Art (American), and stage plays.
Handles: Nonfiction books. Considers these nonfiction areas: travel, fitness; gambling; sports; crime. Considers these fiction areas: erotica; experimental. Send outline/proposal, résumé and SASE.
Terms: Agent receives 10-15% commission on domestic sales; 15% on foreign sales. Offers written contract.
Writers' Conferences: Midwest Writers Conference; International Writers and Translators Conference; ABA.
Tips: Obtains new clients through recommendations. "Do not send dot matrix printed manuscripts. Manuscripts and letters should have a clean professional look, with correct grammar and punctuation." Include SASE or material will be confidentially recycled. No phone calls.

AGENTS INC. FOR MEDICAL AND MENTAL HEALTH PROFESSIONALS, (II), P.O. Box 4956, Fresno CA 93744-4956. Phone/fax: (209)248-0345. Director: Sydney H. Harriet, Ph.D. Estab. 1987. Member of APA. Represents 45 clients. 20% of clients are new/previously unpublished writers. Specializes in "writers who have education and experience in the medical, mental health and legal professions. It is helpful if the writer is licensed, but not necessary. Prior book publication not necessary." Currently handles: 95% nonfiction books; 5% novels.
Handles: Nonfiction books, novels. Considers these nonfiction areas: business; current affairs; health/medicine; how-to; nutrition; psychology; reference; science/technology; self-help/personal improvement; sociology; sports medicine/psychology; mind-body healing. Currently representing only previously published novelists. Query with vita and SASE. Reports in 2 weeks on queries; 1 month on mss.
Recent Sales: *Nobody's Victim,* by Christopher McCullough, Ph. D. (Clarkson Potter); *I'm An Abortion Doctor,* by Suzeanne T. Peppema, M.D. (Prometheus); *What To Eat If You Have Cancer,* by Maureen Keane and Danielle Chase (Contemporary); *The Healthy Gourmet,* by Cherie Calbom (Clarkson Potter).
Terms: Agent receives 15% commission on domestic sales; 20% on foreign sales. Offers written contract, binding for 6-12 months (negotiable).
Writers' Conferences: Scheduled at a number of conferences across the country in 1996-97. Available for conferences by request.
Tips: "Please, please, ask yourself why someone would be compelled to buy your book. If you think the idea is unique, spend the time to create a proposal where every word counts. Please avoid calling to pitch an idea. The only way we can judge the quality of your idea is to see it in writing. We are much in need of business-oriented proposals. Unfortunately, we cannot respond to queries or proposals without receiving a return envelope and sufficient postage."

THE JOSEPH S. AJLOUNY AGENCY, (II), 29205 Greening Blvd., Farmington Hills MI 48334-2945. (810)932-0090. Fax: (810)932-8763. E-mail: agencyajl@aol.com. Contact: Joe Ajlouny. Estab. 1987. Signatory of WGA. "Represents humor and comedy writers, humorous illustrators, cartoonists." Member agents: Joe Ajlouny (original humor, how-to); Elena Pantel (music, popular culture); Gwen Foss (general nonfiction).
Handles: "In addition to humor and titles concerning American popular culture, we will consider general nonfiction in the areas of 'how-to' books, history, joke books, cookbooks, popular reference, trivia, biography and memoirs." Query first with SASE. Reports in 2-4 weeks.
Recent Sales: *Politically Correct American History,* by Edward Moser (Crown); *How to Be a Hollywood Superstar,* by Barry Dutter (General Pub.); *No Chairs Make for Short Meetings,* by Richard Rybolt (NAL/Dutton); *Famous Peoples' Cats,* by Ronna Mogelon (St. Martin's Press).
Terms: Agent receives 15% commission on domestic sales. Charges for postage, photocopying and phone expenses. Foreign and subsidiary rights commission fees established on per-sale basis.
Writers' Conferences ABA (Chicago); Mid-America Publishers Assoc. (Grand Rapids MI, September) Book Fair (Frankfurt, Germany, October).
Tips: Obtains new clients "typically from referrals and by some advertising and public relations projects. We also frequently speak at seminars for writers on the process of being published. Just make

sure your project is clever, marketable and professionally prepared. We see too much material that is limited in scope and appeal. It helps immeasurably to have credentials in the field or topic being written about. Please do not submit material that is not within our areas of specialization."

LEE ALLAN AGENCY, (II), P.O. Box 18617, Milwaukee WI 53218-0617. (414)357-7708. Fax: call for number. Contact: Lee Matthias. Estab. 1983. Signatory of WGA. Represents 15 clients. 50% of clients are new/previously unpublished writers. Specializes in suspense fiction. Currently handles: 95% novels; 5% movie scripts; 5% TV scripts. Member agents: Lee A. Matthias (all types of genre fiction and screenplays; Andrea Knickerbocker (fantasy, science fiction, romance); (Mr.) Chris Hill (fantasy).
  ● This agency reports that it is closed to queries and submissions for books through 12/96. See the expanded listing for this agency in Script Agents.

JAMES ALLEN, LITERARY AGENCY, (III), P.O. Box 278, Milford PA 18337-0278. Estab. 1974. Signatory of WGA. Represents 40 clients. 10% of clients are new/previously unpublished writers. "I handle all kinds of genre fiction (except westerns) and specialize in science fiction and fantasy." Currently handles: 2% nonfiction books; 8% juvenile books; 90% novels.
Handles: Novels. Considers these nonfiction areas: history; true crime/investigative. Considers these fiction areas: action/adventure; detective/police/crime; family saga; fantasy; glitz; historical; horror; mainstream; mystery/suspense; romance (contemporary historical); science fiction; young adult. Query. Responds in 1 week on queries; 2 months on mss. "I prefer first contact to be a query letter with two-three page plot synopsis and SASE with a response time of 1 week. If my interest is piqued, I then ask for the first four chapters, response time two weeks. If I'm impressed by the writing, I then ask for the balance of the manuscript, response time about two months."
Recent Sales: *As the Wolf Loves Winter*, by David Poyer (Tor/Forge); *Down to a Sunless Sea*, by David Poyer (St. Martin's Press); *Wish List*, by Jeane Renick (HarperMonogram); *Cataract*, by Tara Harper (Del Rey); *Black Water*, by Doug Allyn (St. Martin's Press).
Terms: Agent receives 10% commission on domestic print sales; 20% on film sales; 20% on foreign sales. Offers written contract, binding for 3 years "automatically renewed. No reading fees or other up-front charges. I reserve the right to charge for extraordinary expenses. I do not bill the author, but deduct the charges from incoming earnings."
Writers' Conferences: First Coast Writers Festival (Jacksonville FL); California Writers Club Conference (Pacific Grove CA); Writing on the Sea (Bahamas, October).
Tips: *"First time at book length need NOT* apply—only taking on authors who have the foundations of their writing careers in place and can use help in building the rest. A cogent, to-the-point query letter is necessary, laying out the author's track record and giving a brief blurb for the book. The response to a mere 'I have written a novel, will you look at it?' is universally 'NO!' "

LINDA ALLEN LITERARY AGENCY, (II), 1949 Green St., Suite 5, San Francisco CA 94123. (415)921-6437. Contact: Linda Allen or Amy Kossow. Estab. 1982. Represents 35-40 clients. Specializes in "good books and nice people."
Handles: Nonfiction, novels (adult and juvenile). Considers these nonfiction areas: anthropology/archaeology; art/architecture/design; biography/autobiography; business; child guidance/parenting; computers/electronics; ethnic/cultural interests; gay/lesbian issues; government/politics/law; history; juvenile nonfiction; music/dance/theater/film; nature/environment; New Age/metaphysics; popular culture; psychology; sociology; true crime/investigative; women's issues/women's studies. Considers these fiction areas: action/adventure; contemporary issues; detective/police/crime; ethnic; fantasy; feminist; gay; glitz; horror; juvenile; lesbian; literary; mainstream; mystery/suspense; psychic/supernatural; regional; romance (regency); science fiction; thriller/espionage; young adult. Query with SASE. Reports in 2-3 weeks on queries.
Terms: Agent receives 15% commission. Charges for photocopying.
Tips: Obtains new clients "by referral mostly."

MIRIAM ALTSHULER LITERARY AGENCY, (II), 5 Old Post Rd., RR#1 Box 5, Red Hook NY 12571. (914)758-9408. Fax: (914)758-3118. Contact: Miriam Altshuler. Estab. 1994. Member of AAR. Represents 35 clients. 20% of clients are new/previously unpublished writers. Specializes in literary and commercial fiction and nonfiction. Mostly adult, a few young adult and children's books. Currently handles: 45% nonfiction; 10% juvenile books; 45% novels.
Handles: Nonfiction books, novels. Considers these nonfiction areas: biography/autobiography; current affairs; ethnic/cultural interests; gay/lesbian issues; history; nature/environment; psychology; women's issues/women's studies. Considers these fiction areas: ethnic; feminist; gay; literary; mainstream. Query. Must send SASE. Reports in 2 weeks on queries; 3 weeks on mss.
Recent Sales: *Ansel Adams: A Biography*, by Mary Street Alinder (Henry Holt).
Terms: Agent receives 15% commission on domestic sales; 20% on foreign sales; 15% on motion picture sales.
Tips: Obtains new clients through recommendations from others.

MARCIA AMSTERDAM AGENCY, (II), 41 W. 82nd St., New York NY 10024-5613. (212)873-4945. Contact: Marcia Amsterdam. Estab. 1970. Signatory of WGA. Currently handles: 5% nonfiction books; 80% novels; 10% movie scripts; 5% TV scripts.
Handles: Novels. Considers these fiction areas: action/adventure; detective; glitz; historical; horror; humor; mainstream; mystery/suspense; romance (contemporary, historical); science fiction; thriller/espionage; westerns/frontier; young adult. Send outline plus first 3 sample chapters and SASE. Reports in 1 month on queries.
Recent Sales: *Free Fall*, by Joyce Sweeney (Dell); *Children of the Dawn*, by Patricia Rowe (Warner); *Back Slash*, by William Lovejoy (Kensington).
Also Handles: Movie scripts (feature film), TV scripts (TV mow, sitcom).
Terms: Agent receives 15% commission on domestic sales; 20% on foreign sales. Offers written contract, binding for 1 year, "renewable." Charges for extra office expenses, foreign postage, copying, legal fees (when agreed upon).
Tips: "We are always looking for interesting literary voices."

BART ANDREWS & ASSOCIATES INC., (III), 7510 Sunset Blvd., Suite 100, Los Angeles CA 90046. (213)851-8158. Contact: Bart Andrews. Estab. 1982. Represents 25 clients. 25% of clients are new/previously unpublished authors. Specializes in nonfiction only, and in the general category of entertainment (movies, TV, biographies, autobiographies). Currently handles: 100% nonfiction books.
Handles: Nonfiction books. Considers these nonfiction areas: biography/autobiography; music/dance/theater/film; TV. Query. Reports in 1 week on queries; 1 month on mss.
Recent Sales: *Roseanne*, by J. Randy Taraborrelli (G.P. Putnam's Sons); *Out of the Madness*, by Rose Books (packaging firm) (HarperCollins).
Terms: Agent receives 15% commission on domestic sales; 15% on foreign sales (after subagent takes his 10%). Offers written contract, "binding on a project-by-project basis." Author/client is charged for all photocopying, mailing, phone calls, postage, etc.
Writers' Conferences: Frequently lectures at UCLA in Los Angeles.
Tips: "Recommendations from existing clients or professionals are best, although I find a lot of new clients by seeking them out myself. I rarely find a new client through the mail. Spend time writing a query letter. Sell yourself like a product. The bottom line is writing ability, and then the idea itself. It takes a lot to convince me. I've seen it all! I hear from too many first-time authors who don't do their homework. They're trying to get a book published and they haven't the faintest idea what is required of them. There are plenty of good books on the subject and, in my opinion, it's their responsibility—not mine—to educate themselves before they try to find an agent to represent their work. When I ask an author to see a manuscript or even a partial manuscript, I really must be convinced I want to read it—based on a strong query letter—because I have no intention of wasting my time reading just for the fun of it."

‡APOLLO ENTERTAINMENT, (II), 1646 W. Julian, Unit C, Chicago IL 60622. (312)862-7864. Fax: (312)862-7974. Contact: Bruce Harrington. Estab. 1993. Signatory of WGA. Represents 8 clients. 20% of clients are new/previously unpublished writers. Specializes in feature screenplays of unordinary topics. Currently handles: 10% nonfiction books; 80% movie scripts, 10% TV scripts.
  • See the expanded listing for this agency in Script Agents.

APPLESEEDS MANAGEMENT, (II), 200 E. 30th St., Suite 302, San Bernardino CA 92404. (909)882-1667. For screenplays and teleplays only, send to 1870 N. Vermont, Suite 560, Hollywood CA 90027. Executive Manager: S. James Foiles. Estab. 1988. Signatory of WGA, licensed by state of California. 40% of clients are new/previously unpublished writers. Currently handles: 25% nonfiction books; 60% novels; 10% movie scripts; 5% teleplays (mow).
  • This agency reports that it is not accepting unsolicited screenplays and teleplays at this time.
Handles: Nonfiction books, novels. Considers these nonfiction areas: business; health/medicine; money/finance/economics; music/dance/theater/film; psychology; self-help/personal improvement; true crime/investigative. Considers these fiction areas: detective/police/crime; fantasy; horror; mystery/suspense; psychic/supernatural; science fiction; true crime/investigative. Query. Reports in 2 weeks on queries; 2 months on mss.
Also Handles: Movie scripts. Specializes in materials that could be adapted from book to screen; and in screenplays and teleplays. TV scripts (TV mow, no episodic).
Terms: Agent receives 10-15% commission on domestic sales; 20% on foreign sales. Offers written contract, binding for 1-7 years.

Tips: "In your query, please describe your intended target audience and distinguish your book/script from similar works."

‡THE AUTHOR'S AGENCY, (I, II), 3555 N. Five Mile Rd., Suite 332, Boise ID 83713-3925. (208)376-5477. Contact: (Ms.) R.J. Winchell. Estab. 1995. Represents 30 clients. 35% of clients are new/previously unpublished writers. "We specialize in high concepts which have a dramatic impact." Currently handles: 30% nonfiction books; 40% novels; 30% movie scripts.
Handles: Nonfiction books, novels, movie scripts, TV scripts. Considers these nonfiction areas: animals; anthropology/archaeology; biography/autobiography; business; child guidance/parenting; cooking/food/nutrition; crafts/hobbies; current affairs; education; ethnic/cultural interests; government/politics/law; health/medicine; history; how-to; humor; interior design/decorating; language/literature/criticism; military/war; money/finance/economics; music/dance/theater/film; nature/environment; New Age/metaphysics; photography; popular culture; psychology; religious/inspirational; science/technology; self-help/personal improvement; sociology; sports; translations; true crime/investigative; women's issues/women's studies. Considers "any fiction supported by the author's endeavor to tell a story with excellent writing." Query or send entire ms with SASE. Reports in 1 month on mss.
Terms: Agent receives 15% commission on domestic sales; 15% on foreign sales. Offers written contract on project-by-project basis.
Also Handles: Movie scripts (feature film); TV scripts (TV mow). "We consider all types of scripts." Query or send entire script with SASE. Reports in 1 month on mss.
Terms: Agent receives 10% commission on domestic sales; 10% on foreign sales.
Fees: Charges for expenses (photocopying, etc.). 100% of business is derived from commissions on sales.
Tips: "We obtain writers through speaking engagements, and referrals such as this book. We believe that writers make a valuable contribution to society. As such, we offer encouragement and support to writers, whether we represent them or not."

AUTHORS' LITERARY AGENCY, (III), P.O.Box 610582, DFW Airport TX 73069-2103. Phone: (817)267-1078. Fax: (817)571-4656. Contact: Dick Smith. Estab. 1992. Represents 19 clients. 70% of clients are new/previously unpublished writers. Currently handles: 70% nonfiction books; 30% novels. Member agents: Dick Smith; Jim Campise.
Handles: Nonfiction. Considers most nonfiction areas, especially how-to; psychology; spiritual; self-help/personal improvement; true crime/investigative; women's issues/women's studies. Considers these fiction areas: detective/police/crime; mystery/suspense; thriller/espionage. Query first always. Unsolicited mss will be returned unread. Reports in 1 month on queries; 2 months on mss.
Recent Sales: *Fourth and Long: The Kent Waldrep Story*, by Kent Waldrep and Susan Malone (Crossroads); *Sessions: A Self-Help Guide Through Psychotherapy*, by Dr. Ann P. Wildemann, Ph. D. (Crossroad).
Terms: Agent receives 15% commission on domestic sales; 25% on foreign sales. Offers written contract.
Tips: Obtains new clients through recommendations, networking at conferences. "For fiction, always send query letter first with: 1) a synopsis or outline of your work, 2) an author's bio, 3) the first three chapters of your work, and 4) SASE. *Do not send entire manuscript* until the agency requests it. For nonfiction, submit a query letter first with 1) a bio stating your experience and credentials to write the work, 2) a book proposal (we suggest using Michael Larsen's *How To Write A Book Proposal* as a guideline), and 3) SASE. Always send SASE with all queries. We cannot respond to work submitted without SASE and adequate postage for return to you."

THE AXELROD AGENCY, (III), 54 Church St., Lenox MA 01240. (413)637-2000. Fax: (413)637-4725. Contact: Steven Axelrod. Estab. 1983. Member of AAR. Represents 30 clients. Specializes in commercial fiction, nonfiction. Currently handles: 40% nonfiction books; 60% fiction.
● Prior to opening his agency, Mr. Axelrod served as an associate editor with The Literary Guild.
Handles: Considers these nonfiction areas: art; business; computers; government/politics/law; health/medicine; history; money/finance/economics; music/dance/theater/film; nature/environment; science/technology. Considers these fiction areas: cartoon/comic; detective/police/crime; family saga; glitz; historical; literary; mainstream; mystery/suspense; picture book; romance (contemporary, historical, regency); thriller/espionage. Query. Reports in 10 days on queries; 2-3 weeks on mss.

ALWAYS include a self-addressed, stamped envelope (SASE) for reply or return of your manuscript.

Terms: Agent receives 10% commission on domestic sales; 20% on foreign sales. Charges for photocopying.
Writers' Conferences: Romance Writers of America, Novelists, Inc.
Tips: Obtains new clients through referrals.

MALAGA BALDI LITERARY AGENCY, (II), P.O. Box 591, Radio City Station, New York NY 10101-5078. (212)222-1221. Contact: Malaga Baldi. Estab. 1985. Represents 40-50 clients. 80% of clients are new/previously unpublished writers. Specializes in quality literary fiction and nonfiction. Currently handles: 60% nonfiction books; 30% novels; 5% novellas; 5% short story collections.
Handles: Nonfiction books, novels, novellas, short story collections. Considers any well-written nonfiction, but do *not* send child guidance, crafts, juvenile nonfiction, New Age/metaphysics, religious/inspirational or sports material. Considers any well-written fiction, but do *not* send confessional, family saga, fantasy, glitz, juvenile, picture book, psychic/supernatural, religious/inspirational, romance, science fiction, western or young adult. Query first, but prefers entire ms for fiction. Reports within a minimum of 10 weeks. "Please enclose self-addressed stamped jiffy bag with submission and self-addressed stamped postcard for acknowledgement of consideration of manuscript."
Recent Sales: *Like People in History*, by Felice Picano (Viking/Penguin); *Dark Carnival*, by David J. Skal (Anchor/Doubleday); *Wild Ride*, by Bia Love (HarperCollins).
Terms: Agent receives 15% commission on domestic sales; 20% on foreign sales. Offers written contract. Charges "initial $50 fee to cover photocopying expenses. If the manuscript is lengthy, I prefer the author to cover expense of photocopying."
Tips: "From the day I agree to represent the author, my role is to serve as his or her advocate in contract negotiations and publicity efforts. Along the way, I wear many different hats. To one author I may serve as a nudge, to another a confidante, and to many simply as a supportive friend. I am also a critic, researcher, legal expert, messenger, diplomat, listener, counselor and source of publishing information and gossip. I work with writers on developing a presentable submission and make myself available during all aspects of a book's publication."

BALKIN AGENCY, INC., (III), P.O. Box 222, Amherst MA 01004. (413)548-9835. Fax: (413)548-9836. President: R. Balkin. Estab. 1972. Member of AAR. Represents 50 clients. 10% of clients are new/previously unpublished writers. Specializes in adult nonfiction. Currently handles: 85% nonfiction books; 5% scholarly books; 5% reference books; 5% textbooks.
• Prior to opening his agency, Mr. Balkin served as an editor with Bobbs-Merrill Company.
Handles: Nonfiction books, textbooks, reference, scholarly books. Considers these nonfiction areas: animals; anthropology/archaeology; biography; current affairs; health/medicine; history; how-to; language/literature/criticism; music/dance/theater/film; nature/environment; pop culture; science/technology; social science; translations; travel; true crime/investigative. Query with outline/proposal. Reports in 2 weeks on queries; 3 weeks on mss.
Recent Sales: *A Natural History of Glacier National Park*, by David Rockwell (Houghton-Mifflin); *Hiroshima: Why We Dropped the A-Bomb*, by Takaki (Little-Brown); *Consumer's Guide to Generic Drugs*, by D. Sullivan (Putnam/Berkley); *The Spirits Speak: One Woman's Mystical Journey Into the African Spirit World*, by Nicky Arden (Holt).
Terms: Agent receives 15% commission on domestic sales; 20% on foreign sales. Offers written contract, binding for 1 year. Charges for photocopying, trans-Atlantic long-distance calls or faxes and express mail.
Writers' Conferences: Jackson Hole Writers Conference (WY, April and July).
Tips: Obtains new clients through referrals. "I do not take on books described as bestsellers or potential bestsellers. Any nonfiction work that is either unique, paradigmatic, a contribution, truly witty or a labor of love is grist for my mill."

VIRGINIA BARBER LITERARY AGENCY, INC., 101 Fifth Ave., New York NY 10003. Member of AAR. This agency did not respond to our request for information. Query before submitting.

LORETTA BARRETT BOOKS INC., (II), 101 Fifth Ave., New York NY 10003. (212)242-3420. Fax: (212)691-9418. President: Loretta A. Barrett. Associate: Gary Morris. Estab. 1990. Member of AAR. Represents 70 clients. Specializes in general interest books. Currently handles: 20% fiction; 80% nonfiction.
Handles: Considers all areas of nonfiction and fiction. Query first, then send partial ms and synopsis. Reports in 4-6 weeks on queries and mss.
Terms: Agent receives 15% commission on domestic sales; 20% on foreign sales. Offers written contract. Charges for "all professional expenses."

‡THE WENDY BECKER LITERARY AGENCY, (I), 530-F Grand St., #11-H, New York NY 10002. Phone/fax: (212)228-5940. Estab. 1994. Represents 15 clients. 75% of clients are new/previously unpublished writers. Specializes in business/investment/finance, due to agent's background as acquisitions editor in these areas. Currently handles: 90% nonfiction books; 10% novels (genre fiction: romance, mystery/thriller, science fiction).

Handles: Nonfiction books, novels (genre fiction only). Considers these nonfiction areas: animals; anthropology/archaeology; art/architecture/design; biography/autobiography, business; child guidance/parenting; cooking/food/nutrition; crafts/hobbies; current affairs; ethnic/cultural interests; government/politics/law; health; history; how-to; humor; interior design/decorating; military/war; money/finance/economics; music/dance/theater/film; nature/environment; New Age/metaphysics; photography; popular culture; psychology; science/technology; self-help/personal improvement; sociology; sports; women's issues/women's studies. Considers these fiction areas: fantasy; mystery/suspense; romance (gothic, historical, regency); science fiction; thriller/espionage. For nonfiction, send outline/proposal and résumé. For fiction, send outline and up to 3 sample chapters. Reports in 6 weeks on queries and partial mss.

Terms: Agent receives 15% commission on domestic sales; 20% on foreign sales. Offers written contract, binding for 3 months, with 90 day cancellation clause. 100% of business is derived from commissions on sales.

Writers' Conferences: RWA (July); ABA (Chicago, June).

Tips: Obtains new clients through referrals and recommendations from editors, existing clients, meeting at conferences, unsolicited submittals. "Do your homework. Understand as much as you can (before contacting an agent) of the relationship between authors and agents, and the role an agent plays in the publishing process."

JOSH BEHAR LITERARY AGENCY, (I), Empire State Bldg., 350 Fifth Ave., Suite 3304, New York NY 10118. (212)826-4386. Contact: Josh Behar. Estab. 1993. Represents 12 clients. 90% of clients are new/previously unpublished writers. "I specialize in new and unpublished authors." Currently handles: 10% nonfiction books; 90% novels.

Handles: Nonfiction books, novels. Considers these nonfiction areas: biography/autobiography; business; money/finance/economics; New Age/metaphysics; self-help/personal improvement; women's issues/women's studies. Considers these fiction areas: action/adventure; detective/police/crime; fantasy; literary; psychic/supernatural; romance (contemporary, gothic, historical, regency); science fiction; thriller/espionage. Query. Reports in 1 week on queries; 1 month on mss.

Terms: Agent receives 15% commission on domestic sales; 20% on foreign sales. Offers written contract "only after sale has been made."

Writers' Conferences: RWA (NYC); MWA (NY); SciFi (TBA).

Tips: Obtains new clients through "conferences, editors and former agent I worked for. Tell me a good story."

‡PAM BERNSTEIN, (II), 790 Madison Ave., Suite 310, New York NY 10021. (212)288-1700. Fax: (212)288-3054. Contact: Pam Bernstein or Donna Dever. Estab. 1992. Member of AAR. Represents 50 clients. 20% of clients are new/previously published writers. Specializes in commercial fiction and nonfiction. Currently handles: 60% nonfiction books; 40% fiction.

Handles: Considers these nonfiction areas: biography/autobiography; child guidance/parenting; cooking/food/nutrition; current affairs; government/politics/law; health/medicine; how-to; New Age/metaphysics; popular culture; psychology; religious/inspirational; science/technology; self-help/personal improvement; sociology; true crime/investigative; women's issues/women's studies. Considers these fiction areas: action/adventure; contemporary issues; detective/police/crime; ethnic; historical; mainstream; mystery/suspense; romance (contemporary); thriller/espionage. Query. Reports in 2 weeks on queries; 1 month on mss. Include postage for return of ms.

Terms: Agent receives 15% commission on domestic sales; 20% on foreign sales. Offers written contract, binding for 3 years, with 30 day cancellation clause. 100% of business is derived from commissions on sales.

Tips: Obtains new clients through referrals from published authors.

DAVID BLACK LITERARY AGENCY, INC., (II), 156 Fifth Ave., New York NY 10001. (212)242-5080. Fax: (212)924-6609. Contact: David Black, owner. Estab. 1990. Member of AAR. Represents 150 clients. Specializes in sports, politics, novels. Currently handles: 80% nonfiction; 20% novels. Member agent, Susan Raihofer.

Handles: Nonfiction books, literary and commercial fiction. Considers these nonfiction areas: politics; sports. Query with outline, first chapter and SASE. Reports in 2 months on queries.

Recent Sales: *The Heart of the Game*, by Paul Hemphill (Simon & Schuster); *Nest of Vipers*, by Linda Davies (Doubleday); *Third and Indiana*, by Steve Lopez (Viking).

Terms: Agent receives 15% commission. Charges for photocopying and books purchased for sale of foreign rights.

BLASSINGAME SPECTRUM CORP., (II), 111 Eighth Ave., Suite 1501, New York NY 10011. (212)691-7556. Contact: Eleanor Wood, president. Represents 50 clients. Currently handles: 95% fiction; 5% nonfiction books. Member agent: Lucienne Diver.
Handles: Considers these fiction areas: fantasy; historical; literary; mainstream; mystery/suspense; science fiction. Considers select nonfiction. Query with SASE. Reports in 2 months on queries.
Terms: Agent receives 10% commission on domestic sales.
Tips: Obtains new clients through recommendations from authors and others.

REID BOATES LITERARY AGENCY, (II), P.O. Box 328, 274 Cooks Crossroad, Pittstown NJ 08867. (908)730-8523. Fax: (908)730-8931. Contact: Reid Boates. Estab. 1985. Represents 45 clients. 15% of clients are new/previously unpublished writers. Specializes in general fiction and nonfiction, investigative journalism/current affairs; bios and autobiographies; serious self-help; literary humor; issue-oriented business; popular science; "no category fiction." Currently handles: 85% nonfiction books; 15% novels; "very rarely accept short story collections."
Handles: Nonfiction books, novels. Considers these nonfiction areas: animals; anthropology/archaeology; art/architecture/design; biography/autobiography; business; child guidance/parenting; current affairs; ethnic/cultural interests; government/politics/law; health/medicine; history; language/literature/criticism; nature/environment; psychology; science/technology; self-help/personal improvement; sports; true crime/investigative; women's issues/women's studies. Considers these fiction areas: contemporary issues; crime; family saga; mainstream; mystery/suspense; thriller/espionage. Query. Reports in 2 weeks on queries; 6 weeks on mss.
Terms: Agent receives 15% commission on domestic sales; 20% on foreign sales. Offers written contract, binding "until terminated by either party." Charges for photocopying costs above $50.
Tips: Obtain new clients through recommendations from others.

GEORGES BORCHARDT INC., (III), 136 E. 57th St., New York NY 10022. (212)753-5785. Fax: (212)838-6518. Estab. 1967. Member of AAR. Represents 200 clients. 10% of clients are new/previously unpublished writers. Specializes in literary fiction and outstanding nonfiction. Currently handles: 60% nonfiction books; 1% juvenile books; 37% novels; 1% novellas; 1% poetry books. Member agents: Denise Shannon, Cindy Klein, Anne Borchardt, George Borchardt.
Handles: Nonfiction books, novels. Considers these nonfiction areas: anthropology/archaeology; biography/autobiography; current affairs; history; women's issues/women's studies. Considers literary fiction. "Must be recommended by someone we know." Reports in 1 week on queries; 3-4 weeks on mss.
Recent Sales: *Snow Falling on Cedars*, by David Guterson (Harcourt Brace, Vintage, rights sold in England, France, Germany, Italy, Holland, Sweden, Denmark, Norway, Brazil, Greece); *John's Wife*, by Robert Coover (Simon & Schuster); *The Here and Now*, by Robert Cohen (Scribner). Also new books by John Lahr, Stanley Crouch, Richard Rodriguez, Ned Rorem, George Steiner and first novels by Pearl Abraham, Michael Jaffe and Kate Phillips.
Terms: Agent receives 15% commission on domestic and British sales; 20% on foreign sales (translation). Offers written contract. "We charge cost of (outside) photocopying and shipping mss or books overseas."
Tips: Obtains new clients through recommendations from others.

THE BARBARA BOVA LITERARY AGENCY, (II), 3951 Gulfshore Blvd., PH1-B, Still Naples FL 33940. (941)649-7237. Fax: (941)649-0757. Estab. 1974. Represents 35 clients. Specializes in fiction and nonfiction hard and soft science. Currently handles: 35% nonfiction books; 65% novels.
Handles: Considers these nonfiction areas: biography; business; cooking/food/nutrition; how-to; money/finance/economics; self-help/personal improvement; social sciences; true crimes/investigative; women's issues/women's studies. Considers these fiction areas: action/adventure; contemporary issues; detective/police/crime; family saga; glitz; mainstream; mystery/suspense; regional; romance (contemporary); science fiction; thrillers/espionage. Query with SASE. Reports in 1 month on queries.
Recent Sales: *Gray Matter*, by Shirley Kennett (Kensington); *Treasure Box*, by Orson Scott Card (HarperCollins); *Riding Towards Home*, by Borto Milan (Bantam).
Terms: Agent receives 15% commission on domestic sales; handles foreign rights, movies, television, CDs.
Tips: Obtains new clients through recommendations from others.

Agents ranked I and II are most open to both established and new writers. Agents ranked III are open to established writers with publishing-industry references.

BRANDENBURGH & ASSOCIATES LITERARY AGENCY, (III), 24555 Corte Jaramillo, Murrieta CA 92562. (909)698-5200. Contact: Don Brandenburgh. Estab. 1986. Represents 20 clients. "We prefer previously published authors, but will evaluate submissions on their own merits." Works with a small number of new/unpublished authors. Specializes in adult nonfiction for the religious market; limited fiction for religious market. Currently handles: 70% nonfiction books; 20% novels.

 • Prior to opening his agency, Mr. Brandenburgh served as the founder and executive director of the Evangelical Christian Publishers Association.

Handles: Nonfiction books, novels for the religious market only. Query with outline. Reports in 2 weeks on queries. No response without SASE.

Recent Sales: *The Search for Meaning in the Workplace*, by Naylor/Willimon/Osterberg (Abingdon); *Secret Wars of Christian Men*, by Means (Fleming/Revell); *Sons of Fresh Oil*, by Scott/Younce (Thomas Nelson).

Terms: Agent receives 10% commission on domestic sales; 20% on dramatic sales; 20% on foreign sales. Charges $35 mailing/materials fee with signed agency agreement.

THE JOAN BRANDT AGENCY, (II), 788 Wesley Dr. NW, Atlanta GA 30305. (404)351-8877. Contact: Joan Brandt or Alan Schwartz. Estab. 1990. Represents 100 clients. Also handles movie rights for other agents.

 • Prior to opening her agency, Ms. Brandt served as an agent with Sterling Lord Literistic.

Handles: Novels, nonfiction books. Considers these fiction areas: contemporary issues; detective/police/crime; literary; mainstream; mystery/suspense; thriller/espionage; "also will consider popular, topical nonfiction." Query with SAE. Reports in 2 weeks on queries.

Terms: Agent receives 15% commission on domestic sales; 20% on foreign sales (co-agents in all major marketplaces). Charges for photocopying and long-distance postage.

Tips: Obtains new clients through recommendations from others and over-the-transom submissions.

BRANDT & BRANDT LITERARY AGENTS INC., (III), 1501 Broadway, New York NY 10036. (212)840-5760. Fax: (212)840-5776. Contact: Carl Brandt, Gail Hochman, Marianne Merola, Charles Schlessiger. Estab. 1913. Member of AAR. Represents 200 clients.

Handles: Nonfiction books, scholarly books, juvenile books, novels, novellas, short story collections. Considers these nonfiction areas: agriculture/horticulture; animals; anthropology/archaeology; art/architecture/design; biography/autobiography; business; child guidance/parenting; cooking/food/nutrition; crafts/hobbies; current affairs; ethnic/cultural interests; gay/lesbian issues; government/politics/law; health/medicine; history; interior design/decorating; juvenile nonfiction; language/literature/criticism; military/war; money/finance/economics; music/dance/theater/film; nature/environment; psychology; science/technology; self-help/personal improvement; sociology; sports; true crime/investigative; women's issues/women's studies. Considers these fiction areas: action/adventure; contemporary issues; detective/police/crime; erotica; ethnic; experimental; family saga; feminist; gay; historical; humor/satire; lesbian; literary; mainstream; mystery/suspense; psychic/supernatural; regional; romance; science fiction; sports; thriller/espionage; westerns/frontier; young adult. Query. Reports in 1 month on queries.

Recent Sales: *Life on the Tennis Highway*, by Eliot Berry (Holt).

Terms: Agent receives 15% commission on domestic sales; 20% on foreign sales. Charges for "manuscript duplication or other special expenses agreed to in advance."

Tips: Obtains new clients through recommendations from others or "upon occasion, a really good letter. Write a letter which will give the agent a sense of you as a professional writer, your long-term interests as well as a short description of the work at hand."

MARIE BROWN ASSOCIATES INC., (II,III), 625 Broadway, New York NY 10012. (212)533-5534. Fax: (212)533-0849. Contact: Marie Brown. Estab. 1984. Represents 100 clients. Specializes in multicultural African-American writers. Currently handles: 50% nonfiction books; 25% juvenile books; 25% other. Member agents: Joanna Blankson, Lesley Ann Brown, Janell Walden Agyeman.

Handles: Considers these nonfiction areas: art; biography; business; child guidance/parenting; cooking/food/nutrition; ethnic/cultural interests; gay/lesbian issues; history; juvenile nonfiction; money/finance/economics; music/dance/theater/film; New Age; psychology; religious/inspirational; self-help/personal improvement; sociology; women's issues/women's studies. Considers these fiction areas: contemporary issues; ethnic; feminist; gay; historical; humor/satire; juvenile; literary; mainstream; picture book; regional; science fiction. Query with SASE. Reports in 10 weeks on queries.

Recent Sales: *In the Spirit*, by Susan Taylor (Imtad); *Lessons in Living*, by Susan Taylor (Doubleday); *Brother Man*, by Boyd & Allen (Ballantine).

Terms: Agent receives 15% commission on domestic sales; 25% on foreign sales. Offers written contract.

Tips: Obtains new clients through recommendations from others.

CURTIS BROWN LTD., (II), 10 Astor Place, New York NY 10003-6935. (212)473-5400. Member of AAR; signatory of WGA. Perry Knowlton, Chairman & CEO. Peter L. Ginsberg, President. Member agents: Laura J. Blake; Ellen Geiger; Emilie Jacobson, Vice President; Virginia Knowlton; Timothy Knowlton, COO (film, screenplays, plays); Marilyn Marlow, Executive Vice President; Jess Taylor (film, screenplays, plays); Maureen Walters, Queries to Laura J. Blake.
Handles: Nonfiction books, juvenile books, novels, novellas, short story collections, poetry books. All categories of nonfiction and fiction considered. Query. Reports in 3 weeks on queries; 3-5 weeks on mss (only if requested).
Recent Sales: *Good News About High Blood Pressure*, by Thomas Pickering, MD (Simon & Schuster); *Exorcising Your Ex*, by Elizabeth Kuster (Fireside/Simon & Schuster); *The Last Judgment*, by Iain Pears (Scribner).
Also Handles: Movie scripts (feature film), TV scripts (TV mow), stage plays. Considers these script subject areas: action/adventure; comedy; detective/police/crime; ethnic; feminist; gay; historical; horror; lesbian; mainstream; mystery/suspense; psychic/supernatural; romantic comedy and drama; thriller; westerns/frontier.
Terms: Offers written contract. Charges for photocopying, some postage.
Tips: Obtains new clients through recommendations from others, solicitation, at conferences and query letters.

ANDREA BROWN LITERARY AGENCY, INC., (III,IV), P.O. Box 429, El Granada CA 94018-0429. (415)728-1783. Contact: Andrea Brown. Estab. 1981. Member of AAR, WNBA. 10% of clients are new/previously unpublished writers. Specializes in "all kinds of children's books—illustrators and authors including multimedia writers and designers." Currently handles: 98% juvenile books; 2% novels.
  • Prior to opening her agency, Ms. Brown served as an editorial assistant at Random House and Dell Publishing and as an editor with Alfred A. Knopf.
Handles: Juvenile books and multimedia projects. Considers these nonfiction areas: animals; anthropology/archaeology; art/architecture/design; biography/autobiography; current affairs; ethnic/cultural interests; history; how-to; juvenile nonfiction; nature/environment; photography; popular culture; science/technology; sociology; sports. Considers these fiction areas: historical; juvenile; picture book; romance (historical); science fiction; young adult. Query. Reports in 1-3 weeks on queries; 1-3 months on mss.
Recent Sales: *Happily Ever Laughter* series, by Mike Thaler (Scholastic); *Cinnamon Bear*, by Ellen Jackson (Lothrop, Lee & Shepherd); *Who Killed Mr. Chippendale?*, by Mel Glenn (Lodestar, Penguin); *CyberSurfers*, by Mel Gilden and Ted Pedersen (Price Stern Sloan).
Terms: Agent receives 15% commission on domestic sales; 20% on foreign sales. Written contract.
Writers' Conferences: Austin Writers League (Austin TX, Spring '96); SCBWI, Orange County Conferences; Mills College Children's Literature Conference (Oakland CA); Asilomar (Pacific Grove CA).
Tips: Usually obtains new clients through recommendations, editors, clients, agents and slush pile. "Taking on very few picture books. Must be unique—no rhyme, no anthropomorphism. Do not fax queries or manuscripts."

HOWARD BUCK AGENCY, (II), 80 Eighth Ave., Suite 1107, New York NY 10011. (212)807-7855. Contact: Howard Buck or Mark Frisk. Estab. 1981. Represents 75 clients. "All-around agency." Currently handles: 75% nonfiction books; 25% novels.
Handles: Nonfiction, novels. Considers all nonfiction and fiction areas except children's, juvenile, picture book or young adult. Query with SASE. Reports in 6 weeks on queries.
Terms: Agent receives 15% commission on domestic sales. Offers written contract. Charges for office expenses, postage and photocopying.
Tips: Obtains new clients through recommendations from others.

JANE BUTLER, ART AND LITERARY AGENT, (II, III), P.O. Box 33, Matamoras PA 18336-1530. Estab. 1981. "Prefers published credits, but all queries are welcome; no SASE, no reply." Specializes in fiction. Currently handles: 15% nonfiction books; 80% novels; 5% juvenile books. Member agent: Stephen K. Butler (all fiction unsolicited queries).
  • Prior to opening her agency, Ms. Butler served as an associate agent with Virginia Kidd.
Handles: Nonfiction books, novels. Considers nonfiction on Buddhism, Taoism, Shamanism. Considers these fiction areas: science fiction; fantasy; romantic fantasy; romantic suspense; historical fantasy; dark fantasy. Query with first chapter and SASE.
Recent Sales: *Epona Sequence I, II, & III*, by Judith Tarr (TDA, Inc/Forge, 1997-1999); *Orobouros* (tentative title), by S. Andrew Swann (DAW Books, 1997); *Pillar of Fire*, by Judith Tarr (Blackstone Audio Books, Inc., 1997); *Forests of the Night*, by S. Andrew Swann (Media Works Ltd. (Japanese translation), 1997).

Terms: Agent receives 10% commission on domestic sales; 15% on dramatic sales in association with Scovil Chicak Galen Literary Agency, Inc.; 25% on foreign sales in association with Baror International, Inc.

SHEREE BYKOFSKY ASSOCIATES, (IV), 211 E. 51st St., Suite 11-D, Box WD, New York NY 10022. Estab. 1984. Member of AAR, ASJA, WNBA. Represents "a limited number of" clients. Specializes in popular reference nonfiction. Currently handles: 80% nonfiction; 20% fiction.
● Prior to opening her agency, Ms. Bykofsky served as the manager of Chiron Press.
Handles: Nonfiction books. Considers all nonfiction areas, especially biography/autobiography; business; child guidance/parenting; cooking/foods/nutrition; current affairs; ethnic/cultural interests; gay/ lesbian issues; health/medicine; history; how-to; humor; music/dance/theater/film; popular culture; psychology; religious/inspirational; self-help/personal improvement; true crime/investigative; women's issues/women's studies. "I have wide-ranging interests, but it really depends on quality of writing, originality, and how a particular project appeals to me (or not). I take on very little fiction unless I completely love it—it doesn't matter what area or genre." Query with SASE. No unsolicited mss or phone calls. Reports in 1 month on queries.
Recent Sales: *The Encyclopedic Dictionary of Food and Nutrition*, by Ken and Lois Anderson (Wiley); *Handbook for the Soul*, by Richard Carlson and Benjamin Shield (Little Brown); *A Biography of Ezra Jack Keats*, by Dean Engel and Florence Freedman (Silver Moon); *Speaking Your Mind in 101 Difficult Situations*, by Don Gabor (Fireside); *All Aboard: The Comprehensive Guide to North American Train Travel*, by Jim Loomis (Prima); *Life's Little Frustration Book*, by G. Gaynor McTigue (St. Martins).
Terms: Agent receives 15% commission on domestic sales; 15% on foreign sales. Offers written contract, binding for 1 year "usually." Charges for postage, photocopying and fax.
Writers' Conferences: ASJA (NYC); Asilomar (Pacific Grove CA).
Tips: Obtains new clients through recommendations from others. "Read the agent listing carefully and comply with guidelines."

CANTRELL-COLAS INC., LITERARY AGENCY, (II), 229 E. 79th St., New York NY 10021. (212)737-8503. Estab. 1980. Represents 80 clients. Currently handles: 45% nonfiction books; 10% juvenile books; 45% mainstream. Member agent: Maryanne Colas.
Handles: Considers these nonfiction areas: anthropology; art; biography; child guidance/parenting; cooking/food/nutrition; current affairs; ethnic/cultural interests; government/politics/law; health/medicine; history; juvenile nonfiction; language/literature/criticism; military/war; money/finance/economics; nature/environment; New Age/metaphysics; psychology; science/technology; self-help/personal improvement; sociology; true crime/investigative; women's issues/women's studies. Considers these fiction areas: contemporary issues; detective/police/crime; ethnic; experimental; family saga; feminist; historical; humor/satire; juvenile; literary; mainstream; mystery/suspense; psychic/supernatural; science fiction; thriller/espionage; young adult. Query with outline, 2 sample chapters, SASE and "something about author also." Reports in 2 months on queries.
Recent Sales: *Homecoming*, by Kasey Michaels (Pocket Books); *Roosevelt and De Gaulle*, by Raoul Aglion; *Miami: A Saga*, by Evelyn Wilde-Mayerson (Viking); *Bride of the Unicorn*, by Kasey Michaels (Pocket Books).
Terms: Agent receives 15% commission on domestic sales; commission varies on foreign sales. Offers written contract. Charges for foreign postage and photocopying.
Tips: Obtains new clients through recommendations from others. "Make sure your manuscript is in excellent condition both grammatically and cosmetically. Check for spelling, typing errors and legibility."

MARIA CARVAINIS AGENCY, INC., (II), 235 West End Ave., New York NY 10023. (212)580-1559. Fax: (212)877-3486. Contact: Maria Carvainis. Estab. 1977. Member of AAR, Authors Guild, signatory of WGA. Represents 35 clients. 10% of clients are new/previously unpublished writers. Currently handles: 25% nonfiction books; 15% juvenile books; 55% novels; 5% poetry books.
● Maria Carvainis is a member of the AAR Board of Directors, AAR Treasurer and Board Liaison to the AAR Contracts Committee.
Handles: Nonfiction books, scholarly books, novels, poetry books. Considers these nonfiction areas: biography/autobiography; business; current affairs; government/politics/law; health/medicine; history; military/war; money/finance/economics; psychology; true crime/investigative; women's issues/women's studies; popular science. Considers these fiction areas: action/adventure; detective/police/crime; family saga; fantasy; glitz; historical; humor/satire; juvenile; literary; mainstream; mystery/suspense;

> *To find an agent near you, check the Geographic Index.*

romance; thriller/espionage; westerns/frontier; children's; young adult. Query first with SASE. Reports within 2 weeks on queries; within 3 months on solicited mss.

Recent Sales: *The Witness*, by Sandra Brown (Warner Books); *Due Diligence*, by Michael A. Kahn (Dutton); *Zoe Rising*, by Pam Conrad (HarperCollins); *Beyond Workplace 2000*, by Joseph H. Boyett and Jimmie T. Boyett (Dutton).

Terms: Agent receives 15% commission on domestic sales; 20% on foreign sales. Offers written contract, binding for 2 years "on a book-by-book basis." Charges for foreign postage and bulk copying.

Tips: "75% of new clients derived from recommendations or conferences. 25% of new clients derived from letters of query."

MARTHA CASSELMAN LITERARY AGENT, (III), P.O. Box 342, Calistoga CA 94515-0342. (707)942-4341. Estab. 1978. Member of AAR, IACP, NWBA. Represents 30 clients. Specializes in "nonfiction, especially food books; limited YA, children's. Do not send any submission without query." Member agent: Judith Armenta (New Age and alternative medicine nonfiction).

Handles: Nonfiction proposals only, food-related proposals and cookbooks. Considers these nonfiction areas: agriculture/horticulture; anthropology/archaeology; biography/autobiography; cooking/food/nutrition; health/medicine; women's issues/women's studies. Considers only young adult fiction. Send proposal with outline, plus 3 sample chapters. Reports in 2-4 weeks on queries.

Terms: Agent receives 15% commission on domestic sales; 20% on foreign sales (if using subagent). Offers contract review for hourly fee, on consultation with author. Charges for photocopying, overnight and overseas mailings.

Writers' Conferences: IACP (Philadelphia, April 1996).

Tips: Obtains new clients through referrals. "No tricky letters; no gimmicks; *always* include SASE or mailer."

CASTIGLIA LITERARY AGENCY, (II), 1155 Camino Del Mar, Suite 510, Del Mar CA 92014. (619)753-4361. Fax: (619)753-5094. Contact: Julie Castiglia. Estab. 1993. Member of AAR, PEN. Represents 50 clients. 25% of clients are new/previously unpublished writers. Currently handles: 60% nonfiction books; 35% novels; 5% short story collections. Member agent: Moira Coyne (fiction: literary & mainstream; nonfiction: pop culture, music, spirituality/mysticism, film).

• Prior to opening her agency, Ms. Castiglia served as an agent with Waterside Productions, as well as working as a freelance editor and published writer of three books.

Handles: Nonfiction books, novels, short story collections. Considers these nonfiction areas: animals; anthropology/archaeology; biography/autobiography; business; child guidance/parenting; cooking/food/nutrition; current affairs; ethnic/cultural interests; finance; health/medicine; history; language/literature/criticism; nature/environment; New Age/metaphysics; psychology; religious/inspirational; science/technology; self-help/personal improvement; sociology; women's issues/women's studies. Considers these fiction areas: contemporary issues; ethnic; family saga; feminist; gay; glitz; literary mainstream; mystery/suspense; women's fiction especially. Send outline/proposal plus 2 sample chapters; send synopsis with chapters for fiction. Reports in 6-8 weeks on mss.

Recent Sales: *Serafina's Wild Horse Ballet*, by Margarita Engle (Harmony Books); *The Shaman's Bulldog*, by Renaldo Fischer (Warner Books); *Jesus In Blue Jeans*, by Laurie Beth Jones (Disney/Hyperion); *Night Train*, by Jess Mowry (Holt); *Babylon Boyz*, by Jess Mowry (Simon & Schuster); *Dreamscape*, (interactive), by Nicholas Heyneman (Simon & Schuster).

Terms: Agent receives 15% commission on domestic sales; 20% on foreign sales. Offers written contract, 6 week termination. Charges for excessive postage and copying for first-time authors.

Writers' Conferences: Southwestern Writers Conference (Albuquerque NM, August); National Writers Conference; Wilamette Writers Conference Association (OR); San Diego State University.

Tips: Obtains new clients through solicitations, conferences, referrals. "Be professional with submissions. Attend workshops and conferences before you approach an agent."

‡CHARISMA COMMUNICATIONS, LTD., (IV), 210 E. 39th St., New York NY 10016. (212)832-3020. Fax: (212)772-0393. Contact: James W. Grau. Estab. 1972. Represents 10 clients. 20% of clients are new/previously unpublished writers. Specializes in organized crime, Indian casinos, FBI, CIA, secret service, NSA, corporate and private security, casino gaming, KGB. Currently handles: 50% nonfiction books; 20% movie scripts; 20% TV scripts; 10% other. Member agent: Phil Howart.

Handles: Nonfiction books, novels, movie scripts, TV scripts. Considers these nonfiction areas: biography/autobiography; current affairs; government/politics/law; military/war; true crime/investigative. Considers these fiction areas: contemporary issues; detective/police/crime; mystery/suspense; religious/inspirational; sports; cult issues. Send outline/proposal. Reports in 1 month on queries; 2 months on mss.

Terms: Agent receives 10% commission on domestic sales; variable commission on foreign sales. Offers variable written contract. 100% of business is derived from commissions on sales.

Tips: New clients are established writers.

‡JAMES CHARLTON ASSOCIATES, (II), 680 Washington St., #2A, New York NY 10014. (212)691-4951. Fax: (212)691-4952. Contact: Lisa Friedman. Estab. 1983. Specializes in military history, sports. Currently handles: 100% nonfiction books.
Handles: Nonfiction books. Considers these nonfiction areas: child guidance/parenting; cooking/food/nutrition; health/medicine; how-to; humor; military/war; popular culture; self-help/personal improvement; sports. Query with SASE for response. Reports in 2 weeks on queries.
Recent Sales: *The Safe Child Book*, by Kraizer (Simon & Schuster); *West Point Atlas of American Wars*, compiled by West Point (Holt).
Terms: Agent receives 15% commission on domestic sales. Offers written contract, with 60 day cancellation clause.
Tips: Obtains new clients through recommendations from others.

CIRCLE OF CONFUSION LTD., (II), 666 Fifth Ave., Suite 3035, New York NY 10103. (212)969-0653. Fax: (718)997-0521. Contact: Rajeev K. Agarwal, Lawrence Mattis. Estab. 1990. Signatory of WGA. Represents 70 clients. 70% of clients are new/previously unpublished writers. Specializes in screenplays for film and TV. Currently handles: 15% novels; 5% novellas; 80% movie scripts. Member agents: Rageev Agarwal, Lawrence Mattis, Annmarie Negretti.
  • See the expanded listing for this agency in Script Agents.

CISKE & DIETZ LITERARY AGENCY, (II), NE Office: P.O. Box 193, Greenleaf WI 54126. (414)864-7702. Contact: Patricia Dietz. Also: P.O. Box 555, Neenah WI 54957. (414)722-5944. Contact: Fran Ciske. Represents 20 clients. Estab. 1993. Member of RWA. Specializes in romance, women's fiction. Currently handles: 80% fiction; 20% nonfiction. Member agents: Patricia Dietz (action/adventure, thrillers, young adult); Fran Ciske (romance).
Handles: Considers these nonfiction areas: cooking/food/nutrition; religious/inspirational; self-help/personal improvement; true crime; women's issues/women's studies. Considers these fiction areas: mystery/suspense; religious/inspiration; romance (contemporary, historical, regency, time travel); thriller; westerns/frontier. Query. No unsolicited mss. Reports in 2 weeks on queries; 2 months on mss.
Terms: Agent receives 15% commission on domestic sales; 20% on foreign sales. Offers non-binding terms agreement. Expenses for photocopying will be agreed upon in advance.
Writers' Conferences: RWA national conference, Wisconsin RWA conferences and workshops.
Tips: Obtains new clients through recommendation, solicitation and conferences. No phone queries, please. "Agency handles religious/inspirationals for the Evangelical Christian market. No New Age or occult. No reply without SASE. Target a market."

CONNIE CLAUSEN ASSOCIATES, (II), 250 E. 87th St., New York NY 10128. (212)427-6135. Fax: (212)996-7111. Contact: Connie Clausen. Estab. 1976. 10% of clients are new/previously unpublished writers. Specializes in nonfiction with a strong backlist. Member agents: Elyse Cheney, Lisa Kaiser.
Handles: Considers these nonfiction areas: biography; gardening; health/nutrition; how-to; personal finance; psychology; self-help; spirituality; academic works with mass-market potential. Considers literary fiction. Send outline/proposal with return postage. Reports in 3 weeks on queries; 4-6 on mss.
Recent Sales: *I Love Him But . . .* , by Mery Bloch Jones (Workman); *The Rules*, by Fein & Schneider (Warner); *What the IRS Doesn't Want You to Know*, by Kaplan & Weiss (Villard); *The Common Sense Kitchen Advisor*, by Deborah Krasner (HarperCollins); *Who's Insane*, by Barbara Kirwin (Little, Brown); *The Potted Garden*, by Rebecca Cole (Clarkson Potter); *Dress Like a Million*, by Leah Feldon (Villard); *Looking for Mom & Other Mysteries*, by Sherry Suib Cohen (Crown); *Estrogen*, by Heilman & Nachtigall (HarperPerennial); *The Way of the Scout*, by Tom Brown, Jr. (Berkley).
Terms: Agent receives 15% commission on sales. Offers written contract.
Tips: "Research proposal writing and the publishing process; always study your book's competition; send a proposal and outline instead of complete manuscript for faster response; always pitch books in writing, not over the phone."

DIANE CLEAVER INC., 55 Fifth Ave., New York NY 10003.
  • Ms. Cleaver passed away in early 1995. Sanford J. Greenburger Associates continues to represent many of her clients.

RUTH COHEN, INC. LITERARY AGENCY, (II), P.O. Box 7626, Menlo Park CA 94025. (415)854-2054. Contact: Ruth Cohen or associates. Estab. 1982. Member of AAR, Authors Guild, SCBWI. Represents 75 clients. 20% of clients are new/previously unpublished writers. Specializes in "quality writing in juvenile fiction; mysteries; regency and historical romances, adult women's fiction." Currently handles: 15% nonfiction books; 40% juvenile books; 45% novels.
  • Prior to opening her agency, Ms. Cohen served as directing editor at Scott Foresman & Company (now HarperCollins).
Handles: Juvenile books, adult novels. Considers these nonfiction areas: ethnic/cultural interests; juvenile nonfiction; true crime/investigative; women's issues/women's studies. Considers these fiction

areas: detective/police; ethnic; regencies; family saga; historical; juvenile; literary; mainstream; mystery/suspense; picture books; romance (historical, regency); young adult. Send outline plus 2 sample chapters and SASE. Reports in 1 month on queries. No unsolicited mss.

Terms: Agent receives 15% commission on domestic sales; 20% on foreign sales, "if a foreign agent is involved." Offers written contract, binding for 1 year "continuing to next." Charges for foreign postage and photocopying for submissions.

Tips: Obtains new clients through recommendations from others. "A good writer cares about the words he/she uses—so do I. Also, if no SASE is included, material will not be read."

HY COHEN LITERARY AGENCY LTD., (II), 111 W. 57th St., #1400, New York NY 10019. (212)757-5237. Contact: Hy Cohen. Mail ms to P.O. Box 743, Upper Montclair NJ 07043. Estab. 1975. Represents 25 clients. 50% of clients are new/previously unpublished writers. Currently handles: 20% nonfiction books; 5% juvenile books; 75% novels.

Handles: Nonfiction books, novels. All categories of nonfiction and fiction considered. Send 100 pages with SASE. Reports in about 2 weeks (on 100-page submission).

Terms: Agent receives 10% commission.

Tips: Obtains new clients through recommendations from others and unsolicited submissions. "Send double-spaced, legible scripts and SASE. Good writing helps."

FRANCES COLLIN LITERARY AGENT, (III), P.O. Box 33, Wayne PA 19087-0033. (610)254-0555. Estab. 1948. Member of AAR. Represents 90 clients. 5% of clients are new/previously unpublished writers. Currently handles: 48% nonfiction books; 1% textbooks; 50% novels; 1% poetry books.

Handles: Nonfiction books, novels. Considers these nonfiction areas: anthropology/archaeology; biography/autiobiography; business; health/medicine; history; nature/environment; true crime/investigative. Considers these fiction areas: detective/police/crime; ethnic; family saga; fantasy; historical; literary; mainstream; mystery/suspense; psychic/supernatural; regional; romance (historical); science fiction. Query with SASE. Reports in 1 week on queries; 2 months on mss.

Recent Sales: *The Body's Edge*, by Marc Lappé, PhD (Holt).

Terms: Agent receives 15% commission on domestic sales; 20% on foreign sales. Offers written contract. Charges for overseas postage for books mailed to foreign agents; photocopying of mss, books, proposals; copyright registration fees; registered mail fees; pass along cost of any books purchased.

Tips: Obtains new clients through recommendations from others.

‡COLLINS PURVIS, LTD., (I,II), P.O. Box 626, East Amherst NY 14051. (716)639-0713. Fax: (716)639-4017. E-mail: litagency@aol.com. Contact: Michael C. Purvis. Estab. 1995. Represents 10 clients. 100% of clients are new/previously unpublished writers. Currently handles: 60% nonfiction books; 10% scholarly books; 30% novels. Member agents: Michael C. Purvis; Nancy L. Collins, PhD.

• Prior to opening his agency, Mr. Purvis was associated with the Walt Disney Company as an attorney.

Handles: Nonfiction books, scholarly books, textbooks, novels, syndicated material, software and multimedia works. Considers these nonfiction areas: animals; anthropology/archaeology; art/architecture/design; biography/autobiography; business; current affairs; education; ethnic/cultural interests; gay/lesbian issues; government/politics/law; history; how-to; humor; interior design/decorating; juvenile nonfiction; military/war; money/finance/economics; music/dance/theater/film; nature/environment; photography; popular culture; psychology; science/technology; self-help/personal improvement; sociology; true crime/investigative; women's issues/women's studies. Considers these fiction areas: action/adventure; cartoon/comic; contemporary issues; detective/police/crime; family saga; fantasy; feminist; historical; horror; humor/satire; juvenile; mainstream; mystery; picture book; psychic/supernatural; science fiction; thriller/espionage; young adult. Query with SASE. For nonfiction, send outline/proposal and résumé. For fiction, send brief synopsis and 2 sample chapters. Material cannot be returned without a SASE. No faxed queries. Reports in 2 weeks.

Terms: Agent receives 15% commission on domestic sales; 20% on foreign sales. Offers written contract, binding for an open-ended length of time, with 30 day cancellation clause. Charges for photocopying, postage, long distance calls and faxes, overnight deliveries. 100% of business is derived from commissions on sales.

Also Handles: Movie scripts (feature film, documentary); TV scripts (TV mow, miniseries). Considers these script subject areas: action/adventure; comedy; contemporary issues; detective/police/crime; family saga; historical; horror; humor; juvenile; mainstream; mystery/suspense; psychic/supernatural; romantic drama; science fiction; teen; thriller. Query. Reports in 2 weeks.

Terms: Agent receives 10% commission on script sales.

Writers' Conferences: ABA (Chicago, June).

Tips: Obtains new clients through solicitation and queries. "The form and content of your query letter tells an agent a lot about you. Make sure it is well-thought-through and looks professional. Don't give up! If your work is good and has a commercial hook to it, you will find an agent."

COLUMBIA LITERARY ASSOCIATES, INC., (II,IV), 7902 Nottingham Way, Ellicott City MD 21043-6721. (410)465-1595. Fax: Call for number. Contact: Linda Hayes, Kathryn Jensen. Estab. 1980. Member of AAR, IACP, RWA, WRW. Represents 40 clients. 10% of clients are new/previously unpublished writers. Specializes in women's fiction (mainstream/genre), commercial nonfiction, especially cookbooks. Currently handles: 40% nonfiction books; 60% novels.

Handles: Nonfiction books, novels. Considers these nonfiction areas: cooking/food/nutrition; health/medicine; self-help. Considers these fiction areas: mainstream; commercial women's fiction; suspense; contemporary romance; psychological/medical thrillers. Reports in 2-4 weeks on queries; 6-8 weeks on mss; "rejections faster."

Recent Sales: *Running From The Law,* by Lisa Scottoline (HarperCollins); *Face to Face,* by Rebecca York (Harlequin Intrigue); *Skinny Italian Cooking,* by Glick/Baggett (Surrey Books); *White Fury,* by Beth Amos (Harper Paperbacks); *Deja Vu,* by Marie Fiorelli (Kensington).

Terms: Agent receives 15% commission on domestic sales. Offers single- or multiple-book written contract, binding for 6-month terms. "Standard expenses are billed against book income (e.g., books for subrights exploitation, toll calls, UPS)."

Writers' Conferences: Romance Writers of America; International Association of Culinary Professionals; Novelists, Inc.

Tips: "CLA's list is very full; we're able to accept only a rare few top-notch projects." Submission requirements: "For fiction, send a query letter with author credits, narrative synopsis, first chapter or two, manuscript word count and submission history (publishers/agents); self-addressed, stamped mailer mandatory for response/ms return. (When submitting romances, note whether manuscript is mainstream or category—if category, say which line(s) manuscript is targeted to.) Same for nonfiction, plus include table of contents and note audience, how project is different and better than competition (specify competing books with publisher and publishing date.) Please note that we do *not* handle: historical fiction, regencies, futuristics, westerns, science fiction/fantasy, military books, poetry, short stories or screenplays."

DON CONGDON ASSOCIATES INC., (III), 156 Fifth Ave., Suite 625, New York NY 10010-7002. (212)645-1229. Fax: (212)727-2688. E-mail: doncongdon@aol.com. Contact: Don Congdon, Michael Congdon, Susan Ramer. Estab. 1983. Member of AAR. Represents 100+ clients. Currently handles: 50% fiction; 50% nonfiction books.

Handles: Nonfiction books, novels. Considers all nonfiction and fiction areas, especially literary fiction. Query. "If interested, we ask for sample chapters and outline." Reports in 3-4 weeks on mss.

Recent Sales: *Rhoda: A Life in Stories,* by Ellen Gilchrist (Little, Brown); Clint Eastwood biography, by Richard Schickel (Knopf); *A Cottage in Portugal,* by Richard Hewitt (Simon & Schuster).

Terms: Agent receives 10% commission on domestic sales.

Tips: Obtains new clients through referrals from other authors. "Writing a query letter is a must."

THE DOE COOVER AGENCY, (II), 58 Sagamore Ave., Medford MA 02155. (617)488-3937. Fax: (617)488-3153. President: Doe Coover. Agent: Colleen Mohyde. Estab. 1985. Represents 60 clients. Specializes in serious nonfiction and fiction. Currently handles: 80% nonfiction; 20% fiction. Member agents: Doe Coover (cooking, general nonfiction); Colleen Mohyde (fiction, general nonfiction).

Handles: Nonfiction books, fiction. Considers these nonfiction areas: anthropology; biography/autobiography; business; child guidance/parenting; cooking/food; ethnic/cultural interests; finance/economics; health/medicine; history; language/literature/criticism; nature/environment; psychology; religious/inspirational; science/technology; sociology; true crime; women's issues/women's studies. Query with outline. All queries must include SASE and should be addressed to Ms. Mohyde. Reporting time varies on queries.

Recent Sales: *Unplanned Parenthood,* by Liz Carpenter (Random House); *The Hiding Room,* by Jonathan Wilson (Viking); *The Money Diet,* by Ginger Applegarth (Viking).

Terms: Agent receives 15% commission on domestic sales; 15% on foreign sales.

Writers' Conferences: ABA (Chicago).

Tips: Obtains new clients through recommendations from others and solicitation.

ROBERT CORNFIELD LITERARY AGENCY, (II), 145 W. 79th St., New York NY 10024-6468. (212)874-2465. Fax: (212)872-2641. Contact: Robert Cornfield. Estab. 1979. Member of AAR. Represents 60 clients. 20% of clients are new/previously unpublished writers. Specializes in film, art, literary,

> *Agents who specialize in a specific subject area such as computer books or in handling the work of certain writers such as gay or lesbian writers are ranked IV.*

music criticism, food, fiction. Currently handles: 60% nonfiction books; 20% scholarly books; 20% novels.

Handles: Nonfiction books, novels. Considers these nonfiction areas: animals; anthropology/archaeology; art/architecture/ design; biography/autobiography; cooking/food/nutrition; history; language/literature/criticism/ music/dance/theater/film. Considers literary fiction. Query. Reports in 2-3 weeks on queries.

Recent Sales: *Arthur Evans & The Minoans*, by J.A. Mae Gillivray (HarperCollins); *The Tavern on The Green Cookbook*, by Moira Hodgson (Clarkson Potter); *Parenting Cookbook*, by Kathy Gunst & *Parenting* magazine (Holt); *Bean Cookbook*, by Melanie Barnard (Harper); *Adam's Task*, by Vicki Hearne (Harper).

Terms: Agent receives 10% commission on domestic sales; 20% on foreign sales. No written contract. Charges for postage, excessive photocopying.

Tips: Obtains new clients through recommendations.

CRAWFORD LITERARY AGENCY, (III), 198 Evans Rd., Barnstead NH 03218. (603)269-5851. Fax: (603)269-2533. Contact: Susan Crawford. Estab. 1988. Represents 40 clients. 10% of clients are new/previously unpublished writers. Currently handles: 50% nonfiction books; 50% novels. Member agents: Lorne Crawford, Scott Neister.

Handles: Nonfiction books. Considers these nonfiction areas: biography/autobiography; business; child guidance/parenting; cooking/food/nutrition; how-to; true crime/investigative; women's issues/women's studies. Query with SASE. Reports in 3 weeks on queries.

Recent Sales: *So Far*, by Kelsey Grammer (Dutton); *Bogart: In Search of My Father*, Stephen Humphrey Bogart with Gary Provost (Dutton); *Huntress*, by Christopher Keane (Donald I Fine, Inc.); *Doc Holliday's Woman*, by Jane Candia Coleman (Warner Books); *Play It Again*, by Stephen Humphrey Bogart (Forge Books); *The Skelly Man*, by David Daniel (St. Martin's Press).

Terms: Agent receives 15% commission on domestic sales; 20% on foreign sales. Offers written contract, binding for 90 days. 100% of business is derived from commissions on sales.

Writers' Conferences: Hemingway Festival/Writers' Conference (Key West FL); International Film & Writers Workshop (Rockport ME).

Tips: Obtains new clients through recommendations and at conferences.

BONNIE R. CROWN INTERNATIONAL LITERATURE AND ARTS AGENCY, (II, IV), 50 E. Tenth St., New York NY 10003-6221. (212)475-1999. Contact: Bonnie Crown. Estab. 1976. Member of Association of Asian Studies. Represents 14 clients. 10% of clients are previously published writers. Specializes in Asian cross-cultural and translations of Asian literary works, American writers influenced by one or more Asian culture. Currently handles: 5% scholarly books; 80% novels; 10% short story collectors; 5% poetry.

Handles: Nonfiction books, novels, short story collections (if first published in literary magazines). Considers these nonfiction areas: ethnic/cultural interests; nature/environment; translations from Asian languages; women's issues/women's studies. Considers these fiction areas: ethnic; experimental; family saga; historical; humor/satire; literary. Query with SASE. Reports in 2 weeks on queries; 2-4 weeks on mss.

Terms: Agent receives 15% commission on domestic sales; 20% on foreign sales. Charges for processing, usually $35, on submission of ms.

Tips: Obtains new clients through "referrals through other authors and listings in reference works. If interested in agency representation, send brief query with SASE."

RICHARD CURTIS ASSOCIATES, INC., (III), 171 E. 74th St., New York NY 10021. (212)772-7363. Fax: (212)772-7393. Contact: Richard Curtis. Estab. 1969. Member of AAR, signatory of WGA. Represents 150 clients. 5% of clients are new/previously unpublished writers. Specializes in genre paperback fiction such as science fiction, women's romance, horror, fantasy, action-adventure. Currently handles: 9% nonfiction books; 1% juvenile books; 90% novels. Member agents: Amy Victoria Meo, Laura Tucker.

• Mr. Curtis is the current President of the AAR.

Handles: Nonfiction books, novels. Considers these nonfiction areas: biography/autobiography; business; child guidance/parenting; history; military/war; money/finance/economics; music/dance/theater/film; science/technology; self-help/personal improvement; sports; true crime/investigative. Considers these fiction areas: action/adventure; detective/police/crime; family saga; fantasy; feminist; historical; horror; mainstream; mystery/suspense; romance; science fiction; thriller/espionage; westerns/frontier. Query, must be accompanied by SASE. Reports in 2 weeks on queries.

Recent Sales: *Hidden Latitudes*, by Alison Anderson (Scribner); *After Miranda*, by Susan Wiggs (Harper); *Notorious*, by Janet Dailey (Harper); *Tigress In The Night*, by Jennifer Blake (Fawcett); *Dr. Scott's Knee Book*, by Dr. W. Norman Scott with Carol Colman (Fireside/Simon & Schuster).

Terms: Agent receives 15% commission on domestic sales; 20% on foreign sales. Charges for photocopying, express, fax, international postage, book orders.

Writers' Conferences: World Fantasy (Baltimore MD, October 1995); Romance Writers of America (Dallas TX, July 1996); Nebula Science Fiction Conference (San Diego CA, April 1996).
Tips: Obtains new clients through recommendations from others.

‡JAMES R. CYPHER, AUTHOR'S REPRESENTATIVE, (II), 616 Wolcott Ave., Beacon NY 12508-4247. Phone/fax: (914)831-5677. E-mail: jimcypher@aol.com. Estab. 1993. Represents 26 clients. 58% of clients are new/previously unpublished writers. Currently handles: 58% nonfiction books; 42% novels.
• Mr. Cypher is a special contributor to Prodigy Service Books and writing bulletin board.
Handles: Nonfiction books, novels. Considers these nonfiction areas: biography/autobiography; business; computers/electronics; current affairs; ethnic/cultural interests; gay/lesbian issues; government/politics/law; health/medicine; history; how-to; humor; language/literature/criticism; military/war; money/finance/economics; music/dance/theater/film; nature/environment; popular culture; psychology; science/technology; self-help/personal improvement; sociology; sports; true crime/investigative; women's issues/women's studies; travel memoirs. Considers these fiction areas: action/adventure; contemporary issues; detective/police/crime; ethnic; family saga; feminist; gay; historical; horror; humor/satire; lesbian; literary; mainstream; mystery/suspense; psychic/supernatural; sports; thriller/espionage. For nonfiction, send outline proposal, 2 sample chapters and SASE. For fiction, send synopsis, 3 sample chapters and SASE. Reports in 2 weeks on queries; 6 weeks on mss.
Recent Sales: *Living with Chronic Fatigue Syndrome*, by Timothy Kenny (Thunder's Mouth Press); *Open Lands: Travels in Russia's Forbidden Zones*, by Mark A. Taplin (Steerforth Press).
Terms: Agent receives 15% commission on domestic sales; 20% on foreign sales. Offers written contract, with 30 day cancellation clause. Charges for postage, photocopying, overseas phone calls and faxes. 100% of business is derived from commissions on sales.
Tips: Obtains new clients through referrals from others and networking on online computer services. "I especially enjoy character-driven fiction. Make me, acquiring editors and, ultimately, your readers, really care about your protagonist and his or her adventures or misadventures. Horror, thriller or suspense novels *must* be genuine 'page turners.' "

DARHANSOFF & VERRILL LITERARY AGENTS, (II), 179 Franklin St., 4th Floor, New York NY 10013. (212)334-5980. Fax: (212)334-5470. Estab. 1975. Member of AAR. Represents 100 clients. 10% of clients are new/previously unpublished writers. Specializes in literary fiction. Currently handles: 25% nonfiction books; 60% novels; 15% short story collections. Member agents: Liz Darhansoff, Charles Verrill, Leigh Feldman.
Handles: Nonfiction books, novels, short story collections. Considers these nonfiction areas: anthropology/archaeology; biography/autobiography; current affairs; health/medicine; history; language/literature/criticism; nature/environment; science/technology. Considers literary and thriller fiction. Query letter only. Reports in 2 weeks on queries.
Recent Sales: *Water From the Well*, by Myra McLarey (Atlantic Monthly Press).
Tips: Obtains new clients through recommendations from others.

‡JOAN DAVES AGENCY, (II), 21 W. 26th St., New York NY 10010. (212)685-2663. Fax: (212)685-1781. Contact: Jennifer Lyons, director. Estab. 1960. Member of AAR. Represents 100 clients. 10% of clients are new/previously unpublished writers. Specializes in literary fiction and nonfiction, also commercial fiction.
Handles: Nonfiction books, novels. Considers these nonfiction areas: biography/autobiography; gay/lesbian issues; popular culture; translations; women's issues/women's studies. Considers these fiction areas: ethnic, family saga; gay; literary; mainstream; thriller/espionage. Query. Reports in 3 weeks on queries; 6 weeks on mss.
Recent Sales: *Fire on the Mountain*, by John Maclean (William Morrow); Bruno Bettelhelm biography, by Nina Sutton (Basic Books); *Entertaining Angels*, by Marita Van der Vyr (Dutton); *Ruby Tear*, by Suzy Charnas (TOR/St. Martin's).
Terms: Agent receives 15% commission on domestic sales; 20% on foreign sales. Offers written contract, on a per book basis. Charges for office expenses. 100% of business is derived from commissions on sales.
Tips: Obtains new clients through editors' and author clients' recommendations. "A few queries translate into representation."

THE LOIS DE LA HABA AGENCY INC., (III), 1123 Broadway, Suite 810, New York NY 10010. (212)929-4838. Fax: (212)924-3885. Contact: Lois de la Haba. Estab. 1978. Represents 100 clients. Currently handles: 50% nonfiction books; 3% scholarly books; ½% textbooks; 10% juvenile books; 21% novels; ½% poetry; ½% short story collections; 10% movie scripts; 2% stage plays; 2% TV scripts; ½% syndicated material.
Handles: Nonfiction books, scholarly books, juvenile books, novels, movie scripts, TV scripts, stage plays. Considers these nonfiction areas: anthropology/archaeology; art/architecture/design; biography/

INSIDER REPORT

Author Writes Dog Book; Publisher Bites

It's a fairy tale of sorts. An author takes a gamble and publishes her own work. The book succeeds, and, attracts attention. Then it attracts an agent, then a major publisher, and, finally, national distribution. That's what happened when former advertising writer Beth Fowler wrote *Could You Love Me Like My Dog?*, a witty and whimsical look at the unconditional love that dogs show their owners. It was published by Fireside, an imprint of Simon & Schuster, for Valentine's Day 1996, and Fowler already has a contract with Fireside for a follow-up book, *Could You Love Me Like My Cat?*, to be released for Valentine's Day, 1997. And agent David Smith says it's a fairy tale that's coming true for more and more self-published writers.

"Self-publishing has definitely become a viable alternative for people who want to make a mark and get noticed," says Smith, who owns DHS Literary Agency, Inc. in Dallas, Texas. "The major houses do so much gambling; they have to roll the dice every time they take on a new project." Smith says the enormous expense of editing and designing a book means more publishers are looking at self-published books. "When they find a book with quality that has had a little test market, it minimizes their risk."

Smith says that Fowler, who owns a Texas greeting card company, published a print run of 500 copies of *Could You Love Me* . . . . When that run promptly sold out, Fowler ran a larger printing of 10,000 copies. Within six months she sold nearly half, becoming a holiday sensation in Austin. The book became Austin's 1994's #2 Christmas bestseller and 1995's Valentine's Day #1 bestseller. At that point she began to think of national distribution, and contacted Smith.

Smith says having a self-published book picked up by a major publisher is still a long shot, but there are some things authors can do to increase their projects' appeal. Attention to all the details of packaging and production are important. That's what paid off for Beth Fowler. He notes, "Most self-published books are not done very professionally. This book looked like it was done by a professional . . . it was a perfect trim size, and the cover art was simple, but very eye-catching." Even the simple typeface complemented the text.

Smith recommends authors have a clear sense of the potential market for their work. "You need to have a good platform to sell from," he advises. Be prepared to capitalize on those strengths by researching possible outlets for your work. Smith feels *Could You Love Me* . . . has a broad audience. "It appeals to dog owners," he says, "but it's also a book about love." Smith says Fowler decided to take advantage of this by placing her book with bookstores that carried similar "warm, fuzzy" books, and arranged tie-ins with local pet outlets.

Self-published authors can learn, even from rejection. Smith tells hopeful authors to be open to suggestions and willing to revise. "If [authors] haven't been able to place their work with a publisher, they need to listen to what publishers say about *why* the book is not marketable."

Even after a self-published book has attracted a publisher's attention, authors need to keep an open mind about revisions. Strategies that prove successful in small markets may not work for a major publisher, Smith points out. "Authors need to remember that the big trade houses are looking to publish a book with national appeal," and need to be flexible about making changes that might make the book more appealing to a wider audience. The ultimate goal is the same for both a self-published author and a national publisher: "To sell as many copies as humanly possible!"

Some formats are more successful than others, Smith believes. Although he represents many fiction writers, a self-published novel would have more difficulty attracting a major publisher. "But then again," he adds, "there are no absolutes. Anything works if it works!" And sometimes, fairy tales *do* come true.
—*Alison Holm*

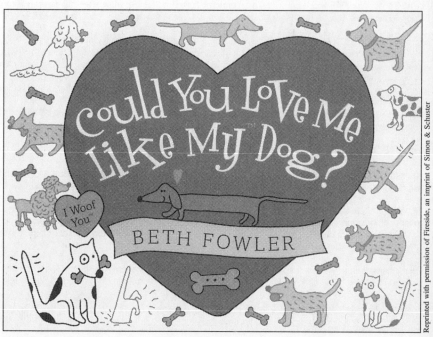

autobiography; business; cooking/food/nutrition; current affairs; ethnic/cultural interests; gay/lesbian issues; government/politics/law; health/medicine; history; juvenile nonfiction; money/finance/economics; music/theater/dance/film; nature/environment; New Age/metaphysics; psychology/healing; religious/inspirational; self-help/personal improvement; women's issues/women's studies. Considers these fiction areas: contemporary issues; detective/police/crime; erotica; ethnic; experimental; fantasy; feminist; gay; glitz; historical; humor/satire; juvenile; literary; mainstream; mystery/suspense; religious/inspirational; young adult. Query with outline/proposal and SASE. Reports in 5 weeks on queries; 2 months on mss.
Recent Sales: *Out of the Blue*, by Mark Hansen (HarperCollins).
Terms: Agent receives 15% commission on domestic sales; 25% on foreign sales. Offers written contract, binding for 3 years. Charges for "photocopying, long-distance calls, etc."
Writers' Conferences: Mystery Writers of America.
Tips: Obtains new clients through recommendations from others.

DH LITERARY, INC., (I, II), (formerly David Hendin Literary), P.O. Box 990, Nyack NY 10960-0990. (212)753-7942. E-mail: dhendin@aol.com. Contact: David Hendin. Estab. 1993. Member of AAR. Represents 25 clients. 75% of clients are new/previously unpublished writers. Specializes in trade fiction, nonfiction and newspaper syndication of columns or comic strips. Currently handles: 60% nonfiction books; 10% scholarly books; 20% novels; 10% syndicated material.
   • Prior to opening his agency, Mr. Hendin served as president and publisher for Pharos Books/
   World Almanac as well as senior VP and COO at sister company United Feature Syndicate.
Handles: Nonfiction books, scholarly books, novels, syndicated material. Considers these nonfiction areas: agriculture/horticulture; animals; anthropology/archaeology; art/architecture/design; biography/autobiography; business; child guidance/parenting; cooking/food/nutrition; current affairs; education; ethnic/cultural interests; gay/lesbian issues; government/politics/law; health/medicine; history; how-to; humor; language/literature/criticism; military/war; money/finance/economics; music/dance/theater/film; nature/environment; New Age/metaphysics; photography; popular culture; psychology; religious/inspirational; science/technology; self-help/personal improvement; sociology; sports; true crime/investigative; women's issues/women's studies. Considers these fiction areas: action/adventure; cartoon/comic; contemporary issues; detective/police/crime; ethnic; feminist; gay; glitz; historical; horror; humor/satire; lesbian; literary; mainstream; psychic/supernatural; thriller/espionage; westerns/frontier. Reports in 2 weeks on queries; 1 month on mss.
Recent Sales: *The Thin You Within You*, by Abraham Twerski, MD (St. Martin's); *The Exodus Enigma*, by Gary Greenburg (Carol Publishing); *Miss Manners Tells You How To Run The World*, by Judith Martin (Crown); *Experiencing The Deceased*, by Dr. Eda Devers (Andrews & McMeel); *His Promised Land: the Memoir of John P. Parker*, by John Parker with Stewart Sprague (W. W. Norton).
Terms: Agent receives 15% commission on domestic sales; 20% on foreign sales. Offers written contract, binding for 1 year. Charges for out of pocket expenses for postage, photocopying manuscript, and overseas phone calls specifically related to a book.
Tips: Obtains new clients through referrals from others (clients, writers, publishers). "Have your project in mind and on paper before you submit. Too many writers/cartoonists say 'I'm good . . . get me a project.' Publishers want writers with their own great ideas and their own unique voice. No faxed submissions."

‡DHS LITERARY, INC., (II, IV), 6060 N. Central Expwy., Suite 624, Dallas TX 75206. (214)363-4422. Fax: (214)363-4423. E-mail: dhslit@computek.net. Contact: David Hale Smith or V. Michele Lewis, submissions director. Estab. 1994. Represents 30 clients. 50% of clients are new/previously unpublished writers. Specializes in commercial fiction and nonfiction for adult trade market. Currently handles: 50% nonfiction books; 50% novels.
   • Prior to opening his agency, Mr. Smith served as an agent with Dupree/Miller & Associates.
Handles: Nonfiction books, novels. Considers these nonfiction areas: biography/autobiography; business; child guidance/parenting; computers/electronics; cooking/food/nutrition; current affairs; ethnic/cultural interests; gay/lesbian issues; popular culture; sports; true crime/investigative. Considers these fiction areas: action/adventure; detective/police/crime; erotica; ethnic; feminist; gay; historical; horror; literary; mainstream; mystery/suspense; sports; thriller/espionage; westerns/frontier. Query for fiction; send outline/proposal and sample chapters for nonfiction. Reports in 2 weeks on queries; 10 weeks on mss.
Recent Sales: *New Wave Diary*, by George Gimarc (St. Martin's Press); *The Winter Wolf* (and 2 untitled fiction), by Richard Parry (TOR Books); *Could You Love Me Like My Dog?*, by Beth Fowler (Simon & Schuster); *The Poison Tree*, by F.M. O'Rourke (Simon & Schuster); *A Flash of Red*, by Clay Harvey (Putnam/Berkley).
Terms: Agent receives 15% commission on domestic sales; 25% on foreign sales. Offers written contract, with 30 days cancellation clause or upon mutual consent. Charges for client expenses, i.e., postage, photocopying. 100% of business is derived from commissions on sales.

Writers' Conferences: Pike's Peak Writers Conference, (Colorado Springs CO, April); University of Texas-Dallas "Craft of Writing" (Dallas TX, September); University of Oklahoma "Short Course on Professional Writing" (Norman OK, June).

Tips: Obtains new clients through referrals from other clients, editors and agents, presentations at writers conferences and via unsolicited submissions. "Remember to be courteous and professional, and to treat marketing your work and approaching an agent as you would any formal business matter. When in doubt, always query first—in writing—with SASE."

ANITA DIAMANT, THE WRITER'S WORKSHOP, INC., (II), 310 Madison Ave., New York NY 10017-6009. (212)687-1122. Contact: Anita Diamant. Estab. 1917. Member of AAR. Represents 125 clients. 25% of clients are new/previously unpublished writers. Currently handles: 20% nonfiction books; 80% novels. Member agents: Robin Rue (fiction and nonfiction); Ashley Kraas (fiction); John Riley (fiction and nonfiction).

● Prior to opening her agency, Ms. Diamant worked as a reporter, writer, magazine editor and journalism professor. See Ms. Diamant's article, A Monday in the Life of an Agent, in this edition of the *Guide*.

Handles: Nonfiction books, young adults, novels. Considers these nonfiction areas: animals; art/architecture/design; biography/autobiography; business; child guidance/parenting; cooking/food/nutrition; crafts/hobbies; current affairs; government/politics/law; health/medicine; history; juvenile nonfiction; money/finance/economics; nature/environment; New Age/metaphysics; psychology; religious/inspirational; science/technology; self-help/personal improvement; sports; true crime/investigative; women's issues/women's studies. Considers these fiction areas: action/adventure; contemporary issues; detective/police/crime; experimental; family saga; feminist; gay; historical; juvenile; literary; mainstream; mystery/suspense; psychic/supernatural; religious/inspiration; romance; thriller/espionage; westerns/frontier; young adult. Query. Reports "at once" on queries; 3 weeks on mss.

Recent Sales: *All That Glitters*, by V.C. Andrews (Pocket); *Why Smart People Do Dumb Things*, by John Tarrand (Fireside); *Jacqueline Kennedy Onassis*, by Lester David (Carol); *Old Ways in the New World*, by Richard Conroy (St. Martin's); *Death of Love*, by Bartholomew Gill (Morrow).

Terms: Agent receives 15% commission on domestic sales; 20% on foreign sales. Offers written contract.

Writers' Conferences: RWA; ABA.

Tips: Obtains new clients through "recommendations from publishers and clients, appearances at writers' conferences, and through readers of my written articles."

DIAMOND LITERARY AGENCY, INC., (III), P.O. Box 117, Arvada CO 80001. (303)759-0291. President: Pat Dalton. Contact: Jean Patrick. Estab. 1982. Represents 20 clients. 10% of clients are new/previously unpublished writers. Specializes in romance, romantic suspense, women's fiction, thrillers, mysteries. Currently handles: 20% nonfiction books; 80% novels.

Handles: Nonfiction books, novels. Considers these nonfiction areas with mass market appeal: business; health/medicine; money/finance/economics; psychology; self-help/personal improvement. Considers these fiction areas: action/adventure; contemporary issues; detective/police/crime; family saga; glitz; historical; mainstream; mystery/suspense; romance; thriller/espionage. Reports in 1 month on mss (partials).

Recent Sales: Specializes in romance, including sales to Harlequin and Silhouette. Specifics on request if representation offered.

Terms: Agent receives 15% commission on domestic sales; 20% on foreign sales. Offers written contract, binding for 2 years "unless author is well established." Charges a "$15 submission fee for writers who have not previously published the same type of book." Charges for express and foreign postage. "Writers provide the necessary photostat copies."

Tips: Obtains new clients through "referrals from writers, or someone's submitting saleable material. We represent only clients who are professionals in writing quality, presentation, conduct and attitudes—whether published or unpublished. Send a SASE for agency information and submission procedures. People who are not yet clients should not telephone. We consider query letters a waste of time—most of all the writer's, secondly the agent's. Submit approximately first 50 pages and complete synopsis for books, along with SASE and standard-sized audiocassette tape for possible agent comments. Non-clients who haven't sold the SAME TYPE of book or script within five years must include a $15 submission fee by money order or cashier's check. Material not accompanied by SASE is not returned. Until mid-1997 only considering new clients who are previously published and romance suspense or contemporary romance writers (series or single title). Previously unpublished writers with completed romance suspense or contemporary romance manuscripts must have a letter of recommendation from a client, editor or other published author personally known to us."

SANDRA DIJKSTRA LITERARY AGENCY, (II), 1155 Camino del Mar, #515, Del Mar CA 92014. (619)755-3115. Contact: Debra Ginsberg. Estab. 1981. Member of AAR, Authors Guild, PEN West, Poets and Editors, MWA. Represents 100 clients. 30% of clients are new/previously unpublished writers. "We specialize in a number of fields." Currently handles: 60% nonfiction books; 5% juvenile books; 35% novels. Member agent: Sandra Dijkstra.
Handles: Nonfiction books, novels. Considers these nonfiction areas: anthropology; biography/autobiography; business; child guidance/parenting; nutrition; current affairs; ethnic/cultural interests; government/politics; health/medicine; history; literary studies (trade only); military/war (trade only); money/finance/economics; nature/environment; psychology; science/technology; self-help/personal improvement; sociology; sports; true crime/investigative; women's issues/women's studies. Considers these fiction areas: contemporary issues; detective/police/crime; ethnic; family saga; feminist; literary; mainstream; mystery/suspense; thriller/espionage. Send "outline/proposal with sample chapters for nonfiction, synopsis and first 50 pages for fiction and SASE." Reports in 2-4 weeks on queries; 1-6 weeks on mss.
Recent Sales: *Dear Zoe*, by Max DePree (Harper San Francisco); *Momma's Girl*, by Veronica Chambers (Riverhead, Putnam); *How One of You Can Bring the Two of You Together*, by Susan Page (Broadway Books, BDD); *The Falconer*, by Elaine Clark McCarthy (Random House); untitled, by Janell Cannon (children's—Harcourt Brace); *Why Good Girls Don't Get Ahead But Gutsy Girls Do*, by Kate White (Warner Books).
Terms: Agent receives 15% commission on domestic sales; 20% on foreign sales. Offers written contract, binding for 1 year. Charges for expenses years we are *active* on author's behalf) to cover domestic costs so that we can spend time selling books instead of accounting expenses. We also charge for the photocopying of the full manuscript or nonfiction proposal and for foreign postage."
Writers' Conferences: "Have attended Squaw Valley, Santa Barbara, Asilomar, Southern California Writers Conference, Rocky Mountain Fiction Writers, to name a few. We also speak regularly for writers groups such as PEN West and the Independent Writers Association."
Tips: Obtains new clients "primarily through referrals/recommendations, but also through queries and conferences and often by solicitation. Be professional and learn the standard procedures for submitting your work. Give full biographical information on yourself, especially for a nonfiction project. Always include SASE with correct return postage for your own protection of your work. Query with a 1 or 2 page letter first and always include postage. Nine page letters telling us your life story, or your book's, are unprofessional and usually not read. Tell us about your book and write your query well. It's our first introduction to who you are and what you can do! Call if you don't hear within a reasonable period of time. Be a regular patron of bookstores and study what kind of books are being published. READ. Check out your local library and bookstores—you'll find lots of books on writing and the publishing industry that will help you! At conferences, ask published writers about their agents. Don't believe the myth that an agent has to be in New York to be successful—we've already disproved it!"

THE JONATHAN DOLGER AGENCY, (II), 49 E. 96th St., Suite 9B, New York NY 10128. (212)427-1853. President: Jonathan Dolger. Contact: Tom Wilson. Estab. 1980. Member of AAR. Represents 70 clients. 25% of clients are new/unpublished writers. Writer must have been previously published if submitting fiction. Prefers to work with published/established authors; works with a small number of new/unpublished writers. Specializes in adult trade fiction and nonfiction, and illustrated books.
Handles: Nonfiction books, novels, illustrated books. Query with outline and SASE.
Terms: Agent receives 15% commission on domestic and dramatic sales; 25% on foreign sales. Charges for "standard expenses."

DONADIO AND ASHWORTH, INC., (II), 121 W. 27th St., Suite 704, New York NY 10011. (212)691-8077. Fax: (212)633-2837. Contact: Candida Donadio, Neil Olson. Estab. 1970. Member of AAR. Represents 100 clients. Specializes in literary fiction and nonfiction. Currently handles: 40% nonfiction; 50% novels; 10% short story collections. Member agent: Edward Hibbert (literary fiction).
Handles: Nonfiction books, novels, short story collections. Query with 50 pages and SASE. Reports in 1 month on queries; 2 months on mss.

The publishing field is constantly changing! If you're still using this book and it is 1997 or later, buy the newest edition of Guide to Literary Agents *at your favorite bookstore or order directly from* Writer's Digest Books.

Terms: Agent receives 15% commission on domestic sales; 20% on foreign sales.

DOYEN LITERARY SERVICES, INC., (II), 1931 660th St., Newell IA 50568-7613. (712)272-3300. President: (Ms.) B.J. Doyen. Estab. 1988. Member of RWA, SCBA. Represents 50 clients. 20% of clients are new/previously unpublished writers. Specializes in nonfiction and handles all genre and mainstream fiction mainly for adults (some children's). Currently handles: 70% nonfiction books; 5% juvenile books; 25% novels. No poetry books.

• See B.J. Doyen's article, Know Your Rights, in the 1994 edition of the *Guide*.

Handles: Nonfiction books, juvenile books, novels. Considers most nonfiction areas. No gay/lesbian issues, religious/inspirational, or translations. Considers these fiction areas: action/adventure; contemporary issues; detective/police/crime; ethnic; experimental; family saga; fantasy; glitz; historical; horror; humor/satire; juvenile; literary; mainstream; mystery/suspense; psychic/supernatural; romance (contemporary, historical, regency); science fiction; thriller/espionage; westerns/frontier; young adult. Query first with SASE. Reports immediately on queries; 6-8 weeks on mss.

Recent Sales: *Homemade Money*, by Barbara Brabec (Betterway); *Megahealth*, by Sorenson (Evans); *The Family Guide to Financial Aid for Higher Education*, by Black (Putnam/Perigee).

Terms: Agent receives 15% commission on domestic sales; 20% commission on foreign sales. Offers written contract, binding for 1 year.

Tips: "We are very interested in nonfiction book ideas at this time; will consider most topics. Many writers come to us from referrals, but we also get quite a few who initially approach us with query letters. Do *not* use phone queries unless you are successfully published or a celebrity. It is best if you do not collect editorial rejections prior to seeking an agent, but if you do, be up-front and honest about it. Do not submit your manuscript to more than one agent at a time—querying first can save you (and us) much time. We're open to established or beginning writers—just send us a terrific letter with SASE!"

DRAGON LITERARY, INC., (II), 1822 New York Dr., Salt Lake City UT 84116. Contact: Bruce D. Richardson. Estab. 1991. 80% of clients are new/previously unpublished writers. Currently handles: 60% novels; 20% movie scripts; 20% TV scripts.

Handles: Novels, movie scripts, TV scripts. Open to all nonfiction and fiction areas on a case-by-case basis. "We'll look at anything; if it's too entertaining to put down, it'll get a good read." Send *detailed* synopsis (not mss) with reference to writer's guide. Reports in approximately 2 weeks on queries.

Terms: Agent receives 10% commission on all sales. Offers written contract, binding for 1 year, with 90-day "no sale" clause.

Tips: "Approximately 300 submissions per year. Don't be overanxious or annoying; we're all busy and being overbearing won't help. Writing exceptional material is the best way to find an agent."

ROBERT DUCAS, (II), 350 Hudson St., New York NY 10014. (212)924-8120. Fax: (212)924-8079. Contact: R. Ducas. Estab. 1981. Represents 55 clients. 15% of clients are new/previously unpublished writers. Specializes in nonfiction, journalistic exposé, biography, history. Currently handles: 70% nonfiction books; 2% scholarly books; 28% novels.

Handles: Nonfiction books, novels, novellas. Considers these nonfiction areas: animals; biography/autobiography; business; current affairs; gay/lesbian issues; government/politics/law; health/medicine; history; military/war; money/finance/economics; nature/environment; science/technology; sports; true crime/investigative. Considers these fiction areas: action/adventure; contemporary issues; detective/police/crime; family saga; literary; mainstream; mystery/suspense; sports; thriller/espionage. Send outline/proposal and SASE. Reports in 2 weeks on queries; 2 months on mss.

Terms: Agent receives 15% commission on domestic sales; 20% on foreign sales. Charges for photocopying and postage. "I also charge for messengers and overseas couriers to subagents."

Tips: Obtains new clients through recommendations.

DUPREE/MILLER AND ASSOCIATES INC. LITERARY, (II), 100 Highland Park Village, Suite 350, Dallas TX 75205. (214)559-BOOK. Fax: (214)559-PAGE. E-mail: dupreemiller@i-link.net. President: Jan Miller. Estab. 1984. Member of ABA. Represents 100 clients. 20% of clients are new/previously unpublished writers. Specializes in commercial fiction, nonfiction. Currently handles: 75% nonfiction books; 25% novels. Member agents: Jan Miller; Dean Williamson (president); Kay Olsen (submission director); Ashley Carroll (assistant to president).

Handles: Nonfiction books, scholarly books, novels, syndicated material. Considers all nonfiction areas. Considers these fiction areas: action/adventure; cartoon/comic; contemporary issues; detective/police/crime; ethnic; experimental; family saga; fantasy; feminist; gay; glitz; historical; horror; humor/satire; lesbian; literary; mainstream; mystery/suspense; picture book; psychic/supernatural; religious/inspirational; romance (contemporary, historical); science fiction; sports; thriller/espionage; westerns/frontier. Send outline plus 3 sample chapters. Reports in 1 week on queries; 8-12 weeks on mss.

Recent Sales: *First Things First*, by Dr. Stephen Covey; *Food*, by Susan Powter (Simon & Schuster); untitled, by Ken Hamblin (Simon & Schuster); *A Millionaire's Notebook*, by Steven Scott (Fireside/ Simon & Schuster).
Terms: Agent receives 15% commission on domestic sales. Offers written contract, binding for "no set amount of time. The contract can be cancelled by either agent or client, effective 30 days after cancellation." Charges $20 processing fee and express mail charges.
Writers' Conferences: Southwest Writers (Albuqurque NM); Brazos Writers (College Station TX).
Tips: Obtains new client through conferences, lectures, clients and "very frequently through publisher's referrals." If interested in agency representation "it is vital to have the material in the proper working format. As agents' policies differ, it is important to follow their guidelines. The best advice I can give is to work on establishing a strong proposal that provides sample chapters, an overall synopsis (fairly detailed) and some bio information on yourself. Do not send your proposal in pieces; it should be complete upon submission. Remember you are trying to sell your work and it should be in its best condition."

JANE DYSTEL LITERARY MANAGEMENT, (I, II), One Union Square West, New York NY 10003. (212)627-9100. Fax: (212)627-9313. Contact: Miriam Goderich. Estab. 1994. Member of AAR. Presently represents 150 clients. 50% of clients are new/previously unpublished writers. Specializes in commercial and literary fiction and nonfiction plus cookbooks. Currently handles: 80% nonfiction books; 15% novels; 1% short story collections; 4% cookbooks, photo books, collections.
● Prior to opening her agency, Ms. Dystel was a principal agent in Acton, Dystel, Leone and Jaffe. See her article, Building a Client List, in the 1995 edition of the *Guide*.
Handles: Nonfiction books, novels, cookbooks. Considers these nonfiction areas: animals; anthropology/archaeology; biography/autobiography; business; child guidance/parenting; cooking/food/nutrition; current affairs; education; ethnic/cultural interests; gay/lesbian issues; government/politics/law; health/medicine; history; humor; military/war; money/finance/economics; New Age/metaphysics; popular cultures; psychology; religious/inspirational; science/technology; true crime/investigative; women's issues/women's studies. Considers these fiction areas: Action/adventure; contemporary issues; detective/police/crime; ethnic; family saga; gay; lesbian; literary; mainstream; thriller/espionage. Query. Reports in 2 weeks on queries; 1 month on mss.
Recent Sales: *What the Deaf Mute Heard*, by Dan Gearino (Simon & Schuster); *Tiger's Tale*, by Gus Lee (Knopf); *I Never Forget A Meal*, by Michael Tucker (Little Brown); *Entries From a Hot Pink Diary*, by Todd Brown (Pocket Books).
Terms: Agent receives 15% commission on domestic sales; 19% of foreign sales. Offers written contract on a book to book basis. Charges for photocopying. Galley charges and book charges from the publisher are passed on to the author.
Writers' Conferences: West Coast Writers Conference (Whidbey Island WA, Columbus Day weekend); University of Iowa Writers' Conference.
Tips: Obtains new clients through recommendations from others, solicitation, at conferences.

EDUCATIONAL DESIGN SERVICES, INC., (II, IV), P.O. Box 253, Wantagh NY 11793-0253. (718)539-4107 or (516)221-0995. President: Bertram L. Linder. Vice President: Edwin Selzer. Estab. 1979. Represents 17 clients. 70% of clients are new/previously unpublished writers. Specializes in textual material for educational market. Currently handles: 100% textbooks.
Handles: Textbooks, scholarly books. Considers these nonfiction areas: anthropology/archaeology; business; child guidance/parenting; current affairs; ethnic/cultural interests; government/politics/law; history; juvenile nonfiction; language/literature/criticism; military/war; money/finance/economics; science/technology; sociology; women's issues/women's studies. Query with outline/proposal or outline plus 1-2 sample chapters. Reports in 1 month on queries; 4-6 weeks on mss.
Recent Sales: *New York and The Nation*, by McCarthy & Wattman (Amsco); *American History Worktext*, by Shakofsky (Minerva); *Nueva Historia de los Estados Unidos (Teachers Guide)*, (Minerva).
Terms: Agent receives 15% commission on domestic sales; 25% on foreign sales. Offers written contract. Charges for photocopying.
Tips: Obtains new clients through recommendations; at conferences; queries.

PETER ELEK ASSOCIATES, (II, IV), Box 223, Canal Street Station, New York NY 10013-2610. (212)431-9368. Fax: (212)966-5768. E-mail: 713714.2515@CompuServe.com. Contact: Jonathan Wurtzel. Estab. 1979. Represents 20 clients. Specializes in children's picture books, adult nonfiction. Currently handles: 30% juvenile books. Staff includes Gerardo Greco (Director of Project Development/Multimedia); Josh Feder (curriculum specialist).
Handles: Juvenile books (nonfiction, picture books). Considers anthropology; parenting; juvenile nonfiction; nature/environment; popular culture; science; true crime/investigative. Considers juvenile picture books. Query with outline/proposal and SASE. Reports in 2 weeks on queries; 3 weeks on mss.

Recent Sales: *Natural Worlds*, by Robert Bateman (Simon & Schuster); *I Was There* series, by various authors (Hyperion); *Lost Liners*, by Spencer Dunmore (Hyperion); *Parts*, by Tedd Arnold (Dial Books).
Terms: Agent receives 15% commission on domestic sales; 20% on foreign sales. If required, charges for photocopying, typing, courier charges.
Writers' Conferences: Internet (Atlanta GA); Frankfurt Book Fair (Frankfurt Germany, October); Milia (Cannes France); Bologna Children's Book Fair (Italy); Seybold (Boston, September).
Tips: Obtains new clients through recommendations and studying consumer and trade magazines. "No work returned unless appropriate packing and postage is remitted. Actively seeking intellectual property/content, text and images for strategic partnering for multimedia. We are currently licensing series and single projects (juvenile, YA and adult) for electronic platforms such as CD-ROM, CD-I and WWW. Our subsidiary company for this is The Content Company Inc.—contact Gerardo Greco, at the same address."

ETHAN ELLENBERG LITERARY AGENCY, (II), 548 Broadway, #5-E, New York NY 10012. (212)431-4554. Fax: (212)941-4652. Contact: Ethan Ellenberg. Estab. 1983. Represents 70 clients. 10% of clients are new/previously unpublished writers. Specializes in commercial and literary fiction, fantasy, including first novels, thrillers, mysteries, science fiction, all categories of romance fiction, quality nonfiction, including biography, history, health, spirituality, business and popular science. Currently handles: 25% nonfiction books; 75% novels.
• See Ethan Ellenberg's article, Understanding Your Book Contract, in this edition of the *Guide*.
Handles: Nonfiction books, novels. Considers these nonfiction areas: biography/autobiography; business; child guidance/parenting; cooking/food/nutrition; current affairs; health/medicine; history; juvenile nonfiction; New Age/metaphysics; psychology; religious/inspirational; science/technology; self-help/personal improvement; true crime/investigative. Considers these fiction areas: detective/police/crime; family saga; fantasy; historical; humor; juvenile; literary; mainstream; mystery/suspense; picture book; romance; science fiction; thriller/espionage; westerns/frontier; young adult. Send outline plus 3 sample chapters. Reports in 10 days on queries; 3-4 weeks on mss.
Recent Sales: 3 books illustrated by Julia Noonan (HarperCollins); *Dreamland*, by Mary Chapin Carpenter (HarperCollins); *Emma and Mommy Talk to God* and *Emma and Mommy and Angel Jane*, by Marianne Williamson (HarperCollins); sequel to *Fields and Pastures New*, by John McCormack (Crown); 2 new picture books by Eric Rohmann (winner of Caldecott Silver Medal for *Time Flies*) *(Crown); The Line* and untitled thriller by Bob Mayer (St. Martin's); 3 fantasy novels by Sharon Shinn (Berkley); 4 untitled westerns by Johnny Quarles (Avon).
Terms: Agent receives 15% on domestic sales; 10% on foreign sales. Offers written contract, "flexible." Charges for "direct expenses only: photocopying, postage."
Writers' Conferences: Attends a number of other RWA conferences (including Hawaii) and Novelists, Inc.
Tips: "We do consider new material from unsolicited authors. Write a good clear letter with a succinct description of your book. We prefer the first three chapters when we consider fiction. For all submissions you must include SASE for return or the material is discarded. It's always hard to break in, but talent will find a home. We continue to see natural storytellers and nonfiction writers with important books."

‡ELLIOTT AGENCY, (I, II), 130 Garth Rd., Suite 506, Scarsdale NY 10583. (914)725-7701. Fax: (914)472-7334. Contact: Elaine Elliott. Estab. 1995. Represents 15 clients. 40% of clients are new/previously unpublished writers. Currently handles: 10% nonfiction books; 80% novels; 10% short story collections.
Handles: Nonfiction books, novels, short story collections. Considers these nonfiction areas: anthropology/archaeology; humor; nature/environment; popular culture; science/technology; true crime/investigative. Considers these fiction areas: action/adventure; contemporary issues; detective/police/crime; ethnic; experimental; horror; humor/satire; literary; mainstream; regional; thriller/espionage. Query. Reports in 2 weeks on queries; 2 months on mss.
Terms: Agent receives 15% commission on domestic sales. No written contract. Agreement may be terminated by either party, at any time, for any reason. 100% of business is derived from commissions on sales.

For explanation of symbols, see the Key to Symbols and Abbreviations. For translation of an organization's acronym, see the Table of Acronyms. For unfamiliar words, check the Glossary.

Writers' Conferences: ABA (Chicago, June).
Tips: Obtains new clients through recommendations from editors and other agents, CompuServe writers forums.

NICHOLAS ELLISON, INC., (II), 55 Fifth Ave., 15th Floor, New York NY 10003. (212)206-6050. Affiliated with Sanford J. Greenburger Associates. Contact: Elizabeth Ziemska. Estab. 1983. Represents 70 clients. Currently handles: 25% nonfiction books; 75% novels. Member agent: Christina Harcar (foreign rights).
Handles: Nonfiction, novels. Considers most nonfiction areas. No biography, gay/lesbian issues or self-help. Considers literary and mainstream fiction. Query with SASE. Reporting time varies on queries.
Recent Sales: *Bloody Waters* and *Bloody Shame*, by Carolina Garcia-Aguilera (Riverhead/Putnam; TV rights to dePasse Entertainment; Shinchosa [Japan]; Bruna [Holland]).
Terms: Agent receives 15% commission on domestic sales; 20% commission on foreign sales.
Tips: Usually obtains new clients from word-of-mouth referrals.

ANN ELMO AGENCY INC., (III), 60 E. 42nd St., New York NY 10165. (212)661-2880, 2881. Fax: (212)661-2883. Contact: Lettie Lee. Estab. 1961. Member of AAR, MWA, Authors Guild. Member agents: Lettie Lee, Mari Cronin (plays).
Handles: Nonfiction, novels. Considers these nonfiction areas: anthropology/archaeology; art/architecture/design; biography/autobiography; business; child guidance/parenting; computers/electronics; cooking/food/nutrition; crafts/hobbies; current affairs; education; health/medicine; history; how-to; juvenile nonfiction; money/finance/economics; music/dance/theater/film; photography; popular culture; psychology; self-help/personal improvement; true crime/investigative; women's issues. Considers these fiction areas: action/adventure; contemporary issues; detective/police/crime; ethnic; family saga; feminist; glitz; historical; juvenile; literary; mainstream; mystery/suspense; psychic/supernatural; regional; romance (contemporary, gothic, historical, regency); thriller/espionage; young adult. Query with outline/proposal. Reports in 6-8 weeks "average" on queries.
Terms: Agent receives 15% commission on domestic sales; 20% on foreign sales. Offers written contract (standard AAR contract).
Tips: Obtains new clients through referrals. "Query first, and when asked please send properly prepared manuscript. A double-spaced, readable manuscript is the best recommendation. Include SASE, of course."

EMERALD LITERARY AGENCY, (I, II), 1212 N. Angelo Dr., Beverly Hills CA 90210. (310)247-0488. (310)247-0885. Contact: Debra Rodman. Estab. 1994. Represents 20 clients. 50% of clients are new/previously published writers. Currently handles: 75% nonfiction books; 25% novels.
Handles: Nonfiction books, scholarly books, novels, novellas. Considers these nonfiction areas: art; biography/autobiography; business; child guidance; computers/electronics; current affairs; finance/economics; literature/criticism; politics; popular culture; psychology; religious/inspirational; self-help/personal improvement; women's and men's issues. Considers these fiction areas: fantasy; literary; cutting edge fiction. Query with 3 sample chapters and SASE. Does not report on queries; 3 weeks on mss.
Recent Sales: *My Life With Elvis*, by Jim Dickerson and Scotty Moore, ed. by Richard Carlin (Schirmer Books, Simon & Schuster); *Story*, by Robert McKee, ed. by Judith Regan (Regan Books, HarperCollins Publishers); *Licking Our Wounds*, by Elise D'L Ihene (The Permanent Press); *Jack and Charlie*, by Howard Shanks (Commonwealth Publications, Canada).
Also Handles: Television and feature film writers who have had their films produced and who are currently working or have worked as staff writers on popular shows. Query. Reports in 10 days on queries; 3 weeks on mss.
Terms: Agent receives 15% commission on domestic sales; 10% on dramatic sales; 20% on foreign sales. Offers written contract. Charges for postage, photocopying.
Writers' Conferences: Maui.
Tips: Obtains new clients through referrals, luck, conferences and listings in *LMP* and *Hollywood Directory*.

ESQ. LITERARY PRODUCTIONS, (II), 1492 Cottontail Lane, La Jolla CA 92037-7427. (619)551-9383. Fax: (619)551-9382. E-mail: fdh161@aol.com. Contact: Sherrie Dixon, Esq. Estab. 1993. Represents 12 clients. 50% of clients are new/previously unpublished writers. Currently handles: 20% nonfiction books; 80% novels. Agency specializes in adult mainstream fiction. Member agent: D.S. Lada (mainstream fiction.)
Handles: Nonfiction books, novels. Considers these nonfiction areas: health/medicine; sports. Considers these fiction areas: action/adventure; contemporary issues; detective/police/crime; family saga; mainstream; mystery/suspense; thriller/espionage. Send outline, SASE and 3 sample chapters. Reports in 1-2 weeks on queries; 1 month on mss.

Recent Sales: Two untitled suspense novels, by Jodie Larsen (Dutton/Signet); *Strange Matter* series, by Engle & Barnes (Montage Publications); *Totally Fit: Mind, Body and Spirit*, By Lori "Ice"Fetrick and Dr. Robert Epstein (Masters Press).
Terms: Agent receives 15% commission on domestic sales; 20% on foreign sales. Offers written contract.

FELICIA ETH LITERARY REPRESENTATION, (II), 555 Bryant St., Suite 350, Palo Alto CA 94301-1700. (415)375-1276. Fax: (415)375-1277. Contact: Felicia Eth. Estab. 1988. Member of AAR. Represents 25-35 clients. Works with established and new writers; "for nonfiction, established expertise is certainly a plus, as is magazine publication—though not a prerequisite. I specialize in provocative, intelligent, thoughtful nonfiction on a wide array of subjects which are commercial and high-quality fiction; preferably mainstream and contemporary. I am highly selective, but also highly dedicated to those projects I represent." Currently handles: 85% nonfiction; 15% adult novels.
Handles: Nonfiction books, novels. Considers these nonfiction areas: animals; anthropology; biography/autobiography; business; child guidance/parenting; current affairs; ethnic/cultural interests; gay/lesbian issues; government/politics/law; health/medicine; history; nature/environment; popular culture; psychology; science/technology; sociology; true crime/investigative; women's issues/women's studies. Considers these fiction areas: ethnic; feminist; gay; lesbian; literary; mainstream; thriller/espionage. Query with outline. Reports in 3 weeks on queries; 1 month on proposals and sample pages.
Recent Sales: *Caught Up In Rapture*, by Sheneska Jackson (Simon & Schuster); *Courage to Compete: Competition and Intimacy in Women's Lives*, by Mariah Nelson (William Morrow); *The Kitty "CAT"a-log*, by Reed Huegel (Crown).
Terms: Agent receives 15% commission on domestic sales; 20% on dramatic sales; 20% on foreign sales. Charges for photocopying, express mail service—extraordinary expenses.
Writers' Conferences: Independent Writers of Southern California (LA); Conference of National Coalition of Independent Scholars (Berkeley CA); Writers Guild.

FARBER LITERARY AGENCY INC., (II), 14 E. 75th St., #2E, New York NY 10021. (212)861-7075. Fax: (212)861-7076. Contact: Ann Farber. Estab. 1989. Represents 30 clients. 84% of clients are new/previously unpublished writers. Currently handles: 65% fiction; 5% scholarly books; 20% stage plays.
Handles: Nonfiction books, textbooks, juvenile books, novels, stage plays. Considers these nonfiction areas: child guidance/parenting; cooking/food/nutrition; music/dance/theater/film; psychology. Considers these fiction areas: action/adventure; contemporary issues; humor/satire; juvenile; literary; mainstream; mystery/suspense; thriller/espionage; young adult. Send outline/proposal, 3 sample chapters and SASE. Reports in 1 week on queries; 1 month on mss.
Recent Sales: *Live A Little*, by Colin Neenan (Harcourt Brace); several books by Gloria Houston with various publishers.
Terms: Agent receives 15% commission on domestic sales; 20% on foreign sales. Offers written contract, binding for 2 years.
Tips: Obtains new clients through recommendations from others. Client must furnish copies of ms. "Our attorney, Donald C. Farber, is the author of many books. His services are available to the clients of the agency as part of the agency service."

FLORENCE FEILER LITERARY AGENCY, (III), 1524 Sunset Plaza Dr., Los Angeles CA 90069. (213)652-6920. Fax: (213)652-0945. Associate: Joyce Boorn. Estab. 1976. Member of PEN American Center, Women in Film, California Writers Club, MWA. Represents 40 clients. No unpublished writers. "Quality is the criterion." Specializes in fiction, nonfiction, screenplays, TV. No short stories.
● See the expanded listing for this agency in Script Agents.

‡FIRST BOOKS, (II), 2040 N. Milwaukee Ave., Chicago IL 60647. (312)276-5911. Estab. 1988. Represents 50 clients. 50% of clients are new/previously unpublished writers.
Handles: Nonfiction books, juvenile books, novels. Query. Reports in 1 month on queries.
Terms: Agent receives 15% commission on domestic sales; 20% on foreign sales. Offers written contract, binding for no specific length of time, with cancellation on demand by either party.
Tips: Obtains new clients through recommendations from others.

*JOYCE A. FLAHERTY, LITERARY AGENT, (II, III), 816 Lynda Court, St. Louis MO 63122-5531. (314)966-3057. Contact: Joyce or John Flaherty. Estab. 1980. Member of AAR, RWA, MWA, Author's Guild. Represents 50 clients. 5% of clients are new/previously unpublished writers. Currently handles: 25% nonfiction books; 75% novels. Member agents: Joyce A. Flaherty (women's fiction, romance, mystery and suspense, general fiction and nonfiction); John Flaherty (thrillers, male-oriented mysteries and espionage novels; also military fiction and nonfiction).
Handles: Nonfiction books, novels. Considers these nonfiction areas: collectibles; Americana; animals; biography/autobiography (celebrity); child guidance/parenting; crafts/hobbies; health/medicine; history (Americana); how-to; military/war; nature/environment; popular culture; psychology; self-help/personal improvement; sociology; true crime/investigative; women's issues/women's studies. Consid-

ers these fiction areas: contemporary issues; crime; family saga; feminist; frontier; historical; literary; mainstream; military/aviation/war; mystery/suspense; psychic/supernatural; romance (contemporary, regency); thriller/espionage; women's fiction. Send outline plus 1 sample chapter and SASE. No unsolicited mss. Reports in 6 weeks on queries; 2 months on mss unless otherwise agreed on.

Recent Sales: *Bride Of The Lion*, by Elizabeth Stuart (St. Martin's Press); *Shawnee Moon*, by Judith French (Avon Books); *Splendor*, by Charlene Cross (Pocket Books); *Riverbend*, by Marcia Martin (Penguin-Onyx).

Terms: Agent receives 15% commission on domestic sales; 25-30% on foreign sales. Charges $50 marketing fee for new clients unless currently published book authors.

Writers' Conferences: Attends Romance Writers of America; Virginia Romance Writers (Williamsburg VA); Moonlight & Magnolias (Atlanta GA); California Writers Club (Asilomar Conference Center, Pacific Grove CA); Lowcountry Romance Writers of America (Charleston SC, April 1996).

Tips: Obtains new clients through recommendations from editors and clients, writers' conferences and from queries. "Be concise in a letter or by phone and well focused. Always include a SASE as well as your phone number. If you want an agent to return your call, leave word to call you collect if you're not currently the agent's client. If a query is a multiple submission, be sure to say so and mail them all at the same time so that everyone has the same chance. Know something about the agent beforehand so that you're not wasting each other's time. Be specific about word length of project and when it will be completed if not completed at the time of contact. Be brief!"

FLAMING STAR LITERARY ENTERPRISES, (II), 320 Riverside Dr., New York NY 10025. Contact: Joseph B. Vallely or Janis C. Vallely. Estab. 1985. Represents 50 clients. 25% of clients are new/previously unpublished writers. Specializes in upscale commercial fiction and nonfiction. Currently handles: 75% nonfiction books; 25% novels.

● Prior to opening his agency, Mr. Vallely served as national sales manager for Dell.

Handles: Nonfiction books, novels. Considers these nonfiction areas: current affairs; government/politics/law; health/medicine; nature/environment; New Age/metaphysics; science/technology; self-help/personal improvement; sports. Considers only upscale commercial fiction. Query with SASE. Reports in 1 week on queries.

Terms: Agent receives 15% commission on domestic sales; 20% on foreign sales. Offers written contract. Charges for photocopying, postage, long distance phone calls only.

Tips: Obtains new clients over the transom and through referrals.

FLANNERY LITERARY, (II), 34-36 28th St., #5, Long Island City NY 11106-3516. (718)472-0523. Fax: (718)482-0718. Contact: Jennifer Flannery. Estab. 1992. Represents 25 clients. 75% of clients are new/previously unpublished writers. Specializes in children's and young adult, juvenile fiction and nonfiction. Currently handles: 5% nonfiction books; 95% juvenile books.

Handles: Nonfiction books, juvenile books. Considers these nonfiction areas: child guidance/parenting; juvenile nonfiction. Considers these fiction areas: action/adventure; contemporary issues; ethnic; experimental; family saga; historical; humor/satire; juvenile; literary; mainstream; mystery/suspense; picture book; sports; western/frontier; young adult. Query. Reports in 2 weeks on queries; 6 weeks on mss.

Also Handles: Movie scripts (feature film, animation), TV scripts (TV mow, miniseries, animation). Considers these script subject areas: action/adventure; comedy; ethnic; family saga; historical; humor; juvenile; mainstream; mystery/suspense; teen. Query. Reports in 2 weeks on queries; 6 weeks on scripts.

Terms: Agent receives 15% commission on domestic sales; 20% on foreign sales. Offers written contract, binding for life of book in print, with 30 day cancellation clause. 100% of business is derived from commissions on sales.

Writers' Conferences: SCBWI Fall Conference (Alabama/Georgia region, October).

Tips: Obtains new clients through referrals. "Write an engrossing succinct query describing your work."

PETER FLEMING AGENCY, (IV), P.O. Box 458, Pacific Palisades CA 90272. (310)454-1373. Contact: Peter Fleming. Estab. 1962. Specializes in "nonfiction books: innovative, helpful, contrarian, individualistic, pro-free market . . . with bestseller big market potential." Currently handles: 100% nonfiction books.

Handles: Nonfiction books. Considers "any nonfiction area with a positive, innovative, helpful, professional, successful approach to improving the world (and abandoning special interests, corruption and patronage)." Query with SASE.

Recent Sales: *How to Stop Foreclosure*, by Lloyd Segal (Nolo Press).

Terms: Agent receives 15% commission on domestic sales; 25% on foreign sales. Offers written contract, binding for 1 year. Charges "only those fees agreed to *in writing*, i.e., NY-ABA expenses shared. We may ask for a TV contract, too."

Tips: Obtains new clients "through a *sensational*, different, one of a kind idea for a book usually backed by the writer's experience in that area of expertise. If you give seminars, you can begin by self-publishing, test marketing with direct sales. One of my clients sold 70,000 copies through his speeches and travels."

B.R. FLEURY AGENCY, (I, II), 1228 E. Colonial Dr., Orlando FL 32803. (407)896-4976. Contact: Blanche or Margaret. Estab. 1994. Signatory of WGA. Currently handles: 50% books; 50% scripts.
● See the expanded listing for this agency in Script Agents.

FOGELMAN LITERARY AGENCY, (I), 7515 Greenville Ave., Suite 712, Dallas TX 75231. (214)361-9956. Fax: (214)361-9553. Contact: Evan Fogelman or Linda Diehl Kruger. Estab. 1990. Member of AAR. Represents 85-100 clients. Specializes in romance fiction and nonfiction. Currently handles: 40% nonfiction books; 60% novels.
Handles: Considers these nonfiction areas: biography; business; current affairs; government/politics/law; money; nutrition; parenting; popular culture; self-help; true crime; contemporary women's issues/women's studies. Query with SASE. Reports in 1-2 working days on 1-page query. Unsolicited mss not accepted.
Terms: Agent receives 15% commission on domestic sales; varying on foreign sales.
Writers' Conferences: Many RWA and multi-genre conferences throughout the world.
Tips: Obtains new clients through referrals, through writers conferences and solicited submissions. Published authors may call; unpublished authors please query.

‡THE FOLEY LITERARY AGENCY, (III, V), 34 E. 38th St., New York NY 10016. (212)686-6930. Contact: Joan or Joseph Foley. Estab. 1956. Represents 15 clients. 5% of clients are new/previously unpublished writers. Currently handles: 75% nonfiction books; 25% novels.
Handles: Nonfiction books, novels. Query with letter, brief outline and SASE. Reports in 2 weeks on queries.
Terms: Agent receives 10% commission on domestic sales; 20% on foreign sales. Charges for photocopying, messenger service and unusual expenses (international phone, etc.). 100% of business is derived from commissions on sales.
Tips: Obtains new clients through recommendations from others. Desires brevity in querying. Include SASE.

‡LYNN C. FRANKLIN ASSOCIATES, LTD., (II), 386 Park Ave. S., #1102, New York NY 10016. (212)689-1842. Fax: (212)213-0649. Contact: Masha Alexander. Estab. 1987. Member of PEN America. Represents 25 clients. 50% of clients are new/previously unpublished writers. Specializes in general nonfiction with a special interest in health, biography, international affairs and spirituality. Currently handles: 90% nonfiction books; 10% novels.
Handles: Nonfiction books, novellas. Considers these nonfiction areas: biography/autobiography; current affairs; health/medicine; history; New Age/metaphysics; psychology; religious/inspirational; self-help/personal improvement. Considers literary and mainstream commercial fiction. Query with SASE. No unsolicited mss. Reports in 2 weeks on queries; 6 weeks on mss.
Recent Sales: *At The Still Point*, by Carol Buckley (Simon & Schuster).
Terms: Agent receives 15% commission on domestic sales; 20% on foreign sales. Offers written contract, with 60 days cancellation clause. Charges for postage, photocopying, long distance telephone if significant. 100% of business is derived from commissions on sales.
Tips: Obtains new clients through recommendations from others and from solicitation.

JAY GARON-BROOKE ASSOC. INC., (II), 101 W. 55th St., Suite 5K, New York NY 10019. (212)581-8300. Vice President: Jean Free. Estab. 1952. Member of AAR, signatory of WGA. Represents 80 clients. 10% of clients are new/previously unpublished writers. Specializes in mainstream fiction and nonfiction. Currently handles: 15% nonfiction books; 75% novels; 5% movie scripts; 3% TV scripts. Member agents: Nancy Coffey, Dick Duane, Bob Thixton.
● Mr. Garon passed away in 1995. The agency will continue to operate under the direction of his associates.
Handles: Nonfiction books, novels, movie scripts, TV scripts, stage plays. Considers these nonfiction areas: biography/autobiography; child guidance/parenting; gay/lesbian issues; health/medicine; history; military/war; music/dance/theater/film; psychology; self-help/personal improvement; true crime/investigative. Considers these fiction areas: contemporary issues; detective/police/crime; family saga; fantasy; gay; literary; mainstream; mystery/suspense; romance; science fiction. Query with SASE. Reports in 3 weeks on queries; 2 months on mss.
Recent Sales: *The Runaway Jury*, by John Grisham (Doubleday-Dell); *Arc Light*, by Eric Harry (Simon & Schuster); *Judgement Day*, by Patrick Reinken (Simon & Schuster); *Intimate*, by Elizabeth Gage (Pocket Book—hardcover & paperback).

Terms: Agent receives 15% on domestic sales; 30% on foreign sales. Offers written contract, binding for 3-5 years. Charges for "photocopying if author does not provide copies."
Tips: Obtains new clients through referrals and from queries. "Send query letter first giving the essence of the manuscript and a personal or career bio with SASE."

MAX GARTENBERG, LITERARY AGENT, (II,III), 521 Fifth Ave., Suite 1700, New York NY 10175-0105. (212)860-8451. Contact: Max Gartenberg. Estab. 1954. Represents 30 clients. 5% of clients are new writers. Currently handles: 90% nonfiction books; 10% novels.
Handles: Nonfiction books. Considers these nonfiction areas: agriculture/horticulture; animals; art/architecture/design; biography/autobiography; child guidance/parenting; current affairs; health/medicine; history; military/war; money/finance/economics; music/dance/theater/film; nature/environment; psychology; science/technology; self-help/personal improvement; sports; true crime/investigative; women's issues/women's studies. Query. Reports in 2 weeks on queries; 6 weeks on mss.
Recent Sales: *Unorthodox Methods of a Hundred Battles*, by Ralph D. Sawyer (Westview Press); *Answers to Lucky*, by Howard Owen (HarperCollins); *Wild Life*, by Edward Kanze (Crown Publishers); *In Search of the Old Ones*, by David Roberts (Simon & Schuster).
Terms: Agent receives 15% commission on first domestic sale, 10% commission on subsequent domestic sales; 15% on foreign sales.
Tips: Obtains new clients "primarily by recommendations from others, but often enough by following up on good query letters. However, this is a small agency serving established writers, and new writers whose work it is able to handle are few and far between. Nonfiction is more likely to be of interest here than fiction, and category fiction not at all."

RICHARD GAUTREAUX—A LITERARY AGENCY (II), 2742 Jasper St., Kenner LA 70062. (504)466-6741. Contact: Jay Richards. Estab. 1985. Represents 6 clients. 75% of clients are new/previously unpublished writers. Currently handles: 45% novels; 25% movie scripts; 20% TV scripts; 5% short story collections.
   • See the expanded listing for this agency in Script Agents.

‡THE SEBASTIAN GIBSON AGENCY, (I), 125 Tahquitz Canyon Way, Suite 200, Palm Springs CA 92262. (619)322-2200. Fax: (619)322-3857. Contact: Sebastian Gibson. Estab. 1995. Member of the California Bar Association and Desert Bar Association. 100% of clients are new/previously unpublished writers. Specializes in fiction, movie scripts, stage musicals. Currently handles: 50% novels; 25% movie scripts; 25% stage plays.
Handles: Nonfiction books, juvenile books, movie scripts, novels, TV scripts. Considers these nonfiction areas: animals; anthropology/archaeology; art/architecture/design; biography/autobiography; business; cooking/food/nutrition; current affairs; ethnic/cultural interests; government/politics/law; health/medicine; history; humor; military/war; money/finance/economics; music/dance/theater/film; nature/environment; New Age/metaphysics; photography; popular culture; psychology; religious/inspirational; science/technology; self-help/personal improvement; sociology; sports; translations; true crime/investigative; women's issues/women's studies. Considers these fiction areas: action/adventure; cartoon/comic; contemporary issues; detective/police/crime; ethnic; family saga; fantasy; feminist; glitz; historical; horror; humor/satire; juvenile; literary; mainstream; picture book; psychic/supernatural; regional; religious/inspirational; romance (contemporary, gothic, historical, regency); science fiction; sports; thriller/espionage; westerns/frontier; young adult. Send outline and 3 sample chapters; SASE required for a response. Reports in 3 weeks.
Terms: Agent receives 10% commission on domestic sales; 20% on foreign sales. Offers written contract, with 30 days cancellation notice. Charges for postage, photocopying and express mail fees charged only against sales.
Writers' Conference: ABA (Chicago, June); Book Fair (Frankfurt); London Int'l Book Fair.
Tips: Obtains new clients through advertising, queries and book proposals, and through the representation of entertainment clients. "Consider hiring a freelance editor to make corrections and assist you in preparing book proposals. Try to develop unusual characters in your novels, and novel approaches to nonfiction. Manuscripts should be clean and professional looking and without errors. Do not send unsolicited manuscripts or disks. Save your money and effort for redrafts. Don't give up. We want to help you become published. But your work must be very readable without plot problems or grammatical

Agents ranked I-IV are actively seeking new clients. Those ranked V or those who prefer not to be listed have been included to inform you they are not currently looking for new clients.

errors. Do not send sample chapters or book proposals until you've completed at least your fourth draft. Unless you're famous, don't send autobiographies."

GODDARD BOOK GROUP, (II), (formerly Connie Goddard Book Development), 203 N. Wabash Ave., Chicago IL 60601-2415. (312)759-5822. Contact: Connie Goddard. Estab. 1992. Represents 25 clients. 30% of clients are new/previously unpublished writers. Specializes in Chicago-area writers and projects with Midwest origins. Currently handles: 85% nonfiction books; 15% novels.
● Prior to opening her agency, Ms. Goddard served as an editor and writer for various publishing houses and as a correspondent for *Publishers Weekly*.
Handles: Nonfiction books, novels. Considers these nonfiction areas: agriculture/horticulture; animals; anthropology/archaeology; art/architecture/design; biography/autobiography; business; child guidance/parenting; cooking/food/nutrition; current affairs; ethnic/cultural interests; government/politics/law; health/medicine; history; interior design/decorating; language/literature/criticism; money/finance/economics; nature/environment; psychology; science/technology; self-help/personal improvement; sociology; true crime/investigative; women's issues/women's studies. Considers these fiction areas: detective/police/crime; historical; mainstream; mystery/suspense; thriller/espionage. Query with letter before sending ms or proposal. Always include SASE. Reports in 1 month.
Recent Sales: *The Recipes of Madison County*, by Jane Heminger and Courtney Work (Oxmoor House); *Chicago: A Pictorial Guide*, by Marilyn D. Clancy and Ron Schramm (Voyageur Press).
Terms: Agent receives 10-20% commission on domestic sales. Offers written contract. Charges for express postage, long distance phone calls, and photocopying.
Writers Conferernces: ABA (Chicago); Printer's Row Book Fair (Chicago).
Tips: Obtains new clients mainly by referral. "I want to work with people who want to work; writing books is a business as well as all the other fine things it might be."

GOLDFARB & GRAYBILL, ATTORNEYS AT LAW, (II), 918 16th St. NW, Washington DC 20006-2902. (202)466-3030. Contact: Nina Graybill. Estab. 1966. Represents "hundreds" of clients. "Minority" of clients are new/previously unpublished writers. Specializes in nonfiction and books with movie and TV tie-ins. Currently handles: 80% nonfiction books; 15% fiction; 5% other. Member agents: Ronald Goldfarb, Nina Graybill.
● Both principals of this agency are published authors. Ron Goldfarb's latest book (his tenth), *Perfect Villans, Imperfect Heroes*, will be published by Random House. Nina Graybill's sixth book, *Pasta Salad Light*, will be published by Farragut Publishing Co.
Handles: Nonfiction books, fiction. Considers all nonfiction areas except children's books. No poetry. Considers these fiction areas: action/adventure; contemporary issues; detective/police/crime; ethnic; feminist; gay; glitz; historical; literary; mainstream; mystery/suspense; thriller/espionage. Send outline or synopsis plus 1-2 sample chapters. Reports in 1 month on queries; 2 months on mss.
Recent Sales: *Breaking Free*, by Susan Eisenhower (Farrar, Straus & Giroux, Inc.); *The Buying of the President*, by Charles Lewis (Avon); *Father Coughlin, Father of Hate Radio*, by Donald Warren (Free Press); *First Principles*, by Marcus Raskin (Free Press); *Crusade of the Spirit Women*, by Mary Gabriel (Algonquin); *The First Citizens Band*, by Adele Alexander (Pantheon); *Breaking Through God's Silence*, and *Ten Thoughts to Take Into Eternity*, by David Yount (Simon & Schuster); *Democracy in the Information Age*, by Morley Winograd and Dudley Buffa (Holt).
Writers' Conferences: Attends Washington Independent Writers Conference (May 1996); Medical Writers Conference; ABA (June); VCCA.
Tips: Obtains new clients mostly through recommendations from others. "We are a law firm which can help writers with related problems, Freedom of Information Act requests, libel, copyright, contracts, etc. We are published writers."

CHARLOTTE GORDON AGENCY, (II), 235 E. 22nd St., New York NY 10010-4633. (212)679-5363. Contact: Charlotte Gordon. Estab. 1986. Represents 30 clients. 10% of clients are new/unpublished writers. "I'll work with writers whose work is interesting to me. Specializes in books (not magazine material, except for my writers, and then only in special situations). My taste is eclectic." Currently handles: 40% nonfiction; 40% novels; 20% juvenile.
● Prior to opening her agency, Ms. Gordon served as an editor with Harper, Fawcett and Grossett.
Handles: Nonfiction books, novels; juvenile fiction and nonfiction. Considers these nonfiction areas: anthropology/archaeology; business; health/medicine; history; juvenile nonfiction; money/finance/economics; nature/environment; psychology; sociology; women's issues/women's studies. Considers these fiction areas: contemporary issues; family saga; gay; juvenile; lesbian; literary; mystery/suspense; romance (regency); young adult. Must query first with first chapter. No unsolicited mss. Reports in 2 weeks on queries. SASE essential.
Recent Sales: *One Mississippi*, (mystery/suspense novel), by Tima Smith (Ballantine).
Terms: Agent receives 15% commission on domestic sales; 10% on dramatic sales; 10% on foreign sales, if another agent involved.

‡GRAHAM LITERARY AGENCY, INC., (II, IV), P.O. Box 1051, Alpharetta GA 30239. (770)569-9755. E-mail: slgraham@mindspring.com. Contact: Susan L. Graham. Estab. 1994. Represents 28 clients. 86% of clients are new/previously unpublished writers. Specializes in science fiction, fantasy, mystery, thrillers, computer, political exposé, popular science, CD-ROMs. Currently handles: 6% nonfiction books; 6% juvenile books; 72% novels; 4% movie scripts; 8% short story collections; 3% CD-ROM.
Handles: Nonfiction books, novels, CD-ROM. Considers these nonfiction subjects: computers/electronics; government/politics/law; nature/environment; science/technology; true crime/investigative. Considers these fiction areas: detective/police/crime; fantasy; mystery/suspense; science fiction; thriller/espionage. Send outline and 3 sample chapters. Reports in 2 months on queries; 3 months on mss.
Recent Sales: *Trouble No More*, by Anthony Grooms (La Questa Press; *Kingmaker's Sword*, by Ann Marston (HarperCollins); *Ladylord*, by Sasha Miller (TOR Books).
Terms: Agent receives 15% commission on domestic sales; 20% on foreign sales. Offers written contract, with 30 day cancellation clause. 100% of business is derived from commissions on sales.
Writers' Conferences: Magic Carpet Con (Dalton GA, May 3-5); Dragon Con (Atlanta, July); World Con (CA, August); World Fantasy Con (CA, October).
Tips: Obtains new clients through recommendations, advertising and conferences. "Finish your book first, make sure to follow all of the formatting rules, then send the agency what they ask for. Be polite, and expect delays, but follow up."

SANFORD J. GREENBURGER ASSOCIATES, INC., (II), 55 Fifth Ave., New York NY 10003. (212)206-5600. Fax: (212)463-8718. Contact: Heide Lange. Estab. 1945. Member of AAR. Represents 500 clients. Member agents: Heide Lange, Faith Hamlin, Beth Vesel, Theresa Park.
Handles: Nonfiction books, novels. Considers all nonfiction areas. Considers these fiction areas: action/adventure; contemporary issues, detective/police/crime; ethnic; family saga; feminist; gay; glitz; historical; humor/satire; juvenile; lesbian; literary; mainstream; mystery/suspense; psychic/supernatural; regional; sports; thriller/espionage. Query first. Reports in 3 weeks on queries; 2 months on mss.
Recent Sales: *Let Me Hear Your Voice*, by Catherine Maurice (Knopf); *The Beast: A Reckoning With Depression*, by Tracy Thompson (Putnam).
Terms: Agent receives 15% commission on domestic sales; 20% on foreign sales. Charges for photocopying, books for foreign and subsidiary rights submissions.

‡ARTHUR B. GREENE, (III), 101 Park Ave., New York NY 10178. (212)661-8200. Fax: (212)370-7884. Contact: Arthur Greene, Esq. Estab. 1980. Represents 20 clients. 10% of clients are new/previously unpublished writers. Specializes in movies, TV and fiction. Currently handles: 25% novels; 10% novellas; 10% short story collections; 25% movie scripts; 10% TV scripts; 10% stage plays; 10% other.
● See the expanded listing for this agency in Script Agents.

RANDALL ELISHA GREENE, LITERARY AGENT, (II), 620 S. Broadway, Suite 210, Lexington KY 40508-3140. (606)225-1388. Contact: Randall Elisha Greene. Estab. 1987. Represents 20 clients. 30% of clients are new/previously unpublished writers. Specializes in adult fiction and nonfiction only. No juvenile or children's books. Currently handles: 50% nonfiction books; 50% novels.
● Prior to opening his agency, Mr. Greene worked at Doubleday & Co. as an editor.
Handles: Nonfiction books, novels. Considers these nonfiction areas: agriculture/horticulture; biography/autobiography; business; current affairs; government/politics/law; history; how-to; language/literature/criticism; psychology; religious/inspirational; true crime/investigative. Considers these fiction areas: action/adventure; contemporary issues; detective/police/crime; family saga; humor/satire; literary; mainstream; regional; romance (contemporary); thriller/espionage. Query with SASE only. No unsolicited mss. Reports in 1 month on queries; 2 months on mss.
Terms: Agent receives 15% commission on domestic sales; 20% on foreign sales and performance rights. Charges for extraordinary expenses such as photocopying and foreign postage.

MAIA GREGORY ASSOCIATES, (II), 311 E. 72nd St., New York NY 10021. (212)288-0310. Contact: Maia Gregory. Estab. 1978. Represents 10-12 clients. Currently handles: 98% nonfiction books.
Handles: Considers these nonfiction areas: art; history; language; music/dance/theater/film. Query with outline, 1 sample chapter and SASE. Reports in 2 weeks on queries.

Agents ranked I and II are most open to both established and new writers. Agents ranked III are open to established writers with publishing-industry references.

Terms: Agent receives 15% commission on domestic sales; varies on foreign sales.
Writers' Conferences: PEN.
Tips: Obtains new clients through recommendations and queries.

LEW GRIMES LITERARY AGENCY, (II), 250 W. 54th St., Suite 800, New York NY 10019-5586. (212)974-9505. Fax: (212)974-9525. Contact: Lew Grimes. Estab. 1991. 25% of clients are new/previously unpublished writers. Currently handles: 50% nonfiction books; 5% scholarly books; 1% textbooks; 43½% novels; ½% poetry books.
Handles: Nonfiction books, novels. Query. Reports in 2 months on queries; 3 months on mss.
Recent Sales: *Style*, by Elsa Kensch (Putnam); *Speed Tribes*, by Karl Taro Greenfeld (HarperCollins).
Terms: Agent receives 15% commission on domestic sales; 20% on foreign sales. Offers written contract. Charges $15 postage and handling for return of ms. "Expenses are reimbursed for unpublished authors and for non-commercial projects."
Tips: Obtains new clients through referral and by query. "Provide brief query and resume showing publishing history clearly. Always put phone number and address on correspondence and enclose SASE. No faxed queries."

MAXINE GROFFSKY LITERARY AGENCY, 2 Fifth Ave., New York NY 10011. Member of AAR. This agency did not respond to our request for information. Query before submitting.

THE CHARLOTTE GUSAY LITERARY AGENCY, (II, IV), 10532 Blythe, Suite 211, Los Angeles CA 90064. (310)559-0831. Fax: (310)559-2639. Contact: Charlotte Gusay. Estab. 1988. Member of SPAR, signatory of WGA. Represents 30 clients. 50% of clients are new/previously unpublished writers. Specializes in fiction, nonfiction, children's (multicultural, nonsexist), children's illustrators, screenplays, books to film. "Percentage breakdown of the manuscripts different at different times."
Handles: Nonfiction books, scholarly books, juvenile books, travel books, novels, movie scripts. Considers all nonfiction and fiction areas. No romance, short stories, science fiction or horror. SASE always required for response. Query. Reports in 4-6 weeks on queries; 6-10 weeks on mss.
Recent Sales: *A Garden Story*, by Leon Whiteson (Faber & Faber).
Terms: Agent receives 15% commission on domestic sales; 10% on dramatic sales; 25% on foreign sales. Offers written contract, binding for "usually 1 year." Charges for out-of-pocket expenses for long distance phone, fax, express mail, postage, etc.
Writers' Conferences: Attends Writers Connection, in San Jose, California; Scriptwriters Connection, in Studio City, California; National Women's Book Association, in Los Angeles.
Tips: Usually obtains new clients through referrals, queries. "Please be professional."

REECE HALSEY AGENCY, (II, III), 8733 Sunset Blvd., Suite 101, Los Angeles CA 90069. (310)652-2409. Fax: (310)652-7595. Contact: Dorris Halsey. Also: Reece Halsey North, 98 Main St., #704, Tiburon CA 94920. (415)789-9191. Fax: (415)789-9177. Contact: Kimberley Cameron. Estab. 1957. Signatory of WGA. Represents 30 clients. 20% of clients are new/previously unpublished writers. Specializes mostly in books/excellent writing. Currently handles: 20% nonfiction books; 60% novels; 20% movie scripts. Member agents: Dorris Halsey; Kimberley Cameron.
  ● The Reese Halsey Agency has an illustrious client list largely of established writers, including the estate of Aldous Huxley and has represented Upton Sinclair, William Faulkner and Henry Miller. Ms. Cameron has recently opened a Northern California office and most queries should be addressed to her at the Tiburon office.
Handles: Nonfiction books, novels. Considers these nonfiction areas: biography/autobiography; current affairs; history; language/literature/criticism; popular culture; true crime/investigative; women's issues/women's studies. Considers these fiction areas: action/adventure; contemporary issues; detective/police/crime; ethnic; family saga; historical; literary; mainstream; mystery/suspense; science fiction; thriller/espionage; women's fiction. Query with SASE. Reports in 1 week on queries; 3 months on mss.
Also Handles: Movie scripts to Los Angeles office only.
Terms: Agent receives 15% commission on domestic sales of books, 10% commission on script sales. Offers written contract, binding for 1 year. Requests four copies of ms if representing an author.
Writers' Conferences: ABA and various writer conferences.
Tips: Obtains new clients through recommendations from others and solicitation. "Always send a well-written query and include a SASE with it!"

THE MITCHELL J. HAMILBURG AGENCY, (II), 292 S. La Cienega Blvd., Suite 312, Beverly Hills CA 90211. (310)657-1501. Contact: Michael Hamilburg. Estab. 1930. Signatory of WGA. Represents 70 clients. Currently handles: 70% nonfiction books; 30% novels.
Handles: Nonfiction, novels. Considers all nonfiction areas and most fiction areas. No romance. Send outline, 2 sample chapters and SASE. Reports in 3-4 weeks on mss.

Recent Sales: *A Biography of the Leakey Family,* by Virginia Morrell (Simon & Schuster); *A Biography of Agnes De Mille,* by Carol Easton (Little, Brown).
Terms: Agent receives 10-15% commission on domestic sales.
Tips: Usually obtains new clients through recommendations from others, at conferences or personal search. "Good luck! Keep writing!"

THE HAMPTON AGENCY, (II, IV), P.O. Box 1298, Bridgehampton NY 11932. (516)537-2828. Fax: (516)537-7272. E-mail: hampton@i-2000.com. Contact Ralph Schiano or Leslie Jennemann. Estab. 1992. Signatory of WGA. Represents 53 clients. 50% of clients are new/previously unpublished writers. Specializes in science fiction, horror, fantasy. Currently handles: 5% nonfiction books; 10% juvenile books; 60% novels; 20% movie scripts; 5% short story collections.
Handles: Considers these fiction areas: action/adventure; contemporary issues; ethnic (juvenile multicultural); experimental; fantasy; feminist; gay; glitz; historical; horror; humor/satire; juvenile; literary; picture book; psychic/supernatural; romance (with science fiction twist); science fiction; young adult. Query with outline/proposal and/or 1 sample chapter and SASE.
Terms: Agent receives 10-15% commission on domestic sales. Offers written contract with cancellation clause. Charges for photocopying and postage.
Tips: Obtains new clients through referrals. "Keep it in the mail and don't give up!"

THE HARDY AGENCY, (II), 3020 Bridgeway, Suite 204, Sausalito CA 94965. (415)380-9985. Contact: Anne Sheldon, Michael Vidor. Estab. 1990. Represents 30 clients. 75% of clients are new/previously unpublished writers. Specializes in literary fiction and nonfiction. Currently handles: 30% nonfiction books; 70% novels. Member agents: Anne Sheldon (fiction); Michael Vidor (nonfiction, media, marketing and PR).
Handles: Nonfiction books, novels. Considers these nonfiction areas: biography/autobiography; current affairs; government/politics/law; health/medicine; New Age/metaphysics. Considers these fiction areas: contemporary; literary. Send outline plus 5 sample chapters. Reports in 1 month on queries and mss.
Terms: Agent receives 15% commission on domestic sales; 20% on foreign sales. Offers written contract, binding for 1 year. Charges for postage, copying. 100% of business is derived from commissions on sales.
Tips: Obtains new clients from recommendations. Welcomes new authors.

‡ROSE HASS LITERARY AGENCY, (II), 2302 Lucaya Lane, Apt. J-4, Coconut Creek FL 33066. (305)973-6844. Contact: Rose Hass. Estab. 1984. Specializes in biographies, art, music, a little fiction. Currently handles: 50% nonfiction books; 25% juvenile books; 25% novels.
Handles: Nonfiction books, juvenile books, novels. Considers these nonfiction areas: art/architecture/design; biography/autobiography; music/dance/theater/film; women's issues/women's studies. Considers these fiction areas: feminist, literary. Query. Reports in 3 weeks on queries.
Terms: Agent receives 10% commission on domestic sales. Charges for postage. 100% of business is derived from commissions on sales.
Tips: Obtains new clients from *LMP* listing and referrals.

JOHN HAWKINS & ASSOCIATES, INC., (II), 71 W. 23rd St., Suite 1600, New York NY 10010. (212)807-7040. Fax: (212)807-9555. Contact: John Hawkins, William Reiss, Sharon Friedman. Estab. 1893. Member of AAR. Represents 100+ clients. 5-10% of clients are new/previously unpublished writers. Currently handles: 40% nonfiction books; 20% juvenile books; 40% novels.
Handles: Nonfiction books, juvenile books, novels. Considers all nonfiction areas except computers/electronics; religion/inspirational; translations. Considers all fiction areas except confessional; erotica; fantasy; romance. Query with outline/proposal. Reports in 1 month on queries.
Recent Sales: *Irongate,* by Richard Herman Jr. (Simon & Schuster); *Zombie,* by Joyce Carol Oates (Penguin).
Terms: Agent receives 15% commission on domestic sales; 20% on foreign sales. Charges for photocopying.
Tips: Obtains new clients through recommendations from others.

HEACOCK LITERARY AGENCY, INC., (II), 1523 Sixth St., Suite #14, Santa Monica CA 90401-2514. (310)393-6227. Fax: (310)451-8524. E-mail: gracebooks@aol.com. Contact: Rosalie Heacock. Estab. 1978. Member of AAR, ATA, SCBWI; signatory of WGA. Represents 60 clients. 30% of clients are new/previously unpublished writers. Currently handles: 85% nonfiction books; 5% juvenile books; 5% novels; 5% movie scripts. Member agents: Rosalie Heacock (psychology, philosophy, women's studies, alternative health, new technology, futurism, new idea books, art and artists); Bill Miller-Jones (general trade fiction and nonfiction).
Handles: Adult nonfiction books, juvenile books. Considers these nonfiction areas: anthropology; art/architecture/design; biography (contemporary celebrity); business; child guidance/parenting; cooking/

food/nutrition; crafts/hobbies; current affairs; education; ethnic/cultural interests; gay/lesbian issues; government/politics; health/medicine (including alternative health); history; how-to; humor; juvenile nonfiction (no beginners); language/literature/criticism; military/war; money/finance/economics; music/dance/theater/film; nature/environment; New Age/metaphysics; popular culture; psychology; religious/inspirational; science/technology; self-help/personal improvement; sociology; sports; true crime; women's issues/women's studies. Considers limited selection of top children's book authors; no beginners. Query with sample chapters. Reports in 2 weeks on queries; 2 months on mss.

Recent Sales: *Making the World*, by Alan Chinen, MD (Tarcher/Putnam); *Under the Influence*, by John Goldhammer, Ph. D. (Prometheus); *A Tangle Tale*, by Audrey & Don Wood (Harcourt Brace); *Owner's Guide to the Skin*, by Joseph Bark, MD (Simon & Schuster).

Also Handles: Movie scripts (feature film, documentary, animation), TV scripts (TV mow). Prefers submissions by Writers Guild members. Considers these script subject areas: action/adventure; contemporary issues; detective/police/crime; family saga; feminist; horror; humor; mainstream; mystery/suspense; psychic/supernatural; sports; thriller.

Recent Sales: *MOW sold: Adrift*, by Terry Gerritsen (Blue Andre); *Movie in development: Weird Parents*, by Audrey Wood (Turner Pictures/Spanish Creek Productions); *Never Live Twice*, by Dan Marlow (film rights to Nikki Marvin Productions).

Terms: Agent receives 15% commission on domestic sales; 25% on foreign sales, "if foreign agent used; if sold directly, 15%." Offers written contract, binding for 1 year. Charges for actual expense for telephone, postage, packing, photocopying. We provide copies of each publisher submission letter and the publisher's response." 95% of business is derived from commission on ms sales. "We provide consultant services to authors who do their own marketing and only need assistance in negotiating their contracts. Charge is $125/hour and no commission charges (5% of our business).

Writers' Conferences: Santa Barbara City College Annual Writer's Workshop; Pasadena City College Writer's Forum; UCLA Symposiums on Writing Nonfiction Books; Society of Children's Book Writers and Illustrators.

Tips: Obtains new clients through "referrals from present clients and industry sources as well as mail queries. Take time to write an informative query letter expressing your book idea, the market for it, your qualifications to write the book, the 'hook' that would make a potential reader buy the book. Always enclose SASE, compare your book to others on similar subjects and show how it is original."

GARY L. HEGLER LITERARY AGENCY, (III), P.O. Box 890101, Houston TX 77289-0101. (713)333-0173. Contact: Gary L. Hegler or Nikki Cane. Estab. 1985. 10% of clients are new/previously unpublished writers. Specializes in young adult, nonfiction and adult westerns. Currently handles: 50% nonfiction books; 40% juvenile books; 10% novels.

Handles: Nonfiction books, textbooks, juvenile books. Considers these nonfiction areas: animals; biography/autobiography; health/medicine; juvenile nonfiction; military/war; money/finance/economics; nature/environment; psychology; religious/inspirational; true crime/investigative; science/technology; self-help/personal improvement. Considers these fiction areas: action/adventure; detective/police/crime; juvenile; mainstream; mystery/suspense; regional (Texas only); westerns; young adult. Query with outline plus 3 sample chapters. "First query; then we'll ask for the outline." Reports in 1 week on queries; 2 months on mss.

Recent Sales: *The Whiskey City* series, by Robin Gibson (Avalon Books); *Blue Hills Robbery*, by Leola Kahrimanis (Eakin Press).

Terms: Agent receives 10% commission on domestic sales; 10% on foreign sales. Offers written contract, binding for 1 year.

Writers' Conferences: Bay Area Writers Conference; Golden Triangle Writers Guild Conference.

Tips: Obtains new clients through recommendations from authors, from WGA referral listing and conferences. "Be sure the submission is the best you can do, this includes its neatness, accuracy and suspense (if fictional). We will not represent writers who won't actively promote their books."

HENDERSON LITERARY REPRESENTATION, (I, II), P.O. Box 476, Sicklerville NJ 08081. Contact: Rita Elizabeth Henderson. Estab. 1994. Specializes in autobiography and biography, especially celebrity bios. Currently handles: 100% nonfiction books.

Handles: Nonfiction books. Considers these nonfiction areas: art/architecture/design; biography/autobiography; biography (celebrity); business; child guidance/parenting; computers/electronics; cooking/food/nutrition; current affairs; education; ethnic/cultural interests; gay/lesbian issues; government/politics/law; health/medicine; history; how-to; humor; interior design/decorating; juvenile nonfiction; money/finance/economics; music/dance/theater/film; photography; popular culture; psychology; religious/inspirational; science/technology; self-help/personal improvement; sociology; sports; true crime/investigative; women's issues/women's studies. Query by mail with outline/proposal and 3 sample chapters. Reports in 1 month.

Recent Sales: *The Boyz II Men Success Story: Defying the Odds*, by Rita Elizabeth Henderson (Anderson Press Publishing).

Terms: Agent receives 10% commission on domestic sales; 20% on foreign sales. Offers written contract, binding for life of book or until mutually terminated. 100% of business derived from commissions on book sales.
Writers' Conferences: Meet the Agents (New York City, October).
Tips: Obtains new clients through conferences, solicitation and referrals from others. "Please be organized in your proposal. If you think you have a good manuscript, and know that there is a marketplace for it, continue to work diligently to get it sold and don't give up. Have patience because some books sell quickly and others can take more time. In preparing your manuscript, please follow the Chicago Manual of Style."

‡RICHARD HENSHAW GROUP, (II, III), 264 W. 73rd St., New York NY 10023. (212)721-4721. Fax: (212)721-4208. E-mail: rhgagents@aol.com. Contact: Rich Henshaw. Estab. 1995. Member of AAR, SinC, MWA, HWA. Represents 25 clients. 20% of clients are new/previously unpublished writers. Specializes in thrillers, mysteries, science fiction, fantasy and horror. Currently handles: 20% nonfiction books; 10% juvenile books; 70% novels.
   • Prior to opening his agency, Mr. Henshaw served as an agent with Richard Curtis Associates, Inc.
Handles: Nonfiction books, juvenile books, novels. Considers these nonfiction areas: animals; biography/autobiography; business; child guidance/parenting; computers/electronics; cooking/food/nutrition; current affairs; gay/lesbian issues; government/politics/law; health/medicine; how-to; humor; juvenile nonfiction; military/war; money/finance/economics; music/dance/theater/film; nature/environment; New Age/metaphysics; popular culture; psychology; science/technology; self-help/personal improvement; sociology; sports; true crime/investigative; women's issues/women's studies. Considers these fiction areas: action/adventure; detective/police/crime; ethnic; family saga; fantasy; glitz; historical; horror; humor/satire; juvenile; literary; mainstream; psychic/supernatural; science fiction; sports; thriller/espionage; young adult. Query. Reports in 3 weeks on queries; 6 weeks on mss.
Recent Sales: *Blood Will Tell*, by Dana Stabenow (Putnam); *Dropshot*, by Harlan Coben (Dell); *The Lost Guardian*, by Ronald Anthony Cross (TOR).
Terms: Agent receives 15% commission on domestic sales; 20% on foreign sales. No written contract. Charges for photocopying manuscripts and book orders. 100% of business is derived from commission on sales.
Tips: Obtains new clients through recommendations from others, solicitation, conferences and query letters. "Always include SASE with correct return postage."

THE JEFF HERMAN AGENCY INC., (II), 500 Greenwich St., #501C, New York NY 10013. (212)941-0540. Contact: Jeffrey H. Herman. Estab. 1985. Member of AAR. Represents 100 clients. 10% of clients are new/previously unpublished writers. Specializes in adult nonfiction. Currently handles: 85% nonfiction books; 5% scholarly books; 5% textbooks; 5% novels. Member agents: Deborah Adams (vice president, nonfiction book doctor); Jamie Forbes (fiction).
   • Prior to opening his agency, Mr. Herman served as a public relations executive.
Handles: Considers these nonfiction areas: business, computers; health; history; how-to; politics; popular psychology; popular reference; recovery; self-help; spirituality. Query. Reports in 2 weeks on queries; 1 month on mss.
Recent Sales: *Joe Montana On The Magic of Making Quarterback*, by Joe Montana (Henry Holt); *The Aladdin Factor*, by Jack Canfield and Mark Victor Hansen (Putnam); *The Ice Myth*, by Bob Stevenberg (Simon & Schuster); *All You Need to Know About the Movie and TV Business*, by Gail Resnick and Scott Trost (Fireside/Simon & Schuster).
Terms: Agent receives 15% commission on domestic sales. Offers written contract.

SUSAN HERNER RIGHTS AGENCY, (II), P.O. Box 303, Scarsdale NY 10583. (914)725-8967. Fax: (914)725-8969. Contact: Susan Herner or Sue Yuen. Estab. 1987. Represents 75 clients. 30% of clients are new/unpublished writers. Eager to work with new/unpublished writers. Currently handles: 60% nonfiction books; 40% novels. Member agent: Sue Yuen (commercial genre fiction).
Handles: Adult nonfiction books, novels. Consider these nonfiction areas: anthropology/archaeology; biography/autobiography; business; child guidance/parenting; cooking/food/nutrition; current affairs; ethnic/cultural interests; gay/lesbian issues; government/politics/law; health/medicine; history; how-to; language/literature/criticism; nature/environment; New Age/metaphysics; popular culture; psychology;

If you're looking for a particular agent, check the Agents Index to find at which agency the agent works. Then check the listing for that agency in the appropriate section.

religious/inspirational; science/technology; self-help/personal improvement; sociology; true crime/investigative; women's issues/women's studies. "I'm particularly interested in women's issues, popular science, and feminist spirituality." Considers these fiction areas: action/adventure; contemporary issues; detective/police/crime; ethnic; family/saga; fantasy; feminist; glitz; historical; horror; literary; mainstream; mystery; romance (contemporary, gothic, historical, regency); science fiction; thriller; "I'm particularly looking for strong women's fiction." Query with outline, sample chapters and SASE. Reports in 1 month on queries.
Recent Sales: *Everything You Need to Know About Latino History*, by Himilce Novas (Dutton); *Something's Cooking*, by Joanna Pence (Harper); *Until Spring*, by Libby Sydes (Dell).
Terms: Agent receives 15% commission on domestic sales; 20% on dramatic sales; 20% on foreign sales. Charges for extraordinary postage, handling and photocopying. "Agency has two divisions: one represents writers on a commission-only basis; the other represents the rights for small publishers and packagers who do not have inhouse subsidiary rights representation. Percentage of income derived from each division is currently 70-30."
Writers' Conferences: Vermont League of Writers (Burlington, Vt); Gulf States Authors League (Mobile, AL).

FREDERICK HILL ASSOCIATES, (II), 8446½ Melrose Place, Los Angeles CA 90069-5308. (213)852-0830. Fax: (213)852-0426. Contact: Bonnie Nadell. Estab. 1979. Represents 100 clients. 50% of clients are new/unpublished writers. Specializes in general nonfiction, fiction.
Handles: Nonfiction books, novels. Considers these nonfiction areas: biography/autobiography; current affairs; government/politics/law; language/literature/criticism; women's issues/women's studies. Considers literary and mainstream fiction.
Recent Sales: *Infinite Jest*, by David Foster Wallace (Little, Brown); *The Inhabited Woman*, by Gioconda Belli (Warner Books); *Gender Shock*, by Phyllis Burke (Anchor Books).
Terms: Agent receives 15% commission on domestic sales; 15% on dramatic sales; 20% on foreign sales. Charges for overseas airmail (books, proofs only).

JOHN L. HOCHMANN BOOKS, (III, IV), 320 E. 58th St., New York NY 10022-2220. (212)319-0505. President: John L. Hochmann. Estab. 1976. Represents 23 clients. Member of AAR, PEN. Specializes in nonfiction books. Writers must have demonstrable eminence in field or previous publications. Prefers to work with published/established authors. Currently handles: 80% nonfiction; 20% textbooks. Member agent: Theodora Eagle (popular medical and nutrition books).
Handles: Nonfiction trade books, college textbooks. Considers these nonfiction areas: anthropology/archaeology; art/architecture/design; biography/autobiography; cooking/food/nutrition; current affairs; gay/lesbian issues; government/politics/law; health/medicine; history; military/war; music/dance/theater/film; sociology. Query first with outline, titles and sample reviews of previous books and SASE. Reports in 1 week on queries; 1 month on solicited mss.
Recent Sales: *Granite and Rainbow: A Life of Virginia Woolf*, by Mitchell A. Leaska (Farrar, Straus); *Olmsted's America*, by Lee Hall (Little, Brown); *What Makes a Picasso a Picasso*, by Richard Mühlberger (Metropolitan Museum of Art).
Terms: Agent receives 15% commission on domestic sales; 25% on foreign sales.
Tips: Obtains new clients through recommendations from authors and editors. "Detailed outlines are read carefully; letters and proposals written like flap copy get chucked. We make multiple submissions to editors, but we do not accept multiple submissions from authors. Why? Editors are on salary, but we work for commission, and do not have time to read manuscripts on spec."

BERENICE HOFFMAN LITERARY AGENCY, (III), 215 W. 75th St., New York NY 10023. (212)580-0951. Fax: (212)721-8916. Contact: Berenice Hoffman. Estab. 1978. Member of AAR. Represents 55 clients.
Handles: Nonfiction, novels. Considers all nonfiction areas and most fiction areas. No romance. Query with SASE. Reports in 3-4 weeks on queries.
Terms: Agent receives 15% on domestic sales. Sometimes offers written contract. Charges of out of the ordinary postage, photocopying.
Tips: Usually obtains new clients through referrals from people she knows.

BARBARA HOGENSON AGENCY, (III), 19 W. 44th St., Suite 1000, New York NY 10036. (212)730-7306. Fax: (212)730-8970. Estab. 1994. Member of AAR, signatory of WGA. Represents 60 clients. 5% of clients are new/previously unpublished writers. Currently handles: 35% nonfiction books; 15% novels; 15% movie scripts; 35% stage plays.
• See the expanded listing for this agency in Script Agents.

HOLUB & ASSOCIATES, (II), 24 Old Colony Rd., North Stonington CT 06359. (203)535-0689. Contact: William Holub. Estab. 1967. Specializes in Roman Catholic publications. Currently handles: 100% nonfiction books.

Handles: Nonfiction books. Considers these nonfiction areas: biography; religious/inspirational; self-help; spirituality; theology. Query with outline, 2 sample chapters and SASE.
Terms: Agent receives 15% commission on domestic sales. Charges for postage and photocopying.
Tips: Obtains new clients through recommendations from others.

‡**HELANE HULBURT LITERARY AGENCY, (III)**, 1616 W. Cullom St., Chicago IL 60613. (312)244-6456. Fax: (312)244-6457. Contact: Helane Hulburt. Estab. 1992. Member of Midland Author's Association. Represents 36 clients. 50% of clients are new/previously unpublished writers. Specializes in nonfiction in the areas of religion, New Age, self-help, education and gay/lesbian studies. Currently handles: 90% nonfiction books; 5% juvenile books; 5% novels. Member agents: Benjamin Woodworth.
Handles: Nonfiction books, juvenile books, novels. Considers these nonfiction areas: biography/autobiography; business; child guidance/parenting; computers/electronics; cooking/food/nutrition; current affairs; education; ethnic/cultural interests; gay/lesbian issues; government/politics/law; health/medicine; history; how-to; money/finance/economics; nature/environment; New Age/metaphysics; psychology; religious/inspirational; science/technology; self-help/personal improvement; sociology; true crime/investigative; women's issues/women's studies. Considers these fiction areas: contemporary issues; ethnic; experimental; feminist; gay; lesbian; literary; mainstream; religious/inspirational. Query. SASE must be included for return of mss. Reports in 2 weeks on queries; 6 weeks on mss.
Recent Sales: *Nothing To Lose*, by Cheri Erdman (HarperCollins); *The Squared Circle*, by James Bennett (Scholastic); *Live Large*, by Cheri Erdman (HarperCollins).
Terms: Agent receives 15% commission on domestic sales; 20% on foreign sales. Offers written contract, with 30 day cancellation clause. Charges for photocopying and overnight mail. 100% of business is derived from commissions on sales.
Writers' Conferences: Taste of Chicago Writers Conference (Chicago, July).
Tips: Obtains new clients through referrals from other clients "and fantastic query letters. I usually reject about 99% of the material I see. Make sure your work is polished, on the cutting-edge and that you have the credentials for writing it in the first place."

HULL HOUSE LITERARY AGENCY, (II), 240 E. 82nd St., New York NY 10028-2714. (212)988-0725. Fax: (212)794-8758. President: David Stewart Hull. Associate: Lydia Mortimer. Estab. 1987. Represents 38 clients. 15% of clients are new/previously unpublished writers. Specializes in military and general history, true crime, mystery fiction, general commercial fiction. Currently handles: 60% nonfiction books; 40% novels. Member agents: David Stewart Hull (history, biography, military books, true crime, mystery fiction, commercial fiction by published authors); Lydia Mortimer (new fiction by unpublished writers, nonfiction of general nature including women's studies).
● Prior to opening his agency, Mr. Hull served as an editor with Coward-McCann Publishers.
Handles: Nonfiction books, novels. Considers these nonfiction areas: anthropology/archaeology; art/architecture/design; biography/autobiography; business; current affairs; ethnic/cultural interests; government/politics/law; history; military/war; money/finance/economics; music/dance/theater/film; sociology; true crime/investigative. Considers these fiction areas: detective/police/crime; literary; mainstream; mystery/suspense. Query with SASE. Reports in 1 week on queries; 1 month on mss.
Recent Sales: *Under the Beetle's Cellar*, by Mary Willis Walker (Bantam; HarperCollins UK; Calmann-Lévy [France]; Kodansha [Japan]; De Bookerij [Holland]; Goldmann [Germany]; Fremad [Denmark]; Grijalbo [Spain]; Forum [Sweden]).
Terms: Agent receives 15% commission on domestic sales; 10% on foreign sales. Written contract is optional, "at mutual agreement between author and agency." Charges for photocopying, express mail, extensive overseas telephone expenses.
Tips: Obtains new clients through "referrals from clients, listings in various standard publications such as *LMP*, *Guide to Literary Agents*, etc. If interested in agency representation, send a single-page letter outlining your project, always accompanied by an SASE. If nonfiction, sample chapter(s) are often valuable. A record of past publications is a big plus."

‡**THE IEVLEVA LITERARY AGENCY, (II)**, 7095 Hollywood Blvd., #832, Hollywood CA 90028. (213)993-6048. Contact: Julie Ievleva. Estab. 1991. Represents 25 clients. 50% of clients are new/previously unpublished writers. Currently handles: 32% nonfiction books; 35% novels; 15% movie scripts; 10% TV scripts; 8% other.
Handles: Nonfiction books, scholarly books, poetry books, juvenile books, novels, novellas, movie scripts, TV scripts, stage plays, syndicated material. Considers these nonfiction areas: animals; art/architecture/design; biography/autobiography; business; child guidance/parenting; cooking/food/nutrition; crafts/hobbies; current affairs; education; ethnic/cultural interests; government/politics/law; health/medicine; history; how-to; humor; interior design/decorating; juvenile nonfiction; language/literature/criticism; military/war; money/finance/economics; music/dance/theater/film; New Age/metaphysics; popular culture; psychology; religious/inspirational; science/technology; self-help/personal improvement; sports; translations; true crime/investigative; women's issues/women's studies. Considers these fiction areas: action/adventure; confessional; contemporary issues; detective/police/crime;

ethnic; experimental; family saga; fantasy; glitz; historical; horror; humor/satire; juvenile; literary; mainstream; mystery/suspense; psychic/supernatural; religious/inspirational; romance (contemporary, gothic, historical, regency); science fiction; sports; thriller/espionage; westerns/frontier; young adult. Query with outline/proposal or send entire ms. Reports in 10 days on queries; 3 weeks on mss.
Recent Sales: *In Pursuit of Reality*, by Charles Giordan, (Sunlight Press); *Russkie Business*, by Applethorn, (Johnson and Associates); *Broken Bones*, by Tony Kondo (Perestroika Press).
Terms: Agent receives 15% commission on domestic sales; 20% on foreign sales. Offers written contract, binding for no specific amount of time, with 30 days cancellation clause. Charges for photocopying and overseas postage. "Any expense must be approved by client before incurred."
Writers' Conferences: San Diego State University Conference; Santa Barbara Writer's Conference.
Tips: Obtains new clients through query letters, proposals, recommendations, writer's conferences and phone calls. "We are very interested in hearing from new writers. We know how hard it is to break in, but if you have a fresh voice and a unique slant, you can make it. Whatever you do, don't give up and send us your material with confidence."

IMG-JULIAN BACH LITERARY AGENCY, (II), 22 E. 71st St., New York NY 10021. (212)772-8900. Fax: (212)772-2617. Contact: Julian Bach. Estab. 1956. Member of AAR. Represents 300 clients. Currently handles: 60% nonfiction books; 40% novels. Member agents: Julian Bach, Carolyn Krupp. Contact: Ann Torrago.
Handles: Nonfiction books, novels. Considers these nonfiction areas: anthropology/archaeology; biography; business; cooking/food/nutrition; current affairs; government/politics; history; language/literature/criticism; military/war; music/dance/theater/film; nature/environment; psychology; self-help/personal improvement; sports; true crime/investigative; women's issues/women's studies. Considers these fiction areas: detective/police/crime; literary; mainstream. Query.
Terms: No information provided. Offers written contract.

INTERNATIONAL CREATIVE MANAGEMENT, (III), 40 W. 57th St., New York NY 10019. (212)556-5600. Fax: (212)556-5665. West Coast office: 8942 Wilshire Blvd., Beverly Hills CA 90211. (310)550-4000. Member of AAR, signatory of WGA. Member agents: Esther Newberg and Amanda Urban, department heads; Lisa Bankoff; Kristine Dahl; Mitch Douglas; Suzanne Gluck; Sloan Harris; Gordon Kato; Heather Schroder.
Terms: Agent receives 10% commission on domestic sales; 15% on UK sales; 20% on translations.

INTERNATIONAL PUBLISHER ASSOCIATES INC., (II), 304 Guido Ave., Lady Lake FL 32159-9014. Contact: Joseph De Rogatis. Estab. 1983. Represents 15 clients. Currently handles: 60% nonfiction books; 40% fiction.
    ● Prior to opening his agency, Mr. De Rogatis served for 18 years with New American Library and has held various management positions in publishing for the past 25 years.
Handles: Nonfiction books. Considers all nonfiction areas. Considers "mostly" mainstream fiction. Query with full ms, outline and SASE. Reports in 3 weeks on queries.
Recent Sales: *The Pocket Pediatrician*, by Dr. David Ziggelman (Doubleday).
Terms: Agent receives 15% commission on domestic sales; 20% on foreign sales. Offers written contract, binding for life of book. Charges for postage and photocopying.
Tips: Obtains new clients through word of mouth and *Guide to Literary Agents*. "We do read unsolicited queries, encourage new writers and read material from unpublished authors. We are seeking fiction and nonfiction in the centres and categories. No poetry."

J DE S ASSOCIATES INC., (II), 9 Shagbark Rd., Wilson Point, South Norwalk CT 06854. (203)838-7571. Contact: Jacques de Spoelberch. Estab. 1975. Represents 50 clients. Currently handles: 50% nonfiction books; 50% novels.
Handles: Nonfiction books, novels. Considers these nonfiction areas: biography/autobiography; business; current affairs; ethnic/cultural interests; government/politics/law; health/medicine; history; military/war; New Age; self-help/personal improvement; sociology; sports; translations. Considers these fiction areas: detective/police/crime; historical; juvenile; literary; mainstream; mystery/suspense; New Age; westerns/frontier; young adult. Query with SASE. Reports in 2 months on queries.
Terms: Agent receives 15% commission on domestic sales; 20% on foreign sales. Charges for foreign postage and photocopying.
Tips: Obtains new clients through recommendations from others, authors and other clients.

‡JABBERWOCKY LITERARY AGENCY, (II), P.O. Box 4558, Sunnyside NY 11104-0558. (718)392-5985. Contact: Joshua Bilmes. Estab. 1994. Represents 40 clients. 25% of clients are new/previously unpublished writers. "Agency represents quite a lot of genre fiction writers and is actively seeking to increase amount of nonfiction projects." Currently handles: 25% nonfiction books; 5% scholarly books; 5% juvenile books; 60% novels; 5% short story collections.

Handles: Nonfiction books, scholarly books, juvenile books, novels. Considers these nonfiction areas: biography/autobiography; business; cooking/food/nutrition; current affairs; gay/lesbian issues; government/politics/law; health/medicine; history; humor; language/literature/criticism; military/war; money/finance/economics; music/dance/theater/film; nature/environment; popular culture; science/technology; sociology; sports; true crime/investigative; women's issues/women's studies. Considers these fiction areas: action/adventure; cartoon/comic; contemporary issues; detective/police/crime; ethnic; family saga; fantasy; gay; glitz; historical; horror; humor/satire; juvenile; lesbian; literary; mainstream; picture book; psychic/supernatural; regional; romance; science fiction; sports; thriller/espionage; young adult. Query. Reports in 2 weeks on queries.

Recent Sales: *Dead Over Heels*, by Charlaine Harris (Scribner); *Anatomy Of A Miracle*, by Mickey Eisenberg (Oxford University Press); *Winning Colors*, by Elizabeth Moon (Baen); *Hot Blood 6: Stranger by Night*, ed. by Jeff Gelbt and Michael Garrett (Pocket).

Terms: Agent receives 10% commission on domestic sales; 20% on foreign sales. Offers written contract, binding for 1 year. Charges for book purchases, ms photocopying, international book/ms mailing, international long distance.

Writers' Conferences: Malice Domestic (Bethesda MD, April); World SF Convention (Los Angeles, August).

Tips: Obtains new clients through recommendation by current clients, solicitation, "and through intriguing queries by new authors. In approaching with a query, the most important things to me are your credits and your biographical background to the extent its relevant to your work. I (and most agents I believe) will ignore the adjectives you may choose to describe your own work."

MELANIE JACKSON AGENCY, 250 W. 57th St., Suite 1119, New York NY 10107. This agency did not respond to our request for information. Query before submitting.

JAMES PETER ASSOCIATES, INC., (II), P.O. Box 772, Tenafly NJ 07670-0772. (201)568-0760. Fax: (201)568-2959. ATT Easylink: BHOLTJE. Contact: Bert Holtje. Estab. 1971. Member of AAR. Represents 84 clients. 15% of clients are new/previously unpublished writers. Specializes in nonfiction, all categories. "We are especially interested in trade and general reference projects." Currently handles: 100% nonfiction books.
   • Prior to opening his agency, Mr. Holtje was a book packager, and before that, president of an advertising agency with book publishing clients.

Handles: Nonfiction books. Considers these nonfiction areas: anthropology/archaeology; art/architecture/design; biography/autobiography; business; child guidance/parenting; current affairs; ethnic/cultural interests; gay/lesbian issues; government/politics/law; health/medicine; history; language/literature/criticism; military/war; money/finance/economics; music/dance/theater/film; popular culture; psychology; self-help/personal improvement; women's issues/women's studies. Send outline/proposal and SASE. Reports in 3-4 weeks on queries.

Recent Sales: *Power, People and Presidents*, by Jim Wright, former Speaker, U.S. House of Representatives (Turner Publishing, 1995); *Field of the Spirit—An Ancient World Revealed*, by Alan Kolata, Ph.D. (Wiley, 1996); *Dictionary of Military Biography*, by Charles Phillips and Alan Axelrod, Ph.D. (Macmillan, 1997); *Women in Film*, by Dawn Sova, Ph.D. (Birch Lane, 1996); *Word Watch*, by Anne Soukhanov (Henry Holt, 1995).

Terms: Agent receives 15% commission on domestic sales; 20% on foreign sales. Offers written contract on a per book basis. Charges for foreign postage.

Tips: Obtains new clients through recommendations from other clients and editors, contact people who are doing interesting things, and over-the-transom queries. "Phone me! I'm happy to discuss book ideas any time."

JANKLOW & NESBIT ASSOCIATES, 598 Madison Ave., New York NY 10022. This agency did not respond to our request for information. Query before submitting.

LAWRENCE JORDAN LITERARY AGENCY, (II), A Division of Morning Star Rising, Inc., 250 W. 57th St., Suite 1527, New York NY 10107-1599. (212)662-7871. Fax: (212)662-8138. President: Lawrence Jordan. Estab. 1978. Represents 50 clients. 25% of clients are new/unpublished writers. Works with a small number of new/unpublished authors. Specializes in general adult fiction and nonfiction. Currently handles: 60% nonfiction; 25% novels; 3% textbooks; 2% juvenile books; 3% movie scripts; 7% stage plays.
   • Prior to opening his agency, Mr. Jordan served as an editor with Doubleday & Co.

Handles: Nonfiction books, novels, textbooks, juvenile books, movie scripts, stage plays. Handles these nonfiction areas: autobiography; business; computer manuals; health; religion; science; self-help; sports. Query with outline. Reports in 3 weeks on queries; 6 weeks on mss.

Recent Sales: *Jeffrey Lyons' 100 Great Movies for Kids*, by Jeffrey Lyons (Fireside/Simon & Schuster); *The Lazy Man's Way to Riches*, by Richard G. Nixon (Viking Penguin); *An Easy Burden: Redeeming the Soul of America*, by Andrew Young (HarperCollins).

Terms: Agent receives 15% commission on domestic sales; 20% on dramatic sales; 20% on foreign sales. Charges long-distance calls, photocopying, foreign submission costs, postage, cables and messengers. Makes 99% of income from commissions.
Writers' Conferences: ABA (Chicago, June); Frankfurt (Germany, October); Miami.

THE KELLOCK COMPANY INC., (III), 222 Park Ave. S., New York NY 10003-1504. (212)529-7122. Fax: (212)982-7573. E-mail: alkellock@aol.com or 73313.2302@compuserve.com. Contact: Alan C. Kellock. Estab. 1990. Represents 60 clients. 25% of clients are new/previously unpublished writers. Specializes in a broad range of practical and informational nonfiction, including illustrated works. Represents authors, packagers, and smaller publishers to larger print and electronic publishers and third party sponsors. Currently handles: 100% nonfiction books. Member agents: Loren Kellock (licensing).
 • Prior to opening his agency, Mr. Kellock served as director of sales and marketing with Harcourt Brace, vice president, marketing with Waldenbooks and president and publisher for Viking Penguin.
Handles: Nonfiction books. Considers these nonfiction areas: anthropology/archaeology, art/architecture/design, biography/autobiography, business, child guidance/parenting, computers/electronics, cooking/food/nutrition; crafts/hobbies, current affairs, education; ethnic/cultural interests, government/politics/law, health/medicine, history, how-to; humor, interior design/decorating, juvenile nonfiction, military/war, money/finance/economics, music/dance/theater/film, nature/environment, photography, popular culture; religious/inspirational; psychology; science/technology; self-help/personal improvement; sociology; sports; women's issues/women's studies. Query. Reports in 2 weeks on queries, 1 month on mss.
Recent Sales: *Fat-Free Meetings In The Digital Age*, by Burton Albert (Peterson's); *Lawyers And Other Reptiles: The Appeal*, by Jess Brallier (Contemporary); *The American Garden Guides*, Layla Productions (Knopf & Microsoft); *The Women*, by Bill Dobbins (Workman); *How To Sell Your Home In 5 Days*, by Bill Effros (Workman); *The Autobiography Of Glenn Seaborg*, (Farrar, Straus & Giroux).
Terms: Agent receives 15% commission on domestic sales; 25% on foreign and multimedia sales. Offers written contract. Charges for postage, photocopying.
Worker's Conferences ABA (Chicago, May); Frankfurt (Germany, October).
Tips: Obtains most new clients through referrals, but all queries are carefully considered.

LOUISE B. KETZ AGENCY, (II), 1485 First Ave., Suite 4B, New York NY 10021. (212)535-9259. Contact: Louise B. Ketz. Estab. 1983. Represents 25 clients. 15% of clients are new/previously unpublished writers. Specializes in science, business, sports, history and reference. Currently handles: 100% nonfiction books.
Handles: Nonfiction books. Considers these nonfiction areas: anthropology/archaeology; biography/autobiography; business; current affairs; history; military/war; money/finance/economics; science/technology; sports; true crime/investigative. Send outline and 2 sample chapters. Reports in 6 weeks.
Recent Sales: *Science Revealed*, by Sidney Harris, Charles Wym and Art Wiggins (Wiley).
Terms: Agent receives 10-15% commission on domestic sales; 10% on foreign sales. Offers written contract.
Tips: Obtains new clients through recommendations, idea development.

VIRGINIA KIDD LITERARY AGENT, (V), 538 E. Harford St., P.O. Box 278, Milford PA 18337-0278. (717)296-6205. Fax: (717)296-7266. E-mail: 73107.3311@compuserve. Contact: Virginia Kidd. Estab. 1965. Member of Authors Guild, SFWA, NWU, SFRA. Represents 80 clients. Very small percentage of clients are new previously unpublished writers. Specializes in speculative fiction. Currently handles: 15% juvenile books; 75% novels; 5% short story collections; 4% novellas; 1% poetry. Member agents: Linn Prentis (mainstream novels).
Handles: Fiction. Considers science fiction, but only from previously published writers. Query. Reports immediately on queries; a month or more on mss.
Recent Sales: "I sell regularly to Berkley, Ballantine/Del Rey, HarperCollins etc."
Terms: Agent receives 10% commission on domestic sales; 20% on foreign sales; 20% on dramatic sales. Offers written contract, binding until canceled by either party.
Tips: Seldom takes on new clients. "Never forget the SASE."

KIDDE, HOYT & PICARD, (III), 335 E. 51st St., New York NY 10022. (212)755-9461. Contact: Katharine Kidde, Laura Langlie. Estab. 1980. Member of AAR. Represents 50 clients. Specializes in mainstream fiction and nonfiction. Currently handles: 15% nonfiction books; 5% juvenile books; 80% novels. Member agents: Kay Kidde (mainstream fiction, romances, mysteries, suspense, literary fiction); Laura Langlie (mainstream fiction, trade nonfiction).
Handles: Nonfiction books, novels. Considers these nonfiction areas: African studies; the arts; biography; current events; dance; ethnic/cultural interests; gay/lesbian issues; government/politics/law; history; language/literature/criticism; popular culture; psychology; self-help/personal improvement; sociology; women's issues. Considers these fiction areas: action/adventure; contemporary issues; detective/

Possibilities Blossom in the Electronic Age

Ask any gardener what the secret to a beautiful garden is, and he'll tell you it's a lot of experience, a lot of hard work, and a little bit of luck. Literary agent Alan Kellock, of the New York-based Kellock Company could say the same thing about a successful contract negotiation. Using his familiarity with book packagers, his knowledge of electronic media, and over 20 years of experience in the publishing business, Kellock helped the *American Garden Guides* (Pantheon/Alfred A. Knopf & Microsoft), grow from a one-book concept to a ground-breaking 12-volume series and interactive CD-ROM with an online component. Kellock says that, like all good things, the *American Garden Guides* started out small, with a phone call from a New York book packager.

Lori Stein, of Layla Productions, called Kellock with an idea for a book on gardening. "She told me, 'I am a terrific book packager, but a lousy salesperson,' " Kellock recalls. Book packagers take a project beyond the manuscript stage, doing the pre-press work of design, typesetting, even laying in illustrations. Stein had just finished books with the Brooklyn Botanical Garden and the New York Botanical Garden, two of the most respected gardening institutions in the country, and she was interested in doing a third.

"I told her from the beginning to think series," Kellock says. He envisioned an authoritative series on the American garden that could offset the heavy influence of British books. And so they began their collaboration.

After discussing various possibilities, Kellock and Stein decided on a 12-book set that would focus on different topics in gardening such as perennials, herbs and roses, and cover the diverse regions of the country, with the staff of one botanical garden as the principal author of each book. Each manuscript would then be reviewed by two other botanical gardens, to ensure the regional variations were accurately and adequately treated. The response was overwhelming.

"As word got out that the project was under way, we started getting unsolicited requests from gardens all over the country to participate," Kellock says. "There was a sense that this series was emerging as a sort of collective statement from the botanical community to America's backyard gardeners."

Initially Kellock and Stein secured verbal commitments from 12 botanical gardens who were interested in participating in the project. At that point, Kellock began looking for a suitable publisher. Although he considered several houses known for their books on gardening, he entered into negotiations with Alfred A. Knopf, a division of Random House (the book was eventually published under the Knopf imprint Pantheon). He says Knopf's legendary attention to detail was one of the key factors.

"Knopf is held in an esteem in the book industry comparable to Mercedes Benz in the automotive industry," he notes. Although Knopf had not published many books on gardening, Kellock says that they are well known for their superior series on subjects like antiques and birds. And Knopf was willing to make a commitment to 12 volumes.

"That was essential to us," Kellock says. "We didn't want to publish just a few books and, in essence, leave the other gardens dangling." Eventually Kellock and Stein developed a consortium of 42 botanical gardens to write and review the series.

With the contract signed and the plans laid out, the hard work began. Kellock says the participation of 42 institutions all over the country created an extraordinarily complex process, and he credits the packager with a phenomenal job. Commissioning thousands of new photos, coordinating subjects, reworking the text for a uniform style was "a marvel of trafficking," Kellock says. As production of the print series got underway, Kellock began to consider marketing the electronic rights to the *American Guides*.

Electronic rights are an increasingly tricky area, Kellock warns, as more and more publishing houses are owned by media conglomerates, and there is pressure to acquire both print and electronic rights. From the start he was firm that the electronic rights should be negotiated separately, "if for no other reason than the future is so hard to read," he states. "Nobody really has a clear fix on what the value of those rights may be, down the road." Kellock began discussing selling the electronic rights to Knopf, but became frustrated with the slow pace of negotiations. And that's where a little bit of luck came in.

Beginning a three-week West Coast vacation, Kellock arranged a meeting at Microsoft, the computer industry giant. Because of his long-standing interest in computers, and his company's reputation as "The Nonfiction Agency for the Digital Age," Kellock had become interested in the Seattle-based company. It was a simple contact call, he says, with no agenda. Until he casually mentioned that he held the rights to the *American Guides*.

"And suddenly, the person I was talking with completely changed his demeanor," Kellock recalls. "He sat up in his chair and stared at me and said, 'You mean *you* control the electronic rights to that series?' " Unbeknownst to Kellock, Microsoft had long considered doing a garden project for its CD-ROM division, Microsoft Home. In a meeting the day before, the project managers had decided that the best gardening books in the United States were the *American Guides*, and concluded that the electronic rights were probably held by Knopf, and sadly out of reach. "And 24 hours later, I walk into the office and casually mention that I control the rights, and they're free and clear!" Within a week, Kellock was back in Seattle, this time accompanied by Stein, and within three weeks, the deal was done—not to simply re-release the *American Guides* in electronic form, but to expand the project beyond its original scope, with additional text and photos. In addition to the CD-ROM, released in early 1996, Microsoft also plans to introduce an online version of the *American Guides* as a part of their Microsoft Network. Kellock says that points to an interesting issue for authors and agents.

Had Knopf kept the electronic rights and done the same deal with Microsoft, he says, they would not have been in a position to provide the additional information. And the world of electronic publishing is changing so rapidly that agents need to stay one step ahead of the technology, to understand all the possibilities. "We're long past the point of taking a book and simply putting it on a computer screen and calling it an electronic publication," Kellock says.

As any good gardener, Kellock is quick to credit others in the success of the *American Guides*. Without the eager interest of the botanical community, or the hard work of the book packager, the project would not have become such a success. But he admits that his own background and a willingness to experiment were also key elements. He says that, "for clients who are involved in projects that make sense in both traditional and newer media, I'm a pretty good stop on their agent-shopping route."

—*Alison Holm*

Reprinted with permission of Pantheon/Alfred A. Knopf

police/crime; ethnic; feminist; gay; glitz; historical; humor; lesbian; literary; mainstream; mystery/ suspense; regional; romance (contemporary, historical, regency); thriller/espionage. Query. Reports in a few weeks on queries; 3-4 weeks on mss.
Recent Sales: *The Kindness of Mike McIntyre*, (Boulevard); *Strangers* (Berkley); *The Judas Glass*, by Michael Cadnum (Carroll & Graf); *Mind Games*, by C.J. Koehler (Carroll & Graf); *See How They Run*, by Bethany Campbell (Bantam).
Terms: Agent receives 15% commission on domestic sales; 15% on foreign sales. Charges for photocopying.
Tips: Obtains new clients through query letters, recommendations from others, "former authors from when I was an editor at NAL, Harcourt, etc.; listings in *LMP*, writers' guides."

KIRCHOFF/WOHLBERG, INC., AUTHORS' REPRESENTATION DIVISION, (II), 866 United Nations Plaza, #525, New York NY 10017. (212)644-2020. Fax: (212)223-4387. Director of Operations: John R. Whitman. Estab. 1930s. Member of AAR, AAP, Society of Illustrators, SPAR, Bookbuilders of Boston, New York Bookbinders' Guild, AIGA. Represents 50 authors. 10% of clients are new/ previously unpublished writers. Specializes in juvenile through young adult trade books and textbooks. Currently handles: 5% nonfiction books; 80% juvenile books; 5% novels; 5% novellas; 5% young adult. Member agent: Elizabeth Pulitzer-Voges (juvenile and young adult authors); Julie Alperen (juvenile and young adult authors).
Handles: "We are interested in any original projects of quality that are appropriate to the juvenile and young adult trade book markets. Send a query that includes an outline and a sample; SASE required." Reports in 1 month on queries; 6 weeks on mss. Please send queries to the attention of Liza Pulitzer-Voges or Julie Alperen.
Recent Sales: *Snowballs*, by Lois Ehlert (Harcourt Brace); *Chicka Chicka Sticka Sticka*, by John Archambault & Bill Martin Jr. (Simon & Schuster); *From The Notebooks Of Melanin Sun*, by Jacqueline Woodson (Scholastic); *A Baby's Journal: A Book Of Firsts*, by Lizi Boyd (Chronicle); *Taking Flight: My Story, By Vicki Van Meter*, by Dan Gutman (Viking);' *Hold Fast To Dreams*, by Andrea Davis Pinkney (Morrow Junior Books).
Terms: Agent receives standard commission "depending upon whether it is an author only, illustrator only, or an author/illustrator book." Offers written contract, binding for not less than 1 year.

Writers' Conferences: International Children's Books Fair (Bologna Italy, Spring 1996); International Reading Association (New Orleans, April 28-May 2 1996); American Booksellers Association (Chicago, June 1996).
Tips: "Usually obtains new clients through recommendations from authors, illustrators and editors. Kirchoff/Wohlberg has been in business for over 50 years."

HARVEY KLINGER, INC., (III), 301 W. 53rd St., New York NY 10019. (212)581-7068. Fax: (212)315-3823. Contact: Harvey Klinger. Estab. 1977. Member of AAR. Represents 100 clients. 25% of clients are new/previously unpublished writers. Specializes in "big, mainstream contemporary fiction and nonfiction." Currently handles: 50% nonfiction books; 50% novels. Member agents: Carol McCleary (mysteries, science fiction, fantasy, category fiction, all general categories); Laurie Liss (politics, women's issues).
Handles: Nonfiction books, novels. Considers these nonfiction areas: biography/autobiography; cooking/food/nutrition; health/medicine; psychology; science/technology; self-help/personal improvement; sports; true crime/investigative; women's issues/women's studies. Considers these fiction areas: action/adventure; detective/police/crime; family saga; glitz; horror (dark); literary; mainstream; mystery/suspense; romance (contemporary); science fiction; thriller/espionage; western. Query. Reports in 2 weeks on queries; 2 months on mss.
Recent Sales: *Timepiece*, by Richard Paul (Simon & Schuster); untitled, by Stephen Collins (Bantam); *Blue Crystal*, by Philip Lee Williams (Grove); *Run with the Hunted*, by Charles Bukowski (HarperCollins); *You Can Look Younger at Any Age: A Leading Dermatologist's Guide*, by Nelson Lee Novick, MD (Holt).
Terms: Agent receives 15% commission on domestic sales; 25% on foreign sales. Offers written contract. Charges for photocopying manuscripts, overseas postage for mss.
Tips: Obtains new clients through recommendations from others.

BARBARA S. KOUTS, LITERARY AGENT, (II), P.O. Box 560, Bellport NY 11713. (516)286-1278. Contact: Barbara Kouts. Estab. 1980. Member of AAR. Represent 50 clients. 10% of clients are new/previously unpublished writers. Specializes in adult fiction and nonfiction and children's books. Currently handles: 20% nonfiction books; 40% juvenile books; 40% novels.
Handles: Nonfiction books, juvenile books, novels. Considers these nonfiction areas: biography/autobiography; business; child guidance/parenting; current affairs; ethnic/cultural interests; health/medicine; history; juvenile nonfiction; music/dance/theater/film; nature/environment; psychology; self-help/personal improvement; women's issues/women's studies. Considers these fiction areas: contemporary issues; family saga; feminist; historical; juvenile; literary; mainstream; mystery/suspense; picture book; romance (gothic, historical); young adult. Query. Reports in 2-3 days on queries; 4-6 weeks on mss.
Recent Sales: *Voice Lessons*, by Nancy Mairs (Beacon); *The Faithful Friend*, by Robert San Souci (Simon & Schuster).
Terms: Agent receives 10% commission on domestic sales; 20% on foreign sales. Charges for photocopying.
Tips: Obtains new clients through recommendations from others, solicitation, at conferences, etc. "Write, do not call. Be professional in your writing."

EDITE KROLL LITERARY AGENCY, (II), 12 Grayhurst Park, Portland ME 04102. (207)773-4922. Fax: (207)773-3936. Contact: Edite Kroll. Estab. 1981. Represents 40 clients. Currently handles: 60% adult books; 40% juvenile books.
Handles: Nonfiction, juvenile books, humor, novels. Considers these nonfiction areas: current affairs; social and political issues (especially feminist). Considers these fiction areas: contemporary issues; feminist; literary; mystery/suspense; juvenile; picture books by author/artists. Query in writing only with SASE; no phone or fax. For nonfiction, send outline and proposal. For fiction, send outline and 1 sample chapter. For picture books, send dummy. Reports in 1 month on queries; 6 weeks on mss.

‡THE CANDACE LAKE AGENCY, (II, IV), 822 S. Robertson Blvd., #200, Los Angeles CA 90035. (310)289-0600. Fax: (310)289-0619. Contact: Elizabeth Thomas. Estab. 1977. Signatory of WGA. 50% of clients are new/previously unpublished writers. Specializes in screenplay and teleplay writers. Currently handles: 20% novels; 40% movie scripts; 40% TV scripts.
   • See the expanded listing for this agency in Script Agents.

 The double dagger before a listing indicates the listing is new in this edition.

PETER LAMPACK AGENCY, INC., (II), 551 Fifth Ave., Suite 1613, New York NY 10176-0187. (212)687-9106. Fax: (212)687-9109. Contact: Deborah T. Brown. Estab. 1977. Represents 50 clients. 10% of clients are new/previously unpublished writers. Specializes in commercial fiction, male-oriented action/adventure, contemporary relationships, distinguished literary fiction, nonfiction by a recognized expert in a given field. Currently handles: 15% nonfiction books; 85% novels. Member agents: Peter Lampack (psychological suspense, action/adventure, literary fiction, nonfiction, contemporary relationships); Sandra Blanton (contemporary relationships, psychological thrillers, mysteries, literary fiction, nonfiction including literary and theatrical biography); Deborah Brown (literary and commercial fiction, mystery, suspense, historical fiction, nonfiction, especially interested in history, art, contemporary culture [not pop] and women's issues).
Handles: Nonfiction books, novels. Considers these nonfiction areas: anthropology/archaeology; art/architecture/design; biography/autobiography; business; current affairs; government/politics/law; health/medicine; history; money/finance/economics; music/dance/theater/film; popular culture; high profile true crime/investigative; women's issues. Considers these fiction areas: action/adventure; contemporary relationships; detective/police/crime; family saga; glitz; historical; literary; mainstream; mystery/suspense; thriller/espionage. Query. No unsolicited mss. Reports in 3 weeks on queries; 2 months on mss.
Recent Sales: *Shockwave* and *Diamonds*, by Clive Cussler (Simon & Schuster); *Fly Away Home*, by Judith Kelman (Bantam); *Eye of the Beholder*, by Brian Lysaght (Simon & Schuster); *James Thurber: His Life & Times*, by Harrison Kinney (Henry Holt); *Magnificent Savages*, by Fred Neustard Stewart (TOR Books); *True Colors*, by Doris Mortman (Crown/Ballantine); *How to Argue and Win Every Time*, by Gerry Spence, Esq. (St. Martin's Press); *The Master of Petersburg*, by J.M. Coetzee (Viking/Penguin); *The Living Trust Workbook*, by Robert A. Esperti, Esq. and Renno L. Peterson, Esq. (Viking/Penguin).
Terms: Agent receives 15% commission on domestic sales; 20% on foreign sales. "Writer is required to furnish copies of his/her work for submission purposes."
Writers' Conferences: ABA (Chicago, June).
Tips: Obtains new clients from referrals made by clients. "Submit only your best work for consideration. Have a very specific agenda of goals you wish your prospective agent to accomplish for you. Provide the agent with a comprehensive statement of your credentials—educational and professional."

THE ROBERT LANTZ-JOY HARRIS LITERARY AGENCY INC., (II), 156 Fifth Ave., Suite 617, New York NY 10010. (212)924-6269. Fax: (212)924-6609. Contact: Joy Harris. Member of AAR. Represents 150 clients. Currently handles: 50% nonfiction books; 50% novels.
Handles: Considers "adult-type books, not juvenile." Considers all fiction areas except fantasy; juvenile; science fiction; westerns/frontier. Query with outline/proposal and SASE. Reports in 2 months on queries.
Recent Sales: *The Magic Bullet*, by Harry Stein (Delacorte, film rights to Ruddy-Morgan Productions).
Terms: Agent receives 15% commission on domestic sales; 20% on foreign sales. Offers written contract. Charges for extra expenses.
Tips: Obtains new clients through recommendations from clients and editors. "No unsolicited manuscripts, just query letters."

MICHAEL LARSEN/ELIZABETH POMADA LITERARY AGENTS, (II), 1029 Jones St., San Francisco CA 94109-5023. (415)673-0939. Contact: Mike Larsen or Elizabeth Pomada. Estab. 1972. Member of AAR, Authors Guild, ASJA, NWA, PEN, WNBA, California Writers Club. Represents 100 clients. 40-45% of clients are new/unpublished writers. Eager to work with new/unpublished writers. "We have very diverse tastes and do not specialize. We look for fresh voices with new ideas. We handle literary, commercial and genre fiction, and the full range of nonfiction books." Currently handles: 60% nonfiction books; 40% novels. Member agents: Michael Larsen (nonfiction), Elizabeth Pomada (fiction, women's issues).
   ● Prior to opening their agency, both Mr. Larsen and Ms. Pomada were promotion executives for major publishing houses. Mr. Larsen worked for Morrow, Bantam and Pyramid (now part of Berkley), Ms. Pomada worked at Holt, David McKay, and The Dial Press.
Handles: Adult nonfiction books, novels. Considers these nonfiction areas: anthropology/archaeology; art/architecture/design; biography/autobiography; business; parenting; cooking/food/nutrition; crafts/hobbies; current affairs; ethnic/cultural interests; futurism; gay/lesbian issues; government/politics/law; health/medicine; history; how-to; humor; interior design/decorating; language/literature/criticism; money/finance/economics; music/dance/theater/film; nature/environment; New Age/metaphysics; photography; popular culture; psychology; religious/inspirational; science/technology; self-help/personal improvement; sociology; sports; true crime/investigative; women's issues/women's studies. Considers these fiction areas: action/adventure; contemporary issues; detective/police/crime; ethnic; experimental; family saga; fantasy; feminist; gay; glitz; historical; horror; humor/satire; lesbian; literary; mainstream; mystery/suspense; psychic/supernatural; religious/inspirational; romance (contemporary,

gothic, historical, regency). Query with synopsis and first 30 pages of completed novel. Reports in 2 months on queries. For nonfiction, call first. "Always include SASE. Send SASE for brochure."
Recent Sales: *Palace*, by Katharine Kerr (Bantam, 1996); *Guerilla Marketing Weapons on the Internet*, by Jay Conrad Levinson (Houghton Mifflin, 1994); *Your Next 50 Years*, by Ginita Wall (Henry Holt); *TV Dinners*, by Pat & Barry Katzmann (Boulevard/Berkley); *Cobra Dane*, by John T. Campbell (Avon, 1995); *The Girls with the Grandmother Faces*, (Hyperion, 1996); *The Water Book, The Sierra Club Guide to Safe Drinking Water*, by Scott Alan Lewis (Sierra Club Books, 1996).
Terms: Agent receives 15% commission on domestic sales; 15% on dramatic sales; 20% on foreign sales. May charge writer for printing, postage for multiple submissions, foreign mail, foreign phone calls, galleys, books, and legal fees.
Writers' Conferences: ABA (Chicago); Santa Barbara Writers Conference (Santa Barbara); Maui Writers Conference (Maui); Ozark Writers Conference (Eureka Springs, October); ASJA (Los Angeles, February).

THE MAUREEN LASHER AGENCY, (II, III), P.O. Box 888, Pacific Palisades CA 90272. (310)459-8415. Contact: Ann Cashman. Estab. 1980.
Handles: Nonfiction books, novels. Considers these nonfiction areas: animals; anthropology/archaeology; art/architecture/design; biography/autobiography; business; child guidance/parenting; cooking/food/nutrition; current affairs; ethnic/cultural interests; govenment/politics/law; health/medicine; history; how-to; nature/environment; popular culture; psychology; science/technology; self-help/personal improvement; sociology; sports; true crime/investigative; women's issues/women's studies. Considers these fiction areas: action/adventure; contemporary issues; detective/police/crime; family saga; feminist; historical; literary; mainstream; sports; thriller/espionage. Send outline/proposal and 1 sample chapter.
Terms: No information provided. Does not charge a reading fee or offer criticism service.

LAZEAR AGENCY INCORPORATED, (II), 430 First Ave., Suite 416, Minneapolis MN 55401. (612)332-8640. Fax: (612)332-4648. Contact: Editorial Board. Estab. 1984. Represents 250 clients. Currently handles: 40% nonfiction books; 20% juvenile books; 29% novels; 1% short story collections; 5% movie scripts; 2.5% TV scripts; 2.5% syndicated material. Member agents: Jonathon Lazear (president); Eric Vrooman (agent); Dennis Cass (director of subsidiary rights); Susie Moncur (agent).
Handles: Nonfiction books, juvenile books, novels, movie scripts, TV scripts, syndicated material, new media with connection to book project. Considers all nonfiction areas. Considers all fiction areas. Query with outline/proposal and SASE. Reports in 3 weeks on queries; 2 months on ms. Highly selective. No phone calls or faxes.
Terms: Agent receives 15% commission on domestic sales; 20% on foreign sales. Offers written contract, binding "for term of copyright." Charges for "photocopying, international express mail."
Tips: Obtains new clients through recommendations from others, "through the bestseller lists, word-of-mouth. The writer should first view himself as a salesperson in order to obtain an agent. Sell yourself, your idea, your concept. Do your homework. Notice what is in the marketplace. Be sophisticated about the arena in which you are writing."

LESCHER & LESCHER LTD., (II), 67 Irving Place, New York NY 10003. (212)529-1790. Fax: (212)529-2716. Contact: Robert or Susan Lescher. Estab. 1966. Member of AAR. Represents 150 clients. Currently handles: 75% nonfiction books; 13% juvenile books; 12% novels.
Handles: Nonfiction books, novels. Query with SASE.
Terms: Agent receives 15% commission on domestic sales; 20-25% on foreign sales. Charges for photocopying mss and copyrighting fees.
Tips: Usually obtains new clients through recommendations from others.

LEVANT & WALES, LITERARY AGENCY, INC., (II, IV), 108 Hayes St., Seattle WA 98109-2808. (206)284-7114. Fax: (206)284-0190. Contact: Elizabeth Wales or Valerie Griffith. Estab. 1988. Member of AAR, Pacific Northwest Writers' Conference, Book Publishers' Northwest. Represents 50 clients. We are interested in published and not-yet-published writers. Prefers writers from the Pacific Northwest, West Coast, Alaska and Pacific Rim countries. Specializes in nonfiction and mainstream fiction. Currently handles: 75% nonfiction books; 25% novels.
Handles: Nonfiction books, novels. Considers these nonfiction areas: animals; anthropology/archaeology; art/architecture/design; biography/autobiography; business; child guidance/parenting; current affairs; education; ethnic/cultural interests; gardening; gay/lesbian issues; health; language/literature/criticism; lifestyle; memoir; nature; New Age/metaphysics; popular culture; psychology; science; self-help/personal improvement; sports; women's issues/women's studies—open to creative or serious treatments of almost any nonfiction subject. Considers these fiction areas: cartoon/comic/women's; ethnic; experimental; feminist; gay; lesbian; literary; mainstream (no genre fiction). Query first. Reports in 3 weeks on queries; 6 weeks on mss.

Recent Sales: *Disappearance: A Meditation on Death and Loss*, by Sheila Nickerson (Doubleday, 1996); *Autobiography of Benjamin Graham*, by Benjamin Graham (McGraw-Hill, 1996); *The African-American Yellow Pages*, by Stanton F. Biddle, PhD (Holt).
Terms: Agent receives 15% commission on domestic sales. "We make all our income from commissions. We offer editorial help for some of our clients and help some clients with the development of a proposal, but we do not charge for these services. We do charge, after a sale, for express mail, manuscript photocopying costs, foreign postage and outside USA telephone costs."
Writers' Conferences: Pacific NW Writers Conference (Seattle, July 1996).

JAMES LEVINE COMMUNICATIONS, INC., (II), 330 Seventh Ave., 14th Floor, New York NY 10001. (212)268-4846. Fax: (212)465-8637. E-mail: levineja@aol.com. Estab. 1989. Member of AAR. Represents 65 clients. 33⅓% of clients are new/previously unpublished writers. Specializes in business, psychology, parenting, health/medicine, narrative nonfiction. Currently handles: 85% nonfiction books; 10% juvenile books; 5% novels. Member agents: James Levine; Daniel Greensberg, associate agent, (sports, history, fiction); Arielle Eckstut, associate agent (narrative nonfiction, psychology, spirituality, religion, women's issues).
   • Prior to opening his agency, Mr. Levine served as vice president of the Bank Street College of Education.
Handles: Nonfiction books, juvenile books, novels. Considers these nonfiction areas: animals; art/architecture/design; biography/autobiography; business; child guidance/parenting; computers/electronics; cooking/food/nutrition; gardening; gay/lesbian issues; health/medicine; juvenile nonfiction; money/finance/economics; nature/environment; New Age/metaphysics; psychology; religious/inspirational; science/technology; self-help/personal improvement; sociology; sports; women's issues/women's studies. Considers these fiction areas: contemporary issues; juvenile; literary; mainstream; young adult. Send outline/proposal plus 1 sample chapter. Reports in 2 weeks on queries; 1 month on mss.
Recent Sales: *Undercurrents: A Life Beneath the Surface*, by Martha Manning (Harper San Francisco); *Catherine, Called Birdy*, by Karen Cushman (Clarion); *The Genesis of Ethics*, by Barton Visotzky (Crown); *Chasing Grace*, by Martha Manning (Harper San Francisco); *Awakening the Spirit*, by Bradford Keeney (Riverheard, Putnam).
Terms: Agent receives 15% commission on domestic sales; 20% on foreign sales. Offers written contract; length of time varies per project. Charges for out-of-pocket expenses—telephone, fax, postage and photocopying—directly connected to the project.
Writers' Conferences: ASJA Annual Conference (New York City, May); ABA (Chicago, June).
Tips: Obtains new clients through client referrals. "We work closely with clients on editorial development and promotion. We work to place our clients as magazine columnists and have created columnists for *McCall's* and *Child*. We work with clients to develop their projects across various media—video, software, and audio."

ELLEN LEVINE LITERARY AGENCY, INC., (II, III), 15 E. 26th St., Suite 1801, New York NY 10010. (212)889-0620. Fax: (212)725-4501. Contact: Ellen Levine, Elizabeth Kaplan, Diana Finch, Anne Dubuisson. Estab. 1980. Member of AAR. Represents over 100 clients. 20% of clients are new/previously unpublished writers. "My three younger colleagues at the agency (Anne Dubuisson, Diana Finch and Elizabeth Kaplan) are seeking both new and established writers. I prefer to work with established writers, mostly through referrals." Currently handles: 60% nonfiction books; 8% juvenile books; 30% novels; 2% short story collections.
   • Ellen Levine is the current Secretary of the AAR.
Handles: Nonfiction books, juvenile books, novels, short story collections. Considers these nonfiction areas: anthropology; biography; current affairs; health; popular culture; psychology; science; women's issues/women's studies; books by journalists. Considers these fiction areas: literary; mystery; women's thrillers. Query. Reports in 3 weeks on queries, if SASE provided; 6 weeks on mss, if submission requested.
Recent Sales: *Model*, by Michael Gross (William Morrow); *Derby Dugan's Depression Funnies*, by Tom De Haven (Holt); *The Debt to Pleasure*, by John Lancaster (Holt).
Terms: Agent receives 15% commission on domestic sales; 20% on foreign sales. Charges for overseas postage, photocopying, messenger fees, overseas telephone and fax, books ordered for use in rights submissions.
Tips: Obtains new clients through recommendations from others.

‡KAREN LEWIS & COMPANY, (I, II), P.O. Box 741623, Dallas TX 75374. (214)342-3885. Fax: (214)340-8875. Contact: Karen Lewis. Estab. 1995. Represents 12 clients. 25% of clients are new/previously unpublished writers. Currently handles: 50% nonfiction books; 50% novels.
Handles: Nonfiction books, juvenile books, novels. Considers these nonfiction areas: ethnic/cultural interests; gay/lesbian issues; juvenile nonfiction; New Age/metaphysics; self-help/personal improvement; women's issues/women's studies. Considers these fiction areas: action/adventure; detective/

police/crime; erotica; ethnic; literary; mainstream; mystery/suspense; science fiction; thriller/espionage. Query. Reports in 2 weeks on queries; 1 month on mss.
Terms: Agent receives 15% commission on domestic sales; 20% on foreign sales. Offers written contract, binding for 1 year, with 30 day cancellation clause. Charges $35 processing fee. 100% of business is derived from commissions on sales.
Writers' Conferences: Southwest Writers (Albuquerque NM).
Tips: Obtains new clients through "conferences and referrals from people I know. Write a clear letter succinctly describing your book. Be sure to include a SASE. If you receive rejection notices, don't despair. Keep writing! A good book will always find a home."

ROBERT LEWIS, 65 E. 96th St., New York NY 10128.
● Mr. Lewis recently passed away and the agency has been closed.

‡ROBERT LIEBERMAN ASSOCIATES, (II), 400 Nelson Rd., Ithaca NY 14850. (607)273-8801. E-mail: rhl10@cornell.edu. Estab. 1993. Represents 20 clients. 50% of clients are new/previously unpublished writers. Specializes in university/college level textbooks and popular tradebooks in science, math, engineering, economics and others. Currently handles: 20% nonfiction books; 80% textbooks.
Handles: Scholarly books, textbooks. Considers these nonfiction areas: agriculture/horticulture; anthropology/archaeology; art/architecture/design; business; computers/electronics; education; health/medicine; money/finance/economics; music/dance/theater/film; nature/environment; psychology; science/technology; sociology; college level textbooks. Query with outline/proposal. Reports in 2 weeks on queries; 1 month on mss.
Terms: Agent receives 15% commission on domestic sales; 20% on foreign sales. Offers written contract, binding for open-ended length of time, with 30 day cancellation clause. "Fees are changed only when special reviewers are required." 100% of business is derived from commissions on sales.
Tips: Obtains new clients through referrals. Send initial inquiries by mail or E-mail.

RAY LINCOLN LITERARY AGENCY, (II), Elkins Park House, Suite 107-B, 7900 Old York Rd., Elkins Park PA 19027. (215)635-0827. Contact: Mrs. Ray Lincoln. Estab. 1974. Represents 34 clients. 35% of clients are new/previously unpublished writers. Specializes in biography, nature, the sciences, fiction in both adult and children's categories. Currently handles: 30% nonfiction books; 20% juvenile books; 50% novels. Member agent: Jerome A. Lincoln.
Handles: Nonfiction books, scholarly books, juvenile books, novels. Considers these nonfiction areas: horticulture; animals; anthropology/archaeology; art/architecture/design; biography/autobiography; business; child guidance/parenting; cooking/food/nutrition; crafts/hobbies; current affairs; ethnic/cultural interests; gay/lesbian issues; government/politics/law; health/medicine; history; interior design/decorating; juvenile nonfiction; language/literature/criticism; money/finance/economics; music/dance/theater/film; nature/environment; psychology; science/technology; self-help/personal improvement; sociology; sports; women's issues/women's studies. Considers these fiction areas: action/adventure; contemporary issues; detective/police/crime; ethnic; family saga; fantasy; feminist; gay; historical; humor/satire; juvenile; lesbian; literary; mainstream; mystery/suspense; psychic/supernatural; regional; romance (contemporary, gothic, historical); science fiction; sports; thriller/espionage; young adult. Query first, then send outline, 2 sample chapters and SASE. "I send for balance of manuscript if it is a likely project." Reports in 2 weeks on queries; 1 month on mss.
Recent Sales: *Sophie's Masterpiece*, by Eileen Spinelli (Simon & Schuster); *Hostile Witness*, by William Lashner (HarperCollins), *Soulfire*; by Lorri Hewett (Dutton).
Terms: Agent receives 15% commission on domestic sales; 20% on foreign sales. Offers written contract, binding "but with notice, may be cancelled. Charges only for overseas telephone calls. I request authors to do manuscript photocopying themselves. Postage, or shipping charge, on manuscripts accepted for representation by agency."
Tips: Obtains new clients usually from recommendations. "I always look for polished writing style, fresh points of view and professional attitudes."

LINDSTROM LITERARY GROUP, (I), 871 N. Greenbrier St., Arlington VA 22205-1220. (703)522-4730. Fax: (703)527-7624. E-mail: lindlitgrp@aol.com. Contact: Kristin Lindstrom. Estab. 1994. Represents 22 clients. 60% of clients are new/previously unpublished writers. Currently handles: 50% nonfiction books; 30% novels; 10% movie scripts; 10% TV scripts. Member agent: Perry Lindstrom (nonfiction, film/TV scripts).
Handles: Nonfiction books; novels. Considers these nonfiction areas: biography/autobiography; business; computers/electronics; current affairs; ethnic/cultural interests; government/politics/law; health/medicine; history; how-to; money/finance/economics; popular culture; psychology; science/technology; self-help/personal improvement; women's issues/women's studies. Considers these fiction areas: action/adventure; contemporary issues; detective/police/crime; ethnic; family saga; fantasy; historical; horror; mainstream; science fiction; thriller/espionage; westerns/frontier. For fiction, send 3 chapters and outline with SASE to cover return of ms if desired. For nonfiction, send outline/proposal with

INSIDER REPORT

Developing the Person, Not Just the Property

Arielle Eckstut of Levine Communications loves her work. "It's a fun job, a very fun job. There's so much creative work in this company that it makes it a very exciting place. That may be the case other places, but I feel in no way certain that it is."

One of the attributes she feels sets the agency apart is the depth of involvement in developing writers. "We really try to build a partnership with our authors. As an agency our specialty is editorial and creative development, but our efforts don't stop there. We see it as not just 'here's a book that we're going to sell,' but 'here's a career we're going to help build.' We've set writers up with everything from magazine columns to video projects, all different kinds of opportunities that really develop the person and not just the property."

UNDER**CURRENTS**
A Life Beneath the Surface

"This remarkable memoir describes a yearlong descent into, and eventually out of, the unbearable hell of depression— and does so with eloquence, grace, and humor."

MARTHA MANNING

Reprinted with permission of HarperCollins/San Francisco

The agency has a special interest in parenting and psychology, largely due to James Levine's background as vice president of the Bank Street College of Education. While the agency list includes a wide array of nonfiction books, Eckstut feels that narrative nonfiction has been a highlight for her. "A project with someone who has a personal knowledge of the subject and a wonderful voice is really special to work on."

One recent project, Martha Manning's intimate account of her battle with depression entitled *Undercurrents: A Life Beneath the Surface* (Harper San Francisco), illustrates the wide range of activities Ms. Eckstut becomes involved in. The book began as an article in the *Family Therapy Networker*, an award-winning small circulation magazine the agency subscribes to for the family therapy community. "Martha had written a very small piece on her experience going through electroconvulsive therapy (ECT). It was her actual diary going through this time. It was beautifully written but it wasn't in any way a book as it stood."

Recognizing the writer's potential, Ms. Eckstut contacted Ms. Manning about working together. "We sat down for hours and just brainstormed on the possibilities for a book like this. Did she keep any journals up to this time, after this time? Just what did we have to work with? Once we established that there was quite a bit of material, we talked about the structure. The book ended up being about the year before her treatment, that year and the year after. She is a woman who is a mother, a professor, a therapist, many things. It is about a woman in her many roles going through the struggles so many women go through. It just happened that she had a very extreme circumstance."

After settling on the direction and material for the book, Eckstut and Manning put together a book proposal. "We used the article as a basis, but we developed it. We had 25 pages of sample writing, and we clearly delineated who the audience was and what the marketing possibilities were." Eckstut sent the proposal to several publishers and set up an auction with five of them. After a few frenetic days, a "hefty" sale was made to Harper San Francisco.

"Martha worked very closely with her editor; she has a great editor and they work well together. It's a wonderful book, a beautiful read. It's very funny, even though it's about a serious topic. The publisher was thrilled with what came out. They did a full color preprint of the book which went out to 3,000 booksellers, and set her up with great publicity to begin with, an interview with Dateline NBC and all sorts of things. They did a really wonderful job.

"But at the same time, we tell people they have to have the 'Martha Stewart' attitude, which is that the publisher can do a lot, but it doesn't mean the book is going to sell. Authors really have to do as much as they can themselves. So we helped her think about what she could bring to the project, such as her connections to the psychiatric community, her teaching and lecturing skills, and networking in her area, which is just outside of DC. She travels doing as many impromptu book signings as she can.

"The publisher set up a book tour which went incredibly well. They analyzed the sales data and found that sales were highest where she had appeared. So she's going back out for a second 'mini-tour' of the East Coast where she had been before she got the great reviews. Once the publicity started there wasn't much we had to do, but we worked in partnership. Now that she's going back on tour I'm going to New York bookstores to help set up readings for her."

In addition, Eckstut lined up other opportunities to highlight the author and her book. "I negotiated several pieces for *Mirabella*, *Harper's Bazaar*, as well as articles for *New Woman* and *Glamour*. We've worked together, the publisher and I, to get the biggest blast we can."

Eckstut sold dramatic rights for a TV movie, directed by a Hallmark Hall of Fame award-winning director, through a co-agent in Hollywood and negotiated a consultation fee for Ms. Manning. "Even before we signed the contract, Martha and the producer had several meetings. He really sees it as a collaborative effort," she adds.

"All in all, it started out with something that wasn't clearly a book. If we had sent just the article to a publisher, I think we would have gotten very little money and who knows where the book would have gone. Now it's doing very well. It's a combination of the author putting everything she had into it, developing what turned out to be a really wonderful book, and the publisher meeting all together. Our efforts bridge all these aspects into one very strong force. It's been a very successful project for all involved."
—*Kirsten Holm*

SASE. Reports in 1 month on queries; 6 weeks on mss. "No comments given on most rejections."

Recent Sales: *The Last Family*, by John Ramsey Miller (Bantam Books); *Genellan II* Sequel, by Scott Gier (Del Rey) (first *Genellan* was the Del Rey Discovery of Year '95).

Also Handles: Movie scripts (feature film), TV scripts (TV mow, miniseries). Considers these script subject areas: action/adventure; comedy; detective/police/crime; ethnic; family saga; historical; horror; mainstream; mystery/suspense; romantic comedy and drama; thriller.

Recent Sales: *Movie/TV Mow optioned/sold: The Last Family*, by John Ramoy Miller (C. Gordon); *Movie/TV Mow in development: The Rose Trap*, by Elsa Houtz (Columbia Tri-Star TV).

Terms: Agent receives 15% commission on domestic sales; 15% on foreign sales. Offers written contract. Charges for marketing and mailing expense, express mail, UPS, etc.

Tips: Obtains new clients through references, guides, electronic mail. "Include biography of writer. Send enough material for an overall review of project scope."

WENDY LIPKIND AGENCY, (II), 165 E. 66th St., New York NY 10021. (212)628-9653. Fax: (212)628-2693. Contact: Wendy Lipkind. Estab. 1977. Member of AAR. Represents 60 clients. Specializes in adult nonfiction. Currently handles: 80% nonfiction books; 20% novels.

Handles: Nonfiction, novels. Considers these nonfiction areas: biography; current affairs; health/medicine; history; science; social history. Considers mainstream and mystery/suspense fiction. No mass market originals. For nonfiction, query with outline/proposal. For fiction, query with SASE only. Reports in 1 month on queries.

Recent Sales: *Where's The Baby* and *Animal's Lullaby*, both by Tom Paxton (Morrow Junior Books).

Terms: Agent receives 15% commission on domestic sales; 20% on foreign sales. Sometimes offers written contract. Charges for foreign postage and messenger service.

Tips: Usually obtains new clients through recommendations from others. "Send intelligent query letter first. Let me know if you sent to other agents."

LITERARY AND CREATIVE ARTISTS AGENCY INC., (III), 3543 Albemarle St. NW, Washington DC 20008. (202)362-4688. Fax: (202)362-8875. Contact: Muriel Nellis, Jane Roberts, Deborah Grosvenor. Estab. 1982. Member of Authors Guild, associate member of American Bar Association. Represents over 75 clients. "While we prefer published writers, it is not required if the proposed work has great merit." Requires exclusive review of material; no simultaneous submissions. Currently handles: 70% nonfiction books; 15% novels; 10% audio/video; 5% film/TV.

Handles: Nonfiction, novels, audio, film/TV rights. Considers these nonfiction areas: business; cooking; health; how-to; human drama; lifestyle; memoir; philosophy; politics. Query with outline, bio and SASE. No unsolicited mss. Reports in 3 weeks on queries.

Recent Sales: *The Return of Merlin*, by D. Chopra (Harmony); *To Teach a Child to Be Kind*, by L. Baldrige (Scribner); *The Web*, by G. Oliphant (Crown); *Witness*, by L. Borger (Pocket); *A Home for the Soul*, by A. Lawlor (Carol Southern Books).

Terms: Agent receives 15% commission on domestic sales; 20% on dramatic sales; 25% on foreign sales. Charges for long-distance phone and fax, photocopying and shipping.

THE LITERARY GROUP, (II), 270 Lafayette St., #1505, New York NY 10012. (212)274-1616. Fax: (212)274-9876. Contact: Frank Weimann. Estab. 1985. Represents 90 clients. 75% of clients are new/previously unpublished writers. Specializes in nonfiction (true crime; biography; sports; how-to). Currently handles: 80% nonfiction books; 20% novels. Member agents: Frank Weimann (nonfiction in all areas); Jessica Wainwright (women's issues, romance); Scott Waxman (sports, politics, inspirational).

Handles: Nonfiction books, novels. Considers these nonfiction areas: animals; anthropology/archaeology; biography/autobiography; business; child guidance/parenting; cookbooks; crafts/hobbies; current affairs; education; ethnic/cultural interests; gay/lesbian issues; government/politics/law; health/medicine; history; how-to; humor; juvenile nonfiction; language/literature/criticism; military/war; money/finance/economics; music/dance/theater/film; nature/environment; New Age/metaphysics; popular culture; psychology; religious/inspirational; science/technology; self-help/personal improvement; sociology; sports; true crime/investigative; women's issues/women's studies. Considers these fiction areas: action/adventure; cartoon/comic; contemporary issues; detective/police/crime; ethnic; family saga; fantasy; feminist; gay; historical; horror; humor/satire; lesbian; mystery/suspense; psychic/supernatural; romance (contemporary, gothic, historical, regency); science fiction; sports; thriller/espionage; westerns/frontier; young adult. Query with outline plus 3 sample chapters. Reports in 1 week on queries; 1 month on mss.

To find an agent near you, check the Geographic Index.

Recent Sales: *Himpressions*, by Valerie Shaw (HarperCollins); *Selena*, by Clint Richmond (Pocket); *I Love Being the Enemy*, by Reggie Miller (Simon & Schuster); *Celestial Bar*, by Tom Youngholm (Dell); *Cooking for Jack*, by Tommy Baratta (Pocket).
Terms: Agent receives 15% commission on domestic sales; 20% on foreign sales. Offers written contract, which can be cancelled after 30 days.
Writers' Conferences: Detroit Women's Writers (MI); Kent State University (OH); San Diego Writers Conference (CA).
Tips: Obtains new clients through referrals, writers conferences, query letters.

STERLING LORD LITERISTIC, INC., (III), 65 Bleecker St., New York NY 10012. (212)780-6050. Fax: (212)780-6095. Contact: Peter Matson. Estab. 1952. Signatory of WGA. Represents 500+ clients. Specializes in "nonfiction and fiction." Currently handles: 50% nonfiction books, 50% novels. Member agents: Peter Matson, Sterling Lord; Joseph Hotchkiss (film scripts); Philippa Brophy; Elizabeth Grossman, Chris Calhoun; Jennifer Hengen, Charlotte Sheedy.
Handles: Nonfiction books, novels. Considers "mainstream nonfiction and fiction." Query. Reports in 1 month on mss.
Recent Sales: *Come To Grief*, by Dick Francis (Putnam); *In Retrospect*, by Robert MacNamara (Times Books); *King of Hearts*, by Susan Moody (Scribner).
Terms: Agent receives 15% commission on domestic sales; 20% on foreign sales. Offers written contract. Charges for photocopying.
Tips: Obtains new clients through recommendations from others.

NANCY LOVE LITERARY AGENCY, (III), 250 E. 65th St., New York NY 10021-6614. (212)980-3499. Fax: (212)308-6405. Contact: Nancy Love. Estab. 1984. Member of AAR. Represents 60-80 clients. Specializes in adult nonfiction. Currently handles: 90% nonfiction books; 10% novels.
Handles: Nonfiction books, novels. Considers these nonfiction areas: animals, biography/autobiography; child guidance/parenting; cooking/food/nutrition; current affairs; ethnic/cultural interests; gay/lesbian issues; government/politics/law; health/medicine; history; how-to; nature/environment; New Age/metaphysics; popular culture; psychology; science/technology; self-help/personal improvement; sociology; true crime/investigative; women's issues/women's studies. Considers these fiction areas: action/adventure; contemporary issues; detective/police/crime; erotica; ethnic; gay; glitz; literary; mystery/suspense; thriller/espionage. "For nonfiction, send a proposal, chapter summary and sample chapter. For fiction, send the first 40-50 pages plus summary of the rest (will consider only *completed* novels)." Reports in 3 weeks on queries; 1 month on mss.
Recent Sales: *The Language of Fertility*, by Niravi Payne (Villard, Crown); *How to Raise a Sexually Healthy Child*, by Beverly Engel (Simon & Schuster).
Terms: Agent receives 15% commission on domestic sales; 20% on foreign sales. Offers written contract. Charges for photocopying, "if it runs over $20."
Tips: Obtains new clients through recommendations and solicitation. Needs an exclusive on fiction. Nonfiction author and/or collaborator must be an authority in subject area. Submissions will be returned only if accompanied by a SASE.

LOWENSTEIN ASSOCIATES, INC., (II), 121 W. 27th St., Suite 601, New York NY 10001. (212)206-1630. Fax: (212)727-0280. President: Barbara Lowenstein. Estab. 1976. Member of AAR. Represents 150 clients. 20% of clients are new/unpublished writers. Specializes in multicultural books (fiction and nonfiction), medical experts, commercial fiction, especially suspense, crime and women's issues. Currently handles: 53% nonfiction books; 45% novels; 1% juvenile books; 1% short story collections. Member agents: Barbara Lowenstein (serious nonfiction, multicultural issues); Nancy Yost (commercial fiction, light nonfiction); Eileen Cope, associate (spirituality, serious fiction and nonfiction).
Handles: Nonfiction books, novels. Considers these nonfiction areas: animals; anthropology/archaeology; art/architecture/design; biography/autobiography; business; child guidance/parenting; craft/hobbies; current affairs; education; ethnic/cultural interests; gay/lesbian issues; government/politics/law; health/medicine; history; how-to; humor; language/literature/criticism; money/finance/economics; music/dance/theater/film; nature/environment; New Age/metaphysics; popular culture; psychology; religious/inspirational; science/technology; self-help/personal improvement; sociology; sports; true crime/investigative; women's issues/women's studies. Considers these fiction areas: contemporary issues; detective/police/crime; erotica; ethnic; feminist; gay; historical; humor/satire; lesbian; mainstream; mystery/suspense; romance (contemporary, historical, regency); medical thrillers. Query. For fiction, send outline and 1st chapter. No unsolicited mss. Reports in 3 weeks on queries.
Recent Sales: *Accentuate the Positive*, by Carolynn Hillman (Fireside/Simon & Schuster); *Juba This and Juba That*, by Dr. Darlene Powell and Derek Hopson (Fireside/Simon & Schuster); *Still Life With Rice*, Helie Lee (Scribner); *The Messiah Stones: A Novel for the Millennium*, by Irving Benig (Villard); *The Melatonin Miracle*, by Regelson & Pierpaoli (Simon & Schuster); *Motion to Suppress*, by Perri O'Shaughnessy (Delacorte); *Different Tongues*, by Lily Pond (Anchor); *The Substance of Things Hoped For*, by S. Proctor (Putnam).

Terms: Agent receives 15% commission on domestic and dramatic sales; 20% on foreign sales. Offers written contract, binding for 2 years, with 60 day cancellation clause. Charges for photocopying, foreign postage, messenger expenses.
Writers' Conferences: Malice Domestic (Bethesda, Spring); Novelists, Inc.; RWA.
Tips: Obtains new clients through recommendations from others. "Know the genre you are working in and READ!"

LYCEUM CREATIVE PROPERTIES, INC., (I, II), P.O. Box 12370, San Antonio TX 78212. (210)732-0200. President: Guy Robin Custer. Estab. 1992. Signatory of WGA. Represents 25 clients. 50% of clients are new/previously unpublished writers. Currently handles: 20% nonfiction books; 5% scholarly books; 40% novels; 25% movie scripts; 5% stage plays; 5% TV scripts. Member agents: Guy Robin Custer (novels, nonfiction, some screenplays); Dave Roy (novels, screenplays, stage plays); Geoff Osborne (nonfiction, screenplays, stage plays).
Handles: Nonfiction books, textbooks, scholarly books, juvenile books, novels, novellas, movie scripts, stage plays, features for TV (no episodics). Considers these nonfiction areas: anthropology/archaeology; art/architecture/design; biography/autobiography; business; child guidance/parenting; computers/electronics; cooking/food/nutrition; current affairs; ethnic/cultural interests; gay/lesbian issues; government/politics/law; history; juvenile nonfiction; language/literature/criticism; music/dance/theater/film; nature/environment; New Age/metaphysics; psychology; sociology; translations; travel; true crime/investigative; exposé. Considers these fiction areas: action/adventure; cartoon/comic; contemporary issues; detective/police/crime; erotica; ethnic; experimental; fantasy; feminist; gay; historical; humor/satire; juvenile; lesbian; literary; mainstream; mystery/suspense; picture book; psychic/supernatural; science fiction; thriller/espionage; westerns/frontier; political satire. Query. Reports in 2 weeks on queries; 2 months on solicited mss.
Terms: Agent receives 10% commission on domestic sales; 20% on foreign sales. Offers written contract, binding for 6 months-2 years. "Some editorial support is available to our signed clients." Writer offsets expenses for long distance tolls, postage, photocopying and any unusual expenses, all agreed upon in advance.
Tips: Obtains new clients through well-written queries and referrals. "Always include SASE with your letter of query. All our agents will consider a new writer. We'd rather not read first drafts or unfinished work. Please, no phone queries."

DONALD MAASS LITERARY AGENCY, (III), 157 West 57th St., Suite 1003, New York NY 10019. (212)757-7755. Contact: Donald Maass. Estab. 1980. Member of AAR, SFWA, MWA. Represents 75 clients. 5% of clients are new/previously unpublished writers. Specializes in commercial fiction, especially science fiction, fantasy, mystery, suspense. Currently handles: 100% novels. Member agent: Jennifer Jackson.
● Prior to opening his agency, Mr. Maass served as an editor at Dell Publishing and as an agent with The Scott Meredith Literary Agency. See Mr. Maass's article, Career Planning for Novelists, in this edition of the Guide.
Handles: Novels. Considers these fiction areas: detective/police/crime; family saga; fantasy; historical; horror; literary; mainstream; mystery/suspense; psychic/supernatural; science fiction; thriller/espionage. Query with SASE. Reports in 2 weeks on queries, 3 months on mss (if requested following query).
Recent Sales: *Pentecost Alley*, by Anne Perry (Fawcett Columbine); *Weighed in the Balance*, by Anne Perry (Fawcett Columbine); *Prisoner's Hope*, by David Feintuch (Warner/Aspect); *Fisherman's Hope*, by David Feintuch (Warner/Aspect); *God's Fires*, by Patricia Anthony (Berkley/Ace).
Terms: Agent receives 15% commission on domestic sales; 20% on foreign sales. "Manuscript copying for auction charged separately."
Writers' Conferences: World Science Fiction Convention (Los Angeles); Bouchercon.
Tips: "Most new clients are established authors referred by clients, publishers and other writers. We are fiction specialists. Few new clients are accepted, but interested authors should query with SASE. Subagents in all principle foreign countries and Hollywood. No nonfiction or juvenile works considered."

MARGRET MCBRIDE LITERARY AGENCY, (II), 7744 Fay Ave., Suite 201, La Jolla CA 92037. (619)454-1550. Fax: (619)454-2156. Contact: Clare Horn. Estab. 1980. Member of AAR, Authors Guild. Represents 50 clients. 15% of clients are new/unpublished writers. Specializes in mainstream fiction and nonfiction. Member agents: Winifred Golden (associate agent); Clare Horn; Kim Sauer (submissions manager).
● Prior to opening her agency, Ms. McBride served in the marketing departments of Random House and Ballantine Books and the publicity departments of Warner Books and Pinnacle Books.
Handles: Nonfiction books, novels, audio, video film rights. Considers these nonfiction areas: biography/autobiography; business; child guidance/parenting; cooking/food/nutrition; current affairs; ethnic/

cultural interests; gay/lesbian issues; government/politics/law; health/medicine; history; how-to; money/finance/economics; music/dance/theater/film; popular culture; psychology; religious/inspirational; science/technology; self-help/personal improvement; sociology; sports; true crime/investigative; women's issues/women's studies. Considers these fiction areas: action/adventure; detective/police/crime; ethnic; historical; literary; mainstream; mystery/suspense; thriller/espionage; westerns/frontier. Query with synopsis or outline. No unsolicited mss. Reports in 6 weeks on queries.

Recent Sales: *Everyone's A Coach*, by Dan Shula and Ken Blanchard (Zondervan); *Maiden Voyage*, by Cynthia Bass (Villard); *From Panic to Power*, by Lucinda Bassett (HarperCollins); *The Max Strategy*, by Dale Danten (Morrow); *Ain't Gonna Be The Same Fool Twice*, by April Sinclair (Hyperion); *The Scout*, by Harry Combs (Dell); *Empowerment Takes More Than A Minute*, by Ken Blanchard, John Carlos and Alan Randolph (Berrett-Koehler).

Terms: Agent receives 15% commission on domestic sales; 10% on dramatic sales; 25% on foreign sales.

DONALD MACCAMPBELL INC., (III), Park West Station, P.O. Box 20191, New York NY 10025-1518. (212)683-5580. E-mail: memoran@delphi.com. Contact: Maureen Moran. Estab. 1940. Represents 50 clients. "The agency does not handle unpublished writers." Specializes in women's book-length fiction in all categories. Currently handles: 100% novels.

● Mr. MacCampbell passed away in December 1994. Ms. Moran has taken over the agency.

Handles: Novels. Query; does not read unsolicited mss. Reports in 1 week on queries.

Recent Sales: *Iron Lace*, by Emilie Richards (Mira).

Terms: Agent receives 10% commission on domestic sales; 20% on foreign sales.

GINA MACCOBY LITERARY AGENCY, (II), 1123 Broadway, Suite 1009, New York NY 10010. (212)627-9210. Contact: Gina Maccoby. Estab. 1986. Represents 35 clients. Currently handles: 33% nonfiction books; 33% juvenile books; 33% novels. Represents illustrators of children's books.

Handles: Nonfiction, juvenile books, novels. Considers these nonfiction areas: biography; current affairs; ethnic/cultural interests; juvenile nonfiction; women's issues/women's studies. Considers these fiction areas: juvenile; literary; mainstream; mystery/suspense; thriller/espionage; young adult. Query with SASE. Reports in 2 months.

Recent Sales: *City of the Century*, by Donald Miller (Simon & Schuster); *Snapshot*, by Linda Barnes (Delacorte); *The Old Woman & Her Pig*, by Rosanne Litzinger (Harcourt Brace Jovanovich).

Terms: Agent receives 15% commission on domestic sales; 25% on foreign sales. May recover certain costs such as airmail postage to Europe or Japan or legal fees.

Tips: Usually obtains new clients through recommendations from own clients.

RICHARD P. MCDONOUGH, LITERARY AGENT, (II), 1950 Franklin St., Cambridge MA 02138. (617)522-6388. Contact: Richard P. McDonough. Estab. 1986. Represents 30 clients. 50% of clients are new/unpublished writers. Works with unpublished and published writers "whose work I think has merit and requires a committed advocate." Specializes in nonfiction for general contract and fiction. Currently handles: 80% nonfiction books; 20% novels.

Handles: Nonfiction books, novels. Query with outline and SASE or send 3 chapters and SASE. Reports in 2 weeks on queries; 2 months on mss.

Recent Sales: *Many Rivers to Cross*, by M.R. Montgomery (Fireside/Simon & Schuster); *Parents Who Love Reading, Kids Who Don't*, by M. Leonhardt (Crown); *We Will Gather at the River*, by M.R. Montgomery (Simon & Schuster).

Terms: Agent receives 15% commission on domestic sales; 15% on dramatic sales; 15% on foreign sales. Charges for photocopying, phone beyond 300 miles; postage for sold work only.

HELEN MCGRATH, (III), 1406 Idaho Ct., Concord CA 94521. (510)672-6211. Contact: Helen McGrath. Estab. 1977. Currently handles: 50% nonfiction books; 50% novels. Member agent: Doris Johnson.

Handles: Nonfiction books, novels. Considers these nonfiction areas: biography; business; current affairs; health/medicine; history; how-to; military/war; psychology; self-help/personal improvement; sports; women's issues/women's studies. Considers these fiction areas: contemporary issues; detective/police/crime; family saga; literary; mainstream; mystery/suspense; psychic/supernatural; romance; sci-

The publishing field is constantly changing! If you're still using this book and it is 1997 or later, buy the newest edition of Guide to Literary Agents *at your favorite bookstore or order directly from* Writer's Digest Books.

ence fiction; thriller/espionage; westerns/frontier. Query with proposal and SASE. No unsolicited mss. Reports in 2 months on queries.
Terms: Agent receives 15% commission on domestic sales. Sometimes offers written contract. Charges for photocopying.
Tips: Usually obtains new clients through recommendations from others.

ROBERT MADSEN AGENCY, (II), 1331 E. 34th St., Suite #1, Oakland CA 94602. (510)223-2090. Agent: Robert Madsen. Senior Editor: Kim Van Nguyen. Estab. 1992. Represents 5 clients. 100% of clients are new/previously unpublished writers. Currently handles: 25% nonfiction books; 25% fiction books; 25% movie scripts; 25% TV scripts.
Handles: Nonfiction books, fiction, TV scripts, radio script, video, stage plays. Considers all nonfiction and fiction areas. Considers all script subject areas. "Willing to look at subject matter that is specialized, controversial, even unpopular, esoteric and outright bizarre. However, it is strongly suggested that authors query first, to save themselves and this agency time, trouble and expense." Query. Reports in 1 month on queries; 2-3 months on mss.
Terms: Agent receives 10% commission on domestic sales; 20% on foreign sales. Offers written contract, binding for 3 years.
Tips: Obtains new clients through recommendations, or by query. "Be certain to take care of business basics in appearance, ease of reading and understanding proper presentation and focus. Be sure to include sufficient postage and SASE with all submissions."

RICIA MAINHARDT AGENCY, (II), 612 Argyle Rd., #L5, Brooklyn NY 11230. (718)434-1893. Fax: (718)434-2157. Contact: Ricia. Estab. 1987. 40% of clients are new/previously unpublished writers. Currently handles: 20% nonfiction books; 30% juvenile books; 50% novels.
Handles: Nonfiction books, juvenile books, novels. Considers these nonfiction areas: agriculture/horticulture; animals; anthropology/archaeology; biography/autobiography; business; child guidance/parenting; cooking/food/nutrition; crafts/hobbies; current affairs; ethnic/cultural interests; government/politics/law; health/medicine; history; how-to; humor; interior design/decorating; juvenile nonfiction; money/finance/economics; nature/environment; New Age/metaphysics; popular culture; psychology; science/technology; self-help/personal improvement; sociology; sports; true crime/investigative; women's issues/women's studies. Considers these fiction areas: action/adventure; contemporary issues; detective/police/crime; erotica; ethnic; family saga; fantasy; feminist; glitz; historical; horror; humor/satire; juvenile; literary; mainstream; picture book; psychic/supernatural; romance (contemporary, gothic, historical, regency); science fiction; sports; thriller/espionage; westerns/frontier; young adult. Send outline and 3 sample chapters. Reports in 1 month on queries; 2-3 months on mss.
Terms: Agent receives 15% commission on domestic sales; 20% on foreign sales. No written contract. Charges new writers $10 to cover postage and handling. Charges for photocopying.
Writers' Conferences: "I attend the major genre conferences—World Fantasy, Bouchercon, Malice Domestic, Romance Writers."
Tips: Obtains most new clients through recommendations of established writers and editors.

CAROL MANN AGENCY, (II,III), 55 Fifth Ave., New York NY 10003. (212)206-5635. Fax: (212)463-8718. Contact: Carol Mann. Estab. 1977. Member of AAR. Represents 100+ clients. 25% of clients are new/previously unpublished writers. Specializes in current affairs; self-help; psychology; parenting; history. Currently handles: 80% nonfiction books; 15% scholarly books; 5% novels. Member agent: Gareth Esersky (contemporary nonfiction).
Handles: Nonfiction books. Considers these nonfiction areas: anthropology/archaeology; art/architecture/design; biography/autobiography; business; child guidance/parenting; current affairs; ethnic/cultural interests; government/politics/law; health/medicine; history; interior design/decorating; money/finance/economics; psychology; self-help/personal improvement; sociology; true crime/investigative; women's issues/women's studies. Considers literary fiction. Query with outline/proposal and SASE. Reports in 3 weeks on queries.
Recent Sales: *The Good Marriage*, by Judith Wallerstein and Sandra Blakeslee (Houghton-Mifflin); *All God's Children*, by Fox Butterfield (Knopf); *What Your Boss Doesn't Tell You Until It's Too Late*, by Robert Bramson, PhD (Fireside/Simon & Schuster); *Mockery of Justice: The True Story of the Sheppard Murder Case*, by Cynthia L. Cooper and Sam Reese Sheppard (Northeastern Univ. Press).
Terms: Agent receives 15% commission on domestic sales; 20% on foreign sales. Offers written contract.

MANUS & ASSOCIATES LITERARY AGENCY, INC., (II), 417 E. 57th St., Suite 5D, New York NY 10022. (212)644-8020. Fax: (212)644-3374. Contact: Janet Wilkens Manus. Also 430 Cowper St., Palo Alto CA 94301. (415)617-4556. Fax: (415)617-4546. Contact: Jillian Manus. Estab. 1985. Member of AAR. Represents 75 clients. 15% of clients are new/previously unpublished writers. Specializes in quality fiction, mysteries, thrillers, true crime, health, pop psychology. Currently handles: 60% nonfiction books; 10% juvenile books; 20% novels; 25% film rights, TV and feature films.

Handles: Nonfiction books, novels. Considers these nonfiction areas: biography/autobiography; business; child guidance/parenting; current affairs; ethnic/cultural interests; health/medicine; how-to; nature/environment; popular culture; psychology; self-help/personal improvement; true crime/investigative; women's issues/women's studies. Considers these fiction areas: action/adventure; confessional; contemporary issues; detective/police/crime; ethnic; family saga; feminist; mainstream; mystery/suspense; thriller/espionage. Send outline and 2-3 sample chapters with SASE. Reports in 3 weeks on queries; 6 weeks on mss.
Recent Sales: *A Natural Death*, by Ruth Furie (Avon); *New Hope*, by Dr. Richard Marrs, etc. (Delacorte); *Pink & Blue Baby PP*, by Waldstein & Zinberg (Contemporary); *Requiem for Renee*, by Carlton Stowers (St. Martin's).
Also Handles: Movie scripts (feature film); TV scripts (TV mow). Considers these script subject areas: contemporary issues; detective/police/crime; family saga; feminist; mainstream; mystery/suspense; romantic comedy; thriller. Query with outline/proposal and 3 sample scenes. Reports in 3 weeks on queries; 1 month on scripts.
Terms: Agent receives 15% commission on domestic sales; 20% on foreign sales. Offers written contract, binding for 2 years, with 45 days cancellation clause. 100% of business is derived from commissions on sales.
Writers' Conferences Squaw Valley Community of Writers; San Diego State University Writers Conference; Writer's Connection/Agent's Day Conference; Maui Writers Conference; ABA (Chicago).
Tips: Obtains new clients through recommendations from others, at conferences, and from editors.

MARCH TENTH, INC., (III), 4 Myrtle St., Haworth NJ 07641. (201)387-6551. Fax: (201)387-6552. President: Sandra Choron. Estab. 1982. Represents 40 clients. 30% of clients are new/unpublished writers. "Writers must have professional expertise in the field in which they are writing." Prefers to work with published/established writers. Currently handles: 75% nonfiction books; 25% fiction.
Handles: Nonfiction books, fiction. Considers these nonfiction areas: biography/autobiography; current affairs; health/medicine; history; humor; language/literature/criticism; music/dance/theater/film; popular culture. Considers these fiction areas: confessional; ethnic; family saga; historical; horror; humor/satire; literary; mainstream; mystery/suspense; thriller/espionage. Query. Does not read unsolicited mss. Reports in 1 month.
Recent Sales: *Schindler's Legacy*, by Elinor Brecher (Dutton); *Louie Louie: A Social History Of The Song*, by Dave Marsh (Hyperion); *The Big Book of Blues*, by Robert Santelli (Penguin).
Terms: Agent receives 15% commission on domestic sales; 20% on dramatic sales; 20% on foreign sales. Charges writers for postage, photocopying, overseas phone expenses.

BARBARA MARKOWITZ LITERARY AGENCY, (II), 117 N. Mansfield Ave., Los Angeles CA 90036-3020. (213)939-5927. Literary Agent/President: Barbara Markowitz. Estab. 1980. Represents 14 clients. Works with a small number of new/unpublished authors. Specializes in mid-level and YA; contemporary fiction; adult trade fiction and nonfiction. Currently handles: 25% nonfiction books; 25% novels; 50% juvenile books. Member agent: Judith Rosenthal (psychology, current affairs, women's issues, biography).
- Prior to opening her agency, Ms. Markowitz owned the well-known, independent Barbara's Bookstores in Chicago.
Handles: Nonfiction books, novels, juvenile books. Considers these nonfiction areas: biography/autobiography; current affairs; juvenile nonfiction; music/dance/theater/film; nature/environment; popular culture; sports; women's issues/women's studies. Considers these fiction areas: contemporary issues; detective/police/crime; ethnic; humor/satire; juvenile; mainstream; mystery/suspense; sports; thriller/espionage; young adult. No illustrated books. Query with outline. SASE required for return of any material. Reports in 3 weeks.
Recent Sales: *How Far Would You Have Gotten*, by Valerie Hobbs (Orchard, Dick Jackson); *Stowaway*, by Kristiana Gregory (Scholastic Books).
Terms: Agent receives 15% commission on domestic sales; 15% on dramatic sales; 15% on foreign sales. Charges writers for mailing, postage.
Tips: "We do *not* agent pre-school or early reader books. Only mid-level and YA contemporary fiction and historical fiction. We receive an abundance of pre-school and early reader mss, which our agency returns if accompanied by SASE."

ELAINE MARKSON LITERARY AGENCY, (II), 44 Greenwich Ave., New York NY 10011. (212)243-8480. Estab. 1972. Member of AAR. Represents 200 clients. 10% of clients are new/unpublished writers. Specializes in literary fiction, commercial fiction, trade nonfiction. Currently handles: 35% nonfiction books; 55% novels; 10% juvenile books; 5% movie scripts. Member agents: Geri Thoma, Sally Wofford-Girand, Elaine Markson.
Handles: Quality fiction and nonfiction. Query with outline (must include SASE). SASE is required for the return of any material.

Recent Sales: *George Burns*, by Martin Gottfried (Simon & Schuster); *The Sword of General Eng-lund*, by Donald Honig (Scribner).
Terms: Agent receives 15% commission on domestic sales; 10% on dramatic sales; 20% on foreign sales. Charges for postage, photocopying, foreign mailing, faxing, long-distance telephone and other special expenses.

THE MARTELL AGENCY, (III), 555 Fifth Ave., Suite 1900, New York NY 10017. (212)692-9770. Contact: Victoria Pasquale or Alice Fried Martell. Estab. 1984. Represents 75 clients. Currently handles: 65% nonfiction books; 35% novels.
Handles: Nonfiction books, novels. Considers all nonfiction areas. Considers most fiction areas. No science fiction or poetry. Query with outline plus 2 sample chapters and SASE. Reports in 3 weeks on queries, only if interested. Does *not* return submitted material.
Recent Sales: Untitled history of rise and fall of Schwinn, by Glenn Coleman and Judith Crown (Holt).
Terms: Agent receives 15% commission on domestic sales; 20% on foreign sales. Offers written contract, binding for 1 year. Charges for foreign postage, photocopying, messenger services.
Tips: Usually obtains new clients by recommendations from agents and editors.

HAROLD MATSON CO. INC., 276 Fifth Ave., New York NY 10001. Member of AAR. This agency did not respond to our request for information. Query before submitting.

‡METROPOLITAN TALENT AGENCY, (III), 4526 Wilshire Blvd., Los Angeles CA 90010. (213)857-4500. Fax: (213)857-4599. Contact: Paul Kelmenson. Estab. 1990. Signatory of WGA. 20% of clients are new/previously unpublished writers. Specializes in feature film, TV rights, novels, screenplays, stories for the big screen or TV. Currently handles: 10% nonfiction books; 10% novels; 10% novellas; 50% movie scripts; 10% TV scripts; 10% short story collections.
  • See the expanded listing for this agency in Script Agents.

‡DORIS S. MICHAELS LITERARY AGENCY, INC., (I), 20 W. 64th St., Apt. 29-R, New York NY 10023. Phone/fax: (212)769-2430. Contact: Doris S. Michaels. Estab. 1994. Member of WNBA. Represents 15 clients. 50% of clients are new/previously unpublished writers. Currently handles: 40% nonfiction books; 60% novels.
Handles: Nonfiction books, novels. Considers these nonfiction areas: art/architecture/design; biography/autobiography; business; computers/electronics (CD-ROM); current affairs; ethnic/cultural interests; health/medicine; history; how-to; money/finance/economics; music/dance/theater/film; nature/environment; self-help/personal improvement; sports; women's issues/women's studies. Considers these fiction areas: action/adventure; contemporary issues; family saga; feminist; historical; literary; mainstream; thriller/espionage. Query with SASE. No phone calls or unsolicited mss. Reports ASAP on queries with SASE; no answer without SASE.
Recent Sales: *The Dollar Bill Knows No Sex*, by Wendy Rue and Karin Abarbanes (McGraw-Hill, Inc.); *The Heart Asks Pleasure*, by Anna Villegas (St. Martin's Press).
Terms: Agent receives 15% commission on domestic sales; 20% on foreign sales. Offers written contract, binding for 1 year, with 30 day cancellation clause. Charges for office expenses including postage, photocopying and fax. 100% of business is derived from commissions on sales.
Writers' Conferences: ABA (Chicago, June); Frankfurt Book Fair (Germany, October).
Tips: Obtains new clients through recommendations from others, solicitation and conferences.

‡THE MILLER AGENCY, (III), 801 West End Ave., New York NY 10025. (212)866-6110. Fax: (212)866-0068. E-mail: 74123.726@compuserve.com. Contact: Angela Miller. Estab. 1990. Represents 100 clients. 5% of clients are new/previously unpublished writers. Specializes in nonfiction, arts, psychology, self-help, cookbooks, biography, travel, memoir, sports. Currently handles: 100% nonfiction books.
Handles: Nonfiction books. Considers these nonfiction areas: anthropology/archaeology; art/architecture/design; biography/autobiography; business; child guidance/parenting; cooking/food/nutrition; current affairs; ethnic/cultural interests; gay/lesbian issues; health/medicine; language/literature/criticism; New Age/metaphysics; psychology; self-help/personal improvement; sports; women's issues/women's studies. Send outline and sample chapters. Reports in 1 week on queries.
Recent Sales: *Sparring with Charlie*, by Christopher Hunt (Anchor/Doubleday); *A Boy Named Phyllis*, by Frank DeCass (Viking); *I.M. Pei: Mandarin of Modernism*, by Michael Cannell (Crown Publishers); *Mother of Immortal Bliss*, by Naomi Mann (Houghton Mifflin).
Terms: Agent receives 15% commission on domestic sales; 20-25% on foreign sales. Offers written contract, binding for 2-3 years, with 60 day cancellation clause. Charges for postage (express mail or messenger services) and photocopying. 100% of business is derived from commissions on fees.
Tips: Obtains new clients through referrals.

ROBERTA MILLER ASSOCIATES, (II), 42 E. 12th St., New York NY 10003-4640. Contact: Roberta Miller. Estab. 1991. Represents 9 clients. 60% of clients are new/previously unpublished writers. Specializes in literary fiction, young adult. Currently handles: 75% adult fiction and nonfiction; 25% young adult. Member agents: Roberta Miller; Elisabeth Whelan (young adult).
 • Prior to opening her agency, Ms. Miller served as an editor with Western Publishing Company, magazine publisher for Children's Television Workshop, and rights director for United Media.
Handles: Nonfiction books, juvenile books, novels. Considers these nonfiction areas: art/architecture/design; biography/autobiography; current affairs; ethnic/cultural interests; language/literature/criticism. Considers these fiction areas: contemporary issues; detective/police/crime; humor/satire; literary; mainstream; young adult. Query with outline plus 2 sample chapters. Reports in 1 month on mss.
Recent Sales: *Red Ice*, by Nick Barker (St. Martin's Press).
Terms: Agent receives 15% commission on domestic sales; 25% on foreign sales. Offers written contract. Charges for photocopying, courier delivery, long distance telephone and fax.
Tips: Obtains new clients from recommendations, agent listings, editors. "U.S. authors only, please."

MOORE LITERARY AGENCY, (IV), 4 Dove St., Newburyport MA 01950. (508)465-9015. Contact: Claudette Moore. Estab. 1989. 20% of clients are new/previously unpublished writers. Specializes in trade computer books. Currently handles: 100% computer-related books.
Handles: Computer books only. Send outline/proposal. Reports in 3 weeks on queries.
Recent Sales: *How to Use Windows*, by Douglas Hergert (Ziff-Davis Press); *The Windows Scanning Book*, by Luisa Simone (John Wiley & Sons).
Terms: Agent receives 15% commission on all sales. Offers written contract.
Writers' Conferences: ABA (Chicago); Comdex (Las Vegas).
Tips: Obtains new clients through recommendations/referrals and conferences.

WILLIAM MORRIS AGENCY, (III), 1350 Avenue of the Americas, New York NY 10019. (212)586-5100. Estab. 1898. Contact: Literary Department. West Coast office: 151 El Camino Dr., Beverly Hills CA 90212. (310)274-7451. Member of AAR. Works with a small number of new/unpublished authors. Specializes in novels, nonfiction. Member agents: Mel Berger, Matthew Bialer, Michael Carlisle, Peter Franklin, Robert Gottlieb, Owen Laster, Samuel Liff, Gilbert Parker, Marcy Posner, James Stein, Dan Strone.
Terms: Agent receives 10% commission on domestic sales; 10% on dramatic sales; 20% on foreign sales.

HENRY MORRISON, INC., (II, III), 105 S. Bedford Rd., Suite 306A, Mt. Kisco NY 10549. (914)666-3500. Fax: (914)241-7846. Contact: Henry Morrison. Estab. 1965. Signatory of WGA. Represents 48 clients. 5% of clients are new/previously unpublished writers. Currently handles: 5% nonfiction books; 5% juvenile books; 85% novels; 5% movie scripts.
Handles: Nonfiction books, novels. Considers these nonfiction areas: anthropology/archaeology; biography; government/politics/law; history; juvenile nonfiction. Considers these fiction areas: action/adventure; detective/police/crime; family saga. Query. Reports in 2 weeks on queries; 3 months on mss.
Recent Sales: *The Apocalypse Watch*, by Robert Ludlum; *Extreme Denial*, by David Morrell; *Choosers of the Slain*, by James Cobb (G.P. Putnam's Sons).
Terms: Agent receives 15% commission on domestic sales; 20% on foreign sales. Charges for ms copies, bound galleys and finished books for submission to publishers, movie producers, foreign publishers.
Tips: Obtains new clients through recommendations from others.

MULTIMEDIA PRODUCT DEVELOPMENT, INC., (III), 410 S. Michigan Ave., Suite 724, Chicago IL 60605-1302. (312)922-3063. Fax: (312)922-1905. President: Jane Jordan Browne. Estab. 1971. Member of AAR, RWA, MWA, SCBWI. Represents 150 clients. 5% of clients are new/previously unpublished writers. "We are generalists." Currently handles: 60% nonfiction books; 8% juvenile books; 30% novels; 1% scholarly books; 1% textbooks. Member agent: Danielle Egan-Miller.
 • Prior to opening her agency Ms. Jordan Browne served as the managing editor, the then head of the juvenile department for Hawthorn Books, senior editor for Thomas Y. Crowell, adult trade department and general editorial and production manager for Macmillan Educational Services, Inc.

The double dagger before a listing indicates the listing is new in this edition.

Handles: Nonfiction books, novels. Considers these nonfiction areas: agriculture/horticulture; animals; anthropology/archaeology; biography/autobiography; business; child guidance/parenting; cooking/food/nutrition; crafts/hobbies; current affairs; ethnic/cultural issues; health/medicine; how-to; humor; juvenile nonfiction; money/finance; nature; popular culture; psychology; religious/inspirational; science/technology; self-help/personal improvement; sociology; sports; true crime/investigative; women's issues/women's studies. Considers these fiction areas: contemporary issues; detective/police/crime; ethnic; family saga; glitz; historical; horror; juvenile; literary; mainstream; mystery/suspense; picture book; religious/inspirational; romance (contemporary, gothic, historical, regency, western); sports; thriller/espionage. Query "by mail with SASE required." Reports within 1 week on queries; 6 weeks on mss.

Recent Sales: *The Persian Pickle Club*, by Sandra Dallas (St. Martin's Press); *Best of Friends*, by Jae-Ha Kim (HarperCollins); *Say It In Six*, by Ron Hoff (Andrews & McMeel); *Poems of Virtue: An Anthology*, by Myrna Grant (Doubleday Book Music Club); *The Scarlet Thread*, by Francine Rivers (Tyndale House); *Deadly Care*, by Leonard Goldberg (New American Library); *Better with Buttermilk*, by Lee Edwards Benning (Holt).

Terms: Agent receives 15% commission on domestic sales; 20% on foreign sales. Offers written contract, binding for 2 years. Charges for photocopying, overseas postage, faxes, phone calls.

Writers' Conferences: ABA (Chicago, June); Frankfurt Book Fair (Frankfurt, October); RWA (Anaheim CA, July).

Tips: Obtains new clients through "referrals, queries by professional, marketable authors. If interested in agency representation, be well informed."

DEE MURA ENTERPRISES, INC., (II), 269 West Shore Dr., Massapequa NY 11758-8225. (516)795-1616. Fax: (516)795-8797. E-mail: samurai5@ix.netcom.com. Contact: Dee Mura. Estab. 1987. Signatory of WGA. 50% of clients are new/previously published writers. "We work on everything, but are especially interested in true life stories, true crime and women's stories and issues." Currently handles: 20% nonfiction books; 15% scholarly books; 15% juvenile books; 20% novels; 15% movie scripts; 15% TV scripts.

Handles: Nonfiction books, scholarly books, juvenile books. Considers these nonfiction areas: agriculture/horticulture; animals; anthropology/archaeology; biography/autobiography; business; child guidance/parenting; computers/electronics; current affairs; education; ethnic/cultural interests; gay/lesbian issues; government/politics/law; health/medicine; history; how-to; humor; juvenile nonfiction; military/war; money/finance/economics; nature/environment; science/technology; self-help/personal improvement; sociology; sports; true crime/investigative; women's issues/women's studies. Considers these fiction areas: action/adventure; contemporary issues; detective/police/crime; ethnic; experimental; family saga; fantasy; feminist; gay; glitz; historical; humor/satire; juvenile; lesbian; literary; mainstream; mystery/suspense; psychic/supernatural; regional; romance (contemporary, gothic, historical, regency); science fiction; sports; thriller/espionage; westerns/frontier; young adult. Query. Reports in approximately 2 weeks on queries.

Also Handles: Movie scripts (feature film, documentary, animation), TV scripts (TV mow, miniseries, episodic drama, sitcom, variety show, animation). Considers these script subject areas: action/adventure; cartoon/animation; comedy; contemporary issues; detective/police/crime; family saga; fantasy; feminist; gay; glitz; historical; horror; humor; juvenile; mainstream; mystery/suspense; psychic/supernatural; religious/inspirational; romantic comedy and drama; science fiction; sports; teen; thriller; western/frontier.

Terms: Agent receives 15% commission on domestic sales; 20-25% on foreign sales. Offers written contract. Charges for photocopying and mailing expenses directly pertaining to writer.

Tips: Obtains new clients through recommendations from others. Query solicitation. "Please include a paragraph on writer's background even if writer has no literacy background and a brief synopsis of the project. We enjoy well-written query letters that tell us about the project and the author."

JEAN V. NAGGAR LITERARY AGENCY, (III), 216 E. 75th St., Suite 1E, New York NY 10021. (212)794-1082. Contact: Jean Naggar. Estab. 1978. Member of AAR. Represents 100 clients. 20% of clients are new/previously unpublished writers. Currently handles: 35% general nonfiction books; 5% scholarly books; 15% juvenile books; 40% novels; 5% short story collections. Member agents: Frances Kuffel; agent-at-large: Anne Engel (nonfiction).

Handles: Nonfiction books, some juvenile books, novels. Considers these nonfiction areas: biography/autobiography; business; child guidance/parenting; cooking/food/nutrition; current affairs; government/politics/law; health/medicine; history; interior design/decorating; juvenile nonfiction; money/finance/economics; music/dance/theater/film; New Age/metaphysics; psychology; religious/inspirational; self-help/personal improvement; sociology; true crime/investigative; women's issues/women's studies. "We would, of course, consider a query regarding an exceptional mainstream manuscript touching on any area." Considers these fiction areas: action/adventure; contemporary issues; detective/police/crime; ethnic; family saga; fantasy; feminist; historical; juvenile; literary; mainstream; mystery/

suspense; psychic/supernatural; regional; science fiction; thriller/espionage. Query. Reports in 24 hours on queries; approximately 2 months on mss.

Recent Sales: *The Return*, by Joe De Mers (Dutton/Signet); *Cheevey*, by Gerald de Pego (Little Brown) *Breach of Trust*, by Bonnie MacDougal (Pocket Books); *The Virus Hunters* (nonfiction) by Ed Gegis (Pocket Books).

Terms: Agent receives 15% commission on domestic sales; 20% on foreign sales. Offers written contract. Charges for overseas mailing; messenger services; book purchases; long-distance telephone; photocopying. "These are deductible from royalties received."

Writers' Conferences: Willamette Writers Conference; Pacific Northwest Writers Conference; Breadloaf Writers Conference; Virginia Women's Press Conference (Richmond VA).

Tips: Obtains new clients through "recommendations from publishers, editors, clients and others, and from writers' conferences. Use a professional presentation. Because of the avalanche of unsolicited queries that flood the agency every week, we have had to modify our policy. We will now only guarantee to read and respond to queries from writers who come recommended by someone we know. Our areas are general fiction and nonfiction, no children's books by unpublished writers, no multimedia, no screenplays, no formula fiction, no mysteries by unpublished writers."

RUTH NATHAN, (II), 80 Fifth Ave., Room 706, New York NY 10011. Phone/fax: (212)675-6063. Estab. 1980. Represents 12 clients. 5% of clients are new/previously unpublished writers. Specializes in art, decorative arts, fine art; theater; film; show business. Currently handles: 90% nonfiction books; 10% novels.

Handles: Nonfiction books, novels. Considers these nonfiction areas: art/architecture/design; biography/autobiography; theater/film; true crime/investigative. Considers some historical fiction. Query. Reports in 2 weeks on queries; 1 month on mss.

Recent Sales: *A Book of Days*, by Stephen Risulle (Macmillan London); *A Dangerous Gift*, by Claudia Crawford (Dutton); *Faking It*, by K.J. Lane (Harry Abrams).

Terms: Agent receives 15% commission on domestic sales; 20% on foreign sales. Charges for office expenses, postage, photocopying, etc.

Tips: "Read carefully what my requirements are before wasting your time and mine."

KAREN NAZOR LITERARY AGENCY, (II, III), Opera Plaza, 601 Van Ness Ave., Suite E3124, San Francisco CA 94102. (415)648-2281. Fax: (415)648-2348. E-mail: AgentNazor@aol.com or agentKN @well.com. (queries only). Contact: Karen Nazor. Estab. 1991. Represents 35 clients. 15% of clients are new/previously unpublished writers. Specializes in "good writers! Mostly nonfiction—arts, culture, politics, technology, civil rights, etc." Currently handles: 75% nonfiction books; 10% electronic; 10% fiction.

Handles: Nonfiction books, novels, novellas. Considers these nonfiction areas: biography; business; computers/electronics; cooking/food; current affairs; ethnic/cultural interests; gay/lesbian issues; government/politics/law; history; how-to; music/dance/theater/film; nature/environment; photography; popular culture; science/technology; sociology; sports; travel; women's issues/women's studies. Considers these fiction areas: action/adventure; cartoon/comic; contemporary issues; erotica; ethnic; feminist; literary; regional. Query (preferred) or send outline/proposal (accepted). Reports in 2 weeks on queries; up to 2 months on mss.

Recent Sales: *Net Chick*, by Carla Sinclair (Henry Holt); *Imagine Nations*, by Michael Rowley (Macmillan); *The International Internet Directory*, by Mitzi Waltz (Ziff-Davis); *Moving to San Francisco*, by Christina Guinot (Prima); *Ebbets Field*, by Bob McGee (W.W. Norton).

Terms: Agent receives 15% commission on domestic sales; 20% on foreign sales. Offers written contract. Charges for express mail services and photocopying costs.

Tips: Referrals from editors and writers; online; teaching classes on publishing; newspaper article on agency. "I'm interested in writers that want a long term, long haul relationship. Not a one-book writer, but a writer who has many ideas, is productive, professional, passionate and meets deadlines!"

‡NEW BRAND AGENCY GROUP, (I), (a division of Alter Entertainment LLC), 205 Wildberry Lane, Nashville TN 37209. (615)353-8829. Fax: (615)353-0372. E-mail: agentnb@aol.com. Contact: Eric Alterman. Estab. 1994. Represents 5 clients. 80% of clients are new/previously unpublished writers. "Focus is on topical and cutting edge materials." Currently handles: 100% novels.

Handles: Novels. Considers these nonfiction areas: biography/autobiography; education; how-to; humor; military/war; popular culture; religious/inspirational; sports. Considers these fiction areas: action/adventure; contemporary issues; detective/police/crime; fantasy; horror; humor/satire; literary; mainstream; mystery/suspense; religious/inspirational; romance; science fiction; sports; thriller/espionage. Query with outline and 3 sample chapters. Reports in 3 weeks.

Terms: Agent receives 15% commission on domestic sales; 15-20% on foreign sales. Offers written contract, binding for 4-12 months, with 30 day cancellation clause. 100% of business is derived from commissions on sales.

Tips: Obtains new clients from recommendations, online discussions and magazine advertisements. "Don't let negative experiences influence your new relationships, particularly with respect to agents."

NEW ENGLAND PUBLISHING ASSOCIATES, INC., (II), P.O. Box 5, Chester CT 06412-0645. (203)345-READ and (203)345-4976. Fax: (203)345-3660. E-mail: nepa@nepa.com. Contact: Elizabeth Frost Knappman, Edward W. Knappman. Estab. 1983. Member of AAR. Represents over 100 clients. 15% of clients are new/previously unpublished writers. Specializes in adult nonfiction books of serious purpose.
Handles: Nonfiction books. Considers these nonfiction areas: biography/autobiography; business; child guidance/parenting; government/politics/law; health/medicine; history; language/literature/criticism; military/war; money/finance/economics; nature/environment; psychology; science/technology; self-help/personal improvement; sociology; true crime/investigative; women's issues/women's studies. Send outline/proposal. Reports in 3 weeks on queries; 5 weeks on mss.
Recent Sales: *Eudora Welty*, by Ann Waldron (Doubleday); *The Importance of Being Different*, by Robert Sherril (Crown); *Dictionary of Art*, by Nancy Frazier (Penguin); A Detective Lane Frank Mystery Series (Bantam); *Christie Whitman: A Political Biography for the People*, Sandy McClure (Prometheus).
Terms: Agent receives 15% commission on domestic sales; 20% foreign sales (split with overseas agent). Offers written contract, binding for 6 months.
Writers' Conferences: ABA (Chicago, June); ALA (San Antonio, January); ALA (New York, July).
Tips: "Send us a well-written proposal that clearly identifies your audience—who will buy this book and why."

NINE MUSES AND APOLLO, INC., (II), 2 Charlton St., New York NY 10014-4909. (212)243-0065. Contact: Ling Lucas. Estab. 1991. Represents 100 clients. 50% of clients are new/previously unpublished writers. Specializes in nonfiction. Currently handles: 90% nonfiction books; 10% novels. Member agents: Ling Lucas, Ed Vesneske, Jr.
 • Prior to opening his agency, Mr. Lucas served as a vice president, sales & marketing director and associate publisher.
Handles: Nonfiction books. Considers these nonfiction areas: animals; biography/autobiography; business; current affairs; ethnic/cultural interests; gay/lesbian issues; government/politics/law; health/medicine; history; humor/satire; language/literature/criticism; psychology; science/technology; spirituality; women's issues/women's studies. Considers these fiction areas: commercial; ethnic; literary; mainstream. Send outline and 2 sample chapters. Reports in 1 month on mss.
Recent Sales: *The Unofficial X-Philes Comparison*, by N.E. Genge (Crown Publishing); *Tracks in the Wilderness of Dreaming*, by Robert Bosnak (Delacorte).
Terms: Agent receives 15% commission on domestic sales; 20-25% on foreign sales. Offers written contract. Charges for photocopying proposals and mss.
Tips: "Your outline should already be well developed, cogent, and reveal clarity of thought about the general structure and direction of your project."

THE BETSY NOLAN LITERARY AGENCY, (II), 224 W. 29th St., 15th Floor, New York NY 10001. (212)967-8200. Fax: (212)967-7292. President: Betsy Nolan. Estab. 1980. Member of AAR. Represents 200 clients. 10% of clients are new/unpublished writers. Works with a small number of new/unpublished authors. Currently handles: 90% nonfiction books; 10% novels. Member agents: Donald Lehr, Corrina Wright, Carla Glasser.
Handles: Nonfiction books. Query with outline. Reports in 3 weeks on queries; 2 months on mss.
Recent Sales: *Why I Am A Democrat*, by Theodore Sorenson (Holt).
Terms: Agent receives 15% commission on domestic sales; 20% on foreign sales.

THE NORMA-LEWIS AGENCY (II), 360 W. 53rd St., Suite B-A, New York NY 10019-5720. (212)664-0807. Fax: (212)664-0462. Contact: Norma Liebert. Estab. 1980. 50% of clients are new/previously unpublished writers. Specializes in juvenile books (pre-school-high school). Currently handles: 60% juvenile books; 40% adult books.
Handles: Juvenile and adult nonfiction and fiction, movie scripts, TV scripts, radio scripts, stage plays. Considers these nonfiction areas: art/architecture/design; biography/autobiography; child guidance/parenting; cooking/food/nutrition; crafts/hobbies; current affairs; ethnic/cultural interests; government/politics/law; health/medicine; history; juvenile nonfiction; music/dance/theater/film; nature/environment; photography; popular culture; self-help/personal improvement; true crime/investigative; women's issues/women's studies. Considers these fiction areas: action/adventure; contemporary issues; detective/police/crime; family saga; historical; horror; humor/satire; juvenile; mainstream; mystery/suspense; picture book; romance (contemporary, gothic, historical, regency); thriller/espionage; westerns/frontier; young adult.
Recent Sales: *Viper Quarry* and *Pitchfork Hollow*, both by Dean Feldmayer (Pocket Books).
Terms: Agent receives 15% commission on domestic sales; 20% on foreign sales.

NUGENT LITERARY, (III), 170 Tenth St. N, Naples FL 33940. Phone/fax: (813)262-3683. Contact: Ray Nugent. Estab. 1976. Represents 15 clients. No new previously unpublished writers. Specializes in nonfiction. Currently handles: 100% nonfiction books.
Handles: Nonfiction books. Considers these nonfiction areas: biography/autobiography; health/medicine; true crime/investigative. Query. Reports in 1 month on queries; 2 months on mss.
Recent Sales: *Evil Web*, by Jose (New Horizon); *Winning with Arthritis*, by Debbie Bruce (John Wiley).
Terms: Agent receives 20% commission on domestic sales; 25% on foreign sales. Offers written contract, binding for 1 year. 100% of business derived from commission on sales.
Tips: Obtains new clients through referrals.

HAROLD OBER ASSOCIATES, (III), 425 Madison Ave., New York NY 10017. (212)759-8600. Fax: (212)759-9428. Estab. 1929. Member of AAR. Represents 250 clients. 10% of clients are new/previously unpublished writers. Currently handles: 35% nonfiction books; 15% juvenile books; 50% novels. Member agents: Claire Smith, Phyllis Westberg, Henry Dunow, Wendy Schmalz.
Handles: Nonfiction books, juvenile books, novels. Considers all nonfiction and fiction subjects. Query letter *only*; faxed queries are not read. Reports in 1 week on queries; 3 weeks on mss.
Terms: Agent receives 10-15% commission on domestic sales; 15-20% on foreign sales. Charges for photocopying and express mail or package services.
Tips: Obtains new clients through recommendations from others.

‡ALICE ORR AGENCY, INC., (V), 305 Madison Ave., Suite 1166, New York NY 10165. (718)204-6673. Fax: (718)204-6023. Contact: Alice Orr. Estab. 1988. Member of AAR. Represents 14 clients. Specializes in women's popular fiction, especially romance, both category and mainstream. Currently handles: 5% nonfiction books; 5% juvenile books; 90% novels.
  • This agency reports that it is not taking on new clients at this time.
Handles: Considers popular culture nonfiction. Considers these fiction areas: Considers family saga; glitz; mainstream; romance (contemporary, historical). Send outline and 3 sample chapters. Reports in 2 months on ms.
Terms: Agent receives 15% commission on domestic sales; 20% on foreign sales. No written contract.
Writers' Conferences: New York City RWA Conference (Melville NY, March); Vancouver RWA Conference (Vancouver Canada, April); Provost Writer's Retreat (Kentucky, May); National RWA Convention (Dallas TX July); Annual Booklovers Convention (Baton Rouge LA, Fall).
Tips: Obtains new clients through recommendations from others.

FIFI OSCARD AGENCY INC., (II), 24 W. 40th St., New York NY 10018. (212)764-1100. Contact: Ivy Fischer Stone, Literary Department. Estab. 1956. Member of AAR, signatory of WGA. Represents 108 clients. 5% of clients are new/unpublished writers. "Writer must have published articles or books in major markets or have screen credits if movie scripts, etc." Specializes in literary novels, commercial novels, mysteries and nonfiction, especially celebrity biographies and autobiographies. Currently handles: 40% nonfiction books; 40% novels; 5% movie scripts; 5% stage plays; 10% TV scripts.
Handles: Nonfiction books, novels, movie scripts, stage plays. Query with outline. Reports in 1 week on queries if SASE enclosed.
Recent Sales: *Tek Money*, by William Shatner (G.P. Putnam's); *Mudville Diaries*, by Michael Schacht (Avon Books); *Autopsy On An Empire*, by Jack Matlock, Jr. (Random House).
Terms: Agent receives 15% commission on domestic sales; 10% on dramatic sales; 20% on foreign sales. Charges for photocopying expenses.

OTITIS MEDIA, (II), 1926 DuPont Ave. S., Minneapolis MN 55403. (612)377-4918. Fax: (612)377-3096. Contact: Richard Boylan or Hannibal Harris. Signatory of WGA. Currently handles: novels; movie scripts; stage plays; TV scripts. Member agents: B.R. Boylan (novels, nonfiction, screenplays, stage plays); Hannibal Harris (queries, evaluation of proposals, books); Greg Boylan (screenplays, TV scripts); Ingrid DiLeonardo (script and ms evaluation, story development).
  • See the expanded listing for this agency in Script Agents.

Agents ranked I-IV are actively seeking new clients. Those ranked V or those who prefer not to be listed have been included to inform you they are not currently looking for new clients.

‡**THE PALMER & DODGE AGENCY, (III)**, 1 Beacon St., Boston MA 02108. (617)573-0100. Fax: (617)227-4420. Contact: Sharon Silva. Estab. 1990. Represents 100 clients. 5% of clients are new/ previously unpublished writers. Specializes in trade nonfiction and quality fiction for adults. No genre fiction. Dramatic rights for books and life story rights only. Currently handles: 80% nonfiction books; 20% novels. Member agents: John Taylor (Ike) Williams, director (books, film, TV); Jill Kneerim, managing director (books); Lane Zachary (books); Elaine Rogers, director of subsidiary rights (dramatic rights, foreign, audio). Currently handles: nonfiction books; novels.
Handles: Nonfiction books, novels. Considers these nonfiction areas: anthropology/archaeology; biography/autobiography; business; child guidance/parenting; current affairs; education; ethnic/cultural interests; gay/lesbian issues; government/politics/law; health/medicine; history; language/literature/ criticism; money/finance/economics; music/dance/theater/film; nature/environment; New Age/metaphysics; popular culture; psychology; religous/inspirational; science/technology; self-help/personal improvement; sociology; women's issues/women's studies. Considers these fiction areas: contemporary issues; ethnic; feminist; gay; literary; mainstream. Query with outline/proposal. Reports in 2 weeks on queries; 3 months on mss.
Terms: Agent receives 15% commission on domestic sales; 20% on foreign sales. Offers written contract, with 4 month cancellation clause. Charges for direct expenses (postage, phone, photocopying, messenger service). 100% of business is derived from commissions on sales.
Tips: Obtains new clients through recommendations from others. "We are taking very few new clients for representation."

THE RICHARD PARKS AGENCY, (III), 138 E. 16th St., 5th Floor, New York NY 10003. (212)254-9067. Contact: Richard Parks. Estab. 1988. Member of AAR. Currently handles: 50% nonfiction books; 5% young adult books; 40% novels; 5% short story collections.
  ● Prior to opening his agency, Mr. Parks served as an agent with Curtis Brown, Ltd.
Handles: Nonfiction books, novels. Considers these nonfiction areas: horticulture; animals; anthopology/archaeology; art/architecture/design; biography/autobiography; business; child guidance/parenting; cooking/food/nutrition; crafts/hobbies; current affairs; ethnic/cultural interests; gay/lesbian issues; government/politics; health/medicine; history; how-to; humor; language/literature/criticism; military/war; money/finance/economics; music/dance/theater/film; nature/environment; popular culture; psychology; science/technology; self-help/personal improvement; sociology; women's issues/women's studies. Considers fiction by referral only. Query with SASE. "We will not accept any unsolicited material." Reports in 2 weeks on queries.
Recent Sales: *Where There's Smoke There's Flavor*, by Richard W. Langer (Little, Brown); *A Killing In Real Estate*, by Tierney McClellan (Signet); *The Scoliosis Handbook*, by Michael Neuwirth, M.D. & Kevin Osborn (Harcourt Brace); *The Wall of the Sky, The Wall of the Eye*, by Jonathan Lethem (Harcourt Brace); *Touched*, by Scott Campbell (Bantam Books).
Terms: Agent receives 15% commission on domestic sales; 20% on foreign sales. Charges for photocopying or any unusual expense incurred at the writer's request.
Tips: Obtains new clients through recommendations and referrals.

KATHI J. PATON LITERARY AGENCY, (II), 19 W. 55th St., New York NY 10019-4907. (212)265-6586. Fax: call first. Contact: Kathi Paton. Estab. 1987. Specializes in adult nonfiction. Currently handles: 65% nonfiction books; 35% fiction.
Handles: Nonfiction, novels, short story collections. Considers these nonfiction areas: business; child guidance/parenting; how-to; nature/environment; psychology; sociology; women's issues/women's studies. Considers literary and mainstream fiction; short stories. For nonfiction, send proposal, sample chapter and SASE. For fiction, send first 40 pages and plot summary or 3 short stories.
Recent Sales: *Total Customer Service*, by Bro Uttal (HarperCollins); *The Myth of the Bad Mother*, by Jane Swigart (Doubleday); *White Trash, Red Velvet*, by Donald Secreast (HarperCollins); *The Home Environmental Checklist*, by Andrew Davis and Paul Schuffman (Holt).
Terms: Agent receives 15% commission on domestic sales; 20% on foreign sales. Offers written contract. Charges for photocopying.
Writers' Conferences: Attends International Womens Writing Guild panels and the Pacific Northwest Writers Conference.
Tips: Usually obtains new clients through recommendations from other clients. "Write well."

‡**THE RICHARD PAUL AGENCY, (IV)**, 126 Wayne St., Suite 3A, Jersey City NJ 07302-3406. (201)433-1100. Fax: (201)433-1623. E-mail: rpliterary@aol.com. Contact: Richard Aloia Jr. Estab. 1993. Represents 7 clients. 100% of clients are new/previously unpublished writers. "Must have advanced writing degree or referral." Specializes in aggressively written fiction. Currently handles: 5% nonfiction books; 95% novels.
Handles: Nonfiction books, novels. Considers these nonfiction areas: biography/autobiography; music/dance/theater/film; "nonfiction should be related to writers or the arts." Considers these fiction areas: contemporary issues; erotica; ethnic; experimental; family saga; gay; humor/satire; lesbian;

literary; mainstream; regional. Exclusive query with SASE. Reports within 1 month on queries; 2 months on mss.

Terms: Agent receives 15% commission on domestic sales; 20% on foreign sales. Offers written contract. Charges for international postage and phone charges. 100% of business is derived from commissions on sales.

Tips: Obtains new clients through recommendations from professional writing instructors and queries. "This is a very small, highly selective agency, specializing in outstanding fiction."

‡PELHAM LITERARY AGENCY, (I), 2290 E. Fremont Ave., Suite C, Littleton CO 80122. (303)347-0623. Contact: Howard Pelham. Estab. 1994. Represents 5 clients. 50% of clients are new/previously unpublished writers. Specializes in genre fiction. Owner has published 14 novels in these categories. Currently handles: 10% nonfiction books; 30% juvenile books; 30% novels; 10% short story collections; 10% movie scripts; 10% TV scripts.

Handles: Juvenile books, novels, short story collections. Considers these fiction areas: action/adventure; detective/police/crime; fantasy; horror; juvenile; literary; mainstream; romance (contemporary, gothic, historical); science fiction; sports; thriller/espionage; westerns/frontier; young adult. Send outline and sample chapters or entire ms. Reports in 3 weeks on queries; 2 months on mss.

Recent Sales: *Foreign Adoption*, by Barbara Bascom and Carole McKelvey (Pocket Books); *Brotherhood of Thieves*, by Howard Pelham (Thomas Bouregy & Co.).

Terms: Agent receives 15% commission on domestic sales; 20% on foreign sales. Offers written contract, with 30-day cancellation clause. Charges $50 processing free for copying, postage. 100% of business is derived from commissions on sales.

Writers' Conferences: Rocky Mountain Book Fair.

Tips: "Most of my clients have been from recommendation by other writers. Don't submit a manuscript until you have written it as professionally as possible."

RODNEY PELTER, (II), 129 E. 61st St., New York NY 10021. (212)838-3432. Contact: Rodney Pelter. Estab. 1978. Represents 10 clients. Currently handles: 25% nonfiction books; 75% novels.

Handles: Nonfiction books, novels. Considers all nonfiction areas. Considers most fiction areas. No juvenile, romance, science fiction. Query with SASE. No unsolicited mss. Reports in 3 months.

Terms: Agent receives 15% commission on domestic sales; 20% on foreign sales. Offers written contract. Charges for foreign postage, photocopying.

Tips: Usually obtains new clients through recommendations from others.

L. PERKINS ASSOCIATES, (IV), 5800 Arlington Ave., Riverdale NY 10471-1419. (718)543-5354. Fax: (718)543-5355. Contact: Lori Perkins, Peter Rubie. Estab. 1990. Member of AAR, HWA. Represents 100 clients. 15% of clients are new/previously unpublished writers. Perkins specializes in horror, dark thrillers, literary fiction, pop culture, Latino and gay issues (fiction and nonfiction). Rubie specializes in science fiction, fantasy, off-beat mysteries, history, literary fiction dark thrillers, journalistic nonfiction. Currently handles: 60% nonfiction books; 40% novels.

● See Lori Perkins' article, How to Find (and Keep) the Right Agent, in the 1994 edition of the *Guide*.

Handles: Nonfiction books, novels. Considers these nonfiction areas: art/architecture/design; current affairs; ethnic popular science/cultural interests; music/dance/theater/film; "subjects that fall under pop culture—TV, music, art, books and authors, film, current affairs etc." Considers these fiction areas: detective/police/crime; ethnic; horror; literary; mainstream; mystery/suspense; psychic/supernatural; dark thriller. Query with SASE. Reports immediately on queries with SASE; 10 weeks on mss.

Recent Sales: *Song of the Banshee*, by Greg Kihn (Forge); *The Anne Rice Reader*, by K. Ranslaud (Ballantine); *Godzilla; The Unofficial Biography*, by S. Ryfle (Delta); *Keeper*, by Gregory Rucka (Bantam); *Rambo Reagan*, by Arsen & Werden (Contemporary); *How the Tiger Lost Its Stripes*, by C. Meacham (Harcourt Brace).

Terms: Agent receives 15% commission on domestic sales; 20% on foreign sales. Offers written contract, only "if requested." Charges for photocopying.

Writers' Conferences: Horror Writers of America Conference; World Fantasy Conference; Necon and Lunacon; Southwest Writers Conference; MidAtlantic Writers Conference; ABA; Cape Cod Writers Conference, Oklahoma short course (Norman OK); Midwest Writers (Muncie IN).

Tips: Obtains new clients through recommendations from others, solicitation, at conferences, etc. "Sometimes I come up with book ideas and find authors (*Coupon Queen*, for example). Be professional. Read *Publishers Weekly* and genre-related magazines. Join writers' organizations. Go to conferences. Know your market."

‡STEPHEN PEVNER, INC., (II), 248 W. 73rd St., 2nd Floor, New York NY 10023. (212)496-0474. Fax: (212)496-0796. E-mail: spevner@aol.com. Contact: Stephen Pevner. Estab. 1991. Signatory of WGA. Represents under 50 clients. 75% of clients are new/previously unpublished writers. Specializes in motion pictures, novels, pop culture, urban fiction, independent filmmakers. Currently handles: 25%

nonfiction books; 25% movie scripts; 25% novels; TV scripts; stage plays.
Handles: Nonfiction books, novels, movie scripts, TV scripts, stage plays. Considers these nonfiction areas: art/architecture/design; biography/autobiography; business; computers/electronics; cooking/food/nutrition; current affairs; ethnic/cultural interests; gay/lesbian issues; government/politics/law; history; humor; language/literature/criticism; money/finance/economics; music/dance/theater/film; New Age/metaphysics; photography; popular culture; religious/inspirational; science/technology; sociology. Considers these fiction areas: action/adventure; cartoon/comic; contemporary issues; detective/police/crime; erotica; ethnic; experimental; gay; glitz; horror; humor/satire; lesbian; literary; mainstream; psychic/supernatural; science fiction; thriller/espionage; urban. Query with outline/proposal. Reports in 1 week on queries; 2 weeks on mss.
Recent Sales: *Fruit Cocktail Diaries*, by Brian and Gretchen Hayduk Carmody (St. Martin's Press); *Noise From the Underground: The Secret History of Alternative Rock*, by Michael Lavine, Henry Rollins and Pat Blashill (Simon & Schuster); *Living in Oblivion*, by Tom DiCillo (Plume).
Terms: Agent receives 15% commission on domestic sales; 20% on foreign sales. Offers written contract, binding for 1 year, with 6 weeks cancellation clause. 100% of business is derived from commissions on sales.
Also Handles: Movie scripts (feature film); TV scripts (TV mow, sitcom); theatrical stage plays. Considers these script subject areas: action/adventure; comedy; contemporary issues; detective/police/crime; gay; glitz; horror; humor; lesbian; mainstream; mystery/suspense; romantic comedy and drama; science fiction; teen; thriller. Query with outline/proposal and SASE. Reports in 1 week on queries; 2 weeks on mss.
Represents: Writer/directors: Richard Linklater (*Slacker, Dazed & Confused, Before Sunrise*); Gregg Araki (*The Living End, Doom Generation*); Tom DiCillo (*Living in Oblivion*); Genvieve Turner/Rose Troche (*Go Fish*).
Terms: Agent receives 10% commission on domestic sales; 10% on foreign sales.
Writers' Conferences: Sundance Film Festival; Independent Feature Market; Cannes; ABA.
Tips: Obtains new clients through recommendations from others. "Be persistent, but civilized."

ARTHUR PINE ASSOCIATES, INC., (III), 250 W. 57th St., New York NY 10019. (212)265-7330. Estab. 1966. Represents 100 clients. 25% of clients are new/previously unpublished writers. Specializes in fiction and nonfiction. Currently handles: 75% nonfiction; 25% novels. Member agents: Richard Pine; Arthur Pine; Lori Andiman; Sarah Piel.
Handles: Nonfiction books, novels. Considers these nonfiction areas: business; current affairs; health/medicine; money/finance/economics; psychology; self-help/personal improvement. Considers these fiction areas: action/adventure; detective/police/crime; family saga; literary; mainstream; romance; thriller/espionage. Send outline/proposal. Reports in 3 weeks on queries. "All correspondence must be accompanied by a SASE. Will not read manuscripts before receiving a letter of inquiry."
Recent Sales: *The Exchange Students*, by Marc Olden (Random House); *The Third Pandemic*, by Pierre Ouelette (Pocketbooks); *Kiss The Girls*, by James Patterson (Little, Brown & Warner Books); *The Optimistic Child*, by Dr. Martin Seligman (Houghton Mifflin).
Terms: Agency receives 15% commission on domestic sales; 25% on foreign sales. Offers written contract, which varies from book to book.
Tips: Obtains new clients through recommendations from others. "Our agency will only look at submissions that have not been submitted to any other agent or publisher simultaneously or at any time whatsoever and must be accompanied by a self-addressed, stamped envelope for return purposes . . . otherwise materials will not be returned."

POCONO LITERARY AGENCY, INC., (II), Box 69, Saylorsburg PA 18353-0069. (610)381-4152. Contact: Carolyn Hopwood Blick, president. Estab. 1993. Represents 20 clients. 80% of clients are new/previously unpublished writers. Specializes in young adult/juvenile novels and romance (all categories). Currently handles: 50% juvenile books; 50% novels.
Handles: Nonfiction books, juvenile books, novels, poetry books (for children). Considers these nonfiction areas: education, history, how-to, interior design/decorating, juvenile nonfiction, sports. Considers these fiction areas: action/adventure; family saga; historical; horror; juvenile; picture book; romance (contemporary, gothic, historical, regency); science fiction; sports; thriller/espionage; westerns/frontier; young adult. Query with 1 page synopsis. Reports in 2 weeks on queries; 1 month on mss.
Recent Sales: *Visions of the Fantastic*, by Alliene Becker (Greenwood).
Terms: Agent receives 15% commission on domestic sales; 20% on foreign sales. Offers written contract, binding for 6 months. Charges for photocopying, postage, long-distance telephone, UPS, and all other reasonable expenses.
Tips: Obtains clients through recommendations from others and direct submissions from authors.

‡POM INC., (II, III), 21 Vista Dr., Great Neck NY 11021. (212)522-6612. Fax: (212)522-4971. Contact: Simon Green. Estab. 1990. Represents 27 clients. 15% of clients are new/previously unpublished

writers. Currently handles: 50% nonfiction books; 5% scholarly books; 35% novels; 10% syndicated material. Member agents: Dan Green; Simon Green.
Handles: Nonfiction books, novels, short story collections, syndicated material. Considers these nonfiction areas: biography/autobiography; business; cooking/food/nutrition; current affairs; ethnic/cultural interests; health/medicine; history; money/finance/economics; music/dance/theater/film; popular culture; sports; women's issues/women's studies. Considers these fiction areas: action/adventure; contemporary issues; detective/police/crime; erotica; fantasy; feminist; glitz; historical; horror; humor/satire; literary; mainstream; mystery/suspense; sports; thriller/espionage. Query. Reports in 2 weeks on queries.
Terms: Agent receives 15% commission on domestic sales; 15% on foreign sales. No written contract. Charges "if a publishing entertainment electronic lawyer is needed to review a contract." 100% of business is derived from commissions on sales.
Tips: Obtains new clients through referrals.

JULIE POPKIN, (II), 15340 Albright St., #204, Pacific Palisades CA 90272-2520. (310)459-2834. Estab. 1989. Represents 26 clients. 40% of clients are new/unpublished writers. Specializes in selling book-length mss including fiction and nonfiction. Especially interested in social issues. Currently handles: 50% nonfiction books; 50% novels; some scripts.
Handles: Nonfiction books, novels. Considers these nonfiction areas: art; criticism; feminist; history; politics. Considers these fiction areas: literary; mainstream; mystery. Reports in 1 month on queries; 2 months on mss.
Recent Sales: *We Are Cows, They Are Pigs*, by Carmen Boullosa (Grave/Atlantic); *The Flight*, by Horacco Verbitsky (The New Press); *Land of a Thousand Dances*, by Tom Waldman and David Reyes (University of New Mexico); *Messianic Revolution*, by David Katz and Richard H. Popkin (Hill & Wang/Farrar Straus Group).
Terms: Agent receives 15% commission on domestic sales; 10% on dramatic sales; 25% on foreign sales.
Fees: Does not charge a reading fee. Charges $100/year for photocopying, mailing, long distance calls.
Writers' Conferences: Frankfurt (October); ABA (Chicago, June).

THE POTOMAC LITERARY AGENCY, (II), 19062 Mills Choice Rd., Suite 5, Gaithersburg MD 20879-2835. (301)208-0674. Fax: (301)869-7513. Contact: Thomas F. Epley. Estab. 1993. Represents 14 clients. 60% of clients are new/previously unpublished writers. Currently handles: 80% novels; 20% nonfiction. Currently handling novels—mostly literary fiction, but will consider commercial fiction, novellas, and general nonfiction.
• Prior to opening his agency, Mr. Epley was director of the Naval Institute Press.
Handles: Nonfiction books, literary and commercial fiction (novels, novellas). Considers these nonfiction areas: biography/autobiography; business; current affairs; ethnic/cultural interests; gay/lesbian issues; history; language/literature/criticism; military/war; money/finance/economics; nature/environment; psychology; science/technology; self-help/personal improvement; sports; true crime/investigative. Considers these fiction areas: action/adventure; contemporary issues; detective/police/crime; ethnic; experimental; family saga; feminist; gay; historical; humor/satire; lesbian; literary; mainstream; sports; thriller/espionage; westerns/frontier. Query with brief synopsis (no more than 1 page), first chapter and SASE. Reports in 2 weeks on queries; 6 weeks on mss.
Recent Sales: *Something to Hide*, by Peter Levine (St. Martin's Press); *In a Heartbeat*, by Eril Stone (Presidio Press); *Walking West*, by Noelle Sickels (St. Martin's Press); *The Rickover Effect*, by T. Rockwell (John Wiley & Sons).
Terms: Agents receive 15% commission on domestic sales; 20% on foreign sales (if co-agent used). Offers written contract.
Tips: Obtains new clients through referrals.

AARON M. PRIEST LITERARY AGENCY, (II), 708 Third Ave., 23rd Floor, New York NY 10017. (212)818-0344. Contact: Aaron Priest or Molly Friedrich. Member of AAR. Currently handles: 25% nonfiction books; 75% fiction. Member agents: Lisa Erbach Vance, Sheri Holman.
• See the interview with Ms. Erbach Vance in the article, How Things Work: Foreign Rights, in this edition of the *Guide*.
Handles: Nonfiction books, fiction. Query only (must be accompanied by SASE). Unsolicited mss will be returned unread.

Check the Subject Index to find the agents who are interested in your nonfiction or fiction subject area.

Recent Sales: *Moo*, by Jane Smiley; *Absolute Power*, by David Baldacci; *Two for the Dough*, by Janet Evanovich (Scribner); *The Juror*, by George Green; Robert James Waller; *Waiting to Exhale*, by Terry McMillan; *Day After Tomorrow*, by Allan Folsom; *Nathan's Run*, by John Gilstrap (HarperCollins).

Terms: Agent receives 15% commission on domestic sales. Charges for photocopying, foreign postage expenses.

PRINTED TREE INC., (II), 2357 Trail Dr., Evansville IN 47711. (812)476-9015. Fax: (812)476-9015 (*51). Contact: Jo Frohbieter-Mueller. Estab. 1990. Represents 45 clients. 60% of clients are new/previously unpublished writers. Currently handles: 30% nonfiction books; 20% scholarly books; 30% novels; 20% textbooks. Member agents: Janet McCormick (novels, juvenile books).

Handles: Nonfiction books, scholarly books, textbooks, juvenile books, novels. Considers these nonfiction areas: business; child guidance/parenting; cooking/food/nutrition; crafts/hobbies; education; how-to; juvenile nonfiction; military/war; religious/inspirational; self-help/personal improvement; women's issues/women's studies. Considers these fiction areas: action/adventure; contemporary issues; family saga; horror; juvenile; mainstream; religious/inspirational; science fiction; thriller/espionage; young adult. Query. Reports in 2 weeks on queries; 2 months on mss.

Terms: Agent receives 15% commission on domestic sales; 20% on foreign sales. Offers written contract. Charges $50 upon acceptance for marketing expenses; taken from commission when book sold.

Writers' Conferences: "I speak at libraries throughout the country on the subject of 'getting into print.' This is an ongoing commitment—I lecture at approximately 50-75 libraries each year. I'm always amazed at the crowds that gather to learn about this subject."

Tips: Obtains new clients from lectures, listing in references. "Write a good query letter that includes 1) target readers of proposed book, 2) brief synopsis of proposed book, 3) explain how it differs from others on market, 4) your qualification for writing book."

SUSAN ANN PROTTER LITERARY AGENT, (II), 110 W. 40th St., Suite 1408, New York NY 10018. (212)840-0480. Contact: Susan Protter. Estab. 1971. Member of AAR. Represents 40 clients. 10% of clients are new/unpublished writers. Writer must have book-length project or ms that is ready to be sold. Works with a very small number of new/unpublished authors. Currently handles: 40% nonfiction books; 60% novels; occasional magazine article or short story (for established clients only).

Handles: Nonfiction books, novels. Considers these nonfiction areas: general nonfiction; biography; child guidance/parenting; health; medicine; psychology; science. Considers these fiction areas: detective/police/crime; mystery; science fiction, thrillers. Send short query with brief description of project/novel, publishing history and SASE. Reports in 3 weeks on queries; 2 months on solicited mss. "Please do not call; mail queries only."

Recent Sales: *Freeware*, by Rudy Rucker (Morrow/AvoNova); *Dr. Nightingale* and *Alice Nestleton* (mystery series), by Lydia Adamson (Signet); *Northern Stars*, by David G. Hartwell and Glenn Grent (TOR); *20 Teachable Virtues*, by Barbara C. Unell and Jerry L. Wyckoff, PhD (Perigee Berkley); *Life Happens*, by Kathleen McCoy, PhD, and Charles Wibbelsmen, MD (Perigee/Berkley); *Pirates of the Universe*, by Terry Bisson (TOR).

Terms: Agent receives 15% commission on domestic sales; 15% on TV, film and dramatic sales; 25% on foreign sales. Charges for long distance, photocopying, messenger, express mail, airmail expenses.

Tips: "Please send neat and professionally organized queries. Make sure to include an SASE or we cannot reply. We receive up to 100 queries a week and read them in the order they arrive. We usually reply within two weeks to any query. Do not call. If you are sending a multiple query, make sure to note that in your letter."

ROBERTA PRYOR, INC., (II), 24 W. 55th St., New York NY 10019-5311. (212)245-0420. Fax: (212)757-8030. President: Roberta Pryor. Estab. 1985. Member of AAR. Represents 50 clients. Prefers to work with published/established authors; works with a small number of new/unpublished writers. Specializes in serious nonfiction and (tends toward) literary fiction. Special interest in natural history, good cookbooks, media studies. Currently handles: 60% nonfiction books; 20% novels; 10% textbooks; 10% juvenile books.

● Prior to opening her agency, Ms. Pryor served as head of Subsidiary Rights for E.P. Dutton, editor with Trident Press (Simon & Schuster), and as an agent (VP) with International Creative Management.

Handles: Nonfiction books, novels, textbooks, juvenile books. Considers these nonfiction areas: animals; anthropology/archaeology; art/architecture/design; biography/autobiography; cooking/food; current affairs; ethnic/cultural interests; gay/lesbian issues; government/politics/law; history; juvenile nonfiction; literature/criticism; military/war; nature/environment; photography; popular culture; sociology; theater/film; true crime/investigative; women's issues/women's studies. Considers these fiction areas: contemporary issues; detective/police/crime; historical; literary; mainstream; mystery/suspense; young adult. Query. SASE required for any correspondence. Reports in 10 weeks on queries.

Recent Sales: *Eagles of Fire*, (techno-thriller), by Timothy Rizzi (Donald I. Fine); new vegetarian cookbook, by Anna Thomas (Knopf); *Jerusalem*, (historical novel), by Cecelia Holland (TOR-Forge/ St. Martin's); *A Memoir*, by Paul Fussell (Little, Brown); *The Gulf War*, (media study), by Mark Crispin Miller (WW Norton).
Terms: Charges 15% commission on domestic sales; 10% on film sales; 20% on foreign sales. Charges for photocopying, and often express mail and messenger service.

PUBLISHING SERVICES, (II), 525 E. 86th St., New York NY 10028-7554. (212)535-6248. Fax: (212)988-1073. Contact: Amy Goldberger. Estab. 1993. Represents 20 clients. 50% of clients are new/ previously unpublished writers. Currently handles: 75% nonfiction books; 25% novels.
Handles: Nonfiction books, novels. Considers these nonfiction areas: biography/autobiography; child guidance/parenting; cooking/food/nutrition; education; ethnic/cultural interests; health/medicine; New Age/metaphysics; popular culture; self-help/personal improvement; women's issues/women's studies. Considers these fiction areas: contemporary issues; ethnic; feminist; historical; literary; mainstream. Query with SASE. Reports in 2 weeks on queries.
Terms: Agent receives 15% commission on domestic sales; 20% on foreign sales. Offers written contract. Charges for photocopying, postage, long distance calls.
Tips: Obtains new clients from queries and referrals. Query first and always include a SASE.

QUICKSILVER BOOKS-LITERARY AGENTS, (II), 50 Wilson St., Hartsdale NY 10530-2542. (914)946-8748. Contact: Bob Silverstein. Estab. 1973 as packager; 1987 as literary agency. Represents 50 clients. 50% of clients are new/previously unpublished writers. Specializes in literary and commercial mainstream fiction and nonfiction (especially psychology, New Age, holistic healing, consciousness, ecology, environment, spirituality). Currently handles: 75% nonfiction books; 25% novels.
  ● Prior to opening his agency, Mr. Silverstein served as senior editor at Bantam Books and Dell Books/Delacorte Press.
Handles: Nonfiction books, novels. Considers these nonfiction areas: anthropology/archaeology; biography; business; child guidance/parenting; cooking/food/nutrition; current affairs; ethnic/cultural interests; health/medicine; history; how-to; literature; nature/environment; New Age/metaphysics; popular culture; psychology; inspirational; science/technology; self-help/personal improvement; sociology; sports; true crime/investigative; women's issues/women's studies. Considers these fiction areas: action/adventure; glitz; mystery/suspense. Query, "always include SASE." Reports in up to 2 weeks on queries; up to 1 month on mss.
Recent Sales: *Deadly Impression*, by Dennis Asen (Bantam Books); *The New Gambler's Bible*, by Arthur Reber (Crown); *Panther*, by Melvin Van Peebles (Thunder's Mouth Press); *Secrets of Better Sex*, by Block & Bakos (Prentice-Hall/Simon & Schuster); *Healing With Ayurveda*, by Vasant Lad (Harmony).
Terms: Agent receives 15% commission on domestic sales; 20% on foreign sales. Offers written contract, "only if requested. It is open ended, unless author requests time frame." Charges for postage. Authors are expected to supply SASE for return of mss and for query letter responses.
Writers' Conferences: National Writers Union Conference (Dobbs Ferry NY, April).
Tips: Obtains new clients through recommendations, listings in sourcebooks, solicitations, workshop participation.

CHARLOTTE CECIL RAYMOND, LITERARY AGENT, (III), 32 Bradlee Rd., Marblehead MA 01945. Contact: Charlotte Cecil Raymond. Estab. 1983. Represents 30 clients. 20% of clients are new/previously unpublished writers. Currently handles: 70% nonfiction books; 10% juvenile books; 20% novels.
Handles: Nonfiction books, juvenile/young adult books, novels. Considers these nonfiction areas: biography; current affairs; ethnic/cultural interests; gay/lesbian issues; history; juvenile nonfiction; nature/environment; psychology; sociology; women's issues/women's studies. No self-help/personal improvement. Considers these fiction areas: contemporary issues; ethnic; gay/lesbian; literary; mainstream; regional; young adult. No mysteries, thrillers, historical fiction, science fiction or romance. Query with outline/proposal. Reports in 2 weeks on queries; 6 weeks on mss.
Terms: Agent receives 15% commission on domestic sales. 100% of business derived from commissions on ms sales.

HELEN REES LITERARY AGENCY, (II, III), 308 Commonwealth Ave., Boston MA 02115-2415. (617)262-2401. Fax: (617)262-2401. Contact: Joan Mazmanian. Estab. 1981. Member of AAR. Represents 50 clients. 50% of clients are new/previously unpublished writers. Specializes in general nonfiction, health, business, world politics, autobiographies, psychology, women's issues. Currently handles: 60% nonfiction books; 40% novels.
Handles: Nonfiction books, novels. Considers these nonfiction areas: biography/autobiography; business; current affairs; government/politics/law; health/medicine; history; money/finance/economics; women's issues/women's studies. Considers these fiction areas: contemporary issues; detective/police/

crime; glitz; historical; literary; mainstream; mystery/suspense; thriller/espionage. Query with outline plus 2 sample chapters. Reports in 1 week on queries; 3 weeks on mss.

Recent Sales: *Romeo,* by Elise Title (fiction); *Changing The Game,* by Adam M. Brandenburger (business) and Barry J. Nalebuff; *Thriving In Transition,* by Marcia Perkins-Reed (Fireside/Simon & Schuster).

Terms: Agent receives 15% commission on domestic sales; 20% on foreign sales.

Tips: Obtains new clients through recommendations from others, solicitation, at conferences, etc.

RENAISSANCE—H.N. SWANSON INC., (III), 8523 Sunset Blvd., Los Angeles CA 90069. (310)289-3636. Contact: Joel Gotler. Signatory of WGA; Member of SAG, AFTRA, DGA. Represents 150 clients. 10% of clients are new/previously unpublished writers. Currently handles: 60% novels; 40% movie and TV scripts. Specializes in selling movies and TV rights from books. Member agents: Irv Schwartz, partner (TV writers); Allan Nevins, partner (book publishing); Brian Lipson, associate (motion picture writers); Steven Fisher.
  ● Renaissance acquired H.N. Swanson, recognized as the first Hollywood Literary agency. Mr. Gotler started his agenting career under H.N. Swanson. The new company will be called Renaissance—H.N. Swanson.

Handles: Nonfiction books, novels. Considers these nonfiction areas: biography/autobiography; history; film; true crime/investigative. Considers these fiction areas: action/adventure; contemporary issue; detective/police/crime; ethnic; family saga; fantasy; historical; humor/satire; literary; mainstream; mystery/suspense; science fiction; thriller/espionage. Query with outline and SASE. Reports in 1 month on queries.

Recent Sales: *Black Eagle,* by Larry Collins (Dutton); *Last Tango in Brooklyn,* by Kirk Douglas (Warner Books); *The Deaths of Sybil Bolton,* by Dennis McAuliffe Jr. (Patchett Kaufman Entertainment).

Also Handles: Movie scripts (feature film); TV scripts (TV mow, episodic drama, sitcom and animation). Considers these script subject areas: action/adventure; cartoon/animation; comedy; contemporary issues; detective/police/crime; erotica; ethnic; experimental; family saga; fantasy; feminist; gay; historical; horror; juvenile; lesbian; mainstream; mystery/suspense; psychic/supernatural; regional; romantic comedy and drama; science fiction; sports; teen; thriller/espionage; westerns/frontier. Query with SASE. Reports in 1 month.

Recent Sales: *Two by Two,* by David Golden/Jay Rosen (Byegam-Baer); *In Contempt,* by Ken Nolan (Weintraub Entertainment).

Terms: Agent receives 15% commission on domestic books; 10% on film sales.

Tips: Obtains news clients through recommendations from others.

‡ANGELA RINALDI LITERARY AGENCY, (II), P.O. Box 7877, Beverly Hills CA 90064. (310)287-0356. Fax: (310)837-8143. Contact: Angela Rinaldi. Estab. 1994. Represents 10 clients. Currently handles: 50% nonfiction books; 50% novels.

Handles: Nonfiction books, novels, TV and motion picture rights. Query first with SASE. For fiction, send outline/proposal and 2 sample chapters. For nonfiction, send outline/proposal. Considers these nonfiction areas: anthropology/archaeology; biography/autobiography; business; child guidance/parenting; cooking/food/nutrition; current affairs; health/medicine; money/finance/economics; popular culture; psychology; self-help/personal improvement; sociology; true crime/investigative; women's issues/women's studies. Considers these fiction areas: action/adventure; contemporary issues; detective/police/crime; ethnic; experimental; family saga; feminist; glitz; historical; literary; mainstream; thriller/espionage. Reports in 3 weeks on proposals; 6 weeks on mss.

Terms: Agent receives 15% commission on domestic sales; 20% on foreign sales. Offers written contract. Charges for marketing expenses. 100% of business is derived from commissions on sales.

RIVERSIDE LITERARY AGENCY, (III), Keets Brook Rd., Leyden MA 01337. (413)772-0840. Fax: (413)772-0969. Contact: Susan Lee Cohen. Estab. 1991. Represents 55 clients. 20% of clients are new/previously unpublished writers. Currently handles: 65% nonfiction books; 30% novels; 5% short story collections.

For explanation of symbols, see the Key to Symbols and Abbreviations. For translation of an organization's acronym, see the Table of Acronyms. For unfamiliar words, check the Glossary.

Handles: Nonfiction books, novels. Very selective. Query with outline and SASE. Reports in 2 months.
Terms: Agent receives 15% commission. Offers written contract at request of author.
Recent Sales: *Reviving Ophelia*, by Mary Pipher (Ballantine/Putnam); *Please Kill Me: An Uncensored Oral History of Punk*, by Legs McNeil and Agillian McCain; *What Every Woman Should Know About Heart Disease*, by Dr. Siegfried Krea (Warner Books).
Tips: Only accepts new clients through referrals.

BJ ROBBINS LITERARY AGENCY, (II), 5130 Bellaire Ave., North Hollywood CA 91607. (818)760-6602. Fax: (818)760-6616. Contact: (Ms.) B.J. Robbins. Estab. 1992. Represents 20 clients. 80% of clients are new/previously unpublished writers. Currently handles: 50% nonfiction books; 50% novels.
Handles: Nonfiction books, novels. Considers these nonfiction areas: biography/autobiography; child guidance/parenting; cooking/food/nutrition; current affairs; education; ethnic/cultural interests; gay/lesbian issues; government/politics/law; health/medicine; how-to; humor; music/dance/theater/film; nature/environment; popular culture; psychology; self-help/personal improvement; sociology; sports; true crime/investigative; women's issues/women's studies. Considers these fiction areas: contemporary issues; detective/police/crime; ethnic; family saga; gay; lesbian; literary; mainstream; mystery/suspense; sports; thriller/espionage. Send outline/proposal and 3 sample chapters. Reports in 2 weeks on queries; 6 weeks on mss.
Recent Sales: *Nightland*, by Louis Owens (Dutton); *Wannabe*, by Everett Weinberger (Birch Lane); *Kink: An Autobiography*, by Dave Davies (Hyperion); *Sweet Remedy*, by Linda Phillips Ashour (Simon & Schuster).
Terms: Agent receives 15% commission on domestic sales; 20% on foreign sales. Offers written contract, with 3 months notice to terminate if project is out on submission. Charges for postage and photocopying only. 100% of business is derived from commissions on sales.
Writers' Conferences: Squaw Valley Fiction Writers Workshop (Squaw Valley CA, August); Art of the Wild (Squaw Valley CA, July); Palm Springs Writers Conference (Palm Springs CA, May).
Tips: Obtains new clients mostly through referrals, also at conferences.

THE ROBBINS OFFICE, INC., (II), 405 Park Ave., New York NY 10022. (212)223-0720. Fax: (212)223-2535. Contact: Kathy P. Robbins, owner; Elizabeth Mackey. Specializes in selling mainstream nonfiction, commercial and literary fiction.
Handles: Nonfiction books, novels, magazine articles for book writers under contract. No unsolicited mss.
Recent Sales: *Why Nobody in Politics Gets Respect Anymore*, by E.J. Dionne Jr. (Scribner); *Being Digital*, by Nicholas Negroponte (Knopf); *Maplethorpe*, by Patricia Morris Roe (Random House).
Terms: Agent receives 15% commission on all domestic, dramatic and foreign sales. Bills back specific expenses incurred in doing business for a client.

ROCK LITERARY AGENCY, (II), P.O. Box 625, Newport RI 02840-0006. (401)849-4442. Fax: (401)849-5563. E-mail: rocklit@lobster.com. Contact: Andrew T. Rock. Estab. 1988. Represents 52 clients. Currently handles: 40% nonfiction books; 60% fiction.
Handles: Fiction (literary and mainstream); nonfiction (literary); business (general and professional). Query with SASE. Reports in 10 days on queries.
Terms: Agent receives 15% commission on domestic sales; 20% on foreign sales. Offers written contract. Charges for photocopying, postage, fax, phone and packages.
Tips: Usually obtains new clients through recommendations from editors and other clients.

IRENE ROGERS LITERARY REPRESENTATION, (III), 9454 Wilshire Blvd., Suite 600, Beverly Hills CA 90212. (213)837-3511 or (310)276-7588. Estab. 1977. Currently represents 10 clients. 10% of clients are new/previously unpublished authors. "We are currently accepting new clients." Currently handles: 50% nonfiction; 50% novels.
Handles: Nonfiction, novels. Considers all nonfiction areas, especially medicine and self-help/personal improvement. Considers all areas of fiction. Query. Responds to queries in 6-8 weeks.
Terms: Agent receives 10% commission on domestic sales; 5% on foreign sales.

ROSE AGENCY, (II), 2033 Ontario Circle, Ft. Wayne IN 46802-6737. (219)432-5857. Contact: Lynn Clough. Estab. 1993. Currently handles: 5% nonfiction books; 5% juvenile books; 90% novels.
Handles: Nonfiction books, juvenile books, novels. Considers these nonfiction areas: business; child guidance/parenting; education; health/medicine; juvenile nonfiction; religious/inspirational; self-help/personal improvement. Considers these fiction areas: action/adventure; contemporary issues; family saga; historical; humor/satire; juvenile; mainstream; mystery/suspense; religious/inspiration; romance (contemporary, gothic, historical, regency); thriller/espionage; westerns/frontier; young adult. Query only. No phone calls. Answers queries promptly. Reports in 6 weeks on mss.
Terms: Agent receives 15% commission on domestic sales; 20% on foreign sales. Offers written contract, binding for 1 year.

Tips: "If you have come this far, you probably have what it takes to be a published author. We find that writers are driven by some inner compulsion to put words on paper. Just because you aren't published doesn't mean you aren't a writer. We'd like to read your best work. If you believe in your work, if your idea is fresh and your approach unique, query us. We generally ask to see 90% of the fiction queries we receive."

ROSE LITERARY AGENCY, (II), 215 Park Ave. S., Suite 1403, New York NY 10003. (212)353-9600. Fax: (212)353-9757. Contact: Mitchell Rose. Estab. 1986. Represents 60 clients. 25% of clients are new/previously unpublished writers. "We have a broad list, but do have a few areas in which we specialize: film, exposé, history, politics, psychology, nutrition and innovative literary fiction." Currently handles: 80% nonfiction books; 15% novels; 5% short story collections.
Handles: Nonfiction books, novels, short story collections. Considers these nonfiction areas: anthropology/archaeology; art/architecture/design; biography/autobiography; business; child guidance/parenting; cooking/food/nutrition; current affairs; ethnic/cultural interests; gay/lesbian issues; government/politics/law; health/medicine; history; language/literature/criticism; military/war; money/finance/economics; music/dance/theater/film; nature/environment; psychology; science/technology; self-help/personal improvement; sociology; sports; women's issues/women's studies. Considers these fiction areas: contemporary issues; ethnic; feminist; gay; humor/satire; literary; thriller/espionage. Query. Reports in 2 weeks on queries; 1 month on mss.
Recent Sales: *Toward Amnesia*, by Sarah Van Arsdale (Riverhead, Putnam); *Nixon as President*, by Gerald Strober (HarperCollins); *Healing Through Nutrition*, by Melvyn Werbach (HarperCollins); *A Taste of Heritage*, by Joe Randall (Macmillan); *Love Awaits*, by Courtney Long (Bantam).
Terms: Agent receives 15% commission on domestic sales; 20% on foreign sales. Offers written contract. "For projects and authors that show promise, we offer extensive editorial feedback at no charge. Critiques are written by myself and staff project developers." Charges fees "but only for very high volume photocopying. Any expense would be approved by the client before it is incurred."
Tips: Obtains new clients mostly through recommendations of existing clients and from editors. "We have taken on several clients whose initial contacts were through query letters."

JANE ROTROSEN AGENCY, (II), 318 E. 51st St., New York NY 10022. (212)593-4330. Estab. 1974. Member of AAR. Represents 100 clients. Works with published and unpublished writers. Specializes in trade fiction and nonfiction. Currently handles: 40% nonfiction books, 60% novels.
Handles: Adult fiction, nonfiction. Query with short outline. Reports in 2 weeks.
Terms: Receives 15% commission on domestic sales; 15% on dramatic sales; 20% on foreign sales. Charges writers for photocopying, long-distance/transoceanic telephone, telegraph, Telex, messenger service and foreign postage.

‡THE DAMARIS ROWLAND AGENCY, (I), RR #1, Box 513 A, Wallingford VT 05773. (802)446-3146. Fax: (802)446-3224. Contact: Damaris Rowland or Steve Axelrod. Estab. 1994. Member of AAR. Represents 25 clients. 25% of clients are new/previously unpublished writers. Specializes in women's fiction. Currently handles: 100% novels.
Handles: Nonfiction books, novels. Considers these nonfiction areas: animals; cooking/food/nutrition; health/medicine; nature/environment; New Age/metaphysics; religious/inspirational; women's issues/women's studies. Considers these fiction areas: detective/police/crime; historical; literary; mainstream; psychic/supernatural; romance (contemporary, gothic, historical, regency). Send outline/proposal. Reports in 6 weeks.
Recent Sales: *A Dangerous Man*, by Connie Brockway (Dell); *The Undefeated*, by Heather Graham (NAL); *Heart's Blood*, by Haywood Smith (St. Martin's).
Terms: Agent receives 15% commission on domestic sales; 20% on foreign sales. Offers written contract, with 30 day cancellation clause. Charges only if extraordinary expenses have been incurred, e.g., photocopying and mailing 15 ms to Europe for a foreign sale. 100% of business is derived from commissions on sales.
Writers' Conferences: Novelists Inc. (Denver, October); RWA National (Texas, July).
Tips: Obtains new clients through recommendations from others, at conferences.

PESHA RUBINSTEIN LITERARY AGENCY, INC. (II), 37 Overlook Terrace, #1D, New York NY 10033-2216. (212)781-7845. Contact: Pesha Rubinstein. Estab. 1990. Member of AAR, RWA, MWA, SCBWI. Represents 35 clients. 25% of clients are new/previously unpublished writers. Specializes in women's fiction and romance, and children's books. Currently handles: 20% juvenile books; 80% novels.
   ● Prior to opening her agency, Ms. Rubinstein served as an editor at Zebra and Leisure Books.
Handles: Genre fiction, juvenile books, picture book illustration. Considers these nonfiction areas: child guidance/parenting; juvenile nonfiction; nature/environment. Considers these fiction areas: detective/police/crime; ethnic; glitz; humor; juvenile; mainstream; mystery/suspense; picture book; psychic/supernatural; romance (contemporary, historical); spiritual adventures. "No westerns, science fiction

or poetry." Send query, first 10 pages and SASE. Reports in 2 weeks on queries; 6 weeks on requested mss.

Recent Sales: *Kissed*, by Tanya Crosby (Avon); *Storyteller's Beads*, by Jane Kurtz (Harcourt Brace); *Fox Maiden*, illustrated by Tatsuno Kiuchi (Simon & Schuster).

Terms: Agent receives 15% commission on domestic sales; 20% on foreign sales. Offers written contract. Charges for photocopying. No collect calls accepted.

Writers' Conferences: Romantic Times (Fort Worth, TX).

Tips: "Keep the query letter and synopsis short. Please send first ten pages of manuscript rather than selected chapters from the manuscript. The work speaks for itself better than any description can. Never send originals. A phone call after one month is acceptable. Always include a SASE covering return of the entire package with the material."

RUSSELL-SIMENAUER LITERARY AGENCY INC., (II), P.O. Box 43267, Upper Montclair NJ 07043-7267. (201)746-0539, (201)992-4198. Fax: (201)746-0754. Contact: Jacqueline Simenauer or Margaret Russell. Estab. 1990. Member of Authors Guild, Authors League, NASW. Represents 45-50 clients. 60% of clients are new/previously unpublished writers. Specializes in popular health/medicine, popular psychology/psychichiatry, self-help/personal inprovement, women's issues, how-to. Currently handles: 90% nonfiction books; 10% novels. Member agents: Jacqueline Simenauer (popular psychology/psychiatry, self-help/personal improvement); Margaret Russell (fiction, women's issues, popular health/medicine).

● Prior to opening their agency, Ms. Russell served as associate director of publicity for Simon & Schuster and director of publicity for Basic Books, and Ms. Simenauer co-authored several books for Doubleday and Times Books.

Handles: Nonfiction books, novels. Considers these nonfiction areas: biography/autobiography; business; child guidance/parenting; current affairs; education; health/medicine; how-to; money/finance; New Age/metaphysics; nutrition; popular culture; psychology; religious/inspirational; self-help/personal improvement; sports; true crime/investigative; women's issues/women's studies. Considers these fiction areas: contemporary issues; family saga; feminist; gay; glitz; historical; literary; mainstream; mystery/suspense; psychic/supernatural; romance (contemporary); thriller/espionage. Query with outline/proposal. Reports in 1 month on queries; 6 weeks on mss.

Recent Sales: *The Benzo Blues*, by Edward Drummond MD (NAL/Dutton); *The Trouble With Mutual Funds*, by Herbert Ringold (Amacom); *Is There a Doctor in the House*, by Samuel Wong (Prima Publishing); *The Endometriosis Source Book*, by Mary Lou Ballweg (Contemporary Books).

Terms: Agent receives 15% commission on domestic sales; 25% on foreign sales. "There are no reading fees." Charges for postage, photocopying, phone, fax. 100% of business is derived from commissions on ms sales.

Worker's Conferences: The American Psychological Association (NYC, August).

Tips: Obtains new clients through recommendations from others; advertising in various journals, newsletters, publications, etc. and professional conferences.

‡ST. CLAIR LITERARY AGENCY, (II), 4501 Colonial Ave., Norfolk VA 23508. Phone/fax: (804)623-0288. Contact: Kelly St. Clair. Estab. 1993. Member of RWA. Represents 20 clients. 99% of clients are new/previously unpublished writers. Specializes in romance novels. Currently handles: 100% novels.

Handles: Novels. Considers these fiction areas: historical; mainstream; romance (contemporary, gothic, historical, regency). Send outline/proposal. Reports in 2 months on queries; 3 months on mss.

Terms: Agent receives 5% commission on domestic sales; 10% on foreign sales. Offers written contract, binding for 1 year, with 30 day cancellation clause.

Tips: Obtains new clients through recommendations from others, at conferences and from the Romance Writers' Pink Pages. "Always be sure to submit your best work to an agent."

VICTORIA SANDERS LITERARY AGENCY, (II), 241 Avenue of the Americas, New York NY 10014-4822. (212)633-8811. Fax: (212)633-0525. Contact: Victoria Sanders and/or Diane Dickensheid. Estab. 1993. Member of AAR, signatory of WGA. Represents 50 clients. 25% of clients are new/previously unpublished writers. Currently handles: 50% nonfiction books; 40% novels; 10% movie scripts.

Handles: Nonfiction, novels. Considers these nonfiction areas: biography/autobiography; current affairs; ethnic/cultural interests; gay/lesbian issues; govenment/politics/law; history; humor; language/literature/criticism; music/dance/theater/film; popular culture; psychology; translations; women's issues/women's studies. Considers these fiction areas: action/adventure; contemporary issues; family saga; feminist; gay; lesbian; literary; thriller/espionage. Query and SASE. Reports in 1 week on queries; 1 month on mss.

Recent Sales: *Bertice: The World According To Me*, by Bertice Berry (Scribner); *The Children Bob Moses Led*, by William Heath (Milkweed); *Big Girls Don't Cry*, by Connie Briscoe (HarperCollins); *America's Good News Almanac*, by Bill Bailey (Pocket Books); *How To Stay Single Forever*, by Jenny Lombard (Warner); *Jumpstart—A Love Story*, by Robb Armstrong (HarperCollins); *Go the Way Your*

Blood Beats: An Anthology of Gay and Lesbian Writings by African Americans, by Shawn Stewart Ruff (Holt).
Also Handles: Movie scripts (feature film); TV scripts (TV mow, miniseries). Considers these script subject areas: action/adventure; comedy; contemporary issues; family saga; romantic comedy and drama; thriller. Query. Reports in 1 week on queries; 1 month on scripts.
Terms: Agent receives 15% commission on domestic sales; 20% on foreign sales. Offers written contract binding at will. Charges for photocopy, messenger, express mail and extraordinary fees. If in excess of $100, client approval is required.
Tips: Obtains new clients through recommendations, "or I find them through my reading and pursue. Limit query to letter, no calls and give it your best shot. A good query is going to get good responses."

SANDUM & ASSOCIATES, (II), 144 E. 84th St., New York NY 10028-2035. (212)737-2011. Fax number on request. Managing Director: Howard E. Sandum. Estab. 1987. Represents 35 clients. 20% of clients are new/unpublished writers. Specializes in general nonfiction—all categories of adult books; commercial and literary fiction. Currently handles: 80% nonfiction books; 20% novels.
Handles: Nonfiction books, novels. Query with proposal, sample pages and SASE. Do not send full ms unless requested. Reports in 2 weeks on queries.
Terms: Agent receives 15% commission. Agent fee adjustable on dramatic and foreign sales. Charges writers for photocopying, air express, long-distance telephone/fax.

HAROLD SCHMIDT LITERARY AGENCY, (II), 343 W. 12th St., #1B, New York NY 10014. (212)727-7473. Fax: (212)807-6025. Contact: Harold Schmidt. Estab. 1983. Member of AAR. Represents 35 clients. 10% of clients are new/previously unpublished writers. Currently handles: 40% nonfiction books; 5% scholarly books; 55% novels.
Handles: Nonfiction books, scholarly books, novels, short story collections. Considers these nonfiction areas: anthropology/archaeology; art/architecture/design; biography/autobiography; business; current affairs; ethnic/cultural interests; gay/lesbian issues; government/politics/law; health/medicine; history; language/literature/criticism; military/war; money/finance/economics; music/dance/theater/film; nature/environment; New Age/metaphysics; psychology; science/technology; self-help/personal improvement; sociology; translations; true crime/investigative; women's issues/women's studies. Considers these fiction areas: action/adventure; contemporary issues; detective/police/crime; ethnic; family saga; feminist; gay; glitz; historical; horror; lesbian; literary; mainstream; mystery/suspense; psychic/supernatural; thriller/espionage. Query before sending any material. Endeavors to report 2 weeks on queries; 4-6 weeks on mss.
Recent Sales: *The Gangster of Love*, by Jessica Hagedorn (Houghton Mifflin); *Coming Out of Shame*, by Gershon Kaufman, PhD and Leu Raphael, PhD (Doubleday); *The Gifts of the Body*, by Rebecca Brown (HarperCollins); *The Other World*, by John Wynne (City Lights Books); *Growing Your Own Business*, by Gregory and Patricia Kishel (Putnam's).
Terms: Agent receives 15% commission on domestic sales; 20% commission on foreign sales. Offers written contract "on occasion—time frame always subject to consultation with author." Charges for "photocopying, long distance telephone calls and faxes, ms submission postage costs."
Tips: Obtains new clients through recommendations from others and solicitation. "I cannot stress enough how important it is for the new writer to present a clear, concise and professionally presented query letter. And, please, NEVER send material until requested. Also, please don't call to pitch your material. We cannot answer any phone queries. The information on how to acquire representation is clearly stated in this entry. Thanks."

SUSAN SCHULMAN, A LITERARY AGENCY, (III), 454 W. 44th St., New York NY 10036-5205. (212)713-1633/4/5. Fax: (212)586-8830. President: Susan Schulman. Estab. 1979. Member of AAR, Dramatists Guild, Women's Media Group, signatory of WGA. 10-15% of clients are new/unpublished writers. Prefers to work with published/established authors; works with a small number of new/unpublished authors. Currently handles: 70% nonfiction books; 20% novels; 10% stage plays. Member agent: Holly Frederick (foreign rights).
Handles: Nonfiction, fiction, plays, emphasizing contemporary women's fiction and nonfiction books of interest to women. Considers these nonfiction areas: anthropology/archaeology; biography/autobiography; business; child guidance/parenting; current affairs; education; ethnic/cultural interests; gay/lesbian issues; government/politics/law; health/medicine; history; how-to; juvenile nonfiction; military/war; money/finance/economics; music/dance/theater/film; nature/environment; New Age/metaphysics; popular culture; psychology; religious/inspirational; self-help/personal improvement; sociology; trans-

---

ALWAYS include a self-addressed, stamped envelope (SASE) for reply or return of your manuscript.

lations; true crime/investigative; women's issues/women's studies. Considers these fiction areas: contemporary issues; detective/police/crime; historical; lesbian; literary; mainstream; mystery/suspense; young adult. Query with outline. Reports in 2 weeks on queries; 6 weeks on mss. SASE required.
Recent Sales: *The Psychic Pathway*, by Sonia Choquette (Crown Publishing); *The Vein of Gold*, by Julia Cameron.
Also Handles: Movie scripts (feature film), stage plays. Considers these script subject areas: comedy; contemporary issues; detective/police/crime; feminist; historical; mainstream; mystery/suspense; teen. Query with outline/proposal and SASE. Reports in 2 weeks on queries; 2 months on mss.
Recent Sales: *Mockingbird*, by Walter Tenis (New Line); *The English Patient*, by Michael Ondaate (Saul Zaentz); *Voodoo Dreams*, by Jewell Parker Rhodes (Steve Tisch Co.); *Evelyn & the Polka King*, by John Olive (Amblin Entertainment).
Terms: Agent receives 15% commission on domestic sales; 10-20% on dramatic sales; 7½-10% on foreign sales (plus 7½-10% to co-agent). Charges for special messenger or copying services, foreign mail and any other service requested by client.

LAURENS R. SCHWARTZ AGENCY, (II), 5 E. 22nd St., Suite 15D, New York NY 10010-5315. (212)228-2614. Contact: Laurens R. Schwartz. Estab. 1984. Represents 100 clients. "General mix of nonfiction and fiction. Also handles movie and TV tie-ins, all licensing and merchandising. Works world-wide. *Very* selective about taking on new clients. Only takes on 2-3 new clients per year."
Handles: No unsolicited mss. Reports in 1 month.
Terms: Agent receives 15% commission on domestic sales; up to 25% on foreign sales. "No fees except for photocopying, and that fee is avoided by an author providing necessary copies or, in certain instances, transferring files on diskette—must be IBM compatible." Where necessary to bring a project into publishable form, editorial work and some rewriting provided as part of service. Works with authors on long-term career goals and promotion.
Tips: "Do not like receiving mass mailings sent to all agents. Be selective—do your homework. Do not send *everything* you have ever written. Choose *one* work and promote that. *Always* include an SASE. *Never* send your only copy. *Always* include a background sheet on yourself and a *one*-page synopsis of the work (too many summaries end up being as long as the work)."

SEBASTIAN LITERARY AGENCY, (III), 333 Kearny St., Suite 708, San Francisco CA 94108. (415)391-2331. Fax: (415)391-2377. Owner Agent: Laurie Harper. Estab. 1985. Member of AAR. Represents approximately 50 clients. Specializes in business, sociology and current affairs. Taking new clients selectively; mainly by referral.
Handles: Nonfiction only at this time. "No children's or YA." Considers these nonfiction areas: anthropology/archaeology; art/architecture/design; biography; business; child guidance/parenting; computers/electronics; consumer reference; current affairs; ethnic/cultural interests; government/politics/law; health/medicine; history; money/finance/economics; psychology; self-help/personal improvement; sociology; sports; true crime/investigative; women's issues/women's studies. Reports in 3 weeks on queries; 6 weeks on mss.
Recent Sales: *David Copperfield's "Tales of the Impossible,"* created and edited by Janet Berliner and David Copperfield (HarperCollins); *The Frugal Investor*, by Scott Spiering (AMACOM); *Natural Beauty All Year Long*, by Janice Cox (Henry Holt/Owl); *The Consumer's Quick Guide to Diet and Nutrition*, by James Marti (Houghton Mifflin); *The Dance Theatre of Harlem*, by Mary C. Kerner (Dutton).
Terms: Agent receives 15% commission on domestic sales; 20% on foreign sales. Offers written contract.
Fees: No reading fees. Charges a $100 annual administration fee for clients and charges for photocopies of ms for submission to publisher. No reading fees.
Writers' Conferences: ASJA (Los Angeles, February).
Tips: Obtains new clients mostly through "referrals from authors and editors, but some at conferences and some from unsolicited queries from around the country."

LYNN SELIGMAN, LITERARY AGENT, (II), 400 Highland Ave., Upper Montclair NJ 07043. (201)783-3631. Contact: Lynn Seligman. Estab. 1985. Member of Women's Media Group. Represents 32 clients. 15% of clients are new/previously unpublished writers. Currently handles: 75% nonfiction books; 15% novels; 10% photography books.
- Prior to opening her agency, Ms. Seligman worked in the subsidiary rights department of Doubleday and Simon & Schuster and served as an agent with Julian Bach Literary Agency (now IMG-Julian Bach).
Handles: Nonfiction books, novels, photography books. Considers these nonfiction areas: anthropology/archaeology; art/architecture/design; biography/autobiography; business; child guidance/parenting; cooking/food/nutrition; current affairs; education, ethnic/cultural interests; government/politics/law; health/medicine; history; how-to; humor; interior design/decorating; language/literature/criticism; money/finance/economics; music/dance/theater/film; nature/environment; photography; popular cul-

ture; psychology; science/technology; self-help/personal improvement; sociology; translations; true crime/investigative; women's issues/women's studies. Considers these fiction areas: contemporary issues; detective/police/crime; ethnic; fantasy; feminist; gay; historical; horror; humor/satire; lesbian; literary; mainstream; mystery/suspense; romance (contemporary, gothic, historical, regency); science fiction. Query with letter or outline/proposal, 1 sample chapter and SASE. Reports in 2 weeks on queries; 2 months on mss.
Recent Sales: *Raising A Thinking Child Workbook*, by Myrna B. Shure & Theresa di Geronimo (Henry Holt); *A Game Of Universe* and *Dry Water*, by Eric Nylund (Avon Books); *20 Strategies to Make You Successful in Business*, by Susan Bixley (Ballantine).
Terms: Agent receives 15% commission on domestic sales; 25% on foreign sales. Charges for photocopying, unusual postage or telephone expenses (checking first with the author), express mail.
Writers' Conferences: Attends Dorothy Canfield Fisher Conference.
Tips: Obtains new clients usually from other writers or from editors.

THE SEYMOUR AGENCY, (II), 17 Rensselaer Ave., Heuvelton NY 13654. Phone/fax: (315)344-7223. Contact: Mike Seymour/Mary Sue Seymour. Estab. 1992. Member of RWA, New York State Outdoor Writers, OWAA. 50% of clients are new/previously unpublished writers. Specializes in women's fiction. Member agents: Mary Sue Seymour (fiction); Mike Seymour (nonfiction).
Handles: Considers these nonfiction areas: art/architecture/design; juvenile nonfiction; religious/inspirational. Considers these fiction areas: action/adventure; detective/police/crime; ethnic; glitz; historical; horror; humor/satire; mainstream; mystery/suspense; religious/inspirational; romance (contemporary, gothic, historical, medieval, regency); westerns/frontier. Accepts a few young adult horror or humor or upbeat romance or adventure. Will read well thought out nonfiction proposals, and any good fiction in any genre. Query with first chapter and synopsis. No certified mail, please. Reports in 2 weeks on queries; 1 month on mss.
Recent Sales: *Fool's Paradise*, by Tori Phillips (Harlequin Historicals); *Whispers of the River*, *Whispers of the Mountain*, and *Whispers of the Wind*, by Tom Hron (Dutton/Signet); *Saxon Bride*, by Tamara Leigh (Bantam).
Terms: Agent receives 15% commission on domestic sales; 15% on foreign sales. Offers written contract, binding for 1 year. Offers criticism service for prospective clients only. Postage fee refundable when/if ms sells. 99% of business derived from commissions on ms sales.
Tips: "Send query, synopsis and first 50 pages. If you don't hear from us, you didn't send SASE. We are looking for westerns and romance—women in jeopardy, suspense, contemporary, historical, some regency and any well written fiction and nonfiction. Both agents are New York state certified teachers who have taught writing and are published authors."

CHARLOTTE SHEEDY LITERARY AGENCY, INC.
   ● Ms. Sheedy has joined Sterling Lord Literistic, Inc.

THE SHEPARD AGENCY, (II), Pawling Savings Bank Bldg., Suite 3, Southeast Plaza, Brewster NY 10509. (914)279-2900 or (914)279-3236. Fax: (914)279-3239. Contact: Jean or Lance Shepard. Specializes in "some fiction; nonfiction: business, biography, homemaking; inspirational; self-help." Currently handles: 75% nonfiction books; 5% juvenile books; 20% novels.
Handles: Nonfiction books, scholarly books, novels. Considers these nonfiction areas: agriculture; horticulture; animals; biography/autobiography; business; child guidance/parenting; computers/electronics; cooking/food/nutrition; crafts/hobbies; current affairs; government/politics/law; health/medicine; history; interior design/decorating; juvenile nonfiction; language/literature/criticism; money/finance/economics; music/dance/theater/film; nature/environment; psychology; religious/inspirational; self-help/personal improvement; sociology; sports; women's issues/women's studies. Considers these fiction areas: contemporary issues; family saga; historical; humor/satire; literary; regional; sports; thriller/espionage. Query with outline, sample chapters and SASE. Reports in 6 weeks on queries; 2 months on mss.
Recent Sales: *Crane's Wedding Blue Book*, by Steven Feinberg (Simon & Schuster).
Terms: Agent receives 15% on domestic sales. Offers written contract. Charges for extraordinary postage, photocopying and long-distance phone calls.
Tips: Obtains new clients through referrals and listings in various directories for writers and publishers. "Provide info on those publishers who have already been contacted, seen work, accepted or rejected same. Provide complete bio and marketing info."

‡THE SHUKAT COMPANY LTD., (III), 340 W. 55th St., Suite 1A, New York NY 10019-3766. (212)582-7614. Fax: (212)315-3752. Estab. 1972. Member of AAR. Currently handles: literary and dramatic works. Query with outline/proposal or 30 pages and SASE.

‡ROSALIE SIEGEL, INTERNATIONAL LITERARY AGENCY, INC., (III), 1 Abey Dr., Pennington NJ 08534. (607)737-1007. (609)737-3708. Contact: Rosalie Siegel or Hill Haas. Estab. 1977. Member of

AAR. Represents 35 clients. 10% of clients are new/previously unpublished writers. Specializes in foreign authors, especially French, though diminishing. Currently handles: 45% nonfiction books; 45% novels; 10% juvenile books and short story collections for current clients.
Terms: Agent receives 15% commission on domestic sales; 20% on foreign sales. Offers written contract, with 60 day cancellation clause. Charges for photocopying. 100% of business is derived from commissions.
Tips: Obtains new clients through referrals from writers and friends. "I'm not looking for new authors in an active way."

BOBBE SIEGEL LITERARY AGENCY, (II), 41 W. 83rd St., New York NY 10024-5246. (212)877-4985. Fax: (212)877-4985. Contact: Bobbe Siegel. Estab. 1975. Represents 60 clients. 30% of clients are new/previously unpublished writers. Currently handles: 65% nonfiction books; 35% novels.
Handles: Nonfiction books, novels. Considers these nonfiction areas: archaeology; biography/autobiography; child guidance/parenting; current affairs; nutrition; ethnic; health/medicine; history; juvenile nonfiction; literature; music/dance/theater/film; nature/environment; psychology; self-help/personal improvement; sports; true crime/investigative; women's issues. Considers these fiction areas: action/adventure; contemporary issues; detective/police/crime; ethnic; family saga; fantasy; feminist; glitz; historical; horror; literary; mainstream; mystery/suspense; psychic/supernatural; thriller/espionage. Query. Reports in 2 weeks on queries; 2 months on mss.
Recent Sales: *The Historical Society Mystery*, by Graham Landrum (St. Martin's); *Sisters & Strangers*, by Eileen Curtis (HarperCollins); *Travellin'*, by John Nordall (Macmillan).
Terms: Agent receives 15% on domestic sales; 20% on foreign sales. Offers written contract. Charges for photocopying; long-distance or overseas telephone calls or fax messages; airmail postage, both foreign and domestic.
Writers' Conferences: Vermont Writer's Conference (Burlington).
Tips: Obtains new clients through "word of mouth; editors' and authors' recommendations; through conferences and from people who see my name in publications. Write clear and neat letters of inquiry; always remember to include SASE. Never use dot matrix. In your letter never tell the agent why your book is great. Letters should be spaced and paragraphed so they are easy to read and should not be more than two pages."

SIERRA LITERARY AGENCY, (II), P.O. Box 1090, Janesville CA 96114-1090. (916)253-3250. Contact: Mary Barr. Estab. 1988. Specializes in contemporary women's novels, mainstream fiction and nonfiction, self-help, self-esteem books.
Handles: Fiction, nonfiction books, novels. Considers these nonfiction areas: gay/lesbian issues; government/politics/law; how-to; nature/environment; self-help/personal improvement; women's issues/women's studies. Considers these fiction areas: action/adventure; detective/police/crime; feminist; mainstream. Query with outline or entire ms. Reports in 2 weeks on queries; 6 weeks on mss.
Recent Sales: *A Matter of Time*, by Bud Egeland (I Love Movies, Inc.).
Terms: Agent receives 10% commission on domestic sales; 15% on dramatic sales; 20% on foreign sales. Charges writers for photocopying, phone and overseas postage.
Writers' Conferences: Surrey Writers' Conference (Surrey, British Columbia, Canada).

EVELYN SINGER LITERARY AGENCY INC., (III), P.O. Box 594, White Plains NY 10602-0594. Contact: Lynn Regnis. Estab. 1951. Represents 30 clients. 25% of clients are new/previously unpublished writers. Specializes in nonfiction (adult/juvenile, adult suspense). Member agent: Evelyn Singer (suspense, juveniles).
● Prior to opening her agency, Ms. Singer served as an associate in the Jeanne Hale Literary Agency.
Handles: Nonfiction books, juvenile books, novels. (No textbooks). Considers these nonfiction areas: anthropology/archaeology; biography; business; child guidance; current affairs; ethnic/cultural interests; government/politics/law; health/medicine; how-to; juvenile nonfiction; money/finance/economics; nature/environment; psychology; religious/inspirational; science; self-help/personal improvement; women's issues/women's studies. Considers these fiction areas: contemporary issues; detective/police/crime; ethnic; feminist; historical; literary; mainstream; mystery/suspense; regional; thriller/espionage. Query. Reports in 2 weeks on queries; 6-8 weeks on mss. "SASE must be enclosed for reply or return of manuscript."

 A bullet introduces comments by the editor of the Guide indicating special information about the listing.

Recent Sales: *Destiny*, by Nancy Covert Smith (Avon); *Homecoming For Murder*, by John Armistead (Carroll & Graf); *Indian Uprising on the Rio Grande*, by Franklin Fosom (Univ. of New Mexico Press).

Terms: Agent receives 15% commission on domestic sales; 20% on foreign sales. Offers written contract, binding for 3 years. Charges for long-distance phone calls, overseas postage ("authorized expenses only").

Tips: Obtains new clients through recommendations. "I am accepting writers who have earned at least $20,000 from freelance writing. SASE must accompany all queries and material for reply and or return of manuscript." Enclose biographical material and double-spaced book outline or chapter outline.

VALERIE SMITH, LITERARY AGENT, (III), 1746 Rt. 44/55, Modena NY 12548-5205. (914)883-5848. Contact: Valerie Smith. Estab. 1978. Represents 30 clients. 1% of clients are new/previously unpublished writers. Specializes in science fiction and fantasy. Currently handles: 2% nonfiction books; 96% novels; 1% novellas; 1% short story collections.

Handles: Novels. Considers these fiction areas: fantasy; literary; mainstream; science fiction; young adult. Query. Reports in 2 weeks on queries; 2 months on mss.

Recent Sales: *The Enchanted Forest*, by Patricia C. Wrede (Harcourt Brace); *Freedom and Necessity*, by Steven Brust & Emma Bull (TOR).

Terms: Agent receives 15% commission on domestic sales; 20% on foreign sales. Offers written contract. Charges for "extraordinary expenses by mutual consent."

Tips: Obtains new clients through recommendations from other clients, various respected contacts.

MICHAEL SNELL LITERARY AGENCY, (II), P.O. Box 1206, Truro MA 02666-1206. (508)349-3718. Contact: Michael Snell. Estab. 1980. Represents 200 clients. 25% of clients are new/previously unpublished authors. Specializes in how-to, self-help and all types of business and computer books, from low-level how-to to professional and reference. Currently handles: 90% nonfiction books; 10% novels. Member agents: Michael Snell (nonfiction); Patricia Smith (fiction and children's books).

● Prior to opening his agency, Mr. Snell served as an editor at Wadsworth and Addison-Wesley for 13 years.

Handles: Nonfiction books. Open to all nonfiction categories, especially business, health, law, medicine, psychology, science, women's issues. Query with SASE. Reports in 1 week on queries; 2 weeks on mss.

Recent Sales: *The Third Agenda: Working Women on the Edge of Change*, by Deborah Swiss (Peterson's); *The Art of Achievement*, by Emmitt Murphy (John Wiley & Sons); *River Teeth*, by David J. Duncan (Doubleday/Bantam); *The Woman Manager's Troubleshooter*, by Vickie Montgomery (Prentice-Hall); *Reinventing the Business Meeting*, by Ava Butler (McGraw-Hill).

Terms: Agent receives 15% on domestic sales; 15% on foreign sales.

Tips: Obtains new clients through unsolicited mss, word-of-mouth, *LMP* and *Guide to Literary Agents*. "Send a half- to a full-page query, with SASE. Brochure 'How to Write a Book Proposal' available on request and SASE."

ELYSE SOMMER, INC., (II), P.O. Box 1133, Forest Hills NY 11375. (718)263-2668. President: Elyse Sommer. Estab. 1952. Member of AAR. Represents 20 clients. Works with a small number of new/unpublished authors. Specializes in nonfiction: reference books, dictionaries, popular culture. Currently handles: 90% nonfiction books; 5% novels; 5% juvenile.

Handles: Nonfiction books, novels (some mystery but no science fiction), juvenile (no pre-school). Query with outline. Reports in 2 weeks on queries.

Terms: Agent receives 15% commission on domestic sales (when advance is under 5,000, 10% over); 5% on dramatic sales; 20% on foreign sales. Charges for photocopying, long distance, express mail, extraordinary expenses.

F. JOSEPH SPIELER, (II, III), 154 W. 57th St., 13th Floor, Room 135, New York NY 10019. (212)757-4439. Fax: (212)333-2019. Contact: Joe Spieler, Lisa Ross or John Thornton. West Coast office: contact Victoria Shoemaker, principal agent, 1328 Sixth Street, #3, Berkeley CA 94710. (510)528-2616. Fax: (510)528-8117. Estab. 1981. Represents 47 clients. 2% of clients are new/previously unpublished writers. Member agents: John Thornton (nonfiction); Lisa M. Ross (fiction/nonfiction); Ginger Wade (fiction).

Handles: Nonfiction books, novels. Considers these nonfiction areas: biography/autobiography; business; child guidance/parenting; cooking/food/nutrition; current affairs; ethnic/cultural interests; gay/lesbian issues; government/politics/law; history; money/finance/economics; sociology; women's issues/women's studies. Considers these fiction areas: ethnic; family saga; feminist; gay; humor/satire; lesbian; literary; mainstream. Query. Reports in 2 weeks on queries; 5 weeks on mss.

Recent Sales: *The Fifth Discipline Fieldbook*, by Bryan Smith/Peter Senge (Doubleday); *Blindside*, by Eamonn Fingelton (Houghton Mifflin).

Terms: Agent receives 15% commission on domestic sales. Charges for long distance phone/fax, photocopying, postage.
Writers' Conferences: Frankfurt Bookfair (October); ABA (Chicago, June).
Tips: Obtains new clients through recommendations and *Literary Market Place* listing.

PHILIP G. SPITZER LITERARY AGENCY, (III), 50 Talmage Farm Lane, East Hampton NY 11937. (516)329-3650. Fax: (516)329-3651. Contact: Philip Spitzer. Estab. 1969. Member of AAR. Represents 60 clients. 10% of clients are new/previously unpublished writers. Specializes in mystery/suspense, literary fiction, sports, general nonfiction (no how-to). Currently handles: 50% nonfiction books; 50% novels.
  ● Prior to opening his agency, Mr. Spitzer served at New York University Press, McGraw Hill and the John Cushman Associates literary agency.
Handles: Nonfiction books, novels. Considers these nonfiction areas: biography/autobiography; business; current affairs; ethnic/cultural interests; government/politics/law; health/medicine; history; language/literature/criticism; military/war; music/dance/theater/film; nature/environment; psychology; popular culture; sociology; sports; true crime/investigative. Considers these fiction areas: contemporary issues; detective/police/crime; literary; mainstream; mystery/suspense; sports; thriller/espionage. Send outline plus 1 sample chapter and SASE. Reports in 1 week on queries; 6 weeks on mss.
Recent Sales: *The Poet*, by Michael Connelly (Little, Brown); *Burning Angel*, by James Lee Burke (Hyperion); *Transforming The Corporation*, by Francis Gonillart & James Kelly (McGraw-Hill); *Dancing After Hours*, Andre Dubus (Knopf); *What We Know So Far: The Wisdom of Women*, by Beth Benatorich (St. Martin's Press); *The Game of Their Lives*, by Geoffrey Douglas (Holt).
Terms: Agent receives 15% commission on domestic sales; 20% on foreign sales. Charges for photocopying.
Writers' Conferences: ABA (Chicago).
Tips: Usually obtains new clients on referral.

NANCY STAUFFER ASSOCIATES, (II, III), 171 Newbury St., Boston MA 02116-2839. (617)247-0356. Fax: (617)267-2412. Contact: Nancy Stauffer Cahoon. Estab. 1989. Member of PEN Center USA West; Boston Literary Agents Society; and Advisory Board Member, Writers At Work. 10% of clients are new/previously unpublished writers. Currently handles: 50% nonfiction books; 50% fiction.
Handles: Nonfiction books, novels, novellas, short story collections. Considers these nonfiction areas: animals; biography/autobiography; business; current affairs; ethnic/cultural interests; nature/environment; popular culture; self-help/personal improvement; sociology; translations. Considers these fiction areas: contemporary issues; literary; mainstream; regional. No unsolicited queries.
Recent Sales: *Indian Killer*, by Sherman Alexie (Grove/Atlantic); *Hole In Our Soul*, by Martha Bayles (Univ. of Chicago Press); *Vendetta*, by Arthur Hailey (Crown).
Terms: Agent receives 15% commission on domestic sales; 20% on foreign sales. Charges for messenger and express delivery; photocopying."
Writers' Conferences: Authors of the Flathead (Whitefish MT, October); Writers At Work (Park City UT, July); "I teach a seminar at the UCLA Extension Writers' Program titled 'Getting Published: A One Day Tour Through the World of New York Publishing,' and participate in writers conferences around the country."
Tips: Obtains new clients primarily through referrals from existing clients.

LYLE STEELE & CO., LTD., (II), 511 E. 73rd St., Suite 6, New York NY 10021. (212)288-2981. Contact: Lyle Steele. Estab. 1985. Signatory of WGA. Represents 125 clients. 20% of clients are new/previously unpublished writers. "In nonfiction we are particularly interested in current events, biography and autobiography, popular business, true crime, health, parenting and children's activities, personal growth and psychological self-help. In fiction we are interested in good mysteries not of the hard-boiled type, horror and occult of all types, thrillers and historical novels. We are also open to quality fiction." Currently handles: 90% nonfiction books; 10% novels. Member agents: Jim Kepler (Chicago, nonfiction).
Handles: Nonfiction books, novels. Considers these nonfiction areas: anthropology/archaeology; biography/autobiography; business; child guidance/parenting; cooking/food/nutrition; current affairs; ethnic/cultural interests; gay/lesbian issues; government/politics/law; health/medicine; history; money/finance/economics; nature/environment; New Age/metaphysics; psychology; science/technology; self-help/personal improvement; sociology; sports; true crime/investigative. Considers these fiction areas: detective/police/crime; family saga; gay; historical; horror; lesbian; literary; mystery/suspense; psychic/supernatural; thriller/espionage; horror. Send outline plus 2 sample chapters. Reports in 10 days on queries; 2 weeks on mss.
Recent Sales: *Testament to Truth*, by Arun Gundhi (Harper); *Show and Sell*, by Margit Weisgul (Amacom); *More Healthy Snacks for Kids* (Contemporary).
Terms: Agent receives 15% commission on domestic sales. Offers written contract, binding for 1 year.

Tips: Obtains new clients through recommendations and solicitations. "Our goal is to represent books that provide readers with solid information they can use to improve and change their personal and professional lives. In addition, we take the long view of an author's career. A successful writing career is built step by step, and our goal is to provide the long-term professional management required to achieve it. Be prepared to send your material quickly once an agent has responded. Frequently, we'll have room to take on only a few new clients and a slow response may mean the openings will be filled by the time your material arrives."

STEPPING STONE, (IV), 59 W. 71st St., New York NY 10023. (212)362-9277. Fax: (212)501-8240. Contact: Sarah Jane Freymann. Member of AAR. Represents 75 clients. 20% of clients are new/previously unpublished writers. Currently handles: 75% nonfiction books; 2% juvenile books; 23% novels.
Handles: Nonfiction books, novels, lifestyle-illustrated. Considers these nonfiction areas: animals; anthropology/archaeology; art/architecture/design; biography/autobiography; business; child guidance/parenting; cooking/food/nutrition; current affairs; ethnic/cultural interests; gay/lesbian issues; health/medicine; history; interior design/decorating; nature/environment; New Age/metaphysics; psychology; religious/inspirational; self-help/personal improvement; women's issues/women's studies. Considers these fiction areas: contemporary issues; ethnic; literary; mainstream; mystery/suspense; thriller/espionage. Query with SASE. Reports in 2 weeks on queries; 6 weeks on mss.
Recent Sales: *Rena's Promise*, by Rena Gillissen (Beacon Press); *A Woman in Amber*, by Agate Nesaule (Soho Press); *Mediterranean Pantry*, by A. Kremezi (Workman/Artisan); *Rituals for the Bath*, by K. Corey & L. Blackmen (Warner Books); *Find a Quiet Corner: A Simple Guide to Self Peace*, by Nancy O'Hara (Warner Books); *Burning Time* and *Hanging Time*, by Leslie Glass (Bantam).
Terms: Agent receives 15% commission on domestic sales; 20% on foreign sales. Offers written contract. Charges for long distance, overseas postage, photocopying. 100% of business is derived from commissions on ms sales.
Tips: Obtains new clients through recommendations from others. "I love fresh new passionate works by authors who love what they are doing and have both natural talent and carefully honed skill."

GLORIA STERN LITERARY AGENCY, (II,III,IV), 2929 Buffalo Speedway, Houston TX 77098-1707. (713)963-8360. Fax: (713)963-8460. Contact: Gloria Stern. Estab. 1976. Member of AAR. Represents 35 clients. 20% of clients are new/previously unpublished writers. Specializes in history, biography, women's studies, child guidance, parenting, business, cookbooks, health, cooking, finance, sociology, true crime. Currently handles: 80% nonfiction books; 5% scholarly books; 15% novels.
   • This agency is not affiliated with the Gloria Stern Agency located in California.
Handles: Nonfiction books, scholarly books, novels. Considers these nonfiction areas: anthropology/archaeology; art/architecture/design; biography; business; child guidance/parenting; cooking/food/nutrition; current affairs; ethnic/cultural interests; government/politics/law; health/medicine; history; how-to; language/literature/criticism; money/finance/economics; psychology; science/technology; self-help/personal improvement; sociology; sports; true crime/investigative; women's issues/women's studies. Considers these fiction areas: contemporary issues; detective/police/crime; ethnic; experimental; family saga; feminist; literary; mainstream; mystery/suspense; thriller/espionage. Query with outline plus 2 sample chapters and SASE. No unsolicited mss. Reports in 1 week on queries; 1 month on mss.
Recent Sales: *Stefan in Love*, by Joseph Machlis (W.W. Norton); *Breaking the Science Barrier*, by Sheila Tobias and Carl Tomizoka (College Board); *Big Noise from Winnetka*, by Jeanne N. Clark (biography of Harold Ikes).
Terms: Agent receives 15% commission on domestic sales; 20% on foreign sales (shared). Offers written contract, binding for 60 days.
Tips: Obtain new clients through editors, previous clients, listings. "I prefer fiction authors that have some published work such as short stories in either commercial or literary magazines or come recommended by an editor or writer. I need a short outline of less than a page, one or two chapters and SASE. For nonfiction, I need credentials, an outline, competitive books, one or two chapters and SASE."

‡ROSLYN TARG LITERARY AGENCY, INC., (III), 105 W. 13th St., New York NY 10011. (212)206-9390. Fax: (212)989-6233. Contact: Roslyn Targ. Original agency estab. 1945; name changed to Roslyn Targ Literary Agency, Inc. in 1970. Member of AAR. Represents approximately 100 clients.
Handles: Nonfiction books, juvenile books, novels, self-help, genre fiction. No mss without queries first. Query with outline, proposal, curriculum vitae, and SASE.
Recent Sales: *Mercy of a Rude Stream: From Bondage* (Vol. 3), by Henry Roth (St. Martin's Press); *Zenzele: A Letter From My Daughter*, by Nozipo Maraire (Crown); *The Passion of Isis & Osiris*, by Jean Houston (Ballantine); *Handyman*, by Jean Heller (Forge); *Natchez*, by Pamela Jekel (Kensington); *The Three Faces of the Mind*, by Elaine Debeauport (Quest); *Mindgames*, by Robert Masters (Quest).

Terms: Agent receives 10-15% commission on domestic sales; 20% on foreign sales. Charges standard agency fees (bank charges, long distance fax, postage, photocopying, shipping of books, etc.).
Tips: Obtains new clients through recommendations, solicitation, queries. "This agency reads on an exclusive basis only."

‡SANDRA TAYLOR LITERARY ENTERPRISES, (II), 38 Fairfield Rd., Hancock NH 03449. (603)525-4436. (603)525-4654. Contact: Sandra Taylor. Estab. 1992. Member of the Boston Literary Agents' Society. Represents 20 clients. 30% of clients are new/previously unpublished writers. Specializes in adult nonfiction. Currently handles: 100% nonfiction books.
Handles: Nonfiction books. Considers these nonfiction areas: animals; cooking/food/nutrition; health/medicine; horticulture; how-to; nature/environment. Send outline/proposal. Reports in 1 month on queries; 6 weeks on mss.
Recent Sales: *Fly-Fishing Guide*, by Gary Lewis and Marnie Crowell (Stackpole Books); *Minnowknits*, by Jil Eaton (Lark Books/Sterling); *Cooking for Friends*, by Susan and Gordon Perry (Alan Hood Publishing).
Terms: Agent receives 15% commission on domestic sales; 20% on foreign sales. Offers written contract. 100% of business is derived from commissions on sales.
Tips: Obtains new clients through recommendations from others, solicitation and conferences.

TCA, (III), 111 W. 57th St., New York NY 10019. Contact: David Chalfant. Estab. 1991. Represents 40 clients. No new/previously unpublished writers. Specializes in general nonfiction. Currently handles: 95% nonfiction books; 5% novels.
Handles: Nonfiction books. Considers these nonfiction areas: biography/autobiography; business; cooking/food/nutrition; current affairs; history; money/finance/economics; true crime/investigative; women's issues/women's studies.
Terms: Agent receives 15% commission on domestic sales; 20% on foreign sales. No written contract.
Tips: Obtains new clients through solicitation by the agent, referrals from existing clients.

PATRICIA TEAL LITERARY AGENCY, (III), 2036 Vista Del Rosa, Fullerton CA 92631-1336. (714)738-8333. Contact: Patricia Teal. Estab. 1978. Member of AAR, RWA, Authors Guild. Represents 60 clients. Published authors only. Specializes in category fiction and commercial, how-to and self-help nonfiction. Currently handles: 10% nonfiction books; 90% novels.
Handles: Nonfiction books, novels. Considers these nonfiction areas: animals; biography/autobiography; child guidance/parenting; health/medicine; how-to; psychology; self-help/personal improvement; true crime/investigative; women's issues. Considers these fiction areas: glitz, mainstream, mystery/suspense, romance (contemporary, historical, regency). Query. Reports in 10 days on queries; 6 weeks on requested mss.
Recent Sales: Historicals by Jill Marie Landis (Berkley/Jove); mystery series by Sherry Lewis (Berkley/PrimeCrime); mainstream woman's novel by Taylor Smith (Mira Books); spiritual nonfiction by Albert Gaulden (Warner); series category romances by Marie Ferrarella (Silhouette Books).
Terms: Agent receives 10-15% commission on domestic sales; 20% on foreign sales. Offers written contract, binding for 1 year. Charges for postage, photocopying.
Writers' Conferences: Romance Writers of America conferences; Asilomar (California Writers Club); Bouchercon; Emerald City (Seattle); ABA (Chicago, June); Romance Writers of America (Dallas TX July); California State University San Diego (January).
Tips: Usually obtains new clients through recommendations from authors and editors or at conferences. "Include SASE with all correspondence."

‡TOAD HALL, INC., (IV), RR 2, Box 16B, Laceyville PA 18623. (717)869-2942. Fax: (717)869-1031. E-mail: toadhall@epix.net. Contact: Sharon Jarvis, Anne Pinzow. Estab. 1982. Member of AAR. Represents 55 clients. 15% of clients are new/previously unpublished writers. Specializes in popular nonfiction, some category fiction. Prefers New Age, paranormal, unusual but popular approaches. Currently handles: 40% nonfiction books; 50% novels; 5% movie scripts; 5% ancillary projects.
Handles: Nonfiction books. Considers these nonfiction areas: animals; anthropology/archaeology; business; child guidance/parenting; cooking/food/nutrition; crafts/hobbies; health/medicine; how-to; nature/environment; New Age/metaphysics; popular culture; religious/inspirational; self-help/personal improvement. Considers these fiction areas: historical; mystery/suspense; romance (contemporary,

---

Agents who specialize in a specific subject area such as computer books or in handling the work of certain writers such as gay or lesbian writers are ranked IV.

historical, regency); science fiction. Query. Reports in 3 weeks on queries; 3 months on mss.
Recent Sales: *Ablaze!*, by Larry Arnold (M. Evans); *Daemons*, by Camille Bacon-Smith (DAW); UFO model kit, by McDonald, Randle & Schmitt (Testor).
Terms: Agent receives 15% commission on domestic sales; 15% on foreign sales. Offers written contract, binding for 1 year. Charges for photocopying and special postage (i.e., express mail). 100% of business is derived from commissions on sales.
Tips: Obtains new clients through recommendations from others, solicitation, conferences. "Pay attention to what is getting published. Show the agent you've done your homework!"

‡SUSAN TRAVIS LITERARY AGENCY, (I), 1317 N. San Fernando Blvd., #175, Burbank CA 91504. (818)557-6538. Fax: (818)557-6549. Contact: Susan Travis. Estab. 1995. Represents 10 clients. 60% of clients are new/previously unpublished writers. Specializes in mainstream fiction and nonfiction. Currently handles: 70% nonfiction books; 30% novels.
   • Prior to opening her agency, Ms. Travis served as an agent with the McBride Agency.
Handles: Nonfiction books, novels. Considers these nonfiction areas: agriculture/horticulture; biography/autobiography; business; child guidance/parenting; cooking/food/nutrition; crafts/hobbies; ethnic/cultural interests; gay/lesbian issues; health/medicine; how-to; interior design/decorating; money/finance/economics; nature/environment; popular culture; psychology; religious/inspirational; self-help/personal improvement; women's issues/women's studies. Considers these fiction areas: action/adventure; contemporary issues; detective/police/crime; erotica; ethnic; feminist; gay; historical; lesbian; literary; mainstream; mystery/suspense; romance (historical); thriller/espionage. Query. Reports in 2 weeks on queries; 1 month on mss.
Terms: Agent receives 15% commission on domestic sales; 20% on foreign sales. Offers written contract, binding for 1 year, with 60 day cancellation clause. Charges for photocopying of mss and proposals if copies not provided by author. 100% of business is derived from commissions on sales.
Tips: Obtains new clients through referrals from existing clients, and mss requested from query letters.

2M COMMUNICATIONS LTD., (II), 121 W. 27 St., #601, New York NY 10001. (212)741-1509. Fax: (212)691-4460. Contact: Madeleine Morel. Estab. 1982. Represents 40 clients. 20% of clients are new/previously unpublished writers. Specializes in adult nonfiction. Currently handles: 100% nonfiction books.
Handles: Nonfiction books. Considers these nonfiction areas: biography/autobiography; child guidance/parenting; ethnic/cultural interests; gay/lesbian issues; health/medicine; music/dance/theater/film; self-help/personal improvement; women's issues/women's studies. Query. Reports in 1 week on queries, weeks on outlines.
Recent Sales: *Contemporary Catholicism*, by P. Ryan, PhD (Henry Holt); *Passover Dessert Cookbook*, by Penny Eisenberg (Macmillan); *American Folk Remedies*, by Elena Oumano (Avon).
Terms: Agent receives 15% commission on domestic sales; 20% on foreign sales. Offers written contract, binding for 2 years. Charges for postage, photocopying, long distance calls and faxes.
Tips: Obtains new clients through recommendations from others, solicitation.

‡ROBERT UBELL ASSOCIATES, (II, IV), 111 Eighth Ave., Suite 1503, New York NY 10011. (212)645-3303. Fax: (212)645-5988. E-mail: 73303.111@CompuServe.com. Contact: Robert Ubell, president. Estab. 1988. Represents 12 clients. 20% of clients are new/previously unpublished writers. Specializes in science, technology, medicine for general audiences. Currently handles: 95% nonfiction books; 4% scholarly books; 1% textbooks.
Handles: Nonfiction books, scholarly books, textbooks. Considers these nonfiction areas: animals, anthropology/archaeology; biography/autobiography; computers/electronics; health/medicine; nature/environment; psychology; science/technology. Query with outline and 2 sample chapters. Reports in 6 weeks on queries; 2 months on mss.
Recent Sales: *Scientific American Focus Series*, by various authors (Henry Holt/Owl); *Earl Ubell's Parade Family Guide to Health*, by Earl Ubell (Prima); *Encyclopedia of Revolutions*, by J.C. Suares (Congressional Quarterly); *Manual of Scientific Style*, by H. Rabinowitz (Springer Verlag).
Terms: Agent receives 15% commission on domestic sales; commission varies on foreign sales. Offers written contract, binding for variable length of time. Charges for phone, postage, fax, photocopying, etc., only in the event of a sale and deducted from advance. 100% of business is derived from commissions on sales.
Tips: Obtains new clients through referrals from others.

*SUSAN P. URSTADT INC. AGENCY, (II), P.O. Box 1676, New Canaan CT 06840-4208. (203)966-6111. Contact: Susan P. Urstadt. Estab. 1975. Member of AAR. Represents 45 clients. 10% of clients are new/previously unpublished authors. Specializes in history, biography, current affairs and journalism, natural history and environment, illustrated books, popular reference, art, antiques, decorative arts, gardening, travel, horses, armchair cookbooks, business, medical, self-help, crafts, hobbies, collectibles. Currently handles: 95% nonfiction books.

Handles: Nonfiction books and select quality commercial literary fiction. Considers these nonfiction areas: agriculture/horticulture; animals; anthropology/archaeology; art/architecture/design; biography/autobiography; business; child guidance/parenting; cooking/food/nutrition; crafts/hobbies; current affairs; education; ethnic/cultural interests; health/medicine; history; how-to; interior design/decorating; juvenile nonfiction; military/war; money/finance/economics; music/dance/theater/film; nature/environment; photography; popular culture; self-help/personal improvement; sports; women's issues/women's studies. "No unsolicited fiction please." Send outline, 2 sample chapters, short author bio and SASE. "Tell us 'why this book'." Reports in 3 weeks on queries.
Recent Sales: *Book of Traditions*, by Emyl Jenkins (Crown); *New England Fish Tales*, by Martha Murphy (Holt); *Roses for Cold Climates*, by Doug Green (Chapters); *Riding the Dragon*, (business), by Donald Krause (Putnam).
Terms: Agent receives 15% commission on domestic sales; 20% on foreign sales. Offers written contract.
Writers' Conferences: ABA (Chicago, June).
Tips: Obtains new clients through recommendations from others and from high quality proposals. "We are interested in building a writer's career through the long term and only want dedicated writers with special knowledge, which they share in a professional way."

‡THE RICHARD R. VALCOURT AGENCY, (I, II), 177 E. 77th St., PHC, New York NY 10021. Phone/fax: (212)570-2340. Contact: Richard R. Valcourt. Estab. 1995. Represents 20 clients. 1% of clients are new/previously unpublished writers. Specializes in intelligence and other national security affairs; domestic and international politics; current events and biographies. Currently handles: 90% nonfiction books; 10% novels.
Handles: Nonfiction books, scholarly books, novels. Considers these nonfiction areas: biography; business; current affairs; education; ethnic/cultural interests; government/politics/law; health/medicine; history; language/literature/criticism; military/war; money/finance/economics; sociology. Considers these fiction areas: contemporary issues; historical; thriller/espionage. Query with SASE. Reports in 1 week on queries; 1 month on mss.
Terms: Agent receives 15% commission on domestic sales; 20% on foreign sales. Offers written contract. Charges for photocopying, express mail and extensive overseas telephone expenses.
Writers' Conferences: Frankfurt Book Fair (Germany, October).
Tips: Obtains new clients through active recruitment and recommendations from others. "Newly established firm seeks works on government, politics, journalism and academics."

VAN DER LEUN & ASSOCIATES, (II), 22 Division St., Easton CT 06612. (203)259-4897. Contact: Cathie Ricci. Estab. 1984. Represents 30 clients. Specializes in fiction, science, biography. Currently handles: 60% nonfiction books; 40% novels. Member agent: Patricia Van der Leun.
Handles: Nonfiction books, novels. Considers all nonfiction areas. Considers these nonfiction areas: art/architecture/design; contemporary issues; ethnic; history; literary; mainstream. Query. Reports in 2 weeks on queries; 1 month on mss.
Recent Sales: *Zen Physics*, by David Darling (HarperCollins); *From Beginning to End*, by Robert Fulghum (Villard Books); *Wherever You Go, There You Are*, by Jon Kabat-Zinn (Hyperion).
Terms: Agent receives 15% on domestic sales; 25% on foreign sales. Offers written contract.
Tips: "We are interested in high-quality, serious writers only."

‡ANNETTE VAN DUREN AGENCY, (III), 925 N. Sweetzer Ave., #12, Los Angeles CA 90069. (213)650-3643. Fax: (213)654-3893. Contact: Annette Van Duren or Patricia Murphy. Estab. 1985. Signatory of WGA. Represents 12 clients. No clients are new/previously unpublished writers. Currently handles: 10% novels; 50% movie scripts; 40% TV scripts.
  • See the expanded listing for this agency in Script Agents.

‡THE VINES AGENCY, INC. (II), 409 E. Sixth St., #4, New York NY 10009. (212)777-5522. Fax: (212)777-5978. Contact: Jimmy Vines. Estab. 1995. Represents 21 clients. 2% of clients are new/previously unpublished writers. Specializes in mystery, suspense, science fiction, mainstream novels, graphic novels, CD-ROMS, screenplays, teleplays. Currently handles: 10% nonfiction books; 2% scholarly books; 10% juvenile books; 50% novels; 15% movie scripts; 5% TV scripts; 1% stage plays; 5% short story collections; 2% syndicated material.
  • Prior to opening his agency, Mr. Vines served as an agent with the Literary Group.
Handles: Nonfiction books, juvenile books, novels, movie scripts, TV scripts. Considers these nonfiction areas: business; child guidance/parenting; how-to; humor; juvenile nonfiction; money/finance/economics; music/dance/theater/film; popular culture; psychology; true crime/investigative; women's issues/women's studies. Considers these fiction areas: action/adventure; cartoon/comic; contemporary issues; detective/police/crime; ethnic; fantasy; feminist; horror; humor/satire; juvenile; literary; mainstream; mystery/suspense; picture book; psychic/supernatural; regional; romance (contemporary, gothic, historical, regency); science fiction; sports; thriller/espionage; westerns/frontier; young adult.

Send outline and first 3 chapters with SASE. Reports in 2 weeks on queries; 1 month on mss.

Recent Sales: *Pest Control*, by Bill Fitzhugh, film rights to Spring Creek Productions for Warner Bros.).

Terms: Agent receives 15% commission on domestic sales; 20% on foreign sales. Offers written contract, binding for 1 year, with 30 days cancellation clause. Charges for foreign postage and photocopying. 100% of business is derived from commissions on sales.

Writers' Conferences: Kent State Writer's Conference (Kent State University OH).

Tips: Obtains new clients through recommendations from others, reading short stories in magazines and soliciting conferences. "Do not follow up on submissions with phone calls to the agency. The agency will read and respond by mail only. Do not pack your manuscript in plastic 'peanuts' that will make us have to vacuum the office after opening the package containing your manuscript. Always enclose return postage."

MARY JACK WALD ASSOCIATES, INC., (III), 111 E. 14th St., New York NY 10003. (212)254-7842. Contact: Danis Sher. Estab. 1985. Member of Authors Guild, SCBWI. Represents 55 clients. 5% of clients are new/previously unpublished writers. Specializes in literary works, juvenile. Currently handles: adult and juvenile fiction and nonfiction, including some original film/TV scripts. Member agents: Danis Sher, Lem Lloyd. Foreign rights representative: Lynne Rabinoff, Lynne Rabinoff Associates.

Handles: Nonfiction books, juvenile books, novels, novellas, short story collections, movie scripts, TV scripts. Considers these nonfiction areas: biography/autobiography; current affairs; ethnic/cultural interests; history; juvenile nonfiction; language/literature/criticism; music/dance/theater/film; nature/environment; photography; sociology; translations; true crime/investigative. Considers these fiction areas: action/adventure; contemporary issues; detective/police/crime; ethnic; experimental; family saga; feminist; gay; glitz; historical; juvenile; literary; mainstream; mystery/suspense; picture book; satire; thriller; young adult. Query with SASE. Will request more if interested. Reports in 2 months.

Recent Sales: *Tombstones*, by John Peel (Pocket Book series/Simon & Schuster).

Terms: Agent receives 15% commission on domestic sales; 15-30% on foreign sales. Offers written contract, binding for 1 year.

Tips: Obtains new clients through recommendations from others.

WALLACE LITERARY AGENCY, INC., (III), 177 E. 70 St., New York NY 10021. (212)570-9090. Contact: Lois Wallace, Thomas C. Wallace. Estab. 1988. Member of AAR. Represents 125 clients. 5% of clients are new/previously unpublished writers. Specializes in fiction and nonfiction by good writers. Currently handles: 60% nonfiction books; 35% novels; 5% magazine articles and short stories. "We handle poetry, movie scripts, juveniles and stage plays ONLY if written by clients who write trade books."

Handles: Nonfiction books, novels. Considers these nonfiction areas: anthropology/archaeology, biography/autobiography, current affairs, history, literature, military/war, science; true crime/investigative. Considers these fiction areas: literary, mainstream, mystery/suspense. Send outline, 1-2 sample chapters, reviews of previously published books, curriculum vitae, return postage. Reports in 2 weeks on queries; 3 weeks on mss.

Terms: Agent receives 10-15% commission on domestic sales; 20% on foreign sales. Offers written contract; binding until terminated with notice. Charges for photocopying, book shipping (or ms shipping) overseas, legal fees (if needed, with writer's approval), galleys and books needed for representation and foreign sales.

Tips: Obtains new clients through "recommendations from editors and writers we respect."

JOHN A. WARE LITERARY AGENCY, (II), 392 Central Park West, New York NY 10025-5801. (212)866-4733. Fax: (212)866-4734. Contact: John Ware. Estab. 1978. Represents 60 clients. 40% of clients are new/previously unpublished writers. Currently handles: 75% nonfiction books; 25% novels.

● Prior to opening his agency, Mr. Ware served as a literary agent with James Brown Associates/Curtis Brown, Ltd. and as an editor for Doubleday & Company.

Handles: Nonfiction books, novels. Considers these nonfiction areas: animals; anthropology; biography/autobiography (memoirs); current affairs; ethnic/cultural interests; gay/lesbian issues; government/politics/law; health/medicine; history (including oral history, Americana and folklore); investigative journalism; language/literature/criticism; military/war; music/dance/theater/film; nature/environment; popular culture; psychology and health (academic credentials required); science; sports; true crime/

 The double dagger before a listing indicates the listing is new in this edition.

investigative; women's issues/women's studies; 'bird's eye' views of phenomena. Considers these fiction areas: accessible literate noncategory fiction; detective/police/crime; literary; mystery/suspense; thriller/espionage. Query by mail first, include SASE. Reports in 2 weeks on queries.
Recent Sales: *Undaunted Courage*, by Stephen E. Ambrose (Simon & Schuster); *A Crack In Nature: Living and Dying in the Christian Science Church*, by Caroline Fraser (Metropolitan Books/Henry Holt); *Four Corners*, by Kenneth A. Brown (HarperCollins); *Into The Wild*, by Jon Krakauer (Villard/Random House).
Terms: Agent receives 15% commission on domestic sales; 15% on dramatic sales; 20% on foreign sales. Charges for messenger service, photocopying, extraordinary expenses.
Writers' Conferences: Austin Writers' Conference (Austin TX); Southern Connecticut Writer's Conference (Greenwich CT); Southwest Writers' Workshop (Albuquerque NM).
Tips: "Writers must have appropriate credentials for authorship of proposal (nonfiction) or manuscript (fiction); no publishing track record required. Open to good writing and interesting ideas by new or veteran writers."

HARRIET WASSERMAN LITERARY AGENCY, (III), 137 E. 36th St., New York NY 10016. (212)689-3257. Contact: Harriet Wasserman. Member of AAR. Specializes in fiction and nonfiction, some young adult and children's.
Handles: Nonfiction books, novels. Considers "mostly quality fiction (novels)." Referrals only. No unsolicited material.
Terms: Information not provided.

WATERSIDE PRODUCTIONS, INC., (II), 2191 San Elijo Ave., Cardiff-by-the-Sea CA 92007-1839. (619)632-9190. Fax: (619)632-9295. E-mail: 75720.410@CompuServe.com or http://www.waterside.com/waterside. President: Bill Gladstone. Contact: Matt Wagner, Margot Maley. Estab. 1982. Represents 300 clients. 20% of clients are new/previously unpublished writers. Currently handles: 100% nonfiction. Member agents: Bill Gladstone (trade computer titles, business); Margot Maley (women's issues, serious nonfiction, trade computer titles); Matthew Wagner (trade computer titles, nonfiction); Carole McClendon (trade computer titles); David Fugate (trade computer titles, business, multimedia); Chris Van Buren (spirituality, self-help).
Handles: Nonfiction books. Considers these nonfiction areas: anthropology/archaeology; art/architecture/design; biography/autobiography; business; child guidance/parenting; computers/electronics; ethnic/cultural interests; health/medicine; money/finance/economics; nature/environment; New Age/metaphysics; psychology; sociology; sports; true crime/investigative; women's issues/women's studies. Query with outline/proposal. Reports in 2 weeks on queries; 2 months on mss.
Recent Sales: *The Internet Business Book*, by Jill Ellsworth (Wiley); *Parenting For Dummies*, by Sandy Gookin (IDG).
Terms: Agent receives 15% commission on domestic sales; 25% on foreign sales. Offers written contract. Charges for photocopying and other unusual expenses.
Writers' Conferences: Waterside Computer Book Conference (San Diego, CA).
Tips: Usually obtains new clients through recommendations from others. "Be professional. The more professional a submission, the more seriously it's viewed. Beginning writers should go to a writers workshop and learn how a presentation should be made."

WATKINS LOOMIS AGENCY, INC., (II), 133 E. 35th St., Suite 1, New York NY 10016. (212)532-0080. Contact: Lily Oei. Estab. 1908. Represents 150 clients. Specializes in literary fiction, London/UK translations. Member agent: Nicole Aragi.
Handles: Nonfiction books, novels. Considers these nonfiction areas: art/architecture/design; biography/autobiography; cooking/food/nutrition; current affairs; ethnic/cultural interests; gay/lesbian issues; history; nature/environment; popular culture; science/technology; translations; true crime/investigative; women's issues/women's studies; journalism. Considers these fiction areas: contemporary issues; detective/police/crime; ethnic; gay; literary; mainstream; mystery/suspense; young adult. Query with SASE. Reports within 3 weeks on queries.
Recent Sales: *Johnny Critelli*, by Frank Lentricchia (Scribner). *Wilder*, by Nina Bernstein (Pantheon); *If Mama Ain't Happy*, by Helen Prejean (Random House).
Terms: Agent receives 15% commission on domestic sales; 15% on foreign sales.

SANDRA WATT & ASSOCIATES, (II), 8033 Sunset Blvd., Suite 4053, Hollywood CA 90046-2427. (213)851-1021. Contact: Davida South. Estab. 1977. Signatory of WGA. Represents 55 clients. 15% of clients are new/previously unpublished writers. Specializes in scripts: film noir; family; romantic comedies; books: women's fiction, mystery, commercial nonfiction. Currently handles: 40% nonfiction books; 35% novels; 25% movie scripts. Member agents: Sandra Watt (scripts, nonfiction, novels); Davida South (scripts).
Handles: Nonfiction books, novels. Considers these nonfiction areas: agriculture/horticulture; animals; anthropology/archaeology; art/architecture/design; crafts/hobbies; current affairs; how-to; hu-

mor; language/literature/criticism; nature/environment; New Age/metaphysics; popular culture; psychology; reference; religious/inspirational; self-help/personal improvement; sports; true crime/investigative; women's issues/women's studies. Considers these fiction areas: contemporary issues; detective/police/crime; family saga; mainstream; mystery/suspense; regional; religious/inspirational; thriller/espionage; women's mainstream novels. Query. Reports in 1 week on queries; 2 months on mss.

Recent Sales: *Doing Good*, by Raymond Obstfeld (Morrow); *Documents of Greece and Rome*, by Ken Atchity (Holt).

Also Handles: Movie scripts (feature film); TV scripts (TV mow). Considers these script subject areas: contemporary issues; detective/police/crime; family saga; psychic/supernatural; religious/inspirational; romantic comedy and drama.

Recent Sales: *Movie/TV mow optional/sold: Love Bite*, Sherry Gottlist (Lifetime); *Afraid of the Dark*, by Mick Strawser (Citadel); *Ladies of Parkwood Lane*, by Andy Gross (Citadel); *Movie/TV mow in development; Northstar*, by Emily Gaydos (Disney).

Terms: Agent receives 15% commission on domestic sales; 25% on foreign sales. Offers written contract, binding for 1 year.

Fees: Does not charge a reading fee. Charges one-time nonrefundable marketing fee of $100 *for unpublished authors.*

Tips: Obtains new clients through recommendations from others, referrals and "from wonderful query letters. Don't forget the SASE!"

WECKSLER-INCOMCO, (II), 170 West End Ave., New York NY 10023. (212)787-2239. Fax: (212)496-7035. Contact: Sally Wecksler. Estab. 1971. Represents 20 clients. 50% of clients are new/previously unpublished writers. Specializes in nonfiction with illustrations (photos and art). Currently handles: 50% nonfiction books; 15% novels; 35% juvenile books. Member agents: Joann Amparan (general), S. Wecksler (foreign rights/co-editions).

Handles: Nonfiction books, novels, juvenile books. Considers these nonfiction areas: art/architecture design; biography/autobiography; business; current affairs; history; juvenile nonfiction; literary; music/dance/theater/film; nature/environment; photography. Considers these fiction areas: contemporary issues; historical; juvenile; literary; mainstream; picture book. Query with outline plus 3 sample chapters. Reports in 1 month on queries; 2 months on mss.

Recent Sales: *Do's & Taboos-English Around the World*, by Roger Axtell (Wiley).

Terms: Agent receives 12-15% commission on domestic sales; 20% on foreign sales. Offers written contract, binding for 3 years.

Tips: Obtains new clients through recommendations from others and solicitations. "Make sure a SASE is enclosed. Send a clearly typed or word processed manuscript, double-spaced, written with punctuation and grammar in approved style."

THE WENDY WEIL AGENCY, INC. (V), 232 Madison Ave., Suite 1300, New York NY 10016. Member of AAR. This agency did not respond to our request for information. Query before submitting.

CHERRY WEINER LITERARY AGENCY, (IV,V), 28 Kipling Way, Manalapan NJ 07726-3711. (908)446-2096. Fax: (908)446-20963*. Contact: Cherry Weiner. Estab. 1977. Represents 40 clients. 10% of clients are new/previously unpublished writers. Specializes in science fiction, fantasy, westerns, all the genre romances. Currently handles: 2-3% nonfiction books; 97% novels.

● This agency is not currently looking for new clients except by referral or by contact at writers' conferences.

Handles: Nonfiction books, novels. Considers self-help/improvement, sociology nonfiction. Considers these fiction areas: action/adventure; contemporary issues; detective/police/crime; family saga; fantasy; glitz; historical; mainstream; mystery/suspense; psychic/supernatural; romance; science fiction; thriller/espionage; westerns/frontier. Query. Reports in 1 week on queries; 2 months on mss.

Recent Sales: *Strands of Strands* and two more, by Gael Boudino (ROC/NAL); *Lord Meren* series, by Lynda S. Robinson (Walker); *The White Abacus*, by Damien Broderick (Avon/Morrow); *Love and Honor*, by Susan Amarillas (Harlequin); *The Hard Land*, by Jack Ballas (Berkley)..

Terms: Agent receives 15% on domestic sales; 15% on foreign sales. Offers written contract. Charges for extra copies of mss "but would prefer author do it"; 1st class postage for author's copies of books; Express Mail for important document/manuscripts.

Writers' Conferences: Western Writers Convention (Albuquerque, June); Golden Triangle; Fantasy Convention.

Tips: "Meet agents and publishers at conferences. Establish a relationship, then get in touch with them reminding them of meetings and conference."

THE WEINGEL-FIDEL AGENCY, (III), 310 E. 46th St., 21E, New York NY 10017. (212)599-2959. Contact: Loretta Fidel. Estab. 1989. Specializes in commercial, literary fiction and nonfiction. Currently handles: 50% nonfiction books; 50% novels.

Handles: Nonfiction books, novels. Considers these nonfiction areas: art/architecture/design; biography/autobiography; investigative; music/dance/theater/film; psychology; science; sociology; women's issues/women's studies. Considers these fiction areas: contemporary issues; literary; mainstream. Referred writers only. No unsolicited mss.
Recent Sales: *Sleepers*, by Lorenzo Carcaterra (Ballantine, film rights to Propaganda Films).
Terms: Agent receives 15% on domestic sales; 20% on foreign sales. Offers written contract, binding for 1 year automatic renewal. Bills back to clients all reasonable expenses such as UPS, express mail, photocopying, etc.
Tips: Obtains new clients through referrals.

RHODA WEYR AGENCY, (II, III), 151 Bergen St., Brooklyn NY 11217. (718)522-0480. President: Rhoda A. Weyr. Estab. 1983. Member of AAR. Prefers to work with published/established authors; works with a small number of new/unpublished authors. Specializes in general nonfiction and fiction.
Handles: Nonfiction books, novels. Query with outline, sample chapters and SASE.
Terms: Agent receives 15% commission on domestic sales; 20% on foreign sales.

WIESER & WIESER, INC., (III), 118 E. 25th St., 7th Floor, New York NY 10010-2915. (212)260-0860. Contact: Olga Wieser. Estab. 1975. 30% of clients are new/previously unpublished writers. Specializes in mainstream fiction and nonfiction. Currently handles: 50% nonfiction books; 50% novels. Member agents: Jake Elwell (history, contemporary, sports); George Wieser (contemporary fiction, thrillers, current affairs); Olga Wieser (psychology, fiction, historicals, translations, literary fiction).
Handles: Nonfiction books, novels. Considers these nonfiction areas: business; cooking/food/nutrition; current affairs; health/medicine; history; money/finance/economics; nature/environment; psychology; translations; true crime/investigative. Considers these fiction areas: contemporary issues; detective/police/crime; family saga; historical; literary; mainstream; mystery/suspense; thriller/espionage. Query with outline/proposal. Reports in 1 week on queries.
Recent Sales: *Pandora's Clock*, by John Nance (Doubleday) including 4 hour miniseries (Citadel Entertainment and cassette edition (Dore Audio); *HMS Cockerel*, by Dewey Lambdin (Donald I. Fine, Inc.); *Marilyn: Her Life in Her Own Words*, by George Barris (Birch Lane Press).
Terms: Agent receives 15% commission on domestic sales; 20% on foreign sales. Offers written contract. Offers criticism service. "No charge to our clients or potential clients." Charges for duplicating of ms and overseas mailing of ms or promotional material.
Writers' Conferences: ABA (Chicago, June); Frankfurt Book Fair (Frankfurt, October).
Tips: Obtains new clients through author's recommendations and industry professionals.

WITHERSPOON & ASSOCIATES, INC., (II), 157 W. 57th St., Suite 700, New York NY 10019. (212)757-0567. Fax: (212)757-2982. Contact: Michele Geminder. Estab. 1990. Represents 100 clients. 20% of clients are new/previously unpublished writers. Currently handles: 50% nonfiction books; 45% novels; 5% short story collections. Member agent: Maria Massie (subsidiary rights).
Handles: Nonfiction books, novels. Considers these nonfiction areas: anthropology/archaeology; biography/autobiography; business; current affairs; ethnic/cultural interests; gay/lesbian issues; government/politics/law; health/medicine; history; money/finance/economics; music/dance/theater/film; science/technology; self-help/personal improvement; true crime/investigative; women's issues/women's studies. Considers these fiction areas: contemporary issues; detective/police/crime; ethnic; family saga; feminist; gay; glitz; historical; humor/satire; lesbian; literary; mainstream; mystery/suspense; romance (contemporary); thriller/espionage. Query. Reports in 3 weeks on queries; 2 months on mss.
Recent Sales: *Sister to Sister*, by P. Foster (Doubleday/Anc); *Raptor Red*, by R. Bakker (Bantam); *Interstate*, by S. Dixon (Holt); *Open Water*, by M. Flook (Pantheon); *Dreamboat*, by D. Swanson (HarperCollins); *Will My Name Be Shouted Out?*, by Stephen O'Connor (Simon & Schuster).
Terms: Agent receives 15% commission on domestic sales; 20% on foreign sales. Offers written contract.
Writers' Conferences: ABA (Chicago, June); Frankfort (Germany, October).
Tips: Obtains new clients through recommendations from others, solicitation and conferences.

RUTH WRESCHNER, AUTHORS' REPRESENTATIVE, (II, III), 10 W. 74th St., New York NY 10023-2403. (212)877-2605. Fax: (212)595-5843. Contact: Ruth Wreschner. Estab. 1981. Represents 80 clients. 70% of clients are new/unpublished writers. "In fiction, if a client is not published yet, I prefer writers who have written for magazines; in nonfiction, a person well qualified in his field is acceptable." Prefers to work with published/established authors; works with new/unpublished authors. "I will always pay attention to a writer referred by another client." Specializes in popular medicine, health, how-to books and fiction (no pornography, screenplays or dramatic plays). Currently handles: 80% nonfiction books; 10% novels; 5% textbooks; 5% juvenile books.
● Prior to opening her agency, Ms. Wreschner served as an administrative assistant and associate editor at John Wiley & Sons for 17 years.

Handles: Nonfiction books, textbooks, adult and young adult fiction. Considers these nonfiction areas: biography/autobiography; business; child guidance/parenting; cooking/food/nutrition; crafts/hobbies; current affairs; ethnic/cultural interests; gay/lesbian issues; government/politics/law; health/medicine; history; how-to; juvenile nonfiction; money/finance/economics; popular culture; psychology; religious/inspirational; science/technology; self-help/personal improvement; true crime/investigative; women's issues/women's studies. Considers these fiction areas: action/adventure; contemporary issues; detective/police/crime; ethnic; family saga; gay; glitz; historical; horror; juvenile; lesbian; literary; mainstream; mystery/suspense; romance (contemporary, historical, regency); thriller/espionage; young adult. Particularly interested in literary, mainstream and mystery fiction. Query with outline. Reports in 2 weeks on queries.
Recent Sales: *Puppy Love*, by Chris Walkowicz (Howell/Macmillan); *Skin Healthy*, by Norman Levine, MD (Taylor Publishing Co.); *Winning On The Edge*, by Wayne Burkan (John Wiley & Sons); *Pirouette Club* (4-book y/a series), by Isabelle Hall (Avon Books for Young Readers)..
Terms: Agent receives 15% commission on domestic sales; 20% on foreign sales. Charges for photocopying expenses. "Once a book is placed, I will retain some money from the second advance to cover airmail postage of books, long-distance calls, etc. on foreign sales. I may consider charging for reviewing contracts in future. In that case I will charge $50/hour plus long-distance calls, if any."
Writers' Conference: ABA (Chicago, June); New Jersey Romance Writers (September).

ANN WRIGHT REPRESENTATIVES, (II), 165 W. 46th St., New York NY 10036-2501. (212)764-6770. Fax: (212)764-5125. Head of Literary Department: Dan Wright. Estab. 1961. Signatory of WGA. Represents 45 clients. 40% of clients are new/unpublished writers. Prefers to work with published/established authors; works with a small number of new/unpublished authors. "Eager to work with any author with material that we can effectively market in the motion picture business worldwide." Specializes in "book or screenplay with strong motion picture potential." Currently handles: 50% novels; 40% movie scripts; 10% TV scripts.
• See the expanded listing for this agency in Script Agents.

WRITERS HOUSE, (III), 21 W. 26th St., New York NY 10010. (212)685-2400. Fax: (212)685-1781. Contact: John Abrahams. Estab. 1974. Member of AAR. Represents 280 clients. 50% of clients were new/unpublished writers. Specializes in all types of popular fiction and nonfiction, as well as the writing for multimedia projects such as "The Seventh Guest." No scholarly, professional, poetry or screenplays. Currently handles: 25% nonfiction books; 35% juvenile books; 40% novels. Member agents: Albert Zuckerman (major novels, thrillers, women's fiction, important nonfiction); Amy Berkower (major juvenile authors, women's fiction, art and decorating, psychology); Merrillee Heifetz (science fiction and fantasy, popular culture, literary fiction); Susan Cohen (juvenile and young adult fiction and nonfiction, Judaism, women's issues); Susan Ginsberg (serious and popular fiction, true crime, narrative nonfiction, personality books, cookbooks); Fran Lebowitz (juvenile and young adult, mysteries, computer-related books, popular culture); Michele Rubin (serious nonfiction); Liza Landsman (multimedia); Karen Solem (contemporary and historical romance, women's fiction, narrative nonfiction, horse and animal books).
• See Liza Landman's article, New Media and the Agent, in the 1995 edition of the *Guide*.
Handles: Nonfiction books, juvenile books, novels, proposals for multimedia project. Considers these nonfiction areas: animals; art/architecture/design; biography/autobiography; business; child guidance/parenting; cooking/food/nutrition; health/medicine; history; interior design/decorating; juvenile nonfiction; military/war; money/finance/economics; music/dance/theater/film; nature/environment; psychology; science/technology; self-help/personal improvement; true crime/investigative; women's issues/women's studies. Considers any fiction area. "Quality is everything." Query. Reports in 1 month on queries.
Recent Sales: *A Place Called Freedom*, by Ken Follett (Crown); *The Babysitters Club*, by Ann Martin, (Scholastic); *Born In Ice*, by Nora Roberts (Jove); *Writing The Blockbuster Novel*, by Albert Zuckerman (Writers Digest Books).
Terms: Agent receives 15% commission on domestic sales; 20% on foreign sales. Offers written contract, binding for 1 year.
Tips: Obtain new clients through recommendations from others. "Do not send manuscripts. Write a compelling letter. If you do, we'll ask to see your work."

Agents ranked I and II are most open to both established and new writers. Agents ranked III are open to established writers with publishing-industry references.

WRITERS' PRODUCTIONS, (II), P.O. Box 630, Westport CT 06881-0630. (203)227-8199. Contact: David L. Meth. Estab. 1982. Represents 25 clients. Specializes in literary-quality fiction and nonfiction, with a special interest in Asia. Currently handles: 40% nonfiction books; 60% novels.
Handles: Nonfiction books, novels. "Literary quality fiction." Send outline plus 2-3 sample chapters (30-50 pages). Reports in 1 week on queries; 1 month on mss.
Terms: Agent receives 15% on domestic sales; 25% on foreign sales; 25% on dramatic sales; 25% on new media or multimedia sales. Offers written contract. Charges for electronic transmissions, long-distance calls, express or overnight mail, courier service, etc.
Tips: Obtain new clients through word of mouth. "Send only your best, most professionally prepared work. Do not send it before it is ready. We must have SASE for all correspondence and return of manuscripts. No telephone calls, please."

WRITERS' REPRESENTATIVES, INC., (II), 25 W. 19th St., New York NY 10011-4202. (212)620-9009. Contact: Glen Hartley or Lynn Chu. Estab. 1985. Represents 100 clients. 5% of clients are new/previously unpublished writers. Currently handles: 90% nonfiction books; 10% novels.
   • See How Things Work: Book Auctions, an interview with Glen Hartley, in the 1995 edition of the *Guide*.
Handles: Nonfiction books, novels. Considers literary fiction. "Nonfiction submissions should include book proposal, detailed table of contents and sample chapter(s). For fiction submissions send sample chapters, not synopses. All submissions should include author biography and publication list. SASE required." Does not accept unsolicited mss.
Recent Sales: *The Assault on Parenthood*, by Dana Mack (Simon & Schuster); *A Gentle Madness*, by Nicholas A. Basdanes (Henry Holt); *How We Die*, by Sherwin Nuland (Alfred A. Knopf); *The Real Anita Hill*, by David Brock (Free Press); *The Divorce Culture*, by Barbara DaFoe Whitehead; *The Western Canon*, by Harold Bloom (Harcourt Brace); *The Moral Sense*, by James Q. Wilson (Free Press).
Terms: Agent receives 15% commission on domestic sales; 20% on foreign sales. "We charge for out-of-house photocopying as well as messengers, courier services (e.g., Federal Express), etc."
Tips: Obtains new clients "mostly on the basis of recommendations from others. Always include a SASE that will ensure a response from the agent and the return of material submitted."

KAREN GANTZ ZAHLER LITERARY AGENCY, (III), 860 Fifth Ave., New York NY 10021. Contact: Karen Gantz Zahler. Estab. 1990. Represents 40 clients. Specializes in nonfiction, cookbooks. Currently handles: 70% nonfiction books; 20% novels; 10% movie scripts.
Handles: Nonfiction books, novels, movie scripts. Considers all nonfiction and fiction areas; "anything great." Query. Reports in 2 months.
Recent Sales: *The Whole Truth*, by Kato Kaelin (HarperCollins); *Rosa Mexicano Cookcook*, by Josephina Howard (Penguin); *Faxes to God*, by Joyce Starr (Harper San Francisco).
Terms: Agent receives 15% commission on domestic sales; 20% commission on foreign sales. Offers written contract, binding for 1 year.
Writers' Conferences: ABA.
Tips: Obtains new clients through recommendations from others. "I'm a literary property lawyer and provide excellent negotiating services and exploitation of subsidiary rights."

SUSAN ZECKENDORF ASSOC. INC., (II), 171 W. 57th St., New York NY 10019. (212)245-2928. Contact: Susan Zeckendorf. Estab. 1979. Member of AAR. Represents 35 clients. 25% of clients are new/previously unpublished writers. Currently handles: 50% nonfiction books; 50% fiction.
Handles: Nonfiction books, novels. Considers these nonfiction areas: art/architecture/design; biography/autobiography; child guidance/parenting; health/medicine; history; music/dance/theater/film; psychology; science; sociology; true crime/investigative; women's issues/women's studies. Considers these fiction areas: action/adventure; contemporary issues; detective/police/crime; ethnic; family saga; glitz; historical; literary; mainstream; mystery/suspense; thriller/espionage. Query. Reports in 10 days on queries; 3 weeks mss.
Recent Sales: *Held Accountable*, by Karen Stuyek (Berkley); *A History of Fifth Avenue*, by Jerry E. Patterson (Harry Abrams); *Morning Glory: The Mary Lou Williams Story*, by Linda Dahl (Schirmer Books).
Terms: Agent receives 15% commission on domestic sales; 20% on foreign sales. Charges for photo-copying, messenger services.
Writers' Conferences: Central Valley Writers Conference; the Tucson Publishers Association Conference; Writer's Connection; Frontiers in Writing Conference (Amarillo TX); Golden Triangle Writers Conference (Beaumont TX); Oklahoma Festival of Books (Claremont OK).
Tips: Obtains new clients through recommendations, listings in writer's manuals.

GEORGE ZIEGLER LITERARY AGENCY, (II), 160 E. 97th St., New York NY 10029. (212)348-3637. Contact: George Ziegler. Estab. 1977. Represents 25 clients. 50% of clients are new/previously unpublished writers. Specializes in nonfiction. Currently handles: 80% nonfiction books; 15% novels; 5% stage plays.

Handles: Nonfiction books, novels. Considers these nonfiction areas: animals; anthropology/archaeology; biography/autobiography; cooking/food/nutrition; crafts/hobbies; gay/lesbian issues; health/medicine; history; music/dance/theater/film; nature/environment; religious/inspirational; self-help/personal improvement. Considers these fiction areas: contemporary issues; family saga; gay; historical; horror; lesbian; literary; mainstream; psychic/supernatural. Query. Reports in 2 weeks on queries.

Recent Sales: *Child of Two Worlds*, by Norman Reyes (Three Continents Press); *Portrait of a Woman*, by Joseph Roccasalvo (Ignatius Press); *Democracy & the Dictator*, by Robert Amerson (American University Press).

Terms: Agent receives 15% commission on domestic sales; 20% on foreign sales if subagent is used. No written contract.

Tips: Obtains new clients through mail queries and recommendations. "Be professional."

Additional Nonfee-charging Agents

The following nonfee-charging agencies have indicated that they are *primarily* interested in handling the work of scriptwriters, but also handle less than ten to fifteen percent book manuscripts. After reading the main listing (you can find the page number in the Listings Index), send them a query to obtain more information on their needs and manuscript submission policies.

All-Star Talent Agency
Cinema Talent International
The Coppage Company
Douroux & Co.
Legacies
Lenhoff/Robinson Talent and

Literary Agency, Inc.
Media Artists Group
Montgomery Literary Agency
Montgomery-West Literary
 Agency
Producers & Creatives Group

Jack Scagnetti Talent & Literary
 Agency
The Tantleff Office
A Total Acting Experience
The Turtle Agency

Nonfee-charging Agents/'95-'96 changes

The following agencies appeared in past editions of *Guide to Literary Agents* but are absent from the 1996 edition. These agencies failed to respond to our request for an update of their listing, or were left out for the reasons indicated in parentheses following the agency name.

The Beekman Literary Agency
 (unable to contact)
Patti Breitman (removed by re-
 quest)
Elaine Davie Literary Agency
 (editorial decision)
Thomas C. Donlan (agency
 closed)
Mary Evans Inc. (removed by re-
 quest)
Goodman Assoc.
Jet Literary Assoc.

Lucy Kroll Agency (agency
 closed)
Lichtman, Trister, Singer & Ross
 (removed by request)
Gerard McCauley
Anita D. McClellan Associates
 (unable to contact)
Mildred Marmur Associates Ltd.
 (removed by request)
Howard Morhaim Literary
 Agency (not accepting new
 clients)

The Otte Company (removed by
 request)
Alison J. Picard Literary Agent
 (editorial decision)
Jean Rosenthal Literary Agency
 (removed by request)
Blanche Schlessinger Agency
Gretchen Spieler Literary Agency
Westchester Literary Agency
 (moved to fee-charging)
Gary S. Wohl Literary Agency

Literary Agents:
Fee-charging

This section contains literary agencies that charge a fee to writers in addition to taking a commission on sales. The sales commissions are the same as those taken by nonfee-charging agents: 10 to 15 percent for domestic sales, 20 to 25 percent for foreign and dramatic sales, with the difference going to the subagent.

Several agencies charge fees only under certain circumstances, generally for previously unpublished writers. These agencies are indicated by an asterisk (*). Most agencies will consider you unpublished if you have subsidy publishing, local or small press publication credits only; check with a prospective agency before sending material to see if you fit its definition of published.

Agents who charge one-time marketing fees in excess of $100 are also included in this section. Those who charge less than $100 and do not charge for other services appear in the Literary Agents: Nonfee-charging section.

Reading fees and critique services

The issue of reading fees is as controversial for literary agents as for those looking for representation. While some agents dismiss the concept as inherently unethical and a scam, others see merit in the system, provided an author goes into it with his eyes open. Some writers spend hundreds of dollars for an "evaluation" that consists of a poorly written critique full of boilerplate language that says little, if anything, about their individual work. Others have received the helpful feedback they needed to get their manuscript in shape and have gone on to publish their work successfully.

Effective January 1, 1996, however, all members of the AAR were prohibited from directly or indirectly charging reading fees. Until that time some members were allowed to continue to do so, provided they adhered to guidelines designed to protect the client. A copy of the AAR's Canon of Ethics may be obtained for $5 and a SASE. The address is listed in Professional Organizations toward the end of the book.

Be wary of an agent who recommends a specific book doctor. While the relationship may be that the agent trusts the work that professional editor produces, it is too hard to tell if there are other reasons an agent is working with him. The Writers Guild of America, which franchises literary agencies dealing largely in scripts, prohibits their signatories from such recommendations simply because it is open to abuse.

In discussing consideration of a fee-charging agent, we must underscore the importance of research. Don't be bowled over by an impressive brochure or an authoritative manner. At the same time, overly aggressive skepticism may kill your chances with a legitimate agent. Business-like, professional behavior will help you gather the material you need to make an informed decision.

● Obtain a fee schedule and ask questions about the fees. Be sure you understand what the fees cover and what to expect for your money.

● Request a sample critique the agent has done for another person's manuscript. Are the suggestions helpful and specific? Do they offer advice you couldn't get elsewhere, such as in writing groups, conferences and seminars or reference books?

● Ask for recent sales an agent has made. Many agents have a pre-printed list of sales they can send you. If there haven't been any sales made in the past two years, what is the agent living on? An agent's worth to you, initially, is who they know and work with. In the listings we provide information on the percentage of income an agency receives from commissions on sales, and the percentage from reading or critique fees.

● Verify a few of these sales. To verify that the publisher has a book by that title, check *Books in Print*. To verify that the agent made the sale, call the contracts department of the publisher and ask who the agent of record is for a particular title.

Recently, there has been a trend among a few agents to recommend contracts with subsidy publishers that ask the writer to pay from $3,500 to $6,000 toward the cost of publication. These deals are open to writers directly, without the intermediating "assistance" of an agent. Your best defense is to carefully examine the list of an agent's recent sales and investigate some of the publishers.

Don't hesitate to ask the questions that will help you decide. The more you know about an agent and her abilities, the fewer unpleasant surprises you'll receive.

Fees range from one agency to another in nomenclature, price and purpose. Here are some of the more frequent terms and their generally-accepted definitions.

● *Reading fee*. This is charged for reading a manuscript (most agents do not charge to look at queries alone). Often the fee is paid to outside readers. It is generally a one-time, nonrefundable fee, but some agents will return the fee or credit it to your account if they decide to take you on as a client. Often an agent will offer to refund the fee upon sale of the book, but that isn't necessarily a sign of good faith. If the agency never markets your manuscript no sale would ever be made and the fee never refunded.

● *Evaluation fee*. Sometimes a reading fee includes a written evaluation, but many agents charge for this separately. An evaluation may be a one-paragraph report on the marketability of a manuscript or a several-page evaluation covering marketability along with flaws and strengths.

● *Marketing fees*. Usually a one-time charge to offset the costs of handling work, marketing fees cover a variety of expenses and may include initial reading or evaluation. Beware of agencies charging a monthly marketing fee; there is nothing to compel them to submit your work in a timely way if they are getting paid anyway.

● *Critiquing service*. Although "critique" and "evaluation" are sometimes used interchangeably, a critique is usually more extensive, with suggestions on ways to improve the manuscript. Many agents offer critiques as a separate service and have a standard fee scale, based on a per-page or word-length basis. Some agents charge fees based on the extent of the service required, ranging from overall review to line-by-line commentary.

● *Editing service*. While we do not list businesses whose primary source of income is from editing, we do list agencies who also offer this service. Many do not distinguish between critiques and edits, but we define editing services as critiques that include detailed suggestions on how to improve the work and reduce weaknesses. Editing services can be charged on similar bases as critiquing services.

● *Consultation services*. Some agents charge an hourly rate to act as a marketing consultant, a service usually offered to writers who are not clients and who just want advice on marketing. Some agents are also available on an hourly basis for advice on publishers' contracts.

● *Other services*. Depending on an agent's background and abilities, the agent may offer a variety of other services to writers including ghostwriting, typing, copyediting, proofreading, translating, book publicity, and legal advice.

Be forewarned that payment of a critique or editing fee does not ensure that an agent will take you on as a client. However, if you feel you need more than sales help and would not mind paying for an evaluation or critique from a professional, the agents listed in this section may interest you.

Special indexes and additional help

To help you with your search, we've included a number of special indexes in the back of the book. The Subject Index is divided into sections for nonfee-charging and fee-charging literary agents and script agents. Each of these sections in the index is then divided by nonfiction and fiction subject categories. Some agencies indicated that they were open to all nonfiction or fiction topics. These have been grouped under the subject heading "open" in each section. This year we have added a number of new topics, including education, how-to, humor and popular culture in nonfiction, and horror in fiction. Many agents have indicated additional areas of interest that were not represented in their listings last year.

We've included an Agents Index as well. Often you will read about an agent who is an employee of a larger agency and may not be able to locate her business phone or address. We asked agencies to list the agents on staff, then listed the names in alphabetical order along with the name of the agency they work for. Find the name of the person you would like to contact and then check the agency listing. You will find the page number for the agency's listing in the Listing Index.

A Geographic Index lists agents state by state, for those authors looking for an agent close to home. A Client Acceptance Policies index ranks agencies according to their openness to new clients.

Many literary agents are also interested in scripts; many script agents will also consider book manuscripts. Fee-charging agents who primarily sell scripts but also handle at least 10 to 15 percent book manuscripts appear among the listings in this section, with the contact information, breakdown of work currently handled and a note to check the full listing in the script section, if they are a signatory of the WGA or report a sale. Those fee-charging script agencies that sell scripts and less than 10 to 15 percent book manuscripts appear in "Additional Fee-charging Agents" at the end of this section. Complete listings for these agents appear in the Script Agent section.

Before contacting any agency, check the listing to make sure it is open to new clients. Those designated (V) are currently not interested in expanding their rosters.

For more information on approaching agents and the specifics of the listings, read How to Use Your Guide to Literary Agents and How to Find (and Keep) the Right Agent. Also see the various articles at the beginning of the book for explorations of different aspects of the author/agent relationship.

We've ranked the agencies listed in this section according to their openness to submissions. Below is our ranking system:

I Newer agency actively seeking clients.
II Agency seeking both new and established writers.
III Agency prefers to work with established writers, mostly obtains new clients through referrals.
IV Agency handling only certain types of work or work by writers under certain circumstances.
V Agency not currently seeking new clients. We have included mention of agencies rated **V** to let you know they are currently not open to new clients. In addition to those ranked **V**, we have included a few well-known agencies' names who have declined the opportunity to receive full listings at this time. *Unless you have a strong recommendation from someone well respected in the field, our advice is to approach only those agents ranked I-IV.*

*ACACIA HOUSE PUBLISHING SERVICES LTD. (II, III), 51 Acacia Rd., Toronto, Ontario M4S 2K6 Canada. Phone/fax: (416)484-8356. Contact: (Ms.) Frances Hanna. Estab. 1985. Represents 30 clients. "I prefer that writers be previously published, with at least a few articles to their credit. Strongest consideration will be given to those with, say, three or more published books. However, I *would* take on an unpublished writer of outstanding talent." Works with a small number of new/unpublished authors. Specializes in contemporary fiction: literary or commercial (no horror, occult or science fiction); nonfiction: all categories but business/economics—in the trade, not textbook area; children's: very few picture books. Currently handles: 30% nonfiction books; 70% novels.

- Prior to opening her agency, Ms. Hanna had been in the publishing business for 25 years as a fiction editor with Barrie & Jenkins and Pan Books, and as a senior editor with a packager of mainly illustrated books. She was condensed books editor for 6 years for Reader's Digest in Montreal, senior editor and foreign rights manager for (the then) Wm. Collins & Sons (now HarperCollins) in Toronto.

Handles: Nonfiction books, novels. Considers these nonfiction areas: animals; biography/autobiography; cooking/food/nutrition; crafts/hobbies; current affairs; health/medicine; language/literature/criticism; military/war; music/dance/theater/film; nature/environment; popular culture; psychology. Considers these fiction areas: action/adventure; detective/police/crime; historical; literary; mainstream; mystery/suspense; romance (historical); thriller/espionage. Query with outline. No unsolicited mss. Reports in 3 weeks on queries.

Recent Sales: *Chicken Little Was Right* and sequel, *Whatever Happened to Jennifer Steele?*, (St. Martin's Press, USA); *Stonekiller*, by J. Robert Janes (Constable); *Our Bravest & Best*, by Arthur Bishop (McGraw-Hill Ryerson).

Terms: Agent receives 15% commission on English language sales; 20% on dramatic sales; 30% on foreign language sales.

Fees: Charges reading fee on mss over 200 pages (typed, double-spaced) in length; $200/200 pages. 4% of income derived from reading fees. "If a critique is wanted on a manuscript under 200 pages in length, then the charge is the same as the reading fee for a longer manuscript (which incorporates a critique)." 5% of income derived from criticism fees. Critique includes 2-3-page overall evaluation "which will contain any specific points that are thought important enough to detail. Marketing advice is not usually included, since most manuscripts evaluated in this way are not considered to be publishable." Charges writers for photocopying, courier, postage, telephone/fax "if these are excessive."

Writer's Conferences: LIBER (Barcelona); London International Book Fair (England); Bologna Book Fair (Spain); ABA (Chicago); Frankfurt Book Fair (Germany).

‡*AEI/ATCHITY EDITORIAL/ENTERTAINMENT INTERNATIONAL, (I), 9601 Wilshire Blvd., Box 1202, Beverly Hills CA 90210. (213)932-0407. Fax: (213)932-0321. E-mail: aeikja@lainet.com. Contact: Kenneth Atchity. Estab. 1994. Represents 20 clients. 90% of clients are new/previously unpublished writers. Specializes in novel-film tie-ins. Currently handles: 30% nonfiction books; 5% scholarly books; 30% novels; 25% movie scripts; 10% TV scripts. Member agents: Chi-Li Wong; Andrea McKeown; Rosemary McKenna; Sidney Kiwitt (business affairs, NY).

Handles: Nonfiction books, novels, movie scripts, TV scripts. Considers these nonfiction areas: anthropology/archaeology; biography/autobiography; business; child guidance/parenting; computers/electronics; government/politics/law; health/medicine; how-to; humor; language/literature/criticism; money/finance/economics; music/dance/theater/film; nature/environment; New Age/metaphysics; popular culture; psychology; science/technology; self-help/personal improvement; translations; true crime/investigative; women's issues/women's studies. Considers these fiction areas: action/adventure; contemporary issues; erotica; historical; horror; literary; mainstream; mystery/suspense; science fiction; thriller/espionage. Send outline and 2 sample chapters. Reports in 2 weeks on queries; 2 months on mss.

Recent Sales: *The Rag Street Journal*, by Liz Mason (Owl Books); *The Hong Kong Sanction*, by Sam Aston (Pinnacle); *Chokecherry Roots*, by Floyd Martinez (Arte Publico); *The Hollywood Facelift*, by Nola Rocco (Barclay House); *Aphrodisia*, by Ken Atchity (Macmillan); *Simply Heavenly*, by Abbott George Burke (Macmillan); *Writing Treatments to Sell*, by Chi-Li Wong (Owl); *Achieving Sexual Ecstasy*, by Milt Lyles (Barclay House).

Terms: Agent receives 15% commission on domestic sales; 25% on foreign sales. Offers written contract, binding for 18 months, with 30 day cancellation clause.

Also Handles: Movie scripts (feature film); TV scripts (TV mow); no episodic. Considers these script subject areas: action/adventure; comedy; contemporary issues; detective/police/crime; erotica; horror; mainstream; mystery/suspense; psychic/supernatural; romantic comedy and drama; science fiction; teen; thriller. Send outline and 25 sample pages with SASE. Reports in 2 weeks on queries; 2 months on mss.

Recent Sales: *TV script(s) optioned/sold:* *Blood Witness*, by Alexander Viespi (Susan Cooper [Saban Entertainment]); *Shadow of Obsession*, based on K.K. Beck's *Unwanted Attention* (NBC); *Amityville: The Evil Escapes*, based on John Jones' novel (NBC).

Terms: Agent receives 10% commission on domestic sales; ("0% if we produce").
Fees: Offers criticism service. Clients receive a 10-20 page letter, written by Kenneth Atchity. Charges $150 one-time fee for expenses for previously unpublished writers. 20% of business is derived from reading fees or criticism service. Payment of criticism or reading fee does not ensure representation.
Tips: Obtains new clients through referrals, directories. "No 'episodic' scripts, treatments, or ideas; no 'category' fiction of any kind. Please send a professional return envelope and sufficient postage. No: children's literature, category, poetry, religious literature. We are always looking for true, heroic, *contemporary* women's stories for both book and television. We perform the same function as a literary agent, but also produce films. Take writing seriously as a career, which requires disciplined time and full attention (as described in *The Mercury Transition* and *A Writer's Time* by Kenneth Atchity). Make your cover letter to the point and focused, your synopsis compelling and dramatic. Most submissions, whether fiction or nonfiction, are rejected because the writing is not at a commercially competitive dramatic level. We have a fondness for Louisiana subjects, and for thrillers (both screenplays and novels), as well as for mainstream nonfiction appealing to everyone today. We rarely do 'small audience' books. Our favorite client is one who has the desire and talent to develop both a novel and a film career and who is determined to learn everything possible about the business of writing, publishing, and producing. Dream big. Risk it. Never give up. Go for it!"

*THE AHEARN AGENCY, INC. (I), 2021 Pine St., New Orleans LA 70118-5456. (504)861-8395. Fax: (504)866-6434. E-mail: pahearn@aol.com. Contact: Pamela G. Ahearn. Estab. 1992. Member of RWA. Represents 25 clients. 20% of clients are new/previously unpublished writers. Specializes in historical romance; also very interested in mysteries and suspense fiction. Currently handles: 10% nonfiction books; 10% juvenile books; 80% novels.
 • Prior to opening her agency, Ms. Ahearn was an agent for eight years and an editor with Bantam Books.
Handles: Nonfiction books, juvenile books, novels, short story collections (if stories previously published), young adult (no picture books). Considers these nonfiction areas: animals; biography; business; child guidance/parenting; current affairs; ethnic/cultural interests; gay/lesbian issues; health/medicine; history; juvenile nonfiction; music/dance/theater/film; popular culture; self-help/personal improvement; true crime/investigative; women's issues/women's studies. Considers these fiction areas: action/adventure; contemporary issues; detective/police/crime; ethnic; family saga; fantasy; feminist; gay; glitz; historical; horror; humor/satire; juvenile; lesbian; literary; mainstream; mystery/suspense; psychic/supernatural; regional; romance (contemporary, gothic, historical, regency); science fiction; thriller/espionage; westerns/frontier; young adult. Query. Reports in 1 month on queries; 10 weeks on mss.
Recent Sales: *Dejima*, by Laura Joh Rowland (Villard/Random House); *Skin Deep, Blood Red*, by Robert Skinner (Kensington); *The Rose of Rowdene*, by Kate Moore (Avon Books); *Someone Like You*, by Susan Sawyer (Avon Books).
Terms: Agent receives 15% commission on domestic sales; 20% on foreign sales. Offers written contract, binding for 1 year; renewable by mutual consent.
Fees: "I charge a reading fee to previously unpublished authors, based on length of material. Fees range from $125-400 and are non-refundable. When authors pay a reading fee, they receive a three to five single-spaced-page critique of their work, addressing writing quality and marketability." Critiques written by Pamela G. Ahearn. Charges for photocopying. 90% of business derived from commissions; 10% derived from reading fees or criticism services. Payment of reading fee does not ensure representation.
Writers' Conferences: Attends Midwest Writers Workshop, Moonlight & Magnolias, RWA National conference (Dallas); Virginia Romance Writers (Williamsburg, VA); Florida Romance Writers (Ft. Lauderdale, FL), Golden Triangle Writers Conference; Bouchercon (Minneapolis, Octber).
Tips: Obtains new clients "usually through listings such as this one and client recommendations. Sometimes at conferences. Be professional! Always send in exactly what an agent/editor asks for, no more, no less. Keep query letters brief and to the point, giving your writing credentials and a very brief summary of your book. If one agent rejects you, keep trying—there are a lot of us out there!"

‡ALLEGRA LITERARY AGENCY, (I), 2806 Pine Hill Dr. NW, Kennesaw GA 30144. (770)795-8318. Fax: (770)795-8318. Contact: Cynthia Lambert. Estab. 1994. Represents 5 clients. 10% of clients are new/previously unpublished writers. Specializes in Christian fiction (mainstream, romance, mystery, science fiction); also some secular. Currently handles: 25% nonfiction books; 5% juvenile books; 70% novels.

The double dagger before a listing indicates the listing is new in this edition.

Handles: Nonfiction books, juvenile books, novels. Considers these nonfiction areas: religious/inspirational. Considers these fiction areas: detective/police/crime; juvenile; mainstream; mystery/suspense; religious/inspirational; romance. Query with 3 consecutive chapters. Reports in 2 weeks on queries; 2 months on mss.

Terms: Agent receives 12% commission on domestic sales; 16% on foreign sales. Offers written contract, binding for 1 year, with 60 day cancellation clause.

Fees: No reading fee. Charges $150 retainer, fully refundable upon the sale of the ms for postage, faxing, copying and long distance phone calls. Authors receive itemized monthly statements.

Tips: Obtains new clients through recommendations.

ALP ARTS CO., (I, II), 221 Fox Rd., Golden CO 80403. Phone/fax: (303)642-0916. E-mail: sffuller@-alparts.com. Contact: Ms. Sandy Ferguson Fuller. Estab. 1994. Represents 30 clients. 80% of clients are new/previously unpublished writers. "Specializes in children's books. Works with picture book authors and illustrators, also middle-grade and YA writers, nonfiction and fiction." Currently handles: 100% juvenile books.

Handles: Juvenile books, all types. Considers juvenile nonfiction. Considers juvenile and young adult fiction, picture books. Query. For picture books and easy readers send entire ms. Reports in 3 weeks on queries; 6 weeks on mss.

Terms: 10% commission on domestic sales. Offers written contract, with 30 day cancellation clause.

Fees: Criticism service: $25/hour for critique and consulting session. Basic consultation is $25/hour or $25/submission. Contract varies upon client's needs. Charges for postage, photocopying costs. Long-distance phone consultation at $25/hour plus phone bill. Receipts supplied to client for all of the above. 50% of business derived from criticism fees.

Writers' Conferences: ABA (Chicago, June); SCBWI (October).

Tips: Obtains new clients from referrals, solicitation and at conferences. "Several mailings per year through advertising services, workshops and seminars. Referrals. Networking in publishing industry. Society of Children's Book Writers and Illustrators. Usually establish a working relationship via consulting or workshop prior to agenting. Agency representation is not for everyone. Some aspiring or published authors and/or illustrators have more confidence in their own abilities to target and market work. Others are 'territorial' or prefer to work directly with the publishers. The best agent/client relationships exist when complete trust is established prior to representation. I recommend at least one (or several) consultations via phone or in person with a prospective agent. References are important. Also, the author or illustrator should have a clear idea of the agent's role i.e., editorial/critiquing input, 'post-publication' responsibilities, exclusive or non-exclusive representation, fees, industry reputation, etc. Each author or illustrator should examine his or her objectives, talents, time constraints, and perhaps more important, personal rapport with an individual agent prior to representation."

‡*AUTHENTIC CREATIONS LITERARY AGENCY, (I, II), 911 Duluth Highway, Suite D3-241, Lawrenceville GA 30243. (770)339-3774. Fax: (770)513-3322. Contact: Mary Lee Laitsch. Estab. 1993. Represents 15 clients. 85% of clients are new/previously unpublished writers. Currently handles: 40% nonfiction books; 10% juvenile books; 50% novels. Member agents: Mary Lee Laitsch; Jason Laitsch; Ronald E. Laitsch.

Handles: Nonfiction books, scholarly books, juvenile books, novels. Considers these nonfiction areas: agriculture/horticulture; animals; anthropology/archaeology; biography/autobiography; business; child guidance/parenting; cooking/food/nutrition; crafts/hobbies; current affairs; education; government/politics/law; health/medicine; history; how-to; humor; interior design/decorating; juvenile nonfiction; military/war; money/finance/economics; nature/environment; popular culture; psychology; religious/inspirational; science/technology; self-help/personal improvement; sports; true crime/investigative; women's issues/women's studies; Considers these fiction areas: action/adventure; contemporary issues; detective/police/crime; erotica; family saga; fantasy; historical; horror; humor/satire; literary; mainstream; mystery/suspense; picture book; religious/inspirational; romance (contemporary, gothic, historical, regency); science fiction; sports; thriller/espionage; westerns/frontier; young adult. Query. Reports in 2 weeks on queries; 6 weeks on mss.

Terms; Agent receives 15% commission on domestic sales; 15% on foreign sales.

Fees: Charges reading fee for unpublished authors: $100 up to 100,000 words; $150 over 100,000 words. Charges for photocopying.

Tips: Obtains new clients through advertising in magazines and word of mouth. "Authentic Creations concentrates on promoting the works of conservative writers. We are actively seeking writers who produce works that do not reflect the liberal philosophy in their manuscripts. Come and join the new wave in literature."

*AUTHOR AID ASSOCIATES, (II), 340 E. 52nd St., New York NY 10022. (212)758-4213; 980-9179. Editorial Director: Arthur Orrmont. Estab. 1967. Represents 185 clients. Specializes in aviation, war, biography, novels, autobiography. Currently handles: 5% magazine fiction; 35% nonfiction books; 38% novels; 5% juvenile books; 5% movie scripts; 2% stage plays; 10% other. Member agent: Leonie

Rosenstiel, vice president, "a musicologist and authority on New Age subjects and nutrition; Ed McCartan (military nonfiction, intelligence/espionage); Annette Bitterman (romance)."
● Prior to opening his agency, Mr. Orrmont served in the editorial department with Farrar, Straus, and as senior editor for Popular Library and executive editor with Fawcett Books.
Handles: Magazine fiction, nonfiction books, novels, juvenile books, movie scripts, stage plays, TV scripts. Considers these nonfiction areas: animals; anthropology/archaeology; biography/autobiography; current affairs; ethnic/cultural interests; health/medicine; history; how-to; humor; juvenile nonfiction; language/literature/criticism; military/war; music/dance/theater/film; nature/environment; New Age/metaphysics; popular culture; psychology; religious/inspirational; science/technology; self-help/personal improvement; sociology; sports; translations; true crime/investigative; women's issues/women's studies. Considers these fiction areas: action/adventure; confessional; contemporary issues; detective/police/crime; erotica; ethnic; experimental; family saga; fantasy; glitz; historical; horror; humor/satire; juvenile; lesbian; literary; mainstream; mystery/suspense; picture book; psychic/supernatural; regional; religious/inspirational; romance (contemporary, gothic, historical, regency); science fiction; sports; thriller/espionage; westerns/frontier; young adult. Query with outline. No unsolicited mss. "Short queries answered by return mail." Reports within 6 weeks on mss.
Recent Sales: *World Series*, by John S. Snyder (Chronicle Books); *Guide to Alaska*, by Larry Ludmer (Hunter Publishers).
Terms: Agent receives 15% commission on domestic and dramatic sales; 20% on foreign sales.
Fees: Charges a reading fee to new authors, refundable from commission on sale. Charges for cable, photocopying and messenger express. Offers consultation service through which writers not represented can get advice on a contract. 80% of income from commissions on sales; 20% of income derived from reading fees.
Tips: Publishers of *Literary Agents of North America* (5th edition).

THE AUTHORS RESOURCE CENTER/TARC LITERARY AGENCY, (II), 4725 E. Sunrise, #219, Tucson AZ 85718. (520)577-7751. Contact: Martha R. Gores. Estab. 1984. Represents 30 clients. Specializes in mainstream adult fiction and nonfiction books. Currently handles: 80% nonfiction books; 20% novels.
Handles: Nonfiction books, novels. Considers all nonfiction areas except essays, autobiography (unless celebrity) and journals. "Especially interested in how-to or self-help books by professionals; parenting books by psychologists or MDs." Query with outline. Does not read unsolicited mss. Reports in 2 months if SASE included.
Recent Sales: *Walker of Time* (Harbinger House).
Terms: Agent receives 15% commission on domestic sales; 20% on dramatic sales; 20% on foreign sales.
Fees: Does not charge a reading fee. Criticism service "only if is requested by the author." No set fee. "Each critique is tailored to the individual needs of the writer. We hire working editors who are employed by book publishers to do critiquing, editing, etc." Charges writers for mailing, photocopying, faxing, telephone calls.
Tips: "We do ghosting for professional people. In order to do ghosting, you must be published by a professional, reputable publisher. To be considered, send a business card with your résumé to our Arizona address."

ELIZABETH H. BACKMAN, (II), 86 Johnnycake Hollow Rd., Pine Plains NY 12567. (518)398-6408. Fax: (518)398-6368. Contact: Elizabeth H. Backman. Also: 337 E. 50th St., #1, New York NY 10022. (212)755-4924. Contact: Louise Gault. Estab. 1981. Represents 50 clients. Specializes in nonfiction, women's interest and positive motivation. Currently handles: 33-66% nonfiction books; 33% fiction.
Handles: Considers these nonfiction areas: biography/memoirs; business; child guidance/parenting; cooking/food/nutrition; current affairs; dance; ethnic/cultural interests; government/politics/law; health/medicine; history; photography; pop science; psychology; religious/inspirational; self-help/personal improvement; sports; women's issues/women's studies. Considers these fiction areas: ethnic; fantasy; historical; mystery/suspense; regional; science fiction; sports; thriller/espionage; men's adventure and suspense; women's contemporary fiction. Query with sample ms. Reports in 3 weeks on queries; 6 weeks on mss.
Recent Sales: *Toughness Training for Business*, by James Loehr; *A Voice Of Her Own: Women and the Journal Writing Journey*, by Marlene Schiwy (Simon & Schuster).
Terms: Agent receives 15% commission on domestic sales; commission varies on foreign sales. Offers written contract on request, binding for 1-3 years.
Fees: Charges $25 reading fee for proposal/3 sample chapters, $50 for complete ms. Offers criticism service. Charges for photocopying, postage, telephone, fax, typing, editing, special services.
Writers' Conferences: International Women's Writing Guild.
Tips: Obtains new clients through referrals from other editors. "I help writers prepare their proposals in best possible shape so they can get best possible deal with publisher. May not be the highest advance, but best overall deal."

INSIDER REPORT

A Rescue Story

"People who are doing interesting things, where they're making a difference, are of significant interest to me personally. It's the kind of book I really respond to and look for," says Meredith Bernstein. Her list of clients includes Patricia Ireland, president of the National Organization for Women; Miep Gies, who hid Anne Frank and her family; Lady Borton, who devoted her life to the people of Vietnam before, during and after the war; and most recently Terri Crisp, head of United Animal Nations.

Ms. Bernstein's instinctive feeling for what makes a good writer, a good story, and a good book, led to the upcoming *Out of Harm's Way*, by Terri Crisp and Samantha Glen (Pocket Books), in which Ms. Glen collaborates with Ms. Crisp to chronicle the courageous animal rescues from natural and man-made disasters ranging from Hurricane Andrew and the Missouri floods to the *Exxon-Valdez* oil spill.

Samantha Glen met Meredith Bernstein in Washington, where she interviewed her for an article. "She originally interviewed me for this story and we just took a liking to each other. Periodically she would show me some romance fiction she was writing, and I thought it was okay, but it wasn't grabbing me. One day we were having lunch in New York and she happened to mention that she'd heard about a woman named Terri Crisp who went into disaster situations and rescued animals."

Ms. Bernstein immediately recognized the potential of a project that paired Crisp's dramatic story with Glen's journalistic skills. "I told her, 'That's the woman to track down. You should do a book with her.' So she called Terri Crisp up, they met, hit it off and found their commitment to animals a true bond. They decided to work together. Now they share a book."

As with most nonfiction books, the project started with a good proposal. "We showed the first draft of the proposal around and there was some interest, but not a great deal. Samantha said, 'I think that I should probably redo the proposal, and I really think it would be important for people to meet Terri, because she's so dynamic,' " to which Bernstein agreed.

They went back to the proposal and worked up a stronger package which included an overview of the book, sample chapters, the intended market, photographs, bios of Glen and Crisp and demographics of the impact of disasters on animals. Meanwhile, Bernstein went back to the publishers who had seen the original material to convince them to view it again. "Sometimes I will go back and say, 'Look, this has been redone and I really think you ought to take a look at it.' I think it has to do with people trusting my opinion. I'll say, 'This is really worth it. Take a second look, they've done a better job. They were on the right track to begin with, but now they've gotten it much better.' "

With the revised proposal in hand, Crisp flew in to New York from California and Bernstein took her around to the meetings she had set up. "As we were in the meetings she would tell the rescue stories about the animals. People would literally be reaching for the tissue boxes and crying. That's when the excitement began to grow. After reading what was by then a very good proposal and seeing the dynamic personality involved, the publishers became extremely interested." A multiple submission took on the character of a heated auction with two publishers, Pocket Books and Berkley, in a very close race at the end. "Although Berkley really wanted it, it went to Pocket."

With an eclectic mix of fiction and nonfiction, Bernstein does not like to characterize her agency's interests in any one direction. But her personal preferences guide the manuscripts she takes on, as well as the projects she develops and packages. "In the end, I am looking for a fresh voice, a compelling story, an expert in one's field—or a creative spin on an interesting topic . . . That is what excites me."
—*Kirsten Holm*

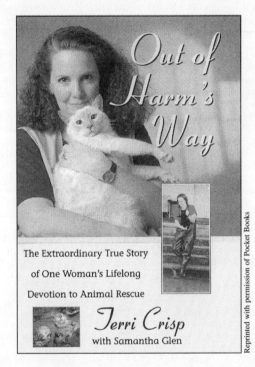

Out of Harm's Way

The Extraordinary True Story
of One Woman's Lifelong
Devotion to Animal Rescue

Terri Crisp
with Samantha Glen

Reprinted with permission of Pocket Books

*GENE BARTCZAK ASSOCIATES INC., (II), Box 715, North Bellmore NY 11710-0766. (516)781-6230. President: Sue Bartczak. Estab. 1980. Represents 18 clients. 100% of clients are new/previously unpublished writers. Currently handles: 33% nonfiction books; 50% juvenile books; 17% novels.
Handles: Nonfiction books, juvenile books, middle readers and up. "No picture books." Considers these nonfiction areas: animals; biography/autobiography; how-to; juvenile nonfiction (middle readers and up); women's issues/women's studies. Considers these fiction areas: contemporary issues; feminist; juvenile (no picture books); mainstream; young adult. Query only. Must have SASE. Reports in 2 weeks on queries; 6 weeks on mss.
Recent Sales: *American Diaries (Books I-IV)*, by Duey (Simon & Schuster); *Crow's Graveyard*, by Duey (Avon Books).
Terms: Agent receives 15% commission on domestic sales; 20% on foreign sales. Offers written contract, binding for 1 year; automatic renewal for 1-year terms unless given 90 days prior written notice to terminate by either party.
Fees: Charges reading fee for unpublished book writers.
Tips: Obtains new clients through recommendations and agency listings. "Be sure to include SASE with any material sent to an agent if you expect to get an answer. If you want the material you sent returned to you, be sure that your SASE has enough postage to take care of that."

*MEREDITH BERNSTEIN LITERARY AGENCY, (II), 2112 Broadway, Suite 503 A, New York NY 10023. (212)799-1007. Fax: (212)799-1145. Contact: Elizabeth Cavanaugh. Estab. 1981. Member of AAR. Represents approximately 85 clients. 20% of clients are new/previously unpublished writers. Does not specialize, "very eclectic." Currently handles: 50% nonfiction books; 50% fiction. Member agents: Meredith Bernstein, Elizabeth Cavanaugh.

● Prior to opening her agency, Ms. Bernstein served in another agency for five years.

Handles: Fiction and nonfiction books. Query first.

Recent Sales: *Gray Matter*, by David Jacobs (Simon & Schuster); *Things I Wish I'd Known Sooner*, by Jaroldeen Edwards (Pocket Books); *Jungleland*, by Sharon Zukowski (NAL); *What Women Want*, by Patricia Ireland (Dutton/NAL); *Out Of Harm's Way*, by Terri Crisp and Samantha Glen (Pocket); *Deep Water Passage*, by Ann Linnea (Little, Brown).

Terms: Agent receives 15% commission on domestic sales; 20% on foreign sales.

Fees: Occasionally charges reading fee of up to $100 for unpublished writers only. Charges $75 disbursement fee per year. 98% of business is derived from commissions on ms sales; 2% is derived from reading fees. Payment of fees does not ensure representation.

Writers' Conferences: Southwest Writers Conference (Albuquerque, August); Rocky Mountain Writers Conference (Denver, September); Golden Triangle (Beaumont TX, October).

Tips: Obtains new clients through recommendations from others, solicitation and at conferences; also develops and packages own ideas.

‡THE BLAKE GROUP LITERARY AGENCY, (II, III), 8609 Northwest Plaza Dr., Suite 300, Dallas TX 75225-4214. (214)373-2221. President: Albert H. Halff, D.Eng. Estab. 1979. Member of Texas Publishers Association (TPA) and Texas Booksellers Association (TBA). Works with published/established authors; works with a small number of new/unpublished authors. Currently handles: 30% fiction; 30% nonfiction; 10% juvenile; 30% poetry.

Handles: Nonfiction books, novels, juvenile books. Query with synopsis and 2 sample chapters. Reports within 3 months. SASE must be included or mss will not be read.

Recent Sales: *Life on the King Ranch*, by Frank Goodwin (Texas A&M University Press); *A Patient's Guide to Surgery*, by Dr. Edward Bradley, MD (Consumer's Digest in conjunction with the University of Pennsylvania); *The Blue Cat*, by Pamela Sanchez (SRA).

Terms: Agent receives 15% commission on domestic sales; 20% on foreign sales.

THE BRINKE LITERARY AGENCY, (II), 4498 B Foothill Rd., Carpinteria CA 93013-3075. (805)684-9655. Contact: Jude Barvin. Estab. 1988. Represents 24 clients. Currently handles: 30% nonfiction books; 60% novels; 10% movie scripts.

Handles: Considers these nonfiction areas: animals; anthropology/archaeology; biography/autobiography; child guidance/parenting; history; how-to; New Age/metaphysics; religious/inspirational; self-help/personal improvement. Considers these fiction areas: action/adventure; detective/police/crime; fantasy; mystery/suspense; psychic/supernatural; religious/inspirational; romance (contemporary); science fiction; thriller/espionage; New Age; meditation. Query with SASE.

Also Handles: Movie scripts (feature film). Considers these script subject areas: action/adventure; contemporary issues; detective/police/crime; mystery/suspense; psychic/supernatural; religious/inspirational; science fiction; thriller.

Terms: Agent receives 15% commissions on domestic sales; 20% on foreign sales. Offers written contract, binding for 1 year.

Fees: Charges $125 reading fee for novel ms; $100 for screenplays. No charges for office expenses, postage, photocopying.

Writers' Conferences: Santa Barbara Writers Conference; ABA (Chicago, June).

Tips: Obtains new clients through recommendations from others, queries, mail. Offers complete critique/evaluation or a contract.

‡RUTH HAGY BROD LITERARY AGENCY, (III), 15 Park Ave., New York NY 10016. (212)683-3232. Fax: (212)269-0313. President: A.T. Brod. Estab. 1975. Represents 10 clients. 10-15% of clients are new/unpublished authors. Prefers to work with published/established authors. Specializes in trade books. Currently handles: 95% nonfiction books; 5% novels.

Handles: Nonfiction books. Query or send entire manuscript. Reports in 5 weeks on queries; 2 months on mss.

Terms: Agent receives 15% commission on domestic sales; 20% on foreign sales.

Fees: Charges a reading fee; waives reading fee when representing writer. 5% of income derived from reading fees. Charges a criticism fee. 5% of income derived from criticism fees.

‡ANTOINETTE BROWN, LITERARY AGENT, (II), P.O. Box 6454, Alexandria VA 22306. (703)768-9583. Contact: A. Brown. Estab. 1991. Member of RWA. Represents 5 clients. 75% of clients are new/

previously unpublished writers. Currently handles: 20% nonfiction books; 60% novels; 20% short story collections.

Handles: Nonfiction books, novels. Considers these nonfiction areas: business; ethnic/cultural interests; health/medicine; history; religious/inspirational (Buddhism); self-help/personal improvement; women's issues/women's studies. Considers these fiction areas: action/adventure; historical; mystery/suspense; romance (historical); thriller/espionage. Query. Reports in 2 weeks on queries; 2 months on mss.

Terms: Agent receives 15% commission on domestic sales; 20% on foreign sales. Offers written contract, with 60 day cancellation clause.

Fees: Charges reading fee: $25 (up to 250 pages); $35 (251-400 pages); $40 (401-500 pages); $50 (over 500 pages). Brief criticism of ms is offered in rejection letter.

Tips: Obtains new clients through recommendations, queries. "Unsolicited manuscripts will be returned unopened. No returns without SASE. The Dalai Lama says 'religion is kindness.' I am looking especially for writers of all backgrounds who consider themselves secular humanists."

*PEMA BROWNE LTD., (II), HCR Box 104B, Pine Rd., Neversink NY 12765-9603. (914)985-2936. Contact: Perry Browne or Pema Browne. Estab. 1966. Member of SCBWI, RWA. Represents 50 clients. Handles any commercial fiction, nonfiction, romance, juvenile and children's picture books. Currently handles: 25% nonfiction books; 25% juvenile books; 45% novels; 5% movie scripts. Member agents: Pema Browne (juvenile, nonfiction); Perry Browne (romance, nonfiction).

Handles: Nonfiction books, scholarly books, juvenile books, novels. Considers these nonfiction areas: anthropology/archaeology; art/architecture/design; biography/autobiography; business; child guidance/parenting; cooking/food/nutrition; current affairs; education; ethnic/cultural interests; gay/lesbian issues; government/politics/law; health/medicine; how-to; juvenile nonfiction; military/war; money/finance/economics; nature/environment; New Age/metaphysics; popular culture; psychology; religious/inspirational; science/technology; self-help/personal improvement; sports; true crime/investigative; women's issues/women's studies. Considers these fiction areas: action/adventure, contemporary issues; detective/police/crime; ethnic; feminist; gay; glitz; historical; humor/satire; juvenile; lesbian; literary; mainstream; mystery/suspense; picture book; psychic/supernatural; religious/inspiration; romance (contemporary, gothic, historical, regency); science fiction; thriller/espionage; westerns/frontier; young adult. Query with SASE. Reports in 1 week on queries; 2 weeks on mss.

Recent Sales: *Top Ten Fears of Job Seekers*, by Gary Grappo (Berkley); *Landing Your First Career*, by Linda Linn (McGraw-Hill Professional Book Group); *101 Grade A Resumes*, by Anthony & Roe (Barron's); *Pool Party*, by Linda Cargill (Scholastic); *Hang Loose*, by Linda Cargill (HarperCollins); *Benni and Victoria*, by Patricia Aust (Child Welfare League of America); *Red Bird*, illustrated by Todd Doney (Lothrop Lee Shepard); *Moonstick*, illustrated by John Sandford (Joanna Cotler Books/HarperCollins); *Miracle In A Shoe Box*, illustrated by Dileen Marsh (Thomas Nelson); *Taste of the Ton*, by Dorothea Donley (Regency Anthology/Kensington); *Only In My Arms*, by Joanne Goodman (Historical/Kensington); *Sleeping Tigers*, by Sandra Dark (Contemporary/Silhouette).

Terms: Agent receives 15% commission on domestic sales; 20% on foreign sales.

Fees: Charges reading fee *only* on *selective adult* novels by unpublished authors.

Tips: Obtains new clients through "editors, authors, *LMP*, *Guide to Literary Agents* and as a result of longevity! If writing romance, be sure to receive guidelines from various romance publishers. In nonfiction, one must have credentials to lend credence to a proposal. Make sure of margins, double-space and use clean, dark type."

‡CAMBRIDGE LITERARY ASSOCIATES, (II), 8 Swan Pond Rd., North Reading MA 01864. Phone/fax: (508)664-8659. E-mail: mrmv@aol.com. Contact: Michael Valentino. Estab. 1990. Represents 30 clients. 50% of clients are new/previously unpublished writers. Currently handles: 20% nonfiction books; 5% juvenile books; 60% novels; 15% short story collections.

Handles: Nonfiction books, scholarly books, textbooks, juvenile books, novels, novellas, short story collections. Considers these nonfiction areas: biography/autobiography; business; current affairs; government/politics/law; history; how-to; humor; juvenile nonfiction; military/war; popular culture; religious/inspirational; sports; true crime/investigative. Considers these fiction areas: action/adventure; contemporary issues; detective/police/crime; erotica; family saga; fantasy; historical; horror; juvenile; literary; mainstream; mystery/suspense; regional; religious/inspirational; romance (contemporary, historical); science fiction; sports; thriller/espionage; westerns/frontier; young adult. Send outline and 3 sample chapters or send entire ms. Reports in 1 week on queries; 3 weeks on mss.

Recent Sales: *Christopher C. Kidd*, by Gwen Starcher (Telcraft Books); *Return of the Matriarchs*, by Gilbert B. Dickey (Blue Moon Press).

Terms: Agent receives 15% commission on domestic sales; 20% on foreign sales. Offers written contract.

Fees: No reading fee. Criticism service: $1/page (includes full blue line editing and analysis or market potential, characterization, plot, etc.) 30% of business is derived from criticism fees. Payment of criticism fee does not ensure representation.

Tips: Obtains new clients through advertising, networking and recommendations from others.

THE CATALOG™ LITERARY AGENCY, (II), P.O. Box 2964, Vancouver WA 98668. (360)694-8531. Contact: Douglas Storey. Estab. 1986. Represents 70 clients. 50% of clients are new/previously unpublished writers. Specializes in business, health, psychology, money, science, how-to, self-help, technology, parenting, women's interest. Currently handles: 50% nonfiction books; 20% juvenile books; 30% novels.
Handles: Nonfiction books, textbooks, juvenile books, novels. Considers these nonfiction areas: agriculture/horticulture; animals; anthropology/archaeology; business; child guidance/parenting; computers/electronics; cooking/food/nutrition; crafts/hobbies; current affairs; education; ethnic/cultural interests; government/politics/law; health/medicine; how-to; juvenile nonfiction; military/war; money/finance/economics; nature/environment; photography; popular culture; psychology; science/technology; self-help/personal improvement; sociology; sports; women's issues/women's studies. Considers these fiction areas: action/adventure; family saga; horror; juvenile; mainstream; romance; science fiction; thriller/espionage; young adult. Query. Reports in 2 weeks on queries; 3 weeks on mss.
Recent Sales: *You Bet Your Assets*, by Don Brown (Amacom Books); *The Video Producers Notebook*, by Aleks Matza (Focal Press).
Terms: Agent receives 15% on domestic sales; 20% on foreign sales. Offers written contract, binding for about 9 months.
Fees: Does not charge a reading fee. Charges an upfront handling fee from $85-250 that covers photocopying, telephone and postage expense.

CHADD-STEVENS LITERARY AGENCY, (II), P.O. Box 2218, Granbury TX 76048. (817)326-4892. Fax: (817)326-3290. Contact: Lee F. Jordan. Estab. 1991. Represents 45 clients. Specializes in working with previously unpublished authors.
Handles: Novels, novellas, short story collections. Considers all nonfiction areas. Considers all fiction areas except feminist. Send entire ms or 3 sample chapters and SASE. Reports within 6 weeks on mss.
Recent Sales: *The Joy of Books*, by Eric Burns (Prometheus); *A Brief Education*, by Maren Sobar (Blue Moon); *The Cretaceous Paradox*, by Frank J. Carradine (Royal Fireworks).
Terms: Agent receives 15% commission on domestic sales; 15% on foreign sales. Offers written contract, binding for 3 months.
Fees: Charges $35 handling fee for entire ms only. Charges $50 per month for expenses. Payment of handling fee does not ensure agency representation.
Writers' Conferences: Regional (Texas and Southwest) writers' conferences including Southwest Writers Conference (Houston, June).
Tips: "I prefer a query letter and I answer all of them with a personal note. My goal is to look at 80% of everything offered to me. I'm interested in working with people who have been turned down by other agents and publishers. I'm interested in first-time novelists—there's a market for your work if it's good. Don't give up. I think there is a world of good unpublished fiction out there and I'd like to see it."

‡LINDA CHESTER LITERARY AGENCY, (II), 666 Fifth Ave., No. 37FL New York NY 10103-0001. (212)439-0881. Contact: Linda Chester. Estab. 1978. Represents 60 clients. 25% of clients are new/previously unpublished writers. Specializes in quality fiction and nonfiction. Currently handles: 70% nonfiction books; 30% novels. Member agents: Laurie Fox (associate agent).
Handles: Nonfiction books, novels, especially literary fiction. Considers these nonfiction areas: art/architecture; biography/autobiography; business; child guidance/parenting; current affairs; health/medicine; history; literature; money/finance/economics; performing arts; environment; psychology; true crime/investigative; women's issues. Considers these fiction areas: contemporary issues; ethnic; feminist; literary; mainstream; mystery/suspense. Query first, then send outline/proposal. Reports in 2 weeks on queries; 3 weeks on mss.
Recent Sales: *She's Come Undone*, by Wally Comb (Pocket Books); *Two Halves of New Haven*, by Martin Schecter (Crown Publishers Inc.); *Juggernaut: The Germaning of Business*, by Philip Glouchevitch (Simon & Schuster); *Investing From the Heart: A Guide to Socially Responsible Investment*, by Jack Brill and Alan Reder (Crown); *The Breathing Book: Good Health and Vitality Through Breath Work*, by Donna Farhi (Holt).

 An asterisk indicates those agents who only charge fees to new or previously unpublished writers or to writers only under certain conditions.

Terms: Agent receives 15% commission on domestic sales; 30% on foreign sales. Offers written contract, binding for 1 year.

Fees: Does not charge a reading fee. Criticism service: $350 for manuscripts up to 400 pages. Consists of a 3-5 page critique/evaluation of manuscripts in terms of presentation, marketability, writing quality, voice, plot, characterization, style, etc. In-house professional editors write the critiques. Charges for photocopying of manuscript and other office expenses. 95% of business is derived from commissions on ms sales; 5% is derived from criticism services. Payment of criticism fee does not ensure representation.

Writers' Conferences: Santa Barbara Writers' Conference.

Tips: Obtains new clients through recommendations from others and solicitation.

*SJ CLARK LITERARY AGENCY, (IV), 56 Glenwood, Hercules CA 94547. (510)741-9826. Fax: (510)236-1052. Contact: Sue Clark. Estab. 1982. Represents 12 clients. 95% of clients are new/previously unpublished writers. Specializes in mysteries/suspense, children's books. Currently handles: 35% juvenile books; 65% novels.

Handles: Juvenile books, novels. Considers these nonfiction areas: New Age/metaphysics; true crime/investigative. Considers these fiction areas: detective/police/crime; juvenile; mystery/suspense; picture book; psychic/supernatural; thriller/espionage; young adult. Query with entire ms. Reports in 1 month on queries; 3 months on mss.

Recent Sales: *Five Alarm Fire*, by D.B. Borton (Berkley); *Jeremy*, by Tatiana Strelkoff (Rebecca House).

Terms: Agent receives 20% commission on domestic sales. Offers written contract.

Fees: "I specialize in working with previously unpublished writers. If the writer is unpublished, I charge a reading fee of $50 which includes a detailed two to three page single-spaced critique. Fee is nonrefundable. If the writer is published, the reading fee is refundable from commission on sale if I agree to represent author. I also offer an editing service for unpublished or published authors. Payment of criticism fee does not ensure representation. Clients are asked to keep all agreed upon amounts in their account to cover postage, phone calls, fax, etc. (Note: Since February 1995, 40% of income from commissions, 60% from reading and critiquing fees from unpublished authors.)"

Tips: Obtains new clients by word of mouth, listing in *Guide to Literary Agents*.

COAST TO COAST TALENT AND LITERARY, (II), 4942 Vineland Ave., Suite 200, North Hollywood CA 91601. (818)762-6278. Fax: (818)762-7049. Estab. 1986. Signatory of WGA. Represents 20 clients. 35% of clients are new/previously unpublished writers. Specializes in "true stories and true crime books that can be packaged into movies/scripts." Currently handles: 25% nonfiction books; 50% movie scripts; 25% TV scripts.

• See the expanded listing for this agency in Script Agents.

COLBY: LITERARY AGENCY, (I), 2864-20 Jefferson Ave., Yuba City CA 95993. (916)674-3378. Contact: Pat Colby. Estab. 1990. Represents 15 clients. 93% of clients are new/previously unpublished writers. Specializes in fiction—mystery and comedy. Currently handles: 100% novels. Member agent: Richard Colby.

Handles: Novels, novellas, short story collections. Considers these fiction areas: cartoon/comic; detective/police/crime; humor/satire; mystery/suspense; sports; thriller/espionage; westerns/frontier. Query or send entire ms. Reports within 1 week on queries; 2 months on mss.

Terms: Agent receives 12% commission on domestic sales; 15% commission on foreign sales. Offers written contract, binding for 1 year.

Fees: No reading fee. Offers criticism service. Send query or 30 pages of ms for a prompt reply with full explanation of any charges. Critiques are done by Pat or Richard Colby. Charges for editing, photocopying, postage. Payment of criticism fee does not ensure representation.

*COLLIER ASSOCIATES, (III), P.O. Box 21361, Palm Beach FL 33416-1361. (407)697-3541. Contact: Dianna Collier. Estab. 1976. Represents 75+ clients. 10% of clients are new/previously unpublished writers. Specializes in "adult fiction and nonfiction books only." Currently handles: 50% nonfiction books; 50% novels. Member agents: Dianna Collier (food, history, self help, women's issues, most fiction); Oscar Collier (financial, biography, autobiography, most fiction). "This is a small agency that rarely takes on new clients because of the many authors it represents already."

Handles: Nonfiction, novels. Considers these nonfiction areas: biography/autobiography; business; computers/electronics; cooking/food/nutrition; crafts/hobbies; history; how-to; self-help/personal improvement; true crime/investigative; women's issues/women's studies. Considers these fiction areas: action/adventure; detective/police/crime; fantasy; historical; mainstream; mystery/suspense; romance (contemporary, gothic, historical, regency); science fiction; thriller/espionage; westerns/frontier. Query with SASE. Reports in 2 months on queries; 4 months "or longer" on mss.

Recent Sales: *The Secret War for the Union*, by Edwin Fischel (Houghton Mifflin); *The Cinema of Oliver Stone*, by Norman Kagan (Continuum); *Glass Cockpit*, by Robert Davis (Readers Condensed Books/Worldwide); *Taboo*, by Ellen Archer (Kensington).
Terms: Agent receives 10-15% commission on domestic sales; 20% on foreign sales. Offers written contract.
Fees: Charges $50 reading fee for unpublished trade book authors. "Reserves the right to charge a reading fee on longer fiction of unpublished authors." Charges for mailing expenses, photocopying and express mail, "if requested, with author's consent, and for copies of author's published books used for rights sales."
Writer's Conferences: ABA (Chicago, June); Florida Mystery Writers (Ft. Lauderdale, March).
Tips: Obtains new clients through recommendations from others. "Send biographical information with query; must have SASE. Don't telephone. Read Oscar Collier's books *How to Write and Sell Your First Novel* and *How to Write and Sell Your First Nonfiction Book*."

*CONNOR LITERARY AGENCY, (III, IV), 640 W. 153rd St., New York NY 10031. (212)491-5233. Also: 7333 Gallagher Dr., #221D, Edina MN 55435. Phone/fax: (612)835-7251. Contact: Marlene K. Connor. Estab. 1985. Represents 50 clients. 30% of clients are new/previously unpublished writers. Specializes in popular fiction and nonfiction. Currently handles: 50% nonfiction books; 50% novels. Member agents: Deborah Connor Coker (children's books); John Lynch (sports, success/inspiration).
  ● Prior to opening her agency, Ms. Connor served at the Literary Guild of America, Simon and Schuster and Random House.
Handles: Nonfiction books, novels, children's books (especially with a minority slant). Considers these nonfiction areas: business; child guidance/parenting; cooking/food/nutrition; crafts/hobbies; current affairs; ethnic/cultural interests; government/politics/law; health/medicine; how-to; humor; interior decorating; language/literature/criticism; money/finance/economics; photography; popular culture; self-help/personal improvement; sports; true crime/investigative; women's issues/women's studies. Considers these fiction areas: contemporary issues; detective/police/crime; ethnic; experimental; family saga; horror; literary; mystery/suspense; thriller/espionage. Query with outline/proposal. Reports in 1 month on queries; 6 weeks on mss.
Recent Sales: *Essence: 25 Years of Celebrating the Black Woman* (Abrams); *The Marital Compatibility Test*, by Susan Adams (Carol Publishing Group); *We Are Overcome*, by Bonnie Allen (Crown); *TLC*, by Maria Corley (Kensington); *Black Sun Signs*, by Thelma Balfour (Fireside/Simon & Schuster).
Terms: Agent receives 15% commission on domestic sales; 25% on foreign sales. Offers written contract, binding for 1 year.
Fees: Charges a reading fee. "Nominal reading fee charged only when absolutely necessary."
Writers' Conferences: Howard University Publishing Institute; ABA; Oklahoma Writer's Federation.
Tips: Obtains new clients through queries, recommendations, conferences, grapevine, etc. "Seeking previously published writers with good sales records and new writers with real talent."

DORESE AGENCY LTD., (III), 37965 Palo Verde Dr., Cathedral City CA 92234. (619)321-1115. Fax: (619)321-1049. Contact: Alyss Barlow Dorese. Estab. 1977. Represents 30 clients. Currently handles: 65% nonfiction books; 35% novels.
Handles: Considers these nonfiction areas: art; biography/autobiography; business; child guidance/parenting; cooking/food/nutrition; crafts/hobbies; current affairs; gay/lesbian issues; government/politics/law; health/medicine; history; interior design/decorating; language/literature/criticism; military/war; money/finance/economics; music/dance/theater/film; New Age/metaphysics; photography; psychology; self-help/personal improvement; sociology; sports; true crime/investigative; women's issues/women's studies. Considers these fiction areas: action/adventure; contemporary issues; detective/police/crime; ethnic; family saga; feminist; gay; glitz; historical; lesbian; literary; mainstream; mystery/suspense; psychic/supernatural; regional; inspirational; sports; young adult. Send outline/proposal and SASE. Reports in 6 weeks on queries.
Recent Sales: *Rape of Kuwait*, by Jean Sassoon (Knightsbridge); *Get Married Now*, by Hilary Rich (Bob Adams).
Terms: Agent receives 15% commission on domestic sales; 20% on foreign sales. Offers written contract, binding for 2 years.
Fees: Does not charge a reading fee. Offers criticism service, cost depends on length of book.
Tips: Obtains new clients through referrals from past clients. "Don't say, 'I've written The Great American Novel.' It's an immediate turnoff."

EVANS & ASSOCIATES, 14330 Caves Rd., Novelty OH 44072-9503. Phone/fax: (216)338-3264. Contact: Bryan Evans. Estab. 1987. Represents 6 clients. 50% of clients are new/previously published writers. Currently handles: 20% nonfiction books; 20% scholarly books; 10% juvenile books; 30% novels; 20% short story collections. Member agents: Bryan Evans (scholarly books, nonfiction, short story collections, juvenile); Clyde Evans (mysteries, self-help).

Handles: Nonfiction books, scholarly books, juvenile books, novels, short story collections. Considers all nonfiction and fiction areas. Query. Send outline and 3 sample chapters. Reports in 2 months on queries; 4 months on mss.
Recent Sales: Recently returned from sabbatical.
Terms: Agent receives 15% commission on domestic sales; 20% on foreign sales (with 10% to foreign agent). Offers written contract, binding for 1 year, but negotiable.
Writers' Conferences: 12th Annual Western Reserve Writers Conference (Cleveland, September).
Tips: Listings such as the *Guide to Literary Agents* and recommendations from other agents, publishers, writers. "Clyde Evans is an attorney and also will review publisher contracts and/or negotiate with them at the rate of $75 per hour for review (usual total fee $75 to $150) and $125 per hour for negotiating with publisher. Initial consultation—no charge."

EXECUTIVE EXCELLENCE, (IV), 1344 E. 1120 South, Provo UT 84606. (801)375-4060. Fax: (801)377-5960. President: Ken Shelton. Agent: Trent Price. Estab. 1984. Represents 35-50 clients. Specializes in nonfiction trade books/management and personal development—books with a special focus such as ethics in business, managerial effectiveness, organizational productivity. Currently handles: 100% nonfiction. Member agents: Ken Shelton (president, editor); Trent Price (literary agent, acquisitions and sales); Noelle Oertle (assistant editor).
Handles: Nonfiction books, magazine articles, some foreign and multimedia rights. Considers these nonfiction areas: business; religious/inspirational; self-help/personal improvement.
Recent Sales: *In God We Trust,* by Norman Vincent Peale (Thomas Nelson); *The Commonsense MBA,* by Richard Astle (St. Martin's); *High Octane Selling,* (AMACOM Books); *Wave 3,* by Richard Poe (Prima); *The Complete Idiot's Guide to Winning Back Your Time,* by Jeff Davidson (Macmillan General Reference/Alpha).
Terms: Agent receives 15% commission on domestic sales. 75% of business is derived from commissions on ms sales; 10% from reading and review fees; 15% from book packaging/assisted self-publishing services.
Fees: "Charges critical reading and review fee. $500 taken from initial advance to cover expenses (phone, mail, travel, etc.)
Writers' Conferences: ABA (Chicago); ASTD; CBA (Denver).

*FRIEDA FISHBEIN LTD., (II), 2556 Hubbard St., Brooklyn NY 11235-6223. (212)247-4398. Contact: Janice Fishbein. Estab. 1928. Represents 32 clients. 50% of clients are new/previously unpublished writers. Currently handles: 10% nonfiction books; 5% young adult; 60% novels; 10% movie scripts; 10% stage plays; 5% TV scripts. Member agents: Heidi Carlson (literary and contemporary); Douglas Michael (play and screenplay scripts).
Handles: Nonfiction books, young adult books, novels. Considers these nonfiction areas: animals; biography/autobiography; cooking/food/nutrition; current affairs; juvenile nonfiction; military/war; nature/environment; self-help/personal improvement; true crime/investigative; women's issues/women's studies. Considers these fiction areas: action/adventure; contemporary issues; detective/police/crime; family saga; fantasy; feminist; historical; humor/satire; mainstream; mystery/suspense; romance (contemporary, historical, regency); science fiction; thriller/espionage; young adult. Query letter a must before sending ms. Reports in 3 weeks on queries; 6 weeks on mss accepted for evaluation.
Also Handles: Movie scripts, TV scripts ("not geared to a series"), stage plays.
Recent Sales: *Ghost in The Machine,* by David Gilman (play and screenplay).
Terms: Agent receives 10% commission on domestic sales; 15% on foreign sales. Offers written contract, binding for 30 days, cancellable by either party, except for properties being marketed or already sold.
Fees: Charges $80 reading fee up to 50,000 words, $1 per 1,000 words thereafter for new authors in a new genre; $80 for plays, TV, screenplays. Criticism service included in reading fee. Offers "an overall critique. Sometimes specific staff readers may refer to associates for no charge for additional readings if warranted." 60% of business is derived from commissions on ms sales; 40% is derived from reading fees or criticism services. Payment of criticism fee does not ensure representation.
Tips: Obtains new clients through recommendations from others. "*Always* submit a query letter first with an SASE. Manuscripts should be done in large type, double-spaced and one and one-half-inch margins, clean copy and edited for typos, etc."

*FLANNERY, WHITE AND STONE, (II), 1675 Larimer St., Suite 410, Denver CO 80202. (303)592-1233. Fax: (303)534-0577. Contact: Robin Barrett. Estab. 1987. Represents 45 clients. 40% of clients are new/previously unpublished writers. Specializes in mainstream, literary and genre fiction and unique nonfiction. Currently handles: 40% nonfiction books; 20% juvenile books; 40% fiction. Member agents: Robin Barrett (mainstream, genre and literary fiction, juvenile); Constance Solowiej (mainstream and literary fiction, nonfiction, business); Robert FitzGerald (business, medical).
Handles: Nonfiction books, juvenile books; novels; short story collections. Considers these nonfiction areas: business; child guidance/parenting; current affairs; ethnic/cultural interests; gay/lesbian issues;

government/politics/law; health/medicine; juvenile nonfiction; money/finance/economics; nature/environment; New Age/metaphysics; psychology; religious/inspirational; self-help/personal improvement; sociology; sports; women's issues/women's studies. Considers these fiction areas: action/adventure; ethnic; family saga; feminist; gay; historical; humor/satire; juvenile; lesbian; literary; mainstream; mystery/suspense; picture book; psychic/supernatural; romance (contemporary, historical); science fiction; thriller/espionage; young adult. Send outline/proposal and 2 sample chapters. Reports in 1 month on queries; 2 months on mss.
Recent Sales: *Waking From the Dream*, by Detong Cho Yin (Charles Tuttle, Inc.); *Risk Your Own Nightmare* and *More Six Minute Mysteries*, by Don Wulffson (Lowell House [juvenile]); *Prize in the Snow*, by Bill Easterling (Storytime [PBS], original sale to Little, Brown).
Terms: Agent receives 15% on domestic sales; 20% on foreign sales. Offers written contract.
Fees: "Due to the overwhelming number of manuscripts we receive, we now charge a reading and analysis fee for new and unpublished writers. The fee includes a five to seven-page overall evaluation report." 90% of business is derived from commissions; 10% from critiques. Payment of reading fee does not ensure representation.
Writers' Conferences: Aspen Writers' Conference (Aspen); ABA (Chicago, June); Rocky Mountain Book Festival (Denver, October).
Tips: "Make your nonfiction proposals professional and publisher-ready; let your fiction speak for itself."

*FOLLENDORE & IKEYAMA LITERARY AGENCY, (II), 298 Country Club Dr., San Luis Obispo CA 93401-8908. (805)545-9297. Fax: (805)545-9297. Contact: Joan Follendore, Carolyn Ikeyama or William Brown. Estab. 1988. Represents 70 clients. 50% of clients are new/previously unpublished writers. Currently handles: 55% nonfiction books; 12% scholarly books; 20% juvenile books; 10% novels; 1% poetry books; 2% short story collections. Member agents: Joan Follendore (adult nonfiction); Carolyn Ikeyama (children's books and adult fiction); William Brown (art and architecture).
Handles: Nonfiction books, textbooks, scholarly books, religious books, juvenile books, novels, picture books, poetry, short story collections. No scripts for stage or screen. Considers these nonfiction areas: agriculture/horticulture; animals; art/architecture/design; biography/autobiography; business; child guidance/parenting; crafts/hobbies; current affairs; education; ethnic/cultural interests; government/politics/law; health/medicine; history; how-to; humor; interior design/decorating; juvenile nonfiction; language/literature/criticism; military/war; money/finance/economics; nature/environment; New Age/metaphysics; popular culture; psychology; religious/inspirational; science/technology; self-help/personal improvement; sociology; true crime/investigative; women's issues/women's studies. Considers all fiction areas. Query first. Reports in 1 week on queries.
Recent Sales: *Peterson's Tennis Camps & Clinics*, by Brown & Thompson (Peterson Publishing Co.); *Point of Power: A Relationship With Your Soul*, by Kay Snow-Davis (Element Books).
Terms: Agent receives 15% on domestic sales; 20% on foreign sales. Offers written contract.
Fees: "No fee to authors who've been published in the prior few years by a major house. Other authors are charged a reading fee and our editing service is offered. For nonfiction, we completely edit the proposal/outline and sample chapter; for fiction and children's, we need the entire manuscript. Editing includes book formats, questions, comments, suggestions for expansion, cutting and pasting, etc." Also offers other services: proofreading, rewriting, proposal development, authors' public relations, etc. 65% of business is derived from commissions on ms sales; 35% is derived from reading or editing fees. Payment of fees does not ensure representation unless "revisions meet our standards."
Writer's Conferences: ABA (Chicago).
Tips: Obtains new clients through recommendations from others and personal contacts at literary functions. "Study and make your query as perfect and professional as you possibly can."

FORTHWRITE LITERARY AGENCY, (II), 3579 E. Foothill Blvd., Suite 327, Pasadena CA 91107. Phone: (818)798-0793. Fax: (818)798-5653. E-mail: literaryag@aol.com. Contact: Wendy L. Zhorne. Estab. 1989. Member of WNBA, National Speakers Association, Publisher's Marketing Association. Represents 50 clients. 10% of clients are new/previously unpublished writers. Specializes in nonfiction. Currently handles: 70% nonfiction books; 5% novels; 25% foreign & electronic rights. Member agent: Nick Griffin (new writers, fiction and nonfiction).
Handles: Considers commercial nonfiction in these areas: self-help and how-to on psychology, pop psychology, health, alternative health, business, child care/parenting, theology, inspirational, spirituality, home maintenance and management, cooking, crafts, interior design, art, biography, writing, film, consumer reference, ecology, coffee table and art books, current affairs, women's studies, economics and history. Considers these adult fiction areas: historical fiction; also literary, romantic suspense, religious, mainstream, mystery/suspense/thriller, metaphysical. "Exemplary fiction from new or established authors." Query with first 30 pages and SASE only. No unsolicited mss. Reports in 1 month on queries; 6 weeks on ms.
Recent Sales: *Self Esteem in the Workplace*, by Jack Canfield & Jackie Miller (McGraw Hill); *Promote Yourself Through Visibility Marketing*, by Raleigh Pinskey (Avon); *Larry Wilde, King of*

Humor, by Larry Wilde (Multimedia Development Corp.); *Japanese Vegetarian Cooking*, by Max Jacobson (Prima Publishing); *Price Wars!*, by Tom Winninger (Prima Publishing).

Also Handles: CD-& disk based rights; foreign, ancillary, upselling (selling a previously published book to a larger publisher) & other secondary & subsidiary rights.

Fees: Does not charge a reading fee. Offers criticism service.

Writers' Conferences: ABA, CBA, Frankfurt Booksellers' Convention, many regional conferences and regularly lectures at local colleges and universities on finding an agent, how to write nonfiction, creativity enhancement.

Tips: Obtains new clients through referrals, recommendations by editors, chambers of commerce, satisfied authors, conferences etc. "Please check your material, including query and cover letter, for spelling and typing errors before sending. If you are worried whether your material will arrive, send a postcard to return to you dated; don't search area codes for agent's home number; always send a SASE with queries. Never tell an agent, 'My grandmother loved it.' Know your subject and your competition."

FRAN LITERARY AGENCY, (I, II), 7235 Split Creek, San Antonio TX 78238-3627. (210)684-1659. Contact: Fran Rathmann. Estab. 1993. Represents 25 clients. 55% of clients are new/previously unpublished writers. "Very interested in Star Trek novels/screenplays." Currently handles: 15% nonfiction books; 10% juvenile books; 30% novels; 5% novellas; 5% poetry books; 15% movie scripts; 20% TV scripts.

Handles: Nonfiction books, novels. Considers these nonfiction areas: agriculture/horticulture; animals; biography/autobiography; business; child guidance/parenting; cooking/food/nutrition; crafts/hobbies; ethnic/cultural interests; health/medicine; history; how-to; humor; interior design/decorating; juvenile nonfiction; military/war; nature/environment; religious/inspirational; self-help/personal improvement. Considers these fiction areas: action/adventure; cartoon/comic; contemporary issues; detective/police/crime; fantasy; historical; horror; humor/satire; juvenile; mainstream; mystery/suspense; picture book; regional; romance (contemporary, historical); science fiction; thriller/espionage; westerns/frontier; young adult. Send outline plus 3 sample chapters. For picture books and poetry send entire ms. Reports in 2 weeks on queries; 2 months on mss.

Recent Sales: *Unaccountable*, by Robert McDonald (HarperCollins); *101 Ways to Raise a Good Kid*, by Albert Santos (Globe).

Also Handles: Movie scripts (feature film, documentary, animation), TV scripts (TV mow, episodic drama). Considers these script subject areas: action/adventure; cartoon/animation; comedy; contemporary issues; detective/police/crime; family saga; historical; horror; humor; juvenile; mainstream; mystery/suspense; romantic comedy and drama; science fiction; thriller; westerns/frontier. Send entire ms.

Recent Sales: *TV Script*: *Family Tree* (Star Trek Deep Space 9), by Patricia Dahlin (Paramount).

Terms: Agent receives 15% commission on domestic sales; 20% on foreign sales. Needs "letter of authorization," usually binding for 6 months.

Fees: Charges $25 processing fee, nonrefundable. Criticism service: $100. 80% of business is derived from commissions on mss sales; 20% from criticism services. Payment of fee does not ensure representation.

Writers' Conferences: SAWG (San Antonio, spring).

Tips: Obtains clients through recommendations, listing in telephone book. "Please send SASE or box!"

GELLES-COLE LITERARY ENTERPRISES, (II), 12 Turner Rd., Pearl River NY 10965. (914)735-1913. President: Sandi Gelles-Cole. Estab. 1983. Represents 50 clients. 25% of clients are new/unpublished writers. "We concentrate on published and unpublished, but we try to avoid writers who seem stuck in mid-list." Specializes in commercial fiction and nonfiction. Currently handles: 50% nonfiction books; 50% novels.

Handles: Nonfiction books, novels. "We're looking for more nonfiction—fiction has to be complete to submit—publishers buying fewer unfinished novels." No unsolicited mss. Reports in 3 weeks.

Terms: Agent receives 15% commission on domestic and dramatic sales; 20% on foreign sales.

Fees: Charges $100 reading fee for proposal; $150/ms under 250 pages; $250/ms over 250 pages. "Our reading fee is for evaluation. Writer receives total evaluation, what is right, what is wrong, is book 'playing' to market, general advice on how to fix." Charges writers for overseas calls, overnight

For explanation of symbols, see the Key to Symbols and Abbreviations. For translation of an organization's acronym, see the Table of Acronyms. For unfamiliar words, check the Glossary.

mail, messenger. 5% of income derived from fees charged to writers. 50% of income derived from commissions on sales; 45% of income derived from editorial service.

‡GEM LITERARY SERVICES, (II), 13042 W. 130th St., Strongsville OH 44136-4672. (216)237-1750. Contact: Darla Pfenninger. Estab. 1992. Represents 9 clients. 70% of clients are new/previously unpublished writers. Currently handles: 10% nonfiction books; 20% juvenile books; 60% novels; 10% movie scripts.
Handles: Nonfiction books, scholarly books, textbooks, juvenile books, novels, movie scripts. Considers these nonfiction areas: biography/autobiography; business; child guidance/parenting; computers/electronics; cooking/food/nutrition; current affairs; gay/lesbian issues; government/politics/law; how-to; humor; juvenile nonfiction; money/finance/economics; music/dance/theater/film; New Age/metaphysics; religious/inspirational; science/technology; self-help/personal improvement; true crime/investigative; women's issues/women's studies. Considers these fiction areas: action/adventure; detective/police/crime; family saga; fantasy; feminist; historical; horror; humor/satire; juvenile; literary; mainstream; mystery; picture book; psychic/supernatural; regional; romance (gothic, historical); science fiction; thriller/espionage; westerns/frontier; young adult. Send outline/proposal with SASE for response. Reports in 2 weeks on queries; 1 month on mss.
Recent Sales: *Vanessa*, by Mary Pfenninger (G&G Publishing).
Terms: Agent receives 10% commission on domestic sales; 15% on foreign sales. Offers written contract, binding for 6 months, with 30 day cancellation clause.
Fees: Charges $175 for office expenses, refunded upon sale of property.
Writers' Conference: Midwest Writers Conference (Canton OH, September/October).
Tips: Obtains new clients through recommendations and solicitations. "Looking for well thought out plots, not run-of-the-mill story lines."

THE GISLASON AGENCY, (II), 219 Main St. SE, Suite 506, Minneapolis MN 55414-2160. (612)331-8033. Fax: (612)331-8115. Attorney/Agent: Barbara J. Gislason. Estab. 1992. Member of Minnesota State Bar Association, Art & Entertainment Law Section, MIPLA Copyright Committee, The Loft, Midwest Fiction Writers, UMBA. 70% of clients are new/previously unpublished writers. Specializes in fiction and nonfiction. Currently handles: 30% nonfiction books; 70% novels. Member agents: Dara Moskowitz, Wendy Valentine.
Handles: Nonfiction books, novels. Considers these nonfiction areas: how-to; law; self-help/personal improvement; true crime/investigative. Considers these fiction areas: fantasy; mystery/suspense; romance (contemporary, gothic, historical, regency); science fiction; law-related. Query with outline plus 3 sample chapters. Reports in 1 month on queries, 2 months on mss.
Terms: Agent receives 15% commission on domestic sales; 20% on foreign sales. Offers written contract, binding for 1 year with option to renew.
Fees: Client pays for all submission costs.
Writer's Conferences: Midwest Fiction Writers; ABA.
Tips: Obtains half of new clients through recommendations from others and half from *Guide to Literary Agents* and *Literary Market Place*. "Cover letter should be well written and include a detailed synopsis of the work, the first three chapters and author information. If the work was written with a specific publisher in mind, this should be communicated. In addition to owning an agency, Ms. Gislason practices law in the area of Art and Entertainment and has a broad spectrum of industry contacts."

GLADDEN UNLIMITED, (II), 3742 Curtis St., San Diego CA 92106. (619)224-5051. Contact: Carolan Gladden. Estab. 1987. Represents 20 clients. 95% of clients are new/previously unpublished writers. Currently handles: 30% nonfiction; 70% novels.
Handles: Novels, nonfiction. Considers these nonfiction areas: celebrity biography; business; how-to; self-help; true crime/investigative. Considers these fiction areas: action/adventure; detective/police/crime; ethnic; glitz; horror; mainstream; thriller. "No romance or children's." Query with synopsis. Reports in 2 weeks on queries; 2 months on mss.
Terms: Agent receives 15% commission on domestic sales; 20% on foreign sales.
Fees: Does not charge a reading fee. Marketability evaluation: $100 (manuscript to 400 pages.) $200 (over 400 pages.) "Offers six to eight pages of diagnosis and specific recommendations to turn the project into a saleable commodity. Also includes a copy of handy guide 'Be a Successful Writer.' Dedicated to helping new authors achieve publication."

LUCIANNE S. GOLDBERG LITERARY AGENTS, INC., (II), 255 W. 84th St., Suite 6-A, New York NY 10024. (212)799-1260. Editorial Director: Jonah Goldberg. Estab. 1974. Represents 65 clients. 10% of clients are new/unpublished writers. "Any author we decide to represent must have a good idea, a good presentation of that idea and writing skill to compete with the market. Representation depends solely on the execution of the work whether writer is published or unpublished." Specializes in nonfiction works, "but will review a limited number of novels." Currently handles: 75% nonfiction books; 25% novels. Member agents: Cyril Hiltebrand (editorial); Jane Moseley (editorial).

Handles: Nonfiction books, novels. Query with outline. Reports in 2 weeks on queries; 3 weeks on mss. "If our agency does not respond within 1 month to your request to become a client, you may submit requests elsewhere."

Recent Sales: *Death Row Women*, by Tom Kuncl (Simon & Schuster); *The Immigrants*, by Dylan Ross (HarperCollins).

Terms: Agent receives 15% commission on domestic sales; 25% on dramatic and foreign sales.

Fees: Charges reading fee on unsolicited mss: $150/full-length ms. Criticism service included in reading fee. "Our critiques run three or four pages, single-spaced. They deal with the overall evaluation of the work. Three agents within the organization read and then confer. Marketing advice is included." Payment of fee does not ensure the agency will represent a writer. Charges for phone expenses, cable fees, photocopying and messenger service after the work is sold. 80% of income derived from commission on ms sales.

*ANDREW HAMILTON'S LITERARY AGENCY (II), P.O. Box 604118, Cleveland OH 44104-0118. (216)881-1032. E-mail: rgbw22a@prodigy.com. Contact: Andrew Hamilton. Estab. 1991. Represents 15 clients. 60% of clients are new/previously unpublished writers. Currently handles: 50% nonfiction books; 7% scholarly books; 3% juvenile books; 40% novels. Member agent: Andrew Hamilton (music, business, self-help, how-to, sports).

● Prior to opening his agency, Mr. Hamilton served as editor at several legal publications.

Handles: Nonfiction books, juvenile books, novels, novellas. Considers these nonfiction areas: animals; biography/autobiography; business; child guidance/parenting; cooking/food/nutrition; current affairs; ethnic/cultural interests; government/politics/law; health/medicine; history; juvenile nonfiction; money/finance/economics; music/dance/theater/film; psychology; religious/inspirational; self-help/personal improvement; sociology; sports; true crime/investigative; women's issues/women's studies; minority concerns; pop music. Considers these fiction areas: action/adventure; cartoon/comic; confessional; contemporary issues; detective/police/crime; erotica; ethnic; family saga; humor/satire; juvenile; mystery/suspense; psychic/supernatural; religious/inspiration; romance (contemporary); sports; thriller/espionage; westerns/frontier; young adult. Send entire ms. Reports in 1 week on queries; 3 weeks on mss.

Terms: Agent receives 15% commission on domestic sales; 20% on foreign sales. Offers written contract.

Fees: "Reading fees are for new authors and are nonrefundable. My reading fee is $50 for 60,000 words or less and $100 for manuscripts over 60,000 words. I charge a one-time marketing fee of $200 for manuscripts." 70% of business derived from commissions on ms sales; 30% from reading fees or criticism services.

Tips: Obtains new clients through recommendations, solicitation and writing seminars. "Be patient: the wheels turn slowly in the publishing world."

*ALICE HILTON LITERARY AGENCY, (II), 13131 Welby Way, North Hollywood CA 91606. (818)982-2546. Fax: (818)765-8207. Contact: Alice Hilton. Editor: David Kinzie. Estab. 1986. Eager to work with new/unpublished writers. "Interested in any quality material, although agent's personal taste runs in the genre of 'Cheers.' 'L.A. Law,' 'American Playhouse,' 'Masterpiece Theatre' and Woody Allen vintage humor."

Handles: Nonfiction, fiction, juvenile. Considers these fiction areas: action/adventure; confessional; contemporary issues; detective/police/crime; erotica; ethnic; fantasy; historical; horror; humor/satire; juvenile; literary; mainstream; mystery/suspense; picture book; psychic/supernatural; romance (contemporary, gothic, historical, regency); science fiction; sports; thriller/espionage; westerns/frontier; young adult.

Recent Sales: *The Next Streetcar*, by Mina Mann (New Saga Press); *The Fair Tax—Now is Our Time*, by Larry Singer (Tomorrow Now Press).

Also Handles: Movie scripts (feature film, documentary); TV scripts (TV mow, sitcom). Considers all script subject areas.

Terms: Agent receives 10% commission. Brochure available with SASE. Preliminary phone call appreciated.

Fees: Charges evaluation fee of $3/1,000 words. Charges for phone, postage and photocopy expenses.

Agents ranked I and II are most open to both established and new writers. Agents ranked III are open to established writers with publishing-industry references.

THE EDDY HOWARD AGENCY, (III), % 37 Bernard St., Eatontown NJ 07724-1906. (908)542-3525. Contact: Eddy Howard Pevovar, N.D., Ph.D. Estab. 1986. Signatory of WGA. Represents 110 clients. 16% of clients are new/previously unpublished writers. Specializes in film, sitcom and literary. Currently handles: 5% nonfiction books; 5% scholarly books; 2% textbooks; 5% juvenile books; 5% novels; 2% novellas; 25% movie scripts; 30% TV scripts; 10% stage plays; 5% short story collections; 1% syndicated material; 5% other. Member agents: Eddy Howard Pevovar, N.D., Ph.D. (agency executive); Francine Gail (director of comedy development).
 ● See the expanded listing for this agency in Script/Agents.

*YVONNE TRUDEAU HUBBS AGENCY, (II), 32371 Alipaz, #101, San Juan Capistrano CA 92675-4147. (714)496-1970. Contact: Yvonne Hubbs. Estab. 1983, temporarily closed 1990, reopened 1993. Member of RWA. Represents 20 clients. 10% of clients are new/previously unpublished writers. Member agents: Thomas D. Hubbs, journalist (radio broadcasting/public relations); Yvonne Hubbs, agent, lecturer, writer.
Handles: Nonfiction books, novels. Considers these nonfiction areas: current affairs; history; women's issues/women's studies. Considers these fiction areas: action/adventure; contemporary issues; family saga; fantasy; feminist; glitz; historical; mainstream; mystery/suspense; psychic/supernatural; romance (contemporary, gothic, historical, regency); science fiction; thriller/espionage. Query with outline/proposal plus 1 sample chapter. Reports in 2 weeks on queries, 1 month on mss.
Terms: Agent receives 15% commission on domestic sales; 20% on foreign sales. Offers written contract, binding for 1 year, with 30 day cancellation clause.
Fees: Charges $50 reading fee to new writers only; refundable if client is sold within 1 year. Criticism service included in reading fee. "I personally write the critiques after reviewing the manuscript." Charges for travel expenses (if approved), photocopying, telegraph/fax expenses, overseas phone calls. 60% of business is derived from commissions on ms sales; 40% derived from reading fees or criticism services. Payment of criticism fee does not ensure representation.
Writer's Conferences: RWA; Romantic Times.
Tips: Obtains new clients through recommendations, conferences. "Be professional in your query letter. Always include SASE with a query."

INDEPENDENT PUBLISHING AGENCY, (I), P.O. Box 176, Southport CT 06490-0176. Phone/fax: (203)268-4878. E-mail: henryberry@aol.com. Contact: Henry Berry. Estab. 1990. Represents 25 clients. 30% of clients are new/previously unpublished writers. Especially interested in topical nonfiction (historical, political, social topics, cultural studies, health, business) and literary and genre fiction. Currently handles: 70% nonfiction books; 10% juvenile books; 20% novels and short story collections.
Handles: Nonfiction books, juvenile books, novels, short story collections. Considers these nonfiction areas: anthropology/archaeology; art/architecture/design; biography/autobiography; business; child guidance/parenting; cooking/food/nutrition; crafts/hobbies; current affairs; ethnic/cultural interests; government/politics/law; history; juvenile nonfiction; language/literature/criticism; military/war; money/finance/economics; music/dance/theater/film; nature/environment; photography; popular culture; psychology; religious; science/technology; self-help/personal improvement; sociology; sports; true crime/investigative; women's issues/women's studies. Considers these fiction areas: action/adventure; cartoon/comic; confessional; contemporary issues; crime; erotica; ethnic; experimental; fantasy; feminist; historical; humor/satire; juvenile; literary; mainstream; mystery/suspense; picture book; psychic/supernatural; thriller/espionage; young adult. Send synopsis/outline plus 2 sample chapters. Reports in 2 weeks on queries; 6 weeks on mss.
Recent Sales: Available upon request by prospective clients.
Terms: Agent receives 15% commission on domestic sales; 20% on foreign sales. Offers "agreement that spells out author-agent relationship."
Fees: No fee for queries w/sample chapters; $125 reading fee for evaluation/critique of complete ms. Offers criticism service if requested. Charges average $1/page, with $50 minimum for poetry and stories; $100 minimum for novels and nonfiction. Written critique averages 3 pages—includes critique of the material, suggestions on how to make it marketable and advice on marketing it. Charges for postage, photocopying and UPS mailing, legal fees (if necessary). All expenses over $25 cleared with client. 90% of business is derived from commissions on ms sales; 10% derived from criticism services.
Tips: Usually obtains new clients through referrals from clients, notices in writer's publications. Looks for "proposal or chapters professionally presented, with clarification of the distinctiveness of the project and grasp of intended readership."

CAROLYN JENKS AGENCY, (II), 205 Walden St., Cambridge MA 02140-3507. Phone/fax: (617)876-6927. E-mail: caroljenks@aol.com. Contact: Carolyn Jenks. Estab. 1966. 50% of clients are new/previously unpublished writers. Currently handles: 15% nonfiction books; 40% novels; 20% movie scripts; 10% stage plays; 15% TV scripts.
Handles: Nonfiction books, juvenile books, novels. Considers these nonfiction areas: animals; archaeology; biography/autobiography; computers/electronics; gay/lesbian issues; health/medicine; history;

inspirational; nature/environment; New Age/metaphysics; psychology; science/technology; theater/ film; women's issues/women's studies. Considers these fiction areas: action/adventure; contemporary issues; fantasy; feminist; gay; glitz; historical; lesbian; literary; mystery/suspense; regional; romance (contemporary, historical); thriller/espionage; westerns/frontier; young adult. Query. Reports in 2 weeks on queries; 6 weeks on mss.

Also Handles: Movie scripts (feature film, documentary); TV scripts (TV mow, episodic drama); stage plays. Considers these script subject areas: action/adventure; comedy; contemporary issues; family saga; historical; humor; juvenile; mainstream; mystery/suspense; romantic comedy and drama; thriller; westerns/frontier.

Terms: Agent receives 15% commission on domestic sales; 10% on film and TV. Offers written contract.

Fees: Charges reading fee to non-WGA members: 120,000 words $100; screenplay $100. WGA members exempted.

Tips: Query first in writing with SASE.

*JLM LITERARY AGENTS, (III), 5901 Warner Ave., Suite 92, Huntington Beach CA 92649. (714)547-4870. Fax: (714)840-5660. Contact: Judy Semler. Estab. 1985. Represents 25 clients. 5% of clients are new/previously unpublished writers. Agency is "generalist with an affinity for high-quality, spiritual self-help psychology and mystery/suspense." Currently handles: 90% nonfiction books; 10% novels.

Handles: Nonfiction books, novels. Considers these nonfiction areas: biography/autobiography; business (popular); current affairs; music/dance/theater/film; nature/environment; popular culture; psychology; religious/inspirational; self-help/personal improvement; sociology; true crime/investigative; women's issues/women's studies. Considers these fiction areas: glitz; mystery/suspense; psychic/ supernatural; contemporary romance. For nonfiction, send outline with 2 sample chapters. For fiction, query with 3 chapters—except for mystery/suspense, send entire ms. No faxed submissions. Reports in 1 month on queries; 10 weeks on mss.

Recent Sales: *The Blue Angel: The First 50 Years* (Motor Book). *The Breast Cancer Companion*, by Kathy LaTour (Morrow/Avon).

Terms: Agent receives 15% commission on domestic sales; 10% on foreign sales plus 15% to subagent. Offers written contract, binding for 1 year, with 30-day escape clause.

Fees: Does not charge a reading fee. Does not do critiques or editing, but will refer to freelancers. Charges retainer for marketing costs for unpublished authors or to authors changing genres. Charges for routine office expenses associated with the marketing. 100% of business is derived from commissions on ms sales.

Tips: "Most of my clients are referred to me by other clients or editors. If you want to be successful, learn all you can about proper submission and invest in the equipment or service to make your project *look* dazzling. Computers are available to everyone and the competition looks good. You must at least match that to even get noticed."

LARRY KALTMAN LITERARY AGENCY, (II), 1301 S. Scott St., Arlington VA 22204-4656. (703)920-3771. Contact: Larry Kaltman. Estab. 1984. Represents 15 clients. 75% of clients are new/previously unpublished writers. Currently handles: 85% novels; 10% novellas; 5% short story collections.
- Prior to opening his agency. Mr. Kaltman worked as a writer for *The Washington Post* and drama critic for various Washington area papers.

Handles: Novels, novellas, short story collections. Considers all fiction areas except for children's.

Recent Sales: *The Return*, by David London (Simon & Schuster); *When Arm & Hammer Met the Pillsbury Doughboy*, by William Van Wert (Simon & Schuster).

Terms: Agent receives 15% commission on domestic sales; 20% on foreign sales. Offers written contract, binding for 6 months.

Fees: Charges reading fee for all unsolicited ms. "For up to 300 pages, the fee is $250. For each additional page the charge is 50¢/page. Author receives an approximately 1,500-word report commenting on writing quality, structure and organization and estimate of marketability. Larry Kaltman write all critiques." Charges for postage, mailing envelopes and long-distance phone calls.

Writers' Conferences: Washington Independent Writers (Washington DC, Spring); California Writers Club; Romance Writers of Virginia (Williamsburg VA, Spring); Maryland Writers (Fall).

Tips: Obtains new clients through query letters, solicitation. "Plots, presentations, synopses and outlines have very little effect. A sample of the writing is the most significant factor." The agency also sponsors the Washington Prize for Fiction, an annual competition for unpublished works." Awards: $5,000 (1st prize), $2,500 (2nd prize), $1,000 (3rd prize).

*J. KELLOCK & ASSOCIATES, LTD., (II), 11017 80th Ave., Edmonton, Alberta T6G 0R2 Canada. (403)433-0274. Contact: Joanne Kellock. Estab. 1981. Member of Writer's Guild of Alberta. Represents 50 clients. 10% of clients are new/previously unpublished writers. "I do very well with all works for children but do not specialize as such." Currently handles: 30% nonfiction books; 1% scholarly books; 50% juvenile books; 19% novels.

Handles: Nonfiction, juvenile, novels. Considers these nonfiction areas: animals; anthropology/archaeology; art/architecture/design; biography/autobiography; business; child guidance/parenting; cooking/food/nutrition; current affairs; health/medicine; history; juvenile nonfiction; language/literature/criticism; music/dance/theater/film; nature/environment; New Age/metaphysics; self-help/personal improvement; sports; true crime/investigative; women's issues/women's studies. Considers these fiction areas: action/adventure; contemporary issues; detective/police/crime; experimental; family saga; fantasy; feminist; glitz; historical; horror; humor/satire; juvenile; literary; mystery/suspense; picture book; romance; science fiction; sports; thriller/espionage; westerns/frontier; young adult. Query with outline plus 3 sample chapters. Reports in 10 weeks on queries; 5 months on mss.

Recent Sales: *My Rows and Piles of Coins* (picture book), by Tololwa M. Mollel (Clarion Books, New York); *Bed and Roses* (three book juvenile series), by Martyn Godfrey (Avon Books, New York); *Killer Instinct*, by Larry Pike (Zebra Books, New York); *Campfire Yarns* (adult nonfiction), by Andy Russell (McClellenad & Stewart, Toronto, Canada).

Terms: Agent receives 15% commission on domestic sales (English language); 20% on foreign sales. Offers written contract, binding for 2 years.

Fees: Charges $150 reading fee. "Fee under no circumstances is refundable. *New writers only are charged.*" $140 (US) to read 3 chapters plus brief synopsis of any work; $100 for children's picture book material. "If style is working with subject, the balance is read free of charge. Criticism is also provided for the fee. If style is not working with the subject, I explain why not; if talent is obvious, I explain how to make the manuscript work. I either do critiques myself or my reader does them. Critiques concern themselves with use of language, theme, plotting—all the usual. Return postage is always required. I cannot mail to the US with US postage, so always enclose a SAE, plus either IRCs or cash. Canadian postage is more expensive, so double the amount for either international or cash. I do not return on-spec long-distance calls; if the writer chooses to telephone, please request that I return the call collect. However, a query letter is much more appropriate." 70% of business is derived from commissions on ms sales; 30% is derived from reading fees or criticism service. Payment of criticism fee does not ensure representation.

Tips: Obtains new clients through recommendations from others, solicitations. "Do not send first drafts. Always double space. Very brief outlines and synopsis are more likely to be read first. For the picture book writer, the toughest sale to make in the business, please study the market before putting pen to paper. All works written for children must fit into the proper age groups regarding length of story, vocabulary level. For writers of the genre novel, read hundreds of books in the genre you've chosen to write, first. In other words, know your competition. Follow the rules of the genre exactly. For writers of science fiction/fantasy and the mystery, it is important a new writer has many more than one such book in him/her. Publishers are not willing today to buy single books in most areas of genre. Publishers who buy science fiction/fantasy usually want a two/three book deal at the beginning."

*NATASHA KERN LITERARY AGENCY, (II), P.O. Box 2908, Portland OR 97208-2908. (503)297-6190. Contact: Natasha Kern. Estab. 1986. Member of AAR, RWA, MWA, SinC. Specializes in literary and commercial fiction and nonfiction.

Handles: Nonfiction books, novels. Considers these nonfiction areas: agriculture/horticulture; animals; anthropology/archaeology; art/architecture/design; biography/autobiography; business; child guidance/parenting; cooking/food/nutrition; current affairs; education; ethnic/cultural interests; gay/lesbian issues; health/medicine; how-to; language/literature/criticism; money/finance/economics; nature/environment; New Age/metaphysics; popular; psychology; science/technology; self-help/personal improvement; true crime/investigative; women's issues/women's studies; women's spirituality. Considers these fiction areas: contemporary issues; detective/police/crime; ethnic; family saga; feminist; historical; mainstream; mystery/suspense; romance (contemporary, gothic, historical, regency, futuristic); thriller/espionage; westerns/frontier. "Send a detailed, one-page query with a SASE, including the submission history, writing credits and information about how complete the project is. If requested, for fiction send a two to three page synopsis, in addition to the first three chapters, for nonfiction, submit a proposal consisting of an outline, two chapters, SASE, and a note describing market and how project is different or better than similar works. Also send a blurb about the author and information about the length of the manuscript. For category fiction, a five- to ten-page synopsis should be sent with the chapters." Reports in 2 weeks on queries.

Recent Sales: *Black Cross*, by Greg Iles (Dutton); *Oprah*, by George Mair (Carol); *Liberty Blue*, by Robin Hatcher (Harper); *Enchant The Heavens*, by Kathleen Morgan (Kensington); *Direct Descendant*, by Charles Wilson (St. Martin's); *Serpents in the Manger*, by Harris and Milam (Barricade).

Terms: Agent receives 15% commission on domestic sales; 20% on foreign sales.

Fees: Charges $45 reading fee for unpublished novelists. "When your work is sold, your fee will be credited to your account. Please do not send fee unless requested."

Writers' Conference: RWA National Conference; Santa Barbara Writer's Conference; Golden Triangle Writer's Conference.

‡THE KIRKLAND LITERARY AGENCY, (II), P.O. Box 50608, Amarillo TX 79159-0608. (806)356-0216. Fax: (806)356-0452. Contact: Dee Pace, submissions director. Estab. 1993. Represents 60 clients. 50% of clients are new/previously unpublished writers. Specializes in romance and mainstream novels, but represents all categories of novel-length fiction. Currently handles: 15% nonfiction books; 5% juvenile books; 80% novels. Member agent: Jean Price.

Handles: Nonfiction books, juvenile books, novels. Considers these nonficton areas: current affairs; humor; self-help/personal improvement. Considers these fiction areas: action/adventure; contemporary issues; detective/police/crime; ethnic; family saga; fantasy; glitz; historical, horror (extremely selective); humor/satire; literary; mainstream; mystery/suspense; psychic/supernatural; romance (contemporary, gothic, historical, inspirational, regency); science fiction; thriller/espionage; westerns/frontier (extremely selective); young adult. Query with outline and 3 sample chapters. Reports in 6 weeks on queries; 3 months on mss.

Terms: Agent receives 15% commission on domestic sales; 20% on foreign sales. Offers written contract, binding for 1 year, with 30 day cancellation clause.

Fees: Does not charge a reading fee. Criticism service on a limited basis (less than 1% of income): $1 per page. Critique written by Dee Pace covers line edit and overall review of plot strengths and weaknesses. Charges marketing fee to previously unpublished writers of $150 for postage, phone calls, photocopying, if necessary. Balance refunded upon first sale. 1% of business is derived from criticism fees. Payment of criticism fee does not ensure representation.

Writers' Conferences: Duel on the Delta (Memphis TN, March); East Texas Writers Conference (Longview TX, April); National Romance Writers of America (Dallas, July): Haunted by Love (Amarillo TX, October).

Tips: Obtains new clients through referrals and conferences. "Write toward publishers' guidelines, particularly concerning maximum and minimum word count."

LAW OFFICES OF ROBERT L. FENTON PC, (II), 31800 Northwestern Hwy., #390, Farmington Hills MI 48334. (810)855-8780. Fax: (810)855-3302. Contact: Robert L. Fenton. Estab. 1960. Signatory of SAG. Represents 40 clients. 25% of clients are new/previously unpublished writers. Currently handles: 25% nonfiction books; 10% scholarly books; 10% textbooks; 10% juvenile books; 35% novels; 2½% poetry books; 2½% short story collections; 5% movie scripts. Member agents: Robert L. Fenton.

● Mr. Fenton has been an entertainment attorney for 25 years, was a producer at 20th Century Fox and Universal Studios for several years and is a published author himself.

Handles: Nonfiction books, novels, short story collections, syndicated material, movie scripts, TV scripts. Considers these nonfiction areas: biography/autobiography; business; child guidance/parenting; computers/electronics; current affairs; government/politics/law; health/medicine; military/war; money/finance/economics; music/dance/theater/film; religious/inspirational; science/technology; self-help/personal improvement; sports; true crime/investigative; women's issues/women's studies. Considers these fiction areas: action/adventure; contemporary issues; detective/police/crime; ethnic; glitz; historical; humor/satire; mainstream; mystery/suspense; romance; science fiction; sports; thriller/espionage; westerns/frontier. Send 3-4 sample chapters (approximately 75 pages). Reports in 2 weeks on queries.

Recent Sales: *Audacious Stuff* and *Kishka Chronicles*, by Greta Lipson (Simon & Schuster); *23 Degrees North*, by Thomas Morrisey; *Shareholders Rebellion*, George P. Schwartz (Irwin Pub.); *Royal Invitation*, Julia Fenton (Berkley).

Terms: Agent receives 15% on domestic sales. Offers written contract, binding for 1 year.

Fees: Charges reading fee. "To waive reading fee, author must have been published at least 3 times by a mainline New York publishing house." Criticism service: $350. Charges for office expenses, postage, photocopying, etc. 75% of business is derived from commissions on ms sales; 25% derived from reading fees or criticism service. Payment of criticism fee does not ensure representation.

Tips: Obtains new clients through recommendations from others, individual inquiry.

‡LAWYER'S LITERARY AGENCY, INC., (II), 64 Isle of Venice, Ft. Lauderdale FL 33301. (954)524-9422. Contact: H. Allen Etling. Also: P.O. Box 126132, San Diego CA 92112. (619)239-8539. Contact: Ellen Shaw Tufts. Estab. 1994. Represents 10 clients. 50% of clients are new/previously unpublished writers. Specializes in true crime, including trial aspect written by attorneys, and lawyer biographies and autobiographies. Currently handles: 100% nonfiction books.

Handles: Nonfiction books, movie scripts. Considers these nonfiction areas: biography/autobiography (of lawyers); law; true crime/investigative. Query with outline and 3 sample chapters. Reports in 2 weeks.

Recent Sales: *Undying Love: A Key West Love Story*, by Ben Harrison (New Horizon Press).

Also Handles: Movie scripts (feature film); TV scripts (TV mow). Considers these script subject areas: detective/police/crime; mystery/suspense. Send outline and 3 sample scenes. Reports in 2 weeks.

Terms: Agent receives 15% commission on domestic sales; does not handle foreign rights. Offers written contract for 1 year, with 30 day cancellation clause.

Fees: Charges $500 for presentation design, printing, postage, fax and telephone.
Tips: Obtains new clients through recommendations from others and advertisements in attorney trade publications. "Both agents, former newspaper journalists, believe the best stories are real stories. And many of the best real stories are true crime stories—including depiction of the crime, background of the participants, official investigation by authorities, defense/prosecution preparation and the trial. There are hundreds of intriguing cases that occur annually in the U.S. and not all of them are handled by attorneys who are household names. We are looking for the most compelling of these stories where there is also a good chance of selling TV movie/feature movie rights. Manuscripts can entail one case or multiple cases. Those involving multiple cases would probably resemble an attorney's biography. The story or stories can be told by defense and prosecution attorneys alike. Our agency will also arrange for co-authors or ghost writers for those attorneys lacking the time or inclination to write the manuscripts."

L. HARRY LEE LITERARY AGENCY, (II), Box #203, Rocky Point NY 11778-0203. (516)744-1188. Contact: L. Harry Lee. Estab. 1979. Member of Dramatists Guild. Represents 285 clients. 65% of clients are new/previously unpublished writers. Specializes in movie scripts. "Comedy is our strength, both features and sitcoms, also movie of the week, science fiction, novels and TV." Currently handles: 30% novels; 50% movie scripts; 5% stage plays; 15% TV scripts.
   • See the expanded listing for this agency in Script Agents.

*LIGHTHOUSE LITERARY AGENCY, (V), P.O. Box 1002, Mooresville NC 28115-1002. Phone/fax: (704)892-8045. Contact: Sandra Kangas. Estab. 1988. Member of WIF, Authors Guild, ABA. Represents 6 clients. 50% of clients are new/previously unpublished writers. Specializes in fiction and nonfiction juvenile and adult books. Currently handles: 50% nonfiction books; 17% juvenile books; 33% novels; accepting few new clients at time of listing.
Handles: Nonfiction, novels. Considers these nonfiction areas: animals; anthropology/archaeology; art/architecture/design; biography/autobiography; business; child guidance/parenting; computers/electronics; cooking/food/nutrition; crafts/hobbies; current affairs; health/medicine; interior design/decorating; juvenile nonfiction; money/finance/economics; music/dance/theater/film; nature/environment; photography; psychology; self-help/personal improvement; sports (especially running and motorsports); women's issues/women's studies. Considers these fiction areas: action/adventure; contemporary issues; detective/police/crime; juvenile; literary; mainstream; mystery/suspense; picture book; regional; science fiction; sports; thriller/espionage; westerns/frontier; young adult. Query with outline and 3 or more sample chapters. Reports in 2 weeks on queries; 2 months on mss.
Terms: Agent receives 15% commission on domestic sales; 20% on foreign sales. Offers written contract.
Fees: Charges $60 reading fee. "Waived for recent/trade published authors." Criticism service: $1/ms page, minimum $200. Critiques are done by writers who have been published in the field they are asked to judge. Charges for normal marketing expenses. 50% of business is derived from reading or criticism services. Payment of criticism fee does not ensure representation. "If author rewrites the work, we agree to read it again at no charge, no guarantee."
Writers' Conferences: ABA (Chicago, June).
Tips: Obtains new clients through professional organizations and referrals. "Send a short query or cover letter with brief description of the project including where your book will fit in the marketplace. Always enclose a stamped return mailer."

*LITERARY GROUP WEST, (II), 300 W. Shaw, Suite 453, Clovis CA 93612. (209)297-9409. Fax: (209)225-5606. Contact: Ray Johnson. Estab. 1993. Represents 2 clients. 50% of clients are new/previously unpublished writers. Specializes in novels. Currently handles: 20% nonfiction books; 70% novels; 10% novellas. Member agents: B.N. Johnson, Ph.D. (English literature).
Handles: Nonfiction books, novels. Considers these nonfiction areas: current affairs; ethnic/cultural interests; military/war; true crime/investigative. Considers these fiction areas: action/adventure; detective/police/crimes; historical; mainstream; thriller/espionage. Query. Reports in 1 week on queries; 1 months on mss.

The publishing field is constantly changing! If you're still using this book and it is 1997 or later, buy the newest edition of Guide to Literary Agents *at your favorite bookstore or order directly from* Writer's Digest Books.

Recent Sales: *In Vitro Madonna*, by Beverly White (European-Czech).
Terms: Agent receives 20% commission on domestic sales; 25% on foreign sales. Offers written contract.
Fees: Charges expense fees to unpublished authors. Deducts expenses from sales of published authors.
Writers' Conferences: Fresno County Writers Conference (Fresno CA, July).
Tips: Obtains new clients through recommendation. "Query first with strong letter. Please send SASE with query letter."

*TONI LOPOPOLO LITERARY AGENCY, (II), P.O. Box 1484, Manhattan Beach CA 90267-1484. (310)546-6690. Fax: (310)546-2930. Contact: Toni Lopopolo. Estab. 1990. Member of Sisters in Crime. Represents 40 clients. 85% of clients are new/previously unpublished writers. Specializes in true crime. Currently handles: 75% nonfiction books; 10% scholarly books; 15% novels. Member agent: Toni Lopopolo (mysteries, self-help/how-to); Nicole Ballard (science fiction, editorial evaluation).
  • Prior to opening her agency, Ms. Lopopolo served for 20 years in the publishing industry, including as a managing editor with Houghton Mifflin and as executive editor with Macmillan and St. Martin's Press.
Handles: Nonfiction books, novels. Considers these nonfiction areas: animals; anthropology/archaeology; art/architecture/design; biography/autobiography; business; child guidance/parenting; cooking/food/nutrition; ethnic/cultural interests; health/medicine; history; how-to; language/literature/criticism; money/finance/economics; nature/environment; New Age/metaphysics; popular culture; psychology; self-help/personal improvement; true crime/investigative; women's issues/women's studies. Considers these fiction areas: contemporary issues; detective/police/crime; erotica; ethnic; family saga; feminist; glitz; historical; literary; mainstream; mystery/suspense; psychic/supernatural; westerns/frontier. Query. Reports in 1 month on queries; 6 weeks on mss. No certified mail.
Recent Sales: *Leader of the Pack*, by Nancy Baer and Steve Duno (HarperCollins); *Coping with Chaos Culprits*, by Harriet Schechter (Crown); *Showbiz Tricks You Can Teach Your Cat*, by Steve Duno (Adams Publishing).
Terms: Agent receives 15% commission on domestic sales; 10-15% on foreign sales. Offers written contract, binding for 2 years.
Fees: Charges reading and written evaluation fee "for *unrecommended*, first novelists only. Will work with the promising; entire fee refunded upon sale of novel." Offers criticism service: fee depends on length and genre of novel. Charges marketing fee to cover phone, fax, postage and photocopying only. 95% of business is derived from commissions on ms sales; 5% is derived from reading fees or criticism services. Payment of criticism fee does not ensure representation.
Writers' Conferences: San Diego Writers (San Diego, January); Pacific Northwest Writers (Seattle, July).
Tips: Obtains new clients through recommendations from clients, lectures, workshops, conferences, publishers.

M.H. INTERNATIONAL LITERARY AGENCY, (II), 706 S. Superior St., Albion MI 49224. (517)629-4919. Contact: Mellie Hanke. Estab. 1992. Represents 15 clients. 75% of clients are new/previously unpublished writers. Specializes in historical novels. Currently handles: 100% novels. Member agents: Jeff Anderson (detective/police/crime); Martha Kelly (historical/mystery); Costas Papadopoulos (suspense; espionage); Nikki Stogas (confession); Marisa Handaris (foreign language ms reviewer, Greek); Mellie Hanke (Spanish); Erin Jones Morgart (French).
Handles: Novels. Considers these fiction areas: confession; detective/police/crime; historical; mystery. "We also handle Greek and French manuscripts in the above categories, plus classics. No westerns." Send all material to the attention of Mellie Hanke. Reports in 6 weeks on mss.
Terms: Agent receives 10% commission on domestic sales; 15% on foreign sales.
Fees: Charges reading fee and general office expenses. Offers criticism service, translations from above foreign languages into English, editing, evaluation and typing of mss.
Tips: "We provide translation from Greek and French into English, editing and proofreading."

VIRGINIA C. MCKINLEY, LITERARY AGENCY, (I, II), 1830 Roosevelt Ave., #101, Racine WI 53406. (414)637-9590. Contact: Virginia C. McKinley. Estab. 1992. 100% of clients are new/previously unpublished writers. Currently handles: 30% nonfiction books; 20% juvenile books; 40% novels; 10% poetry books. Member agent: Virginia C. McKinley (religious books, biography/autobiography, fiction).
Handles: Nonfiction books, juvenile books, novels, short story collections, poetry books, movie scripts, stage plays, TV scripts. Considers these nonfiction areas: animals; biography/autobiography; business; child guidance/parenting; ethnic/cultural interests; health/medicine; juvenile nonfiction; military/war; money/finance/economics; music/dance/theater/film; nature/environment; psychology; religious/inspirational; self-help/personal improvement; sociology; sports; women's issues/women's studies. Considers these fiction areas: action/adventure; contemporary issues; detective/police/crime;

ethnic; family saga; fantasy; feminist; humor/satire; juvenile; literary; mystery/suspense; religous/inspiration; romance (historical); westerns/frontier. Query with entire ms or 3 sample chapters. Reports in 1 month.

Terms: Agent receives 15% commission on domestic sales; 20% on foreign sales. Offers written contract.

Fees: Criticism service: $125 for 3-page critique. Reports within 2 months. Charges marketing fee—$100 per year for authors under contract, photocopying ms, postage, phone, any unusual expenses. 95% of business is derived from commissions on ms sales; 5% is derived from criticism services. Payment of criticism fee does not ensure representation.

Tips: Obtains new clients through solicitation. "No multiple submissions. We feel a dynamic relationship between author and agent is essential. SASE must be included with ms or 3 chapters; also query. Will work with writer to develop his full potential."

THE DENISE MARCIL LITERARY AGENCY, INC., (II), 685 West End Ave., New York NY 10025. (212)932-3110. Contact: Denise Marcil. Estab. 1977. Member of AAR. Represents 70 clients. 40% of clients are new/previously unpublished authors. Specializes in women's commercial fiction, how-to, self-help and business books, popular reference. Currently handles: 30% nonfiction books; 70% novels.

• Prior to opening her agency, Ms. Marcil served as an editorial assistant with Avon Books and as an editor with Simon & Schuster. See Denise Marcil's article, On the Merits: The Case For Reading Fees, in the 1995 edition of the *Guide*.

Handles: Nonfiction books, novels. Considers these nonfiction areas: business; child guidance/parenting; nutrition; health/medicine; how-to; inspirational; money/finance/economics; New Age/metaphysics; psychology; self-help/personal improvement; spirituality; women's issues/women's studies. Considers these fiction areas: mystery/suspense; romance (contemporary). Query with SASE *only*! Reports in 3 weeks on queries. No unsolicited mss.

Recent Sales: *Children Who Say No When You Want Them to Say Yes*, by James Wendell (Macmillan); *Finding You*, by Carla Neggers (Pocket Books); *Managing Your Inheritance*, by Emily Card Ph.D. and Adam Miller JD/MBA (Times Business Books).

Terms: Agent receives 15% commission on domestic sales; 20% on foreign sales. Offers written contract, binding for 2 years.

Fees: Charges $50 reading fee for 3 chapters and outline "that we request only." Charges $100/year for postage, photocopying, long-distance calls, etc. 99.9% of business is derived from commissions on ms sales; .1% is derived from reading fees and criticism.

Writers' Conferences: Golden Triangle (Beaumont TX, October); Pacific Northwest Writers Conference; RWA (Dallas, July).

Tips: Obtains new clients through recommendations from other authors and "35% of my list is from query letters! Only send a one-page query letter. I read them all and ask for plenty of material; I find many of my clients this way. *Always* send a SASE."

*THE EVAN MARSHALL AGENCY, (III), 6 Tristam Place, Pine Brook NJ 07058-9445. (201)882-1122. Fax: (201)882-3099. E-mail: esmarshall@aol.com. Contact: Evan Marshall. Estab. 1987. Currently handles: 48% nonfiction books; 48% novels; 2% movie scripts; 2% TV scripts.

• Prior to opening his agency, Mr. Marshall served as an editor with New American Library, Everest House, and Dodd, Mead & Co., and then worked as a literary agent at The Sterling Lord Agency.

Handles: Nonfiction books, novels. Considers these nonfiction areas: animals; biography/autobiography; business; child guidance/parenting; cooking/food/nutrition; crafts/hobbies; current affairs; government/politics/law; health/medicine; history; how-to; humor; interior design/decorating; language/literature/criticism; military/war; money/finance/economics; music/dance/theater/film; nature/environment; New Age/metaphysics; psychology; religious/inspirational; science/technology; self-help/personal improvement; true crime/investigative; women's issues/women's studies. Considers these fiction areas: action/adventure; contemporary issues; detective/police/crime; erotica; ethnic; family saga; glitz; historical; horror; humor/satire; literary; mainstream; mystery/suspense; psychic/supernatural; religious/inspirational; romance; (contemporary, gothic, historical, regency); science fiction; thriller/espionage; westerns/frontier. Query. Reports in 1 week on queries; 2 months on mss.

Recent Sales: *Compromises*, by Joan Hohl (Kensington); *Dance of the Flame*, by Elaine Barbieri (Dorchester); *Passion*, by Bobbi Smith (Kensington); *A Wine and Food Guide to the Loire, France's Royal River*, by Jacqueline Friedrich (Holt).

Also Handles: Movie scripts (feature film), TV scripts (TV mow, episodic drama, sitcom). Considers these script subject areas: action/adventure; comedy; contemporary issues; detective/police/crime; erotica; ethnic; family saga; fantasy; glitz; historical; horror; humor; mainstream; mystery/suspense; psychic/supernatural; religious/inspirational; romantic comedy and drama; science fiction; sports; teen; thriller; western/frontier.

Terms: Agent receives 15% on domestic sales; 20% on foreign sales. Offers written contract.
Fees: Charges a fee to consider for representation material by *writers who have not sold a book or script.* "Send SASE for fee schedule. There is no fee if referred by a client or an editor or if you are already published in the genre of your submission."
Tips: Obtains many new clients through referrals from clients and editors.

*MEWS BOOKS LTD., (II, III), 20 Bluewater Hill, Westport CT 06880. (203)227-1836. Fax: (203)227-1144. Contact: Sidney B. Kramer. Estab. 1972. Represents 35 clients. Prefers to work with published/established authors; works with small number of new/unpublished authors "producing professional work." Specializes in juvenile (pre-school through young adult), cookery, self-help, adult nonfiction and fiction, technical and medical and electronic publishing. Currently handles: 20% nonfiction books; 10% novels; 20% juvenile books; 40% electronic; 10% miscellaneous. Member agent: Fran Pollak (assistant).
Handles: Nonfiction books, novels, juvenile books, character merchandising and video use of illustrated published books. Query with precis, outline, character description, a few pages of sample writing and author's bio.
Recent Sales: *Dr. Susan Love's Breast Book*, by Susan M. Love, MD, with Karen Lindsey (Addison-Wesley).
Terms: Agent receives 15% commission on domestic sales; 20% on foreign sales.
Fees: Does not charge a reading fee. "If material is accepted, agency asks for $350 circulation fee (4-5 publishers), which will be applied against commissions (waived for published authors)." Charges for photocopying, postage expenses, telephone calls and other direct costs.
Tips: "Principle agent is an attorney and former publisher. Offers consultation service through which writers can get advice on a contract or on publishing problems."

MONTGOMERY LITERARY AGENCY, (II), P.O. Box 8822, Silver Spring MD 20907-8822. (301)230-1807. Contact: M.E. Olsen. Estab. 1984. Signatory of WGA. Represents 50 clients. 25% of clients are new/previously unpublished writers. Equal interest in scripts (films and TV mainly) and books. Currently handles: 12% nonfiction books; 2% poetry; 5% juvenile books; 25% novels; 30% movie scripts; 20% TV scripts; 1% short story collections; 2% syndicated material; 2% comics, etc.
• See the expanded listing for this agency in Script Agents.

*DAVID H. MORGAN LITERARY AGENCY, INC. (II), P.O. Box 14810, Richmond VA 23221. (804)672-2740. Contact: David H. Morgan. Estab. 1987. Represents 25-35 clients. Currently handles: 60% nonfiction books; 40% novels.
Handles: Nonfiction books, novels. Considers all categories, ages middle-reader through adult. No children's illustrated books. No Harlequin or Silhouette romances; all other romances accepted. Query with SASE. Reports in 1 week on queries.
Recent Sales: *Goddess Ruins*, by P.M.H. Atwater (Avon); *The Love Your Heart Guide for the 1990s*, by Lee Belshin (Contemporary); *Prophecies & Predictions: Everyone's Guide to the Coming Changes*, by Moira Timms (Ballantine).
Terms: Agent receives 15% commission on domestic sales; 20% on foreign sales. Offers written contract.
Fees: Charges a fee to evaluate works by unpublished authors. Fee refunded if ms accepted by agency. "Please query for details." Client must provide photocopies of mss. 95% of business is derived from commissions on ms sales; 5% is derived from reading or criticism fees.

*BK NELSON LITERARY AGENCY & LECTURE BUREAU, (II, III), 84 Woodland Rd., Pleasantville NY 10570-1322. (914)741-1322. Fax: (914)741-1324. Contact: Bonita Nelson, John Benson or Erv Rosenfeld. Estab. 1980. Member of NACA, Author's Guild, NAFE, ABA. Represents 62 clients. 40% of clients are new/previously unpublished writers. Specializes in business, self-help, how-to, novels, biographies. Currently handles: 40% nonfiction books; 5% CD-ROM/electronic products; 40% novels; 5% movie scripts; 5% TV scripts; 5% stage plays. Member agents: Bonita Nelson (business books); John Benson (Director of Lecture Bureau); Erv Rosenfeld (novels and TV scripts); Dave Donnelly (videos); Geisel Ali (self-help); JW Benson (novels); Jean Rejaunier (biography, nonfiction).
• Prior to opening her agency, Ms. Nelson worked for a law firm specializing in entertainment law and at American Play Company, a literary agency.
Handles: Nonfiction books, CD ROM/electronic products, scholarly books, novels. Considers these nonfiction areas: agriculture; animals; anthropology/archaeology; art/architecture/design; biography/autobiography; business; child guidance/parenting; computers/electronics; cooking/food/nutrition; crafts/hobbies; current affairs; education; ethnic/cultural interests; government/politics/law; health/medicine; history; how-to; language/literature/criticism; military/war; money/finance/economics; music/dance/theater/film; nature/environment; popular culture; psychology; religious/inspirational; science/technology; self-help/personal improvement; sociology; sports; true crime/investigative; women's issues/women's studies. Considers these fiction areas: action/adventure; cartoon/comic; contemporary

issues; detective/police/crime; family saga; fantasy; feminist; glitz; historical; horror; literary; mainstream; mystery/suspense; psychic/supernatural; romance (contemporary, historical); science fiction; sports; thriller/espionage; westerns/frontier. Query. Reports in 1 week on queries; 3 weeks on ms.

Recent Sales: *What to Say When . . . You're Dying on the Platform* by Lilly Walters (McGraw-Hill); *The Idiot's Guide to Managing People*, by Dr. Arthur Pell (Macmillan); *Blacklist*, by Congressman Gary Franks (HarperCollins); *Business Communications for Dummies*, by Robert W. Bly (IDG); *Successful Telephone Sales*, by Robert Bly (Holt).

Also Handles: Movie scripts (feature film, documentary, animation), TV scripts (TV mow, episodic drama, sitcom), stage plays. Considers these script subject areas: action/adventure; family saga; fantasy; historical; horror; mainstream; psychic/supernatural; romantic comedy and drama; thriller; westerns/frontier.

Terms: Agent receives 15% on domestic sales; 20% on foreign sales. Offers written contract, exclusive for 8-12 months.

Fees: Charges $325 reading fee for *new clients' material only.* "It is not refundable. We usually charge for the first reading only. The reason for charging in addition to time/expense is to determine if the writer is saleable and thus a potential client."

Writers' Conferences: Frankfurt Book Fair (Frankfurt, October); National NACA (Nashville TN, February); ABA (Chicago, June).

Tips: Obtains new clients through referrals and reputation with editors. "We handle the business aspect of the literary and lecture fields. We handle careers as well as individual book projects. If the author has the ability to write and we are harmonious, success is certain to follow with us handling the selling/business."

*NORTHEAST LITERARY AGENCY, (II), 69 Broadway, Concord NH 03301-2736. (603)225-9162. Contact: Dale Harrington. Estab. 1973. Represents 15 clients. 50% of clients are new/previously unpublished writers. Specializes in popular fiction and nonfiction, children's picture books. Currently handles: 75% nonfiction books; 25% novels. Member agents: Victor A. Levine (fiction, mainstream, serious nonfiction); Dale Harrington (genre fiction and how-to nonfiction); Don Emmons (scholarly nonfiction).

● Prior to opening the agency, Mr. Levine served in the Scott Meredith Literary Agency; Mr. Harrington worked as a freelance writer and editor; and Mr. Emmons was a professor of philosophy.

Handles: Novels, nonfiction books, juvenile books, short story collections, poetry books, movie and TV scripts. Considers all nonfiction subjects, especially biography/autobiography; business; history; how-to; humor; music/dance/theater/film; science/technology; true crime/investigative. Considers all fiction especially cartoon/comic; detective/police/crime; humor/satire; mystery/suspense, picture book; science fiction; thriller/espionage. Query. Reports in 5 days on queries; 10 days on mss.

Recent Sales: *Accepting Ourselves and Others*, by Kominars (Hazelden, Fall 1996); *Monsters' Test*, by Heinz (Milbrook, Fall 1996).

Terms: Agent receives 15% commission on domestic sales; 25% on foreign sales. Offers written contract, with 90 days cancellation clause.

Fees: Charges a reading fee to unpublished writers, refundable following a sale. Criticism service: costs depend on type of criticism and whether conducted by mail or in a seminar or workshop setting. Charges for extraordinary expenses, such as express mail, long-distance phone calls, extensive photocopying but not for marketing or ordinary office expenses."

Writers' Conferences: Underwrites Wells Writers' Workshop, which meets twice yearly in Wells, Maine.

Tips: Obtains new clients through classes, workshops, conferences, advertising in *Writer's Digest*, referrals. "Please be very specific about writing background, published credits and current project(s)." Always include SASE.

*NORTHWEST LITERARY SERVICES, (II), 2699 Decca Rd., Shawnigan Lake, British Columbia V0R 2W0 Canada. (604)743-8236. Contact: Brent Laughren. Estab. 1986. Represents 20 clients. 75% of clients are new/previously unpublished writers. Specializes in working with new writers. Currently handles: 45% nonfiction books; 10% juvenile books; 40% novels; 5% short story collections. Member agent: Jennifer Chapman (juvenile books). Send juvenile queries, etc., to Jennifer Chapman, 1252 A Fifth St., Courtney, British Columbia V9N 1L8 Canada.

An asterisk indicates those agents who only charge fees to new or previously unpublished writers or to writers only under certain conditions.

Handles: Nonfiction books, juvenile books, novels, movie scripts, stage plays, TV scripts. Considers these nonfiction areas: agriculture/horticulture; animals; art/architecture/design; biography/autobiography; child guidance/parenting; cooking/food/nutrition; crafts/hobbies; ethnic/cultural interests; gay/lesbian issues; health/medicine; history; how-to; humor; juvenile nonfiction; language/literature/criticism; music/dance/theater/film; nature/environment; New Age/metaphysics; photography; popular culture; religious/inspirational; self-help/personal improvement; sports; translations; true crime/investigative; women's issues/women's studies. Considers these fiction areas: action/adventure; confessional; contemporary issues; detective/police/crime; erotica; ethnic; experimental; family saga; fantasy; feminist; historical; humor/satire; juvenile; literary; mainstream; mystery/suspense; picture book; psychic/supernatural; romance; science fiction; sports; thriller/espionage; westerns/frontier; young adult. Query with outline/proposal. Reports in 1 month on queries; 2 months on mss.
Terms: Agent receives 15% on domestic sales; 20% on foreign sales. Offers written contract.
Fees: Charges reading fee for unpublished authors. Children's picture books $50; fiction/nonfiction synopsis and first 3 chapters $75. Reading fee includes short evaluation. Criticism service: $100 for book outline and sample chapters up to 20,000 words. Charges 75¢-$1/page for copyediting and content editing; $1/page for proofreading; $10-20/page for research. "Other related editorial services available at negotiated rates. Critiques are two to three page overall evaluations, with suggestions. All fees, if charged, are authorized by the writer in advance." 75% of business is derived from commissions on ms sales; 25% is derived from reading fees or criticism service. Payment of criticism fee does not ensure representation.
Tips: Obtains new clients through recommendations. "Northwest Literary Services is particularly interested in the development and marketing of new and unpublished writers. We are also interested in literary fiction."

EDWARD A. NOVAK III LITERARY REPRESENTATION, (II), 218 Herr St., Harrisburg PA 17102. (717)232-8081. Fax: (717)232-7020. Contact: Ed Novak. Estab. 1991. Represents 30 clients. 65% of clients are new/previously unpublished writers. Currently handles: 80% nonfiction books; 20% novels.
• Prior to opening his agency, Mr. Novak served as editorial director for the Acton and Dystel agency, and as an editor with Charles Scribner's Sons (now Scribner) and Macmillan. See Edward Novak's article, *The Literary Savant, Savior or Svengali?* in the 1995 edition.
Handles: Nonfiction books, novels. Considers these nonfiction areas: art/architecture/design; biography/autobiography; business; child guidance/parenting; current affairs; ethnic/cultural interests; gay/lesbian issues; government/politics/law; health/medicine; history; military/war; money/finance/economics; music/dance/theater/film; nature/environment; science/technology, self-help/personal improvement; sports; true crime/investigative; women's issues/women's studies. Considers these fiction areas: contemporary issues; detective/police/crime; historical; literary; mainstream; mystery/suspense; romance (contemporary, historical); sports; thriller/espionage. Query with 3 chapters and outline.
Recent Sales: *Tim Allen Laid Bare*, by Mike Arkish (Avon Books); *No More Secrets*, by C.S. Troix (St. Martin's Press).
Terms: Agent receives 15% commission on domestic sales; 19% on foreign sales. Offers written contract. Reports within 1 month.
Fees: Charges $50 reading fee for unsolicited works. Manuscripts are read by the agent. Charges for photocopying.
Tips: Obtains new clients "mostly through referrals, some through my own solicitation, very few through unsolicited queries."

PACIFIC LITERARY SERVICES, (I, II), 1220 Club Court, Richmond CA 94803. (510)222-6555. Contact: Victor West. Estab. 1992. Represents 3 clients. 100% of clients are new/previously unpublished writers. Specializes in science fiction, fantasy, horror, military, historical and genre and general fiction and nonfiction. Currently handles: 25% movie scripts; 25% short story collections; 50% novels.
Handles: Nonfiction books, scholarly books, juvenile books, novels, movie scripts, TV scripts, unusual stories and factual subjects. Open to all nonfiction and fiction subject areas. Query. Send brief synopsis and first 2-3 sample chapters. Reports in 1 month on queries; 2-4 months on mss.
Terms: Agent receives 10% commission on domestic sales; 20% on foreign sales. Offers written contract, binding for 4 years.
Fees: Criticism service: book ms up to 100,000 words $300; analysis of screenplay up to 150 pages $200; analysis of treatment, teleplay or sitcom script $100; marketing analysis $50. Critiques done by Victor West and vary from 5-7 pages for book almost ready to submit to 38½ pages for one needing extensive work; average 20-25 enclosed pages. Charges for postage only—clients supply copies. 100% of business is derived from reading or criticism fees.
Tips: Recommendations and queries. "The best way to get an agent and make a sale is to write well and be professional in all areas related to the writing business."

‡PARAVIEW, INC.—THE SANDRA MARTIN LITERARY AGENCY, (II, III), 1674 Broadway, #415, New York NY 10019. (212)489-5343. Fax: (212)489-5371. Contact: Justin Fernandez. Estab. 1988.

Represents 63 clients. 50% of clients are new/previously unpublished writers. Specializes in spiritual and paranormal. Currently handles: 80% nonfiction books; 10% scholarly books. Member agents: Sandra Martin; Justin Fernandez (general); Leonard Belzer (spiritual).

Handles: Nonfiction books. Considers these nonfiction areas: anthropology/archaeology; art/architecture/design; biography/autobiography; business; current affairs; health/medicine; history; how-to; military/war; music/dance/theater/film; New Age/metaphysics; psychology; religious/inspirational; self-help/personal improvement; women's issues/women's studies. Query. Reports in 1 month on queries; 2 months on mss.

Recent Sales: *I Am With You Always*, by S. Sparrow (Bantam); *How to Attract Anyone*, by S. Rabin (Penguin); *Cosmic Voyage*, by C. Brown (Dutton); *Music & Healing*, by C. Bush (Rubra).

Fees: Charges a variable reading fee. Offers criticism service. Critiques written by Justin Fernandez and are usually 4-5 pages. Payment of reading or criticism fee does not ensure representation.

Writers' Conferences: ABA (Chicago, June).

Tips: Obtains new clients mostly through recommendations from editors.

*WILLIAM PELL AGENCY, (II), 300 E. 40th St., Suite 8D, New York NY 10016 and P.O. Box 1049, Bridgehampton NY 11932. (212)490-2845. Contact: Susan Kelly. Estab. 1990. Represents 14 clients. 85% of clients are new/previously unpublished writers. Member agent: Susan Kelly (fiction); Clarissa Katz.

Handles: Novels. Considers these nonfiction areas: biography/autobiography; photography. Considers these fiction areas: action/adventure; detective/police/crime; humor/satire; thriller/espionage. Query with 2 sample chapters. Reports in 1 month on queries; 3 months on mss.

Recent Sales: *Mind-Set*, by Paul Dostor (Penguin USA); *Endangered Beasties*, by Derek Pell (Dover).

Terms: Agent receives 15% commission on domestic sales; 20% on foreign sales. Offers written contract, binding for 1 year.

Fees: Charges $100 reading fee for new writers. 90% of business is derived from commission on ms sales; 10% is derived from reading fees or criticism services. Payment of criticism fees does not ensure representation.

PENMARIN BOOKS, (II), P.O. Box 286, 58 Oak Grove Ave., Woodacre CA 94973-0286. (415)488-1628. Fax: (415)488-1123. President: Hal Lockwood. Estab. 1987. Represents 20 clients. 80% of clients are new/unpublished writers. "No previous publication is necessary. We do expect authoritative credentials in terms of history, politics, science and the like." Handles general trade nonfiction and illustrated books, as well as fiction.

- Prior to opening his agency, Mr. Lockwood served as an editorial assistant at Stanford University Press, an editor with Painter/Hopkins Publishing and in editorial production with Presidio Publishing.

Handles: Nonfiction books, fiction. Nonfiction books, query with outline. For fiction, query with outline and sample chapters. Will read submissions at no charge, but may charge a criticism fee or service charge for work performed after the initial reading. Reports in 2 weeks on queries; 1 month on mss.

Recent Sales: *The Emerging Digital Economy*, by Brian Kirk & Brad Pickar; *The Mena Connection*, by Terry Reed (Clandestine Publishing); *Partners in Transition*, by Roger & Bonnie Nall (Addison-Wesley).

Terms: Agent receives 15% commission on domestic sales; 15% on dramatic sales; 15% on foreign sales.

Fees: "We normally do not provide extensive criticism as part of our reading but, for a fee, will prepare guidance for editorial development. Charges $200/300 pages. Our editorial director writes critiques. These may be two to ten pages long. They usually include an overall evaluation and then analysis and recommendations about specific sections, organization or style."

PMA LITERARY AND FILM MANAGEMENT, INC., 132 W. 22nd St., 12th Floor, New York NY 10011-1817. (212)929-1222. Fax: (212)206-0238. E-mail: pmalitfilm@aol.com. President: Peter Miller. Member agents: Jennifer Robinson (film and fiction); Yuri Skujins (fiction and nonfiction); Harrison McGuigan (foreign rights). Estab. 1975. Represents 80 clients. 50% of clients are new/unpublished writers. Specializes in commercial fiction and nonfiction, thrillers, true crime and "fiction with *real* motion picture and television potential." Currently handles: 50% fiction; 25% nonfiction; 25% screenplays.

Handles: Fiction, nonfiction, film scripts. Considers these nonfiction areas: business; popular culture; true crime/investigative; women's issues/women's studies. Considers these fiction areas: action/adventure; contemporary issues; detective/police/crime; horror; literary; mainstream; mystery/suspense; thriller/espionage; young adult. Query with outline and/or sample chapters. Writer's guidelines for 5 × 8½ SASE with 2 first-class stamps. Reports in 1 week on queries; 1 month on ms. Submissions and queries without SASE will not be returned.

Recent Sales: *The Ultimate Movie Guide*, by Andrea Shaw (Fireside/Simon & Schuster); *Dangerous Attachments*, by Sarah Lovett (Villard/Random House); *The Godforsaken*, by Jay Bonansinga (Simon & Schuster); *The Ten Commandments of Pleasure*, by Dr. Susan Block (St. Martin's); *Authorized Biography of The Chieftains*, by John Glatt (Crown); *Rats Saw God*, by Feb Thomas (Simon & Schuster).
Also Handles: Movie scripts (feature film); TV scripts (TV mow, miniseries). Considers these script subject areas: action/adventure; comedy; contemporary issues; detective/police/crime; erotica; ethnic; feminist; historical; horror; humor; juvenile; mainstream; mystery/suspense; psychic/supernatural; romantic comedy and drama; science fiction; teen; thriller; western/frontier. Query. Reports in 2 weeks on queries; 2 months on mss.
Recent Sales: *Movie scripts optioned/sold*: *Manslayer*, by Jay Bonansinga (Kushner-Locke).
Terms: Agent receives 15% commission on domestic sales; 20-25% on foreign sales.
Fees: Does not charge a reading fee. Paid reading evaluation service available upon request. "The evaluation, usually four to seven pages in length, gives a detailed analysis of literary craft and commercial potential as well as further recommendations for improving the work." Charges for photocopying expenses.
Writers' Conferences: Maui Writer's Conference, Santa Fe Writer's Conference.

‡*SIDNEY E. PORCELAIN, (II,III), 414 Leisure Loop, Milford PA 18337-9568. (717)296-6420. Manager: Sidney Porcelain. Estab. 1952. Represents 20 clients. 50% of clients are new/unpublished writers. Prefers to work with published/established authors; works with a small number of new/unpublished authors. Specializes in fiction (novels, mysteries and suspense) and nonfiction (celebrity and exposé). Currently handles: 2% magazine articles; 5% magazine fiction; 5% nonfiction books; 50% novels; 5% juvenile books; 2% movie scripts; 1% TV scripts; 30% "comments for new writers."
Recent Sales: *Steve McQueen*, by Marshall Terrill (Donald I. Fine).
Handles: Magazine articles, magazine fiction, nonfiction books, novels, juvenile books. Query with outline or entire ms. Reports in 2 weeks on queries; 3 weeks on mss.
Terms: Agent receives 15% commission on domestic sales; 15% on dramatic sales; 15% on foreign sales.
Fees: Does not charge a reading fee. Offers criticism service to new writers. 50% of income derived from commission on ms sales.

***THE PORTMAN ORGANIZATION, (III)**, 7337 N. Lincoln Ave., Suite 283, Chicago IL 60076. (312)509-6421. Fax: (708)982-9386. Contact: Ms. Ludmilla Dudin, Julien John Portman. Estab. 1972. Represents 33 clients. 10-15% of clients are new/previously unpublished writers. Currently handles: 50% nonfiction books; 10% movie scripts; 25% novels; 15% TV scripts. Member agents: Julien Portman (Hollywood); Ludmilla Dudin (novels); Paula Chalk (nonfiction); Phyllis Emer (general).
Handles: Nonfiction books, novels, movie scripts, TV scripts. Considers these nonfiction areas: biography/autobiography; current affairs; history; military/war; music/dance/theater/film; sports; true crime/investigative; women's issues/women's studies. Considers these fiction areas: action/adventure; detective/police/crime; family saga; historical; romance (contemporary, historical); science fiction; sports; thriller/espionage; westerns/frontier. Query. Reports in 10 days on queries; 1 month on mss.
Recent Sales: *Shadow Over China*, by J. Portman/L. Kipfer (Knightsbridge); *Marketing of the President*, by B. Newman (Morrow Publications); *Profile of a Killer*, by Paul Stemm (Doubleday).
Terms: Agent receives 15% commission on domestic sales; 25% on foreign sales. Offers written contract, binding for 1 year.
Fees: Charges reading fee for new writers only, $150 for 350 pages, $200 for 350- 600 pages. Fees refundable if representation offered. Less than 10% of business is derived from reading fees.
Writers' Conferences: "Rarely do we attend writers conferences, but do attend the yearly show, [ABA] which will be in Chicago for the next three years."
Tips: Obtains clients through referrals, recommendations and from referrals. "We have an excellent track record—we're very careful with solicitation. Reputation in the field of war, due to working with CIA for years. Spent time in Vietnam, and played the role in other areas: Australia, Hong Kong, Thailand, Japan and China. We, also, are involved with TV and motion picture projects. Our agent is William Morris Agency. Two properties are presently optioned. Our office has been successful (modestly) through the years. *Shadow Over China*, a book, is optioned for a major motion picture; 75% in China."

PUDDINGSTONE LITERARY AGENCY, (II), Affiliate of SBC Enterprises Inc., 11 Mabro Dr., Denville NJ 07834-9607. (201)366-3622. Contact: Alec Bernard or Eugenia Cohen. Estab. 1972. Represents 25 clients. 80% of clients are new/previously unpublished writers. Currently handles: 10% nonfiction books; 70% novels; 20% movie scripts.
Handles: Nonfiction books, novels, movie scripts. Considers these nonfiction areas: business; howto; language/literature/criticism; military/war; true crime/investigative. Considers these fiction areas: action/adventure; detective/police/crime; horror; science fiction; thriller/espionage. Query first with

SASE including $1 cash processing fee, "which controls the volume and eliminates dilettantism among the submissions." Reports immediately on queries; 1 month on mss "that are requested by us."
Recent Sales: *The Action-Step Plan to Owning And Operating A Small Business*, by E. Toncré (Prentice-Hall).
Terms: Agent receives 10-15% sliding scale (decreasing) on domestic sales; 20% on foreign sales. Offers written contract, binding for 1 year with renewals.
Fees: Reading fee charged for unsolicited mss over 20 pages. Negotiated fees for market analysis available. Charges for photocopying for foreign sales.
Tips: Obtains new clients through referrals and listings.

QCORP LITERARY AGENCY, (I), P.O. Box 8, Hillsboro OR 97123-0008. (800)775-6038. Contact: William C. Brown. Estab. 1990. Represents 14 clients. 75% of clients are new/previously unpublished writers. Currently handles: 40% nonfiction books; 60% fiction books. Member agent: William C. Brown.
Handles: Fiction and nonfiction books, including textbooks, scholarly books, novels, novellas, short story collections. Considers all nonfiction areas. Considers all areas of fiction, excluding cartoon/comic books. Query through critique service. Reports in 2 weeks on queries; 3 months on mss.
Recent Sales: *Introduction to Internet Security*, by Garry Howard (Prima Publishing).
Terms: Agent receives 10% commission on domestic sales; 20% on foreign sales. Offers written contract, binding for 6 months, automatically renewed unless cancelled by author.
Fees: "No charges are made to agency authors if no sales are procured. If sales are generated, then charges are itemized and collected from proceeds up to a limit of $200, after which all expenses are absorbed by agency." Offers criticism service.
Tips: Obtains new clients through recommendations from others and from critique service. "New authors should use our critique service and its free, no obligation first chapter critique to introduce themselves. Call or write for details. Our critique service is serious business, line by line and comprehensive. Established writers should call or send résumé."

*DIANE RAINTREE AGENCY, (II), 360 W. 21st St., New York NY 10011-3305. (212)242-2387. Contact: Diane Raintree. Estab. 1977. Represents 6-8 clients. Specializes in novels, film and TV scripts, plays, poetry and children's books.
 • Prior to opening her agency, Ms. Raintree served as a copyeditor and proofreader for Zebra Books and Charter Books, as a reader for Avon Books and a senior editor for Dial Press.
Handles: Considers all fiction areas and some nonfiction. Phone first.
Terms: Agent receives 10% on domestic sales.
Fees: May charge reading fee. "Amount varies from year to year."

RYDAL, (V), P.O. Box 2247, Santa Fe NM 87504. (505)983-1680. Fax: (505)982-9105. Director: Clark Kimball. Estab. 1986. Represents 15 clients. 20% of clients are new/previously published writers. Currently handles: 40% nonfiction books; 10% scholarly books; 10% juvenile books; 40% novels.
Handles: Nonfiction books, novels. Considers these nonfiction areas: anthropology/archaeology; ethnic/cultural interests; nature/environment; photography. Considers these fiction areas: literary; mainstream; regional; westerns/frontier. Send outline and 3 sample chapters. Reports in 3 weeks on mss.
Recent Sales: *En Divina Luz*, by Wallis/Varjabedian (UNM); *Plane Truth*, by Stevens (New Horizon).
Terms: Agent receives 15% commission on domestic sales; 20% on foreign sales. Offers written contract.
Fees: Charges annual account fee, from $100-400.
Tips: "Obtains new clients through referrals to us by clients, trade connections. Don't try to hype agent—be straight forward and to the point."

SLC ENTERPRISES, (II), 852 Highland Place, Highland Park IL 60035. (708)432-7553. Contact: Ms. Carole Golin. Estab. 1985. Represents 30 clients. 50% of clients are new/previously unpublished writers. Currently handles: 65% nonfiction books; 5% textbooks; 10% juvenile books; 20% novels. Member agents: Stephen Cogil (sports).
Handles: Nonfiction books, poetry books, juvenile books, novels, short story collections. Considers these nonfiction areas: biography/autobiography, business, cooking/food/nutrition; current affairs; his-

Agents ranked I-IV are actively seeking new clients. Those ranked V or those who prefer not to be listed have been included to inform you they are not currently looking for new clients.

tory; sports; women's issues/women's studies; Holocaust studies. Considers these fiction areas: detective/police/crime; feminist; historical; juvenile; literary; picture book; regional; romance (contemporary, historical); sports; young adult. Query with outline/proposal. Reports in 2 weeks on queries; 1 months on mss.
Recent Sales: *Eyeopeners II*, by Kubrin (Scholastic); *Will To Live*, by Adam Starkopt (SUNY).
Terms: Agent receives 15% commission on domestic sales. Offers written contract, binding for 9 months.
Fees: Charges $150 reading fee for entire ms; $75-150 for children's, depending on length and number of stories. Reading fee includes overall critique plus specifics. No line editing for grammar etc. Charges no other fees. 20% of business is derived from reading and criticism fees.
Tips: Recommendations, listings in literary manuals.

‡*SOUTHERN LITERARY AGENCY, (III), 16411 Brookvilla Dr., Houston TX 77059. (713)480-6360. Contact: Michael Doran. Estab. 1980. Represents 58 clients. 20% of clients are new/previously unpublished writers. "We are most interested in popular financial, professional and technical books." Currently handles: 70% nonfiction books; 20% novels; 10% movie scripts. Member agents: Michael Doran (nonfiction); Patricia Coleman (mainstream novels, some nonfiction).
Handles: Nonfiction books, novels, movie scripts. Considers these nonfiction areas: anthropology/ archaeology; biography/autobiography; business; child guidance/parenting; health/medicine; history; money/finance/economics; psychology; self-help/personal improvement. Considers these fiction areas: action/adventure; detective/police/crime; humor/satire; mainstream; mystery/suspense; thriller/espionage. Telephone query. Reports in 1 month on mss.
Recent Sales: *Making the Right Choice*, by Richard Evans (Avery); *How to Invest Today*, by Dr. Lawrence Lymn (Henry Holt); *What They Should Have Taught Me at Big Blue*, by Darryl Tramonae (Heritage).
Terms: Agent receives 15% commission on domestic sales; 20% on foreign sales. Offers written contract.
Fees: "There is a $350 fee for unpublished new novelists, returnable if their manuscript is publishable and we do the selling of it. Refund on first royalties. Offers multi-page critique on manuscripts which can be made marketable; 1-page remarks and suggestions for writing improvements otherwise. Charges cost-per on extraordinary costs, pre-agreed." 90% of business derived from commissions on ms sales; 10% from reading fees or criticism services.
Writers' Conferences: ABA; Texas and other Southern regional conferences.
Tips: Obtains new clients through conferences, yellow pages—mainly referrals. "Learn about the book business through conferences and reading before contacting the agent."

MICHAEL STEINBERG LITERARY AGENCY, (III), P.O. Box 274, Glencoe IL 60027-0274. (708)835-8881. Contact: Michael Steinberg. Estab. 1980. Represents 27 clients. 5% of clients are new/previously unpublished writers. Specializes in business and general nonfiction, mysteries, science fiction. Currently handles: 75% nonfiction books; 25% novels.
Handles: Nonfiction books, novels. Considers these nonfiction areas: biography; business; computers; law; history; how-to; money/finance/economics; self-help/personal improvement. Considers these fiction areas: action/adventure; contemporary issues; detective/police/crime; erotica; mainstream; mystery/suspense; science fiction; thriller/espionage. Query for guidelines. Reports in 2 weeks on queries; 6 weeks on mss.
Recent Sales: *How to Buy Mutual Funds the Smart Way*, by Stephen Littauer (Dearborn Publishing); *The Complete Day Trader*, by Jake Bernstein (McGraw-Hill).
Terms: Agent receives 15% on domestic sales; 15-20% on foreign sales. Offers written contract, which is binding, "but at will."
Fees: Charges $75 reading fee for outline and chapters 1-3; $200 for a full ms to 100,000 words. Criticism included in reading fee. Charges actual phone and postage, which is billed back quarterly. 95% of business is derived from commissions on ms sales; 5% derived from reading fees or criticism services.
Writers' Conferences: ABA (Chicago).
Tips: Obtains new clients through unsolicited inquiries and referrals from editors and authors. "We do not solicit new clients. Do not send unsolicited material. Write for guidelines and include SASE. Do not send generically addressed, photocopied query letters."

GLORIA STERN AGENCY, (II), 1235 Chandler Blvd., #3, North Hollywood CA 91607-1934. Phone/ fax: (818)508-6296. E-mail: af385@lafn.org. Contact: Gloria Stern. Estab. 1984. Member of IWOSC, SCW. Represents 14 clients. 80% of clients are new/unpublished writers. Specializes in consultation, writer's services (ghost writing, editing, critiquing, etc.). Currently handles: 79% fiction; 19% nonfiction books; 8% movie scripts; 2% reality based. Member agent: Gloria Stern (romance, detective, science fiction).
● This agency is not affiliated with the Gloria Stern Literary Agency in Texas.

Handles: Novels, short story collections. Considers these nonfiction areas: biography/autobiography; business; child guidance/parenting; computers/electronics; cooking; current affairs; education; ethnic/ cultural interests; gay/lesbian issues; health/medicine; how-to; language/literature/criticism; money/ finance/economics; music/dance/theater/film; New Age/metaphysical; popular culture; psychology (pop); self-help/personal improvement; sociology; true crime/investigative; women's issues/women's studies. Considers these fiction areas: action/adventure; contemporary issues; detective/police/crime; erotica; fantasy; feminist; glitz; horror; literary; mainstream; romance (contemporary, gothic, historical, regency); science fiction; thriller/espionage; western/frontier. Query with short bio, credits. Reports in 1 month on queries; 5 weeks on mss.
Also Handles: Movie scripts (feature film, TV mow). Considers these script subject areas: action/ adventure; comedy; contemporary issues; detective/police/crime; erotica; ethnic; family saga; fantasy; feminist; glitz; horror; mainstream; mystery/suspense; psychic/supernatural; romance (comedy, drama); science fiction; sports; thriller; westerns/frontier.
Terms: Agent receives 12% commission on domestic sales; 20% on foreign sales. Offers written contract, binding for 1 year.
Fees: Charges reading fee, by project (by arrangement), $35/hour for unpublished writers. Criticism service: $35/hour. Critiques are "detailed analysis of all salient points regarding such elements as structure, style, pace, development, publisher's point of view and suggestions for rewrites if needed." Charges for long-distance, photocopying and postage. 38% of income derived from sales, 29% from reading fees, 26% from correspondence students, 7% from teaching. Payment of criticism fee does not insure representation.
Writers' Conferences: ABA (Chicago, June); Show Biz Expo (Los Angeles, May); SigGraph (Los Angeles, August).
Tips: Obtains new clients from book (*Do the Write Thing: Making the Transition to Professional*), classes, lectures, listings, word of mouth and online column. "To a writer interested in representation: Be sure that you have researched your field and are aware of current publishing demands. Writing is the only field in which all the best is readily available to the beginning writer. Network, take classes, persevere and most of all, write, write and rewrite."

*MARIANNE STRONG LITERARY AGENCY, (III), 65 E. 96th St., New York NY 10128. (212)249-1000. Fax: (212)831-3241. Contact: Marianne Strong. Estab. 1978. Represents 15 clients. 1% of clients are new/previously unpublished writers. Specializes in biographies. Currently handles: 80% nonfiction books; 5% scholarly books; 5% novels; 10% TV scripts. Member agent: Jeanne Toomey (true crime).
Handles: Nonfiction books, novels, TV scripts, syndicated material. Considers these nonfiction areas: art/architecture/design; biography/autobiography; business; child guidance/parenting; cooking/food/ nutrition; current affairs; education; health/medicine; history; how-to; interior design/decorating; juvenile nonfiction; military/war; money/finance/economics; religious/inspirational; self-help/personal improvement; true crime; women's issues/women's studies. Considers these fiction areas: action/adventure; contemporary issues; detective/police/crime; family saga; glitz; historical; literary; mainstream; religious/inspirational; romance (contemporary, gothic, historical, regency); thriller/espionage; western/frontier. Send outline plus 3-4 sample chapters. Reports "fairly soon" on queries; 2 months on mss.
Terms: Agent receives 15% commission on domestic sales; 15% on foreign sales. Offers written contract, binding for the life of book or play.
Fees: Charges a reading fee for new writers only, "refundable when manuscript sold." Offers criticism service. "Fee to read and service a manuscript to six to eight publishers $350. If using outside freelance writers and editors, entire fee goes to them. Critiques prepared by freelance writers and editors who receive entire fee." Charges for long distance calls for established clients, but not for unpublished writers as their fee covers these out-of-pocket expenses.
Tips: Obtains new clients through recommendations from others. "Submit a totally professional proposal with a story line that elucidates the story from A to Z plus several perfectly typed or word processed chapters. No disks, please. Also include background information on the author, especially literary or journalistic references."

DAWSON TAYLOR LITERARY AGENCY, (II), 4722 Holly Lake Dr., Lake Worth FL 33463-5372. (407)965-4150. Fax: (407)641-8765. Contact: Dawson Taylor, Attorney at Law. Estab. 1974. Represents 34 clients. 80% of clients are new/previously unpublished writers. Specializes in nonfiction, fiction, sports, military history. Currently handles: 80% nonfiction; 5% scholarly books; 15% novels.
● Prior to opening his agency, Mr. Taylor served as book editor at the *National Enquirer* from 1976-1983, and book editor at *The Globe* from 1984-1991.
Handles: Nonfiction books, textbooks, scholarly books, novels. Considers all nonfiction areas. Specializes in nonfiction on sports, especially golf. Considers these fiction areas: detective/police/crime; mystery/suspense; thriller/espionage. Query with outline. Reports in 5 days on queries; 10 days on mss.

Recent Sales: *Bowling Strikes*, by Earl Anthony (Contemporary Books); *How to Talk Golf*, by D. Taylor & T. Jones (Microsoft Video Golf); *How to Talk Bowling*, by D. Taylor & T. Jones (Barricade Books).

Terms: Agent receives 15% or 20% commission "depending upon editorial help." Offers written contract, indefinite, but cancellable on 60 days notice by either party.

Fees: "Reading fees are subject to negotiation, usually $100 for normal length manuscript, more for lengthy ones. Reading fee includes critique and sample editing. Criticism service subject to negotiation, from $100. Critiques are on style and content, include editing of manuscript, and are written by myself." 90% of business is derived from commissions on ms sales; 10% is derived from reading fees or criticism services. Payment of reading or criticism fee does not ensure representation.

Tips: Obtains new clients through "recommendations from publishers and authors who are presently in my stable."

*JEANNE TOOMEY ASSOCIATES, (II), 95 Belden St., Falls Village CT 06031. (203)824-0831/ 5469. Fax: (203)824-5460. Contact: Jeanne Toomey. Estab. 1985. Represents 10 clients. 50% of clients are new/previously unpublished writers. Specializes in "nonfiction; biographies of famous men and women; history with a flair—murder and detection. No children's books, no poetry, no Harlequin-type romances." Currently handles: 45% nonfiction books; 20% novels; 35% movie scripts.

Handles: Nonfiction books, novels, short story collections, movie scripts. Considers these nonfiction areas: agriculture/horticulture; animals; anthropology/archaeology; art/architecture/design; biography/ autobiography; government/politics/law; history; interior design/decorating; money/finance/economics; nature/environment; true crime/investigative. Considers these fiction areas: detective/police/crime; psychic/supernatural; thriller/espionage. Send outline plus 3 sample chapters. "Query first, please!" Reports in 1 month.

Recent Sales: *Hostile Witness*, by Vic Clark; *Uncovering the Sources of Love and Hate*, by Dr. Collier Rule; *Unleashed*, by Sam Robins; (all by Sunstone Books).

Terms: Agent receives 15% commission on domestic sales.

Fees: Charges $100 reading fee for unpublished authors; no fee for published authors. "The $100 covers marketing fee, office expenses, postage, photocopying. We absorb those costs in the case of published authors."

‡PHYLLIS TORNETTA AGENCY, (II), Box 423, Croton-on-Hudson NY 10521. (914)737-3464. President: Phyllis Tornetta. Estab. 1979. Represents 22 clients. 35% of clients are new/unpublished writers. Specializes in romance, contemporary, mystery. Currently handles: 90% novels and 10% juvenile.

Handles: Novels and juvenile. Query with outline. No unsolicited mss. Reports in 1 month.

Recent Sales: *Heart of the Wolf*, by Sally Dawson (Leisure); *Jennie's Castle*, by Elizabeth Sinclair (Silhouette).

Terms: Agent receives 15% commission on domestic sales and 20% on foreign sales.

Fees: Charges $100 reading fee for full mss.

A TOTAL ACTING EXPERIENCE, (II), Dept. N.W., 20501 Ventura Blvd., Suite 399, Woodland Hills CA 91364. (818)901-1044. Contact: Dan A. Bellacicco. Estab. 1984. Signatory of WGA, SAG, AFTRA. Represents 30 clients. 50% of clients are new/previously unpublished writers. Specializes in "quality instead of quantity." Currently handles: 5% nonfiction books; 5% juvenile books; 10% novels; 5% novellas; 5% short story collections; 50% movie scripts; 10% TV scripts; 5% stage plays; 5% how-to books and videos.

● See the expanded listing for this agency in Script Agents.

*VISIONS PRESS, (II), P.O. Box 4904, Valley Village CA 91617-0904. (805)285-8174. Contact: Allen Williams Brown. Estab. 1991. Represents 9 clients. 60% of clients are new/previously unpublished writers. "We prefer to support writers who incorporate African-American issues in the storyline. We handle adult romance novels, children's books and consciousness-raising pieces." Currently handles: 50% novels; 50% magazine pieces.

Handles: Novels, magazine pieces. Considers these magazine areas: ethnic/cultural interests; gay/ lesbian issues; religious/inspirational; self-help/personal improvement; women's issues/women's studies. Considers these fiction areas: confessional; contemporary issues; erotica; ethnic; gay; lesbian; mainstream; romance (contemporary); young adult. Send outline and 2 sample chapters and author bio or description of self. Reports in 2 weeks on queries; 1 month on mss.

Recent Sales: "Help for the homebound," by Diana Williams (Los Angeles Times); "African American see O.J. Simpson as family," by Diana Williams (Glendale News Press).

Terms: Agent receives 10% commission on domestic sales; 15% on foreign sales. Offers written contract, specific length of time depends on type of work—novel or magazine piece.

Fees: Charges reading fee. "Reading fees are charged to new writers only. Fee is refunded if agency decides to represent author. Fees are based on length of manuscript ($100 for up to 300 pages; $150 for any length thereafter.)" Offers criticism service. "Same as for the reading fee. Both the reading fee and the criticism fee entitle the author to a critique of his/her work by one of our editors. We are interested in everyone who has a desire to be published . . . to hopefully realize their dream. To that end, we provide very honest and practical advice on what needs to be done to correct a manuscript." Additional fees "will be negotiated with the author on a project by project basis. Often there is a one-time fee charged that covers all office expenses associated with the marketing of a manuscript." 90% of business is derived from commissions on ms sales; 10% is derived from reading fees or criticism services. Payment of criticism fee does not ensure representation.

Writers' Conferences: "We do not usually attend writing conferences. Most of our contacts are made through associations with groups such as NAACP, Rainbow Coalition, Urban League and other such groups that promote consciousness-raising activities by African-Americans. We look for talent among African-American scholars and African-American "common folk" who can usually be found sharing their opinions and visions at an issues-related conference and town hall type meeting."

Tips: Obtains new clients through recommendations from others and through inquiries. "We believe the greatest story ever told has yet to be written! For that reason we encourage every writer to uninhibitedly pursue his/her dream of becoming published. A no from us should simply be viewed as a temporary setback that can be overcome by another attempt to meet our high expectations. Discouraged, frustrated, and demoralized are words we have deleted from our version of the dictionary. An aspiring writer must have the courage to press on and believe in his/her talent."

*THE GERRY B. WALLERSTEIN AGENCY, (II), 2315 Powell Ave., Suite 12, Erie PA 16506-1843. (814)833-5511. Fax: (814)833-6260. Contact: Ms. Gerry B. Wallerstein. Estab. 1984. Member of Authors Guild, Inc., ASJA. Represents 40 clients. 25% of clients are new/previously unpublished writers. Specializes in nonfiction books and "personalized help for new novelists." Currently handles: 52% nonfiction books; 2% scholarly trade books; 2% juvenile books; 35% novels; 2% short story collections; 2% TV scripts; 2% short material. (Note: juvenile books, scripts and short material marketed for *clients only!*)

● Prior to opening her agency, Ms. Wallerstein worked as a writer, editor, publisher, and PR consultant.

Handles: Nonfiction books, scholarly trade books, novels, no textbooks. Considers these nonfiction areas for general trade: agriculture/horticulture; animals; anthropology/archaeology; art/architecture/ design; biography/autobiography (celebrity only); business; child guidance/parenting; cooking/food/ nutrition; crafts/hobbies; current affairs; education; ethnic/cultural interests; gay/lesbian issues; government/politics/law; health/medicine; history; how-to; humor; interior design/decorating; language/literature/criticism; military/war; money/finance/economics; music/dance/theater/film; nature/environment; photography; popular culture; psychology; science/technology; self-help/personal improvement; sociology; sports; true crime/investigative; women's issues/women's studies. Considers these fiction areas: action/adventure; contemporary issues; detective/police/crime; family saga; fantasy; glitz; historical; horror; humor/satire; literary; mainstream; mystery/suspense; romance (contemporary, historical); thriller/espionage; young adult. To query, send entire ms for fiction; proposal (including 3 chapters) for nonfiction books. "No manuscripts are reviewed until writer has received my brochure." Reports in 1 week on queries; 2 months on mss.

Recent Sales: *Surrender The Night*, by Susan P. Teklits (HarperPaperbacks/Monogram); *Racism or Attitude? The First Step Toward Liberation*, by James L. Robinson, Ph.D. (Insight Books/Plenum Publishing Corp.); *The Official Price Guide to Glassware*, by Mark Pickvet (Ballantine/Random House).

Terms: Agent receives 15% on domestic sales; 20% on foreign sales. Offers written contract, which "can be cancelled by either party, with 60 days' notice of termination."

Fees: "To justify my investment of time, effort and expertise in working with newer or beginning writers, I charge a reading/critique fee based on length of manuscript, for example: $400 for each manuscript of 105,000-125,000 words." Critique included in reading fee. "Reports are 1-2 pages for proposals and short material; 2-4 pages for full-length mss; done by agent." Charges clients $25/month for postage, telephone and fax and if required, ms photocopying or typing, copyright fees, cables, attorney fees (if approved by author), travel expense (if approved by author). 50% of business is derived from commissions on ms sales; 50% is derived from reading fees and critique services. Payment of criticism fee does not ensure representation.

Writers' Conferences: Westminster College Conference; Midwest Writers' Conference; National Writers' Uplink; Writer's Center at Chautauqua; Midland Writers' Conference.

Check the Subject Index to find the agents who are interested in your nonfiction or fiction subject area.

Tips: Obtains new clients through recommendations; listings in directories; referrals from clients and publishers/editors. "A query letter that tells me something about the writer and his/her work is more likely to get a personal response."

JAMES WARREN LITERARY AGENCY (II), 13131 Welby Way, North Hollywood CA 91606. (818)982-5423. Fax: (818)765-8207. Agent: James Warren. Editor: Cameron Garcia. Estab. 1969. Represents 60 clients. 60% of clients are new/unpublished writers. "We are willing to work with select unpublished writers." Specializes in fiction, history, textbooks, professional books, craft books, how-to books, self-improvement books, health books and diet books. Currently handles: 40% nonfiction books; 20% novels; 10% textbooks; 5% juvenile books; 10% movie scripts; 15% TV scripts and teleplays.
Handles: Juvenile books, historical romance novels. Query with outline. No unsolicited mss. No reply without SASE. Brochure available for SASE. Reports in 1 week on queries; 1 month on mss.
Recent Sales: *Holistic Revolution*, (update), by Lillian Grant (New Saga Press); *Witty Words*, (2nd edition), by Eileen Mason (Sterling Press); *Harry's Star*, by Malcolm Fitz (New Saga Press).
Also Handles: Movie scripts (especially drama and humor), TV scripts (drama, humor, documentary).
Terms: Agent receives 10% commission on domestic sales; 20% on foreign sales.
Fees: Charges reading fee of $3/1,000 words; refunds reading fee if material sells. 80% of income derived from commission on ms sales; 20% of income derived from fees. Payment of reading fee does not ensure representation.

WEST COAST LITERARY ASSOCIATES, (II), 7960-B Soquel Dr., Suite 151, Aptos CA 95003-3945. (408)685-9548. E-mail: westlit@aol.com. Contact: Richard Van Der Beets. 1986. Member of Authors League of America, Authors Guild. Represents 50 clients. 75% of clients are new/previously unpublished clients. Currently handles: 20% nonfiction books; 80% novels.
• Prior to opening his agency, Mr. Van Der Beets served as a professor of English at San Jose State University.
Handles: Nonfiction books, novels. Considers these nonfiction areas: biography/autobiography; current affairs; ethnic/cultural interests; government/politics/law; history; language/literature/criticism; music/dance/theater/film; nature/environment; psychology; true crime/investigative; women's issues/women's studies. Considers these fiction areas: action/adventure; contemporary issues; detective/police/crime; experimental; historical; literary; mainstream; mystery/suspense; regional; romance (contemporary and historical); science fiction; thriller/espionage; westerns/frontier. Query first. Reports in 2 weeks on queries; 1 month on mss.
Terms: Agent receives 10% commission on domestic sales; 20% commission on foreign sales. Offers written contract, binding for 6 months.
Recent Sales: *Lorien Lost*, by Michael King (St. Martin's/A Wyatt Book); *The Last Client*, by Manuel Ramos (St. Martin's); *The Tears of the Madonna*, by George Herman (Carroll & Graf).
Fees: Does not charge a reading fee. Charges $75-95 marketing and materials fee, depending on genre and length. Fees are refunded in full upon sale of the property.
Writers' Conferences: California Writer's Conference (Asilomar).
Tips: "Query with SASE for submission guidelines before sending material."

WESTCHESTER LITERARY AGENCY, INC., (II), 2533 Egret Lake Dr., West Palm Beach FL 33413. (407)642-2908. Fax: (407)439-2228. Contact: Neil G. McCluskey. Estab. 1991. Represents 55 clients. 30% of clients are new/previously unpublished writers with an academic or school background. Currently handles: 75% nonfiction books; 3% juvenile books; 22% novels and novellas. Member agents: Medved Jeffers (fiction/adventure); Elaine Jacobs (fiction/romance); Eleanor Jeffers (mystery/western); Diann Seagrave (business, how-to, hobbies); Georgia Kent (proposal design).
Handles: Nonfiction books, juvenile books, novels, novellas, short story collections. Considers these nonfiction areas: biography/autobiography; business; child guidance/parenting; current affairs; education; ethnic/cultural interests; gay/lesbian issues; government/politics; health/medicine; history; how-to; humor; juvenile nonfiction; language/literature; nature/environment; popular culture; psychology; religious/inspirational; self-help/personal improvement; sociology; sports; translations; true crime/investigative; women's issues/women's studies. Considers these fiction areas: action/adventure; contemporary issues; detective/police/crime; family saga; historical; juvenile; lesbian; literary; mainstream; mystery/suspense; regional; religious/inspirational; romance (contemporary, gothic, historical, regency); thriller/espionage; westerns/frontier; young adult. Query with outline/proposal. Reports in 1 month on queries; 1 month on mss. "Ordinarily, fiction manuscripts should be submitted only after professional editing by a book doctor."
Recent Sales: *Clearwater Summer*, by John Keegan (Carroll & Graf).
Terms: Agent receives 15% commission on domestic sales; 20% on foreign sales. Offers written contract, binding for 1 year and renewable.
Fees: Does not charge a reading fee. Client pays for all submission costs. Frequently recommends a book doctor.

Writers' Conferences: ABA (Chicago, June); regional and local conferences in the Southeast.
Tips: Obtains new clients through *LMP*, *Guide to Literary Agents*, stories in *WD* and recommendations from clients and editors.

*STEPHEN WRIGHT AUTHORS' REPRESENTATIVE, (III), P.O. Box 1341, FDR Station, New York NY 10150-1341. (212)213-4382. Contact: Stephen Wright. Estab. 1984. Prefers to work with published/established authors. Works with a small number of new/unpublished authors. Member of MWA, signatory of WGA. Currently handles: 20% nonfiction; 60% novels; 10% movie scripts; 10% TV scripts.
Handles: Nonfiction books, novels, young adult and juvenile books, syndicated material. Considers "most if not all" nonfiction and fiction areas. Query first; do *not* send ms. Include SASE with query. Reports in 3 weeks on queries.
Also Handles: Movie scripts (feature films), TV scripts (documentary, episodic drama, TV mow), radio scripts, stage plays. Considers "most if not all" script areas.
Terms: Agent receives 10-15% commission on domestic sales; 10-15% on dramatic sales; 15-20% on foreign sales.
Fees: "When the writer is a beginner or has had no prior sales in the medium for which he or she is writing, we charge a reading criticism fee; does not waive fee when representing the writer. Charges $600/300 pages; or $100/50 pages (double-spaced). We simply do not 'read' a manuscript, but give the writer an in-depth criticism. If we like what we read, we would represent the writer. We tell the writer whether we believe his/her work is marketable. I normally provide the critiques."

*WRITER'S CONSULTING GROUP, (II, III), P.O. Box 492, Burbank CA 91503-0492. (818)841-9294. Director: Jim Barmeier. Estab. 1983. Represents 10 clients. "We will work with established and unestablished writers. We welcome unsolicited queries." Currently handles: 40% nonfiction books; 20% novels; 40% movie scripts.
Handles: Nonfiction books, novels. Considers these nonfiction areas: biography/autobiography; business; current affairs; education; health/medicine; money/finance/economics; music/dance/theater/film; popular culture; psychology; science/technology; self-help/personal improvement; true crime/investigative. Considers these fiction areas: action/adventure; contemporary issues; detective police/crime; family saga; feminist; horror; mainstream; mystery/suspense; thriller/espionage. True stories (for which the author has legal rights) about women and families put in crisis situations overcoming adversities or challenges; finding unusual answers to problems (like tracking down a daughter's rapist when the legal system has failed); true stories of unusual survival and profiles in courage; show biz or celebrity stories; HBO-type stories involving controversial peole in the news (like Mike Tyson) or stories with controversial political overtones (like dramatic trial stories); stories about historical, famous or infamous women; unusual family stories; off-beat mother-daughter, wife-husband, sister-sister stories; death row or prison stories; true crime (especially if the villain is a female); true Christmas stories about family reunions or unusual miracles; little-known stories about the accomplishments of women; hot contemporary stories; Generation X; famous trial cases; health issues; novels (women's, mainstream, contemporary thrillers); movie scripts (comedies, love stories, thrillers, women's stories). Query or send proposal. Include SASE. Reports in 1 month on queries; 3 months on mss.
Recent Sales: *Moment to Moment* (Medical Consumers Publishing).
Also Handles: Movie scripts (feature film), TV scripts (TV mow). Considers these script subject areas: action/adventure; comedy; contemporary issues; detective/police/crime; family saga; feminist; horror; humor; mainstream; mystery/suspense; psychic/supernatural; romantic comedy and drama; thriller.
Recent Sales: "Witness Against My Mother" (CBS Movie of the Week).
Terms: "We will explain our terms to clients when they wish to sign. We receive a 10% commission on domestic sales. We also work with other agencies in the sale of stories."
Fees: Sometimes charges reading fee. "Additionally, we offer ghostwriting and editorial services, as well as book publicity services for authors. Mr. Barmeier is a graduate of Stanford University's Master's Degree in Creative Writing Program."
Tips: "We will help an author from concept to final product—if need be, designing the proposal, creating the package, doing rewrites on the manuscript. We are on the lookout for controversial women's stories that can be turned into movies-of-the-week. These usually involve women who take risks, are involved in jeopardy or crisis situations, and have upbeat endings."

Additional Fee-charging Agents

The following fee-charging agencies have indicated they are *primarily* interested in handling the work of scriptwriters. They also handle less than ten to fifteen percent book manuscripts. After reading the listing (you can find the page number in the Listings Index), send them a query to obtain more information on their needs and manuscript submissions policies.

Client First—A/K/A Leo P. Haffey Agency

Durkin Artists Agency
Dykeman Associates Inc.

Earth Tracks Agency

Fee-charging Agents/'95-'96 changes

The following agencies appeared in the last (1995) edition of *Guide to Literary Agents* but are absent from the 1996 edition. These agencies failed to respond to our request for an update of their listing, or were left out for the reasons indicated in parentheses following the agency name.

A & R Burke Corp. (unable to contact)
The Abacus Group (renamed The Aachen Group) (editorial decision)
Joseph Anthony Agency (editorial decision)
Author Author Literary Agency (editorial decision)
Authors' Marketing Services Ltd. (unable to contact)
Bruce Cook Agency (unable to contact)
Aleta M. Daley/Maximilan Becker

Eastwind Writers (editorial decision)
Eden Literary Agency (editorial decision)
Lee Shore Agency (complaints)
The Literary Bridge (editorial decision)
March Media Inc.
Mid-America Literary Agency (agency closed)
New Writing Agency (editorial decision)
Oceanic Press (book packager/syndicator)
Oceanic Press Service (book

packager/syndicator)
Shoestring Press (editorial decision)
Singer Media Corp. (book packager/syndicator)
Mark Sullivan (editorial decision)
Tiger Moon Enterprises (unable to contact)
Wildstar Associates (editorial decision)
Write Design (editorial decision)
The Write Therapist (editorial decision)

Script Agents

The Ins and Outs of Working with Script Agents

by Gary Salt

Cows don't give milk. As anyone raised on a farm knows perfectly well, you have to get up (usually around dawn) and go out and take it from them. Thus is it also within the film and television industry. No one is waiting at the bus depot or the other end of a modem to give you money, a production commitment, options, assignments, credit, development deals, prestige, glory, or studio parking space. Agents can go out and get some of these things for you—some, but not all. Writers have agents because cows don't give milk. Agents level the playing field. They help minimize (but do not eliminate) the odds that are stacked severely against all but a handful of film and television writers.

What does an agent do?

In simple terms, an agent represents someone else's professional interests in return for a commission. Therefore, the least to expect and demand is that the agent is also a professional: full-time, with an office, business hours and, hopefully, a verifiable reputation. The most common functions undertaken every day by agents are those of introducer, negotiator and advisor; and every good agent should be able to do all three all the time.

Agents can either introduce their clients' work or their clients *to* work and usually they do both. They are constantly searching by every possible means for buyers and customers for existing scripts or treatments and much of their time is spent covering a massive field of potential markets. Moreover, these markets can change from month to month in their signals and writing requirements. In all of this, either by personal contact or by phone, the agent is scanning and evaluating when and to whom to submit which scripts. This process is ongoing and never stops. Like the surf, it can be high or low, cold or warm, but always ceaseless. It goes on over weekends, at social events, on "vacation." Agencies may keep office hours, but no agent punches a clock. There are few professional contacts who are not also possible customers for a client's script. With few exceptions, the bulk of an agent's time is spent reading and evaluating material

Gary Salt entered the agency business in 1972, and joined Paul Kohner, Inc. in 1976. In 1987 he and his partner purchased the firm and he subsequently became president. Paul Kohner, Inc. is one of the oldest continuously-operated agencies in the country, and is a mid-sized full-service agency representing a range of clients including actors, writers, directors, composers and authors. In addition, the firm conducts a substantial rights business in film and television and represents several major publishers in this market.

and then organizing and making submissions of that material to the marketplace. Nearly all of the latter business is done over the phone.

But agents can also introduce their clients to the work and this means setting up personal meetings either to have a client pitch a concept in the hope of securing a deal to write it or to have the client audition for an open writing assignment. In television, such meetings are nearly always with the producers or development staff of a production company if the subject is a film, or with the "show-runners" if it's a 30-minute or 60-minute episodic show. Pilots and TV movies that get past the first step will lead to meetings with network development executives, but the agent will not have to organize these once things get rolling. Feature pitch meetings are usually held at production companies or studio offices with development executives responsible for screening new material. Occasionally, a writer will start out meeting with a director and carry on from there.

Where open writing assignments are at stake, expect merciless competition. There are more qualified writers than there are ever jobs available. Writers who get into these meetings will have already been screened by submission of résumés and, where necessary, writing samples appropriate to the assignment in question. Usually, by the time a meeting is set up, the producer basically wants to get a sense of the writer's "take" on the project and there is also an element of checking the writer out personally. Is he or she someone we can deal with? Does he present himself well? Does he listen? Do we want to spend much time and much money working with this person? While highly personalized, these meetings are always limited to creative matters and no deals or negotiations are discussed. The producer will have already ascertained the writer's availability and his or her "quotes" or current price for similar, recent work.

Aside from introducer, an agent is also a professional advisor with a strong vested interest in putting your best work or best foot forward. Resolve early on that when you challenge the marketplace for position you are going to face consequences that include all forms of rejection both personal and professional and in every conceiveable manner from flat-out hardball passes to soft-soap copouts. Regardless of the type of spoon used to convey the castor oil, brace yourself to swallow it quickly and get on with your work. Let the agent deal with the politics of the situation and if there is anything useful to be gleaned from a pass, the agent will convey it. Spec scripts are sometimes returned with comments worth considering in possible rewrites.

If a personal meeting or pitch fails to deliver a deal or a sale, move on at once unless there is some specific shortcoming that can be corrected for future meetings.

An advisor with knowledge of the market

Part of the advisor's function requires an agent to evaluate your material. This area, more than any other, will determine the kind of relationship you have with an agent, because this is where disagreements about your work will first appear. Agents do not *have* to represent or submit anything you deliver to them. In fact, if you have decided to embark on a new script, the person to call *before* typing the first page is your agent. You may thus discover that two studios have been developing "your" script for several months or, worse, that principal photography just wrapped on the same story only with a Doberman pinscher in the lead role. Use your agent as a sounding board before, during and after writing anything you expect him to put on the market. Aside from knowing how to protect your interests in negotiations, the most frequent and valuable service from good representation is knowing the market, thus often saving the writer time and much wasted effort.

If a first consultation does not shut a project down, give the finished product to your agent before you make any other professional submissions. It can be a scratch draft but should be fairly well proofed. The important thing is to get the best evaluation you can from the agent before you decide to go forward. If there is complete disagreement on the quality of the script and your agent refuses to submit it, you might suggest a limited number (four or five) of selected submissions where a pass does the least harm (therefore, not to the head of production) and thereby test the waters. You can agree to rewrite or abandon for now if these submissions turn up generally negative results. If, after all best efforts and good faith discussion are exhausted, the agent still will not go out with your material, start looking for someone else to represent you.

What agents are not

They are not your mother or father, nor your priest or rabbi. They are not your editor, tax consultant or investment counselor. They are not social secretaries, tennis partners or psychiatrists (except where your aberrant behavior threatens continued employment). Agencies are not banks and agents not loan officers. (Yet I have never talked with an agent who has done the job for more than a couple of years who has not, at one time or another, loaned a client money. But you had better be either a longtime client or have a firm deal coming in the door.)

Agents do not guarantee success; they reduce the odds of complete failure. An agent may become a good friend in the long term, but unless he does, agents are not entitled to love, birthday cards, gifts, gratitude, or public acclaim as you nervously clutch your Oscar. What an agent *is* entitled to is your payment of commissions. All of the other things may come in the fullness of time, but what an agent deserves and has a right to expect for services rendered is commission. Regardless of anything else, the relationship is always fundamentally an economic one and therefore completely predictable and dependable.

What about commissions?

One of your main career goals is to pay as much in commissions as possible. That means you are working frequently and making obscenely high fees. Agents are franchised by the Writers Guild of America (WGA) through the Association of Talent Agents (ATA); agents in California are also licensed by the State Labor Commissioner. These bodies set commission rates at no more than 10% for film and television writers. The ATA is a professional group which bargains with various guilds and unions which have jurisdiction over clients and it also supports quality control on its members. ATA and WGA affiliations are good indicators of professional competence and integrity when seeking representation.

Generally when signing agency contracts you will also be asked to sign authorizations which permit the agency to receive your checks. This is a standard practice among all established agencies. By this method the agency knows if *timely* payments have been made; they can deduct commission and send your check wherever you direct. This also permits the agency to verify the correct amounts are being paid and there are no unauthorized deductions or holdbacks taken by the employer.

Seeking representation

Basically, there are two ways to go about finding an agent to represent you or your work. Either you get a third-party reference (you know someone I know and they've read your work and give me a call), or you contact agents cold through query letters. The first way is better, but the second is far more likely, especially for writers just starting out. Unless you have a personal relationship with an agent, cold calls are virtually useless and can do more harm than good; they place you in about the same category of desirability as a strange stockbroker pushing shares of Montana Smelting.

A few words now about query letters:
- They should be typed, readable and to the point.
- Always include your address and phone number.
- If you expect an answer, include sufficient return postage to send back whatever you want back.
- Avoid sending sample pages or "teaser" scenes which, at best, can represent barely 5% of the finished work.
- State clearly and quickly what type of script you have or are writing and a suitable summary of the plot. Use your own judgment as to how much detail you want to disclose.
- *A query letter is not a résumé.* You are trying to induce a complete stranger to read your script, not applying for a job. Therefore, academic credentials, work history, family tree, awards and honors, and special skills and hobbies have no place in a query *unless* something in them bears *directly* on the subject matter of your script. If you are writing about the murder of a game warden in Kenya and you have lived in Africa or count murder among your special skills, then the agent will certainly want to know about it.
- Before you dispatch scads of letters hither and yon, do some decent research about your targets. Know why and to whom you are sending a query. Some agencies and/or agents represent only TV material and don't really deal very much in the feature market and vice-versa. Check the current *Guide to Literary Agents* and other standard reference guides which list agents' preferences and the correct spelling of their names.
- Queries may be sent at any time. Agents may be busier at certain times of the year than others if they deal in episodic television, but as a practical matter there is no easy way for you to figure that out, so don't worry about it. Start making contacts whenever the script is ready to be seen outside your immediate family.
- If you get a pass from an agent or no answer at all, move on to others.
- If you get a request to send in your script, GREAT! You're off the street and into the lobby, even if you aren't yet through the office door.

What to expect when you're represented

Having secured the interest of an agent(s) in your script, what kind of representation can you expect?

First, an agent can represent you and/or your script. What's the difference? For one thing, representing just your script but not you as a client means the agent does not assume the obligation to solicit and procure employment for you as a writer. In the television markets especially, this is always time-consuming and usually a fruitless task unless you present some existing credentials that an agent can work with. By limiting the representation to your script alone the agent can focus time, energy and resources where they will do the most good; he can concentrate on his main goal: to sell the script to the best customer for the best deal (we will come back to this). Some agencies have developed special contracts called "single project" agreements, specifically designed to lock in an individual script or TV treatment as the client rather than the actual writer. Where the sale of a script is the first career step, there are no "career strategies" to worry about yet. With luck and good writing, those headaches will come later.

If the agent wants to represent you *and* your work and you are a new writer to film and television, then he will inevitably use your best available writing as sample scripts to solicit other work on assignment. Thus, a spec script often serves two functions on the market: as submitted material and as a "calling card" which might land the writer unforeseen employment—"We don't want to make what you wrote, but we like the quality of the work so how about considering what we *do* want to make," etc. It is a commonly heard observation in the film business that some writers' best work has earned them a great deal of money and has never been produced.

What makes the best deal best?

Earlier I said the agent's goal was the best deal from the best customer, so let's look at this concept for a minute.

Why not just go after the best deal? The most money? Writers often read and hear about "auctions" and "bidding wars" for new scripts and deals with breathtaking numbers. Yes, these deals do happen every so often, but they are not the usual course of business. Part of useful representation is having skillful and experienced advice about when and with whom to make deals. Agents know who the good buyers are but they should also be able to discern for you the traps you cannot see for yourself—the wannabe producers, the time-wasters, the energy-vampires who never quite come through with the deal or the money; in short, all of the marginal and lightweight players whose tactics in the marketplace can ruin an otherwise solid script. One of the most essential and valuable parts of any agent's job is to protect you from these types. The most money may not be the best deal if it comes from someone who has no real chance or intention of getting your film or television project into production or to distribute it adequately. Some option money trickles into your checking account, but then a year or more goes by and nothing happens. The option lapses after the script has been shopped to death and worn out its welcome everywhere because nobody wants to make it with the knucklehead who is attached to it like a bad rash.

A bad deal is not better than no deal!

That's because a bad deal can kill a script forever but at least with no deal the script remains available and can still seek out a home. Thus, if the agent is on the ball and has really found the best customer, then it won't ever be a bad deal.

Learning to be a good client

There is more to the agent-writer relationship than just sending in material with the attitude of "call me when it sells." Clients can be their own worst enemy, usually when they decide to take on both the jobs of writer *and* agent. To be a client means you are willing to put your livelihood in someone else's hands. If you take your work seriously, take your agent seriously as well. You can learn to be a good writer and you can learn to be a good client. This requires reasonable diligence, fairness, and cooperation in dealing with your agent. Remember that your agent is the prism through which employers see you and your work. In short, if you have a jerk or a clown for an agent, then you can be mistaken for a jerk or a clown. There is simply no foolproof test to guarantee the success of any agency alliance. Like romance, it is the indefinable chemistry and it either works or it doesn't. Nevertheless, here are a few tips on the elusive problem of how to be a client:

● Try to find someone who sees the agency business as a *profession*, not a way station on a career path to being a producer or a studio executive. If you ever get a whiff of this sort of thing, get out quick and find someone else. You cannot afford to be represented by someone who has one eye cocked on a studio or network office; they will always be willing to satisfy someone other than you and they will always be willing to settle for less.

● The most valuable items an agent can give you are time and judgment, so make the most of both. When in doubt about calling, leave the agent alone. Every ten minutes spent in small talk about smaller issues is ten minutes not spent contacting a possible buyer or setting up a useful meeting. Don't expect or request daily or even weekly briefings on the course of your career. This is the real business world here, not the State Department press room. If there is an agreed program of submissions of material, updates every couple of weeks would be about right.

● If you make any contacts or submissions on your own, notify your agent, especially if you have sent a script on your own. Even better, discuss this upfront. You want to be kept informed and so does your agent. Also, there may be good reasons why you should not submit to or contact a certain party directly at a certain time.

● Find out if there is a preferred time during the business day when you can call.

● Concede the fact that, at least in the early going, the agent's knowledge counts for something and that his job is to set the priorities of what and when to move and to whom. He is making a living doing his job and you may not be.

● For short, informational messages, faxes are best of all. Consider investing in this purchase. Communication can thus be frequent but quick and there is a written record.

● Be as informed about the business as you can be. If you have easy access to the Hollywood trade papers, learn how to read them with sensible skepticism. A good substitute is weekly *Variety* out of New York, which encapsulates most of the previous week's important news from the West Coast's daily edition.

Finally, somewhere around your workspace find a place for these words from Winston Churchill: "Never give up. Never give up. Never, never, never."

Just the FAQs: The Ten Most Frequently Asked Questions About Agents

by Kerry Cox

In my decade as editor/publisher of *Hollywood Scriptwriter*, the international newsletter for scriptwriters, we've published ten Annual Agency Surveys, in which "open" agencies (those who will consider the work of new, uncredited writers) tell us what they're looking for and how they want it submitted.

Invariably, this issue elicits a flurry of questions from our readers. Chances are their questions are similar to the ones you might be asking as you use this book to help you land representation. So, in the hopes of saving you some time and effort, here are the ten most frequently asked questions about agents.

How can I tell if the agent is a "good" agent? How do I know if they've sold anything, or who their clients are?

The obvious way to start is by asking. If the agency has a list of reasonably impressive clients, or some notable sales, they'll be happy to tell you.

There is a small catch, however. As a beginning writer you'll find that the majority of agencies willing to consider your work are just starting out themselves—they may not have much to tell you when you start questioning their track record.

Does this mean you shouldn't give them a shot? Well, everyone has to start somewhere, including agents. It can be argued that a new agency is the hungriest, eager to land quality writers who will allow them to attack the marketplace. That may be just the kind of energy and enthusiasm you want behind your script.

You should also find out if an agency is a signator to the Writers Guild of America. The only agencies taken seriously by the Hollywood community are signators; it means they're aware of the terms of the Guild contract, and they'll function within those parameters.

Do I really need to send a self-addressed, stamped envelope (SASE)? If you ask me, that's just an invitation to send my script back.

Actually, *not* sending a SASE is an invitation to have your script dumped, unread.

When you send a script, synopsis, treatment, or even a query letter to an agency sans SASE, you're sending two messages: (1) I'm a rank amateur; and (2) I consider this material disposable.

Obviously, neither message is desirable.

Agencies large and small are besieged by scripts and queries daily. They would

Kerry Cox *is editor/publisher of* Hollywood Scriptwriter, *the leading international newsletter for scriptwriters. He is co-author (with Jurgen Wolff) of* Successful Scriptwriting, *(Writer's Digest Books) and* Top Secrets: Screenwriting, *(Lone Eagle Publishing). He has had, at one time or another, five different agents. For a sample copy of* Hollywood Scriptwriter, *see the contact information in Recommended Publications.*

quickly go under if they had to foot the bill for the postage to return all the material they receive. SASEs are part of the cost of doing business for all writers, and should be considered as integral to each submission as the material itself.

Should I rewrite a script at the request of an agent if they haven't said they'll represent me?

It depends. Was the feedback good? Did the script need a rewrite anyway, based on that feedback? Or do you completely disagree with the assessment, but figure it's your only shot at an agent and you better do it or you'll lose out?

Rewrite a script when it needs rewriting. If that need was pointed out to you by an agent, and you can see that he has made some good points, then go to it. Or, rewrite a script if you're being paid to. But don't rewrite it against your better judgment, simply out of desperation to land an agent.

What do I do when the agent asks me for money up front for copies, mailing, etc.?

This is a tricky one. Are they asking for $35, or $3,500? If they're just asking you for money for copies, offer instead to supply them with the copies if you're uncomfortable sending the money. We had one writer make this offer, and the agent said, "No, I want to do the copies so I know they're done right." Pretty weak.

It isn't uncommon at all—in fact, it's the rule, not the exception—for your agent to ask you to provide copies. Some will even ask for a deposit against mailing costs (my own book agent does, although I have to admit I'm losing patience with that, since I've sold two books through them). As long as the amounts seem reasonable, there's no cause to suspect that your agent is playing the horses with your hard-earned dollars and leaving your script to rot.

However, if they start asking for big bucks—especially for rewriting services, critiquing services, or other baloney—well, that leads us to the next question . . .

What if the agent responds to my submission by recommending a critiquing or rewriting service?

The Writers Guild has a position on agents referring writers to services such as these. According to an official at the Guild, they will not advertise such agencies on their master list of signatory agents. However, that doesn't mean their signatory status is revoked.

In other words, the Guild doesn't approve, but doesn't really seem interested in doing anything about it.

What should *you* do? Again, you must rely on common sense and not fall victim to desperation. Frankly, I'm suspicious of any agency that comes up with the name of a critiquing service they recommend, or worse, offers to do the work themselves. In the first instance, I have no way of knowing why they favor that particular service, but my cynical and suspicious nature leads me to wonder about such ugly realities as kickbacks. In the second scenario, why would I want an agent who is spending his or her time critiquing scripts, instead of hustling sales?

In *Hollywood Scriptwriter* we run advertisements for critiquing services that I have either used myself (and liked enough to recommend), or whose work I have personally reviewed. This doesn't necessarily mean they're right for you, but at least you can be assured of their professionalism.

Is it okay to make multiple submissions?

Absolutely. If you wait around for one agent to get back to you before you submit to another, you'll die of old age long before you find representation.

Once you sign with an agent, however, you can't send your work to others just because you think your agent isn't pushing hard enough. That's why it's so important to choose your agent wisely: you're making a commitment.

A note: an agent friend showed me one query letter with an opening sentence that went something like, "I'm submitting this same material to a number of other agencies, so if you want to get in on a good thing you'd better act fast!" My friend did act fast. The query letter was back in the SASE within seconds, the remainder unread.

What if an agent says she'll "show my work around?" Does that mean I have an agent?

Some agents will try to avoid a complete commitment by testing the waters with your material. It's not an ideal situation, but it happens. If you give an okay, it means you have an agent for that particular project, for an unspecified amount of time. It doesn't mean the agent will represent everything else you write; but then again, even an agent with whom you have a signed contract will put up a fight if asked to represent something she feels is sub-standard. After all, her reputation is on the line, too. Agents are judged by the caliber of work they send out, just as you are.

Once you sign with an agent, you must notify any others who are "showing your work around," and advise them that you're withdrawing your permission. Don't ever get in the unethical position of having more than one agent shopping the same script.

How long should I wait to get a response before I start calling?

Allow at least a month, then send a short follow-up note. Two or three weeks after that, a polite, professional phone call is in order. If another month goes by and you've heard nothing, it's probably a dead issue, so send a letter requesting the return of the submission. It's tempting at this point to get sarcastic and accusatory—"Hey, I don't mean to wake you, but when you sober up do you think you can send my script back?"—but don't give in. It was never a personal issue, so don't make it one. Just ask for your stuff back, and move on.

Should I submit a complete script when first approaching an agency?

NO. Always begin with a letter of inquiry, in which you *briefly* summarize the story, indicate the genre, and include any pertinent details on your background. The letter should be a page long, no more. If the agent is intrigued by your inquiry and wants to see more, you'll receive a request for the complete script.

Is there any reason to choose a L.A.-based agent over one located elsewhere?

If you have a choice of two agencies, and all else is equal, go with the L.A. agency. It's simply easier for them to make and maintain contacts.

On the other hand, few new writers are fortunate enough to choose between two agencies. So the real question is, "Am I handicapped by having an out-of-town agent?"

A little bit, maybe, but not to the point of being crippled. If your agent has the desire and willingness to hustle, and can afford a few networking trips a year to L.A., you're much better off than you'd be with an L.A.-based agency that devotes most of its efforts to established clients and treats you as an afterthought.

So, there are the Top Ten. I hope among them were some questions that popped into your own mind, and that you now feel better informed and equipped to embark on the rocky journey toward representation. Good luck.

Building a Career in Hollywood

by Jeff Ordway

Hollywood . . . land of dreams. Day after day, huge amounts of money are spent creating films, television programs and interactive entertainment. If you believe what you see in films, the Hollywood agent is the maker of stars, putting deals together on the cellular phone while driving around in a spotless Mercedes convertible, making and breaking careers by the minute.

Actually, careers aren't made in a minute, but are created over time. Granted, there are those few instances where a first-time writer creates a spec script that takes the market by storm, but these are few and far between. A writer's career usually takes a bell-curve shaped path. In most cases, a slower, more solid rise translates into a longer, more prosperous time at the top. The agent's role is to assist the writer in creating the longest and most prosperous career possible. In pursuit of this, the agent's job can be broken down into three different areas: finding new talent, carving out a career for that talent, and nurturing and maintaining the artists to allow them to grow.

A career begins: getting to know you and your script

Everyday I get letters from people with ideas, from writers who have created stories. Some have completed scripts, others have outlines and summaries. Some are film ideas, others for television or interactive projects. Are the letters read? Yes. Every one. Unfortunately, due to the sheer volume coming into my office, I am only able to respond to those that somehow catch my attention.

So what makes a letter stand out? Funky paper? Bright envelopes? Try the writing. You would be surprised at how many poorly written letters I receive, filled with typos, improper sentence structure, and many other problems. The intro letter is the writer's calling card. It must be good. I guarantee I will not read an entire screenplay when I can't even make it through a one- or two-page letter.

Include some personal information in your letter. It helps to know who the writer is. Also send a brief synopsis that adequately represents the story. It might take one sentence, one paragraph, or one page. Put some time into thinking about topic, plot and story. A worthwhile story must be entertaining, interesting and informative. Ask friends if they think it is a good idea. (Make sure to ask people who will respond honestly.) Too many story ideas range from ridiculous to boring to completely unmarketable. It takes a lot of time and energy to create a complete story and put it into script form. That time shouldn't be wasted on something that no one will want to see either on TV or in a theater.

I prefer that writers use their own words to synopsize the story rather than comparing

Jeff Ordway is formerly of Stephen Cannell Productions Feature Film Division, where he was responsible for soliciting and developing screenplays. He is currently at Camden, a boutique talent and literary agency which handles approximately 20-25 writing clients.

it to someone else's work. I would much rather hear about a futuristic thriller than be told that I'm missing out on the next *Blade Runner*. In this case, *Blade Runner* happens to be a personal favorite, but many times I get references to films that I either dislike or didn't see. Obviously, this taints my impression of the writer's work before I even get to read it, and if I dislike the film references, I never will.

I also like it when a writer encloses a short scene from the screenplay. This, coupled with an accurate synopsis and a well-written letter, makes it easier to determine whether I will contact the writer to request the script. Since it is physically impossible to read every script outlined in these letters, the more information I have at my disposal, the better educated I am about the writer, and the better the chance that I will be "caught" by some aspect of the query submission. I am fully aware that because of my limited time, I am missing out on a number of good writers and their creations. I wish I had a hundred people that I could count on, that I could trust completely, and that think like I do. Then I could read everything.

But, I don't have those hundred helpers. As I write this, I have a backlog of approximately 23 scripts to read. They come to me from a number of sources: some from query letters, some referred by producers or other agents, some referred by friends. The writers range from doctors and lawyers to bartenders and teachers. Each of them is waiting to hear whether he is "good" enough to be represented by my agency. Their hopes and dreams are captured in a few words on a few pages. They deserve my full attention and my honest opinion.

Of the multitude of scripts that I do read, the vast majority will be a "pass," and upon request, will be returned to the writer along with a note sending my best wishes. To lessen the chance of having the script sent back, have it read by others before you send it out. Show it to those who will respond honestly about what they think. Give it to a friend, or better yet, ask them to give it to one of their friends who doesn't know you. That person may respond with a more honest opinion about the script.

At some point, the script should be read aloud. The writer needs to hear what his words sound like in the mouths of others. If it doesn't flow, change it until it does. Just because a script has been completed doesn't mean that it is written well enough to be worth sending out. Remember, most times a writer only gets one shot. If I don't like what is sent, chances are I won't read anything the writer creates in the future.

Sometimes I will like a portion or element of a screenplay, but not be excited about the entire work. When this happens, I invite the writer to contact me so we can discuss it further. I know it is difficult to deal with the thought of rejection, but answering my invitation can pay dividends. Currently, I am looking forward to the fourth draft of a screenplay from a writer who was bold enough to call me and ask that very important question: "WHY?" Will his script be what I'm looking for this time? I don't know. So far, each draft has gotten better. I do know that if it isn't, he and I will have another conversation to discuss what is missing, and he will (again) have the choice of rewriting it. If he decides to rework it, I would gladly read it again, and again, and again, until either he gives up on me, or I have the passionate response to the material that I need to go out and sell it.

Building a career step by step

I have a great deal of respect for anyone who can take even the smallest of ideas and bring it to fruition. I know how hard it is to create. At least once a day, either in person or on the phone, I meet with writers to discuss their work. Some of these are writers with whom I am already working. Others are those I'm interested in possibly representing. Each writer has different needs, and subsequently, my working relationships are based on each individual writer. We learn together what it means to be a team.

First step: working together on the script

A large part of my job is helping writers create well-crafted pieces that best display their talents and abilities. We spend a great deal of time working together to bring their creations to market-readiness. I believe that every writer who sits down to create a story sees their creation perfectly. Each scene, sequence, and piece of dialogue flows seamlessly in their imagination. However, sometimes what gets translated to the paper is an inadequate representation of that picture. Thus, I paint my comments in broad colors; what I did or did not like, which sequences seem out of place, how the characters feel, whether it is marketable. The ultimate goal is to create a perfect depiction of the story as envisioned.

Once I have a script that I'm passionate about, I attempt to create in potential buyers the same passion. The spec script market is the highest profile market for writers. Every day, I learn of yet another script or story idea purchased by a production company or studio for hundreds of thousands of dollars. For each of these sales, there are a handful of other deals made for less. But they all have one thing in common: The right script got into the right hands at the right time.

Second step: knowing the market

Every production executive has their own likes and dislikes. The trick is to match a script with someone who can get it made. There are a couple of different approaches to this. One is the shotgun approach, sending the script all over town hoping someone will bite. The other approach is to be very selective about who sees the script, sending it only to people with a history of liking and/or purchasing material of a similar nature or writing style.

I spend a great deal of time cultivating and maintaining relationships with these production executives. We discuss writers, film genres, story ideas, topics that give me insight into what interests them, what passions drive them. Mutual trust is essential for strong relationships. Thus, I continually strive to educate them, not only about the writers I work with, but about myself and the quality of work they can expect from the people I represent.

Having worked in development at a production company, I know how my feelings toward an agent affect my feelings about material he sends to me. Therefore, I never tell anyone "this is the best script I've ever read" unless it is. To help new talent my reputation must be that I will only work with talented writers who are able to tell interesting stories with dynamic characters. This is why I am particular about scripts I allow to be shopped with my name attached. I must be. Otherwise, I am more detrimental than helpful.

Likewise, I expect honest feedback from industry executives about my client's material. It helps me know if there is anything in the script, such as insufficient character development, holes in the plot line, or slow moving sequences, that either I or the writer missed. I don't expect a writer to rewrite their work based on a single executive's opinion, but if there is a consensus, the writer needs to hear it.

Third step: selling ability, not just material

I do more than just try to sell spec material. A large portion of my time and energy goes into getting my clients hired for open writing assignments. Production companies have projects where the existing script doesn't work, and they need the script rewritten. They also purchase the film and television rights to books where they need an adaptation written. The "glory" of rewriting is obviously not the same as that of the large spec script sale, but there is the overall payoff of consistent work. Rewriting can be not only a solid way to create a career but also a great way to earn a living. A writer creates a name for himself by proving capable, skilled and dependable.

Many times, after building a career through rewriting, it is possible to get people to revisit a writer's spec scripts that have not sold. A buyer may be more receptive to a writer's original ideas based on solid working relationships that have been forged in working together on rewrites. These scripts may now be prized possessions in the marketplace. In this industry, as in any other, everybody loves a winner.

Executives become "fans" of writers based on their work. When this happens, we set up a meeting between the writer and the executive so they can meet face to face. In these general meetings the relationship between the writer and the industry is born. After the meeting I receive feedback from the writer about how it went. Just as importantly, I get the executive's opinion as well, letting me know if this is a person they feel they can work with and have confidence in.

Understanding and achieving career goals

The writer's job is to write; mine is to sell that writing ability. Consequently, it is my responsibility to pass on to the writer any information to remove the blocks keeping his work from selling. There must be a high level of trust to adequately relay the feedback that I receive, be it good, bad or indifferent. If we have not yet learned how to act as a team, then we need to do so now.

In pursuit of the team approach, I must know my clients' long-term goals and help them reach those goals. Some want to keep writing all their lives, others want to become a writer/actor, writer/director, or writer/producer. As time goes by, these goals can be reached if we are both committed to them.

Clarity is the key. I try to have a "goals discussion" with my clients regularly to discuss where we started, where we are, and where we want to go. In these discussions we set goals together, collectively and individually, short-term, mid-term and long-term. We work to create a plan of action to drive the writer's career forward. For example, a collective goal I have with one client, who is a college professor, is for him not to teach next fall. Individual goals that move us closer to our collective goal are for me to sell one of his spec scripts by a certain date, and for him to complete his next screenplay by a mutually agreed upon deadline.

Sometimes goals change. One difficult situation I recently faced involved a writing team that decided to split up and pursue different paths. Each writer now wishes to create an individual career. Relationships they have made in the industry as partners must now be reestablished on a new level, including the one between the three of us. It's not as easy as it seems. In discussing the ramifications of this decision, I have to mediate how they will relate to one another in the future. Although it was an amicable parting, a number of issues remain regarding future collaborations and how they will work together if a previously unsold property is acquired.

Helping writers achieve their dreams

These are basic steps toward creating the overall career that each client desires. Each requires a different focus to make it happen. I view my job in very simple terms: to help make other people's dreams come true. I believe that in doing so, I move closer to fulfilling my own dreams and goals. My mentor, David Wardlow, once told me, "If you do this only for the money, you will always be wanting. Do it because you enjoy it and the money will be there." I am lucky in that I love what I do. There is no greater satisfaction than calling a writer who has not yet sold his work and telling him that someone is interested in what he has created. Hearing the response is one of the few great pleasures in life. It costs nothing, and lasts a long time.

Understanding Your Contract: A View from the Other Side of the Table

by Janice Pieroni

"Make a good deal, but don't blow it," was a favorite directive at Universal Studios, where I was a business affairs executive.

Business affairs executives represent studios, production companies, networks and other film and television producers in negotiations with agents about writers. Agents protect writers' interests during such negotiations.

Becoming familiar with the agent-business affairs "tap dance," or knowing a little about how business affairs executives and agents interact while negotiating, can go a long way toward making writers feel in control during the nerve-wracking deal-making process. It may also help keep them focused on what they should be doing: developing new projects.

How the deal-making process begins

Writers submit written material (usually through agents) or verbally "pitch" their ideas to producers, creative affairs executives or development executives in a position to buy material. If producers or executives like the material and decide to proceed, the deal is assigned to a business affairs executive.

The business affairs executive reads the project, finds out whatever she can about the writer and agent, and calls the agent to ask for "quotes"—the amounts of money a writer has earned on previous deals. The business affairs exeutive then calls the agent with a first offer, the agent reacts with outrage, and negotiations are officially underway.

The following are the major deal points business affairs executives and agents representing newer writers hash out with respect to movie and television deals.

Movie deals

Options

A friend recently complained that a major magazine had reported he'd just made a six figure deal with an Oscar-winning producer-director, while he was running around with a check for $1,500 in his pocket.

Welcome to the world of options.

An option is a payment made in exchange for a promise that the producer has the exclusive right to purchase a property at a set price before the expiration of the option period. An option allows a producer time to assess a project's viability with minimal financial risk. He'll approach studios, production companies, directors and actors in an

---

Janice Pieroni *worked as a business affairs attorney for Universal Studios, where she negotiated deals with agents representing writers, producers, directors and actors. She has also written screenplays, television episodes and articles. She broke into the film industry by working in various production and development capacities, including assistant to Martin Scorsese.*

attempt to interest them in making a movie from the script under option.

The general rule of thumb is that option money is 10 percent of the purchase price, but options can be granted for as little as $100. Writers are entitled to keep any option money even if the project is not purchased. Option periods can run for six to twelve months, and are often renewable for another six to twelve months.

"Many are called but few are chosen" is the rule with options. Option money is often the only money a writer will see for a particular project.

Purchase money

Naturally, producers try to minimize risks whenever possible. Consequently they purchase projects only when necessary. This can happen in one of three circumstances: the project is "greenlighted" and is about to go into production; the option period is about to run out and the project is in active development; or the project has received several bids and the only way to beat out the competition is to purchase the property.

Purchasing a project represents a substantial commitment. After purchasing a property, a company is entitled, but not required, to use it to create a film. Some writers considered successful may have optioned or sold a number of projects but have yet to see a single original project produced.

This can happen for many reasons. There is often a long gap between when a movie is sold and when it is produced. Or, a writer's work might be so controversial or unusual that it takes a long time to persuade studios or production companies to back it. Also, movie regimes are distinctly unstable. When a new regime enters, they often bring in their own pet projects and throw the others, no matter how worthwhile, into "turnaround"—another word for releasing them.

Production bonus

Few scripts are optioned, fewer are purchased and even fewer are produced.

To reward writers of scripts that actually get produced, agents frequently negotiate for production bonuses. The amount varies and is often payable 1/3 upon start of principal photography (meaning filming involving the main characters); 1/3 upon completion of principal photography; and 1/3 upon distribution.

Writing services

The WGA requires that writers of original screenplays be offered at least a first rewrite. Unless a scriptwriter is a true novice, the screenplay contains a great idea but terrible execution, or the development pace for the script is greatly accelerated, most studios, production companies or networks also prefer that writers rewrite their own scripts.

Securing at least a first rewrite helps protect writers' screen credits (which has important monetary and other consequences). It also gives writers a chance to work with and learn from top professionals, providing exposure and a chance to build contacts.

Screen credit

Screen credit is not negotiable—the WGA determines this after the producer submits proposed screen credit. The WGA seeks to protect the original writer. More than 50% of original material has to be rewritten before a writer is required to share credit and is guaranteed a minimum of shared story credit.

Consulting services

Agents representing writers with specialized knowledge or training who have written on their area of expertise can often negotiate a consulting deal for their client.

Consulting typically allows producers, directors and actors to draw on writers' expertise to aid with filming a movie story. Consulting is valuable to writers because it assists them in developing relationships with producers and directors who might hire them again. Moreover, consulting provides writers with additional compensation.

Producing

Producing is the least defined of all movie roles. Generally there are two types of producers, with some overlap. Line producers handle the nuts and bolts of everyday production. Creative producers work with writers to develop and sell ideas, raise financing and the like. Sometimes there may be four, five or more producers on a film.

Unless a writer can make a meaningful producing contribution, agents should not drive up costs by negotiating producing credits and fees, particularly for new writers. A producing credit and fee might be appropriate, for example, where the writer secured the rights to a newsworthy nonfiction story.

First time producers will most often receive a co-producer or associate producer credit.

Profits and merchandising

Most agents ask for and receive at least some profit participation. Writers will typically be entitled to between 1 and 5 percent of 100 percent of net (as opposed to gross). For newer writers the amount will probably be 1½ to 2½ percent. However, chances are overwhelming that writers will never see profits even if their projects become hits. Net profits are an industry joke; studio accounting procedures rarely show any profit at all.

Remakes, sequels and spin-offs

A remake is where a movie is remade into another movie, using substantially the same story line and typically the same name. Remakes are often made to update good stories for contemporary audiences. Recent remakes include *Sabrina* and *Little Women*.

A sequel is a continuation of a movie story that was popular, using elements common to both movies, which might but will not necessarily include the same actors, characters, setting or themes. Recent sequels include *Addams Family Values* and *My Girl 2*. The general rule is that writers receive half of what they originally were paid when a sequel is made, and a third for a remake.

A spin-off is when a writer's movie is adapted for a television series or one television series begets another. The WGA requires royalties be paid to a writer in these cases; agents representing experienced writers can generally negotiate higher royalties. Additionally, if a writer winds up working on the series, as often happens, she will receive additional compensation.

Step deals

Producers frequently hire writers to write original scripts on a "step deal" basis. A step deal gives them the option of terminating the project at each successive step (treatment, first draft, etc.), thus minimizing their financial exposure. The WGA provides for minimum payments for each step. Total payments cannot be less than if the writer had been hired at the outset to write a complete script.

Television deals

Television movies

Television movies are substantially similar to feature movie deals, with many of the same deal points. First time television screenplay writers are often paid WGA minimum or close to it. They will receive additional sums for reruns.

Episodic television

This is the land of television writing assignments—sitcoms and dramas. Assignments for existing shows are known in the industry as "one-shots."

Writers hired to write television episodes first write a story in prose instead of script form. Producers have the option of paying the writer for the story and either abandoning it or assigning it to another writer.

If they decide to proceed, they assign a first draft teleplay. A writer is also paid for a second draft, although it is sometimes not required. If the first draft was either very strong or very weak the producers might, under pressure of shooting dates, assign it right away to a staff member for revisions.

The WGA mandates minimum payments for each step. In addition, writers are also entitled to residual, or rerun, payments.

Staffing deals

For writers talented enough to land on or create a hit series, it can be an endless gravy train. Even if the writer has trouble finding work or finds herself unable to work during, for example, a WGA strike, residuals and series royalties alone can often carry her through lean times.

In many ways, writing a television episode for a television series is an audition for a staff position. If you write several good episodes for a show on a freelance basis, you're surely in line for such a position.

Staff writers generally move on to become story editors. After that, they progress to co-producer, producer, supervising producer and, for the lucky few, executive producer (there may be two or three executive producers on any one show). Staff writers generally are paid WGA minimum. Sometimes they are also guaranteed one or two scripts, which can be credited against the staffer's weekly salary.

Staff writing is a tremendous training ground because it gives writers an opportunity to work closely with and learn from a show's story editors and producers. In addition, it also teaches writers to write quickly under the pressure of shooting and air dates.

Much to the chagrin of agents and writers, producers often require a trial period, typically around 14 weeks, at the end of which they have the option of firing writers. Naturally writers (who often sacrifice fulltime day jobs to come aboard) and agents (who are only human and like the steady stream of income staff writing generates) resist such trial periods. Nevertheless, their use is commonplace in the industry.

Producers also require options on writers' services for subsequent years—generally one additional year and up to three or four—that guarantee they will be able to bring needed writers back onto a show at a fixed salary that has been agreed to in advance.

New writers are often dismayed when they learn they will be contractually bound to optional years. Sometimes, writers even think at the outset that it is *they* who have the option of coming back onto the series—not the producers who get to choose whether to bring them on. Producers require options to hold a creative team in place. The ability to point to a stable creative team can be very persuasive to a network on the fence about picking up an option on a show itself.

However, effective agents work with business affairs executives to make sure staff writing deals do not become unduly burdensome. Concessions agents might ask for include keeping the option years to the minimum necessary, making sure that writers can only be assigned to a particular show, and built-in raises that at least somewhat reflect writers' typical rise in their market worth once they gain experience.

Most importantly, agents can request guaranteed promotions to story editor followed by producer in subsequent years. Staff writers' writing assignments are credited against their salaries. Story editors and producers, in addition to having more prestigious positions, earn higher WGA minimum salaries plus are paid independently over and above their salaries for whatever scripts they write.

Caveat

Be forewarned.

Writers should be prepared to live with whatever deals they make. Most producers will not renegotiate, particularly with someone who is not yet a major player. If you refuse to perform under the terms of your contract, they might seek an injunction against you. They can't force you to work for them, but they can prevent you from working for any other company for the duration of your contract with them.

Tightwads and tenderness

A colleague used to describe those who became agents and business affairs executives as the ones who, growing up, were "the bullies on the back of the bus." It's true, in a way.

But it's also true that they're much more well-educated, respectable and even, on occasion, more thoughtful than you might expect.

My department at Universal included law degrees from Stanford and NYU and MBAs from Harvard and UCLA. We all had, if not a true feel for the industry, at least a healthy awe with respect to it. "Graduates" of my department include Sid Sheinberg, who, until very recently was the number two person at powerhouse MCA/Universal Studios, and Wendy Wasserman, producer of the blockbuster, *Forrest Gump*. With that level of opportunity looming, we had a lot to lose. We all aimed to be tough, but in the end, we also wanted to be fair.

Good luck. And remember: Make a good deal—but don't blow it.

Roadmap to a Career: How to Get There from Here

by Michael Straczynski

Every so often, I delight in writing about a subject I haven't discussed before. This topic, selling a television series, is one of them.

I couldn't write about it before in any detail because I have this rule: *Don't write about it if you haven't done it.* There are already enough writing "tutors" and "consultants" and "experts" (some of whom have also written scriptwriting books—I won't name names, it isn't good form) who've never sold a script in their entire lives, or who wouldn't recognize a good one if it bit them. But now that it seems I've accomplished the feat, it's okay for me to talk about it. I'm legit.

This topic is of particular importance to newbies for two reasons: (1) An inordinate number of new scriptwriters spend a lot of time fruitlessly writing spec scripts for series they invent and think are saleable, thus wasting valuable time and energy, and (2) the information can serve as a benchmark for things a selling writer *can* expect down the road.

First, it's important to separate the actual selling of a new series from the Cerberus-like creature known as the *development deal*. I've been involved in many such deals in the past, and have the scars to prove it. The way it usually works is that the producer, network or studio acquires a property, or already owns a property that it wants to revive, and finds a writer to do the pilot script and series bible. Ninety percent of such deals never go into production—which was exactly the case with most of *my* development deals: *Elfquest* for CBS, a revival of the *V* science fiction series for syndication, and others too numerous to go into here.

A couple of shows I developed actually *did* get on the air, but not in a form conducive to my mentioning them here. (In one case, I took my name off the project, which was the only realistic alternative to Plan A, which involved fire-bombing the producer's office and destroying all copies of the film *and* the negative.)

The development deal is an entirely different situation from creating a series concept from scratch and trying to sell it. The latter process is even longer and more tiring, and the standard period required for a writer to sell his first original series is usually about four to five years.

That's four to five years of pitching, re-pitching, promises, deals almost but-not-quite-done, broken promises, changing studios, changing executives, new promises, tense negotiations with business affairs people and antacid by the bucket.

Here's how it works.

The hierarchy of television

When a network or studio commissions a series, it's investing anywhere from $20 million for a full season of a syndicated series (24 to 26 episodes) to $26 million or

J. Michael Straczynski *is executive producer of* Babylon 5, *currently in its third season. He has been a producer on* Murder, She Wrote, *as well as story editor on* The Twilight Zone, *among others. Nominated for WGA, Ace, Gemini and Bram Stoker Awards, he is also the author of* The Complete Book of Scriptwriting, *published by Writer's Digest Books.*

more for a full network season. Not to put too fine a point on it, but that's an *awful* lot of money. When it comes time to hand out that kind of cash, studios and networks have a preference for dealing with people they know, who have proven themselves in the marketplace, and who have shown that they can manage the many facets of a series.

For the writer, that means a shot at a series will typically come only after a long and tedious journey. You start as a freelancer, selling occasional scripts to television series already in production. Then, in time, you'll be lucky enough to get hired as a staff writer. Work at it a year or so, and you move up to story editor or executive story consultant (essentially the same thing), where you learn more about the nuts and bolts of actually putting a show together.

Eventually, you move up to co-producer. You get additional responsibilities, such as sitting in on casting and music scoring sessions and working closely with the director and the editors. Next thing you know, you're a full-fledged producer, the studio knows you and your work personally, and the rest of the climb to supervising producer and executive producer happens a lot faster.

The most coveted title in television these days is the unofficial designation *show-runner*, a position held by one of a show's executive producers. A show-runner is the person at a show's creative heart, giving the stories direction, molding the look of the show, selecting directors and coordinating with the studio and the network.

Becoming a show-runner—or being perceived as a potential show-runner—is the goal for a lot of writers, just as it's been my aim over the years. Sometimes a network or a studio will test you by giving you development deals for projects they currently have in the works to see how you handle them.

And eventually, they get comfortable enough to say, "Okay, we trust you now . . . so what do you have for us?"

That is the point at which you can finally sell something of your own creation. And it can *still* take four to five years to actually get it on the air.

Trust me.

That's how long it's taken to get *Babylon 5* in front of the cameras.

The history of *Babylon 5*

It was around 1987, and I was working as story editor on a science fiction television series that was chronically over budget, a problem common to SF television. "But does it have to be that way?" I wondered. "Why can't a show be designed with enough forethought that it won't run out of control after two episodes?"

This pondering led to a thought-experiment in true Einsteinian fashion: What show would I enjoy watching, and how would I design that show so it wouldn't be a budget-killer?

The image that sprang immediately to mind was a space station, a stable location where the stories come to the characters instead of the characters chasing them all over the universe. (The *sell-line*—the bottom-line description of the show—would eventually become "Imagine Casablanca in space.") The name I gave to that space station was Babylon 5.

Stealing time to work on the project where I could, I eventually wrote a series bible and two-hour script, and in 1988, while story editing *The Twilight Zone*, I took the project to a producer with whom I'd worked before. We formed a partnership to jointly own and produce the show, on which I would be co-executive producer/show-runner. The series bible spelled out every aspect of the show: the characters, the locations, the possible stories and the budgetary requirements. The script was necessary to help executives understand what we had in mind and to show that it would be feasible financially.

Babylon 5 became a space station, five miles long, in a sector of space designated neutral territory among five different governments—four alien, one human. It was a port of call for travelers from every sector of space, containing casinos, nightclubs, a bordello, customs and recreation areas, living quarters and business rooms. It would be run by the Earth Alliance and overseen by an advisory council made up of one ambassador from each of the alien governments.

In 1988, we began pitching the concept. To further expedite explaining a SF concept to those who might not necessarily have a long and intimate familiarity with the genre, I commissioned artwork to represent the station, the characters and the technology we'd use. The first person to see the material was Evan Thompson, CEO of Chris-Craft Television, who announced his full support of the project and asked us to work with him in getting the show on the air.

Then came disappointment. Several attempts to put together international financing with Chris-Craft at the center fell apart, some deals at the last moment. There was the Japanese/American/Italian deal. Then the Japanese/German/American deal. We'd initially decided to go non-network, non-major studio in order to maximize our creative control of the project, but after enough fooling around, in late 1989 we decided to link up with a major American studio.

First stop was Paramount, which loved the series treatment and pilot screenplay, but declined because they already had a SF series on the air, *Star Trek: The Next Generation*. Next was Warner Bros., where executive Dick Robertson pledged his support. We were told that there was something in the works, something big, which *Babylon 5* would be a part of, but we never quite knew what that something big was supposed to be. Nonetheless, trusting in our associates, we stuck with them.

Finally, in November 1991, Warner Bros. announced the formation of the Warner Bros. Television Consortium, a collection of TV stations whose core was Thompson's Chris-Craft station group. The Consortium debuted in early 1993 with one night of programming per week. As time passed, more nights of programming were to be added. The original projects included a revival of the *Kung Fu* series, a SF/action series called *Time Trax*, the documentary miniseries *The Wild West* . . . and *Babylon 5*.

It took more than five years—from 1987 to (early) 1993—to get *Babylon 5* on the air. Which is, again, typical of any first series. The time span from concept to produced program gets consistently shorter the more of these you do. Along the way, as a writer turning into a producer, you have to learn a lot of things you never felt you'd need to know, strictly in self-defense. But now I have to be conversant with budgets, points, profit participation, merchandising, insurance, completion bonds, legal and business affairs, and a hundred other related areas.

That's probably the biggest problem afflicting writers who climb this ladder. You do so to protect your material, and to create the sort of shows you'd want to write for. That was, and is, my sole rationale behind creating *Babylon 5*. But the only way to accomplish that is to spend a lot of time on business stuff, which takes time away from the writing that you were fighting to do in the first place.

None of this would have been possible without support from people with whom I'd worked before, and without the experience I'd picked up during my long progress from freelancer to story editor to producer on another show (in this case, *Murder, She Wrote*), which demonstrated my potential to make the jump to show-runner.

You have to flag down the train and make it stop before you can get on. Once you're aboard, though, it can take you as far as you want to go.

Even as far as a distant space-station called *Babylon 5*.

Script Agents: Nonfee-charging and Fee-charging

A quick test: What do you need to succeed in Hollywood?
  a) Great scripts.
  b) Insecurity.
  c) Confidence.
  d) A good agent.
  e) All of the above.
If you answered "e," you've got a good start.

A good script takes time. It takes time to write. It takes time to rewrite. It takes time to write the four or five scripts that precede the really great one. The learning curve from one script to the next is tremendous and you'll probably have a drawer full of work before you've got a script with which to approach an agent. Your talent has to show on the page, and the page has to excite people.

Once you have a script that says what you want it to say, that is the best idea you've ever had, expressed in the best way you know, put it aside. And get on with the next "best idea you've ever had." Practice and hone your skills until you are ready to enter the race. The more horses you enter, the better your chances to win, place or show.

You'll need both confidence and insecurity at the same time. Confidence to enter the business at all. There are less than 300 television movies and far fewer big screen movies made each year. For a 22-week season, a half-hour sitcom buys two freelance scripts. Every year, thousands of new graduates of film schools and writing programs enter the market. But talent will out. If you're good, and you persevere, you will find work. Believe in yourself and your talent, because if you don't, no one else will either.

Use your insecurity to spur you and your work on to become better. Accept that, at the beginning, you know little. Then go out and learn. Read all the books you can find on scriptwriting, from format to dramatic structure. Learn the formulas, but don't become formulaic. Observe the rules, but don't be predictable. Absorb what you learn and make it your own.

And finally, you'll need a good agent. In this book we call agents handling screenplays or teleplays script agents, but in true West Coast parlance they are literary agents, since they represent writers as opposed to actors or musicians. Most studios, networks and production companies will return unsolicited manuscripts unopened and unread for legal protection. An agent has the entree to get your script in the office and on the desk of a story analyst or development executive.

The ideal agent understands what a writer writes, is able to explain it to others, and has credibility with individuals who are in a position to make decisions. An agent sends out material, advises what direction a career should take and makes the financial arrangements. And how do you get a good agent? By going back to the beginning—great scripts.

The spec script

There are two sides to an agent's representation of a scriptwriter: finding work on an existing project and selling original scripts. Most writers break in with scripts written on "spec," that is, on speculation without a specific sale in mind. A spec script is a calling card that demonstrates skills and gets your name and abilities before influential people. Movie spec scripts are always original, not for a sequel. Spec scripts for TV are always based on existing TV shows, not for an original concept.

More often than not, a spec script will not be made. An original movie spec can either be optioned or bought outright, with the intention of making a movie, or it can attract rewrite work on a script for an existing project. For TV, on the basis of the spec script a writer can be invited in to pitch five or six ideas to the producers. If an idea is bought, the writer is paid to flesh out the story to an outline. If that is acceptable, the writer can be commissioned to write the script. At that point the inhouse writing staff comes in, and in a lot of cases, rewrites the script. But it's a sale, and the writer receives the residuals every time that episode is shown anywhere in the world. The goal is to sell enough scripts so that you are invited to join the writing staff.

What makes a good spec script? Good writing for a start. Write every single day. Talk to as many people you can find who are different from you. Take an acting class to help you really hear dialogue. Take a directing class to see how movies are put together. Live and experience life.

Learn the correct dramatic structure and internalize those rules. Then throw them away and write intuitively. The three act structure is basic and crucial to any dramatic presentation. Act 1—get your hero up a tree. Act 2—throw rocks at him. Act 3—get him down. Some books will tell you that certain events have to happen by a certain page. What they're describing is not a template, but a rhythm. Good scriptwriting is good storytelling.

Spec scripts for movies

If you're writing for movies, explore the different genres until you find one you feel comfortable writing. Read and study scripts for movies you admire to find out what makes them work. Choose a premise for yourself, not "the market." What is it you care most about? What is it you know the most about? Write it. Know your characters and what they want. Know what the movie is about and build a rising level of tension that sucks the reader in and makes her care about what happens.

For feature films, you'll need two or three spec scripts, and perhaps a few long-form scripts (miniseries, movies of the week or episodics) as well. Your scripts should depict a layered story with well-developed characters who feel real, each interaction presenting another facet of their personalities.

Spec scripts for TV

If you want to write for TV, watch a lot of it. Tape four or five episodes of a show and analyze them. Where do the jokes fall? Where do the beats or plot points come? How is the story laid out? Read scripts of a show to find out what professional writers do that works. (Script City, (800)676-2522, and Book City, (800)4-CINEMA, have thousands of movie and TV scripts for sale.)

Your spec script will demonstrate your knowledge of the format and ability to create believable dialogue. Choose a show you like, that has a voice you can speak. Knowing the show is the most important thing you can do, and you should understand the characters as if they are a part of you. Current hot shows for writers include *NYPD Blue*, *Law and Order*, *Mad About You*, *Frasier* and *Friends*. Shows that are newer may also be good bets. If a show has been on three or more years a lot of story lines have already been done, either on camera or in spec scripts. Your spec should be for today's hits, not yesterday's.

You may have a specific program in mind that you want to write for. Paradoxically, to be considered for that show your agent will submit a spec script for a different show. To protect themselves from lawsuits, producers do not read scripts written for their characters. Pick a show that is similar in tone and theme. A *Home Improvement* for *Dave's World*, for example. The hour-long dramatic shows are more individual in nature. You practically would have had to attend med school to write for *ER*, but *Homicide*, *Law and Order* and *NYPD Blue* have a number of things in common that would make them good specs for one another. Half-hour shows generally have a writing staff and only occasionally buy freelance scripts. Hour-long shows are more likely to pick up scripts written by freelancers.

In writing a spec script, you're not just writing an episode. You're writing an *Emmy-winning* episode. You'll write for the show as it is—and then better than it ever has been. You are not on staff yet, you have plenty of time. Make this the episode the staff writers wish they had written.

But at the same time, certain conventions must be observed. The regular characters always have the most interesting story line. Involve all the characters in the episode. Don't introduce important new characters.

Selling yourself to the salespeople

Scriptwriting is an art and craft. Marketing your work is salesmanship, and it's a very competitive world. Give yourself an edge. Read the trades, attend seminars, stay on top of the news. Make opportunities for yourself.

But at the same time, your writing side has to always be working, producing pages for the selling side to hawk. First you sell yourself to an agent. Then the agent sells herself to you. If you both feel the relationship is mutually beneficial, the agent starts selling you to others.

All agents are open to third party recommendations, referrals from a person whose opinion is trusted. To that end, you can pursue development people, producers' assistants, anyone who will read your script. Mail room employees at the bigger agencies are agents in training. They're looking out for the next great script that will earn them a raise, approval and a promotion to the next rung.

The most common path, however, is through a query letter. In one page you identify yourself, what your script is about and why you're contacting this particular agent. Show that you've done some research and make the agent inclined to read your script. Find a connection to the agent—from "my mother hit your sister's car in the parking lot at the mall," to "we both attended the same college," to recent sales you know through your reading the agent has made. Give a three or four line synopsis of your screenplay, with some specific plot elements, not just a generic premise. You can use comparisons as shorthand. *While You Were Sleeping* could be described as "Sleeping Beauty with a twist" and lets the reader into the story quickly, through something she's familiar with already. Be sure to include your name, return address and telephone number in your letter, as well as a SASE. If the response is positive, the agent probably will want to contact you by phone to let you know of her interest, but will need the SASE to send you a release form that must accompany your script.

Your query may not be read by the agent, but by an assistant instead. That's okay. There are few professional secretaries in Hollywood, and the assistants are looking for the material that will earn them the step up they've been working for.

To be taken seriously, your script must be presented as professionally as possible.

Few agents have the time to develop talent. A less than professional script will be read only once. If it's not ready to be seen, you may have burned that bridge. Putting the cart before the horse, or the agent before the script, will not get you to where you want to go. Your script should sound right and look right before you look for an agent.

The basics of script presentation are simple. Keep your query letter succinct. Never send a script unless it is requested. Always include a SASE with a query or script. Study the correct format for your type of script. Cole and Haag's *Complete Guide to Standard Script Formats* is a good source for the various formats.

Read everything you can about scriptwriting and the industry. As in all business ventures, you must educate yourself about the market to be successful. There are a vast number of books to read. Samuel French ((213)876-0570) is a good source, as is The Write Stuff ((800)989-8833). *Lew Hunter's Screenwriting 434* and Richard Walter's *Screenwriting* are both highly recommended books on the art of scriptwriting. Newsletters such as *Hollywood Scriptwriter* are good sources of information. Trade publications such as *The Hollywood Reporter*, *Premiere*, *Variety* and *The WGA Journal* are invaluable as well. A number of smaller magazines have sprung up in the last few years, including *Screenwrite Now!*, *Creative Screenwriting* and *New York Screenwriter*. See the Resources section for information.

The Writers Guild of America

Many of the script agents listed in the book are signatories to the Writers Guild of America Artists' Manager Basic Agreement. This means they have paid a membership fee and agreed to abide by a standard code of behavior. Enforcement is uneven, however. Although a signatory can, theoretically, be stripped of its signatory status, this rarely happens. Contact the WGA for more information on specific agencies or to check if an agency is a signatory. Agents who are signatories are not permitted to charge a reading fee to WGA members, but are allowed to do so to nonmembers. They are permitted to charge for critiques and other services, but may not refer you to a particular script doctor.

The WGA also offers a registration service which is available to members and nonmembers alike. It's a good idea to register your script before sending it out. Membership in the WGA is earned through the accumulation of professional credits and carries a number of significant benefits. Write the Guild for more information on script registration as well as membership requirements.

Help with your search

This section contains agents who sell feature film scripts, teleplays and theatrical stage plays. Many of the agencies in the Literary Agents section also handle scripts, but agencies that primarily handle scripts are listed here.

To help you with your search for an agent, we've included a number of special indexes in the back of the book. The Subject Index is divided into sections for fee-charging and nonfee-charging literary agents and script agents. The script agent index is divided into various subject areas specific to scripts, such as mystery, romantic comedy and teen. Some agencies indicated that they were open to all categories. These have been grouped in the subject heading "open." This year we again index the agents according to script types, such as TV movie of the week (mow), sitcom and episodic drama in the Script Agents Format Index.

We've included an Agents Index as well. Often you will read about an agent who is an employee of a larger agency and may not be able to locate her business phone or address. We asked agencies to list the agents on staff, then listed the names in alphabetical order along with the name of the agency they work for. Find the name of the person you would like to contact and then check the agency listing. You will find the page number for the agency's listing in the Listings Index.

A Geographic Index lists agents state by state for those who are looking for an agent close to home. A Client Acceptance Policies index ranks agencies according to their openness to new clients.

Many script agents are also interested in book manuscripts; many literary agents will also consider scripts. Agents who primarily sell books but also handle at least 10 to 15 percent scripts appear among the listings in this section, with the contact information, breakdown of work currently handled and a note to check the full listing in the literary agents section. Those literary agents that sell mostly books and less than 10 to 15 percent scripts appear in Additional Script Agents at the end of this section. Complete listings for these agents appear in the Literary Agents section.

Before contacting any agency, check the listing to make sure it is open to new clients. Those designated (V) are currently not interested in expanding their rosters. Some agents will only accept new clients through referrals. Read the listings carefully.

For more information on approaching script agents in particular, see the various articles at the beginning of this section. For information on agents in general and the specifics of the listings, read How to Use Your Guide to Literary Agents and How to Find (and Keep) The Right Agent.

About the listings

The listings in this section differ slightly from those in the literary agent sections. A breakdown of the types of scripts each agency handles is included in the listing. Nonfee-charging and fee-charging agencies are listed together. If an agency is a WGA signatory, we include this information in the listing. As noted above, WGA signatories are not permitted to charge reading fees to members, but may do so to nonmembers. However, most signatories do not charge a reading fee across the board. Many agencies do charge for other services—critiques, consultations, promotion, marketing, etc. Those agencies who charge some type of fee have been indicated with a box (□) symbol by their name. The heading "Recent Sales" is also slightly different. Reflecting the different ways scriptwriters work, we asked for movies optioned or sold and scripting assignments procured for clients. We've found the film industry is very secretive about sales, but you may be able to get a list of clients or other references upon request.

We've ranked the agencies listed in this section according to their openness to submissions. Below is our ranking system:

   I Newer agency actively seeking clients.
  II Agency seeking both new and established writers.
 III Agency prefers to work with established writers, mostly obtains new clients through referrals.
 IV Agency handling only certain types of work or work by writers under certain circumstances.
  V Agency not currently seeking new clients. We have included mention of agencies rated **V** to let you know they are currently not open to new clients. In addition to those ranked **V**, we have included a few well-known agencies' names who have declined the opportunity to receive full listings at this time. *Unless you have a strong recommendation from someone well respected in the field, our advice is to approach only those agents ranked I-IV.*

ABOVE THE LINE AGENCY, (III), 9200 Sunset Blvd., #401, Los Angeles CA 90069. (310)859-6115. Contact: Bruce Bartlett. Owner: Rima Bauer Greer. Estab. 1994. Signatory of WGA. Represents 14 clients. 5% of clients are new/previously unpublished writers. Currently handles: 2½% juvenile books; 5% novels; 90% movie scripts; 2½% TV scripts.
• Prior to starting her own agency, Ms. Greer served as an agent with Writers & Artists Agency.
Handles: Movie scripts. Query. Reports in 2 weeks on queries.
Recent Sales: *Movie scripts sold*: *Sorceror's Apprentice* (indieprod). *Scripting assignments*: *Dial M for Murder* (A. Kopelson); *Oliver* (Disney); *The Computer Wore Tennis Shoes* (Disney); *Academic Decathlon* (Fox); *Wild Swans* (Disney); *Deep Space 9* (Paramount TV).
Terms: Agent receives 10% commission on domestic sales; 10% on foreign sales. Offers written contract, binding for 2 years.
Tips: Obtains new clients through referrals.

‡ACT I, (II), 1523 Washington Ave., Miami Beach FL 33139. (305)674-1113. Fax: (305)672-8705. Contact: Peggi McKinley, Arnold Soloway. Estab. 1993. Signatory of WGA. Represents 15 clients. 35% of clients are new/previously unpublished writers. Currently handles: 5% nonfiction books; 10% novels; 30% movie scripts; 30% TV scripts; 5% stage plays; 10% syndicated material; 10% other.
Handles: Movie scripts (feature film); TV scripts (TV mow, miniseries, sitcom, variety show); theatrical stage play. Considers these script subject areas: action/adventure; detective/police/crime; erotica; mystery/suspense; romance; science fiction. Send outline/proposal, then script if interested. Reports in 2 weeks on queries; 6 weeks on mss.
Terms: Agent receives 10% commission on domestic sales; 10% on foreign sales.
Also Handles: Nonfiction books, novels. Considers these nonfiction areas: biography/autobiography; child guidance/parenting; how-to; true crime/investigative; women's issues/women's studies. Considers these fiction areas: action/adventure; detective/police/crime; erotica; mystery; picture book; romance; science fiction. Send outline/proposal. Reports in 2 weeks on queries; 6 weeks on mss.
Terms: Agent receives 15% commission on domestic sales; 13% on foreign sales. Offers written contract. Sometimes charges for photocopying.
Tips: Obtains new clients through referrals. "If you get turned down once, keep writing if you believe in yourself."

‡AEI/ATCHITY EDITORIAL/ENTERTAINMENT INTERNATIONAL, (I), 9601 Wilshire Blvd., Box 1202, Beverly Hills CA 90210. (213)932-0407. Fax: (213)932-0321. E-mail: aeikja@lainet.com. Contact: Kenneth Atchity. Estab. 1994. Represents 20 clients. 90% of clients are new/previously unpublished writers. Specializes in novel-film tie-ins. Currently handles: 30% nonfiction books; 5% scholarly books; 30% novels; 25% movie scripts; 10% TV scripts. Member agents: Chi Li-Wong, Andrea McKeown, Rosemary McKenna; Sidney Kiwitt (business affairs, NY).
• See the expanded listing for this agency in Literary Agents: Fee-charging.

□AGAPÉ PRODUCTIONS, (III), P.O. Box 147, Flat Rock IN 47234. (812)587-5654. Fax: (812)587-0029. Contact: Sue Green or Donna. Estab. 1990. Signatory of WGA. Member of Indiana Film Commission. Represents 55 clients. 30% of clients are new/previously unpublished writers. Specializes in movie scripts, TV scripts, packaging deals. Currently handles: 2% juvenile books; 4% novels; 70% movie scripts; 10% TV scripts; 2% stage plays; 6% syndicated material; 4% animation; 2% poetry. Member agent: (Mr.) Terry D. Porter.
Handles: Movie scripts (feature film); TV scripts; stage plays. Considers these script subject areas: action/adventure; biography/autobiography; cartoon/comic; family saga; humor/satire; psychic/supernatural; science fiction; self-help/personal improvement; thriller/espionage; true crime/investigative; westerns/frontier. Query. Send outline/proposal. Reports in 2 weeks on queries; 1 month on mss.
Recent Sales: *TV script sold*: *Deep Space 9*, by Jeff Morris (Mike Piller).
Also Handles: Novels, syndicated material, animation/cartoon, poetry books.
Terms: Agent receives 10% commission on domestic sales; 15% on foreign sales. Offers written contract, binding for 1 year.
Fees: Charges reading fee: $25 for MP/TV scripts, $50 for novels. "If we represent, half of fee is returned." Offers criticism service at same rates. "Critiques written by agent and professional readers I employ." Charges $50/quarter for all except photocopying. Will provide binders if necessary.

□ *An open box indicates script agents who charge fees to writers. WGA signatories are not permitted to charge for reading manuscripts, but may charge for critiques or consultations.*

Writers' Conferences: Hollywood Scriptwriters (Universal Studios CA, October); Media Focus (NBC Studios CA, October); WGA Awards (Beverly Hills CA, 1996); Heartland Film Fest (Indianapolis); Austin Film Fest.

Tips: Obtains new clients through solicitation, at conferences. "Mr. Porter has numerous contacts within entertainment industry that allow production companies and film executive (director of development) to review/consider purchasing or optioning material. Publishing company contacts very good."

THE AGENCY, (III), 1800 Avenue of the Stars, Suite 400, Los Angeles CA 90067-4206. (310)551-3000. Fax: (310)551-1424. Contact: Walter Morgan. Estab. 1984. Signatory of WGA. Represents 300 clients. No new/previously unpublished writers. Specializes in TV and motion pictures. Currently handles: 45% movie scripts; 45% TV scripts; 10% syndicated material.

Handles: Movie scripts (feature film, animation); TV scripts (TV mow, miniseries, episodic drama, sitcom, animation). Considers these script subject areas: action/adventure; cartoon/animation; comedy; contemporary issues; detective/police/crime; ethnic; family saga; fantasy; historical; horror; humor; juvenile; mainstream; military/war; mystery/suspense; psychic/supernatural; romantic comedy and drama; science fiction; teen; thriller; westerns/frontier; women's issues.

Query: Reports in 2 weeks.

Terms: Agent receives 10% commission on domestic sales; 10% on foreign sales. Offers written contract, binding for 2 years.

Tips: Obtains new clients through recommendations from others.

AGENCY FOR THE PERFORMING ARTS, (II), 9000 Sunset Blvd., Suite 1200, Los Angeles CA 90069. (310)273-0744. Fax: (310)888-4242. Contact: Lee Dinstman. Estab. 1962. Signatory of WGA. Represents 50 clients. Specializes in film and TV scripts. Member agent: Stuart M. Miller.

Handles: Movie scripts (feature film); TV scripts (mow). Considers all nonfiction and fiction areas. Query must include SASE. Reports in 3 weeks on queries.

Terms: Agent receives 10% commission on domestic sales. Offers written contract.

Tips: Obtains new clients through recommendations from others.

LEE ALLAN AGENCY, (II), P.O. Box 18617, Milwaukee WI 53218-0617. (414)357-7708. Contact: Lee Matthias. Estab. 1983. Signatory of WGA. Represents 15 clients. 50% of clients are new/previously unpublished writers. Specializes in suspense fiction. Currently handles: 90% novels; 5% movie scripts; 5% TV scripts. Member agents: Lee A. Matthias (all types of genre fiction and screenplays); Andrea Knickerbocker (fantasy, science fiction, romance); (Mr.) Chris Hill (fantasy).

Handles: Movie scripts (feature film); TV scripts (TV mow, episodeic drama). Considers these script subject areas: action/adventure; comedy; contemporary issues; detective/police/crime; horror; mystery/suspense; psychic/supernatural; romantic comedy and drama; science fiction; thriller; westerns/frontier.

Also Handles: Novels. Considers these fiction areas: action/adventure; detective/police/crime; fantasy; glitz; historical; horror; mystery/suspense; psychic/supernatural; romance (contemporary, historical); science fiction; thriller/espionage.

• This agency reports that it is closed to queries and submissions for books through 12/96.

Terms: Agent receives 15% commission on domestic sales, except where commissions set by WGA; foreign higher. Offers written contract. Charges for photocopying, international telephone calls and/or excessive long-distance telephone calls."

Tips: Obtains new clients mainly through recommendations and solicitations. If interested in agency representation, "read agency listings carefully and query the most compatible. Always query by letter with SASE or IRC with return-addressed envelope. A very brief, straightforward letter (one-two pages, maximum) introducing yourself, describing or summarizing your material will suffice. Avoid patronizing or 'cute' approaches. We *do not reply* to queries *without* SASE; we *do not* consider unsolicited submissions, and we *will not* hold them for later retrieval. Do not expect an agent to sell a manuscript which you know is not a likely sale if nonagented. Agents are not magicians; they serve best to find better and more of the likeliest publishers or producers. And they really do their work after an offer by way of negotiating contracts, selling subsidiary rights, administrating the account(s), advising the writer with objectivity, and acting as the buffer between writer and editor."

ALL-STAR TALENT AGENCY, (I), 7834 Alabama Ave., Canoga Park CA 91304-4905. (818)346-4313. Contact: Robert Allred. Estab. 1991. Signatory of WGA. Represents 8 clients. 100% of clients are new/previously unpublished writers. Specializes in film, TV. Currently handles: movie scripts, TV scripts, 4 books.

Handles: Movie scripts (feature film); TV scripts (TV mow, episodic drama, sitcom). Considers these script subject areas: action/adventure; comedy; detective/police/crime; fantasy; historical; horror; humor; juvenile; mainstream; mystery/suspense; psychic/supernatural; romantic comedy and drama; science fiction; sports; thriller; westerns/frontier; "any mainstream film or TV ideas." Query. Reports in 3 weeks on queries; 2 months on mss.

Also Handles: Novels. Considers these fiction areas: action/adventure; cartoon/comic; contemporary issues; detective/police/crime; family saga; fantasy; historical; humor/satire; mainstream; mystery/suspense; psychic/supernatural; romance (contemporary); science fiction; sports; thriller/espionage; westerns/frontier.

Terms: Agent receives 10% commission on domestic sales; 10% on foreign sales with foreign agent receiving additional 10%. Offers written contract, binding for 1 year. 100% of business derived from commissions on ms.

Tips: Obtains new clients through recommendations and solicitation. "A professional appearance in script format, dark and large type and simple binding go a long way to create good first impressions in this business, as does a professional business manner."

‡THE ALPERN GROUP, (II), 4400 Coldwater Canyon Ave., Suite 125, Studio City CA 91604. (818)752-1877. Fax: (818)752-1859. Contact: Jeff Alpern. Estab. 1994. Signatory of WGA. Represents 25 clients. 10% of clients are new/previously unpublished writers. Currently handles: 20% movie scripts; 70% TV scripts; 10% stage plays. Member agent: Jeff Alpern.
   ● Prior to opening his agency, Mr. Alpern served as an agent with William Morris.
Handles: Movie scripts (feature film); TV scripts (TV mow, miniseries, episodic drama). Query with SASE. Reports in 1 month.
Terms: Agent receives 10% commission on domestic sales. Offers written contract.

MICHAEL AMATO AGENCY (II), 1650 Broadway, Suite 307, New York NY 10019. (212)247-4456-57. Fax: (212)664-0641. Contact: Michael Amato. Estab. 1970. Member of SAG, AFTRA. Represents 6 clients. 2% of clients are new/previously unpublished writers. Specializes in TV. Currently handles nonfiction books; stage plays.
Handles: Novels, movie scripts (feature film, documentary, animation), TV scripts (TV mow, miniseries, episodic drama, animation). Considers action/adventure stories only. Query. Reports within a month on queries. Does not return scripts.
Tips: Obtains new clients through recommentaions.

□AMERICAN PLAY CO., INC. (II), 19 W. 44th St., Suite 1204, New York NY 10036. (212)921-0545. Fax: (212)869-4032. President: Sheldon Abend. Contact: Joan Hrubi. Estab. 1889. Century Play Co. is subsidiary of American Play Co. Specializes in novels, plays, screenplays and film production.
Handles: Novels; movie scripts (feature film, documentary, TV mow, animation); stage plays. Considers all nonfiction and fiction areas. Send entire ms, "double space each page." Reports as soon as possible on ms.
Terms: Agent receives 15% commission on domestic sales; 20% on foreign sales.
Fees: Call or send letter of inquiry.
Tips: Obtains new clients through referrals, unsolicited submissions by authors. "Writers should write novels first before screenplays. They need to know what's going on behind the camera. Before they write or attempt a play, they need to understand the stage and sets. Novels need strong plots, characters who are fully developed."

MARCIA AMSTERDAM AGENCY, (II), 41 W. 82nd St., New York NY 10024-5613. (212)873-4945. Contact: Marcia Amsterdam. Estab. 1970. Signatory of WGA. Currently handles: 5% nonfiction books; 80% novels; 10% movie scripts; 5% TV scripts.
   ● See the expanded listing for this agency in Literary Agents: Nonfee-charging.

APOLLO ENTERTAINMENT, (II), 1646 W Julian, Unit C, Chicago IL 60622. (312)862-7864. Fax: (312)862-7974. Contact: Bruce Harrington. Estab. 1993. Signatory of WGA. Represents 8 clients. 20% of clients are new/previously unpublished writers. Specializes in feature screenplays of unordinary topics. Currently handles: 10% nonfiction books; 80% movie scripts; 10% TV scripts.
Handles: Movie scripts; TV scripts. Considers these script subject areas: action/adventure; contemporary issues; detective/police/crime; family saga; fantasy; feminist; gay; glitz; historical; horror; humor; lesbian; mainstream; psychic/supernatural; romance; science fiction; teen; thriller/espionage. Query. Replies in 2 weeks on queries; 1 month on mss.
Also Handles: Nonfiction books. Considers these nonfiction areas: ethnic/cultural interests; fantasy; gay/lesbian issues; history.

> *Agents who specialize in a specific subject area such as computer books or in handling the work of certain writers such as gay or lesbian writers are ranked IV.*

Terms: Agent receives 10% commission on domestic sales. Offers written contract, binding for 6 months, 1 year or for sale only, with 30 day cancellation clause.
Tips: Obtains new clients through WGA listing, cold readings, through known sources. "Be patient, know your craft and be true to your talent."

THE ARTISTS AGENCY, (II,IV), 10000 Santa Monica Blvd., Suite 305, Los Angeles, CA 90035. (310)277-7779. Fax: (310)785-9338. Contact: Merrily Kane. Estab. 1974. Signatory of WGA. Represents 80 clients. 20% of clients are new/previously unpublished writers. Obtains new clients through referrals. Currently handles: 50% movie scripts; 50% TV scripts.
Handles: Movie scripts (feature film); TV scripts (TV mow). Considers these script subject areas: action/adventure; comedy; contemporary issues; detective/police/crime; mystery/suspense; romantic comedy and drama; thriller. Query. Reports in 2 weeks on queries.
Terms: Agent receives 10% commission. Offers written contract, binding for 1-2 years, per WGA.
Tips: Obtains new clients through recommendations from others.

BDP & ASSOCIATES TALENT AGENCY, (IV), 10637 Burbank Blvd., North Hollywood CA 91601. (818)506-7615. Fax: (818)506-4983. Vice President, Literary: Samuel W. Gelfman. Estab. 1980. Signatory of WGA, DGA, SAG. "Not seeking clients, but will discuss representation with playwrights and screenwriters referred by mutually known professional acquaintance." Specializes in legitimate theater, theatrical motion pictures and long-form TV (mows and miniseries, not episodic).
Handles: Movie scripts (feature film); long-form TV scripts (TV mow, miniseries); stage plays. Will read samples of writing after referral and conversation.
Also Handles: Represents dramatic subsidiary sales for prose material (nonfiction and fiction) referred by literary agents.
Terms: Agent receives 10-15% commission on domestic sales. Charges for postage, photocopying, any other expenses entailed in sale (legal fees, etc.).
Tips: Obtains new clients through "recommendations from known professionals in the entertainment industry only!"

THE BENNETT AGENCY, (II, III), 150 S. Barrington Ave., Suite #1, Los Angeles CA 90035. (310)471-2251. Fax: (310)471-2254. Contact: Carole Bennett. Estab. 1984. Signatory of WGA, DGA. Represents 15 clients. 2% of clients are new/previously unpublished writers. Specializes in TV sitcom. Currently handles: 5% movie scripts; 95% TV scripts. Member agents: Carole Bennett (owner); Tanna Herr (features).
Handles: Movie scripts (features); TV scripts (sitcom). Considers these script subject areas: comedy; family saga; mainstream; young adult. Query. Reports in 10 days on queries; 10 days on mss.
Recent Sales: *Scripting assignments:* "Most of our clients are on staff on such half-hour sitcoms as *Grace Under Fire*.
Terms: Agent receives 10% commission on domestic sales. Offers written contract.
Tips: Obtains new clients through recommendations from others.

BERMAN, BOALS AND FLYNN, (III), (formerly Lois Berman, Writer's Representatives), 225 Lafayette St., Suite 1207, New York NY 10012. (212)966-0339. Contact: Lois Berman or Judy Boals. Estab. 1972. Member of AAR, Signatory of WGA. Represents about 25 clients. Specializes in dramatic writing for stage, film, TV.
Handles: Movie scripts, TV scripts, stage plays. Query first.
Terms: Agent receives 10% commission.
Tips: Obtains new clients through recommendations from others.

‡□BETHEL AGENCY, (II), 360 W. 53rd St., Suite BA, New York NY 10019. (212)664-0455. Contact: Lewis R. Chambers. Estab. 1967. Represents 25 clients.
Handles: Movie scripts, TV scripts. Considers these nonfiction areas: agriculture/horticulture; animals; anthropology/archaeology; art/architecure/design; biography/autobiography; business; child guidance/parenting; cooking/food/nutrition; crafts/hobbies; current affairs; ethnic/cultural interests; gay/lesbian issues; government/politics/law; health/medicine; history; interior design/decorating; juvenile nonfiction; language/literature/criticism; military/war; money/finance/economics; music/dance/theater/film; nature/environment; photography; psychology; religious/inspirational; science/technology; self-help/personal improvement; sociology; sports; translations; true crime/investigative; women's issues/women's studies. Considers these fiction areas: action/adventure; comedy; confessional; contemporary issues; detective/police/crime; ethnic; family saga; fantasy; feminist; gay; glitz; historical; juvenile; lesbian; literary; mainstream; mystery/suspense; picture book; psychic/supernatural; regional; religious/inspiration; romance (contemporary, gothic, historical, regency); sports; teen; thriller/espionage; westerns/frontier. Query with outline plus 1 sample chapter and SASE. Reports in 1-2 months on queries.

Recent Sales: *The Viper Quarry*, by Dean Feldmeyer (Pocket Books) (nominated for an Edgar); *Pitchfork Hollow*, by Dean Feldmeyer (Pocket Books); *Hamburger Heaven*, by Jeffrey Tennyson (Hyperion).
Terms: Agent receives 15% commission on domestic sales; 20% on foreign sales. Offers written contract, binding for 6 months to 1 year.
Fees: Charges reading fee only to unpublished authors; writer will be contacted on fee amount.
Tips: Obtains new clients through recommendations from others. "Never send original material."

CURTIS BROWN LTD., (II), 10 Astor Place, New York NY 10003-6935. (212)473-5400. Member of AAR; signatory of WGA. Perry Knowlton, chairman & CEO. Peter L. Ginsberg, vice president. Member agents: Laura J. Blake; Ellen Geiger; Emilie Jacobson, President; Virginia Knowlton; Timothy Knowlton, COO (films, screenplays, plays); Marilyn Marlow, executive vice president; Jess Taylor (film, screenplays, plays); Maureen Walters. Queries to Laura J. Blake.
• See the expanded listing for this agency in Literary Agents: Nonfee-charging.

DON BUCHWALD AGENCY, (III), 10 E. 44th St., New York NY 10017. (212)867-1070. Contact: Traci Ching Weinstein. Also: 9229 Sunset Blvd., Suite 70, Los Angeles CA 90069. Estab. 1977. Signatory of WGA. Represents 50 literary clients. Talent and literary agency.
Handles: Movie scripts (feature film, documentary, animation); TV scripts (TV mow, miniseries, episodic drama, sitcom, variety show, animation, soap opera); stage play. Query with SASE only.
Tips: Obtains new clients through other authors, agents.

KELVIN C. BULGER AND ASSOCIATES, (I), 123 W. Madison, Suite 905, Chicago IL 60602. (312)280-2403. Fax: (312)922-4221. Contact: Kelvin C. Bulger. Estab. 1992. Signatory of WGA. Represents 25 clients. 90% of clients are new/previously unpublished writers. Currently handles: 75% movie scripts; 25% TV scripts.
Handles: Movie scripts (feature film, documentary); TV scripts (TV mow); syndicated material. Considers these script subject areas: action/adventure; cartoon/animation; contemporary issues; ethnic; family saga; historical; humor; religious/inspirational. Query. Reports in 2 weeks on queries; 2 months on mss. "If material is to be returned, writer must enclose SASE."
Recent Sales: *The Playing Field*, (documentary) by Darryl Pitts (CBS).
Terms: Agent receives 10% commission on domestic sales; 10% on foreign sales. Offers written contract, binding from 6 months-1 year.
Tips: Obtains new clients through solicitations and recommendations. "Proofread before submitting to agent. Only replies to letter of inquiries if SASE is enclosed."

‡CAMDEN, (II), 822 S. Robertson Blvd., Suite 200, Los Angeles CA 90035. (310)289-2700. Fax: (310)289-2718. Contact: Jeff Ordway. Estab. 1980. Signatory of WGA. Represents 60 clients. 5% of clients are new/previously unpublished writers. Currently handles: 50% movie scripts; 50% TV scripts. Member agents: David Wardlow; Jeff Ordway.
• See Mr. Ordway's article, Building a Career in Hollywood, in this edition of the *Guide*.
Handles: Movie scripts (feature film); TV scripts (TV mow, miniseries, episodic drama, sitcom). Considers all script subject areas, particularly: action/adventure; contemporary issues; detective/police/crime; family saga; fantasy; gay; horror; humor; mainstream; mystery/suspense; romance; science fiction; thriller; western/frontier. Query with SASE. Reports in 1 month on queries.
Also Handles: CD-ROM.
Terms: Agent receives 10% commission on domestic sales; 10% on foreign sales. Offers written contract, binding for 1 year.
Tips: Obtains new clients through recommendations from others and solicitation.

□THE MARSHALL CAMERON AGENCY, (II), Rt. 1 Box 125, Lawtey FL 32058. Phone/fax: (904)964-7013. Contact: Margo Prescott. Estab. 1986. Signatory of WGA. Specializes in feature films and TV scripts and true story presentations for MFTS. Currently handles: 95% movie scripts; 5% TV scripts. Member agents: Margo Prescott; Ashton Prescott.
Handles: Movie scripts (feature film); TV scripts (TV mow). No longer represents books. Considers these script subject areas: action/adventure; comedy; contemporary issues; detective/police/crime; drama (contemporary); juvenile; mainstream; mystery/suspense; romantic comedy and drama; thriller/espionage; westerns/frontier. Query. Reports in 1 week on queries; 1-2 months on mss.

 The double dagger before a listing indicates the listing is new in this edition.

Recent Sales: *Syd & Ollie*, by Margo Prescott (Driskill Entertainment); *The Tribe*, by M. Canales (Driskill Entertainment).
Terms: Agent receives 10% commission on domestic sales; 20% on foreign sales. Offers written contract, binding for 1 year.
Fees: No reading fee for screenplays. Charges $85 to review all true story material for TV or film ("maybe higher for extensive material"). Offers criticism service, overall criticism, some on line criticism. "We recommend changes, usually 3-10 pages depending on length of the material (on request only)." Charges nominal marketing fee which includes postage, phone, fax, express mail service. 98% of business is derived from commissions on sales; 2% is derived from reading fees or criticism services. Payment of criticism fee does not ensure representation.
Tips: "Often professionals in film and TV will recommend us to clients. We also actively solicit material. Always enclose SASE with your query."

CINEMA TALENT INTERNATIONAL, (II), 8033 Sunset Blvd., Suite 808, West Hollywood CA 90046. (213)656-1937. Contact: Marie Heckler. Estab. 1976. Represents approximately 23 clients. 3% of clients are new/previously unpublished writers. Currently handles: 1% nonfiction books; 1% novels; 95% movie scripts; 3% TV scripts. Member agents: George Kriton; George N. Rumanes; Maria Heckler (motion pictures); Nicholas Athans (motion pictures).
Handles: Movie scripts; TV scripts. Query with outline/proposal plus 2 sample chapters. Reports in 4-5 weeks on queries and mss.
Terms: Agent receives 10% on domestic sales; 20% on foreign sales. Offers written contract, binding for 2 years.
Tips: Obtains new clients through recommendations from others.

CIRCLE OF CONFUSION LTD., (II), 666 Fifth Ave., Suite 3035, New York NY 10103. (212)969-0653. Fax: (718)997-0521. Contact: Rajeev K. Agarwal, Lawrence Mattis. Estab. 1990. Signatory of WGA. Represents 70 clients. 70% of clients are new/previously unpublished writers. Specializes in screenplays for film and TV. Currently handles: 15% novels; 5% novellas; 80% movie scripts. Member agents: Rajeev Agarwal, Lawrence Mattis, Annmarie Negretti.
Handles: Movie scripts (feature film). Considers all script subject areas. Send entire ms. Reports in 2 weeks on queries; 2 months on mss.
Recent Sales: *Movie/TV mow scripts*: *When Heroes Go Down*, by Chagot/Peter Ka (Fox); *Bound*, by Wachowski/Wachowski (DDLC); *Dust*, by Somonelli/Frumkes (Brigham Park).
Also Handles: Nonfiction books, novels, novellas, short story collections. Considers these nonfiction areas: anthropology/archaeology; biography/autobiography; business; current affairs; gay/lesbian issues; government/politics/law; health/medicine; history; humor; juvenile nonfiction; military/war; New Age/metaphysics; popular culture; sports; true crime/investigative; women's issues/women's studies. Considers all fiction areas.
Terms: Agent receives 10% commission on domestic sales; 10% on foreign sales. Offers written contract, binding for 1 year.
Tips: Obtains new clients through queries, recommendations and writing contests. "We look for screenplays and other material for film and television."

☐CLIENT FIRST—A/K/A LEO P. HAFFEY AGENCY, (II), P.O. Box 795, White House TN 37188. (615)325-4780. Contact: Robin Swensen. Estab. 1990. Signatory of WGA. Represents 21 clients. 60% of clients are new/previously unpublished writers. Specializes in movie scripts and novels for sale to motion picture industry. Currently handles: 30% novels; 70% movie scripts. Member agent: Leo P. Haffey Jr. (attorney/agent to the motion picture industry).
Handles: Movie scripts. Considers these script subject areas: action/adventure; cartoon; animation; comedy; contemporary issues; detective/police/crime; family saga; historical; mystery/suspense; romance (contemporary, historical); science fiction; sports; thriller/espionage; westerns/frontier. Query. Reports in 1 week on queries; 2 months on mss.
Also Handles: Novels, novellas, short story collections.
Terms: Offers written contract, binding for a negotiable length of time.
Fees: Charges $50 reading fee to non-WGA members.
Tips: Obtains new clients through referrals. "The motion picture business is a numbers game like any other. The more you write the better your chances of success. Please send a SASE along with your query letter."

☐COAST TO COAST TALENT AND LITERARY, (II), 4942 Vineland Ave., Suite 200, North Hollywood CA 91601. (818)762-6278. Fax: (818)762-7049. Estab. 1986. Signatory of WGA. Represents 20 clients. 35% of clients are new/previously unpublished writers. Specializes in "true stories and true crime books that can be packaged into movies/scripts." Currently handles: 25% nonfiction books; 50% movie scripts; 25% TV scripts.

Handles: Movie scripts (feature film, documentary, animation), TV scripts (TV mow, miniseries, episodic drama, sitcom, variety show, animation, soap opera), syndicated material, true stories, humor books. Considers these script subject areas: action/adventure; detective/police/crime; erotica; humor/satire; literary; mystery/suspense; psychic/supernatural; romance; thriller/espionage; true crime. Query. Reports in 2 months on queries; 6 months on mss.
Also Handles: Nonfiction books, novels, humor books.
Terms: Agent receives 10% commission on domestic sales; 15% on foreign sales. Offers written contract, binding for 1 year.
Fees: Does not charge a reading fee. Criticism service: for mss only, not screenplays.
Tips: Obtains new clients through recommendations, query letter. "Be concise in what you're looking for. Don't go on and on in your query letter, get to the point."

COMMUNICATIONS AND ENTERTAINMENT, INC., (III), 5902 Mount Eagle Dr., #903, Alexandria VA 22303-2518. (703)329-3796. Fax: (301)589-2222. Contact: James L. Bearden. Estab. 1989. Represents 10 clients. 50% of clients are new/previously unpublished writers. Specializes in TV, film and print media. Currently handles: 5% juvenile books; 40% movie scripts; 10% novels; 40% TV scripts. Member agents: James Bearden (TV/film); Roslyn Ray (literary).
• Prior to opening his agency, Mr. Bearden worked as a producer/director and an entertainment attorney.
Handles: Novels, movie scripts, TV scripts. Considers these nonfiction areas: history; music/dance/theater/film. Considers these fiction areas: action/adventure; cartoon/comic; contemporary issues; fantasy; historical; science fiction; thriller/espionage. Query with outline/proposal or send entire ms. Reports in 1 months on queries; 3 months on mss.
Terms: Agent receives 10% commission on domestic sales; 5% on foreign sales. Offers written contract, varies with project.
Tips: Obtains new clients through referrals and recommendations. "Be patient."

THE COPPAGE COMPANY, (III), 11501 Chandler Blvd., North Hollywood CA 91601. (818)980-1106. Fax: (818)509-1474. Contact: Judy Coppage. Estab. 1984. Signatory of WGA, member of WGA, DGA, SAG. Represents 25 clients. Specializes in "literary novels; writers who do other jobs, i.e., producing, directing, acting."
Handles: Novels; novellas; movie scripts (feature films); TV scripts (episodic drama, sitcoms); stage plays. Considers all script subject areas.
Terms: Agent receives 10% commission on domestic sales; 10% on foreign sales. Offers written contract, binding for 2 years.
Tips: Obtains new clients through recommendation only.

DOUROUX & CO., (II), 445 S. Beverly Dr., Suite 310, Beverly Hills CA 90212-4401. (310)552-0900. Fax: (310)552-0920. Contact: Michael E. Douroux. Estab. 1985. Signatory of WGA, member of DGA. 20% of clients are new/previously unpublished writers. Currently handles: 50% movie scripts; 50% TV scripts. Member agents: Michael E. Douroux (chairman/CEO); Tara T. Thiesmeyer (assistant).
Handles: Movie scripts (feature film); TV scripts (TV mow, episodic drama, sitcom, animation). Considers these script subject areas: action/adventure; comedy; detective/police/crime; family saga; fantasy; historical; humor/satire; mainstream; mystery/suspense; romantic comedy and drama; science fiction; thriller/espionage; westerns/frontier. Query.
Terms: Agent receives 10% commission. Offers written contract, binding for 2 years. Charges for photocopying only.

‡DRAGON LITERARY, INC., (II), 1822 New York Dr., Salt Lake City UT 84116. Contact: Bruce D. Richardson. Estab. 1991. 80% of clients are new/previously unpublished writers. Currently handles: 60% novels; 20% movie scripts; 20% TV scripts.
• See the expanded listing for this agency in Literary Agents: Nonfee-charging.

DRAMATIC PUBLISHING, (IV), 311 Washington, Woodstock IL 60098. (815)338-7170. Fax: (815)338-8981. Contact: Sara Clark. Estab. 1885. Specializes in a full range of stage plays, musicals and instructional books about theater. Currently handles: 2% textbooks; 98% stage plays.
Handles: Stage plays. Reports in 2 weeks on queries; 18 weeks on mss.

‡□DURKIN ARTISTS AGENCY, (II), 127 Broadway, Suite 210, Santa Monica CA 90401. (310)458-5377. Fax: (310)458-5337. Contact: Debbie E. Durkin. Estab. 1979. Signatory of WGA. Specializes in theatrical film. Currently handles: 10% nonfiction books; 90% movie scripts.
Handles: Movie scripts (feature film). Considers these script subject areas: action/adventure; comedy; contemporary issues; ethnic; family saga; horror; juvenile; mystery/suspense; romantic comedy; science fiction; thriller; western/frontier.

Also Handles: Nonfiction books. Considers these nonfiction areas: true crime/investigative; women's issues/women's studies. Send synopsis and SASE. Reports in 6 weeks.
Terms: Commission negotiable. Offers written contract.
Fees: Negotiable.
Tips: Obtains new clients through the mail and referrals. "Please *don't* call the agency at *any* time. Mail us *only!*"

☐**DYKEMAN ASSOCIATES INC., (III),** 4115 Rawlins, Dallas TX 65219. (214)528-2991. Fax: (214)528-0241. E-mail: adykeman@indfw.net. Contact: Alice Dykeman. Estab. 1988. 20% of clients are new/previously unpublished writers. Currently handles: 20% novels; 20% business and other; 60% TV scripts.
Handles: Movie scripts; TV scripts. Considers these script subject areas: action/adventure; biography/autobiography; business; contemporary issues; detective/police/crime; fantasy; money/finance/economics; mystery/suspense; religious/inspirational; thriller/espionage. Query with outline/proposal or outline and 3 sample chapters. Reports in 1 week on queries; 1 month on mss.
Also Handles: Novels, short story collections.
Terms: Agent receives 15% commission on domestic sales; 15% on foreign sales. Offers written contract.
Fees: Charges $250 reading fee. Criticism service included in reading fee. Critiques are written by readers and reviewed by Alice Dykeman. Charges for postage, copies, long distance phone calls. Payment of criticism fee does not ensure representation.
Tips: Obtains new clients through listings in directories and word of mouth.

☐**EARTH TRACKS AGENCY, (I, II),** 4809 Avenue N, Suite 286, Brooklyn NY 11234. Contact: David Krinsky. Estab. 1990. Signatory of WGA. Represents 5 clients. 50% of clients are new/previously unpublished writers. Specializes in "movie and TV script sales of original material." Currently handles: 20% novels; 60% movie scripts; 20% TV scripts. Member agents: David Krinsky (movie scripts); Howard Smith.
Handles: Movie scripts (feature film); TV scripts (TV mow, sitcom). Considers these script subject areas: action/adventure; comedy; contemporary issues; detective/police/crime; erotica; ethnic; experimental; horror; humor; mainstream; teen; thriller/espionage. Query with SASE. Reports in 4-6 weeks on queries; 6-8 weeks on mss (only if requested).
Terms: Agent receives 10-12% commission on domestic sales; 10-12% on foreign sales. Offers written contract, binding for 6-24 months.
Fees: "No fee for TV or movie scriptwriters. For books I charge $100 a book, nonrefundable. Criticism service: $25 per manuscript submitted. I personally write the critiques. An author *must* provide *proper* postage (SASE) if author wants material returned. If no SASE enclosed, material is not returned." 90% of business is derived from commissions on ms sales; 10% is derived from reading fees or criticism service. Payment of criticism fee does not ensure representation.
Tips: Obtains new clients through recommendations and letters of solicitations by mail. "Send a one-page letter describing the material the writer wishes the agency to represent. Do *not* send anything other than query letter with SASE. Unsolicited scripts will not be returned. Do not 'hype' the material—just explain exactly what you are selling. If it is a play, do not state 'screenplay.' If it is a movie script, do not state 'manuscript,' as that implies a book. Be specific, give description (summary) of material."

EPSTEIN-WYCKOFF AND ASSOCIATES, (II), 280 S. Beverly Dr., #400, Beverly Hills CA 90212-3904. (310)278-7222. Fax: (310)278-4640. Contact: Karin Wakefield. Estab. 1993. Signatory of WGA. Represents 20 clients. Specializes in features, TV, books and stage plays. Currently handles: 1% nonfiction books; 1% novels; 80% movie scripts; 25% TV scripts; 2% stage plays.
Handles: Movie scripts (feature film); TV scripts (TV mow, miniseries, episodic drama, sitcom, animation, soap opera); stage plays. Considers these script subject areas: action/adventure; comedy; contemporary issues; detective/police/crime; erotica; family saga; feminist; gay; historical; juvenile; lesbian; mainstream; mystery/suspense; romantic comedy and drama; teen; thriller. Query with SASE. Reports in 1 week on queries; 1 month on mss, if solicited.
Terms: Agent receives 15% commission on domestic sales of books, 10% on scripts; 20% on foreign sales. Offers written contract, binding for 1 year. Charges for photocopying.
Writers' Conferences: ABA.
Tips: Obtains new clients through recommendations, queries.

To find an agent near you, check the Geographic Index.

☐**F.L.A.I.R. or FIRST LITERARY ARTISTS INTERNATIONAL REPRESENTATIVES (II, IV)**, P.O. Box 666, Coram NY 11727-0666. Contact: Jacqulin Chambers. Estab. 1991. Represents 15 clients. Specializes in sitcoms, screenplays, mows. Member agents: Ruth Schulman (TV mow, screenplays), Jacqulin Chambers (new clientele, screenplays).

Handles: Movie scripts (feature film); TV scripts (TV mow, sitcom). Considers these script subject areas: action/adventure; animals; archaeology; child guidance/parenting; comedy; contemporary issues; detective/police/crime; erotica; family saga; fantasy; film; health/medicine; inspirational; juvenile; mainstream; money/finance/economics; mystery/suspense; nature/environment; psychology; psychic/supernatural; romantic comedy and drama; teen; true crime/investigative; women's issues. Query with synopsis. Reports in 2 weeks on queries; 6 months on mss.

Recent Sales: *Movie/TV mow optioned*: *My Dead Neighbor*, by Danny Brockner (Lock-n-Load Productions); *Movie/TV mow in development*: *Witness to Murder*, by Bill Johnston (Stuart Benjamin Productions).

Terms: Agent receives 10% commission on domestic sales; 10% on foreign sales. Offers written contract, binding for 1 year.

Fees: Criticism service: screenplays $150; sitcoms $100. "I give a complete listing of what can be improved within their script, as well as suggested changes. I have compiled an at-home workshop for screen and sitcom writers: screenwriters $25; sitcom writers $15." Charges marketing fee, office expenses, postage, photocopying and phone calls. 70% of business is derived from commissions on ms sales; 30% from reading fees or criticism service. Payment of criticism fee does not ensure representation.

Tips: "Become a member of the Writer's Digest Book Club and you will learn a lot. Learning the format for screenplays and sitcoms is essential. Register all your work with either the copyright office or the WGA. You must send a query letter and synopsis of your script with a SASE. Please do not call."

FLORENCE FEILER LITERARY AGENCY, (III), 1524 Sunset Plaza Dr., Los Angeles CA 90069. (213)652-6920. Fax: (213)652-0945. Associate: Joyce Boorn. Estab. 1976. Member of PEN American Center, Women in Film, California Writers Club, MWA. Represents 40 clients. None are unpublished writers. "Quality is the criterion." Specializes in fiction, nonfiction, screenplays, TV. No short stories.

Handles: Movie scripts (feature film); TV scripts (TV mow, episodic drama); stage plays. Considers these script subject areas: detective/police/crime; family saga; gay; historical; juvenile; lesbian; mystery/suspense; romantic comedy and drama; thriller. Query with outline only. Reports in 2 weeks on queries. "We will not accept simultaneous queries to other agents."

Recent Sales: *A Lantern In Her Hand*, by Bess Streeter Aldrich (Kraft-General Foods); *Cheers For Miss Bishop*, by Bess Streeter Aldrich (Scripps Howard); *The Caryatids* and *The Angelic Avengers*, by Isak Dinesen (Kenneth Madsen).

Also Handles: Nonfiction books, novels, juvenile books. Considers these nonfiction areas: art/architecture/design; cooking/food/nutrition; crafts/hobbies; education; gay/lesbian issues; health/medicine; history; how-to; juvenile nonfiction; military/war; photography; psychology; religious/inspirational; self-help/personal improvement; true crime/investigative; women's issues/women's studies. Consider these fiction areas: contemporary issues; detective/police/crime; family saga; gay; historical; juvenile; lesbian; literary; mainstream; mystery/suspense; religious/inspirational; romance (contemporary, gothic, historical, regency); young adult.

Recent Sales: *Time's Fool*, by Patricia Veryan (St. Martin's); *Passion's Bitter Brew*, by Barbara Jones (Harlequin); *Shadows & Whispers*, by Collin McDonald (Penguin).

Terms: Agent receives 10% commission on domestic sales; 10% on dramatic sales; 20% on foreign sales.

☐**FRIEDA FISHBEIN LTD., (II)**, 2556 Hubbard St., Brooklyn NY 11235-6223. (212)247-4398. Contact: Janice Fishbein. Estab. 1928. Represents 32 clients. 50% of clients are new/previously unpublished writers. Currently handles: 10% nonfiction books; 5% young adult; 60% novels; 10% movie scripts; 10% stage plays; 5% TV scripts. Member agents: Heidi Carlson (contemporary and literary); Douglas Michael (play and screenplay scripts).

• See the expanded listing for this agency in Literary Agents: Fee-charging.

B.R. FLEURY AGENCY, (I, II), 1228 E. Colonial Dr., Orlando FL 32803. (407)896-4976. Contact: Blanche or Margaret. Estab. 1994. Signatory of WGA. Currently handles: 50% books; 50% scripts.

Handles: Movie scripts (feature film/documentary); TV scripts (episodic drama). Considers these script subject areas: action/adventure; comedy; detective/police/crime; ethnic; family saga; fantasy; historical; horror; juvenile; mainstream; mystery/suspense; psychic/supernatural; romantic comedy and drama; science fiction; sports; teen; thriller; western/frontier. Query with SASE or call for information. Reports immediately on queries; 3 months on scripts.

Terms: Agent receives 10% commission on domestic sales; 10% on foreign sales.
Also Handles: Nonfiction books, novels. Considers these nonfiction areas: agriculture/horticulture; animals; anthropology/archaeology; art/architecture/design; biography/autobiography; business; child guidance/parenting; computers/electronics; cooking/food/nutrition; crafts/hobbies; current affairs; education; ethnic/cultural interests; government/politics/law; health/medicine; how-to; humor; interior design/decorating; juvenile; language/literature; military/war; money/finance/economics; film; nature/environment; New Age/metaphysics; photography; popular cultural; psychology; science/technology; self-help/personal improvement; sociology; sports; true crime/investigative. Considers these fiction areas: action; detective/police/crime; ethnic; experimental; family saga; fantasy; historical; horror; humor/satire; juvenile; literary; mainstream; mystery/suspense; psychic/supernatural; regional; romance (contemporary, gothic, historical, regency); science fiction; sports; thriller/espionage; westerns/frontier; young adult. Call or make personal contact.
Terms: Agent receives 15% commission on domestic sales. Offers written contract, binding as per contract.
Fees: Charges for business expenses directly related to work represented.
Tips: Obtains new clients through referrals and listings. "Be creative."

☐**FRAN LITERARY AGENCY, (I, II)**, 7235 Split Creek, San Antonio TX 78238-3627. (210)684-1569. Contact: Fran Rathman. Estab. 1993. Signatory of WGA, ASCAP. Represents 25 clients. 55% of clients are new/previously unpublished writers. "Very interested in Star Trek novels/screenplays." Currently handles: 15% nonfiction books; 10% juvenile books; 30% novels; 5% novellas; 5% poetry books; 15% movie scripts; 20% TV scripts.
• See the expanded listing for this agency in Literary Agents: Fee-charging.

ROBERT A. FREEDMAN DRAMATIC AGENCY, INC., (II, III), 1501 Broadway, Suite 2310, New York NY 10036. (212)840-5760. President: Robert A. Freedman. Vice President: Selma Luttinger. Estab. 1928. Member of AAR, signatory of WGA. Prefers to work with established authors; works with a small number of new authors. Specializes in plays, movie scripts and TV scripts.
• Robert Freedman has served as Vice President of the dramatic division of AAR.
Handles: Movie scripts; TV scripts; stage plays. Query. No unsolicited mss. Usually reports in 2 weeks on queries; 3 months on mss.
Terms: Agent receives 10% on dramatic sales; "and, as is customary, 20% on amateur rights." Charges for photocopying.
Recent Sales: "We will speak directly with any prospective client concerning sales that are relevant to his/her specific script."

SAMUEL FRENCH, INC., (II, III), 45 W. 25th St., New York NY 10010-2751. (212)206-8990. Fax: (212)206-1429. Editors: William Talbot and Lawrence Harbison. Estab. 1830. Member of AAR. Represents plays which it publishes for production rights. Member agents: Pam Newton, Jim Merrilat, Henry Wallengren.
Handles: Stage plays (theatrical stage play, variety show). Considers these script subject areas: comedy; contemporary issues; detective/police/crime; ethnic; experimental; fantasy; horror; mystery/suspense; religious/inspirational; thriller. Query or send entire ms. Replies "immediately" on queries; decision in 2-8 months regarding publication. "Enclose SASE."
Terms: Agent usually receives 10% professional production royalties; 20% amateur production royalties.

THE GARDNER AGENCY, (IV), 4952 New Ross Ave., Richmond VA 23228-6335. (804)747-1871. Fax: (804)649-0475. Contact: Charles G. Meyst. Estab. 1981. Signatory of WGA. 85% of clients are new/previously unpublished writers. Currently handles: 50% movie scripts; 50% TV scripts.
Handles: Movie scripts (feature film, documentary); TV scripts (TV mow, miniseries, episodic drama). Considers these script subject areas: action/adventure; comedy; contemporary issues; detective/police/crime; erotica; experimental; fantasy; feminist; glitz; historical; horror; mainstream; mystery/suspense; psychic/supernatural; romantic comedy and drama; science fiction; teen; thriller/espionage; western/frontier. Send outline/proposal. No unsolicited mss. Reports in 2 months on queries.
Terms: Agent receives 10% commission on domestic sales; 10% on foreign sales. Offers written contract. Charges for unusual expenses.
Tips: Obtains new clients through recommendations from others.

☐**THE GARY-PAUL AGENCY, (II)**, 84 Canaan Court, Suite 17, Stratford CT 06497-4609. Phone/fax: (203)336-0257. Contact: Gary Maynard. Estab. 1989. Represents 54 clients. Specializes in client representation and promotion. Most clients are freelance writers. Member agents: Gary Maynard, Paul Carbonaro, Paul Caravatt.
• Prior to opening his agency, Mr. Maynard was a motion picture writer/director.

Handles: Movie scripts; TV scripts; educational and technical publications; films/videos; products. Considers all script subject areas. Query with letter of introduction. Reports in 10 days on requested submissions.
Recent Sales: *Movie/TV MOW in development: A Laying of Hands,* by Michele Verhoosky (The Onyx Group); *Ms. Wollstonecraft,* by Joanne Netland (Private Investor). *Movie/TV MOW optioned/ sold: The Waters Edge,* by Gary Maynard/Mark Trumbull (Waters Edge Prods.); *Scripting assignments:* sceenplay about Lewis Carroll; documentary about Native American hero Black Elk.
Terms: Agent receives 10% commission.
Fees: No charge for client representation. Charges marketing expenses to circulate ms. Also markets products.
Writers' Conferences: NBC Writers' Workshop (Burbank, CA), Script Festival (Los Angeles, CA), Yale University Writers' Workshop, Media Art Center Writers' Workshop (New Haven, CT), Fairfield University "Industry Profile Symposium" (Fairfield, CT).
Tips: "There is no such thing as a dull story, just dull storytelling. Give us a call."

RICHARD GAUTHREAUX—A LITERARY AGENCY, (II), 2742 Jasper St., Kenner LA 70062. (504)466-6741. Contact: Jay Richards. Estab. 1985. Represents 6 clients. 75% of clients are new/ previously unpublished writers. Currently handles: 45% novels; 25% movie scripts; 20% TV scripts; 5% stage plays; 5% short story.
Handles: Movie scripts, novels, TV scripts, stage plays. Considers these nonfiction areas: sports; true crime/investigative. Considers these fiction areas: horror; thriller/espionage. Query. Reports in 2 weeks on queries; 2 months on mss.
Terms: Agent receives 10% commission on domestic sales; 15% on foreign sales. Offers written contract, binding for 6 months.
Tips: Obtains new listings through guild listing, local referrals.

GEDDES AGENCY, (IV), 1201 Greenacre Ave., Los Angeles CA 90046. (213)878-1155. Contact: Literary Department. Estab. 1983 in L.A., 1967 in Chicago. Signatory of WGA, SAG, AFTRA. Represents 10 clients. 100% of clients are new/previously unpublished writers. "We are mainly representing actors—writers are more 'on the side.' " Currently handles: 100% movie scripts. Member agent: Ann Geddes.
Handles: Movie scripts. Query with synopsis. Reports in 2 months on mss only if interested.
Terms: Agent receives 10% commission on domestic sales. Offers written contract, binding for 1 year. Charges for "handling and postage for a script to be returned—otherwise it is recycled."
Tips: Obtains new clients through recommendations from others and through mailed-in synopses. "Send in query—say how many scripts available for representation. Send synopsis of each one. Mention something about yourself."

THE LAYA GELFF AGENCY, (IV), 16133 Ventura Blvd., Suite 700, Encino CA 91436. (818)713-2610. Estab. 1985. Signatory of WGA. Represents many clients. No new/previously unpublished writers. Specializes in TV and film scripts; WGA members only. Currently handles: 50% movie scripts; 50% TV scripts.
Handles: Movie scripts; TV scripts. Query. Reports in 2 weeks on queries; 1 month on mss.
Terms: Agent receives 10% commission on domestic sales; 10% on foreign sales. Offers standard WGA contract.
Tips: Obtains new clients through recommendations from others.

THE GERSH AGENCY, (II, III), 232 N. Canon Dr., Beverly Hills CA 90210. (310)274-6611. Fax: (310)274-4035. Contact: Laurie Zaifert. Estab. 1962. Less than 10% of clients are new/previously unpublished writers. Special interests: "mainstream—convertible to film and television." Member agent: Ron Bernstein.
Handles: Movie scripts (feature film, animation); TV scripts (TV mow, miniseries, sitcom). Considers all script subject areas. Send query letter with SASE, a brief synopsis and brief personal background. Does not accept any unsolicited material.
Recent Sales: Film rights to *Shot in the Heart,* by Mikal Gilmore; *Pigs in Heaven,* by Barbara Kingsolver.
Terms: Agent receives 10% commission on domestic sales. "We strictly deal in *published* manuscripts in terms of potential film or television sales, on a strictly 10% commission—sometimes split with a New York literary agency or various top agencies."

Check the Subject Index to find the agents who are interested in your nonfiction or fiction subject area.

‡**THE SEBASTIAN GIBSON AGENCY, (I)**, 125 Tahquitz Canyon Way, Suite 200, Palm Springs CA 92262. (619)322-2200. Fax: (619)322-3857. Contact: Sebatian Gibson. Estab. 1995. Member of the California Bar Association and Desert Bar Asociation. 100% of clients are new/previously unpublished writers. Specializes in fiction, movie scripts, stage musicals. Currently handles: 50% novels; 25% movie scripts; 25% stage plays.
  • See the expanded listing for this agency in Literary Agents: Nonfee-charging.

GOLD/MARSHAK & ASSOCIATES, (II), 3500 W. Olive Ave., Suite 1400, Burbank CA 91505. (818)972-4300. Fax: (818)955-6411. Contact: Jenette Jenson. Estab. 1993. Signatory of WGA. Represents 43 literary clients. 40% of clients are new/previously unpublished writers. Currently handles: 40% movie scripts; 40% TV scripts; 10% stage plays; 10% syndicated material. Member agents: Ms. Evan Corday (TV series, mows, features); Mr. Jeff Melnick (mows, features).
  • Prior to joining the agency, both Ms. Corday and Mr. Melnick were development executives. Mr. Melnick has also worked at two other agencies.
Handles: Movie scripts (feature film); TV scripts (TV mows, miniseries, episodic drama, sitcom, soap opera); stage plays; syndicated material. Considers these script subject areas: action/adventure; comedy; contemporary issues; detective/police/crime/family saga; ethnic; family saga; feminist; gay; lesbian; mainstream; mystery/suspense; psychic/supernatural; romantic comedy and drama; science fiction; sports; thriller/espionage; women's issues. Query with outline/proposal. Reports in 1 week on queries; 1 month on mss.
Recent Sales: *Movie/TV MOW optioned/sold: Labor of Love*, by M. Night Shyamalan (M. Manheim, Fox); numerous movie/TV mows in development.
Terms: Agent receives 10% commission on domestic sales; 10% on foreign sales.
Tips: Obtains new clients through recommendations from others, solicitation and at conferences and film schools.

MICHELLE GORDON & ASSOCIATES, (III), 260 S. Beverly Dr., Suite 308, Beverly Hills CA 90212. (310)246-9930. Contact: Michelle Gordon. Estab. 1993. Signatory of WGA. Represents 4 clients. None are new/previously unpublished writers. Currently handles: 100% movie scripts.
Handles: Movie scripts. Considers these script subject areas: biography/autobiography; contemporary issues; detective/police/crime; feminist; government/politics/law; psychology; true crime/investigative; women's issues/women's studies. Query. Reports in 2 weeks on queries.
Terms: Agent receives 10% commission on domestic sales; 10% on foreign sales. Offers written contract, binding for 1 year.
Tips: Obtains new clients through recommendations and solicitation.

GRAHAM AGENCY, (II), 311 W. 43rd St., New York NY 10036. (212)489-7730. Owner: Earl Graham. Estab. 1971. Represents 40 clients. 30% of clients are new/unproduced writers. Specializes in playwrights and screenwriters only. "We're interested in commercial material of quality." Currently handles: 20% movie scripts, 80% stage plays.
Handles: Stage plays, movie scripts. No one-acts, no material for children.   "We consider on the basis of the letters of inquiry." Writers *must* query before sending any material for consideration. Reports 3 months on queries; 6 weeks on mss.
Terms: Agent receives 10% commission. No written contract.
Tips: Obtains new clients through queries and referrals. "Contact appropriate agents, not all of them. Write a concise, intelligent letter giving the gist of what you are offering."

‡**ARTHUR B. GREENE, (III)**, 101 Park Ave., New York NY 10178. (212)661-8200. Fax: (212)370-7884. Contact: Arthur Greene. Estab. 1980. Represents 20 clients. 10% of clients are new/previously unpublished writers. Specializes in movies, TV and fiction. Currently handles: 25% novels; 10% novellas; 10% short story collections; 25% movie scripts; 10% TV scripts; 10% stage plays; 10% other.
Handles: Movie scripts (feature film); TV scripts (TV mow); stage play. Considers these script subject areas: action/adventure; detective/police/crime; horror; mystery/suspense. Query. Reports in 2 weeks on queries. No written contract, 30 day cancellation clause. 100% of business is derived from commissions on sales.
Also Handles: Novels. Considers these nonfiction areas: animals; music/dance/theater/film; sports. Considers these fiction areas: action/adventure; detective/police/crime; horror; mystery/suspense; sports; thriller/espionage. Query. Reports in 2 weeks on queries. No written contract, 30 day cancellation clause.
Terms: Agent receives 10% commission on domestic sales; 20% on foreign sales.
Tips: Obtains new clients through recommendations from others.

THE SUSAN GURMAN AGENCY, (IV), 865 West End Ave., #15A, New York NY 10025-8403. (212)864-5243. Fax: (212)864-5055. Estab. 1993. Signatory of WGA. Represents 5 clients. 50% of

clients are new/previously unpublished writers. Specializes in referred screenwriters and playwrights. Currently handles: 20% movie scripts; 80% stage plays.
Handles: Movie scripts; stage plays. Referral only. Reports in 2 weeks on queries; 2 months on mss.
Terms: Agent receives 10% commission on domestic sales; 10% on foreign sales.
Tips: Obtains new clients *through referral only.* No letters of inquiry.

REECE HALSEY AGENCY, (II, III), 8733 Sunset Blvd., Suite 101, Los Angeles CA 90069. (310)652-2409. Fax: (310)652-7595. Contact: Dorris Halsey. Also: Reece Halsey North, 98 Main St., #704, Tiburon CA 94920. (415)789-9191. Fax: (415)789-9177. Contact: Kimberly Cameron. Address most new queries to Kimberly Cameron. Estab. 1957. Signatory of WGA. Represents 30 clients. 20% of clients are new/previously unpublished writers. Specializes in mostly books and excellent writing. Currently handles: 10% nonfiction books; 60% novels; 30% movie scripts. Member agents: Dorris Halsey, Kimberley Cameron.
  ● See the expanded listing for this agency in Literary Agents: Nonfee-charging.

THE HAMPTON AGENCY, (II, IV), P.O. Box 1298, Bridgehampton NY 11932. (516)537-2828. Fax: (516)537-7272. E-mail: hampton@i-2000.com. Contact Ralph Schiano or Leslie Jennemann. Estab. 1992. Represents 53 clients. 50% of clients are new/previously unpublished writers. Specializes in science fiction, horror, fantasy. Currently handles: 5% nonfiction books; 10% juvenile books; 60% novels; 20% movie scripts; 5% short story collections.
  ● See the expanded listing for this agency in Literary Agents: Nonfee-charging.

HEACOCK LITERARY AGENCY, INC., (II), 1523 Sixth St., Suite #14, Santa Monica CA 90401-2514. (310)393-6227. Fax: (310)451-8524. E-mail: gracebooks@aol.com. Contact: Rosalie Heacock. Estab. 1978. Member of AAR, ATA, SCBWI; signatory of WGA. Represents 60 clients. 30% of clients are new/previously unpublished writers. Currently handles: 85% nonfiction books; 5% juvenile books; 5% novels; 5% movie scripts. Member agents: Rosalie Heacock (psychology, philosophy, women's studies, alternative health, new technology, futurism, new idea books, art and artists); Bill Miller-Jones (general trade fiction and nonfiction).
  ● See the expanded listing for this agency in Literary Agents: Nonfee-charging.

☐ALICE HILTON LITERARY AGENCY, (II), 13131 Welby Way, North Hollywood CA 91606. (818)982-2546. Fax: (818)765-8207. Contact: Alice Hilton. Editor: David Kinzie. Estab. 1986. Eager to work with new/unpublished writers. "Interested in any quality material, although agent's personal taste runs in the genre of 'Cheers.' 'L.A. Law,' 'American Playhouse,' 'Masterpiece Theatre' and Woody Allen vintage humor."
  ● See the expanded listing for this agency in the Literary Agents: Fee-charging.

CAROLYN HODGES AGENCY, (III), 1980 Glenwood Dr., Boulder CO 80304-2329. (303)443-4636. Fax: (303)443-4636. Contact: Carolyn Hodges. Estab. 1989. Signatory of WGA. Represents 18 clients. 90% of clients are new/previously unpublished writers. Represents only screenwriters for film and TV mows. Currently handles: 80% movie scripts; 20% TV scripts.
  ● See Carolyn Hodges's article, What an Agent Really Looks For, in the 1995 edition of the *Guide.* Prior to opening her agency, Ms. Hodges was a freelance writer and founded the Writers In The Rockies Screenwriting Conference that has been held for the past 12 years.
Handles: Movie scripts (feature film); TV scripts (TV mow). Considers these script subject areas: action/adventure; contemporary issues; detective/police/crime; ethnic; experimental; fantasy; feminist; gay; glitz; historical; lesbian; literary; mainstream; mystery/suspense; psychic/supernatural; regional; romance (contemporary); science fiction; thriller/espionage. Query with 1 page synopsis. Reports in 1 week on queries; 10 weeks on mss.
Terms: Agent receives 10% on domestic sales; foreign sales "depend on each individual negotiation." Offers written contract, standard WGA. No charge for criticism. "I always try to offer concrete feedback, even when rejecting a piece of material. I do request that writers supply me with copies of their screenplays. I pay all other expenses."
Recent Sales: *Movie optioned*: *Letters From Home,* by Zambrano (Thompson/Albert); *Cybercide,* by Jan Jones (Fortis Entertainment).
Writers' Conferences: Director and founder of Writers In The Rockies Film Screenwriting Conference (Boulder CO, August).
Tips: Obtains new clients via WGA Agency list or by referral. "Become proficient at your craft. Attend all workshops accessible to you. READ all the books applicable to your area of interest. READ as many 'produced' screenplays as possible. Live a full, vital and rewarding life so your writing will have something to say. Get involved in a writer's support group. Network with other writers. Receive 'critiques' from your peers and consider merit of suggestions. Don't be afraid to re-examine your perspective."

BARBARA HOGENSON AGENCY, (III), 19 W. 44th St., Suite 1000, New York NY 10036. (212)730-7306. Fax: (212)730-8970. Estab. 1995. Member of AAR, signatory of WGA. Represents 60 clients. 5% of clients are new/previously unpublished writers. Currently handles: 35% nonfiction books; 15% novels; 15% movie scripts; 35% stage plays.

● Ms. Hogenson was with the prestigious Lucy Kroll Agency for ten years before starting her own agency.

Handles: Nonfiction books, novels, movie scripts, TV scripts. Query with outline and SASE. No unsolicited mss. Reports in 1 month.

Recent Sales: *Frieda's Fiestas*, by Marie-Pierre Colle and Guadalupe Rivera; *Mittel Europa*, by Slesin & Cliff, et al. (Clarkson N. Potter).

Terms: Agent receives 10% on film and TV sales; 15% commission on domestic sales of books; 20% on foreign sales of books. Offers written contract, binding for 2 years with 90 day cancellation clause. 100% of business derived from commissions on sales.

Tips: Obtains new clients strictly by referral.

□**THE EDDY HOWARD AGENCY (III)**, % 37 Bernard St., Eatontown NJ 07724-1906. (908)542-3525. Contact: Eddy Howard Pevovar, N.D., Ph.D. Estab. 1986. Signatory of WGA. Represents 110 clients. 16% of clients are new/previously unpublished writers. Specializes in film, sitcom and literary. Currently handles: 5% nonfiction books; 5% scholarly books; 2% textbooks; 5% juvenile books; 5% novels; 2% novellas; 25% movie scripts; 30% TV scripts; 10% stage plays; 5% short story collections; 1% syndicated material; 5% other. Member agents: Eddy Howard Pevovar, N.D., Ph.D. (agency executive); Francine Gail (director of comedy development).

Handles: Movie scripts (feature film, documentary, animation); TV scripts (TV mows, miniseries, episodic drama, sitcom, variety show, animation, soap opera, educational); stage plays. Considers these script subject areas: action/adventure; cartoon/animation; comedy; erotica; experimental; family saga; fantasy; historical; humor; juvenile; mainstream; mystery/suspense; psychic/supernatural; religious/inspirational; romantic comedy; science fiction; sports; teen; thriller; western/frontier.

Also Handles: Nonfiction books, scholarly books, textbooks, juvenile books, novels, novellas. Considers these areas: agriculture/horticulture; animals; anthropology/archaeology; cooking/food/nutrition; crafts/hobbies; education; health/medicine; humor; juvenile nonfiction; music/dance/theater/film; nature/environment; New Age/metaphysics; photography; psychology; science/technology; self-help/personal improvement; sports; translations; women's issues/women's studies. Considers these fiction areas: cartoon/comic; erotica; experimental; fantasy; humor/satire; juvenile; literary; mainstream; picture book; psychic/supernatural; regional; young adult. Query with outline and proposal—include phone number. Reports in 5 days on queries; 2 months on mss.

Terms: Agent receives 10% commission on domestic sales; 15% on foreign sales. Offers written contract.

Fees: No fees. Offers criticism service: corrective—style, grammar, punctuation, spelling, format. Technical critical evaluation with fee (saleability, timeliness, accuracy).

Writers' Conferences: Instructor—Writers Workshops at Brookdale College; Community Education Division.

Tips: Obtains new clients through recommendations from others. "I was rejected 12 times before I ever had my first book published and I was rejected 34 times before my first magazine article was published. Stick to what you believe in . . . Don't give up! Never give up! Take constructive criticism for whatever its worth and keep yourself focused. Each rejection a beginner receives is one step closer to the grand finale—acceptance. It's sometimes good to get your manuscript peer reviewed. This is one way to obtain objective analysis of your work, and see what others think about it. Remember, if it weren't for new writers . . . there'd be *no* writers."

HUDSON AGENCY, (I, IV), 3 Travis Lane, Montrose NY 10548. (914)737-1475. Fax: (914)737-1475. Contact: Susan or Pat Giordano. Estab. 1994. Signatory of WGA. Represents 12 clients. 80% of clients are new/previously unpublished writers. Specializes in feature film and TV only. Currently handles: 50% movie scripts; 50% TV scripts. Member agents: Sue Giordano, Pat Giordano.

Handles: Movie scripts (feature film, documentary), TV scripts (TV mow, miniseries); PG or PG-13 only. Considers these script subject areas: action/adventure; comedy; contemporary issues; detective/police/crime; ethnic; family saga; fantasy; historical; juvenile; mainstream; mystery/suspense; romantic comedy and drama; science fiction; sports; teen; thriller/espionage; westerns/frontier. Send outline and sample pages. Reports in 1 week on queries; 3 weeks on mss.

Terms: Agent receives 15% commission on domestic sales; 15% on foreign sales. Offers criticism service. "Free, if we think the script is workable. Critiques done by paid story analysts. Writer receives a critique on story structure, plot development, character development and dialogue, etc."

Tips: Obtains new clients through recommendations from others and listing on WGA agency list. "Yes, we may be small, but we work very hard for our clients. Any script we are representing gets excellent exposure to producers. Our network is over 50 contacts in the business and growing rapidly.

We are GOOD salespeople. Ultimately it all depends on the quality of the writing and the market for the subject matter."

INTERNATIONAL CREATIVE MANAGEMENT, (III), 8942 Wilshire Blvd., Beverly Hills CA 90211. (310)550-4000. Fax: (310)550-4108. East Coast office: 40 W. 57th St., New York NY 10019. (212)556-5600. Signatory of WGA, member of AAR. Member agents: *TV*: Scott Arnovitz; Tricia Davey; Bill Douglass; Paul Haas; Nancy Josephson; Steve Sanford; Jeanne Williams. *Movies*: Diane Cairns; Barbara Dreyfus; Richard Feldman; Ken Kamins; Steve Rabineau; Jeff Robinov; Jim Rosen; David Wirtschafter.

INTERNATIONAL LEONARDS CORP., (II), 3612 N. Washington Blvd., Indianapolis IN 46205-3534. (317)926-7566. Contact: David Leonards. Estab. 1972. Signatory of WGA. Currently handles: 50% movie scripts; 50% TV scripts.
Handles: Movie scripts (feature film, animation); TV scripts (TV mow, sitcom, variety show). Considers these script subject areas: action/adventure; cartoon/animation; comedy; contemporary issues; detective/police/crime; horror; mystery/suspense; romantic comedy; science fiction; sports; thriller. Query. Reports in 1 month on queries; 6 months on mss.
Terms: Agent receives 10% commission on domestic sales; 10% on foreign sales. Offers written contract, "WGA standard," which "varies."
Tips: Obtains new clients through recommendations and queries.

☐**CAROLYN JENKS AGENCY, (II)**, 205 Walden St., Cambridge MA 02140-3507. Phone/fax: (617)876-6927. Contact: Carolyn Jenks. Estab. 1966. 50% of clients are new/previously unpublished writers. Currently handles: 15% nonfiction books; 40% novels; 20% movie scripts; 10% stage plays; 15% TV scripts.
   ● See the expanded listing for this agency in Literary Agents: Fee-charging.

LESLIE KALLEN AGENCY, (III), 15303 Ventura Blvd., Sherman Oaks CA 91401. (818)906-2785. Fax: (818)906-8931. Contact: Andrew McCarthy. Estab. 1988. Signatory of WGA, DGA. Specializes in feature films and mows.
Handles: Movie scripts (feature film); TV scripts (TV mow). Query. "No phone inquiries for representation."
Terms: Agent receives 10% commission on domestic sales.
Tips: "Write a two to three page query that makes an agent excited to read the material."

CHARLENE KAY AGENCY, 901 Beaudry St., Suite 6, St. Jean/Richelieu, Quebec J3A 1C6 Canada. (514)348-5296. Director of Development: Louise Meyers. Estab. 1992. Signatory of WGA; member of BMI. 100% of clients are new/previously unpublished writers. Specializes in teleplays and screenplays. Currently handles: 50% TV scripts; 50% movie scripts.
Handles: Movie scripts (feature film); TV scripts (TV mow). Considers these script subject areas: action/adventure, biography/autobiography; family saga. No thrillers. "Real-life stories and biographical movies or something unique: a story that is out of the ordinary something we don't see too often. A *well-written* and *well-constructed* script." Query with outline/proposal by mail only. Reports in 1 month on queries with SASE (or IRC outside Canada). Reports in 8-10 weeks on mss.
Terms: Agent receives 10% commission on domestic sales; 10% on foreign sales. Offers written contract, binding for 1 year. Returns Canadian scripts if SASE provided; returns scripts from US if 14 IRCs are included with an envelope.
Tips: "My agency is listed on the WGA lists and query letters arrive by the dozens every week. I don't even have to advertise in any magazine. As my present clients understand, success comes with patience. A sale rarely happens overnight, especially when you are dealing with totally unknown writers. Saturated with new talents at the moment. The agency will consider new or professional writers who have been given a firm offer from a producer or production company."

‡**CHARLES KERIN ASSOCIATES, (II, IV)**, 155 E. 55th St., #5D, New York NY 10022. (212)838-7373. Fax: (212)838-0774. Contact: Charles Kerin. Estab. 1984. Signatory of WGA. Represents 29

The publishing field is constantly changing! If you're still using this book and it is 1997 or later, buy the newest edition of Guide to Literary Agents *at your favorite bookstore or order directly from Writer's Digest Books.*

clients. Specializes in theater plays, screenplays, teleplays. Currently handles: 30% movie scripts; 30% TV scripts; 40% stage plays.

Handles: Movie scripts (feature film); TV scripts (TV mow, miniseries, episodic drama, sitcom, variety show, syndicated material); stage plays. Considers all script subject areas. Query. Reports in 1 month on queries; 2 months on scripts.

Terms: Agent receives 10% commission on domestic sales; 10% commission on foreign sales. Offers written contract. 100% of business is derived from commissions on sales.

Tips: Obtains new clients through recommendations from others.

THE JOYCE KETAY AGENCY, (II, III), 1501 Broadway, Suite 1910, New York NY 10036. (212)354-6825. Fax: (212)354-6732. Contact: Joyce Ketay, Carl Mulert. Playwrights and screenwriters only. No novels. Member of AAR. Member agents: Joyce Ketay, Carl Mulert.

Handles: Movie scripts (feature film), TV scripts (TV mow, episodic drama, sitcom). Considers these script subject areas: action/adventure; comedy; contemporary issues; detective/police/crime; ethnic; experimental; family saga; fantasy; feminist; gay; glitz; historical; juvenile; lesbian; mainstream; mystery/suspense; psychic/supernatural; romantic comedy and drama; thriller; westerns/frontier.

Recent Sales: *Angels in America,* by Tony Kushner (Robert Altman and Avenue Pictures).

KICK ENTERTAINMENT, (I), 1934 E. 123rd St., Cleveland OH 44106-1912. Phone/fax: (216)791-2515. Contact: Sam Klein. Estab. 1992. Signatory of WGA. Represents 8 clients. 100% of clients are new/previously unpublished writers. Currently handles: 100% movie scripts. Member agent: Geno Trunzo (director-creative affairs).

Handles: Movie scripts (feature film). Considers these script subject areas: action/adventure; comedy; detective/police/crime; family saga; fantasy; horror; mainstream; military/war; mystery/suspense; psychic/supernatural; romantic comedy and drama; science fiction; thriller/espionage; true crime/investigative; westerns/frontier. Query. Reports in 2 weeks on queries; 6-8 weeks on mss.

Terms: Agent receives 10% commission on domestic sales; 10% on foreign sales. Offers written contract, binding for 1 or 2 years.

Tips: "Always send a query letter first, and enclose a SASE. We now presently represent clients in six states."

☐TYLER KJAR AGENCY, (II), 10643 Riverside Dr., Toluca Lake CA 91602. (818)760-6326. Fax: (818)760-0642. Contact: Tyler Kjar. Estab. 1974. Signatory of WGA. Represents 11 clients. 10% of clients are new/previously unpublished writers. "Seeking youth-oriented screenplays with positive emphasis on personal exchange; no guns or drugs." Currently handles: 50% movie scripts; 50% TV scripts.

Handles: Movie scripts (feature film); TV scripts (TV mow, miniseries, sitcom); stage plays. Considers these script subject areas: action/adventure; family saga; horror; romantic comedy and drama; science fiction; teen; American period pieces (nonwestern); children/8 + with positive roles (no drugs, blood, guns, relating in today's society). Query; do not send outline or script. Reports in 2 weeks on queries; 6 weeks on mss.

Recent Sales: *Movie scripts optioned/sold: Baby on Board,* by Gary Eggers (Lantana Films); *Hollywood Storage,* by Gardner Compton; *Scripting assignment: Empty Nest.*

Fees: Charges reading fee. Criticism service: $100. Critiques done by Tyler Kjar.

Tips: Obtains new clients from recommendations. "Most scripts are poorly written, with incorrect format, too much description, subject matter usually borrowed from films they have seen. Must follow established format."

PAUL KOHNER, INC., (IV), 9300 Wilshire Blvd., Suite 555, Beverly Hills CA 90212-3211. (310)550-1060. Contact: Gary Salt. Estab. 1938. Member of ATA, signatory of WGA. Represents 150 clients. 10% of clients are new/previously unpublished writers. Specializes in film and TV rights sales and representation of film and TV writers.

• See Gary Salt's article, The Ins and Outs of Script Agents, in this edition of the *Guide.*

Handles: Firm/TV rights to published books; movie scripts (feature film, documentary, animation); TV scripts (TV mow, miniseries, episodic drama, sitcom, variety show, animation; soap opera), stage plays. Considers these script subject areas: action/adventure; comedy; detective/police/crime; ethnic; family saga; feminist; historical; mainstream; mystery/suspense; romantic comedy and drama. Query with SASE. Reports in 2 weeks on queries.

Recent Sales: *Damaged Goods,* by Stephen Solomita (Scribner).

Terms: Agent receives 10% commission on domestic sales; 10% on foreign sales. Offers written contract, binding for 1-3 years. "We charge for copying manuscripts or scripts for submission unless a sufficient quantitiy is supplied by the author. All unsolicited material is automatically returned unread."

‡**THE CANDACE LAKE AGENCY, (II, IV)**, 822 S. Robertson Blvd., #200, Los Angeles CA 90035. (310)289-0600. Fax: (310)289-0619. Contact: Elizabeth Thomas. Estab. 1977. Signatory of WGA. 50% of clients are new/previously unpublished writers. Specializes in screenplay and teleplay writers. Currently handles: 20% novels; 40% movie scripts; 40% TV scripts.

Handles: Movie scripts (feature film); TV scripts (TV mow, episodic drama, sitcom). Considers these script subject areas: action/adventure; cartoon/animation; comedy; contemporary issues; detective/police/crime; erotica; ethnic; family saga; fantasy; feminist; gay; glitz; historical; horror; humor; juvenile; lesbian; mainstream; mystery/suspense; psychic/supernatural; religious/inspirational; romantic comedy and drama; science fiction; sports; teen; thriller; western/frontier. Query with SASE. Reports in 1 month on queries; 3 months on scripts.

Also Handles: Novels. Considers all fiction types. Query with SASE. Reports in 1 month on queries; 3 months on mss.

Terms: Agent receives 10% commission on domestic sales; 10% on foreign sales. Offers written contract, binding for 2 years. Charges for photocopying. 100% of business is derived from commissions on sales.

Tips: Obtains new clients through referrals.

□**L. HARRY LEE LITERARY AGENCY, (II)**, Box #203, Rocky Point NY 11778-0203. (516)744-1188. Contact: L. Harry Lee. Estab. 1979. Member of Dramatists Guild. Represents 285 clients. 65% of clients are new/previously unpublished writers. Specializes in movie scripts. "Comedy is our strength, both features and sitcoms, also movie of the week, science fiction, novels and TV. We have developed two sitcoms of our own." Currently handles: 30% novels; 50% movie scripts; 5% stage plays; 15% TV scripts. Member agents: Mary Lee Gaylor (episodic TV, feature films); Charles Rothery (feature films, sitcoms, movie of the week); Katie Polk (features, mini-series, children's TV); Patti Roenbeck (science fiction, fantasy, romance, historical romance); Frank Killeen (action, war stories, American historical, westerns); Hollister Barr (mainstream, feature films, romantic comedies); Edwina Berkman (novels, contemporary, romance, mystery); Sal Senese (motion picture screenplays, mows, original TV episodic series, sitcoms); Judith Faria (all romance, fantasy, mainstream); Charis Biggis (plays, historical novels, westerns, action/suspense/thriller films); Stacy Parker (love stories, socially significant stories/films, time travel science fiction); Jane Breoge (sitcoms, after-school specials, mini-series, episodic TV); Cami Callirgos (mainstream/contemporary/humor, mystery/suspense); Vito Brenna (action/adventure, romantic comedy, feature films); Anastassia Evereaux (feature films, romantic comedies).

Handles: Movie scripts (feature film); TV scripts (TV mow, episodic drama, sitcom); stage plays. Considers these script subject areas: action/adventure; comedy; contemporary issues; detective/police/crime; family saga; fantasy; feel good family stories; foreign intrigue; historical; mainstream; mystery/suspense; psychic/supernatural; reality shows; romantic drama (futuristic, contemporary, historical); science fiction; sports; thriller; westerns/frontier; zany comedies. Query "with a short writing or background résumé of the writer. A SASE is a must. No dot matrix, we don't read them." Reports in "return mail" on queries; 1 month on mss. "We notify the writer when to expect a reply."

Recent Sales: *Movie/TV mow optioned/sold*: The City Island Messenger, by James G. Kingston (Lighthorse); *Who's the Fox? Who's the Hunter?*, by James E. Colaneri (Universal Pictures); *How Dare They . . .* , by James E. Colaneri (Lighthorse Prods.). *Movie/TV MOW in development: Everybody in This Place is Innocent* (sitcom). *Scripting assignments:* The Dr. Reza Story, by Sal Senese.

Also Handles: Novels. Considers these fiction areas: action/adventure; detective/police/crime; erotica; family saga; fantasy; historical; humor/satire; literary; mainstream; mystery/suspense; romance (contemporary, gothic, historical, regency); science fiction; sports; thriller/espionage; westerns/frontier; young adult.

Books: *Forever*, by Patricia Roenbeck (Zebra); *Running Out of Yets*, by Edwina Berkman (Zebra); *I Am Cheyenne*, by Roy Dennis (St. Martin's Press).

Terms: Agent receives 10% on movie/TV scripts and plays; 15% commission on domestic sales; 20% on foreign sales. Offers written contract "by the manuscript which can be broken by mutual consent; the length is as long as the copyright runs."

Fees: Does not charge a reading fee. Criticism service: $215 for screenplays; $165 for movie of the week; $95 for TV sitcom; $215 for a mini-series; $1 per page for one-act plays. "All of the agents and readers write the carefully thought-out critiques, five-page checklist, two to four pages of notes, and a manuscript that is written on, plus tip sheets and notes that may prove helpful. It's a thorough service, for which we have received the highest praise." Charges for postage, handling, photocopying per submission, "not a general fee." 90% of business is derived from commissions on ms sales. 10% is derived from criticism services. Payment of a criticism fee does not ensure representation.

Tips: Obtains new clients through recommendations, "but mostly queries. If interested in agency representation, write a good story with interesting characters and that's hard to do. Learn your form and format. Take courses, workshops. Read *Writer's Digest*; it's your best source of great information."

LEGACIES (I), 501 Woodstock Circle, Perico Bay, Bradenton FL 34209. Phone/fax: (813)792-9159. Executive Director: Mary Ann Amato. Estab. 1993. Signatory of WGA, member of Florida Motion Picture & Television Association, Board of Talent Agents, Dept. of Professional Regulations License No. TA 0000404. 50% of clients are new/previously unpublished writers. Specializes in screenplays. Currently handles: 10% nonfiction books; 80% movie scripts; 10% stage plays.

Handles: Movie scripts (feature film); TV scripts (TV mow, sitcom); stage plays. Considers these script subject areas: contemporary issues; ethnic; family saga; feminist; historical; humor/satire. Query, then send entire ms. Enclose SASE. Reports in 2 weeks on queries; 6 weeks on mss.

Recent Sales: *Movie optioned/sold*: *Journey from the Jacarandas*, by Patricia A. Friedberg (Eva Monley, producer of *A Far Away Place*). *Movie in development*: *Progress of the Sun*, by Patricia A. Friedberg. *TV MOW in development*: *Shillings*, by Gail Griffin & Janet Noel Sadler (Karen Kramer, KNK Productions).

Terms: Agent receives 15% commission on domestic sales; 20% on foreign sales (WGA percentages on member sales). Offers written contract.

Tips: Speaker at the Florida Motion Picture and TV Association conference.

LENHOFF/ROBINSON TALENT AND LITERARY AGENCY, INC., (III), 1728 S. La Cienega Blvd., 2nd Floor, Los Angeles CA 90035. (310)558-4700. Fax: (310)558-4440. Contact: Lloyd Robinson. Estab. 1992. Signatory of WGA, franchised by DGA/SAG. Represents 120 clients. 10% of screenwriting clients are new/previously unpublished writers; all are WGA members. We represent screenwriters, playwrights, novelists and producers, directors. Currently handles: 15% novels; 40% movie scripts; 40% TV scripts; 5% stage plays. Member agents: Charles Lenhoff; Lloyd Robinson; Dan Pasternack.

Handles: Movie scripts (feature film, documentary); TV scripts (TV mow, miniseries, episodic drama, variety show); stage play; CD-ROM. Considers these script subject areas: action/adventure; cartoon/animation; comedy; contemporary issues; detective/police/crime; erotica; ethnic; experimental; family saga; fantasy; mainstream; mystery/suspense; psychic/supernatural; religious/inspirational; romantic comedy and drama; science fiction; sports; teen; thriller; western/frontier. Send outline/proposal, synopsis or log line.

Recent Sales: *Movie scripts optioned/sold*: *Return of Philo T. McGiffen*, by David Poyer; *Silent Partners*, by Burt Prelutsky (Finnegan-Pinchuk); *Scripting assignments*: "Burke's Law," by Stanley Ralph Ross (Spelling & CBS). "We sell or place most of our writers for staff positions in TV and movies. Scripts are sold to individual producing companies and studios."

Terms: Agent receives 10% commission on domestic sales; 10% on foreign sales. Offers written contract, binding for 2 years minimum. Charges for photocopying/messenger when required.

Tips: Obtains new clients only through referral. "We are a talent agency specializing in the copyright business. Fifty percent of our clients generate copyright—screenwriters, playwrights and novelists. Fifty percent of our clients service copyright—producers, directors and cinematographers. We represent only produced, published and/or WGA writers who are eligible for staff TV positions as well as novelists and playwrights whose works may be adapted for film on television."

LINDSTROM LITERARY GROUP, (I), 871 N. Greenbrier St., Arlington VA 22205-1220. (703)522-4730. Fax: (703)527-7624. E-mail: lindlitgrp@aol.com. Contact: Kristin Lindstrom. Estab. 1994. Represents 22 clients. 60% of clients are new/previously unpublished writers. Currently handles: 50% nonfiction books; 30% novels; 10% movie scripts; 10% TV scripts. Member agent: Perry Lindstrom (nonfiction, film/TV scripts).

   • See the expanded listing for this agency in Literary Agents: Nonfee-charging.

LYCEUM CREATIVE PROPERTIES (I, II) P.O. Box 12370, San Antonio TX 78212. (210)732-0200. President: Guy Robin Custer. Estab. 1992. Signatory of WGA. Represents 25 clients. 50% of clients are new/previously unpublished writers. Currently handles: 20% nonfiction books; 5% scholarly books; 40% novels; 25% movie scripts; 5% stage plays; 5% TV scripts. Member agents: Guy Robin Custer (novels, nonfiction, some screenplays); Dave Roy (novels, screenplays, stage plays); Geoff Osborne (nonfiction, screenplays, stage plays).

   • See expanded listing for this agency in Literary Agents: Nonfee-charging.

‡MAJOR CLIENTS AGENCY, (III), 345 N. Maple Dr., #395, Beverly Hills CA 90210. (310)205-5000. Fax: (310)205-5099. Contact: Donna Williams Fontino. Estab. 1985. Signatory of WGA. Represents 200 clients. No clients are new/previously unpublished writers. Specializes in TV writers, creators, directors and film writers/directors. Currently handles: 30% movie scripts; 70% TV scripts.

Handles: Movie scripts (feature films); TV scripts (TV mow, sitcom). Considers these script subject areas: detective/police/crime; erotica; family saga; horror; mainstream; mystery/suspense; sports; thriller/espionage. Send outline/proposal. Reports in 2 weeks on queries; 1 month on scripts.

Terms: Agent receives 10% commission on domestic sales; 10% on foreign sales. Offers written contract.

MANUS & ASSOCIATES LITERARY AGENCY, INC. (II), 417 E. 57th St., Suite 5-D, New York NY 10022. (212)644-8020. Fax: (212)644-3374. Contact: Janet Wilkens Manus. Also: 430 Cowper St., Palo Alto CA 94301. (415)617-4556. Fax: (415)617-4546. Contact: Jillian Manus. Estab. 1985. Member of AAR. Represents 75 clients. 15% of clients are new/previously unpublished writers. Specializes in quality fiction, mysteries, thrillers, true crime, health, pop psychology. Currently handles: 60% nonfiction books; 10% juvenile books; 20% novels; 25% film rights, TV and feature films.
● See the expanded listing for this agency in Literary Agents: Nonfee-charging.

MARBEA AGENCY, (II, IV), 1946 NE 149th St., North Miami FL 33181. (305)949-0615. Fax: (305)949-6104. Contact: Jeffery Hasseler. Estab. 1970. Signatory of WGA. Represents 6 clients. 100% of clients are new/previously unpublished writers. Specializes in screenplays of various genres. Currently handles: 100% movie scripts. Member agents: Phillip Jennings (action/adventure films).
Handles: Movie scripts (feature film). Considers all script subject areas. Query. Reports in 2 weeks.
Terms: Agent receives 10% commission on domestic sales; 10% on foreign sales. Offers written contract, binding for 2 years. Charges for expenses.
Tips: Obtains new clients through WGA list and referrals. "Be polite; write well."

‡MEDIA ARTISTS GROUP, (III), 8383 Wilshire Blvd., Suite 954, Beverly Hills CA 90211. (213)658-7434. Contact: Barbara Alexander. Estab. 1988. Signatory of WGA. Represents 25 clients. 30% of clients are new/previously unpublished writers. Currently handles: 5% novels; 55% movie scripts; 35% TV scripts; 5% stage plays. Member agents: Barbara Alexander; Ken Greenblatt.
Handles: Movie scripts (feature film, documentary, animation); TV scripts (TV mow, miniseries, episodic drama, sitcom, variety show, animation, soap opera, syndicated material); theatrical stage plays. Considers all script subject areas. Query. Reports in 6 weeks.
Recent Sales: *Movie scripts optioned/sold*: *Because You're Mine*, by Williams (Savoy); *TV scripts optioned/sold*: *Cuban Missile Crisis*, by Goldstein (New World); *Staff Writers*, by Engelberg (Disney TV).
Also Handles: Novels. Considers current affairs nonfiction. Considers all fiction areas. Query. Reports in 6 weeks.
Terms: Agent receives 10% commission on domestic sales; 10% on foreign sales. Charges for photocopying. 100% of business is derived from commissions on sales.
Writers' Conferences: Selling to Hollywood (Glendale CA, August).
Tips: Obtains new clients through recommendations from producers.

‡METROPOLITAN TALENT AGENCY, (III), 4526 Wilshire Blvd., Los Angeles CA 90010. (213)857-4500. Fax: (213)857-4599. Contact: Paul Kelmenson. Estab. 1990. Signatory of WGA. 20% of clients are new/previously unpublished writers. Specializes in feature film, TV rights, novels, screenplays, stories for the big screen or TV. Currently handles: 10% nonfiction books; 10% novels; 10% novellas; 50% movie scripts; 10% TV scripts; 10% short story collections.
Handles: Movie scripts (feature film, documentary, animation); TV scripts (TV mow, miniseries, sitcom, animation); theatrical stage plays. Considers these script subject areas: action/adventure; cartoon/animation; comedy; contemporary issues; detective/police/crime; erotica; family saga; fantasy; glitz; horror; juvenile; mainstream; mystery/suspense; psychic/supernatural; religious/inspirational; romantic comedy and drama; science fiction; teen; thriller; western/frontier. Query with outline/proposal. Reports in 3 weeks on queries.
Terms: Agent receives 10% commission on domestic sales; 10% on foreign sales. Offers written contract. 100% of business is derived from commissions on sales.
Also Handles: Nonfiction books, scholarly books, juvenile books, novels, novellas, short story collections. Considers these nonfiction areas: biography/autobiography; current affairs; history; humor; nature/environment; popular culture; true crime/investigative. Considers these fiction areas: action/adventure; cartoon/comic; confessional; contemporary issues; detective/police/crime; family saga; fantasy; glitz; historical; horror; humor/satire; mainstream; mystery/suspense; romance (contemporary, gothic, historical); science fiction; thriller/espionage. Query with outline/proposal.

‡MONTEIRO ROSE AGENCY, (II), 17514 Ventura Blvd., #205, Encino CA 91316. (818)501-1177. Fax: (818)501-1195. Contact: Milissa Brockish. Estab. 1987. Signatory of WGA. Represents 50 clients. Specializes in scripts for animation, TV, film and interactive. Currently handles: 40% movie scripts;

The double dagger before a listing indicates the listing is new in this edition.

20% TV scripts; 40% animation. Member agents: Candace Monteiro (literary); Fredda Rose (literary); Milissa Brockish (literary/interactive).

Handles: Movie scripts (feature film, animation); TV scripts (TV mow, episodic drama, animation). Considers these script subjects: action/adventure; cartoon/animation; comedy; contemporary issues; detective/police/crime; ethnic; family saga; fantasy; historical; humor; juvenile; mainstream; mystery/suspense; psychic/supernatural; romantic comedy and drama; science fiction; teen; thriller; western/frontier. Query with SASE. Reports in 1 week on queries; 6 weeks on mss.

Terms: Agent receives 10% commission on domestic sales. Offers standard WGA 2 year contract, with 120 day cancellation clause. Charges for photocopying. 100% of business is derived from commissions.

Tips: Obtains new clients through recommendations from others in the entertainment business and query letters. "It does no good to call and try to speak to an agent before they have read your material, unless referred by someone we know, and then it's best if the referral calls. The best and only way, if you're a new writer, is to send a query letter with a SASE. If an agent is interested, they will request to read it. Also enclose a SASE with the script if you want it back."

□**MONTGOMERY LITERARY AGENCY, (II),** P.O. Box 8822, Silver Spring MD 20907-8822. (301)230-1807. Contact: M.E. Olsen. Estab. 1984. Signatory of WGA. 25% of clients are new/previously unpublished writers. Equal interest in scripts (films, TV and videos) and books. Currently handles: 12% nonfiction books; 2% poetry; 5% juvenile books; 25% novels; 30% movie scripts; 20% TV scripts; 1% stage plays; 1% short story collections; 2% syndicated material; 2% other (comics, etc.).

Handles: Movie scripts (feature film); TV scripts; stage plays. Considers these script subject areas: action/adventure; comedy; contemporary issues; detective/police/crime; mystery/suspense; romantic comedy; science fiction; western. Send entire script with synopsis. Reports in 1 month on queries; 2 months on mss.

Terms: Agent receives 10% commission on scripts.

Also Handles: Nonfiction books, juvenile books, novels, syndicated material. Considers these nonfiction areas: art/architecture/design; biography; business; child guidance; computers; cooking/food/nutrition; crafts/hobbies; current affairs; education; ethnic/cultural interests; government/politics/law; health; history; how-to; humor; juvenile nonfiction; language/literature/criticism; military/war; money/finance/economics; music/dance/theater/film; nature/environment; New Age; photography; popular culture; psychology; science/technology; self-help/personal improvement; sociology; sports; true crime/investigative. Considers these fiction areas: action/adventure; cartoon/comic; contemporary issues; detective/police/crime; ethnic; historical; horror; humor/satire; juvenile; literary; mainstream; psychic/supernatural; regional; romance (contemporary, historical); science fiction; sports; thriller/espionage; westerns; young adult. Send entire ms with synopsis. Reports in 1 month on queries; 2 months on mss.

Terms: Agent receives 15% commission on books and plays.

Fees: No reading fee. Offers criticism service. Offers written contract.

MONTGOMERY-WEST LITERARY AGENCY, (IV), 7450 Butler Hills Dr., Salt Lake City UT 84121-5008. Contact: Carole Western. Estab. 1989. Signatory of WGA. Represents 30 clients. 80% of clients are new/previously unpublished writers. Specializes in movie and TV scripts. Currently handles: 10% novels; 90% movie scripts. Member agents: Carole Western (movie and TV scripts); Nancy Gummery (novel, consultant and editor).

 • Prior to opening her agency, Ms. Western was a creative writing teacher, holding a Royal Society Arts degree from London University in English Literature, and interned in two talent literary agencies.

Handles: Movie scripts (feature film); TV scripts (TV mow). Considers these script subject areas: action/adventure; comedy; detective/police/crime; family saga; feminist; glitz; juvenile family; mainstream; mystery/suspense; romantic comedy and drama; science fiction; teen; thriller/espionage. Query with outline, 1st act (approximately 26 pages) and SAE. Reports in 2 months on queries; 10 weeks on mss.

Recent Sales: *Movies sold*: *Spaceless* (20th Century Fox), *Long Hello* (Tonque River), *Hardwired* (Warner Bros.), all by Jeff Vintar. *Scripting assignments*: *The Last Hacker* and *Manplus* (Disney).

Also Handles: Novels.

Recent Sales: *Crystal Pyramid*, *Nightmare Cafe*, and *Winds of Karazan*, by Carole Western (Cora Verlag [Germany]).

Terms: Agent receives 10% commission on movie scripts; 15% on foreign sales; 15% on networking sales with other agencies. Charges for telephone, postage and consultations.

Writers' Conferences: Attends 3 workshops a year; WGA west Conference.

Tips: "Send in only the finest product you can and keep synopses and treatments brief and to the point. Have patience and be aware of the enormous competition in the writing field."

DEE MURA ENTERPRISES, INC., (II), 269 West Shore Dr., Massapequa NY 11758-8225. (516)795-1616. Fax: (516)795-8757. E-mail: samurai5@ix.netcom.com. Contact: Dee Mura. Estab. 1987. Signatory of WGA. 50% of clients are new/previously published writers. "We work on everything, but are especially interested in true life stories, true crime and women's stories and issues." Currently handles: 20% nonfiction books; 15% scholarly books; 15% juvenile books; 20% novels; 15% movie scripts; 15% TV scripts.

• See the expanded listing for this agency in Literary Agents: Nonfee-charging.

OTITIS MEDIA, (II), 1926 DuPont Ave. S., Minneapolis MN 55403. (612)377-4918. Fax: (612)377-3096. Contact: Richard Boylan or Hannibal Harris. Signatory of WGA. Currently handles: novels; movie scripts; stage plays; TV scripts. Member agents: B.R. Boylan (novels, nonfiction, screenplays, stage plays); Hannibal Harris (queries, evaluation of proposals, books) Greg Boylan (screenplays, TV scripts); Ingrid DiLeonardo (script and ms evaluation, story development).
Handles: Movie scripts (feature film); TV scripts (TV mow); stage plays. Considers these script subject areas: action/adventure; comedy; historical; mystery/suspense; romantic comedy and drama; thriller. Send proposal.
Also Handles: Nonfiction books, novels. Considers these nonfiction areas: anthropology/archaeology; biography/autobiography; health/medicine; history; humor; military/war; music/dance/theater/film; photography; true crime/investigative. Considers these fiction areas: action/adventure; historical; humor/satire; mainstream; mystery/suspense; thriller/espionage.
Terms: Agent receives 15% on domestic sales; negotiable on foreign sales. Offers written contract. "We prefer that the writer supply whatever additional copies we request."
Tips: "Seminars or classes in creative writing alone are insufficient to attract our attention. You should be constantly writing and rewriting before you submit your first work. Correct format, spelling and grammar are essential. We shall respond quickly to a query letter containing a one page outline, a list of your writing credits, and the opening ten pages of only *one* work at a time . . . plus an SASE. (No SASE means we do not return anything.) Please, in your query letter, try not to be cute, clever, or hardsell. Save us all the time of having to read about what your relatives, friends, teachers, paid 'editors' or gurus think about your story. Nor do we need a pitch about who will want this book or movie, spend money for it and how much it will earn for writer, editor/producer, and agent. You should, in a few short paragraphs, be able to summarize the work to the point where we'll ask for more. You also should indicate your own survey of the market to see what other similar works are available and then demonstrate why yours is better. We are appalled to receive works whose cover page is dated and who indicate that this is a first draft. No producer or editor is likely to read a first draft of anything. Please don't call us the day we receive your manuscript, asking us how much we like it. In fact, please don't call us. We'll contact you if we want more."

DOROTHY PALMER, (III), 235 W. 56 St., New York NY 10019. Phone/fax: (212)765-4280. Estab. 1990. Signatory of WGA. Represents 12 clients. 90% of clients are new/previously unpublished writers. Specializes in screenplays, TV. Currently handles: 70% movie scripts, 30% TV scripts.
Handles: Movie scripts (feature film); TV scripts (TV mow, episodic drama, sitcom, soap opera). Considers these script subject areas: comedy; cooking/food/nutrition; current affairs; detective/police/crime; family saga; health/medicine; mainstream; mystery/suspense; romantic comedy; romantic drama; thriller/espionage; true crime/investigative; women's issues/women's studies. Send entire ms with outline/proposal.
Recent Sales: "Startek," by Manuel Garcia (Paramount).
Terms: Agent receives 10% commission on domestic sales; 10% on foreign sales. Offers written contract, binding for 1 year.
Tips: Obtains new clients through recommendations from others. "Do *not* telephone. When I find a script that interests me, I call the writer. Calls to me are a turn-off because it cuts into my reading time."

PANDA TALENT, (II), 3721 Hoen Ave., Santa Rosa CA 95405. (707)576-0711. Fax: (707)544-2765. Contact: Audrey Grace. Estab. 1977. Signatory of WGA, SAG, AFTRA, Equity. Represents 10 clients. 80% of clients are new/previously unpublished writers. Currently handles: 5% novels; 40% TV scripts; 50% movie scripts; 5% stage plays. Story readers: Steven Grace (science fiction/war/action); Vicki Lima (mysterious/romance); Cleo West (western/true stories).
Handles: Movie scripts (feature film); TV scripts (TV mow, episodic drama, sitcom). Handles these script subject areas: action/adventure; animals; comedy; detective/police/crime; ethnic; family saga; military/war; mystery/suspense; romantic comedy and drama; science fiction; true crime/investigative; westerns/frontier. Query with treatment. Reports in 3 weeks on queries; 2 months on mss. Must include SASE.
Terms: Agent receives 10% commission on domestic sales; 10% on foreign sales.

‡THE PARTOS COMPANY, (II), 6363 Wilshire Blvd., Suite 227, Los Angeles CA 90048. (213)876-5500. Fax: (213)876-7836. Contact: Jim Barquette. Estab. 1991. Signatory of WGA. Represents 20 clients. 50% of clients are new/previously unpublished writers. Specializes in independent features. Currently handles: 90% movie scripts; 10% TV scripts (features only). Member agents: Walter Parkes (below the line and literary); Jim Barquette (literary); Cynthia Guber (actors).
Handles: Movie scripts (feature film); TV scripts (TV mow). Considers these script subject areas: action/adventure; comedy; contemporary issues; detective/police/crime; ethnic; experimental; family saga; fantasy; feminist; gay; horror; humor; juvenile; lesbian; mainstream; mystery/suspense; psychic/supernatural; romantic comedy and drama; science fiction; teen; thriller. Query. Reports in 1 month on queries; 3 months on scripts.
Terms: Agent receives 10% commission on domestic sales; 10% on foreign sales. Offers written contract, binding for 1 year plus WGA Rider W. 100% of business is derived from commissions on sales.

‡PART-TIME PRODUCTIONS, (II, V), 1129 Sixth Ave., #1, Rockford IL 61104. (815)964-0629. Fax: (815)964-3061. Contact: Tom Lee. Estab. 1989. Signatory of WGA. Represents several dozen clients. 95% of clients are new/previously unpublished writers. Currently handles: 10% novels; 80% movie scripts; 8% TV scripts; 2% short story collections.
Handles: Movie scripts, novels. Considers these fiction areas: action/adventure; contemporary issues; detective/police/crime; erotica; fantasy; feminist; gay; historical; horror; lesbian; mainstream; psychic/supernatural; science fiction; thriller/espionage. Query with outline/proposal, 3 sample chapters and a release. Reports in 2 months on queries; 4 months on mss.
Terms: Agent receives 10% commission on domestic sales; 10-15% on foreign sales. Offers written contract, binding for 2 years, with 60 day cancellation clause. Sometimes charges for postage and photocopying.
Writers' Conferences: Northern Illinois Writers Conference.
Tips: Obtains new clients through advertising, listings. "Be respectful and patient with agents, publishers, and producers."

‡PELHAM LITERARY AGENCY, (I), 2290 E. Fremont Ave., Suite C, Littleton CO 80122. (303)347-0623. Contact: Howard Pelham. Estab. 1994. Represents 5 clients. 50% of clients are new/previously unpublished writers. Specializes in genre fiction. Owner has published 14 novels in these categories. Currently handles: 10% nonfiction books; 30% juvenile books; 30% novels; 10% movie scripts; 10% TV scripts; 10% short story collections.
 • See the expanded listing for this agency in Literary Agents: Nonfee-charging.

‡STEPHEN PEVNER, INC., (II), 248 W. 73rd St., 2nd Floor, New York NY 10023. (212)496-0474. Fax: (212)496-0796. E-mail: spevner@aol.com. Contact: Stephen Pevner. Estab. 1991. Member of AAR, signatory of WGA. Represents under 50 clients. 75% of clients are new/previously unpublished writers. Specializes in motion pictures, novels, pop culture, urban fiction, independent filmmakers. Currently handles: 25% nonfiction books; 25% novels; 25% movie scripts; TV scripts; stage plays.
 • Mr. Pevner represents a number of substantial independent writer/directors. See the expanded listing for this agency in Literary Agents: Nonfee-charging.

‡A PICTURE OF YOU, (II), 1176 Elizabeth Dr., Hamilton OH 45013. (513)863-2993. Fax: (513)852-5144. Contact: Lenny Minelli. Estab. 1993. Signatory of WGA. Represents 25 clients. 60% of clients are new/previously unpublished writers. Specializes in screenplays and TV scripts. Currently handles: 70% movie scripts; 20% TV scripts; 10% syndicated material.
Handles: Movie scripts (feature film); TV scripts (miniseries, episodic drama, soap opera, syndicated material). Considers these script subject areas: action/adventure; comedy; detective/police/crime; erotica; family saga; fantasy; gay; horror; mainstream; mystery/suspense; psychic/supernatural; religious/inspirational; romantic drama; thriller; western/frontier. Query with SASE first. Reports in 3 weeks on queries; 1 month on scripts.
Terms: Agent receives 10% commission on domestic sales; 15% on foreign sales. Offers written contract, binding for 1 year, with 90 day cancellation clause. Charges for postage/express mail and some long distance calls. 100% of business is derived from commissions on sales.
Tips: Obtains new clients through recommendations and queries. "Make sure that the script is the best it can be before seeking an agent."

To find an agent near you, check the Geographic Index.

☐**PMA LITERARY AND FILM MANAGEMENT, INC.**, 132 W. 22nd St., 12th Floor, New York NY 10011. (212)929-1222. Fax: (212)206-0238. E-mail: pmalit@aol.com. President: Peter Miller. Member agents: Jennifer Robinson (film and fiction); Yuri Skuins (fiction and nonfiction); Harrison McGuigan (foreign rights). Estab. 1975. Represents 80 clients. 50% of clients are new/unpublished writers. Specializes in commercial fiction and nonfiction, thrillers, true crime and "fiction with *real* motion picture and television potential." Currently handles: 50% fiction; 25% nonfiction; 25% screenplays.

• See the expanded listing for this agency in the Literary Agents: Fee-charging.

‡**PRODUCERS & CREATIVES GROUP, (II)**, 7060 Hollywood Blvd., Suite 1025, Los Angeles CA 90028. (213)465-1600. Fax: (213)461-2967. Contact: George Bailey. Estab. 1992. Represents 54 clients. 10% of clients are new/previously unpublished writers. Specializes in family entertainment. Currently handles: 50% movie scripts; 40% TV scripts; 10% short story collections. Member agents: George Bailey; Jack Pollock; Adam Dearden.

Handles: Movie scripts (feature film); TV scripts (TV mow, miniseries episodic drama, sitcom, soap opera). Considers these script subject areas: action/adventure; comedy; contemporary issues; detective/police/crime; erotica; ethnic; family saga; fantasy; feminist; horror; juvenile; mainstream; mystery/suspense; romantic comedy and drama; psychic/supernatural; science fiction; teen; thriller. Send outline/proposal with SASE. Reports in 2 weeks on queries; 2 months on mss.

Also Handles: Short story collections. Considers these nonfiction areas: biography/autobiography; juvenile nonfiction; popular culture; true crime/investigative. Considers these fiction areas: detective/police/crime; family saga; fantasy; horror; juvenile; mainstream; picture book; romance (contemporary); science fiction; thriller/espionage. Reports in 5 days on queries; 2 months on mss.

Terms: Agent receives 10% commission on domestic sales; 10% on foreign sales. Offers written contract, binding for 1 year, with 30 day cancellation clause. 100% of business is derived from commissions on sales.

Tips: Obtains new clients through recommendation and references.

REDWOOD EMPIRE AGENCY, (II), P.O. Box 1946, Guerneville CA 95446-1146. (707)869-1146. Contact: Jim Sorrells or Rodney Shull. Estab. 1992. Represents 6 clients. 90% of clients are new/previously unpublished writers. Specializes in screenplays, big screen or TV. Currently handles: 100% movie scripts.

Handles: Movie scripts (feature film, TV mow). Considers these script subject areas: comedy; contemporary issues; erotica; family saga; fantasy; feminist; gay; historical; juvenile; lesbian; romance (contemporary). Query with 1 page synopsis. Reports in 1 week on queries; 1 month on mss.

Terms: Agent receives 10% commission on domestic sales; 10% on foreign sales. Offers criticism service: structure, characterization, dialogue, format style. No fee. "Writer must supply copies of script as needed. We ship and handle."

Tips: Obtains new clients through word of mouth, letter in *Hollywood Scriptwriter.* "Most interested in ordinary people confronting real-life situations."

RENAISSANCE—H.N. SWANSON INC., (III), (formerly H.N. Swanson), 8523 Sunset Blvd., Los Angeles CA 90069. (310)289-3636. Contact: Joel Gotter, H.N. Swanson. Estab. 1934. Signatory of WGA. Member of SAG, AFTRA, DGA. Represents over 150 clients. 10% of clients are new/previously unpublished writers. Currently handles: 60% novels; 40% movie and TV scripts. Member agents: Irv Schwartz (TV); Allan Nevins (book publishing); Brian Lipson (motion pictures); Steven Fisher.

• See the expanded listing for this agency in Literary Agents: Nonfee-charging.

STEPHANIE ROGERS AND ASSOCIATES, (III), 3575 Cahuenga Blvd. West, 2nd Floor, Los Angeles CA 90068. (213)851-5155. Owner: Stephanie Rogers. Estab. 1980. Signatory of WGA. Represents 40 clients. 20% of clients are new/unproduced writers. Prefers that the writer has been produced (movies or TV), his/her properties optioned or has references. Prefers to work with published/established authors. Currently handles: 10% novels; 50% movie scripts; 40% TV scripts.

• Prior to opening her agency, Ms. Rogers served as a development executive at Universal TV and Paramount.

Handles: Movie scripts (feature film); TV scripts (TV mow). Considers these script subject areas: action/adventure; dramas (contemporary); romantic comedies; suspense/thrillers. Must be professional in presentation and not over 125 pages. Query. No unsolicited mss. SASE required.

Recent Sales: *TV Mow optioned/sold*: *The Lady*, by Don Henry (Hearst for Lifetime); *Reckoning*, by Bob Hopkins (Movie Vista Productions USA); *Sweetwater Redemption*, by Jeff Elison (Hearst for CBS); *Movie in development*: *Dr. Dazzle*, by Joel Kauffmann and Don Yost (Jones Entertainment); *Pilot/Movie*: *Venice Beach, USA*, by Bob Hopkins (Len Hill Productions); *Scripting assignments*: *October Moon*, by Jeff Elison (Turner Pictures); episodic assignments: *Dr. Quinn, Murder, She Wrote, Hercules, Silk Stalkings*, etc.

Also Handles: Novels (only wishes to see those that have been published and can translate to screen).
Terms: Agent receives 10% commission on domestic sales; 10% on dramatic sales; 20% on foreign sales. Charges for phone, photocopying and messenger expenses.
Tips: "When writing a query letter, you should give a short bio of your background, a thumbnail sketch (no more than a paragraph) of the material you are looking to market and an explanation of how or where (books, classes or workshops) you studied screenwriting." Include SASE for response.

VICTORIA SANDERS LITERARY AGENCY, (II), 241 Avenue of the Americas, New York NY 10014-4822. (212)633-8811. Fax: (212)633-0525. Contact: Victoria Sanders and/or Diane Dickensheid. Estab. 1993. Member of AAR, signatory of WGA. Represents 50 clients. 25% of clients are new/previously unpublished writers. currently handles: 50% nonfiction books; 40% novels; 10% movie scripts.
  • See the expanded listing for this agency in Literary Agents: Nonfee-charging.

JACK SCAGNETTI TALENT & LITERARY AGENCY, (III), 5118 Vineland Ave., #102, North Hollywood CA 91601. (818)762-3871. Contact: Jack Scagnetti. Estab. 1974. Signatory of WGA, member of Academy of Television Arts and Sciences. Represents 40 clients. 50% of clients are new/previously unpublished writers. Specializes in film books with many photographs. Currently handles: 20% nonfiction books; 70% movie scripts; 10% TV scripts. Member agents: Jack Scagnetti (nonfiction and screenplays); Leonard Bloom (men's novels); Beth Brotz (women's novels).
Handles: Movie scripts (feature film); TV scripts (TV mow, episodic drama). Considers these script subject areas: action/adventure; comedy; detective/police/crime; family saga; historical; horror; mainstream; mystery/suspense; romantic comedy and drama; sports; thriller; westerns/frontier. Query with outline/proposal. Reports in 1 month on queries; 2 months on mss.
Also Handles: Nonfiction. Considers these nonfiction areas: biography/autobiography; current affairs; how-to; military/war; music/dance/theater/film; sports; true crime/investigative. Considers these fiction areas: action/adventure; contemporary issues; detective/police/crime; family saga; historical; mainstream; mystery/suspense; picture book; romance (contemporary); sports; thriller/espionage; westerns/frontier.
Recent Sales: *Scripting assignments*: *Star Trek: Voyager* series.
Terms: Agent receives 10% commission on domestic sales; 15% on foreign sales. Offers written contract, binding for 6 months-1 year. Charges for postage and photocopies.
Tips: Obtains new clients through "referrals by others and query letters sent to us. Write a good synopsis, short and to the point and include marketing data for the book."

SUSAN SCHULMAN, A LITERARY AGENCY, (III), 454 W. 44th St., New York NY 10036-5205. (212)713-1633/4/5. Fax: (212)586-8830. President: Susan Schulman. Estab. 1979. Member of AAR, Dramatists Guild, Women's Media Group. 10-15% of clients are new/unpublished writers. Prefers to work with published/established authors; works with a small number of new/unpublished authors. Currently handles: 70% nonfiction books; 20% novels; 10% stage plays. Member agents: Holly Frederick (foreign rights).
  • See the expanded listing for this agency in Literary Agents: Nonfee-charging.

KEN SHERMAN & ASSOCIATES, (III), 9507 Santa Monica Blvd. Beverly Hills CA 90210. (310)273-3840. Fax: (310)271-2875. Contact: Ken Sherman. Estab. 1989. Member of DGA, BAFTA, PEN Int'l, signatory of WGA. Represents 30 clients. 10% of clients are new/previously unpublished writers. Specializes in solid writers for film, TV, books and rights to books for film and TV. Currently handles: nonfiction books; juvenile books, novels, movie scripts, TV scripts.
  • Prior to opening his agency, Mr. Sherman was with the William Morris Agency, The Lantz Office, and Paul Kohner, Inc.
Handles: Nonfiction, novels, movie scripts, TV scripts. Considers all nonfiction and fiction areas. *Contact by referral only please*. Reports in approximately 1 month on mss.
Recent Sales: *Brazil*, by John Updike (film rights to Claucio Carmagos). *Fifth Sacred Thing*, by Starhawk (Bantam); *Questions From Dad*, by Dwight Twilly (Tuttle).
Terms: Agent receives 15% commission on domestic sales. Offers written contract. Charges for office expenses, postage, photocopying, negotiable expenses.
Writers' Conferences: Maui; Squaw Valley; Santa Barbara.
Tips: Obtains new clients through recommendations from others.

□ *An open box indicates script agents who charge fees to writers. WGA signatories are not permitted to charge for reading manuscripts, but may charge for critiques or consultations.*

☐**SILVER SCREEN PLACEMENTS, (II)**, 602 65th St., Downers Grove IL 60516. (708)963-2124. Fax: (708)963-1998. Contact: William Levin. Estab. 1991. Signatory of WGA. Represents 6 clients. 100% of clients are new/previously unpublished writers. Currently handles: 5% juvenile books; 5% novels; 80% movie scripts; 10% TV scripts.
Handles: Movie scripts (feature film); TV scripts. Considers these script subject areas: action/adventure; comedy; contemporary issues; detective/police/crime; family saga; fantasy; historical; juvenile; mainstream; mystery/suspense; science fiction; thriller/espionage; young adult. Brief query with outline/proposal and SASE. Reports in 1 week on queries; 6 weeks on mss.
Also Handles: Juvenile books, novels. Considers these nonfiction areas: education; juvenile nonfiction; language/literature/criticism. Consider these fiction areas: action/adventure; cartoon/comic; contemporary issues; detective/police/crime; family saga; fantasy; historical; humor/satire; juvenile; mainstream; mystery/suspense; science fiction; thriller/espionage; young adult.
Terms: Agent receives 10% commission on domestic sales; 15% on foreign sales. Offers written contract, binding for 2-4 years.
Fees: Criticism service: $195 per script or ms. Critiques written by contract writer, and are 5-7 pages plus partial editing of work.
Tips: Obtains new clients through recommendations from other parties, as well as being listed with WGA and *Guide to Literary Agents*. "Advise against 'cutesy' inquiry letters."

SISTER MANIA PRODUCTIONS, INC., (III, V), 916 Penn St., Brackenridge PA 15014. (412)226-2964. Fax: (412)339-8526. Contact: Literary Department. Estab. 1988. Signatory of WGA. Represents 5 clients. 20% of clients are new/previously unpublished writers. "We also package, develop and produce." Currently handles: 80% movie scripts; 10% TV scripts; 10% syndicated material.
Handles: Movie scripts (feature film); TV scripts; syndicated material. Considers these script subject areas: action/adventure; comedy; detective/police/crime; experimental; family saga; horror; language/literature/criticism; money/finance/economics; romance; thriller/espionage; true crime/investigative. Query. Reports up to 1 month on queries; 1-2 months on mss.
Terms: Offers written contract. Offers criticism service, no fees for clients.
Tips: Usually obtains new clients through "very creative query with project creative and executive appeal in maintaining integrity through quality products."

STANTON & ASSOCIATES LITERARY AGENCY (II), 4413 Clemson Dr., Garland TX 75042. (214)276-5427. Fax: (214)276-5426. Contact: Henry Stanton, Harry Preston. Estab. 1990. Signatory of WGA. Represents 36 clients. 90% of clients are new screenwriters. Specializes in screenplays only. Currently handles: 50% movie scripts; 50% TV scripts.
• Prior to joining the agency, Mr. Preston was with the MGM script department and an author and screenwriter for 40 years.
Handles: Movie scripts (feature film); TV scripts (TV mow). Query. Reports in 1 week on queries; 1 month on screenplays (review).
Recent Sales: *Inner Secrets* (Clarke Entertainment); *For Love and Money* (NBC); *Crossing the Line* (LaMoth Productions); *Splintered Image* (Hearst Entertainment); *Belle and Her Boys* (Bob Banner Associates); *The Body Shop* and *Sisters Revenge* (Esquivel Entertainment).
Terms: Agent receives 15% commission on domestic sales. Offers written contract, binding for 2 years on individual screenplays. Returns scripts with reader's comments.
Tips: Obtains new clients through WGA listing, *Hollywood Scriptwriter*, word of mouth (in Dallas). "We have writers available to edit or ghostwrite screenplays. Fees vary dependent on the writer. All writers should always please enclose a SASE with any queries."

☐**STAR LITERARY SERVICE, (II)**, 1540 N. Louis, Tucson AZ 85712. (520)326-4146. Contact: Marilyn Caponegri. Estab. 1990. Signatory of WGA. Represents 9 clients. 80% of clients are new/previously unpublished writers. Currently handles: 100% movie scripts.
Handles: Movie scripts (feature film); TV scripts (TV mow). Considers these script subject areas: action/adventure; biography/autobiography; detective/police/crime; mystery; psychic/supernatural; romance; thriller/espionage. Query. Reports in 2 weeks on queries; 6 weeks on mss.
Terms: Agent receives 10% commission on domestic sales. Offers written contract, binding for 2 years.
Fees: Criticism service: $100 for a maximum of 150 pages. Agent writes critiques that "point out problems in dialogue, plotting and character development and determines the overall marketability of the project."
Tips: Obtains new clients through queries. "Stick with popular genres such as mystery, comedy, romance. Always include a SASE."

TALENT SOURCE, 237 Dayton St., P.O. Box 14120, Savannah GA 31416. (912)232-9390. Fax: (912)232-8213. Contact: Michael L. Shortt. Estab. 1991. Signatory of WGA. 35% of clients are new/previously unpublished writers. Currently handles: 50% movie scripts; 50% TV scripts.

Handles: Movie scripts (feature film); TV scripts. Send outline with character breakdown. Reports in 6 weeks on queries.
Terms: Agent receives 10% commission on domestic sales; 15% on foreign sales. Offers written contract.
Tips: Obtains new clients through word of mouth.

THE TANTLEFF OFFICE, (II), 375 Greenwich St., Suite 700, New York NY 10013. (212)941-3939. President: Jack Tantleff. Estab. 1986. Signatory of WGA, member of AAR. Specializes in theater, film, TV, fiction and nonfiction. Member agents: John Santoianni (theater); Charmaine Ferenczi (theater); Jill Bock (TV and film); Anthony Gardner (fiction, nonfiction books); Alan Willig (talent); Jay Kane (talent).
Handles: Movie scripts, TV scripts, stage plays, musicals, fiction and nonfiction books. Query with outline.
Terms: Agent receives 10% commission on domestic sales; 10% on dramatic sales; 10% on foreign sales: 15% on book sales.

TAURO BROTHERS MANAGEMENT, (II), 1541 Ocean Ave., #200, Santa Monica CA 90401. (310)458-1505. Fax: (310)393-7777. Contact: Chris Maggiore, Robert Tauro. Estab. 1992. Represents 2 clients. None are new/previously unpublished writers. Currently handles: 25% movie scripts; 75% recording artists.
Handles: Movie scripts. Considers these script subject areas: action/adventure; cartoon/comic; comedy; contemporary issues; current affairs; detective/police/crime; erotica; ethnic; gay; historical; horror; juvenile; lesbian; military/war; photography; religious/inspirational; romance; sports; thriller/espionage; true crime/investigative. Send entire ms. Reports in 10 days.
Terms: Agent receives 10% commission on domestic sales; 10% on foreign sales.
Tips: Obtains new clients through recommendations.

□A TOTAL ACTING EXPERIENCE, (II), Dept. N.W., 20501 Ventura Blvd., Suite 399, Woodland Hills CA 91364. (818)340-9249. Contact: Dan A. Bellacicco. Estab. 1984. Signatory of WGA, SAG, AFTRA. Represents 30 clients. 50% of clients are new/previously unpublished writers. Specializes in "quality instead of quantity." Currently handles: 5% nonfiction books; 5% juvenile books; 10% novels; 5% novellas; 5% short story collections; 50% movie scripts; 5% stage plays; 10% TV scripts; 5% how-to books and videos.
Handles: Movie scripts (feature film, documentary); TV scripts (TV mow, episodic drama, sitcom, variety show, soap opera, animation); stage plays; syndicated material; how-to books, videos. "No heavy drugs." Considers these script subject areas: action/adventure; cartoon/animation; comedy; contemporary issues; detective/police/crime; erotica; ethnic; experimental; family saga; fantasy; historical; horror; juvenile; mainstream; mystery/suspense; psychic/supernatural; religious/inspirational; romantic comedy and drama; science fiction; sports; teen; thriller; westerns/frontier. Query with outline and 3 sample chapters. Reports in 3 months on mss. "We will respond *only* if interested; material will *not* be returned."
Also Handles: Nonfiction books, textbooks, juvenile books, novels, novellas, short story collections, poetry books. Considers these nonfiction areas: animals; art/architecture/design; biography/autobiography; business; child guidance/parenting; computers/electronics; cooking/food/nutrition; crafts/hobbies; current affairs; education; ethnic/cultural interests; government/politics/law; health/medicine; history; how-to; humor; juvenile nonfiction; language/literature/criticism; military/war; money/finance/economics; music/dance/theater/film; nature/environment; New Age/metaphysics; photography; popular culture; psychology; religious/inspirational; science/technology; self-help/personal improvement; sociology; sports; translations; true crime/investigative; women's issues/women's studies; "any well-written work!" Considers these fiction areas: action/adventure; cartoon/comic; confessional; contemporary issues; detective/police/crime; erotica; ethnic; experimental; family saga; fantasy; glitz; historical; horror; humor/satire; juvenile; literary; mainstream; mystery/suspense; picture book; psychic/supernatural; regional; religious/inspirational; romance (contemporary, gothic, historical, regency); science fiction; sports; thriller/espionage; westerns/frontier; young adult.
Terms: Agent receives 10% on domestic sales; 10% on foreign sales. Offers written contract, binding for 2 years or more.
Fees: Offers criticism service (for our clients only at no charge.) 60% of business is derived from commission on ms sales.
Tips: Obtains new clients through mail and conferences. "We seek new sincere, quality writers for long-term relationships. We would love to see film, television, and stage material that remains relevant and provocative 20 years from today; dialogue that is fresh and unpredictable; story, and characters that are enlightening, humorous, witty, creative, inspiring, and, most of all, entertaining. Please keep in mind quality not quantity. Your characters must be well delineated and fully developed with high

contrast. Respond only if you appreciate our old fashioned agency nurturing, strong guidance, and in return: your honesty, loyalty and a quality commitment."

THE TURTLE AGENCY, (III), 12456 Ventura Blvd., Studio City CA 91604. (818)506-6898. Fax: (818)506-1723. Contact: Cindy Turtle, Jeanne Scott. Estab. 1985. Signatory of WGA, member of SAG, AFTRA. Represents 45 clients. Specializes in network TV, features, interactive. Currently handles: 5% novels; 25% movie scripts; 70% TV scripts.
Handles: Movie scripts (feature film); TV scripts (TV mow). Considers these script subject areas: action/adventure; detective/police/crime; erotica; fantasy; historical; mainstream; mystery/suspense; psychic/supernatural; romance; science fiction; thriller/espionage; westerns/frontier; young adult. Query. Reports in 2 weeks on queries; 1 month on mss. "If writer would like material returned, enclose SASE."
Terms: Agent receives 10% commission on domestic sales. Offers written contract, binding for 2 years.
Tips: Obtains new clients through recommendations, usually—on *rare* occassions through query letters.

‡ANNETTE VAN DUREN AGENCY, (III), 925 N. Sweetzer Ave., #12, Los Angeles CA 90069. (213)650-3643. Fax: (213)654-3893. Contact: Annette Van Duren or Patricia Murphy. Estab. 1985. Signatory of WGA. Represents 12 clients. No clients are new/previously unpublished writers. Currently handles: 10% novels; 50% movie scripts; 40% TV scripts.
Handles: Movie scripts (feature film, animation); TV scripts (TV mow, sitcom, animation). Considers these script subject areas: action/adventure; cartoon/animation; comedy; contemporary issues; juvenile; mainstream; romantic comedy and drama; science fiction; thriller. Query with SASE. Reports in 2 weeks on queries.
Also Handles: Novels. Considers these nonfiction areas: true crime/investigative. Considers these fiction areas: action/adventure; cartoon/comic; contemporary issues; detective/police/crime; humor/satire; juvenile; mainstream; science fiction; thriller/espionage; westerns/frontier; young adult. Query. Reports in weeks on queries.
Terms: Agent receives 10% commission on domestic sales. Offers written contract, binding for 2 years.
Tips: Obtains new clients only through recommendations from "clients or other business associates."

‡THE VINES AGENCY, INC, (II), 409 E. Sixth St., #4, New York NY 10009. (212)777-5522. Fax: (212)777-5978. Contact: Jimmy Vines. Estab. 1995. Represents 21 clients. 2% of clients are new/previously unpublished writers. Specializes in mystery, suspense, science fiction, mainstream novels, graphic novels, CD-ROMs, screenplays, teleplays. Currently handles: 10% nonfiction books; 2% scholarly books; 10% juvenile books; 50% novels; 15% movie scripts; 5% TV scripts; 5% short story collections; 2% syndicated material.
 • Mr. Vines has broadened his representation to include writer/directors. See the expanded listing for this agency in Literary Agents: Nonfee-charging.

WARDEN, WHITE & KANE, INC., (II, IV), 8444 Wilshire Blvd., 4th Floor, Beverly Hills CA 90211. Estab. 1990. Signatory of WGA. Represents 100 clients. 10% of clients are new/previously unpublished writers. Specializes in film and TV. Currently handles: 100% movie scripts. Member agents: David Warden, Steve White, Michael Kane.
Handles: Movie scripts (feature film). Only by referral. Reports in 2 months on queries.
Recent Sales: *Mango,* by Miles Millar (New Line); *Bullet Proof,* by Phoebe Dorin and Christian Stoianovich (Universal). "Also sold *Sleepless in Seattle* and represents author of *Batman.*"
Terms: Agent receives 10% commission on domestic sales; 10% on foreign sales. Offers written contract, binding for 2 years. Charges for photocopying.
Tips: Obtains new clients only through referrals.

□SANDRA WATT & ASSOCIATES, (II), 8033 Sunset Blvd., Suite 4053, Hollywood CA 90046. (213)653-2339. Contact: Davida South. Estab. 1977. Signatory of WGA. Represents 55 clients. 15% of clients are new/previously unpublished writers. Specializes in scripts: film noir; family; romantic comedies; books, women's fiction, mystery, commercial nonfiction. Currently handles: 40% nonfiction

Agents ranked I and II are most open to both established and new writers. Agents ranked III are open to established writers with publishing-industry references.

Selling a Script the Wright Way: With Belief and Perseverance

If you really believe in your material, you keep pushing until you make it a success. That's what screen agent Marcie Wright, of The Wright Concept, told herself when a long-time client came into her office with a proposal for a script about two young friends who face the tragedy of AIDS. It was a script written on spec, with no buyers and no stars, about a sensitive subject, but Wright decided to take it on. That script eventually became the movie *The Cure*, released in 1995.

Wright says it was not an easy path from concept to completion, but she believed in the script and the writer from the start.

"I've known Robert Kuhn [the writer] since 1984," Wright says. He had worked for Fox's late show, *The Pat Sajak Show*, and the Fox series *Haywire*. After *Haywire*, Kuhn decided he wanted to write comedy features.

"One morning Robert walked into my office and said 'I have an idea,' " Wright recalls. Wright encouraged him to get started on the script, although she says "it was quite a departure from the cynical, dark comedy I was used to seeing from him." Nonetheless, Wright was deeply impressed with the script.

"It's sort of a modern day *Huckleberry Finn*," Wright says. "About two outcasts who befriend each other at the beginning of a summer. One of the boys is a rebellious teenager, and the other boy has AIDS." By the end of the summer, the rebellious teen is determined to find a cure for his friend.

Dark material, perhaps, but Wright says the writer handled the subject well. "I told people, 'It's a bittersweet comedy,' " she says. "The script had a lot of humor in it. Robert blended the tragedy of the subject with the humor of friendship." Because of the nature of the film, Wright decided to look for a director first. "I try to tailor submissions to producers who have an affinity for the material," she states.

Wright says marketing the script posed a few challenges. In addition to the subject matter, a film focusing on two young boys meant studios couldn't bank on big name stars to sell the movie. "There are parts for the boys' mothers and the doctor," Wright says, but the success of the movie would depend on finding talented young actors to play the leads.

Wright says initial reaction was frustrating. "People were telling us 'We love the script, but . . . I don't want to do a movie about AIDS,' or 'I don't want to direct kids,' or 'I don't want to do a movie where a kid dies,' " she recalls. At the same time, Wright was fielding phone calls from people who had heard about the script, including a call from the vice president of Amblin Productions, who passed the script on to director Steven Spielberg the weekend before *Jurassic Park* opened. The vice president called Wright back on Monday to say that Spielberg loved it, but his schedule was too busy for him to take on additional projects.

Still, Spielberg's praise gave the script an added luster, and Wright was sure to mention the fact with every phone call she made. By the next day Wright received a call from a representative of Warner Pictures, who had received the script from another agency, and wanted to know how much was needed to take the script off the open market. Wright told him the asking price was one million dollars.

"He just laughed, and said 'This is no *Lethal Weapon!*'," Wright says. But she held firm. She returned to the three producers she had contacted, who also had confidence in the script, and they went to work.

"We divided the city between us," Wright recalls. "By the next day a major frenzy had developed," Wright laughs. "I had reporters from *Variety* calling me up, saying 'We understand you have this hot property.' " By the end of the week, the CEO of Island Entertainment called, and a very satisfactory seven-figure deal was struck.

Despite its quick-paced conclusion, Wright says the deal was actually some time in the making. "The script had been on the market for several months," she says, "slowly fanning its way through." Wright feels the positive word-of-mouth helped sell the script to the studio, but she believed in the project from the start and stood behind it. Wright says that it's a good lesson for agents and authors: "If you believe in the material, you just have to keep working."

—Alison Holm

books; 35% novels; 25% movie scripts. Member agents: Sandra Watt (scripts, nonfiction, novels); Davida South (scripts).
• See the expanded listing for this agency in Literary Agents: Nonfee-charging.

□PEREGRINE WHITTLESEY AGENCY, (II), 345 E. 80th St., New York NY 10021. (212)737-0153. Contact: Peregrine Whittlesey. Estab. 1986. Signatory of WGA. Represents 25 English and American clients. 30% of clients are new/previously unpublished writers. Specializes in plays and screenplays; original playwrights who write for screen and TV. Currently handles: 10% movie scripts; 90% stage plays.
Handles: Movie scripts (feature film); stage plays. Query first with SASE. Reports in 1 month.
Recent Sales: Two plays by Nilo Cruz, *Dancing On Her Knees* and *A Park In Our House*.
Terms: Agent receives 10% commission on domestic sales; 10% on foreign sales. Offers written contract, binding for 2 years.
Fees: Offers criticism service. "Critiques are usually 3-4 pages, single-spaced, written by Peregrine Whittlesey." 5% of business is derived from criticism fees.
Tips: Obtains new clients through recommendations from recognized source.

‡THE WRIGHT CONCEPT, (II), 1811 W. Burbank Blvd., Burbank CA 91506. (818)954-8943. Fax: (818)954-9370. Contact: Jason Wright. Estab. 1985. Signatory of WGA. Specializes in TV comedy writers and feature comedy writers. Currently handles: 50% movie scripts; 50% TV scripts. Member agents: Marcie Wright (TV); Jason Wright (features).
Handles: Movie scripts (feature film, animation); TV scripts (TV mow, episodic drama, sitcom, variety show, animation, syndicated material). Considers these script subject areas: action/adventure; cartoon/animation; comedy; detective/police/crime; ethnic; fantasy; humor; juvenile; mystery/suspense; romantic comedy and drama; thriller; western/frontier. Query with SASE. Reports in 2 weeks.
Recent Sales: Movie scripts optioned/sold: *Black Sheep*, by Fred Wolf (Paramount); *The Cure*, by Robert Kuhn (Universal); *Snow White*, by Tom Szollosi (Interscope). **TV scripts optioned/sold:** *If Only.* **Scripting assignments:***The Crew, Saturday Night Live, Dennis Miller Live, The Simpsons, Bike Patrol, Star Trek Voyager, Sea Quest.*
Terms: Agent receives 10% commission on sales. Offers written contract, binding for 1 year, with 90 day cancellation clause. 100% of business is derived from commissions on sales.
Writers' Conferences: Speaks at UCLA 3-4 times a year.
Tips: Obtains new clients through recommendations and queries.

‡MARC WRIGHT, (II), 3284 Barham Blvd., #201, Los Angeles CA 90068-1454. (213)876-7590. Fax: (213)876-4090. E-mail: wfax@aol.com. Contact: Marc Wright. Estab. 1993. Signatory of WGA.

Currently handles: novels, nonfiction books, feature films, TV, stage plays.
Handles: Movie scripts (feature film, documentary, animation); TV scripts (TV mow, miniseries, episodic drama, sitcom, variety show, animation, soap opera, syndicated material); stage plays. Considers all script subject areas. Query with SASE. Reports in 1 week on queries.
Also Handles: Nonfiction books, scholarly books, novels. Considers all nonfiction and fiction areas. "However, no material on child molestation." Query with SASE.
Terms: Agent receives 10% commission on domestic sales; 15% on foreign sales. 100% of business is derived from commissions on sales.
Tips: Obtains new clients through recommendations from others or cold submissions. "Don't write a novel based on the suffering of you or your family."

ANN WRIGHT REPRESENTATIVES, (II), 165 W. 46th St., Suite 1105, New York NY 10036-2501. Dan Wright. Estab. 1961. Signatory of WGA. Represents 45 clients. 40% of clients are new/unpublished writers. Prefers to work with published/established authors; works with a small number of new/unpublished authors. "Eager to work with published/established authors; works with a small number of new/unpublished authors. "Eager to work with any author with material that we can effectively market in the motion picture business worldwide." Specializes in "book or screenplays with strong motion picture potential." Currently handles: 50% novels; 40% movie scripts; 10% TV scripts.
Handles: Movie scripts (feature film); TV scripts (TV mow, episodic drama, sitcom). Considers these script subject areas: action/adventure; comedy; detective/police/crime; gay; historical; horror; humor; lesbian; mainstream; mystery/suspense; psychic/supernatural; romantic comedy and drama; sports; thriller; westerns/frontier. Query with outline and SASE. Does not read unsolicited mss. Reports in 3 weeks on queries; 3 months on mss. "All work must be sent with a SASE to ensure its return."
Recent Sales: *Movie/TV mow scripts optioned/sold*: *Baubles*, by Brian Neich (Jonathan Demme for Tristar); *Movie/TV MOW in development*: *Ride Home*, by Tom Dempsey; *Scripting assignments*: *The Red Zoltaire* by Alex Stirling (Schulz Film Ltd.)..
Also Handles: Novels. Considers these fiction areas: action/adventure; detective/police/crime; family saga; fantasy; feminist; gay; historical; horror; humor/satire; lesbian; literary; mainstream; mystery/suspense; romance (contemporary, historical, regency); sports; thriller/espionage; westerns/frontier; young adult.
Books: *The Bermuda Virus*, by Bob O'Quinn (Bermudiana Publishing); *The Da Vinci Deception*, by Thomas Swan (Bantam Books); *A Wing and A Prayer*, by John Morano (Northwest Publishing).
Terms: Agent receives 10% commission on domestic sales; 10% on dramatic sales; 15-20% on foreign sales; 20% on packaging. Offers written contract, binding for 2 years. Critiques only works of signed clients. Charges for photocopying expenses.
Tips: "Send a letter with SASE. Something about the work, something about the writer."

WRITERS & ARTISTS (III), 19 W. 44th St., Suite 1000, New York NY 10036. (212)391-1112. Fax: (212)398-9877. Contact: Scott Hudson, William Craver or Peter Hagen. Estab. 1970. Member of AAR, signatory of WGA. Represents 100 clients. West Coast location: Suite 900, 924 Westwood Blvd., Los Angeles CA 90024. (310)824-6300. Fax: (310)824-6343. *DON SPRADLIN - ETHAN PHICCI*
Handles: Movie scripts (feature film), TV scripts (TV mow, miniseries, episodic drama), stage plays. Considers all script subject areas. Query with brief description of project, bio and SASE. Reports in 2-4 weeks on queries only when accompanied by SASE. No unsolicited mss accepted.
Recent Sales: *Irreperable Harm*, by Lee Gruenfeld (Warner Books, BOMC alternate, TV rights to Wolper Co. for Warner Bros.); *All Fall Down*, by Lee Gruenfeld (Warner Books, movie rights to Tristar).

☐**WRITER'S CONSULTING GROUP, (II, III)** P.O. Box 492, Burbank CA 91503-0492. (818)841-9294. Director: Jim Barmeier. Estab. 1983. Represents 10 clients. "We will work with established and unestablished writers. We welcome unsolicited queries." Currently handles: 40% nonfiction books; 20% novels; 40% movie scripts.
   • See the expanded listing for this agency in Literary Agents: Fee-charging.

Additional Script Agents

The following agencies have indicated that they are *primarily* interested in handling book manuscripts, but also handle less than ten to fifteen percent scripts. After reading the listing (you can find the page number in the Listings Index), send them a query to obtain more information on their needs and manuscript submission policies.

Linda Allen Literary Agency
The Joan Brandt Agency
The Brinke Literary Agency
Pema Browne Ltd.

The Lois de la Haba Agency Inc.
Emerald Literary Agency
Farber Literary Agency Inc.
Flannery Literary

ForthWrite Literary Agency
Jay Garon-Brooke Assoc. Inc.
Gem Literary Services
Lew Grimes Literary Agency

The Charlotte Gusay Literary
  Agency
Gary L. Hegler Literary Agency
The Ievleva Literary Agency
Lawrence Jordan Literary Agency
Law Offices of Robert L. Fenton
  PC
Lazear Agency Incorporated
Literary and Creative Artists
  Agency Inc.
Virginia C. McKinley, Literary
  Agency

Robert Madsen Agency
Elaine Markson Literary Agency
The Evan Marshall Agency
William Morris Agency
Henry Morrison, Inc.
Nelson Literary Agency & Lec-
  ture Bureau, BK
Northwest Literary Services
Fifi Oscard Agency, Inc.
Julie Popkin
Irene Rogers Literary Representa-
  tion

Russell-Simenauer Literary
  Agency Inc.
Southern Literary Agency
Gloria Stern Agency (CA)
Marianne Strong Literary Agency
Jeanne Toomey Associates
Mary Jack Wald Associates, Inc.
Wallace Literary Agency, Inc.
James Warren Literary Agency
Stephen Wright Authors' Repre-
  sentative
Writer's Consulting Group

Script Agents/'95-'96 changes

The following agencies appeared in the last (1995) edition of *Guide to Literary Agents*
but are absent from the 1996 edition. These agencies failed to respond to our request
for an update of their listings, or were left out for the reasons indicated in parentheses
following the agency name.

The Chandelyn Literary Agency
  (unable to contact)
Gil Hayes & Associates (editorial
  decision)

JNG Entertainment
Brian Keith Moody Management
Panettiere & Co.
Camille Sorice Agency

Erika Wain Agency
Julius Windermere Agency (unable to contact)

Resources

Professional Organizations

Organizations for agents

ASSOCIATION OF AUTHORS' REPRESENTATIVES (AAR), *3rd Floor, 10 Astor Place, New York NY 10003. A list of member agents is available for $5 and SAE with 52 cents for postage.*

Organizations for writers

The following professional organizations publish newsletters and hold conferences and meetings in which they often share information on agents.

AMERICAN SOCIETY OF JOURNALISTS & AUTHORS, *1501 Broadway, Suite 302, New York NY 10036. (212)997-0947.*

THE AUTHORS GUILD INC., *330 W. 42nd St., 29th Floor, New York NY 10036. (212)563-5904.*

THE AUTHORS LEAGUE OF AMERICA, INC., *330 W. 42nd St., New York NY 10036. (212)564-8350.*

CANADIAN AUTHORS ASSOCIATION, *27 Doxsee Ave., Campbellsford, Ontario KOL 1L0 Canada. (705)653-0323. Provides a literary agent list to members.*

COUNCIL OF WRITERS ORGANIZATIONS, *% Michigan Living, 1 Auto Club Dr., Dearborn MI 48126. (313)336-1211.*

THE DRAMATISTS GUILD, *234 W. 44th St., 11th Floor, New York NY 10036. (212)398-9366.*

HORROR WRITERS ASSOCIATION, *Lawrence Watt-Evans, president, 5 Solitaire Court, Gaithersburg MD 20878. (301)926-7687.*

INTERNATIONAL ASSOCIATION OF CRIME WRITERS INC., *North American Branch, JAF Box 1500, New York NY 10016. (212)757-3915.*

THE INTERNATIONAL WOMEN'S WRITING GUILD, *P.O. Box 810, Gracie Station, New York NY 10016. (212)737-7536. Provides a literary agent list to members and holds "Meet the Agents and Editors" in April and October.*

MYSTERY WRITERS OF AMERICA (MWA), *17 E. 47th St., 6th Floor, New York NY 10017.*

NATIONAL LEAGUE OF AMERICAN PEN WOMEN, *1300 17th St. NW, Washington DC 20036. (202)785-1997.*

NATIONAL WRITERS ASSOCIATION, *1450 S. Havana, Suite 424, Aurora CO 80012. (303)751-7844. In addition to agent referrals, also operates an agency for members.*

NATIONAL WRITERS UNION, *873 Broadway, Suite 203, New York NY 10003-1209. (212)254-0279. A trade union, this organization has an agent data base available to members.*

PEN AMERICAN CENTER, *568 Broadway, New York NY 10012. (212)334-1660.*

POETS & WRITERS, *72 Spring St., New York NY 10012. (212)226-3586. Operates an information line, taking calls from 11-3 EST Monday through Friday.*

ROMANCE WRITERS OF AMERICA, *13700 Veterans Memorial Dr., #315, Houston TX 77014. Publishes an annual agent list for members for $10.*

SCIENCE FICTION AND FANTASY WRITERS OF AMERICA, *5 Winding Brook Dr., #1B, Guilderland NY 12084.*

SOCIETY OF CHILDREN'S BOOK WRITERS & ILLUSTRATORS, *22736 Van Owen St., #106, West Hills CA 91307. Provides a literary agents list to members.*

VOLUNTEER LAWYERS FOR THE ARTS, *1 E. 53rd St., 6th Floor, New York NY 10022. (212)319-2787.*

WASHINGTON INDEPENDENT WRITERS, *733 15th St. NW, Room 220, Washington DC 20005.*

WESTERN WRITERS OF AMERICA, *1012 Fair St., Franklin TN 37064. (615)791-1444.*

WOMEN IN COMMUNICATIONS, INC., *2101 Wilson Blvd., Suite 417, Arlington VA 22201.*

WRITERS GUILD OF ALBERTA, *11759 Groat St., Edmonton, Alberta T5M 3K6 Canada. (403)422-8174.*

WRITERS GUILD OF AMERICA-EAST, *555 W. 57th St., New York NY 10019. (212)767-7800. Provides list of WGA signatory agents for $1.29.*

WRITERS GUILD OF AMERICA-WEST, *8955 Beverly Blvd., West Hollywood CA 90048. (213)550-1000. Provides a list of WGA signatory agents for $2 and SASE sent to Agency Department.*

Recommended Books & Publications

ADVENTURES IN THE SCREEN TRADE, by William Goldman, published by Warner Books, 666 Fifth Ave., New York NY 10103. An insider's view of screenwriting and the entertainment business.

THE ART OF DRAMATIC WRITING, by Lajos Egri, published by Touchstone, a division of Simon & Schuster, 1230 Avenue of the Americas, New York, NY 10020.

BEYOND THE BESTSELLER: A LITERARY AGENT TAKES YOU INSIDE PUBLISHING, by Richard Curtis, published by NAL, 375 Hudson St., New York NY 10014. The "inside story" on publishing by a New York agent.

BUSINESS & LEGAL FORMS FOR AUTHORS AND SELF-PUBLISHERS, by Tad Crawford, published by Allworth Press, c/o Writer's Digest Books, 1507 Dana Ave., Cincinnati OH 45207. Forms for all types of agreements and contracts needed in the publishing business.

THE CAREER NOVELIST, by Donald Maass, published by Heinemann, 361 Hanover St., Portsmouth NH 03801-3912. A New York literary agent's detailed overview of fiction writers' careers, from breaking in to breaking out. Demystifies query letters, agents, marketing, numbers, self-promotion, common plot problems, electronic rights, economic forces and more. Of special interest are three "strategy sessions" that help new, mid-career and breakout authors manage their careers.

CHILDREN'S WRITER'S & ILLUSTRATOR'S MARKET, edited by Alice Buening, published by Writer's Digest Books, 1507 Dana Ave., Cincinnati OH 45207. Annual market directory for children's writers and illustrators. Includes information on writing and art business.

THE COMPLETE GUIDE TO STANDARD SCRIPT FORMAT (Parts 1 and 2), by Hillis Cole and Judith Haag, published by CMC Publishing, 11642 Otsego St., N. Hollywood CA 91601. Standard script formats and other information for scriptwriters.

THE COPYRIGHT HANDBOOK: How to Protect and Use Written Works, by Stephen Fishman, published by Nolo Press, 950 Parker St., Berkeley CA 94710.

THE CRAFT OF THE SCREENWRITER, by John Brady, published by Simon & Schuster, 1230 Avenue of the Americas, New York NY 10020.

CREATIVE SCREENWRITING, published by the Creative Screenwriters Group, 816 E St., NE, Suite 201, Washington DC 20002. Quarterly journal publishing critical, theoretical, historical and practical essays on all aspects of writing for the screen. Also publishes a quarterly newsletter.

DAILY VARIETY, 5700 Wilshire Blvd., Los Angeles CA 90036. Publication featuring information on the entertainment business, trade oriented.

DRAMATISTS SOURCEBOOK, edited by Angela E. Mitchell and Gilliam Richards, published by Theatre Communications Group, Inc., 355 Lexington Ave., New York NY 10017. Directory listing opportunities for playwrights. Includes agents.

THE DRAMATIST'S TOOLKIT, by Jeffrey Sweet, published by Heinemann, 361 Hanover St., Portsmouth NH 03801-3912. Guide to the craft of dramatic writing.

EDITOR & PUBLISHER, The Editor & Publisher Co., Inc., 11 W. 19th St., New York NY 10011. Weekly magazine covering latest developments in journalism and newspaper production.

ESSENTIAL SOFTWARE FOR WRITERS, by Hy Bender, published by Writer's Digest Books, 1507 Dana Ave., Cincinnati OH 45207. Examines software suited for book writers, screenwriters and playwrights.

FOUR SCREENPLAYS, by Syd Field, published by Dell, 1540 Broadway, New York NY 10036. A frame-by-frame look at four movies and why they work.

FROM SCRIPT TO SCREEN, by Linda Seger and Edward Jay Whetmore, published by Henry Holt & Co., Inc. 115 W. 18th St., New York NY 10011.

FUNNY BUSINESS, by Sol Saks, published by Lone Eagle Publishing Co., 2337 Roscomare Rd., Suite 9, Los Angeles CA 90077-1851. How to write comedy and sell it.

GETTING YOUR SCRIPT THROUGH THE HOLLYWOOD MAZE, by Linda Stuart, published by Acrobat Books, P.O. Box 870, Venice CA 90294. An insider's guide to writing and marketing movie scripts.

THE GUIDE TO WRITERS CONFERENCES, published by ShawGuides, P.O. Box 1295, New York NY 10023. Directory of writers' conferences. (212)799-6464.

HOLLYWOOD AGENTS & MANAGERS DIRECTORY, published by Hollywood Creative Directory, 3000 Olympic Blvd., Suite 2413, Santa Monica CA 90404. Triannual directory of agents and managers.

HOLLYWOOD CREATIVE DIRECTORY, published by Hollywood Creative Directory, 3000 Olympic Blvd., Suite 2413, Santa Monica CA 90404. Triannual directory of producers, studios, TV and cable networks, and companies with studio deals, listing addresses, phones, produced credits and staff members.

THE HOLLYWOOD JOB-HUNTER'S SURVIVAL GUIDE, by Hugh Taylor, published by Lone Eagle Publishing, 2337 Roscomare Rd., Suite 9, Los Angeles CA 90077-1851. Finding, getting and keeping entry-level jobs in Hollywood.

HOLLYWOOD REPORTER, *Billboard Publications, Inc., 6715 Sunset Blvd., Hollywood CA 90028. Publication covering news and information on the entertainment industry. Includes information on scriptwriters and sales of scripts.*

HOLLYWOOD SCRIPTWRITER, *1626 N. Wilcox, #385, Hollywood CA 90028. E-mail: kerrycox@aol.com. Newsletter featuring information for scriptwriters. Includes an annual agents issue.*

HOW TO BE YOUR OWN LITERARY AGENT, *by Richard Curtis, published by Houghton Mifflin Company, 2 Park St., Boston MA 02108. An insider's guide to contract negotiations, deal-making and the business of publishing.*

HOW TO BREAK IN FROM WHEREVER YOU ARE, *audiotape, by David Dworski, published by Dworski & Associates, 821 Nowita Place, Venice CA 90291. (310)823-5181. $29, including shipping and handling. "The Pitching Workshop" teaches you how to sell your scripts, your ideas, and yourself. "Your Creative Career" gives break-in shortcuts to accelerate your writing life.*

HOW TO FIND AND WORK WITH A LITERARY AGENT *audiotape, by Anita Diamant, published by Writer's AudioShop, 204 E. 35th St., Austin TX 78705. A comprehensive look at the author/agent relationship from a respected agent with over 30 years' experience.*

HOW TO MAKE IT IN HOLLYWOOD, *by Linda Buzzell, published by Harper Perennial, 10 E. 53rd St., New York NY 10022. Opportunities in Hollywood for a wide variety of areas, including writing.*

HOW TO PITCH & SELL YOUR TV SCRIPT, *by David Silver, published by Writer's Digest Books, 1507 Dana Ave., Cincinnati OH 45207. Information on marketing your television scripts. Includes information on working with script agents.*

HOW TO SELL YOUR IDEA TO HOLLYWOOD, *by Robert Kosberg with Mim Eichler, published by HarperCollins, 10 E. 53rd St., New York NY 10022. How to create and develop your own unique movie ideas and sell them to studios.*

HOW TO SELL YOUR SCREENPLAY, *by Carl Sautter, published by New Chapter Press, 381 Park Ave., S., Suite 1122, New York NY 10016. How Hollywood works.*

HOW TO WRITE A BOOK PROPOSAL, *by Michael Larsen, published by Writer's Digest Books, 1507 Dana Ave., Cincinnati OH 45207. How to put together a professional-quality book proposal package.*

HOW TO WRITE IRRESISTIBLE QUERY LETTERS, *by Lisa Collier Cool, published by Writer's Digest Books, 1507 Dana Ave., Cincinnati OH 45207. How to write professional, effective queries.*

LEW HUNTER'S SCREENWRITING 434, *by Lew Hunter, published by Perigee Books, a division of Berkley, 200 Madison Ave,. New York NY 10016. Hunter, chairman of UCLA's Screenwriting Department, outlines the graduate workshop on writing for the movies.*

THE INSIDER'S GUIDE TO BOOK EDITORS, PUBLISHERS & LITERARY AGENTS, *by Jeff Herman, published by Prima Communications, Box 1260, Rocklin CA 95677-1260. An inside look at the publishing industry. Includes information on agents.*

LITERARY AGENTS: A WRITER'S GUIDE, *by Adam Begley, published by Poets & Writer's, 72 Spring St., New York NY 10012. Directory of literary agents with articles on working with agents.*

LITERARY MARKET PLACE (LMP), *R.R. Bowker Company, 121 Chanlon Road, New Providence NJ 07974. Book publishing industry directory. In addition to publishing companies, includes a list of literary agents and a list of art representatives.*

MAKING A GOOD SCRIPT GREAT, *by Dr. Linda Seger, published by Samuel French Trade, 7623 Sunset Blvd., Hollywood CA 90046. Information on improving your script.*

MANUSCRIPT SUBMISSION, *by Scott Edelstein, published by Writer's Digest Books, 1507 Dana Ave., Cincinnati OH 45207. How to prepare submissions for publishers and agents.*

THE NEW SCREENWRITER LOOKS AT THE NEW SCREENWRITER, *by William Froug, published by Silman-James Press, 1181 Angelo Dr., Beverly Hills, CA 90210. A second volume of interviews with Hollywood screenwriters discussing their craft.*

NEW YORK SCREENWRITER, *published by the New York Screenwriter, 548 8th Ave., Suite 401, New York NY 10018. Newsletter published ten times a year featuring interviews and articles of interest to screenwriters, from software reviews to agency profiles. Annual guide to products and services.*

NOVEL & SHORT STORY WRITER'S MARKET, *edited by Robin Gee, published by Writer's Digest Books, 1507 Dana Ave., Cincinnati OH 45207. Annual market directory for fiction writers. Includes information on the writing business, organizations and conferences for fiction writers.*

OPENING THE DOORS TO HOLLYWOOD: HOW TO SELL YOUR IDEA, *by Carlos de Abreu & Howard Jay Smith, published by Custos Morum Publishers, 2049 Century Park East, Suite 1100, Los Angeles CA 90067. Information on how to sell your story, book or screenplay from Hollywood insiders.*

POETS AND WRITERS, *72 Spring St., New York NY 10012. Magazine for writers. Includes interviews and articles of interest to poets and literary writers. Poets and Writers also publishes several books and directories for writers.*

PREMIERE MAGAZINE, *published by K-III Magazines, 2 Park Ave., New York NY 10016. Monthly magazine covering current news on feature films and the personalities involved.*

PROFESSIONAL WRITER'S GUIDE, *revised and expanded edition, edited by Donald Bower and James Lee Young, National Writers Press, 1450 S. Havana, Suite 424, Aurora CO 80012. The basics of starting and building a writing career.*

PUBLISHERS WEEKLY, *249 W. 17th St., New York NY 10011. Weekly magazine covering industry trends and news in the book publishing industry. Contains announcements of new agencies.*

ROSS REPORTS, *published by Television Index, Inc. 40-29 27th St., Long Island City, NY 11101. Monthly booklet listing opportunities for actors, writers, technicians and TV personnel in New York.*

SCREENWRITE NOW!, *published by Forum, P.O. Box 7, Long Green Pike, Baldwin MD 21013-0007.*

Quarterly magazine with articles and interviews on writing and marketing screenplays.

THE SCREENWRITER LOOKS AT THE SCREENWRITER, *by William Froug, published by Silman-James Press, 1191 Angelo Dr., Beverly Hills, CA 90210. Twelve screenwriters discuss their craft.*

THE SCREENWRITER'S WORKBOOK, *by Syd Field, published by Dell, 1540 Broadway, New York NY 10036. Exercises and step-by step instruction in creating a successful screenplay.*

SCREENWRITING TRICKS OF THE TRADE, *by William Froug, published by Silman James Press, 1181 Angelo Dr., Beverly Hills CA 90210. A guide to writing and selling scripts.*

SCREENWRITING, *by Richard Walter, published by Plume, an imprint of Penguin USA, 375 Hudson St., New York NY 10014. The Chairman of Department of Film and Television at UCLA shows how to write a script that sells.*

THE SCRIPT IS FINISHED, NOW WHAT DO I DO?, *by K. Callan, published by Sweden Press, Box 1612, Studio City CA 91614. Numerous interviews with agents on issues such as query letters, meetings, agent/author relationships and what to expect, as well as agency listings.*

SELLING YOUR SCREENPLAY, *by Cynthia Whitcomb, published by Crown, 201 E. 50th St., New York NY 10022. A guide to screenwriting, with information on agents, producers, spec scripts and what to expect.*

SUCCESSFUL SCRIPTWRITING, *by Jurgen Wolff and Kerry Cox, published by Writer's Digest Books, 1507 Dana Ave., Cincinnati OH 45207. Includes information on the movie and television business, as well as tips on marketing and selling scripts.*

THEATRE DIRECTORY, *Theatre Communications Group, Inc., 355 Lexington Ave., New York NY 10017. Directory listing theaters in the U.S.*

TOP SECRETS: SCREENWRITING, *by Jurgen Wolff & Kerry Cox, published by Lone Eagle Publishing, 2337 Roscomare Rd., Suite 9, Los Angeles CA 90077-1851. Interviews with top screenwriters and commentary on their work, with advice and guidance to aspiring screenwriters.*

THE TV SCRIPTWRITER'S HANDBOOK, *by Alfred Brenner, published by Writer's Digest Books, 1507 Dana Ave., Cincinnati OH 45207. Includes all aspects of writing for television including marketing scripts.*

WORKING IN HOLLYWOOD, *by Alexandra Brouwer and Thomas Lee Wright, published by Avon, 1350 Avenue of the Americas, New York NY 10019. Insiders discuss what they do and how they got there.*

THE WRITER, *120 Boylston St., Boston MA 02116. Magazine for writers. Includes articles on technique and writing issues.*

THE WRITER'S BOOK OF CHECKLISTS, *by Scott Edelstein, published by Writer's Digest Books, 1507 Dana Ave., Cincinnati OH 45207. Checklists on topics of concern to writers, from legal matters to qualities of a good agent.*

WRITER'S DIGEST, *1507 Dana Ave., Cincinnati OH 45207. Monthly magazine for writers. Includes technique, lifestyle, business and market information.*

THE WRITER'S DIGEST GUIDE TO MANUSCRIPT FORMATS, *by Dian Dincin Buchman and Seli Groves, published by Writer's Digest Books, 1507 Dana Ave., Cincinnati OH 45207. Models for all types of manuscript formats including query and cover letters to editors, publishers and agents.*

WRITER'S ESSENTIAL DESK REFERENCE *Second Edition, edited by Glenda Tennant Neff, published by Writer's Digest Books, 1507 Dana Ave., Cincinnati OH 45207. Reference guide for writers including business, tax and legal information for both U.S. and Canadian writers.*

A WRITER'S GUIDE TO CONTRACT NEGOTIATIONS, *by Richard Balkin, published by Writer's Digest Books, 1507 Dana Ave., Cincinnati OH 45207. Written by an agent, this is an insider's view of book contract negotiations.*

WRITERS GUILD OF AMERICA, *Membership Directory, published by the Writers Guild of America, 8955 Beverly Blvd., West Hollywood CA 90048. Member writers of WGA east and west, including list of signatory agencies.*

THE WRITER'S LEGAL COMPANION, *by Brad Bunnin and Peter Beren, published by Addison Wesley, Jacob Way, Reading MA 01867. Legal guide for writers. Bunnin is a publishing-industry lawyer.*

WRITER'S MARKET, *edited by Mark Garvey, published by Writer's Digest Books, 1507 Dana Ave., Cincinnati OH 45207. Annual market directory for writers and scriptwriters. Includes information on the writing business.*

WRITING SCREENPLAYS THAT SELL, *by Michael Hauge, published by HarperCollins, 10 E. 53rd St., New York NY 10022.*

Bookstores and Catalogs

BOOK CITY, *Dept. 101, 308 N. San Fernando Blvd., Burbank CA 91502. (800)4-CINEMA. Offers hundreds of movie and TV scripts and books on screenwriting. Catalog $2.50.*

SAMUEL FRENCH THEATRE & FILM BOOKSHOPS, *7623 Sunset Blvd., Hollywood CA 90046. (213)876-0570. Books on film, screenwriting, and making movies, as well as scripts for TV and movies.*

SCRIPT CITY, *8033 Sunset Blvd., Suite 1500, Hollywood CA 90046. (800)676-2522. Offers hundreds of movie and TV scripts, books on writing and screenwriting, as well as movie paraphenalia. Catalog $2.*

THE WRITE STUFF, *21115 Devonshire St., #182, Chatsworth CA 91311. (800)989-8833. Discount catalog of books, audiotapes and computer software for writers of all genres.*

This Could Be the Most Important Decision of Your Career!

You already know an agent can be the key to selling your work. But, how do you know when you're ready to sign on with one? And how do you select an agent that's right for you? To make such crucial decisions you need the most up-to-date information on the agents out there and what they can offer you. That's exactly what you'll find in *Guide to Literary Agents*. Every year this indispensable market resource is 100% updated and verified for accuracy so you'll have the most complete and timely information at your fingertips. You'll find listings of literary agents (fee-charging and non-fee-charging) and script agents (TV, movies and plays), plus, insider articles from writing pros to help you find and work with the right agent.

Through this special offer, you can get a jump on next year today! If you order now, you'll get the *1997 Guide to Literary Agents* at the 1996 price—just $21.99 —no matter how much the regular price may increase! *1997 Guide to Literary Agents* will be published and ready for shipment in January 1997.

Keep on top of the fast-changing publishing industry and get a jump on selling your work with help from the *1997 Guide to Literary Agents*. Order today! You deserve it!

Turn Over for More Great Books to Help You Sell Your Work! ➤

☐ **Yes!** I want the most current edition of *Guide to Literary Agents*. Please send me the 1997 edition at the 1996 price – $21.99. (NOTE: *1997 Guide to Literary Agents* will be ready for shipment in January 1997.) #10495

I also want more great books to help me sell my work!

Book #_____ Price $ _____

Book #_____ Price $ _____

Book #_____ Price $ _____

Book #_____ Price $ _____

Subtotal $ _____

Add $3.50 postage and handling for one book;
$1.00 for each additional book.

Postage and handling $ _____

Payment must accompany order.
Ohioans add 5.5% sales tax.

Total $ _____

VISA/MasterCard orders call
TOLL-FREE 1-800-289-0963

☐ Payment enclosed $ _____ (or)
Charge my: ☐ Visa ☐ MasterCard Exp. _____

Account # _____

Signature _____

Name _____

Address _____

City _____ State _____ Zip _____

Phone Number _____
(will be used only if we must contact you regarding this order.)

30-Day Money Back Guarantee
on every book you buy!

Mail to:
Writer's Digest Books
1507 Dana Avenue
Cincinnati, OH 45207   6866

Get Published with help from these Writer's Digest Books!

Latest Edition!

1996 Writer's Market
edited by Mark Garvey
Get published in 1996! This totally updated edition brings you over 4,000 listings of buyers of freelance work—their names, addresses, submission requirements, contact persons and more! Each listing has been verified for accuracy, updated with critical information changes over last year, and 800 brand new listings have been added! Plus, helpful articles and interviews with top professionals make this your most essential writing resource. #10432/$27.99/1008 pages

New!

Writing to Sell
Let Scott Meredith guide you along the professional writing path, as he has for so many others. You'll find help creating characters, plotting your novel and placing it, formatting your manuscript, deciphering your contract–even combating a slump. #10476/$17.99/240 pages

The Writer's Ultimate Research Guide
Save research time and frustration. These 352 information-packed pages will point you straight to the information you need to create better, more accurate fiction and non-fiction. #10447/$19.99/352 pages

Revised Edition!

Writer's Encyclopedia
You'll find facts, figures, definitions and examples on every discipline connected with writing—editing, contracts, tax forms, copyrights, query letters, advertising, songwriting, film and more. #10464/$22.99/560 pages

Fill out order card on reverse side and mail today!

NO POSTAGE
NECESSARY
IF MAILED
IN THE
UNITED STATES

BUSINESS REPLY MAIL
FIRST CLASS MAIL   PERMIT NO. 17   CINCINNATI, OHIO

POSTAGE WILL BE PAID BY ADDRESSEE

WRITER'S DIGEST BOOKS
1507 DANA AVENUE
CINCINNATI OH 45207-9965

Glossary

Above the line. A budgetary term for movies and TV. The line refers to money budgeted for creative talent, such as actors, writers, directors and producers.

Advance. Money that a publisher pays a writer prior to publication of a book, usually paid in installments, such as one-half upon signing the contract; one-half upon delivery of the complete, satisfactory manuscript. An advance is paid against the royalty money to be earned by the book. Agents take their percentage off the top of the advance as well as from the royalties earned.

Auction. Publishers sometimes bid for the acquisition of a book manuscript with excellent sales prospects. The bids are for the amount of the author's advance, guaranteed dollar amounts, advertising and promotional expenses, royalty percentage, etc.

Backlist. Those books still in print from previous years' publication.

Backstory. The history of what has happened before the action in your script takes place, affecting a character's current behavior.

Beat. Major plot points of a story.

Below the line. A budgetary term for movies and TV, referring to production costs, including production manager, cinematographer, editor and crew members such as gaffers, grips, set designers, make-up etc.

Bible. The collected background information on all characters and storylines of all existing episodes, as well as projections of future plots.

Bio. Brief (usually one page) background information about an artist, writer or photographer. Includes work and educational experience.

Boilerplate. A standardized publishing contract. "Our standard contract" usually means the boilerplate without any changes. Most authors and agents make many changes on the boilerplate before accepting the contract.

Business-size envelope. Also known as a #10 envelope.

Castable. A script with attractive roles for known actors.

Category fiction. A term used to include all various types of fiction. See *genre*.

Client. When referring to a literary or script agent "client" is used to mean the writer whose work the agent is handling.

Clips. Writing samples, usually from newspapers or magazines, of your published work.

Commercial novel. A novel designed to appeal to a broad audience. It often falls into a category or genre such as western, romance, mystery, science fiction and horror. See also *genre*.

Concept. A statement that summarizes a screenplay or teleplay—before the treatment is written.

Contributor's copies. Copies of the author's book sent to the author. The number of contributor's copies is often negotiated in the publishing contract.

Copyediting. Editing of a manuscript for writing style, grammar, punctuation and factual accuracy. Some agents offer this service.

Cover letter. A brief descriptive letter sent with a manuscript submitted to an agent or publisher.

Coverage. A brief synopsis and analysis of a script, provided by a reader to a buyer considering purchasing the work.

Critiquing service. A service offered by some agents in which writers pay a fee for comments on the saleability or other qualities of their manuscript. Sometimes the critique includes suggestions on how to improve the work. Fees vary, as do the quality of the critiques.

D person. Development person. Includes readers and story editors through creative executives who work in development and acquisition of properties for TV and movies.

Deal memo. The memorandum of agreement between a publisher and author that precedes the actual contract and includes the more important issues such as royalty, advance, rights, distribution and option clauses.

Development. The process where writers present ideas to producers overseeing the developing script through various stages to finished product.

Division. An unincorporated branch of a company.

Docudrama. A fictional film rendition of recent newsmaking events or people.

Editing service. A service offered by some agents in which writers pay a fee—either lump sum or per-page—to have their manuscript edited. The quality and extent of the editing varies from agency to agency.

Elements. Actors, directors and producers attached to a project to make an attractive package. Writers are rarely elements.

El-hi. Elementary to high school. A term used to indicate reading or interest level.

Episodic drama. Hour-long continuing TV show, often shown at 10 o'clock.

Evaluation fees. Fees an agent may charge to evaluate material. The extent and quality of this evaluation varies, but comments usually concern the saleability of the manuscript.

Exclusive. Offering a manuscript, usually for a set period of time, to just one agent and guaranteeing that agent is the only one looking at the manuscript.

Floor bid. If a publisher is very interested in a manuscript he may offer to enter a floor bid when the book goes to auction. The publisher sits out of the auction, but agrees to take the book by topping the highest bid by an agreed-upon percentage (usually 10 percent).

Foreign rights agent. An agent who handles selling the rights to a country other than that of the first book agent. Usually an additional percentage (about 5 percent) will be added on to the first book agent's commission to cover the foreign rights agent.

Genre. Refers to either a general classification of writing such as a novel, poem or short story or to the categories within those classifications, such as problem novels or sonnets. Genre fiction is a term that covers various types of commercial novels such as mystery, romance, western, science fiction or horror.

Ghosting or ghost writing. When a writer puts into literary form the words, ideas or knowledge of another person under that person's name it is called ghostwriting. Some agents offer this service. Others will pair ghostwriters with celebrities or experts.

Green light. To give the go-ahead to a movie or TV project.

Half-hour. A 30-minute TV show, also known as a sitcom.

High concept. A story idea easily expressed in a quick, one-line description.

Imprint. The name applied to a publisher's specific line of books (e.g., Lisa Drew, an imprint of Simon & Schuster).

IRC. International Reply Coupons; purchased at a post office to enclose with material sent outside your country to cover the cost of return postage. The recipient can turn in the coupons for stamps in their own country.

Log line. A one-line description of a plot as it might appear in *TV Guide*.

Long-form TV. Movies of the week or miniseries.

Mainstream fiction. Fiction on subjects or trends that transcend popular novel categories such as mystery or romance. Using conventional methods, this kind of fiction tells stories about people and their conflicts.

Marketing fee. Fee charged by some agents to cover marketing expenses. It may be used to cover postage, telephone calls, faxes, photocopying or any other expense incurred in marketing a manuscript.

Mass market paperbacks. Softcover book, usually around 4×7, on a popular subject directed at a general audience and sold in groceries and drugstores as well as bookstores.

MFTS. Made for TV series. A series developed for television also known as episodics.

Middle reader. The general classification of books written for readers 9-11 years old.

Midlist. Those titles on a publisher's list expected to have limited sales. Midlist books are mainstream, not literary, scholarly or genre, and are usually written by new or relatively unknown writers.

Miniseries. A limited dramatic series written for television, often based on a popular novel.

MOW. Movie of the week. A movie script written especially for television, usually seven acts with time for commercial breaks. Topics are often contemporary, sometimes controversial, fictional accounts. Also known as a made-for-TV-movie.

Net receipts. One method of royalty payment based on the amount of money a book publisher receives on the sale of the book after the booksellers' discounts, special sales discounts and returned copies.

Novelization. A novel created from the script of a popular movie, usually called a movie "tie-in" and published in paperback.

Novella. A short novel or long short story, usually 7,000 to 15,000 words. Also called a novelette.

Option clause. A contract clause giving a publisher the right to publish an author's next book.

Outline. A summary of a book's contents in 5 to 15 double-spaced pages; often in the form of chapter headings with a descriptive sentence or two under each one to show the scope of the book. A screenplay's or teleplay's outline is a scene-by-scene narrative description of the story (10-15 pages for a ½-hour teleplay; 15-25 pages for 1-hour; 25-40 pages for 90 minutes and 40-60 pages for a 2-hour feature film or teleplay).

Over-the-transom. Slang for the path of an unsolicited manuscript into the slush pile.

Packaging. The process of putting elements together, increasing the chances of a project being made.

Picture book. A type of book aimed at the preschool to 8-year-old that tells the story primarily or entirely with artwork. Agents and reps interested in selling to publishers of these books often handle both artists and writers.

Pitch. The process where a writer meets with a producer and briefly outlines ideas that could be developed if the writer is hired to write a script for the project.

Proofreading. Close reading and correction of a manuscript's typographical errors. A few agents offer this service for a fee.

Property. Books or scripts forming the basis for a movie or TV project.

Proposal. An offer to an editor or publisher to write a specific work, usually a package consisting of an outline and sample chapters.

Prospectus. A preliminary, written description of a book, usually one page in length.

Query. A letter written to an agent or a potential market, to elicit interest in a writer's work.

Reader. A person employed by an agent or buyer to go through the slush pile of scripts and select those worth considering.

Release. A statement that your idea is original, has never been sold to anyone else and that you are selling negotiated rights to the idea upon payment.

Remainders. Leftover copies of an out-of-print or slow-selling book, which can be purchased from the publisher at a reduced rate. Depending on the author's contract, a reduced royalty or no royalty is paid on remaindered books.

Reporting time. The time it takes the agent to get back to you on your query or submission.

Royalties. A percentage of the retail price paid to the author for each copy of the book that is sold. Agents take their percentage from the royalties earned as well as from the advance.

SASE. Self-addressed, stamped envelope. This or a self-addressed, stamped postcard should be included with all correspondence.

Scholarly books. Books written for an academic or research audience. These are usually heavily researched, technical and often contain terms used only within a specific field.

Screenplay. Script for a film intended to be shown in movie theaters.

Script. Broad term covering teleplay, screenplay or stage play. Sometimes used as a shortened version of the word "manuscript" when referring to books.

Show runner. A TV writer-producer with responsibility over an entire TV series.

Simultaneous submission. Sending the same manuscript to several agents or publishers at the same time. Simultaneous query letters are common, but simultaneous submissions are unacceptable to many agents or publishers.

Sitcom. Situation comedy. Episodic comedy script for a television series. Term comes from the characters dealing with various situations with humorous results.

Slush pile. A stack of unsolicited submissions in the office of an editor, agent or publisher.

Spec script. A script written on speculation without expectation of a sale.

Standard commission. The commission an agent earns on the sales of a manuscript or script. For literary agents, this commission percentage (usually between 10 and 20 percent) is taken from the advance and royalties paid to the writer. For script agents, the commission is taken from script sales; if handling plays, agents take a percentage from the box office proceeds.

Story analyst. See reader.

Storyboards. Series of panels which illustrates a progressive sequence or graphics and story copy for a TV commercial, film or filmstrip.

Subagent. An agent who handles certain subsidiary rights. This agent usually works in conjunction with the agent who has handled the book rights and the percentage paid the book agent is increased to cover paying the subagent.

Subsidiary. An incorporated branch of a company or conglomerate (e.g. Alfred Knopf, Inc., is a subsidiary of Random House, Inc.)

Subsidiary rights. All rights other than book publishing rights included in a book publishing contract, such as paperback rights, bookclub rights, movie rights. Part of an agent's job is to negotiate those rights and advise you on which to sell and which to keep.

Synopsis. A brief summary of a story, novel or play. As a part of a book proposal, it is a comprehensive summary condensed in a page or page and a half, single-spaced. See also *outline*.

Tearsheet. Published samples of your work, usually pages torn from a magazine.

Textbook. Book used in a classroom on the elementary, high school or college level.

Trade book. Either a hard cover or soft cover book; subject matter frequently concerns a special interest for a general audience; sold mainly in bookstores.

Trade paperback. A softbound volume, usually around 5×8, published and designed for the general public, available mainly in bookstores.

Treatment. Synopsis of a television or film script (40-60 pages for a 2-hour feature film or teleplay).

Turnaround. When a script has been in development but not made in the time allotted, it can be put back on the market. Scripts in turnaround can be very desireable to other buyers since some of the problems have already been worked out by previous development personnel.

Unsolicited manuscript. An unrequested manuscript sent to an editor, agent or publisher.

Young adult. The general classification of books written for readers age 12-18.

Young reader. Books written for readers 5-8 years old, where artwork only supports the text.

Table of Acronyms

The organizations and their acronyms listed below are frequently referred to in the listings and are widely used in the industries of agenting and writing.

AAP	American Association of Publishers
AAR	Association of Author's Representatives (1991 merger of ILAA and SAR)
ABA	American Booksellers Association
ABWA	Associated Business Writers of America
AEB	Association of Editorial Businesses
AFTRA	American Federation of TV and Radio Artists
AGVA	American Guild of Variety Artists
AMWA	American Medical Writer's Association
ASJA	American Society of Journalists and Authors
ATA	Association of Talent Agents
AWA	Aviation/Space Writers Association
CAA	Canadian Authors Association
DGA	Director's Guild of America
GWAA	Garden Writers Association of America
HWA	Horror Writers of America
IACP	International Association of Culinary Professionals
ILAA	Independent Literary Agents Association (see AAR)
MWA	Mystery Writers of America, Inc.
NASW	National Association of Science Writers
NLAPW	National League of American Pen Women
NWA	National Writers Association
OWAA	Outdoor Writers Association of America, Inc.
RWA	Romance Writers of America
SAG	Screen Actor's Guild
SAR	Society of Authors' Representatives (see AAR)
SATW	Society of American Travel Writers
SCBWI	Society of Children's Book Writers & Illustrators
SFWA	Science Fiction and Fantasy Writers of America
WGA	Writers Guild of America
WIA	Women in the Arts Foundation, Inc.
WIF	Women in Film
WICI	Women in Communications, Inc.
WIW	Washington Independent Writers
WNBA	Women's National Book Association
WRW	Washington Romance Writers (chapter of RWA)
WWA	Western Writers of America

Indexes

Client Acceptance Policies

We've ranked the agencies according to their openness to submissions. Some agencies are listed under more than one category.

Nonfee-charging literary agents

I—Newer agency actively seeking clients

The Author's Agency
The Wendy Becker Literary
Agency
Josh Behar Literary Agency
Collins Purvis, Ltd.
DH Literary, Inc.
Jane Dystel Literary Management
Elliot Agency

Emerald Literary Agency
B.R. Fleury Agency
Fogelman Literary Agency
The Sebastian Gibson Agency
Henderson Literary Representation
Karen Lewis & Company
Lindstrom Literary Group

Lyceum Creative Properties, Inc.
Doris S. Michaels Literary
Agency, Inc.
New Brand Agency Group
Pelham Literary Agency
The Damaris Rowland Agency
Susan Travis Literary Agency
The Richard R. Valcourt Agency

II—Agency seeking both new and established writers

Dominick Abel Literary Agency,
Inc.
Acton, Leone, Hanson & Jaffe,
Inc.
Adler & Robin Books Inc.
Agency Chicago
Agents Inc. For Medical and
Mental Health Professionals
The Joseph S. Ajlouny Agency
Lee Allan Agency
Linda Allen Literary Agency
Miriam Altshuler Literary
Agency
Marcia Amsterdam Agency
Apollo Entertainment
Appleseeds Management
The Author's Agency
Malaga Baldi Literary Agency
Loretta Barrett Books Inc.
Pam Bernstein
David Black Literary Agency,
Inc.
Blassingame Spectrum Corp.
Reid Boates Literary Agency
The Barbara Bova Literary
Agency
The Joan Brandt Agency
Marie Brown Associates Inc.
Curtis Brown Ltd.
Howard Buck Agency
Jane Butler, Art and Literary
Agent
Cantrell-Colas Inc., Literary
Agency
Maria Carvainis Agency, Inc.

Castiglia Literary Agency
James Charlton Associates
Circle of Confusion Ltd.
Ciske & Dietz Literary Agency
Connie Clausen Associates
Ruth Cohen, Inc. Literary Agency
Hy Cohen Literary Agency Ltd.
Collins Purvis, Ltd.
Columbia Literary Associates,
Inc.
The Doe Coover Agency
Robert Cornfield Literary Agency
Bonnie R. Crown International
Literature and Arts Agency
James R. Cypher, Author Representative
Darhansoff & Verrill Literary
Agents
Joan Daves Agency
DH Literary, Inc.
DHS Literary, Inc.
Anita Diamant, The Writer's
Workshop, Inc.
Sandra Dijkstra Literary Agency
The Jonathan Dolger Agency
Donadio and Ashworth, Inc.
Doyen Literary Services, Inc.
Dragon Literary, Inc.
Robert Ducas
Dupree/Miller and Associates
Inc. Literary
Jane Dystel Literary Management
Educational Design Services, Inc.
Peter Elek Associates
Ethan Ellenberg Literary Agency

Elliot Agency
Nicholas Ellison, Inc.
Emerald Literary Agency
Esq. Literary Productions
Felicia Eth Literary Representation
Farber Literary Agency Inc.
Joyce A. Flaherty, Literary Agent
Flaming Star Literary Enterprises
Flannery Literary
B.R. Fleury Agency
Lynn C. Franklin Associates, Ltd.
Jay Garon-Brooke Assoc. Inc.
Max Gartenberg, Literary Agent
Richard Gautreaux-A Literary
Agency
Gem Literary Services
Goddard Book Group
Goldfarb & Graybill, Attorhneys
at Law
Charlotte Gordon Agency
Graham Literary Agency, Inc.
Sanford J. Greenburger Associates, Inc.
Randall Elisha Greene, Literary
Agent
Maia Gregory Associates
Lew Grimes Literary Agency
The Charlotte Gusay Literary
Agency
Reece Halsey Agency
The Mitchell J. Hamilburg
Agency
The Hampton Agency
The Hardy Agency

Rose Hass Literary Agency
John Hawkins & Associates, Inc.
Heacock Literary Agency, Inc.
Henderson Literary Representation
Richard Henshaw Group
The Jeff Herman Agency Inc.
Susan Herner Rights Agency
Frederick Hill Associates
Hull House Literary Agency
The Ievleva Literary Agency
Img-Julian Bach Literary Agency
International Publisher Associates
J de S Associates Inc.
Jabberwocky Literary Agency
James Peter Associates, Inc.
Lawrence Jordan Literary Agency
Louise B. Ketz Agency
Kirchoff/Wohlberg, Inc., Authors' Representation Division
Barbara S. Kouts, Literary Agent
Edite Kroll Literary Agency
The Candace Lake Agency
Peter Lampack Agency, Inc.
The Robert Lantz-Joy Harris Literary Agency Inc.
Michael Larsen/Elizabeth Pomada Literary Agents
The Maureen Lasher Agency
Lazear Agency Incorporated
Lescher & Lescher Ltd.
Levant & Wales Literary Agency, Inc.
James Levine Communications, Inc.
Ellen Levine Literary Agency, Inc.
Karen Lewis & Company
Robert Lieberman Associates
Ray Lincoln Literary Agency
Wendy Lipkind Agency
The Literary Group

Lowenstein Associates, Inc.
Lyceum Creative Properties, Inc.
Margret Mcbride Literary Agency
Gina Maccoby Literary Agency
Richard P. Mcdonough, Literary Agent
Robert Madsen Agency
Ricia Mainhardt Agency
Carol Mann Agency
Manus & Associates Literary Agency, Inc.
Barbara Markowitz Literary Agency
Elaine Markson Literary Agency
Roberta Miller Associates
Henry Morrison, Inc.
Dee Mura Enterprises, Inc.
Ruth Nathan
Karen Nazor Literary Agency
New England Publishing Associates, Inc.
Nine Muses and Apollo, Inc.
The Betsy Nolan Literary Agency
The Norma-lewis Agency
Fifi Oscard Agency Inc.
Otitis Media
Kathi J. Paton Literary Agency
Rodney Pelter
Stephen Pevner, Inc.
Pocono Literary Agency, Inc.
Pom Inc.
Julie Popkin
The Potomac Literary Agency
Aaron M. Priest Literary Agency
Printed Tree Inc.
Susan Ann Protter Literary Agent
Roberta Pryor, Inc.
Publishing Services
Quicksilver Books-Literary Agents
Helen Rees Liteary Agency
Angela Rinaldi Literary Agency
BJ Robbins Literary Agency
The Robbins Office, Inc.
Rock Literary Agency
Rose Agency

Rose Literary Agency
Jane Rotrosen Agency
Pesha Rubinstein Literary Agency, Inc.
Russell-Simenauer Literary Agency Inc.
St. Clair Literary Agency
Victoria Sanders Literary Agency
Sandum & Associates
Harold Schmidt Literary Agency
Laurens R. Schwartz Agency
Lynn Seligman, Literary Agent
The Seymour Agency
The Shepard Agency
Bobbe Siegel Literary Agency
Sierra Literary Agency
Michael Snell Literary Agency
Elyse Sommer, Inc.
F. Joseph Spieler
Nancy Stauffer Associates
Lyle Steele & Co., Ltd.
Gloria Stern Literary Agency
Sandra Taylor Literary Enterprises
2M Communications Ltd.
Robert Ubell Associates
Susan P. Urstadt Inc. Agency
The Richard R. Valcourt Agency
Van Der Leun & Associates
The Vines Agency, Inc.
John A. Ware Literary Agency
Waterside Productions, Inc.
Watkins Loomis Agency, Inc.
Sandra Watt & Associates
Wecksler-Incomco
Rhoda Weyr Agency
Witherspoon & Associates, Inc.
Ruth Wreschner Authors' Representative
Ann Wright Representatives
Writers' Productions
Writers' Representatives, Inc.
Susan Zeckendorf Assoc. Inc.
George Ziegler Literary Agency

III—Agency pefers to work with established writers, mostly obtains new clients through referrals

Dominick Abel Literary Agency, Inc.
James Allen, Literary Agency
Bart Andrews & Associates Inc.
Authors' Literary Agency
The Axelrod Agency
Balkin Agency, Inc.
Georges Borchardt Inc.
Brandenburgh & Associates Literary Agency
Brandt & Brandt Literary Agents Inc.
Marie Brown Associates Inc.
Andrea Brown Literary Agency, Inc.
Jane Butler, Art and Literary Agent

Martha Casselman Literary Agent
Frances Collin Literary Agent
Don Congdon Associates Inc.
Crawford Literary Agency
Richard Curtis Associates, Inc.
The Lois de la Haba Agency Inc.
Diamond Literary Agency, Inc.
Ann Elmo Agency Inc.
Florence Feiler Literary Agency
Joyce A. Flaherty, Literary Agent
The Foley Literary Agency
Max Gartenberg, Literary Agent
Arthur B. Greene
Reece Halsey Agency
Gary L. Hegler Literary Agency
Richard Henshaw Group
John L. Hochmann Books

Berenice Hoffman Literary Agency
Barbara Hogenson Agency
Helane Hulburt Literary Agency
International Creative Management
The Kellock Company Inc.
Kidde, Hoyt & Picard
Harvey Klinger, Inc.
The Maureen Lasher Agency
Ellen Levine Literary Agency, Inc.
Literary and Creative Artists Agency Inc.
Sterling Lord Literistic, Inc.
Nancy Love Literary Agency
Donald Maass Literary Agency

Donald MacCampbell Inc.
Helen McGrath
Carol Mann Agency
March Tenth, Inc.
The Martell Agency
Metropolitan Talent Agency
The Miller Agency
William Morris Agency
Henry Morrison, Inc.
Multimedia Product Development, Inc.
Jean V. Naggar Literary Agency
Karen Nazor Literary Agency
Nugent Literary
Harold Ober Associates
The Palmer & Dodge Agency
The Richard Parks Agency
Arthur Pine Associates, Inc.
Pom Inc.

Charlotte Cecil Raymond, Literary Agent
Helen Rees Literary Agency
Renaissance-H.N. Swanson Inc.
Riverside Literary Agency
Irene Rogers Literary Representation
Susan Schulman, A Literary Agency
Sebastian Literary Agency
Rosalie Siegel, International Literary Agency, Inc.
Evelyn Singer Literary Agency Inc.
Valerie Smith, Literary Agent
F. Joseph Spieler
Philip G. Spitzer Literary Agency
Nancy Stauffer Associates

Gloria Stern Literary Agency
Roslyn Targ Literary Agency, Inc.
Patricia Teal Literary Agency
Annette Van Duren Agency
Mary Jack Wald Associates, Inc.
Wallace Literary Agency, Inc.
Harriet Wasserman Literary Agency
The Weingel-Fidel Agency
Rhoda Weyr Agency
Wieser & Wieser, Inc.
Ruth Wreschner, Authors' Representative
Writers House
Karen Gantz Zahler Literary Agency

IV—Agency handling only certain types of work or work by writers under certain circumstances

Andrea Brown Literary Agency, Inc.
Sheree Bykofsky Associates
Charisma Communications, Ltd.
Columbia Literary Associates, Inc.
Bonnie R. Crown International Literature and Arts Agency
DHS Literary, Inc.
Educational Design Services, Inc.

Peter Elek Associates
Peter Fleming Agency
Graham Literary Agency, Inc.
The Charlotte Gusay Literary Agency
The Hampton Agency
John L. Hochmann Books
The Candace Lake Agency
Levant & Wales, Literary Agency, Inc.

Moore Literary Agency
The Richard Paul Agency
L. Perkins Associates
Stepping Stone
Gloria Stern Literary Agency
Toad Hall, Inc.
Robert Ubell Associates
Cherry Weiner Literary Agency

V—Agency not currently seeking new clients

The Foley Literary Agency
Virginia Kidd Literary Agent

Alice Orr Agency, Inc.
The Wendy Weil Agency, Inc.

Cherry Weiner Literary Agency

Fee-charging literary agents

I—Newer agency actively seeking clients

AEI/Atchity Editorial/ Entertainment International
The Ahearn Agency, Inc.
Allegra Literary Agency
Alp Arts Co.

Authentic Creations Literary Agency
Colby: Literary Agency
Fran Literary Agency
Independent Publishing Agency

Virginia C. McKinley, Literary Agency
Pacific Literary Services
QCorp Literary Agency

II—Agency seeking both new and established writers

Acacia House Publishing Services Ltd.
Alp Arts Co.
Authentic Creations Literary Agency
Author Aid Associates
The Authors Resource Center/ TARC Literary Agency
Elizabeth H. Backman
Gene Bartczak Associates Inc.
Meredith Bernstein Literary Agency
The Blake Group Literary Agency

The Brinke Literary Agency
Antoinette Brown, Literary Agent
Pema Browne Ltd.
Cambridge Literary Associates
The Catalog Literary Agency
Chadd-Stevens Literary Agency
Linda Chester Literary Agency
Coast to Coast Talent and Literary
Frieda Fishbein Ltd.
Flannery, White and Stone
Follendore & Ikeyama Literary Agency
Forthwrite Literary Agency
Fran Literary Agency

Gelles-Cole Literary Enterprises
The Gislason Agency
Gladden Unlimited
Lucianne S. Goldberg Literary Agents, Inc.
Andrew Hamilton's Literary Agency
Alice Hilton Literary Agency
Yvonne Trudeau Hubbs Agency
Carolyn Jenks Agency
Larry Kaltman Literary Agency
J. Kellock & Associates, Ltd.
Natasha Kern Literary Agency
The Kirkland Literary Agency

Law Offices of Robert L. Fenton PC
Lawyer's Literary Agency, Inc.
L. Harry Lee Literary Agency
Literary Group West
Toni Lopopolo Literary Agency
M.H. International Literary Agency
Virginia C. McKinley, Literary Agency
The Denise Marcil Literary Agency, Inc.
Mews Books Ltd.
Montgomery Literary Agency

David H. Morgan Literary Agency, Inc.
BK Nelson Literary Agency & Lecture Bureau
Northeast Literary Agency
Northwest Literary Services
Edward A. Novak III Literary Representation
Pacific Literary Services
Paraview, Inc.-The Sandra Martin Literary Agency
William Pell Agency
Penmarin Books
Sidney E. Porcelain

Puddingstone Literary Agency
Diane Raintree Agency
SLC Enterprises
Gloria Stern Agency
Dawson Taylor Literary Agency
Jeanne Toomey Associates
Phyllis Tornetta Agency
A Total Acting Experience
Visions Press
The Gerry B. Wallerstein Agency
James Warren Literary Agency
West Coast Literary Associates
Westchester Literary Agency
Writer's Consulting Group

III—Agency pefers to work with established writers, mostly obtains new clients through referrals

Acacia House Publishing Services Ltd.
The Blake Group Literary Agency
Ruth Hagy Brod Literary Agency
Collier Associates
Connor Literary Agency
Dorese Agency Ltd.
The Eddy Howard Agency

JLM Literary Agents
The Evan Marshall Agency
Mews Books Ltd.
BK Nelson Literary Agency & Lecture Bureau
Paraview, Inc.-The Sandra Martin Literary Agency
The Portman Organization

Sidney E. Porcelain
Southern Literary Agency
Michael Steinberg Literary Agency
Marianne Strong Literary Agency
Stephen Wright Authors' Representative
Writer's Consulting Group

IV—Agency handling only certain types of work or work by writers under certain circumstances

SJ Clark Literary Agency

Connor Literary Agency

Executive Excellence

V—Agency not currently seeking new clients

Lighthouse Literary Agency

Rydal

Script agents

I—Newer agency actively seeking clients

AEI/Atchity Editorial/Entertainment International
All-Star Talent Agency
Kevin C. Bulger and Associates
Earth Tracks Agency

B.R. Fleury Agency
Fran Literary Agency
The Sebastian Gibson Agency
Hudson Agency
Kick Entertainment

Legacies
Lindstrom Literary Group
Lyceum Creative Properties
Pelham Literary Agency

II—Agency seeking both new and established writers

Act I
Agency for the Performing Arts
Lee Allan Agency
The Alpern Group
Michael Amato Agency
American Play Co., Inc.
Marcia Amsterdam Agency
Apollo Entertainment
The Artists Agency
The Bennett Agency
Bethel Agency
Curtis Brown Ltd.
Camden
The Marshall Cameron Agency

Cinema Talent International
Circle of Confusion Ltd.
Client First-A/K/A Leo P. Haffey Agency
Coast to Coast Talent and Literary
Douroux & Co.
Dragon Literary, Inc.
Durkin Artists Agency
Earth Tracks Agency
Epstein-Wyckoff and Associates
F.L.A.I.R or First Literary Artists International Representatives
Frieda Fishbein Ltd.
B.R. Fleury Agency

Fran Literary Agency
Robert A. Freedman Dramatic Agency, Inc.
Samuel French, Inc.
The Gary-Paul Agency
Richard Gauthreaux-A Literary Agency
The Gersh Agency
Gold/Marshak & Associates
Graham Agency
Reece Halsey Agency
The Hampton Agency
Heacock Literary Agency, Inc.
Alice Hilton Literary Agency

International Leonards Corp.
Carolyn Jenks Agency
Charles Kerin Associates
The Joyce Ketay Agency
Tyler Kjar Agency
The Candace Lake Agency
L. Harry Lee Literary Agency
Lyceum Creative Properties
Manus & Associates Literary
    Agency, Inc.
Marbea Agency
Monteiro Rose Agency
Montgomery Literary Agency

Dee Mura Enterprises, Inc.
Otitis Media
Panda Talent
The Partos Company
Part-Time Productions
Stephen Pevner, Inc.
A Picture of You
Producers & Creatives Group
Redwood Empire Agency
Victoria Sanders Literary Agency
Silver Screen Placements
Stanton & Associates Literary
    Agency

Star Literary Service
The Tantleff Office
Tauro Brothers Management
A Total Acting Experience
The Vines Agency, Inc.
Warden, White & Kane, Inc.
Sandra Watt & Associates
Peregrine Whittlesey Agency
The Wright Concept
Marc Wright
Ann Wright Representatives
Writer's Consulting Group

III—Agency pefers to work with established writers, mostly obtains new clients through referrals

Above the Line Agency
Agape Productions
The Agency
The Bennett Agency
Berman Boals and Flynn
Don Buchwald
Communications and Entertain-
    ment, Inc.
The Coppage Company
Dykeman Associates Inc.
Florence Feiler Literary Agency
Robert A. Freedman Dramatic
    Agency, Inc.
Samuel French, Inc.
The Gersh Agency

Michelle Gordon & Ass-
    ociates
Arthur B. Greene
Reece Halsey Agency
Carolyn Hodges Agency
Barbara Hogenson Agency
The Eddy Howard Agency
International Creative Manage-
    ment
Leslie Kallen Agency
The Joyce Ketay Agency
Lenhoff/Robinson Talent and
    Literary Agency, Inc.
Major Clients agency
Media Artists Group

Metropolitan Talent
    Agency
Dorothy Palmer
Renaissance—H.N. Swanson Inc.
Stephanie Rogers and Associates
Jack Scagnetti Talent & Literary
    Agency
Susan Schulman, A Literary
    Agency
Ken Sherman & Associates
Sister Mania Productions, Inc.
The Turtle Agency
Annette Van Duren Agency
Writers & Artists
Writer's Consulting Group

IV—Agency handling only certain types of work or work by writers under certain circumstances

The Artists Agency
Dramatic Publishing
F.L.A.I.R. or First Literary Artists
    International Representatives
The Gardner Agency
Geddes Agency

The Laya Gelff Agency
The Susan Gurman Agency
The Hampton Agency
Hudson Agency
Charles Kerin Associates
Paul Kohner, Inc.

The Candace Lake Agency
Marbea Agency
Montgomery-West Literary
    Agency
Warden, White & Kane, Inc.

V—Agency not currently seeking new clients

Part Time Productions

Sister Mania Productions, Inc.

Subject Index

The subject index is divided into nonfiction and fiction subject categories for each section—Nonfee-charging Literary Agents, Fee-charging Literary Agents and Script Agents. To find an agent interested in the type of manuscript you've written, see the appropriate sections under subject headings that best describe your work. Check the Listings Index for the page number of the agent's listing. Agents who are open to most fiction or nonfiction subjects appear in the "Open" heading.

Nonfee-charging agents/Fiction

Action/adventure. Act I; Acton, Leone, Hanson & Jaffe; Allan Agency, Lee; Allen, Literary Agency, James; Amsterdam Agency, Marcia; Baldi Literary Agency, Malaga; Behar Literary Agency, Josh; Bernstein, Pam; Bova Literary Agency, Barbara; Brandt & Brandt Literary Agents; Buck Agency, Howard; Carvainis Agency, Maria; Circle of Confusion; Ciske & Dietz Literary Agency; Collins Purvis, Ltd.; Curtis Associates, Richard; Cypher, Author's Representative, James R.; DH Literary; DHS Literary; Diamant, Anita; Diamond Literary Agency; Doyen Literary Services; Ducas, Robert; Dupree/Miller and Assoc.; Dystel Literary Management, Jane; Elliott Agency; Elmo Agency, Ann; Esq. Literary Productions; Farber Literary Agency; Flannery Literary; Fleury Agency, B.R.; Gibson Agency, Sebastian; Goldfarb & Graybill, Attorneys at Law; Green, Literary Agent, Randall Elisha; Greenburger Assoc., Sanford J.; Greene, Arthur B.; Gusay Literary Agency, Charlotte; Halsey Agency, Reece; Hampton Agency; Hawkins & Assoc., John; Hegler Literary Agency, Gary L.; Henshaw Group, Richard; Herner Rights Agency, Susan; Ievleva Literary Agency; JABberwocky Literary Agency; Kidde, Hoyt & Picard; Klinger, Harvey; Lampack Agency, Peter; Lantz-Joy Harris Literary Agency, Robert; Larsen/Elizabeth Pomada Literary Agents, Michael; Lasher Agency, Maureen; Lewis & Co., Karen; Lincoln Literary Agency, Ray; Lindstrom Literary Group; Literary Group; Love Literary Agency, Nancy; Lyceum Creative Properties; McBride Literary Agency, Margret; Madsen Agency, Robert; Mainhardt Agency, Ricia; Manus & Associates Literary Agency; Metropolitan Talent Agency; Michaels Literary Agency; Morrison, Henry; Mura Enterprises, Dee; Naggar Literary Agency, Jean V.; Nazor Literary Agency, Karen; New Brand Agency Group; Norma-Lewis Agency; Otitis Media; Parks Agency, Richard; Pelham Literary Agency; Pelter, Rodney; Pevner, Stephen; Pine Assoc., Arthur; Pocono Literary Agency; Pom; Potomac Literary Agency; Printed Tree; Quicksilver Books-Literary Agents; Renaissance—H.N. Swanson; Rinaldi Literary Agency, Angela; Rock Literary Agency; Rose Agency; Sanders Literary Agency, Victoria; Schmidt Literary Agency, Harold; Seymour Agency; Siegel Literary Agency, Bobbe; Sierra Literary Agency; Travis Literary Agency, Susan; Van Duren Agency, Annette; Vines Agency; Wald Assoc., Mary Jack; Weiner Literary Agency, Cherry; Wreschner, Authors' Representative, Ruth; Wright Representatives, Ann; Zeckendorf Assoc., Susan

Cartoon/comic. Axelrod Agency; Baldi Literary Agency, Malaga; Buck Agency, Howard; Circle of Confusion; Collins Purvis, Ltd.; DH Literary.; Dupree/Miller and Assoc.; Gibson Agency, Sebastian; Gusay Literary Agency, Charlotte; Hawkins & Assoc., John; JABberwocky Literary Agency; Lantz-Joy Harris Literary Agency, Robert; Levant & Wales, Literary Agency; Literary Group; Lyceum Creative Properties; Mainhardt Agency, Ricia; Metropolitan Talent Agency; Nazor Literary Agency, Karen; Pelter, Rodney; Pevner, Stephen; Rock Literary Agency; Van Der Leun & Assoc.; Van Duren Agency, Annette; Vines Agency

Confessional. Buck Agency, Howard; Circle of Confusion; Gusay Literary Agency, Charlotte; Ievleva Literary Agency; Lantz-Joy Harris Literary Agency, Robert; Manus & Associates Literary Agency; March Tenth; Metropolitan Talent Agency; Pelter, Rodney; Rock Literary Agency

Contemporary issues. Acton, Leone, Hanson & Jaffe; Adler & Robin Books Inc.; Agents Inc. for Medical and Mental Health Professionals; Baldi Literary Agency, Malaga; Bernstein, Pam; Boates Literary Agency, Reid; Bova Literary Agency, Barbara; Brandt Agency, Joan; Brandt & Brandt Literary Agents; Brown Assoc., Marie; Buck Agency, Howard; Cantrell-Colas, Literary Agency; Castiglia Literary Agency; Charisma Communications; Circle of Confusion; Collins Purvis, Ltd.; Cypher, Author's Representative, James R.; de la Haba Agency, Lois; DH Literary; Diamant, Anita; Diamond Literary Agency; Dijkstra Literary Agency, Sandra; Doyen Literary Services; Ducas, Robert; Dupree/Miller and Assoc.; Dystel Literary Management, Jane; Elliott Agency; Elmo Agency, Ann; Esq. Literary Productions; Farber Literary Agency; Feiler Literary Agency, Florence; Flaherty, Literary Agent, Joyce A.; Flannery Literary; Garon-Brooke Assoc., Jay; Gibson Agency, Sebastian; Goldfarb & Graybill, Attorneys at Law; Gordon Agency, Charlotte; Green, Literary Agent, Randall Elisha; Greenburger Assoc., Sanford J.; Gusay Literary Agency, Charlotte; Halsey Agency, Reece; Hampton Agency; Hawkins & Assoc., John; Heacock Literary Agency, Inc.; Herner Rights Agency, Susan; Hulburt Literary Agency, Helane; Ievleva Literary Agency; JABberwocky Literary Agency; Kidde, Hoyt & Picard; Kouts, Literary Agent, Barbara S.; Kroll Literary Agency, Edite; Lampack Agency, Peter; Lantz-Joy Harris Literary Agency, Robert; Larsen/Elizabeth Pomada Literary Agents,

Michael; Lasher Agency, Maureen; Levine Communications, James; Lincoln Literary Agency, Ray; Lindstrom Literary Group; Literary Group; Love Literary Agency, Nancy; Lowenstein Associates; Lyceum Creative Properties; McGrath, Helen; Mainhardt Agency, Ricia; Manus & Associates Literary Agency; Markowitz Literary Agency, Barbara; Metropolitan Talent Agency; Michaels Literary Agency; Miller Assoc., Roberta; Multimedia Product Development; Mura Enterprises, Dee; Naggar Literary Agency, Jean V.; Nazor Literary Agency, Karen; New Brand Agency Group; Norma-Lewis Agency; Palmer & Dodge Agency; Parks Agency, Richard; Paul Agency, The Richard; Pelter, Rodney; Pevner, Stephen; Pom; Potomac Literary Agency; Printed Tree; Pryor, Roberta; Publishing Services; Quicksilver Books-Literary Agents; Raymond, Literary Agent, Charlotte Cecil; Rees Literary Agency, Helen; Rinaldi Literary Agency, Angela; Robbins Literary Agency, BJ; Rock Literary Agency; Rose Agency; Rose Literary Agency; Russell-Simenauer Literary Agency; Sanders Literary Agency, Victoria; Schmidt Literary Agency, Harold; Schulman, Susan; Schwartz Agency, Laurens R.; Seligman, Literary Agent, Lynn; Shepard Agency; Siegel Literary Agency, Bobbe; Singer Literary Agency, Evelyn; Spitzer Literary Agency, Philip G.; Stauffer Assoc., Nancy; Stepping Stone; Stern Literary Agency, Gloria (TX); Travis Literary Agency, Susan; Valcourt Agency, Richard R.; Van Der Leun & Assoc.; Van Duren Agency, Annette; Vines Agency; Wald Assoc., Mary Jack; Watkins Loomis Agency, Inc.; Wecksler-Incomco; Weiner Literary Agency, Cherry; Weingel-Fidel Agency; Wieser & Wieser; Witherspoon & Associates; Wreschner, Authors' Representative, Ruth; Zeckendorf Assoc., Susan; Ziegler Literary Agency, George

Detective/police/crime. Act I; Acton, Leone, Hanson & Jaffe; Adler & Robin Books Inc.; Allan Agency, Lee; Allen, Literary Agency, James; Amsterdam Agency, Marcia; Appleseeds Management; Authors' Literary Agency; Axelrod Agency; Baldi Literary Agency, Malaga; Behar Literary Agency, Josh; Bernstein, Pam; Boates Literary Agency, Reid; Bova Literary Agency, Barbara; Brandt Agency, Joan; Brandt & Brandt Literary Agents; Buck Agency, Howard; Bykofsky Assoc., Sheree; Cantrell-Colas, Literary Agency; Carvainis Agency, Maria; Charisma Communications; Circle of Confusion; Cohen, Literary Agency, Ruth; Collin Literary Agent, Frances; Collins Purvis, Ltd.; Curtis Associates, Richard; Cypher, Author's Representative, James R.; de la Haba Agency, Lois; DH Literary; DHS Literary; Diamant, Anita; Diamond Literary Agency; Dijkstra Literary Agency, Sandra; Doyen Literary Services; Ducas, Robert; Dupree/Miller and Assoc.; Dystel Literary Management, Jane; Ellenberg Literary Agency, Ethan; Elliott Agency; Elmo Agency, Ann; Esq. Literary Productions; Farber Literary Agency; Feiler Literary Agency, Florence; Flaherty, Literary Agent, Joyce A.; Fleury Agency, B.R.; Garon-Brooke Assoc., Jay; Gibson Agency, Sebastian; Goddard Book Group; Goldfarb & Graybill, Attorneys at Law; Graham Literary Agency; Green, Literary Agent, Randall Elisha; Greenburger Assoc., Sanford J.; Greene, Arthur B.; Gusay Literary Agency, Charlotte; Halsey Agency, Reece; Hawkins & Assoc., John; Hegler Literary Agency, Gary L.; Henshaw Group, Richard; Herner Rights Agency, Susan; Hull House Literary Agency; Ievleva Literary Agency; Img-Julian Bach Literary Agency; J de S Assoc.; JABberwocky Literary Agency; Kidde, Hoyt & Picard; Klinger, Harvey; Lampack Agency, Peter; Lantz-Joy Harris Literary Agency, Robert; Larsen/Elizabeth Pomada Literary Agents, Michael; Lasher Agency, Maureen; Lewis & Co., Karen; Lincoln Literary Agency, Ray; Lindstrom Literary Group; Literary Group; Love Literary Agency, Nancy; Lowenstein Associates; Lyceum Creative Properties; Maass Literary Agency, Donald; McBride Literary Agency, Margret; McGrath, Helen; Mainhardt Agency, Ricia; Manus & Associates Literary Agency; Markowitz Literary Agency, Barbara; Metropolitan Talent Agency; Miller Assoc., Roberta; Morrison, Henry; Multimedia Product Development; Mura Enterprises, Dee; Naggar Literary Agency, Jean V.; Norma-Lewis Agency; Parks Agency, Richard; Pelham Literary Agency; Pelter, Rodney; Perkins Assoc., L.; Pevner, Stephen; Pine Assoc., Arthur; Pom; Potomac Literary Agency; Protter Literary Agent, Susan Ann; Pryor, Roberta; Rees Literary Agency, Helen; Renaissance—H.N. Swanson; Rinaldi Literary Agency, Angela; Robbins Literary Agency, BJ; Rock Literary Agency; Rowland Agency, Damaris; Rubenstein Literary Agency, Pesha; Schmidt Literary Agency, Harold; Schulman, Susan; Seligman, Literary Agent, Lynn; Seymour Agency; Siegel Literary Agency, Bobbe; Sierra Literary Agency; Singer Literary Agency, Evelyn; Spitzer Literary Agency, Philip G.; Steele & Co., Lyle; Stern Literary Agency, Gloria (TX); Targ Literary Agency, Roslyn; Travis Literary Agency, Susan; Van Duren Agency, Annette; Vines Agency; Wald Assoc., Mary Jack; Wallace Literary Agency; Watkins Loomis Agency, Inc.; Watt & Assoc., Sandra; Weiner Literary Agency, Cherry; Wieser & Wieser; Witherspoon & Associates; Wreschner, Authors' Representative, Ruth; Wright Representatives, Ann; Zeckendorf Assoc., Susan

Erotica. Act I; Agency Chicago; Baldi Literary Agency, Malaga; Brandt & Brandt Literary Agents; Buck Agency, Howard; Circle of Confusion; de la Haba Agency, Lois; DHS Literary; Gusay Literary Agency, Charlotte; Lantz-Joy Harris Literary Agency, Robert; Lewis & Co., Karen; Love Literary Agency, Nancy; Lowenstein Associates; Lyceum Creative Properties; Mainhardt Agency, Ricia; Nazor Literary Agency, Karen; Paul Agency, The Richard; Pelter, Rodney; Pevner, Stephen; Pom; Rock Literary Agency; Travis Literary Agency, Susan

Ethnic. Altshuler Literary Agency, Miriam; Apollo Entertainment; Baldi Literary Agency, Malaga; Bernstein, Pam; Brandt & Brandt Literary Agents; Brown Assoc., Marie; Buck Agency, Howard; Cantrell-Colas, Literary Agency; Castiglia Literary Agency; Circle of Confusion; Cohen, Literary Agency, Ruth; Collin Literary Agent, Frances; Crown International Literature and Arts Agency, Bonnie R.; Cypher, Author's Representative, James R.; Daves Agency, Joan; de la Haba Agency, Lois; DHS Literary; Dijkstra Literary Agency, Sandra; Doyen Literary Services; Dupree/Miller and Assoc.; Dystel Literary Management, Jane; Elliott Agency; Elmo Agency, Ann; Eth Literary Representation, Felicia; Flannery Literary; Fleury Agency, B.R.; Gibson Agency, Sebastian; Goldfarb & Graybill, Attorneys at Law; Greenburger Assoc., Sanford J.; Gusay Literary Agency, Charlotte; Halsey Agency, Reece; Hampton Agency; Hawkins & Assoc., John; Henshaw Group, Richard; Herner Rights Agency, Susan; Hulburt Literary Agency, Helane; Ievleva Literary Agency; JABberwocky Literary Agency; Kidde, Hoyt & Picard; Lantz-Joy Harris Literary Agency, Robert; Larsen/Elizabeth Pomada Literary Agents, Michael; Levant & Wales, Literary Agency; Lewis & Co., Karen; Lincoln Literary Agency, Ray; Lindstrom Literary Group; Literary Group; Love Literary Agency, Nancy; Lowenstein Associates; Lyceum Creative Properties; McBride Literary Agency, Margret; Mainhardt Agency, Ricia; Manus & Associates Literary Agency; March Tenth; Markowitz Literary Agency, Barbara;

Multimedia Product Development; Mura Enterprises, Dee; Naggar Literary Agency, Jean V.; Nazor Literary Agency, Karen; Nine Muses and Apollo; Palmer & Dodge Agency; Parks Agency, Richard; Paul Agency, The Richard; Pelter, Rodney; Perkins Assoc., L.; Pevner, Stephen; Potomac Literary Agency; Publishing Services; Raymond, Literary Agent, Charlotte Cecil; Renaissance—H.N. Swanson; Rinaldi Literary Agency, Angela; Robbins Literary Agency, BJ; Rock Literary Agency; Rose Literary Agency; Rubenstein Literary Agency, Pesha; Schmidt Literary Agency, Harold; Seligman, Literary Agent, Lynn; Seymour Agency; Siegel Literary Agency, Bobbe; Singer Literary Agency, Evelyn; Spieler, F. Joseph; Stepping Stone; Stern Literary Agency, Gloria (TX); Travis Literary Agency, Susan; Van Der Leun & Assoc.; Vines Agency; Wald Assoc., Mary Jack; Watkins Loomis Agency, Inc.; Witherspoon & Associates; Wreschner, Authors' Representative, Ruth; Zeckendorf Assoc., Susan

Experimental. Agency Chicago; Baldi Literary Agency, Malaga; Brandt & Brandt Literary Agents; Buck Agency, Howard; Cantrell-Colas, Literary Agency; Circle of Confusion; de la Haba Agency, Lois; Diamant, Anita; Doyen Literary Services; Dupree/Miller and Assoc.; Elliott Agency; Flannery Literary; Fleury Agency, B.R.; Gusay Literary Agency, Charlotte; Hampton Agency; Hawkins & Assoc., John; Hulbert Literary Agency, Helane; Ievleva Literary Agency; Lantz-Joy Harris Literary Agency, Robert; Larsen/Elizabeth Pomada Literary Agents, Michael; Levant & Wales, Literary Agency; Lyceum Creative Properties; Mura Enterprises, Dee; Paul Agency, The Richard; Pelter, Rodney; Pevner, Stephen; Potomac Literary Agency; Rinaldi Literary Agency, Angela; Rock Literary Agency; Stern Literary Agency, Gloria (TX); Wald Assoc., Mary Jack

Family saga. Allen, Literary Agency, James; Axelrod Agency; Boates Literary Agency, Reid; Brandt & Brandt Literary Agents; Buck Agency, Howard; Cantrell-Colas, Literary Agency; Carvainis Agency, Maria; Castiglia Literary Agency; Circle of Confusion; Cohen, Literary Agency, Ruth; Collin Literary Agent, Frances; Collins Purvis, Ltd.; Crown International Literature and Arts Agency, Bonnie R.; Curtis Associates, Richard; Cypher, Author's Representative, James R.; Daves Agency, Joan; Diamant, Anita; Diamond Literary Agency; Dijkstra Literary Agency, Sandra; Doyen Literary Services; Ducas, Robert; Dupree/Miller and Assoc.; Dystel Literary Management, Jane; Ellenberg Literary Agency, Ethan; Elmo Agency, Ann; Esq. Literary Productions; Feiler Literary Agency, Florence; Flaherty, Literary Agent, Joyce A.; Flannery Literary; Fleury Agency, B.R.; Garon-Brooke Assoc., Jay; Gibson Agency, Sebastian; Gordon Agency, Charlotte; Green, Literary Agent, Randall Elisha; Greenburger Assoc., Sanford J.; Gusay Literary Agency, Charlotte; Halsey Agency, Reece; Hawkins & Assoc., John; Henshaw Group, Richard; Herner Rights Agency, Susan; Ievleva Literary Agency; JABberwocky Literary Agency; Klinger, Harvey; Kouts, Literary Agent, Barbara S.; Lampack Agency, Peter; Lantz-Joy Harris Literary Agency, Robert; Larsen/Elizabeth Pomada Literary Agents, Michael; Lasher Agency, Maureen; Lincoln Literary Agency, Ray; Lindstrom Literary Group; Literary Group; Maass Literary Agency, Donald; McGrath, Helen; Mainhardt Agency, Ricia; Manus & Associates Literary Agency; March Tenth; Metropolitan Talent Agency; Michaels Literary Agency; Morrison, Henry; Mura Enterprises, Dee; Naggar Literary Agency, Jean V.; Norma-Lewis Agency; Orr Agency, Alice; Parks Agency, Richard; Paul Agency, The Richard; Pelter, Rodney; Pine Assoc., Arthur; Pocono Literary Agency; Potomac Literary Agency; Printed Tree; Renaissance—H.N. Swanson; Rinaldi Literary Agency, Angela; Robbins Literary Agency, BJ; Rock Literary Agency; Rose Agency; Russell-Simenauer Literary Agency; Sanders Literary Agency, Victoria; Schmidt Literary Agency, Harold; Shepard Agency; Siegel Literary Agency, Bobbe; Spieler, F. Joseph; Steele & Co., Lyle; Wald Assoc., Mary Jack; Weiner Literary Agency, Cherry; Wieser & Wieser; Witherspoon & Associates; Wreschner, Authors' Representative, Ruth; Wright Representatives, Ann; Zeckendorf Assoc., Susan; Ziegler Literary Agency, George

Fantasy. Allan Agency, Lee; Allen, Literary Agency, James; Apollo Entertainment; Appleseeds Management; Becker Literary Agency, Wendy; Behar Literary Agency, Josh; Buck Agency, Howard; Butler, Art and Literary Agent, Jane; Carvainis Agency, Maria; Circle of Confusion; Collin Literary Agent, Frances; Collins Purvis, Ltd.; Curtis Associates, Richard; de la Haba Agency, Lois; Doyen Literary Services; Dupree/Miller and Assoc.; Ellenberg Literary Agency, Ethan; Emerald Literary Agency; Fleury Agency, B.R.; Garon-Brooke Assoc., Jay; Gibson Agency, Sebastian; Graham Literary Agency; Gusay Literary Agency, Charlotte; Hampton Agency; Henshaw Group, Richard; Herner Rights Agency, Susan; Ievleva Literary Agency; JABberwocky Literary Agency; Klinger, Harvey; Larsen/Elizabeth Pomada Literary Agents, Michael; Lincoln Literary Agency, Ray; Lindstrom Literary Group; Literary Group; Lyceum Creative Properties; Maass Literary Agency, Donald; Mainhardt Agency, Ricia; Metropolitan Talent Agency; Naggar Literary Agency, Jean V.; New Brand Agency Group; Pelham Literary Agency; Pelter, Rodney; Pom; Renaissance—H.N. Swanson; Rock Literary Agency; Schwartz Agency, Laurens R.; Seligman, Literary Agent, Lynn; Siegel Literary Agency, Bobbe; Smith, Literary Agent, Valerie; Vines Agency; Weiner Literary Agency, Cherry; Wright Representatives, Ann

Feminist. Altshuler Literary Agency, Miriam; Baldi Literary Agency, Malaga; Brandt & Brandt Literary Agents; Brown Assoc., Marie; Buck Agency, Howard; Cantrell-Colas, Literary Agency; Castiglia Literary Agency; Circle of Confusion; Collins Purvis, Ltd.; Curtis Associates, Richard; Cypher, Author's Representative, James R.; de la Haba Agency, Lois; DH Literary; DHS Literary; Diamant, Anita; Dijkstra Literary Agency, Sandra; Dupree/Miller and Assoc.; Eth Literary Representation, Felicia; Flaherty, Literary Agent, Joyce A.; Gibson Agency, Sebastian; Goldfarb & Graybill, Attorneys at Law; Gusay Literary Agency, Charlotte; Hass Literary Agency, Rose; Hawkins & Assoc., John; Herner Rights Agency, Susan; Hulbert Literary Agency, Helane; Kidde, Hoyt & Picard; Kouts, Literary Agent, Barbara S.; Kroll Literary Agency, Edite; Lantz-Joy Harris Literary Agency, Robert; Larsen/Elizabeth Pomada Literary Agents, Michael; Lasher Agency, Maureen; Levant & Wales, Literary Agency; Lincoln Literary Agency, Ray; Literary Group; Lowenstein Associates; Lyceum Creative Properties; Mainhardt Agency, Ricia; Manus & Associates Literary Agency; Michaels Literary Agency; Naggar Literary Agency, Jean V.; Nazor Literary Agency, Karen; Palmer & Dodge Agency; Parks Agency, Richard; Pelter, Rodney; Pom; Potomac Literary Agency; Publishing Services; Rinaldi Literary Agency, Angela; Rock Literary Agency; Rose Literary Agency; Russell-Simenauer Literary Agency; Sanders Literary Agency, Victoria; Schmidt Literary Agency, Harold; Seligman, Literary Agent, Lynn;

Siegel Literary Agency, Bobbe; Sierra Literary Agency; Singer Literary Agency, Evelyn; Spieler, F. Joseph; Stern Literary Agency, Gloria (TX); Travis Literary Agency, Susan; Vines Agency; Wald Assoc., Mary Jack; Watkins Loomis Agency, Inc.; Witherspoon & Associates; Wright Representatives, Ann

Gay. Altshuler Literary Agency, Miriam; Apollo Entertainment; Brandt & Brandt Literary Agents; Brown Assoc., Marie; Buck Agency, Howard; Castiglia Literary Agency; Circle of Confusion; Cypher, Author's Representative, James R.; Daves Agency, Joan; de la Haba Agency, Lois; DH Literary; DHS Literary; Diamant, Anita; Dupree/Miller and Assoc.; Dystel Literary Management, Jane; Eth Literary Representation, Felicia; Feiler Literary Agency, Florence; Garon-Brooke Assoc., Jay; Goldfarb & Graybill, Attorneys at Law; Gordon Agency, Charlotte; Greenburger Assoc., Sanford J.; Gusay Literary Agency, Charlotte; Hawkins & Assoc., John; Hulburt Literary Agency, Helane; JABberwocky Literary Agency; Kidde, Hoyt & Picard; Lantz-Joy Harris Literary Agency, Robert; Larsen/Elizabeth Pomada Literary Agents, Michael; Levant & Wales, Literary Agency; Lincoln Literary Agency, Ray; Literary Group; Love Literary Agency, Nancy; Lowenstein Associates; Lyceum Creative Properties; Mura Enterprises, Dee; Palmer & Dodge Agency; Parks Agency, Richard; Paul Agency, The Richard; Perkins Assoc., L.; Pevner, Stephen; Potomac Literary Agency; Raymond, Literary Agent, Charlotte Cecil; Robbins Literary Agency, BJ; Rock Literary Agency; Rose Literary Agency; Russell-Simenauer Literary Agency; Sanders Literary Agency, Victoria; Seligman, Literary Agent, Lynn; pieler, F. Joseph; Steele & Co., Lyle; Travis Literary Agency, Susan; Wald Assoc., Mary Jack; Watkins Loomis Agency, Inc.; Witherspoon & Associates; Wreschner, Authors' Representative, Ruth; Wright Representatives, Ann; Ziegler Literary Agency, George

Glitz. Allan Agency, Lee; Allen, Literary Agency, James; Amsterdam Agency, Marcia; Axelrod Agency; Bova Literary Agency, Barbara; Buck Agency, Howard; Bykofsky Assoc., Sheree; Carvainis Agency, Maria; Castiglia Literary Agency; Circle of Confusion; de la Haba Agency, Lois; DH Literary; Diamond Literary Agency; Doyen Literary Services; Dupree/Miller and Assoc.; Elmo Agency, Ann; Gibson Agency, Sebastian; Goldfarb & Graybill, Attorneys at Law; Greenburger Assoc., Sanford J.; Gusay Literary Agency, Charlotte; Hawkins & Assoc., John; Henshaw Group, Richard; Herner Rights Agency, Susan; Ievleva Literary Agency; JABberwocky Literary Agency; Kidde, Hoyt & Picard; Klinger, Harvey; Lampack Agency, Peter; Lantz-Joy Harris Literary Agency, Robert; Larsen/Elizabeth Pomada Literary Agents, Michael; Love Literary Agency, Nancy; Mainhardt Agency, Ricia; Metropolitan Talent Agency; Multimedia Product Development; Mura Enterprises, Dee; Orr Agency, Alice; Parks Agency, Richard; Pelter, Rodney; Pevner, Stephen; Pom; Quicksilver Books-Literary Agents; Rees Literary Agency, Helen; Rinaldi Literary Agency, Angela; Rock Literary Agency; Rubenstein Literary Agency, Pesha; Russell-Simenauer Literary Agency; Schmidt Literary Agency, Harold; Seymour Agency; Siegel Literary Agency, Bobbe; Teal Literary Agency, Patricia; Wald Assoc., Mary Jack; Watt & Assoc., Sandra; Weiner Literary Agency, Cherry; Witherspoon & Associates; Wreschner, Authors' Representative, Ruth; Zeckendorf Assoc., Susan

Historical. Allan Agency, Lee; Allen, Literary Agency, James; Amsterdam Agency, Marcia; Apollo Entertainment; Axelrod Agency; Baldi Literary Agency, Malaga; Bernstein, Pam; Blassingame Spectrum; Brandt & Brandt Literary Agents; Brown Assoc., Marie; Brown Literary Agency, Andrea; Buck Agency, Howard; Butler, Art and Literary Agent, Jane; Cantrell-Colas, Literary Agency; Carvainis Agency, Maria; Circle of Confusion; Cohen, Literary Agency, Ruth; Collin Literary Agent, Frances; Collins Purvis, Ltd.; Crown International Literature and Arts Agency, Bonnie R.; Curtis Associates, Richard; Cypher, Author's Representative, James R.; de la Haba Agency, Lois; DH Literary; DHS Literary; Diamant, Anita; Diamond Literary Agency; Doyen Literary Services; Dupree/Miller and Assoc.; Ellenberg Literary Agency, Ethan; Elmo Agency, Ann; Farber Literary Agency; Feiler Literary Agency, Florence; Flaherty, Literary Agent, Joyce A.; Flannery Literary; Fleury Agency, B.R.; Gibson Agency, Sebastian; Goddard Book Group; Goldfarb & Graybill, Attorneys at Law; Greenburger Assoc., Sanford J.; Gusay Literary Agency, Charlotte; Halsey Agency, Reece; Hawkins & Assoc., John; Henshaw Group, Richard; Herner Rights Agency, Susan; Ievleva Literary Agency; J de S Assoc.; JABberwocky Literary Agency; Kidde, Hoyt & Picard; Kouts, Literary Agent, Barbara S.; Lampack Agency, Peter; Lantz-Joy Harris Literary Agency, Robert; Larsen/Elizabeth Pomada Literary Agents, Michael; Lasher Agency, Maureen; Lincoln Literary Agency, Ray; Lindstrom Literary Group; Literary Group; Lowenstein Associates; Lyceum Creative Properties; Maass Literary Agency, Donald; McBride Literary Agency, Margret; Mainhardt Agency, Ricia; March Tenth; Metropolitan Talent Agency; Michaels Literary Agency; Multimedia Product Development; Mura Enterprises, Dee; Naggar Literary Agency, Jean V.; Nathan, Ruth; Norma-Lewis Agency; Otitis Media; Parks Agency, Richard; Pelter, Rodney; Pocono Literary Agency; Pom; Potomac Literary Agency; Pryor, Roberta; Publishing Services; Rees Literary Agency, Helen; Renaissance—H.N. Swanson; Rinaldi Literary Agency, Angela; Rock Literary Agency; Rose Agency; Rowland Agency, Damaris; Russell-Simenauer Literary Agency; St. Clair Literary Agency; Schulman, Susan; Seligman, Literary Agent, Lynn; Seymour Agency; Shepard Agency; Siegel Literary Agency, Bobbe; Singer Literary Agency, Evelyn; Steele & Co., Lyle; Toad Hall; Travis Literary Agency, Susan; Valcourt Agency, Richard R.; Van Der Leun & Assoc.; Wald Assoc., Mary Jack; Wecksler-Incomco; Weiner Literary Agency, Cherry; Wieser & Wieser; Witherspoon & Associates; Wreschner, Authors' Representative, Ruth; Wright Representatives, Ann; Zeckendorf Assoc., Susan; Ziegler Literary Agency, George

Horror. Allan Agency, Lee; Allen, Literary Agency, James; Amsterdam Agency, Marcia; Appleseeds Management; Buck Agency, Howard; Butler, Art and Literary Agent, Jane; Circle of Confusion; Collins Purvis, Ltd.; Curtis Associates, Richard; Cypher, Author's Representative, James R.; DH Literary; DHS Literary; Doyen Literary Services; Dupree/Miller and Assoc.; Elliott Agency; Fleury Agency, B.R.; Gibson Agency, Sebastian; Greene, Arthur B.; Hampton Agency; Henshaw Group, Richard; Herner Rights Agency, Susan; Ievleva Literary Agency; JABberwocky Literary Agency; Klinger, Harvey; Larsen/Elizabeth Pomada Literary Agents, Michael; Lindstrom Literary Group; Literary Group; Maass Literary Agency, Donald; Mainhardt Agency, Ricia; March Tenth; Metropolitan Talent Agency; Multimedia Product Development; New Brand Agency Group; Norma-Lewis Agency; Parks Agency, Richard; Pelham Literary Agency; Perkins Assoc., L.; Pevner, Stephen; Pocono Literary Agency; Pom;

Printed Tree; Schmidt Literary Agency, Harold; Seligman, Literary Agent, Lynn; Seymour Agency; Siegel Literary Agency, Bobbe; Steele & Co., Lyle; Vines Agency; Wreschner, Authors' Representative, Ruth; Ziegler Literary Agency, George

Humor/satire. Agency Chicago; Amsterdam Agency, Marcia; Baldi Literary Agency, Malaga; Brandt & Brandt Literary Agents; Brown Assoc., Marie; Buck Agency, Howard; Cantrell-Colas, Literary Agency; Carvainis Agency, Maria; Crown International Literature and Arts Agency, Bonnie R.; de la Haba Agency, Lois; DH Literary; Doyen Literary Services; Dupree/Miller and Assoc.; Ellenberg Literary Agency, Ethan; Farber Literary Agency; Flannery Literary; Green, Literary Agent, Randall Elisha; Greenburger Assoc., Sanford J.; Greenburger Assoc., Sanford J.; Gusay Literary Agency, Charlotte; Hampton Agency; Hawkins & Assoc., John; Henshaw Group, Richard; Kidde, Hoyt & Picard; Lantz-Joy Harris Literary Agency, Robert; Larsen/Elizabeth Pomada Literary Agents, Michael; Lincoln Literary Agency, Ray; Literary Group; Lyceum Creative Properties; Madsen Agency, Robert; Mainhardt Agency, Ricia; March Tenth; Markowitz Literary Agency, Barbara; Metropolitan Talent Agency; Norma-Lewis Agency; Otitis Media; Pelter, Rodney; Pom; Potomac Literary Agency; Renaissance—H.N. Swanson; Rock Literary Agency; Rose Agency; Rose Literary Agency; Seligman, Literary Agent, Lynn; Seymour Agency; Shepard Agency; Spieler, F. Joseph; Wald Assoc., Mary Jack; Witherspoon & Associates

Juvenile. Allan Agency, Lee; Brown Assoc., Marie; Brown Literary Agency, Andrea; Butler, Art and Literary Agent, Jane; Butler, Art and Literary Agent, Jane; Cantrell-Colas, Literary Agency; Carvainis Agency, Maria; Circle of Confusion; Cohen, Literary Agency, Ruth; Collins Purvis, Ltd.; de la Haba Agency, Lois; Diamant, Anita; Doyen Literary Services; Elek Assoc., Peter; Ellenberg Literary Agency, Ethan; Elmo Agency, Ann; Farber Literary Agency; Feiler Literary Agency, Florence; Flannery Literary; Fleury Agency, B.R.; Gibson Agency, Sebastian; Gordon Agency, Charlotte; Greenburger Assoc., Sanford J.; Gusay Literary Agency, Charlotte; Hampton Agency; Hawkins & Assoc., John; Hegler Literary Agency, Gary L.; Henshaw Group, Richard; Ievleva Literary Agency; J de S Assoc.; JABberwocky Literary Agency; Kirchoff/Wohlberg, Inc., Authors' Representation Division; Kouts, Literary Agent, Barbara S.; Levine Communications, James; Lincoln Literary Agency, Ray; Lyceum Creative Properties; Maccoby Literary Agency, Gina; Mainhardt Agency, Ricia; Markowitz Literary Agency, Barbara; Multimedia Product Development; Mura Enterprises, Dee; Naggar Literary Agency, Jean V.; Norma-Lewis Agency; Pelham Literary Agency; Pocono Literary Agency; Printed Tree; Pryor, Roberta; Rose Agency; Rubenstein Literary Agency, Pesha; Targ Literary Agency, Roslyn; Van Duren Agency, Annette; Vines Agency; Wald Assoc., Mary Jack; Wasserman Literary Agency, Harriet; Wecksler-Incomco; Wreschner, Authors' Representative, Ruth

Lesbian. Baldi Literary Agency, Malaga; Brandt & Brandt Literary Agents; Buck Agency, Howard; Circle of Confusion; Cypher, Author's Representative, James R.; DH Literary; Dupree/Miller and Assoc.; Dystel Literary Management, Jane; Eth Literary Representation, Felicia; Feiler Literary Agency, Florence; Gordon Agency, Charlotte; Greenburger Assoc., Sanford J.; Gusay Literary Agency, Charlotte; Hawkins & Assoc., John; Hulburt Literary Agency, Helane; JABberwocky Literary Agency; Kidde, Hoyt & Picard; Lantz-Joy Harris Literary Agency, Robert; Larsen/Elizabeth Pomada Literary Agents, Michael; Levant & Wales, Literary Agency; Lincoln Literary Agency, Ray; Literary Group; Lowenstein Associates; Lyceum Creative Properties; Mura Enterprises, Dee; Parks Agency, Richard; Paul Agency, The Richard; Pelter, Rodney; Perkins Assoc., L.; Pevner, Stephen; Potomac Literary Agency; Raymond, Literary Agent, Charlotte Cecil; Robbins Literary Agency, BJ; Rock Literary Agency; Sanders Literary Agency, Victoria; Schmidt Literary Agency, Harold; Schulman, Susan; Seligman, Literary Agent, Lynn; Spieler, F. Joseph; Steele & Co., Lyle; Travis Literary Agency, Susan; Witherspoon & Associates; Wreschner, Authors' Representative, Ruth; Wright Representatives, Ann; Ziegler Literary Agency, George

Literary. Acton, Leone, Hanson & Jaffe; Adler & Robin Books Inc.; Agents Inc. for Medical and Mental Health Professionals; Allan Agency, Lee; Altshuler Literary Agency, Miriam; Axelrod Agency; Baldi Literary Agency, Malaga; Behar Literary Agency, Josh; Blassingame Spectrum; Borchardt, Georges; Brandt Agency, Joan; Brandt & Brandt Literary Agents; Associates Inc., Marie; Brown, Curtis; Buck Agency, Howard; Bykofsky Assoc., Sheree; Cantrell-Colas, Literary Agency; Carvainis Agency, Maria; Castiglia Literary Agency; Circle of Confusion; Cohen, Literary Agency, Ruth; Collin Literary Agent, Frances; Congdon Associates, Don; Cornfield Literary Agency, Robert; Crown International Literature and Arts Agency, Bonnie R.; Cypher, Author's Representative, James R.; Darhansoff & Verrill Literary Agents; Daves Agency, Joan; de la Haba Agency, Lois; DH Literary; DHS Literary; Diamant, Anita; Dijkstra Literary Agency, Sandra; Doyen Literary Services; Ducas, Robert; Dupree/Miller and Assoc.; Dystel Literary Management, Jane; Ellenberg Literary Agency, Ethan; Elliott Agency; Ellison, Nicholas; Elmo Agency, Ann; Emerald Literary Agency; Eth Literary Representation, Felicia; Feiler Literary Agency, Florence; Flaherty, Literary Agent, Joyce A.; Flaming Star Literary Enterprises; Flannery Literary; Franklin Assoc., Lynn C.; Garon-Brooke Assoc., Jay; Gibson Agency, Sebastian; Goldfarb & Graybill, Attorneys at Law; Gordon Agency, Charlotte; Green, Literary Agent, Randall Elisha; Greenburger Assoc., Sanford J.; Gregory Assoc., Maia; Gusay Literary Agency, Charlotte; Halsey Agency, Reece; Hampton Agency; Hardy Agency; Hass Literary Agency, Rose; Hawkins & Assoc., John; Heacock Literary Agency, Inc.; Henshaw Group, Richard; Herner Rights Agency, Susan; Hill Associates, Frederick; Hulburt Literary Agency, Helane; Hull House Literary Agency; Ievleva Literary Agency; Img-Julian Bach Literary Agency; J de S Assoc.; JABberwocky Literary Agency; Kidde, Hoyt & Picard; Klinger, Harvey; Kouts, Literary Agent, Barbara S.; Kroll Literary Agency, Edite; Lampack Agency, Peter; Lantz-Joy Harris Literary Agency, Robert; Larsen/Elizabeth Pomada Literary Agents, Michael; Lasher Agency, Maureen; Levant & Wales, Literary Agency; Levine Communications, James; Levine Literary Agency, Ellen; Lewis & Co., Karen; Lincoln Literary Agency, Ray; Love Literary Agency, Nancy; Lowenstein Associates; Lyceum Creative Properties; Maass Literary Agency, Donald; McBride Literary Agency, Margret; Maccoby Literary Agency, Gina; McGrath, Helen; Mainhardt Agency, Ricia; Mann Agency, Carol; March Tenth; Markson Literary Agency, Elaine; Michaels Literary Agency; Miller Assoc., Roberta; Multimedia Product Development; Mura Enterprises, Dee; Naggar Literary Agency, Jean V.; Nazor Literary Agency, Karen; New Brand Agency Group; Nine Muses and Apollo; Nine Muses and Apollo; Palmer & Dodge Agency; Parks Agency, Richard; Paton Literary Agency, Kathi J.; Paul Agency, The Richard; Pelham Literary Agency; Pelter, Rodney; Perkins Assoc., L.; Pevner, Stephen; Pine Assoc., Arthur; Pom; Popkin, Julie; Potomac Literary Agency; Pryor, Roberta; Publishing Services; Quicksilver Books-Literary Agents; Raymond, Literary Agent, Charlotte Cecil; Rees Literary Agency, Helen; Renaissance—H.N. Swanson; Rinaldi Literary Agency, Angela; Robbins Literary Agency, BJ; Rock Literary Agency; Rose Literary Agency; Rowland Agency, Damaris; Russell-Simenauer Literary Agency; Sanders Literary Agency, Victoria; Sandum & Assoc.; Schmidt Literary Agency, Harold; Schulman, Susan; Schwartz Agency, Laurens R.; Seligman, Literary Agent, Lynn; Shepard Agency; Siegel Literary Agency, Bobbe; Singer Literary Agency, Evelyn; Smith, Literary Agent, Valerie; Spieler, F. Joseph; Spitzer Literary Agency, Philip G.; Stauffer Assoc., Nancy; Steele & Co., Lyle; Stepping Stone; Stern Literary Agency, Gloria (TX); Travis Literary Agency, Susan; Van Der Leun & Assoc.; Vines Agency; Wald Assoc., Mary Jack; Wallace Literary Agency; Watkins Loomis Agency, Inc.; Wecksler-Incomco; Weingel-Fidel Agency; Wieser & Wieser; Witherspoon & Associates; Wreschner, Authors' Representative, Ruth; Wright Representatives, Ann; Writers' Productions; Writers' Representatives; Zeckendorf Assoc., Susan; Ziegler Literary Agency, George

Mainstream. Acton, Leone, Hanson & Jaffe; Adler & Robin Books Inc.; Allan Agency, Lee; Allen, Literary Agency, James; Altshuler Literary Agency, Miriam; Amsterdam Agency, Marcia; Axelrod Agency; Baldi Literary Agency, Malaga; Bernstein, Pam; Blassingame Spectrum; Boates Literary Agency, Reid; Bova Literary Agency, Barbara; Brandt Agency, Joan; Brandt & Brandt Literary Agents; Brown Assoc., Marie; Buck Agency, Howard; Bykofsky Assoc., Sheree; Cantrell-Colas, Literary Agency; Carvainis Agency, Maria; Castiglia Literary Agency; Circle of Confusion; Cohen, Literary Agency, Ruth; Collin Literary Agent, Frances; Collins Purvis, Ltd.; Columbia Literary Assoc.; Curtis Associates, Richard; Cypher, Author's Representative, James R.; Daves Agency, Joan; de la Haba Agency, Lois; DH Literary; DHS Literary; Diamant, Anita; Diamond Literary Agency; Dijkstra Literary Agency, Sandra; Doyen Literary Services; Ducas, Robert; Dupree/Miller and Assoc.; Dystel Literary Management, Jane; Ellenberg Literary Agency, Ethan; Elliott Agency; Ellison, Nicholas; Elmo Agency, Ann; Esq. Literary Productions; Eth Literary Representation, Felicia; Farber Literary Agency; Feiler Literary Agency, Florence; Flaherty, Literary Agent, Joyce A.; Flannery Literary; Fleury Agency, B.R.; Franklin Assoc., Lynn C.; Garon-Brooke Assoc., Jay; Gibson Agency, Sebastian; Goddard Book Group; Goldfarb & Graybill, Attorneys at Law; Green, Literary Agent, Randall Elisha; Greenburger Assoc., Sanford J.; Gusay Literary Agency, Charlotte; Halsey Agency, Reece; Hawkins & Assoc., John; Hegler Literary Agency, Gary L.; Henshaw Group, Richard; Herner Rights Agency, Susan; Hill Associates, Frederick; Hulburt Literary Agency, Helane; Hull House Literary Agency; Ievleva Literary Agency; Img-Julian Bach Literary Agency; Int'l Publisher Associates Inc.; J de S Assoc.; Kidde, Hoyt & Picard; Klinger, Harvey; Kouts, Literary Agent, Barbara S.; Lampack Agency, Peter; Lantz-Joy Harris Literary Agency, Robert; Larsen/Elizabeth Pomada Literary Agents, Michael; Lasher Agency, Maureen; Levant & Wales, Literary Agency; Levine Communications, James; Lewis & Co., Karen; Lincoln Literary Agency, Ray; Lindstrom Literary Group; Lipkind Agency, Wendy; Lord Literistic, Inc., Sterling; Lowenstein Associates; Lyceum Creative Properties; Maass Literary Agency, Donald; McBride Literary Agency, Margret; Maccoby Literary Agency, Gina; McGrath, Helen; Mainhardt Agency, Ricia; Manus & Associates Literary Agency; March Tenth; Markowitz Literary Agency, Barbara; Markson Literary Agency, Elaine; Metropolitan Talent Agency; Michaels Literary Agency; Miller Assoc., Roberta; Multimedia Product Development; Mura Enterprises, Dee; Naggar Literary Agency, Jean V.; New Brand Agency Group; Nine Muses and Apollo; Norma-Lewis Agency; Orr Agency, Alice; Otitis Media; Palmer & Dodge Agency; Parks Agency, Richard; Paton Literary Agency, Kathi J.; Paul Agency, The Richard; Pelham Literary Agency; Pelter, Rodney; Perkins Assoc., L.; PPevner, Stephen; Pine Assoc., Arthur; Pom; Popkin, Julie; Potomac Literary Agency; Printed Tree; Pryor, Roberta; Publishing Services; Quicksilver Books-Literary Agents; Raymond, Literary Agent, Charlotte Cecil; Rees Literary Agency, Helen; Renaissance—H.N. Swanson; Rinaldi Literary Agency, Angela; Robbins Literary Agency, BJ; Rock Literary Agency; Rose Agency; Rowland Agency, Damaris; Rubenstein Literary Agency, Pesha; Russell-Simenauer Literary Agency; St. Clair Literary Agency; Sandum & Assoc.; Schmidt Literary Agency, Harold; Schulman, Susan; Schwartz Agency, Laurens R.; Seligman, Literary Agent, Lynn; Seymour Agency; Siegel Literary Agency, Bobbe; Sierra Literary Agency; Singer Literary Agency, Evelyn; Smith, Literary Agent, Valerie; Spieler, F. Joseph; Spitzer Literary Agency, Philip G.; Stauffer Assoc., Nancy; Stepping Stone; Stern Literary Agency, Gloria (TX); Teal Literary Agency, Patricia; Travis Literary Agency, Susan; Van Der Leun & Assoc.; Van Duren Agency, Annette; Vines Agency; Wald Assoc., Mary Jack; Wallace Literary Agency; Ware Literary Agency, John A.; Watkins Loomis Agency, Inc.; Watt & Assoc., Sandra; Wecksler-Incomco; Weiner Literary Agency, Cherry; Weingel-Fidel Agency; Wieser & Wieser; Witherspoon & Associates; Wreschner, Authors' Representative, Ruth; Wright Representatives, Ann; Zeckendorf Assoc., Susan; Ziegler Literary Agency, George

Multimedia. Curtis Associates, Richard; Elek Assoc., Peter; Kellock Company; Larsen/Elizabeth Pomada Literary Agents, Michael; Lazear Agency Inc.; Multimedia Product Development; Nine Muses and Apollo; Renaissance—H.N. Swanson; Writers House; Writers' Productions

Mystery/suspense. Act I; Acton, Leone, Hanson & Jaffe; Adler & Robin Books Inc.; Agents Inc. for Medical and Mental Health Professionals; Allan Agency, Lee; Allen, Literary Agency, James; Amsterdam Agency, Marcia; Appleseeds Management; Authors' Literary Agency; Axelrod Agency; Baldi Literary Agency, Malaga; Becker Literary Agency, Wendy; Bernstein, Pam; Blassingame Spectrum; Boates Literary Agency, Reid; Bova Literary Agency, Barbara; Brandt Agency, Joan; Brandt & Brandt Literary Agents; Brown Assoc., Marie; Brown, Curtis; Buck Agency, Howard; Butler, Art and Literary Agent, Jane; Bykofsky Assoc., Sheree; Cantrell-Colas, Literary Agency; Carvainis Agency, Maria; Castiglia Literary Agency; Charisma Communications; Circle of Confusion; Ciske & Dietz Literary Agency; Cohen, Literary Agency, Ruth; Collin Literary Agent, Frances; Collins Purvis, Ltd.; Columbia Literary Assoc.; Curtis Associates, Richard; Cypher, Author's Representative, James R.; de la Haba Agency, Lois; DHS Literary; Diamant, Anita; Diamond Literary Agency; Dijkstra Literary Agency, Sandra; Doyen

Literary Services; Ducas, Robert; Dupree/Miller and Assoc.; Ellenberg Literary Agency, Ethan; Elmo Agency, Ann; Esq. Literary Productions; Farber Literary Agency; Feiler Literary Agency, Florence; Flaherty, Literary Agent, Joyce A.; Flannery Literary; Garon-Brooke Assoc., Jay; Gibson Agency, Sebastian; Goddard Book Group; Goldfarb & Graybill, Attorneys at Law; Gordon Agency, Charlotte; Graham Literary Agency; Greenburger Assoc., Sanford J.; Greene, Arthur B.; Gusay Literary Agency, Charlotte; Halsey Agency, Reece; Hawkins & Assoc., John; Hegler Literary Agency, Gary L.; Herner Rights Agency, Susan; Hull House Literary Agency; Ievleva Literary Agency; J de S Assoc.; JABberwocky Literary Agency; Kidde, Hoyt & Picard; Klinger, Harvey; Kouts, Literary Agent, Barbara S.; Kroll Literary Agency, Edite; Lampack Agency, Peter; Lantz-Joy Harris Literary Agency, The Robert; Larsen/Elizabeth Pomada Literary Agents, Michael; Levine Literary Agency, Ellen; Lewis & Co., Karen; Lincoln Literary Agency, Ray; Lipkind Agency, Wendy; Literary Group; Love Literary Agency, Nancy; Lowenstein Associates; Lyceum Creative Properties; Maass Literary Agency, Donald; McBride Literary Agency, Margret; Maccoby Literary Agency, Gina; McGrath, Helen; Madsen Agency, Robert; Manus & Associates Literary Agency; March Tenth; Markowitz Literary Agency, Barbara; Metropolitan Talent Agency; Multimedia Product Development; Mura Enterprises, Dee; Naggar Literary Agency, Jean V.; New Brand Agency Group; Norma-Lewis Agency; Otitis Media; Parks Agency, Richard; Pelham Literary Agency; Pelter, Rodney; Perkins Assoc., L.; Pom; Popkin, Julie; Protter Literary Agent, Susan Ann; Pryor, Roberta; Quicksilver Books-Literary Agents; Rees Literary Agency, Helen; Renaissance—H.N. Swanson; Robbins Literary Agency, BJ; Rock Literary Agency; Rose Agency; Rowland Agency, Damaris; Rubenstein Literary Agency, Pesha; Russell-Simenauer Literary Agency; Schmidt Literary Agency, Harold; Schulman, Susan; Seligman, Literary Agent, Lynn; Seymour Agency; Siegel Literary Agency, Bobbe; Singer Literary Agency, Evelyn; Spitzer Literary Agency, Philip G.; Steele & Co., Lyle; Stepping Stone; Stern Literary Agency, Gloria (TX); Targ Literary Agency, Roslyn; Teal Literary Agency, Patricia; Toad Hall; Travis Literary Agency, Susan; Vines Agency; Wald Assoc., Mary Jack; Wallace Literary Agency; Ware Literary Agency, John A.; Watkins Loomis Agency, Inc.; Watt & Assoc., Sandra; Weiner Literary Agency, Cherry; Wieser & Wieser; Witherspoon & Associates; Wreschner, Authors' Representative, Ruth; Wright Representatives, Ann; Zeckendorf Assoc., Susan

Open to all fiction categories. Author's Agency; Barrett Books, Loretta; Brown, Curtis; Bykofsky Assoc., Sheree; Circle of Confusion; Cohen Literary Agency, Hy; Congdon Associates, Don; Dragon Literary; Hamilburg Agency, Mitchell J.; Hoffman Literary Agency, Berenice; Lazear Agency Inc.; Maccampbell, Donald; Madsen Agency, Robert; Martell Agency; Ober Assoc., Harold; Rogers Literary Representation, Irene; Writers House; Zahler Literary Agency, Karen Gantz

Picture book. Act I; Axelrod Agency; Brown Assoc., Marie; Brown Literary Agency, Andrea; Circle of Confusion; Cohen, Literary Agency, Ruth; Collins Purvis, Ltd.; Doyen Literary Services; Dupree/Miller and Assoc.; Elek Assoc., Peter; Ellenberg Literary Agency, Ethan; Flannery Literary; Gibson Agency, Sebastian; Gusay Literary Agency, Charlotte; Hampton Agency; Hawkins & Assoc., John; JABberwocky Literary Agency; Kouts, Literary Agent, Barbara S.; Kroll Literary Agency, Edite; Lantz-Joy Harris Literary Agency, Robert; Lyceum Creative Properties; Mainhardt Agency, Ricia; Multimedia Product Development; Norma-Lewis Agency; Pocono Literary Agency; Rubenstein Literary Agency, Pesha; Vines Agency; Wald Assoc., Mary Jack; Wecksler-Incomco

Psychic/supernatural. Allan Agency, Lee; Appleseeds Management; Behar Literary Agency, Josh; Buck Agency, Howard; Cantrell-Colas, Literary Agency; Circle of Confusion; Collin Literary Agent, Frances; Collins Purvis, Ltd.; Cypher, Author's Representative, James R.; DH Literary; Diamant, Anita; Doyen Literary Services; Dupree/Miller and Assoc.; Elmo Agency, Ann; Flaherty, Literary Agent, Joyce A.; Fleury Agency, B.R.; Gibson Agency, Sebastian; Greenburger Assoc., Sanford J.; Gusay Literary Agency, Charlotte; Hampton Agency; Hawkins & Assoc., John; Heacock Literary Agency, Inc.; Henshaw Group, Richard; Ievleva Literary Agency; JABberwocky Literary Agency; Lantz-Joy Harris Literary Agency, Robert; Larsen/Elizabeth Pomada Literary Agents, Michael; Lincoln Literary Agency, Ray; Literary Group; Lyceum Creative Properties; Maass Literary Agency, Donald; McGrath, Helen; Mainhardt Agency, Ricia; Mura Enterprises, Dee; Naggar Literary Agency, Jean V.; Parks Agency, Richard; Pelter, Rodney; Perkins Assoc., L.; Pevner, Stephen; Rock Literary Agency; Rowland Agency, Damaris; Rubenstein Literary Agency, Pesha; Russell-Simenauer Literary Agency; Schmidt Literary Agency, Harold; Siegel Literary Agency, Bobbe; Steele & Co., Lyle; Vines Agency; Wald Assoc., Mary Jack; Weiner Literary Agency, Cherry; Ziegler Literary Agency, George

Regional. Baldi Literary Agency, Malaga; Bova Literary Agency, Barbara; Brandt & Brandt Literary Agents; Brown Assoc., Marie; Buck Agency, Howard; Circle of Confusion; Collin Literary Agent, Frances; Elliott Agency; Elmo Agency, Ann; Fleury Agency, B.R.; Gibson Agency, Sebastian; Green, Literary Agent, Randall Elisha; Greenburger Assoc., Sanford J.; Gusay Literary Agency, Charlotte; Hawkins & Assoc., John; JABberwocky Literary Agency; Kidde, Hoyt & Picard; Lantz-Joy Harris Literary Agency, Robert; Lincoln Literary Agency, Ray; Mura Enterprises, Dee; Naggar Literary Agency, Jean V.; Nazor Literary Agency, Karen; Paul Agency, The Richard; Pelter, Rodney; Raymond, Literary Agent, Charlotte Cecil; Rock Literary Agency; Shepard Agency; Singer Literary Agency, Evelyn; Vines Agency

Religious/inspiration. Brandenburgh & Assoc. Literary Agency; Buck Agency, Howard; Charisma Communications; Circle of Confusion; Ciske & Dietz Literary Agency; de la Haba Agency, Lois; Diamant, Anita; Dupree/Miller and Assoc.; Emerald Literary Agency; Feiler Literary Agency, Florence; Gibson Agency, Sebastian; Gusay Literary Agency, Charlotte; Hawkins & Assoc., John; Hegler Literary Agency, Gary L.; Hulburt Literary Agency, Helane; Ievleva Literary Agency; Lantz-Joy Harris Literary Agency, Robert; Larsen/Elizabeth Pomada Literary Agents, Michael; Multimedia Product Development; New Brand Agency Group; Pelter, Rodney; Printed Tree; Rock Literary Agency; Rose Agency; Seymour Agency

Romance. Act I; Acton, Leone, Hanson & Jaffe; Adler & Robin Books Inc.; Allan Agency, Lee; Allen, Literary

Agency, James; Amsterdam Agency, Marcia; Axelrod Agency; Becker Literary Agency, Wendy; Behar Literary Agency, Josh; Bernstein, Pam; Bova Literary Agency, Barbara; Brandt & Brandt Literary Agents; Brown Literary Agency, Andrea; Buck Agency, Howard; Carvainis Agency, Maria; Circle of Confusion; Ciske & Dietz Literary Agency; Cohen, Literary Agency, Ruth; Collin Literary Agent, Frances; Columbia Literary Assoc.; Curtis Associates, Richard; Diamant, Anita; Diamond Literary Agency; Doyen Literary Services; Dupree/Miller and Assoc.; Ellenberg Literary Agency, Ethan; Elmo Agency, Ann; Farber Literary Agency; Feiler Literary Agency, Florence; Flaherty, Literary Agent, Joyce A.; Fleury Agency, B.R.; Fogelman Literary Agency; Garon-Brooke Assoc., Jay; Gibson Agency, Sebastian; Gordon Agency, Charlotte; Green, Literary Agent, Randall Elisha; Hampton Agency; Herner Rights Agency, Susan; Ievleva Literary Agency; JABberwocky Literary Agency; Kidde, Hoyt & Picard; Klinger, Harvey; Kouts, Literary Agent, Barbara S.; Lantz-Joy Harris Literary Agency, Robert; Larsen/Elizabeth Pomada Literary Agents, Michael; Lincoln Literary Agency, Ray; Literary Group; Lowenstein Associates; Lyceum Creative Properties; McGrath, Helen; Mainhardt Agency, Ricia; Multimedia Product Development; Mura Enterprises, Dee; New Brand Agency Group; Norma-Lewis Agency; Orr Agency, Alice; Parks Agency, Richard; Pelham Literary Agency; Pine Assoc., Arthur; Pocono Literary Agency; Rock Literary Agency; Rose Agency; Rowland Agency, Damaris; Rubenstein Literary Agency, Pesha; Russell-Simenauer Literary Agency; St. Clair Literary Agency; Seymour Agency; Siegel Literary Agency, Bobbe; Teal Literary Agency, Patricia; Toad Hall; Travis Literary Agency, Susan; Vines Agency; Wald Assoc., Mary Jack; Weiner Literary Agency, Cherry; Witherspoon & Associates; Wreschner, Authors' Representative, Ruth; Wright Representatives, Ann

Science fiction. Act I; Adler & Robin Books Inc.; Allan Agency, Lee; Allen, Literary Agency, James; Amsterdam Agency, Marcia; Appleseeds Management; Becker Literary Agency, Wendy; Behar Literary Agency, Josh; Blassingame Spectrum; Bova Literary Agency, Barbara; Brandt & Brandt Literary Agents; Brown Assoc., Marie; Brown Literary Agency, Andrea; Buck Agency, Howard; Butler, Art and Literary Agent, Jane; Cantrell-Colas, Literary Agency; Circle of Confusion; Collin Literary Agent, Frances; Collins Purvis, Ltd.; Curtis Associates, Richard; Doyen Literary Services; Dupree/Miller and Assoc.; Ellenberg Literary Agency, Ethan; Fleury Agency, B.R.; Garon-Brooke Assoc., Jay; Gibson Agency, Sebastian; Graham Literary Agency; Halsey Agency, Reece; Hampton Agency; Hawkins & Assoc., John; Henshaw Group, Richard; Herner Rights Agency, Susan; Ievleva Literary Agency; JABberwocky Literary Agency; Kidd, Literary Agent, Virginia; Lewis & Co., Karen; Lincoln Literary Agency, Ray; Lindstrom Literary Group; Literary Group; Lyceum Creative Properties; Maass Literary Agency, Donald; McGrath, Helen; Madsen Agency, Robert; Mainhardt Agency, Ricia; Metropolitan Talent Agency; Mura Enterprises, Dee; Naggar Literary Agency, Jean V.; New Brand Agency Group; Pelham Literary Agency; Pevner, Stephen; Pocono Literary Agency; Printed Tree; Protter Literary Agent, Susan Ann; Rees Literary Agency, Helen; Renaissance—H.N. Swanson; Rock Literary Agency; Schmidt Literary Agency, Harold; Siegel Literary Agency, Bobbe; Smith, Literary Agent, Valerie; Targ Literary Agency, Roslyn; Toad Hall; Van Duren Agency, Annette; Vines Agency; Wald Assoc., Mary Jack; Weiner Literary Agency, Cherry

Sports. Acton, Leone, Hanson & Jaffe; Brandt & Brandt Literary Agents; Buck Agency, Howard; Charisma Communications; Charlton Associates, James; Circle of Confusion; Cypher, Author's Representative, James R.; DHS Literary; Ducas, Robert; Dupree/Miller and Assoc.; Flannery Literary; Fleury Agency, B.R.; Gibson Agency, Sebastian; Greenburger Assoc., Sanford J.; Greene, Arthur B.; Gusay Literary Agency, Charlotte; Hawkins & Assoc., John; Henshaw Group, Richard; Ievleva Literary Agency; JABberwocky Literary Agency; Lantz-Joy Harris Literary Agency, Robert; Lasher Agency, Maureen; Lincoln Literary Agency, Ray; Literary Group; Mainhardt Agency, Ricia; Markowitz Literary Agency, Barbara; Multimedia Product Development; Mura Enterprises, Dee; New Brand Agency Group; Pelham Literary Agency; Pelter, Rodney; Pocono Literary Agency; Pom; Potomac Literary Agency; Robbins Literary Agency, BJ; Rock Literary Agency; Shepard Agency; Spitzer Literary Agency, Philip G.; Vines Agency; Wald Assoc., Mary Jack; Wright Representatives, Ann

Thriller/espionage. Acton, Leone, Hanson & Jaffe; Adler & Robin Books; Allan Agency, Lee; Amsterdam Agency, Marcia; Authors' Literary Agency; Axelrod Agency; Baldi Literary Agency, Malaga; Becker Literary Agency, Wendy; Behar Literary Agency, Josh; Bernstein, Pam; Boates Literary Agency, Reid; Bova Literary Agency, Barbara; Brandt Agency, Joan; Brandt & Brandt Literary Agents; Buck Agency, Howard; Cantrell-Colas, Literary Agency; Carvainis Agency, Maria; Circle of Confusion; Ciske & Dietz Literary Agency; Collins Purvis, Ltd.; Columbia Literary Assoc.; Curtis Associates, Richard; Cypher, Author's Representative, James R.; Darhansoff & Verrill Literary Agents; Daves Agency, Joan; DH Literary; DHS Literary; Diamant, Anita; Diamond Literary Agency; Dijkstra Literary Agency, Sandra; Doyen Literary Services; Ducas, Robert; Dupree/Miller and Assoc.; Dystel Literary Management, Jane; Ellenberg Literary Agency, Ethan; Elliott Agency; Elmo Agency, Ann; Esq. Literary Productions; Eth Literary Representation, Felicia; Farber Literary Agency; Flaherty, Literary Agent, Joyce A.; Fleury Agency, B.R.; Gibson Agency, Sebastian; Goddard Book Group; Goldfarb & Graybill, Attorneys at Law; Graham Literary Agency; Green, Literary Agent, Randall Elisha; Greenburger Assoc., Sanford J.; Greene, Arthur B.; Gusay Literary Agency, Charlotte; Halsey Agency, Reece; Hawkins & Assoc., John; Henshaw Group, Richard; Herner Rights Agency, Susan; Ievleva Literary Agency; JABberwocky Literary Agency; Kidde, Hoyt & Picard; Klinger, Harvey; Lampack Agency, Peter; Lantz-Joy Harris Literary Agency, Robert; Lasher Agency, Maureen; Levine Literary Agency, Ellen; Lewis & Co., Karen; Lincoln Literary Agency, Ray; Lindstrom Literary Group; Literary Group; Love Literary Agency, Nancy; Lowenstein Associates; Lyceum Creative Properties; Maass Literary Agency, Donald; McBride Literary Agency, Margret; Maccoby Literary Agency, Gina; McGrath, Helen; Mainhardt Agency, Ricia; Manus & Associates Literary Agency; March Tenth; Markowitz Literary Agency, Barbara; Metropolitan Talent Agency; Michaels Literary Agency; Multimedia Product Development; Mura Enterprises, Dee; Naggar Literary Agency, Jean V.; New Brand Agency Group; Norma-Lewis Agency; Otitis Media; Parks Agency, Richard; Pelham Literary Agency; Pelter, Rodney; Perkins Assoc., L.; Pevner Inc, Stephen; Pine Assoc., Arthur; Pocono Literary Agency; Pom; Potomac Literary Agency; Printed Tree; Protter Literary Agent, Susan Ann; Rees Literary

Agency, Helen; Renaissance—H.N. Swanson; Rinaldi Literary Agency, Angela; Robbins Literary Agency, BJ; Rock Literary Agency; Rose Agency; Rose Literary Agency; Russell-Simenauer Literary Agency; Sanders Literary Agency, Victoria; Schmidt Literary Agency, Harold; Shepard Agency; Siegel Literary Agency, Bobbe; Singer Literary Agency, Evelyn; Spitzer Literary Agency, Philip G.; Steele & Co., Lyle; Stepping Stone; Stern Literary Agency, Gloria (TX); Targ Literary Agency, Roslyn; Travis Literary Agency, Susan; Valcourt Agency, Richard R.; Van Duren Agency, Annette; Vines Agency; Wald Assoc., Mary Jack; Ware Literary Agency, John A.; Watt & Assoc., Sandra; Weiner Literary Agency, Cherry; Wieser & Wieser; Witherspoon & Associates; Wreschner, Authors' Representative, Ruth; Wright Representatives, Ann; Zeckendorf Assoc., Susan

Westerns/frontier. Agency Chicago; Amsterdam Agency, Marcia; Brandt & Brandt Literary Agents; Buck Agency, Howard; Carvainis Agency, Maria; Circle of Confusion; Ciske & Dietz Literary Agency; Curtis Associates, Richard; DH Literary; DHS Literary; Diamant, Anita; Doyen Literary Services; Dupree/Miller and Assoc.; Ellenberg Literary Agency, Ethan; Flaherty, Literary Agent, Joyce A.; Flannery Literary; Fleury Agency, B.R.; Gibson Agency, Sebastian; Gusay Literary Agency, Charlotte; Hawkins & Assoc., John; Hegler Literary Agency, Gary L.; Ievlela Literary Agency; J de S Assoc.; Lindstrom Literary Group; Literary Group; Lyceum Creative Properties; McBride Literary Agency, Margret; McGrath, Helen; Madsen Agency, Robert; Mainhardt Agency, Ricia; Multimedia Product Development; Mura Enterprises, Dee; Norma-Lewis Agency; Parks Agency, Richard; Pelham Literary Agency; Pelter, Rodney; Pocono Literary Agency; Potomac Literary Agency; Rock Literary Agency; Rose Agency; Schmidt Literary Agency, Harold; Seymour Agency; Targ Literary Agency, Roslyn; Vines Agency; Wald Assoc., Mary Jack; Weiner Literary Agency, Cherry; Wright Representatives, Ann

Young adult. Allen, Literary Agency, James; Amsterdam Agency, Marcia; Brandt & Brandt Literary Agents; Brown Literary Agency, Andrea; Butler, Art and Literary Agent, Jane; Cantrell-Colas, Literary Agency; Carvainis Agency, Maria; Casselman Literary Agent, Martha; Circle of Confusion; Ciske & Dietz Literary Agency; Cohen, Literary Agency, Ruth; Collins Purvis, Ltd.; de la Haba Agency, Lois; Diamant, Anita; Doyen Literary Services; Ellenberg Literary Agency, Ethan; Elmo Agency, Ann; Farber Literary Agency; Feiler Literary Agency, Florence; Flannery Literary; Fleury Agency, B.R.; Gibson Agency, Sebastian; Gordon Agency, Charlotte; Gusay Literary Agency, Charlotte; Hampton Agency; Hegler Literary Agency, Gary L.; Henshaw Group, Richard; Ievlela Literary Agency; J de S Assoc.; JABberwocky Literary Agency; Kirchoff/Wohlberg, Inc., Authors' Representation Division; Kouts, Literary Agent, Barbara S.; Lantz-Joy Harris Literary Agency, Robert; Levine Communications, James; Lincoln Literary Agency, Ray; Literary Group; Maccoby Literary Agency, Gina; Mainhardt Agency, Ricia; Markowitz Literary Agency, Barbara; Miller Assoc., Roberta; Mura Enterprises, Dee; Norma-Lewis Agency; Parks Agency, Richard; Pelham Literary Agency; Pocono Literary Agency; Printed Tree; Pryor, Roberta; Raymond, Literary Agent, Charlotte Cecil; Rose Agency; Schulman, Susan; Smith, Literary Agent, Valerie; Van Duren Agency, Annette; Vines Agency; Wald Assoc., Mary Jack; Wasserman Literary Agency, Harriet; Watkins Loomis Agency, Inc.; Wreschner, Authors' Representative, Ruth; Wright Representatives, Ann

Nonfee-charging literary agents/Nonfiction

Agriculture/horticulture. Baldi Literary Agency, Malaga; Brandt & Brandt Literary Agents; Buck Agency, Howard; Casselman Literary Agent, Martha; de la Haba Agency, Lois; DH Literary; Doyen Literary Services; Ellison, Nicholas; Fleury Agency, B.R.; Gartenberg, Literary Agent, Max; Goddard Book Group; Green, Literary Agent, Randall Elisha; Hawkins & Assoc., John; Levant & Wales, Literary Agency; Levine Communications, James; Lieberman Assoc., Robert; Lincoln Literary Agency, Ray; Mainhardt Agency, Ricia; Multimedia Product Development; Mura Enterprises, Dee; Parks Agency, Richard; Shepard Agency; Taylor Literary Enterprises, Sandra; Travis Literary Agency, Susan; Urstadt Agency, Susan P.

Animals. Acton, Leone, Hanson & Jaffe; Author's Agency; Baldi Literary Agency, Malaga; Balkin Agency; Becker Literary Agency, Wendy; Boates Literary Agency, Reid; Brandt & Brandt Literary Agents; Brown Literary Agency, Andrea; Buck Agency, Howard; Castiglia Literary Agency; Collins Purvis, Ltd.; Cornfield Literary Agency, Robert; DH Literary; Diamant, Anita; Doyen Literary Services; Ducas, Robert; Dystel Literary Management, Jane; Ellison, Nicholas; Eth Literary Representation, Felicia; Flaherty, Literary Agent, Joyce A.; Fleury Agency, B.R.; Gartenberg, Literary Agent, Max; Gibson Agency, Sebastian; Goddard Book Group; Greene, Arthur B.; Hawkins & Assoc., John; Hegler Literary Agency, Gary L.; Henshaw Group, Richard; Ievleva Literary Agency; Lasher Agency, Maureen; Levant & Wales, Literary Agency; Levine Communications, James; Lincoln Literary Agency, Ray; Literary Group; Love Literary Agency, Nancy; Lowenstein Associates; Mainhardt Agency, Ricia; Multimedia Product Development; Mura Enterprises, Dee; Nine Muses and Apollo; Parks Agency, Richard; Pryor, Roberta; Rowland Agency, Damaris; Shepard Agency; Stauffer Assoc., Nancy; Stepping Stone; Taylor Literary Enterprises, Sandra; Teal Literary Agency, Patricia; Toad Hall; Ubel Assoc., Robert; Urstadt Agency, Susan P.; Watt & Assoc., Sandra; Writers House; Ziegler Literary Agency, George

Anthropology. Author's Agency; Baldi Literary Agency, Malaga; Balkin Agency; Becker Literary Agency, Wendy; Boates Literary Agency, Reid; Borchardt, Georges; Brandt & Brandt Literary Agents; Brown Literary Agency, Andrea; Buck Agency, Howard; Cantrell-Colas, Literary Agency; Casselman Literary Agent, Martha; Castiglia Literary Agency; Circle of Confusion; Collin Literary Agent, Frances; Collins Purvis, Ltd.; Coover Agency, Doe; Cornfield Literary Agency, Robert; Darhansoff & Verrill Literary Agents; de la Haba Agency, Lois; DH Literary; Dijkstra Literary Agency, Sandra; Doyen Literary Services; Dystel Literary Management, Jane; Educational Design Services; Elek Assoc., Peter; Elliott Agency; Ellison, Nicholas; Elmo Agency, Ann; Eth Literary Representation, Felicia; Fleury Agency, B.R.; Gibson Agency, Sebastian; Goddard Book Group; Gordon Agency, Charlotte; Hawkins & Assoc., John; Heacock Literary Agency, Inc.; Herner Rights Agency, Susan; Hochmann Books, John

L.; Hull House Literary Agency; Img-Julian Bach Literary Agency; James Peter Assoc.; Kellock Company; Ketz Agency, Louise B.; Lampack Agency, Peter; Larsen/Elizabeth Pomada Literary Agents, Michael; Lasher Agency, Maureen; Levant & Wales, Literary Agency; Levine Literary Agency, Ellen; Lieberman Assoc., Robert; Lincoln Literary Agency, Ray; Literary Group; Lowenstein Associates; Lyceum Creative Properties; Mainhardt Agency, Ricia; Mann Agency, Carol; Miller Agency; Morrison, Henry; Multimedia Product Development; Mura Enterprises, Dee; Palmer & Dodge Agency; Parks Agency, Richard; Pryor, Roberta; Quicksilver Books-Literary Agents; Rinaldi Literary Agency, Angela; Rose Literary Agency; Schmidt Literary Agency, Harold; Schulman, Susan; Sebastian Literary Agency; Seligman, Literary Agent, Lynn; Siegel Literary Agency, Bobbe; Singer Literary Agency, Evelyn; Steele & Co., Lyle; Stepping Stone; Stern Literary Agency, Gloria (TX); Toad Hall; Ubel Assoc., Robert; Urstadt Agency, Susan P.; Wallace Literary Agency; Ware Literary Agency, John A.; Waterside Productions; Watt & Assoc., Sandra; Witherspoon & Associates, Inc.; Ziegler Literary Agency, George

Art/architecture/design. Agency Chicago; Author's Agency; Becker Literary Agency, Wendy; Boates Literary Agency, Reid; Brandt & Brandt Literary Agents; Brown Associates Inc., Marie; Brown Literary Agency, Andrea; Buck Agency, Howard; Cantrell-Colas, Literary Agency; Collins Purvis, Ltd.; Cornfield Literary Agency, Robert; de la Haba Agency, Lois; DH Literary; Diamant, Anita; Doyen Literary Services; Ellison, Nicholas; Elmo Agency, Ann; Emerald Literary Agency; Feiler Literary Agency, Florence; Fleury Agency, B.R.; Gartenberg, Literary Agent, Max; Gibson Agency, Sebastian; Goddard Book Group; Gregory Assoc., Maia; Hass Literary Agency, Rose; Hawkins & Assoc., John; Heacock Literary Agency, Inc.; Henderson Literary Representation; Hochmann Books, John L.; Hull House Literary Agency; Ievleva Literary Agency; James Peter Assoc.; Kellock Company; Kidde, Hoyt & Picard; Lampack Agency, Peter; Larsen/Elizabeth Pomada Literary Agents, Michael; Lasher Agency, Maureen; Levant & Wales, Literary Agency; Levine Communications, James; Lieberman Assoc., Robert; Lincoln Literary Agency, Ray; Lowenstein Associates; Lyceum Creative Properties; Mann Agency, Carol; Michaels Literary Agency; Miller Agency; Miller Assoc., Roberta; Nathan, Ruth; Norma-Lewis Agency; Parks Agency, Richard; Perkins Assoc., L.; Pevner, Stephen; Popkin, Julie; Pryor, Roberta; Rose Literary Agency; Schmidt Literary Agency, Harold; Sebastian Literary Agency; Seligman, Literary Agent, Lynn; Seymour Agency; Stepping Stone; Stern Literary Agency, Gloria (TX); Urstadt Agency, Susan P.; Van Der Leun & Assoc.; Waterside Productions; Watkins Loomis Agency; Wecksler-Incomco; Weingel-Fidel Agency; Writers House; Zeckendorf Assoc., Susan

Biography/autobiography. Act I; Acton, Leone, Hanson & Jaffe; Adler & Robin Books; Ajlouny Agency, Joseph S.; Altshuler Literary Agency, Miriam; Andrews & Associates Inc., Bart; Author's Agency; Baldi Literary Agency, Malaga; Balkin Agency; Becker Literary Agency, Wendy; Behar Literary Agency, Josh; Bernstein, Pam; Boates Literary Agency, Reid; Borchardt, Georges; Brandt & Brandt Literary Agents; Brown Associates Inc., Marie; Brown Literary Agency, Andrea; Buck Agency, Howard; Bykofsky Assoc., Sheree; Cantrell-Colas, Literary Agency; Carvainis Agency, Maria; Casselman Literary Agent, Martha; Castiglia Literary Agency; Charisma Communications; Circle of Confusion; Clausen Assoc., Connie; Collin Literary Agent, Frances; Collins Purvis, Ltd.; Coover Agency, Doe; Cornfield Literary Agency, Robert; Crawford Literary Agency; Curtis Associates, Richard; Cypher, Author's Representative, James R.; Darhansoff & Verrill Literary Agents; Daves Agency, Joan; de la Haba Agency, Lois; DH Literary; DHS Literary; Diamant, Anita; Dijkstra Literary Agency, Sandra; Doyen Literary Services; Ducas, Robert; Dystel Literary Management, Jane; Ellenberg Literary Agency, Ethan; Elmo Agency, Ann; Emerald Literary Agency; Eth Literary Representation, Felicia; Flaherty, Literary Agent, Joyce A.; Fleury Agency, B.R.; Fogelman Literary Agency; Franklin Assoc., Lynn C.; Garon-Brooke Assoc. Inc., Jay; Gartenberg, Literary Agent, Max; Gibson Agency, Sebastian; Goddard Book Group; Green, Literary Agent, Randall Elisha; Halsey Agency, Reece; Hardy Agency; Hass Literary Agency, Rose; Hawkins & Assoc., John; Heacock Literary Agency, Inc.; Hegler Literary Agency, Gary L.; Henderson Literary Representation; Henshaw Group, Richard; Herner Rights Agency, Susan; Hill Associates, Frederick; Hochmann Books, John L.; Holub and Assoc.; Hulburt Literary Agency, Helane; Hull House Literary Agency; Ievleva Literary Agency; Img-Julian Bach Literary Agency; J de S Assoc.; JABberwocky Literary Agency; James Peter Assoc.; Jordan Literary Agency, Lawrence; Kellock Company; Ketz Agency, Louise B.; Kidde, Hoyt & Picard; Klinger, Harvey; Kouts, Literary Agent, Barbara S.; Lampack Agency, Peter; Larsen/Elizabeth Pomada Literary Agents, Michael; Lasher Agency, Maureen; Levant & Wales, Literary Agency; Levine Communications, James; Levine Literary Agency, Ellen; Lincoln Literary Agency, Ray; Lindstrom Literary Group; Lipkind Agency, Wendy; Literary Group; Love Literary Agency, Nancy; Lowenstein Associates; Lyceum Creative Properties; McBride Literary Agency, Margret; Maccoby Literary Agency, Gina; McGrath, Helen; Mainhardt Agency, Ricia; Mann Agency, Carol; Manus & Associates Literary Agency; March Tenth; Markowitz Literary Agency, Barbara; Metropolitan Talent Agency; Michaels Literary Agency; Miller Agency; Miller Assoc., Roberta; Morrison, Henry; Multimedia Product Development; Mura Enterprises, Dee; Naggar Literary Agency, Jean V.; Nathan, Ruth; Nazor Literary Agency, Karen; New Brand Agency Group; New England Publishing Associates; Nine Muses and Apollo; Norma-Lewis Agency; Nugent Literary; Otitis Media; Palmer & Dodge Agency; Parks Agency, Richard; Paul Agency, Bill; Pevner, Stephen; Pom; Potomac Literary Agency; Protter Literary Agent, Susan Ann; Pryor, Roberta; Publishing Services; Quicksilver Books-Literary Agents; Raymond, Literary Agent, Charlotte Cecil; Rees Literary Agency, Helen; Renaissance—H.N. Swanson; Rinaldi Literary Agency, Angela; Robbins Literary Agency, BJ; Rose Literary Agency; Russell-Simenauer Literary Agency; Sanders Literary Agency, Victoria; Schmidt Literary Agency, Harold; Schulman, Susan; Sebastian Literary Agency; Seligman, Literary Agent, Lynn; Shepard Agency; Siegel Literary Agency, Bobbe; Singer Literary Agency, Evelyn; Spieler, F. Joseph; Spitzer Literary Agency, Philip G.; Stauffer Assoc., Nancy; Steele & Co., Lyle; Stepping Stone; Stern Literary Agency, Gloria (TX); TCA; Teal Literary Agency, Patricia; Travis Literary Agency, Susan; 2M Comm.; Ubel Assoc., Robert; Urstadt Agency, Susan P.; Valcourt Agency, Richard R.; Wald Assoc., Mary Jack; Wallace Literary Agency; Ware Literary Agency, John A.; Waterside Productions; Watkins Loomis Agency; Wecksler-Incomco; Weingel-Fidel Agency; Witherspoon & Associates, Inc.; esentative, Ruth; Wright Representatives, Ann; Writers House; Zeckendorf Assoc., Susan; Ziegler Literary Agency, George

Business. Acton, Leone, Hanson & Jaffe; Adler & Robin Books; Agents Inc. for Medical and Mental Health Professionals; Appleseeds Management; Author's Agency; Author's Agency; Baldi Literary Agency, Malaga; Becker Literary Agency, Wendy; Behar Literary Agency, Josh; Boates Literary Agency, Reid; Brandt & Brandt Literary Agents; Brown Associates Inc., Marie; Buck Agency, Howard; Bykofsky Assoc., Sheree; Carvainis Agency, Maria; Castiglia Literary Agency; Clausen Assoc., Connie; Collin Literary Agent, Frances; Collins Purvis, Ltd.; Coover Agency, Doe; Crawford Literary Agency; Curtis Associates, Richard; Cypher, Author's Representative, James R.; de la Haba Agency, Lois; DH Literary; DHS Literary; Diamant, Anita; Diamond Literary Agency; Dijkstra Literary Agency, Sandra; Doyen Literary Services; Ducas, Robert; Dystel Literary Management, Jane; Educational Design Services; Ellenberg Literary Agency, Ethan; Ellison, Nicholas; Elmo Agency, Ann; Emerald Literary Agency; Eth Literary Representation, Felicia; Fleury Agency, B.R.; Fogelman Literary Agency; Gibson Agency, Sebastian; Goddard Book Group; Gordon Agency, Charlotte; Green, Literary Agent, Randall Elisha; Hawkins & Assoc., John; Heacock Literary Agency, Inc.; Henderson Literary Representation; Henshaw Group, Richard; Herman Agency, Jeff; Herner Rights Agency, Susan; Hulburt Literary Agency, Helane; Hull House Literary Agency; Ievleva Literary Agency; Img-Julian Bach Literary Agency; J de S Assoc.; JABberwocky Literary Agency; James Peter Assoc.; Jordan Literary Agency, Lawrence; Kellock Company; Ketz Agency, Louise B.; Kouts, Literary Agent, Barbara S.; Lampack Agency, Peter; Larsen/Elizabeth Pomada Literary Agents, Michael; Lasher Agency, Maureen; Levant & Wales, Literary Agency; Levine Communications, James; Lieberman Assoc., Robert; Lincoln Literary Agency, Ray; Lindstrom Literary Group; Literary and Creative Artists Agency; Literary Group; Lowenstein Associates; Lyceum Creative Properties; McBride Literary Agency, Margret; McGrath, Helen; Mainhardt Agency, Ricia; Mann Agency, Carol; Manus & Associates Literary Agency; Michaels Literary Agency; Miller Agency; Multimedia Product Development; Mura Enterprises, Dee; Naggar Literary Agency, Jean V.; Nazor Literary Agency, Karen; New England Publishing Associates; Nine Muses and Apollo; Palmer & Dodge Agency; Parks Agency, Richard; Paton Literary Agency, Kathi J.; Pevner, Stephen; Pine Assoc., Arthur; Pom; Potomac Literary Agency; Printed Tree; Quicksilver Books-Literary Agents; Rees Literary Agency, Helen; Rinaldi Literary Agency, Angela; Rock Literary Agency; Rose Agency; Rose Literary Agency; Russell-Simenauer Literary Agency; Schmidt Literary Agency, Harold; Schulman, Susan; Seligman, Literary Agent, Lynn; Shepard Agency; Singer Literary Agency, Evelyn; Snell Literary Agency, Michael; Spieler, F. Joseph; Spitzer Literary Agency, Philip G.; Stauffer Assoc., Nancy; Steele & Co., Lyle; Stepping Stone; Stern Literary Agency, Gloria (TX); TCA; Toad Hall; Travis Literary Agency, Susan; Urstadt Agency, Susan P.; Valcourt Agency, Richard R.; Vines Agency; Waterside Productions; Wecksler-Incomco; Wieser & Wieser; Witherspoon & Associates, Inc.; Wreschner, Authors' Representative, Ruth; Writers House

Child guidance/parenting. Act I; Acton, Leone, Hanson & Jaffe; Adler & Robin Books; Author's Agency; Becker Literary Agency, Wendy; Bernstein, Pam; Boates Literary Agency, Reid; Brandt & Brandt Literary Agents; Brown Associates Inc., Marie; Buck Agency, Howard; Bykofsky Assoc., Sheree; Cantrell-Colas, Literary Agency; Castiglia Literary Agency; Charlton Assoc., James; Coover Agency, Doe; Crawford Literary Agency; Curtis Associates, Richard; DH Literary; DHS Literary; Diamant, Anita; Doyen Literary Services; Dystel Literary Management, Jane; Educational Design Services; Elek Assoc., Peter; Ellenberg Literary Agency, Ethan; Ellison, Nicholas; Elmo Agency, Ann; Emerald Literary Agency; Eth Literary Representation, Felicia; Farber Literary Agency; Flaherty, Literary Agent, Joyce A.; Flannery Literary; Fleury Agency, B.R.; Fogelman Literary Agency; Garon-Brooke Assoc. Inc., Jay; Gartenberg, Literary Agent, Max; Goddard Book Group; Hawkins & Assoc., John; Heacock Literary Agency, Inc.; Henderson Literary Representation; Henshaw Group Henshaw Group, Richard; Herner Rights Agency, Susan; Hulburt Literary Agency, Helane; Ievleva Literary Agency; James Peter Assoc.; Kellock Company; Kouts, Literary Agent, Barbara S.; Lasher Agency, Maureen; Levant & Wales, Literary Agency; Levine Communications, James; Lincoln Literary Agency, Ray; Literary Group; Love Literary Agency, Nancy; Lowenstein Associates; Lyceum Creative Properties; McBride Literary Agency, Margret; Mainhardt Agency, Ricia; Mann Agency, Carol; Manus & Associates Literary Agency; Miller Agency; Multimedia Product Development; Mura Enterprises, Dee; Naggar Literary Agency, Jean V.; New England Publishing Associates; Norma-Lewis Agency; Palmer & Dodge Agency; Parks Agency, Richard; Paton Literary Agency, Kathi J.; Printed Tree; Protter Literary Agent, Susan Ann; Publishing Services; Quicksilver Books-Literary Agents; Rinaldi Literary Agency, Angela; Robbins Literary Agency, BJ; Rose Agency; Rose Literary Agency; Rubenstein Literary Agency, Pesha; Russell-Simenauer Literary Agency; Schulman, Susan; Sebastian Literary Agency; Seligman, Literary Agent, Lynn; Shepard Agency; Siegel Literary Agency, Bobbe; Singer Literary Agency, Evelyn; Spieler, F. Joseph; Steele & Co., Lyle; Stepping Stone; Stern Literary Agency, Gloria (TX); Teal Literary Agency, Patricia; Toad Hall; Travis Literary Agency, Susan; 2M Comm.; Urstadt Agency, Susan P.; Vines Agency; Waterside Productions; Wreschner, Authors' Representative, Ruth; Writers House; Zeckendorf Assoc., Susan

Computers/electronics. Adler & Robin Books; Author's Agency; Baldi Literary Agency, Malaga; Buck Agency, Howard; Cypher, Author's Representative, James R.; DHS Literary; Doyen Literary Services; Ellison, Nicholas; Elmo Agency, Ann; Emerald Literary Agency; Fleury Agency, B.R.; Graham Literary Agency; Henderson Literary Representation; Henshaw Group, Richard; Herman Agency, Jeff; Hulburt Literary Agency, Helane; Jordan Literary Agency, Lawrence; Kellock Company; Ketz Agency, Louise B.; Levine Communications, James; Lieberman Assoc., Robert; Lindstrom Literary Group; Lyceum Creative Properties; Michaels Literary Agency; Moore Literary Agency; Mura Enterprises, Dee; Nazor Literary Agency, Karen; Pevner, Stephen; Sebastian Literary Agency; Shepard Agency; Ubel Assoc., Robert; Waterside Productions

Cooking/food/nutrition. Adler & Robin Books; Agents Inc. for Medical and Mental Health Professionals; Ajlouny Agency, Joseph S.; Author's Agency; Baldi Literary Agency, Malaga; Becker Literary Agency, Wendy; Bernstein, Pam; Brandt & Brandt Literary Agents; Brown Associates Inc., Marie; Bykofsky Assoc., Sheree; Cantrell-Colas, Literary Agency; Casselman Literary Agent, Martha; Castiglia Literary Agency; Charlton Assoc., James; Ciske & Dietz Literary Agency; Clausen Assoc., Connie; Columbia Literary Assoc., Inc.; Coover Agency, Doe;

Cornfield Literary Agency, Robert; Crawford Literary Agency; de la Haba Agency, Lois; DH Literary; DHS Literary; Diamant, Anita; Dijkstra Literary Agency, Sandra; Doyen Literary Services; Dystel Literary Management, Jane; Ellenberg Literary Agency, Ethan; Ellison, Nicholas; Elmo Agency, Ann; Farber Literary Agency; Feiler Literary Agency, Florence; Fleury Agency, B.R.; Fogelman Literary Agency; Gibson Agency, Sebastian; Goddard Book Group; Hawkins & Assoc., John; Heacock Literary Agency, Inc.; Henderson Literary Representation; Henshaw Group, Richard; Herner Rights Agency, Susan; Hochmann Books, John L.; Hulburt Literary Agency, Helane; Ievleva Literary Agency; Img-Julian Bach Literary Agency; JABberwocky Literary Agency; Kellock Company; Klinger, Harvey; Larsen/Elizabeth Pomada Literary Agents, Michael; Lasher Agency, Maureen; Levine Communications, James; Lincoln Literary Agency, Ray; Literary and Creative Artists Agency; Literary Group; Love Literary Agency, Nancy; Lyceum Creative Properties; McBride Literary Agency, Margret; Mainhardt Agency, Ricia; Miller Agency; Multimedia Product Development; Naggar Literary Agency, Jean V.; Nazor Literary Agency, Karen; Norma-Lewis Agency; Parks Agency, Richard; Pevner, Stephen; Pom; Printed Tree; Publishing Services; Quicksilver Books-Literary Agents; Rinaldi Literary Agency, Angela; Robbins Literary Agency, BJ; Rose Literary Agency; Rowland Agency, Damaris; Russell-Simenauer Literary Agency; Seligman, Literary Agent, Lynn; Shepard Agency; Siegel Literary Agency, Bobbe; Steele & Co., Lyle; Stepping Stone; Stern Literary Agency, Gloria (TX); Taylor Literary Enterprises, Sandra; TCA; Toad Hall; Travis Literary Agency, Susan; Urstadt Agency, Susan P.; Watkins Loomis Agency; Wieser & Wieser; Ziegler Literary Agency, George

Crafts/hobbies. Author's Agency; Becker Literary Agency, Wendy; Brandt & Brandt Literary Agents; Buck Agency, Howard; Diamant, Anita; Doyen Literary Services; Ellison, Nicholas; Elmo Agency, Ann; Feiler Literary Agency, Florence; Flaherty, Literary Agent, Joyce A.; Fleury Agency, B.R.; Hawkins & Assoc., John; Heacock Literary Agency, Inc.; Ievleva Literary Agency; Kellock Company; Larsen/Elizabeth Pomada Literary Agents, Michael; Lincoln Literary Agency, Ray; Literary Group; Lowenstein Associates; Mainhardt Agency, Ricia; Multimedia Product Development; Norma-Lewis Agency; Parks Agency, Richard; Printed Tree; Shepard Agency; Toad Hall; Travis Literary Agency, Susan; Urstadt Agency, Susan P.; Wreschner, Authors' Representative, Ruth; Ziegler Literary Agency, George

Current affairs. Acton, Leone, Hanson & Jaffe; Adler & Robin Books; Agents Inc. for Medical and Mental Health Professionals; Altshuler Literary Agency, Miriam; Author's Agency; Baldi Literary Agency, Malaga; Balkin Agency; Becker Literary Agency, Wendy; Bernstein, Pam; Boates Literary Agency, Reid; Borchardt, Georges; Brandt & Brandt Literary Agents; Brown Literary Agency, Andrea; Buck Agency, Howard; Bykofsky Assoc., Sheree; Cantrell-Colas, Literary Agency; Carvainis Agency, Maria; Castiglia Literary Agency; Charisma Communications; Circle of Confusion; Clausen Assoc., Connie; Collins Purvis, Ltd.; Cypher, Author's Representative, James R.; Darhansoff & Verrill Literary Agents; de la Haba Agency, Lois; DH Literary; DHS Literary; Diamant, Anita; Dijkstra Literary Agency, Sandra; Doyen Literary Services; Ducas, Robert; Dystel Literary Management, Jane; Educational Design Services; Ellenberg Literary Agency, Ethan; Ellison, Nicholas; Elmo Agency, Ann; Emerald Literary Agency; Eth Literary Representation, Felicia; Flaming Star Literary Enterprises; Fleury Agency, B.R.; Fogelman Literary Agency; Franklin Assoc., Lynn C.; Gartenberg, Literary Agent, Max; Gibson Agency, Sebastian; Goddard Book Group; Green, Literary Agent, Randall Elisha; Halsey Agency, Reece; Hardy Agency; Hawkins & Assoc., John; Henderson Literary Representation; Henshaw Group, Richard; Herner Rights Agency, Susan; Hill Associates, Frederick; Hochmann Books, John L.; Hulburt Literary Agency, Helane; Hull House Literary Agency; Ievleva Literary Agency; Img-Julian Bach Literary Agency; J de S Assoc.; JABberwocky Literary Agency; James Peter Assoc.; Kellock Company; Ketz Agency, Louise B.; Kidde, Hoyt & Picard; Kouts, Literary Agent, Barbara S.; Kroll Literary Agency, Edite; Lampack Agency, Peter; Larsen/Elizabeth Pomada Literary Agents, Michael; Lasher Agency, Maureen; Levant & Wales, Literary Agency; Levine Literary Agency, Ellen; Lincoln Literary Agency, Ray; Lindstrom Literary Group; Lipkind Agency, Wendy; Literary Group; Love Literary Agency, Nancy; Lowenstein Associates; Lyceum Creative Properties; McBride Literary Agency, Margret; Maccoby Literary Agency, Gina; McGrath, Helen; Mainhardt Agency, Ricia; Mann Agency, Carol; Manus & Associates Literary Agency; March Tenth; Markowitz Literary Agency, Barbara; Metropolitan Talent Agency; Michaels Literary Agency; Miller Agency; Miller Assoc., Roberta; Multimedia Product Development; Mura Enterprises, Dee; Naggar Literary Agency, Jean V.; Nazor Literary Agency, Karen; Nine Muses and Apollo; Norma-Lewis Agency; Palmer & Dodge Agency; Parks Agency, Richard; Perkins Assoc., L.; Pevner, Stephen; Pine Assoc., Arthur; Pom; Potomac Literary Agency; Quicksilver Books-Literary Agents; Raymond, Literary Agent, Charlotte Cecil; Rees Literary Agency, Helen; Rinaldi Literary Agency, Angela; Robbins Literary Agency, BJ; Rose Literary Agency; Russell-Simenauer Literary Agency; Sanders Literary Agency, Victoria; Schmidt Literary Agency, Harold; Schulman, Susan; Sebastian Literary Agency; Seligman, Literary Agent, Lynn; Shepard Agency; Siegel Literary Agency, Bobbe; Singer Literary Agency, Evelyn; Spieler, F. Joseph; Spitzer Literary Agency, Philip G.; Stauffer Assoc., Nancy; Steele & Co., Lyle; Stepping Stone; Stern Literary Agency, Gloria (TX); TCA; Urstadt Agency, Susan P.; Valcourt Agency, Richard R.; Wald Assoc., Mary Jack; Wallace Literary Agency; Ware Literary Agency, John A.; Watkins Loomis Agency; Wecksler-Incomco; Wieser & Wieser; Witherspoon & Associates, Inc.; Wreschner, Authors' Representative, Ruth

Education. Author's Agency; Brown, Curtis; Buck Agency, Howard; Collins Purvis, Ltd.; DH Literary; Doyen Literary Services; Dystel Literary Management, Jane; Elmo Agency, Ann; Feiler Literary Agency, Florence; Fleury Agency, B.R.; Heacock Literary Agency, Inc.; Henderson Literary Representation; Hulburt Literary Agency, Helane; Ievleva Literary Agency; Kellock Company; Levant & Wales, Literary Agency; Lieberman Assoc., Robert; Literary Group; Lowenstein Associates; Mura Enterprises, Dee; New Brand Agency Group; Palmer & Dodge Agency; Pocono Literary Agency; Printed Tree; Publishing Services; Robbins Literary Agency, BJ; Rose Agency; Russell-Simenauer Literary Agency; Schulman, Susan; Seligman, Literary Agent, Lynn; Urstadt Agency, Susan P.; Valcourt Agency, Richard R.

Ethnic/cultural interests. Acton, Leone, Hanson & Jaffe; Adler & Robin Books; Altshuler Literary

Agency, Miriam; Authors Agency Author's Agency; Baldi Literary Agency, Malaga; Becker Literary Agency, Wendy; Boates Literary Agency, Reid; Brandt & Brandt Literary Agents; Brown Associates Inc., Marie; Brown Literary Agency, Andrea; Buck Agency, Howard; Bykofsky Assoc., Sheree; Cantrell-Colas, Literary Agency; Castiglia Literary Agency; Clausen Assoc., Connie; Cohen, Literary Agency, Ruth; Collins Purvis, Ltd.; Coover Agency, Doe; Crown International Literature and Arts Agency, Bonnie R.; Cypher, Author's Representative, James R.; de la Haba Agency, Lois; DH Literary; DHS Literary; Dijkstra Literary Agency, Sandra; Doyen Literary Services; Dystel Literary Management, Jane; Educational Design Services; Ellison, Nicholas; Eth Literary Representation, Felicia; Fleury Agency, B.R.; Gibson Agency, Sebastian; Goddard Book Group; Hawkins & Assoc., John; Heacock Literary Agency, Inc.; Henderson Literary Representation; Herner Rights Agency, Susan; Hulburt Literary Agency, Helane; Hull House Literary Agency; Ievleva Literary Agency; J de S Assoc.; James Peter Assoc.; Kellock Company; Ketz Agency, Louise B.; Kidde, Hoyt & Picard; Kouts, Literary Agent, Barbara S.; Larsen/Elizabeth Pomada Literary Agents, Michael; Lasher Agency, Maureen; Levant & Wales, Literary Agency; Lewis & Co., Karen; Lincoln Literary Agency, Ray; Lindstrom Literary Group; Literary Group; Love Literary Agency, Nancy; Lowenstein Associates; Lyceum Creative Properties; McBride Literary Agency, Margret; Maccoby Literary Agency, Gina; Mainhardt Agency, Ricia; Mann Agency, Carol; Manus & Associates Literary Agency; Michaels Literary Agency; Miller Agency; Miller Assoc., Roberta; Multimedia Product Development; Mura Enterprises, Dee; Nazor Literary Agency, Karen; Nine Muses and Apollo; Norma-Lewis Agency; Palmer & Dodge Agency; Parks Agency, Richard; Perkins Assoc., L.; Pevner, Stephen; Pom; Potomac Literary Agency; Pryor, Roberta; Publishing Services; Quicksilver Books-Literary Agents; Raymond, Literary Agent, Charlotte Cecil; Robbins Literary Agency, BJ; Rose Literary Agency; Sanders Literary Agency, Victoria; Schmidt Literary Agency, Harold; Sebastian Literary Agency; Seligman, Literary Agent, Lynn; Siegel Literary Agency, Bobbe; Singer Literary Agency, Evelyn; Spieler, F. Joseph; Spitzer Literary Agency, Philip G.; Stauffer Assoc., Nancy; Steele And Company Steele & Co., Lyle; Stepping Stone; Stern Literary Agency, Gloria (TX); Travis Literary Agency, Susan; 2M Comm.; Urstadt Agency, Susan P.; Valcourt Agency, Richard R.; Wald Assoc., Mary Jack; Ware Literary Agency, John A.; Waterside Productions; Watkins Loomis Agency; Witherspoon & Associates, Inc.; Wreschner, Authors' Representative, Ruth

Gay/lesbian issues. Acton, Leone, Hanson & Jaffe; Adler & Robin Books; Altshuler Literary Agency, Miriam; Baldi Literary Agency, Malaga; Brandt & Brandt Literary Agents; Brown Associates Inc., Marie; Brown, Curtis; Buck Agency, Howard; Bykofsky Assoc., Sheree; Circle of Confusion; Clausen Assoc., Connie; Collins Purvis, Ltd.; Cypher, Author's Representative, James R.; Daves Agency, Joan; de la Haba Agency, Lois; DH Literary; DHS Literary; Ducas, Robert; Dystel Literary Management, Jane; Eth Literary Representation, Felicia; Feiler Literary Agency, Florence; Garon-Brooke Assoc. Inc., Jay; Hawkins & Assoc., John; Heacock Literary Agency, Inc.; Henderson Literary Representation; Henshaw Group, Richard; Herner Rights Agency, Susan; Hochmann Books, John L.; Hulburt Literary Agency, Helane; JABberwocky Literary Agency; James Peter Assoc.; Kidde, Hoyt & Picard; Larsen/Elizabeth Pomada Literary Agents, Michael; Levant & Wales, Literary Agency; Levine Communications, James; Lewis & Co., Karen; Lincoln Literary Agency, Ray; Literary Group; Love Literary Agency, Nancy; Lowenstein Associates; Lyceum Creative Properties; McBride Literary Agency, Margret; Miller Agency; Mura Enterprises, Dee; Nazor Literary Agency, Karen; Nine Muses and Apollo; Palmer & Dodge Agency; Parks Agency, Richard; Perkins Assoc., L.; Pevner, Stephen; Potomac Literary Agency; Pryor, Roberta; Raymond, Literary Agent, Charlotte Cecil; Robbins Literary Agency, BJ; Rose Literary Agency; Sanders Literary Agency, Victoria; Schmidt Literary Agency, Harold; Schulman, Susan; Sierra Literary Agency; Spieler, F. Joseph; Steele & Co., Lyle; Stepping Stone; Travis Literary Agency, Susan; 2M Comm.; Ware Literary Agency, John A.; Watkins Loomis Agency; Witherspoon & Associates, Inc.; Wreschner, Authors' Representative, Ruth; Ziegler Literary Agency, George

Government/politics/law. Acton, Leone, Hanson & Jaffe; Adler & Robin Books; Author's Agency; Author's Agency; Baldi Literary Agency, Malaga; Becker Literary Agency, Wendy; Bernstein, Pam; Black Literary Agency, David; Boates Literary Agency, Reid; Brandt & Brandt Literary Agents; Buck Agency, Howard; Cantrell-Colas, Literary Agency; Carvainis Agency, Maria; Charisma Communications; Circle of Confusion; Collins Purvis, Ltd.; Cypher, Author's Representative, James R.; de la Haba Agency, Lois; DH Literary; Diamant, Anita; Dijkstra Literary Agency, Sandra; Doyen Literary Services; Ducas, Robert; Dystel Literary Management, Jane; Educational Design Services; Ellison, Nicholas; Emerald Literary Agency; Eth Literary Representation, Felicia; Flaming Star Literary Enterprises; Fleury Agency, B.R.; Fogelman Literary Agency; Gibson Agency, Sebastian; Goddard Book Group; Graham Literary Agency; Green, Literary Agent, Randall Elisha; Hardy Agency; Hawkins & Assoc., John; Heacock Literary Agency, Inc.; Henderson Literary Representation; Henshaw Group, Richard; Herman Agency, Jeff; Herner Rights Agency, Susan; Hill Associates, Frederick; Hochmann Books, John L.; Hulburt Literary Agency, Helane; Hull House Literary Agency; Ievleva Literary Agency; Img-Julian Bach Literary Agency; J de S Assoc.; JABberwocky Literary Agency; James Peter Assoc.; Kellock Company; Kidde, Hoyt & Picard; Lampack Agency, Peter; Larsen/Elizabeth Pomada Literary Agents, Michael; Lasher Agency, Maureen; Lincoln Literary Agency, Ray; Lindstrom Literary Group; Literary and Creative Artists Agency; Literary Group Literary Group; Love Literary Agency, Nancy; Lowenstein Associates; Lyceum Creative Properties; McBride Literary Agency, Margret; Madsen Agency, Robert; Mainhardt Agency, Ricia; Mann Agency, Carol; Morrison, Henry; Mura Enterprises, Dee; Naggar Literary Agency, Jean V.; Nazor Literary Agency, Karen; New England Publishing Associates; Nine Muses and Apollo; Norma-Lewis Agency; Palmer & Dodge Agency; Parks Agency, Richard; Pevner, Stephen; Popkin, Julie; Pryor, Roberta; Rees Literary Agency, Helen; Robbins Literary Agency, BJ; Rose Literary Agency; Sanders Literary Agency, Victoria; Schmidt Literary Agency, Harold; Schulman, Susan; Sebastian Literary Agency; Seligman, Literary Agent, Lynn; Shepard Agency; Sierra Literary Agency; Singer Literary Agency, Evelyn; Snell Literary Agency, Michael; Spieler, F. Joseph; Spitzer Literary Agency, Philip G.; Steele & Co., Lyle; Stern Literary Agency, Gloria (TX); Valcourt Agency, Richard R.; Ware Literary Agency, John A.; Witherspoon & Associates, Inc.; Wreschner, Authors' Representative, Ruth

Health/medicine. Adler & Robin Books; Agency Chicago; Agents Inc. for Medical and Mental Health Professionals; Ajlouny Agency, Joseph S.; Appleseeds Management; Author's Agency; Author's Agency; Baldi Literary Agency, Malaga; Balkin Agency; Becker Literary Agency, Wendy; Bernstein, Pam; Boates Literary Agency, Reid; Brandt & Brandt Literary Agents; Brown Literary Agency, Andrea; Buck Agency, Howard; Bykofsky Assoc., Sheree; Cantrell-Colas, Literary Agency; Carvainis Agency, Maria; Casselman Literary Agent, Martha; Castiglia Literary Agency; Charlton Assoc., James; Circle of Confusion; Clausen Assoc., Connie; Collin Literary Agent, Frances; Columbia Literary Assoc., Inc.; Coover Agency, Doe; Cypher, Author's Representative, James R.; Darhansoff & Verrill Literary Agents; de la Haba Agency, Lois; DH Literary; Diamant, Anita; Dijkstra Literary Agency, Sandra; Doyen Literary Services; Ducas, Robert; Dystel Literary Management, Jane; Ellenberg Literary Agency, Ethan; Ellison, Nicholas; Elmo Agency, Ann; Esq. Literary Productions; Eth Literary Representation, Felicia; Feiler Literary Agency, Florence; Flaherty, Literary Agent, Joyce A.; Flaming Star Literary Enterprises; Fleury Agency, B.R.; Franklin Assoc., Lynn C.; Garon-Brooke Assoc. Inc., Jay; Gartenberg, Literary Agent, Max; Gibson Agency, Sebastian; Goddard Book Group; Gordon Agency, Charlotte; Hardy Agency; Hawkins & Assoc., John; Heacock Literary Agency, Inc.; Hegler Literary Agency, Gary L.; Henderson Literary Representation; Henshaw Group, Richard; Herman Agency, Jeff; Herner Rights Agency, Susan; Hochmann Books, John L.; Hulburt Literary Agency, Helane; Ievleva Literary Agency; J de S Assoc.; JABberwocky Literary Agency; James Peter Assoc.; Jordan Literary Agency, Lawrence; Kellock Company; Klinger, Harvey; Kouts, Literary Agent, Barbara S.; Lampack Agency, Peter; Larsen/Elizabeth Pomada Literary Agents, Michael; Lasher Agency, Maureen; Levant & Wales, Literary Agency; Levine Communications, James; Levine Literary Agency, Ellen; Lieberman Assoc., Robert; Lincoln Literary Agency, Ray; Lindstrom Literary Group; Lipkind Agency, Wendy; Literary and Creative Artists Agency; Literary Group; Love Literary Agency, Nancy; Lowenstein Associates; McBride Literary Agency, Margret; McGrath, Helen; Mainhardt Agency, Ricia; Mann Agency, Carol; Manus & Associates Literary Agency; March Tenth; Michaels Literary Agency; Miller Agency; Multimedia Product Development; Mura Enterprises, Dee; Naggar Literary Agency, Jean V.; New England Publishing Associates; Nine Muses and Apollo; Norma-Lewis Agency; Nugent Literary; Otitis Media; Palmer & Dodge Agency; Parks Agency, Richard; Pine Assoc., Arthur; Pom; Protter Literary Agent, Susan Ann; Publishing Services; Quicksilver Books-Literary Agents; Rees Literary Agency, Helen; Rinaldi Literary Agency, Angela; Robbins Literary Agency, BJ; Rogers Literary Representation, Irene; Rose Agency; Rose Literary Agency; Rowland Agency, Damaris; Russell-Simenauer Literary Agency; Schmidt Literary Agency, Harold; Schulman, Susan; Sebastian Literary Agency; Seligman, Literary Agent, Lynn; Shepard Agency; Siegel Literary Agency, Bobbe; Singer Literary Agency, Evelyn; Snell Literary Agency, Michael; Spitzer Literary Agency, Philip G.; Steele & Co., Lyle; Stepping Stone; Stern Literary Agency, Gloria (TX); Taylor Literary Enterprises, Sandra; Teal Literary Agency, Patricia; Toad Hall; Travis Literary Agency, Susan; 2M Comm.; Ubel Assoc., Robert; Urstadt Agency, Susan P.; Valcourt Agency, Richard R.; Ware Literary Agency, John A.; Waterside Productions; Wieser & Wieser; Witherspoon & Associates, Inc.; Wreschner, Authors' Representative, Ruth; Writers House; Zeckendorf Assoc., Susan; Ziegler Literary Agency, George

History. Acton, Leone, Hanson & Jaffe; Adler & Robin Books; Ajlouny Agency, Joseph S.; Allen, Literary Agency, James; Altshuler Literary Agency, Miriam; Authors Agency Author's Agency; Author's Agency; Baldi Literary Agency, Malaga; Balkin Agency; Becker Literary Agency, Wendy; Boates Literary Agency, Reid; Borchardt, Georges; Brandt & Brandt Literary Agents; Brown Associates Inc., Marie; Brown, Curtis; Brown Literary Agency, Andrea; Buck Agency, Howard; Bykofsky Assoc., Sheree; Cantrellcolas Inc. Cantrell-Colas, Literary Agency; Carvainis Agency, Maria; Castiglia Literary Agency; Circle of Confusion; Collin Literary Agent, Frances; Collins Purvis, Ltd.; Coover Agency, Doe; Cornfield Literary Agency, Robert; Curtis Associates, Richard; Cypher, Author's Representative, James R.; Darhansoff & Verrill Literary Agents; de la Haba Agency, Lois; DH Literary; Diamant, Anita; Dijkstra Literary Agency, Sandra; Doyen Literary Services; Ducas, Robert; Dystel Literary Management, Jane; Educational Design Services; Ellenberg Literary Agency, Ethan; Ellison, Nicholas; Elmo Agency, Ann; Eth Literary Representation, Felicia; Feiler Literary Agency, Florence; Flaherty, Literary Agent, Joyce A.; Fleury Agency, B.R.; Franklin Assoc., Lynn C.; Garon-Brooke Assoc. Inc., Jay; Gartenberg, Literary Agent, Max; Gibson Agency, Sebastian; Goddard Book Group; Gordon Agency, Charlotte; Green, Literary Agent, Randall Elisha; Gregory Assoc., Maia; Halsey Agency, Reece; Hawkins & Assoc., John; Heacock Literary Agency, Inc.; Henderson Literary Representation; Herman Agency, Jeff; Herner Rights Agency, Susan; Hochmann Books, John L.; Hulburt Literary Agency, Helane; Hull House Literary Agency; Ievleva Literary Agency; Img-Julian Bach Literary Agency; J de S Assoc.; JABberwocky Literary Agency; James Peter Assoc.; Kellock Company; Ketz Agency, Louise B.; Kidde, Hoyt & Picard; Kouts, Literary Agent, Barbara S.; Lampack Agency, Peter; Larsen/Elizabeth Pomada Literary Agents, Michael; Lasher Agency, Maureen; Lincoln Literary Agency, Ray; Lindstrom Literary Group; Lipkind Agency, Wendy; Literary Group; Love Literary Agency, Nancy; Lowenstein Associates; Lyceum Creative Properties; McBride Literary Agency, Margret; McGrath, Helen; Madsen Agency, Robert; Mainhardt Agency, Ricia; Mann Agency, Carol; March Tenth; Metropolitan Talent Agency; Michaels Literary Agency; Morrison, Henry; Mura Enterprises, Dee; Naggar Literary Agency, Jean V.; Nazor Literary Agency, Karen; New England Publishing Associates; Nine Muses and Apollo; Norma-Lewis Agency; Otitis Media; Palmer & Dodge Agency; Parks Agency, Richard; Pevner, Stephen; Pocono Literary Agency; Popkin, Julie; Potomac Literary Agency; Pryor, Roberta; Quicksilver Books-Literary Agents; Raymond, Literary Agent, Charlotte Cecil; Rees Literary Agency, Helen; Renaissance—H.N. Swanson; Rock Literary Agency; Rose Literary Agency; Sanders Literary Agency, Victoria; Schmidt Literary Agency, Harold; Schulman, Susan; Sebastian Literary Agency; Seligman, Literary Agent, Lynn; Shepard Agency; Siegel Literary Agency, Bobbe; Spieler, F. Joseph; Spitzer Literary Agency, Philip G.; Steele & Co., Lyle; Stepping Stone; Stern Literary Agency, Gloria (TX); TCA; Urstadt Agency, Susan P.; Valcourt Agency, Richard R.; Van Der Leun & Assoc.; Wald Assoc., Mary Jack; Wallace Literary Agency; Ware Literary Agency, John A.; Watkins Loomis Agency; Wecksler-Incomco; Wieser & Wieser; Witherspoon & Associates, Inc.; Wreschner, Authors' Representative, Ruth; Writers House; Zeckendorf Assoc., Susan; Ziegler Literary Agency, George

How to. Act I; Adler & Robin Books; Agents Inc. for Medical and Mental Health Professionals; Author's Agency; Authors' Literary Agency; Becker Literary Agency, Wendy; Bernstein, Pam; Bova Literary Agency, Barbara; Brown, Curtis; Brown Literary Agency, Andrea; Buck Agency, Howard; Bykofsky Assoc., Sheree; Charlton Assoc., James; Collins Purvis, Ltd.; Crawford Literary Agency; Cypher, Author's Representative, James R.; DH Literary; Doyen Literary Services; Elmo Agency, Ann; Feiler Literary Agency, Florence; Flaherty, Literary Agent, Joyce A.; Fleury Agency, B.R.; Green, Literary Agent, Randall Elisha; Heacock Literary Agency, Inc.; Henderson Literary Representation; Henshaw Group, Richard; Herner Rights Agency, Susan; Hulburt Literary Agency, Helane; Ievleva Literary Agency; Kellock Company; Larsen/Elizabeth Pomada Literary Agents, Michael; Lasher Agency, Maureen; Lindstrom Literary Group; Literary Group; Love Literary Agency, Nancy; Lowenstein Associates; McBride Literary Agency, Margret; Mainhardt Agency, Ricia; Manus & Associates Literary Agency; Michaels Literary Agency; Multimedia Product Development; Mura Enterprises, Dee; Nazor Literary Agency, Karen; New Brand Agency Group; Parks Agency, Richard; Pocono Literary Agency; Printed Tree; Quicksilver Books-Literary Agents; Robbins Literary Agency, BJ; Russell-Simenauer Literary Agency; Schulman, Susan; Seligman, Literary Agent, Lynn; Sierra Literary Agency; Singer Literary Agency, Evelyn; Stern Literary Agency, Gloria (TX); Taylor Literary Enterprises, Sandra; Teal Literary Agency, Patricia; Toad Hall; Travis Literary Agency, Susan; Urstadt Agency, Susan P.; Vines Agency; Wreschner, Authors' Representative, Ruth

Humor. Acton, Leone, Hanson & Jaffe; Author's Agency; Becker Literary Agency, Wendy; Brown, Curtis; Brown Literary Agency, Andrea; Buck Agency, Howard; Bykofsky Assoc., Sheree; Charlton Assoc., James; Circle of Confusion; Collins Purvis, Ltd.; Cypher, Author's Representative, James R.; DH Literary; Doyen Literary Services; Dystel Literary Management, Jane; Elliott Agency; Gibson Agency, Sebastian; Heacock Literary Agency, Inc.; Henderson Literary Representation; Henshaw Group, Richard; Ievleva Literary Agency; JABberwocky Literary Agency; Kellock Company; Ketz Agency, Louise B.; Larsen/Elizabeth Pomada Literary Agents, Michael; Literary Group Literary Group; Lowenstein Associates; Mainhardt Agency, Ricia; March Tenth; Metropolitan Talent Agency; Multimedia Product Development; Mura Enterprises, Dee; New Brand Agency Group; Nine Muses and Apollo; Otitis Media; Parks Agency, Richard; Pevner, Stephen; Robbins Literary Agency, BJ; Rose Agency; Sanders Literary Agency, Victoria; Seligman, Literary Agent, Lynn; Vines Agency

Interior design/decorating. Author's Agency; Baldi Literary Agency, Malaga; Becker Literary Agency, Wendy; Brandt & Brandt Literary Agents; Buck Agency, Howard; Collins Purvis, Ltd.; Doyen Literary Services; Ellison, Nicholas; Fleury Agency, B.R.; Goddard Book Group; Hawkins & Assoc., John; Henderson Literary Representation; Ievleva Literary Agency; Kellock Company; Larsenelizabeth Pomada Larsen/Elizabeth Pomada Literary Agents, Michael; Lincoln Literary Agency, Ray; Mainhardt Agency, Ricia; Mann Agency, Carol; Naggar Literary Agency, Jean V.; Pocono Literary Agency; Seligman, Literary Agent, Lynn; Shepard Agency; Stepping Stone; Travis Literary Agency, Susan; Urstadt Agency, Susan P.; Writers House

Juvenile nonfiction. Brandt & Brandt Literary Agents; Brown Associates Inc., Marie; Brown Literary Agency, Andrea; Cantrell-Colas, Literary Agency; Circle of Confusion; Cohen, Inc. Literary Agency, Ruth; Collins Purvis, Ltd.; de la Haba Agency, Lois; Diamant, Anita; Doyen Literary Services; Educational Design Services; Elek Assoc., Peter; Ellenberg Literary Agency, Ethan; Elmo Agency, Ann; Feiler Literary Agency, Florence; Flannery Literary; Fleury Agency, B.R.; Gordon Agency, Charlotte; Hawkins & Assoc., John; Heacock Literary Agency, Inc.; Hegler Literary Agency, Gary L.; Henderson Literary Representation; Henshaw Group, Richard; Ievleva Literary Agency; Kellock Company; Kirchoff/Wohlberg, Inc., Authors' Representation Division; Kouts, Literary Agent, Barbara S.; Levine Communications, James; Lewis & Co., Karen; Lincoln Literary Agency, Ray; Literary Group; Lyceum Creative Properties; Maccoby Literary Agency, Gina; Mainhardt Agency, Ricia; Markowitz Literary Agency, Barbara; Morrison, Henry; Multimedia Product Development; Mura Enterprises, Dee; Naggar Literary Agency, Jean V.; Norma-Lewis Agency; Pocono Literary Agency; Printed Tree; Raymond, Literary Agent, Charlotte Cecil; Rubenstein Literary Agency, Pesha; Schulman, Susan; Seymour Agency; Shepard Agency; Siegel Literary Agency, Bobbe; Singer Literary Agency, Evelyn; Targ Literary Agency, Inc., Roslyn; Urstadt Agency, Susan P.; Vines Agency; Wald Assoc., Mary Jack; Wasserman Literary Agency, Harriet; Wreschner, Authors' Representative, Ruth; Writers House

Language/literature/criticism. Ajlouny Agency, Joseph S.; Author's Agency; Baldi Literary Agency, Malaga; Balkin Agency; Boates Literary Agency, Reid; Brandt & Brandt Literary Agents; Buck Agency, Howard; Cantrell-Colas, Literary Agency; Castiglia Literary Agency; Coover Agency, Doe; Cornfield Literary Agency, Robert; Cypher, Author's Representative, James R.; Darhansoff & Verrill Literary Agents; DH Literary; Dijkstra Literary Agency, Sandra; Educational Design Services; Ellison, Nicholas; Emerald Literary Agency; Fleury Agency, B.R.; Goddard Book Group; Green, Literary Agent, Randall Elisha; Gregory Assoc., Maia; Halsey Agency, Reece; Hawkins & Assoc., John; Heacock Literary Agency, Inc.; Herner Rights Agency, Susan; Hill Associates, Frederick; Ievleva Literary Agency; Img-Julian Bach Literary Agency; JABberwocky Literary Agency; James Peter Assoc.; Kidde, Hoyt & Picard; Larsen/Elizabeth Pomada Literary Agents, Michael; Levant & Wales, Literary Agency; Lincoln Literary Agency, Ray; Literary Group; Lowenstein Associates; Lyceum Creative Properties; March Tenth; Miller Agency; Miller Assoc., Roberta; New England Publishing Associates; Nine Muses and Apollo; Palmer & Dodge Agency; Parks Agency, Richard; Pevner, Stephen; Popkin, Julie; Potomac Literary Agency; Quicksilver Books-Literary Agents; Rose Literary Agency; Sanders Literary Agency, Victoria; Schmidt Literary Agency, Harold; Seligman, Literary Agent, Lynn; Shepard Agency; Siegel Literary Agency, Bobbe; Spitzer Literary Agency, Philip G.; Stern Literary Agency, Gloria (TX); Valcourt Agency, Richard R.; Wald Assoc., Mary Jack; Wallace Literary Agency; Ware Literary Agency, John A.

Military/war. Acton, Leone, Hanson & Jaffe; Author's Agency; Baldi Literary Agency, Malaga; Becker Literary Agency, Wendy; Brandt & Brandt Literary Agents; Buck Agency, Howard; Cantrell-Colas, Literary Agency;

Carvainis Agency, Maria; Charisma Communications; Charlton Assoc., James; Circle of Confusion; Collins Purvis, Ltd.; Curtis Associates, Richard; Cypher, Author's Representative, James R.; DH Literary; Dijkstra Literary Agency, Sandra; Doyen Literary Services; Ducas, Robert; Dystel Literary Management, Jane; Educational Design Services; Ellison, Nicholas; Feiler Literary Agency, Florence; Flaherty, Literary Agent, Joyce A.; Garon-Brooke Assoc. Inc., Jay; Gartenberg, Literary Agent, Max; Gibson Agency, Sebastian; Hawkins & Assoc., John; Heacock Literary Agency, Inc.; Hegler Literary Agency, Gary L.; Henshaw Group, Richard; Hochmann Books, John L.; Hull House Literary Agency; Ievleva Literary Agency; Img-Julian Bach Literary Agency; J de S Assoc.; JABberwocky Literary Agency; James Peter Assoc.; Kellock Company; Ketz Agency, Louise B.; Literary Group; McGrath, Helen; Madsen Agency, Robert; Mura Enterprises, Dee; New Brand Agency Group; New England Publishing Associates; Otitis Media; Parks Agency, Richard; Potomac Literary Agency; Printed Tree; Pryor, Roberta; Rose Literary Agency; Schmidt Literary Agency, Harold; Schulman, Susan; Spitzer Literary Agency, Philip G.; Urstadt Agency, Susan P.; Valcourt Agency, Richard R.; Wallace Literary Agency; Ware Literary Agency, John A.; Writers House

Money/finance/economics. Acton, Leone, Hanson & Jaffe; Adler & Robin Books; Appleseeds Management; Author's Agency; Author's Agency; Baldi Literary Agency, Malaga; Becker Literary Agency, Wendy; Behar Literary Agency, Josh; Bova Literary Agency, Barbara; Brandt & Brandt Literary Agents; Brown Associates Inc., Marie; Buck Agency, Howard; Cantrell-Colas, Literary Agency; Carvainis Agency, Maria; Castiglia Literary Agency; Clausen Assoc., Connie; Collins Purvis, Ltd.; Coover Agency, Doe; Curtis Associates, Richard; Cypher, Author's Representative, James R.; de la Haba Agency, Lois; DH Literary; Diamant, Anita; Diamond Literary Agency; Dijkstra Literary Agency, Sandra; Doyen Literary Services; Ducas, Robert; Dystel Literary Management, Jane; Educational Design Services; Ellison, Nicholas; Elmo Agency, Ann; Emerald Literary Agency; Fleury Agency, B.R.; Fogelman Literary Agency; Gartenberg, Literary Agent, Max; Gibson Agency, Sebastian; Goddard Book Group; Gordon Agency, Charlotte; Hawkins & Assoc., John; Heacock Literary Agency, Inc.; Hegler Literary Agency, Gary L.; Henderson Literary Representation; Henshaw Group, Richard; Hulburt Literary Agency, Helane; Hull House Literary Agency; Ievleva Literary Agency; JABberwocky Literary Agency; James Peter Assoc.; Kellock Company; Ketz Agency, Louise B.; Lampack Agency, Peter; Larsen/Elizabeth Pomada Literary Agents, Michael; Levine Communications, James; Lieberman Assoc., Robert; Lincoln Literary Agency, Ray; Lindstrom Literary Group; Literary Group; Lowenstein Associates; McBride Literary Agency, Margret; Mainhardt Agency, Ricia; Mann Agency, Carol; Michaels Literary Agency; Multimedia Product Development; Mura Enterprises, Dee; Naggar Literary Agency, Jean V.; New England Publishing Associates; Palmer & Dodge Agency; Parks Agency, Richard; Pevner, Stephen; Pine Assoc., Arthur; Pom; Potomac Literary Agency; Rees Literary Agency, Helen; Rinaldi Literary Agency, Angela; Rose Literary Agency; Russell-Simenauer Literary Agency; Schmidt Literary Agency, Harold; Schulman, Susan; Sebastian Literary Agency; Seligman, Literary Agent, Lynn; Shepard Agency; Singer Literary Agency, Evelyn; Spieler, F. Joseph; Steele & Co., Lyle; Stern Literary Agency, Gloria (TX); TCA; Travis Literary Agency, Susan; Urstadt Agency, Susan P.; Valcourt Agency, Richard R.; Vines Agency; Waterside Productions; Wieser & Wieser; Witherspoon & Associates, Inc.; Wreschner, Authors' Representative, Ruth; Writers House

Music/dance/theater/film. Acton, Leone, Hanson & Jaffe; Andrews & Associates Inc., Bart; Appleseeds Management; Authors Agency Author's Agency; Author's Agency; Baldi Literary Agency, Malaga; Balkin Agency; Becker Literary Agency, Wendy; Brandt & Brandt Literary Agents; Brown Associates Inc., Marie; Buck Agency, Howard; Bykofsky Assoc., Sheree; Casselman Literary Agent, Martha; Clausen Assoc., Connie; Collins Purvis, Ltd.; Cornfield Literary Agency, Robert; Curtis Associates, Richard; Cypher, Author's Representative, James R.; Dde la Haba Agency, Lois; DH Literary; Doyen Literary Services; Ellison, Nicholas; Elmo Agency, Ann; Farber Literary Agency; Garon-Brooke Assoc. Inc., Jay; Gartenberg, Literary Agent, Max; Gibson Agency, Sebastian; Greene, Arthur B.; Gregory Assoc., Maia; Hass Literary Agency, Rose; Hawkins & Assoc., John; Heacock Literary Agency, Inc.; Henderson Literary Representation; Henshaw Group, Richard; Hochmann Books, John L.; Hull House Literary Agency; Ievleva Literary Agency; Img-Julian Bach Literary Agency; JABberwocky Literary Agency; James Peter Assoc.; Kellock Company; Kouts, Literary Agent, Barbara S.; Lampack Agency, Peter; Larsen/Elizabeth Pomada Literary Agents, Michael; Lieberman Assoc., Robert; Lincoln Literary Agency, Ray; Literary Group; Lowenstein Associates; Lyceum Creative Properties; McBride Literary Agency, Margret; March Tenth; Markowitz Literary Agency, Barbara; Michaels Literary Agency; Naggar Literary Agency, Jean V.; Nathan, Ruth; Nazor Literary Agency, Karen; Norma-Lewis Agency; Otitis Media; Palmer & Dodge Agency; Parks Agency, Richard; Paul Agency, Richard; Perkins Assoc., L.; Pevner, Stephen; Pom; Pryor, Roberta; Renaissance—H.N. Swanson; Robbins Literary Agency, BJ; Rose Literary Agency; Sanders Literary Agency, Victoria; Schmidt Literary Agency, Harold; Schulman, Susan; Seligman, Literary Agent, Lynn; Shepard Agency; Siegel Literary Agency, Bobbe; Spitzer Literary Agency, Philip G.; 2M Comm.; Urstadt Agency, Susan P.; Vines Agency; Wald Assoc., Mary Jack; Ware Literary Agency, John A.; Wecksler-Incomco; Weingel-Fidel Agency; Witherspoon & Associates, Inc.; Writers House; Zeckendorf Assoc., Susan; Ziegler Literary Agency, George

Nature/environment. Acton, Leone, Hanson & Jaffe; Adler & Robin Books; Agency Chicago; Altshuler Literary Agency, Miriam; Author's Agency; Author's Agency; Baldi Literary Agency, Malaga; Balkin Agency; Becker Literary Agency, Wendy; Boates Literary Agency, Reid; Brandt & Brandt Literary Agents; Brown Literary Agency, Andrea; Buck Agency, Howard; Cantrell-Colas, Literary Agency; Castiglia Literary Agency; Clausen Assoc., Connie; Collin Literary Agent, Frances; Collins Purvis, Ltd.; Coover Agency, Doe; Crown International Literature and Arts Agency, Bonnie R.; Cypher, Author's Representative, James R.; Darhansoff & Verrill Literary Agents; de la Haba Agency, Lois; DH Literary; Diamant, Anita; Dijkstra Literary Agency, Sandra; Doyen Literary Services; Ducas, Robert; Elek Assoc., Peter; Elliott Agency; Ellison, Nicholas; Eth Literary Representation, Felicia; Flaherty, Literary Agent, Joyce A.; Flaming Star Literary Enterprises; Fleury Agency, B.R.; Gartenberg, Literary Agent, Max; Gibson Agency, Sebastian; Goddard Book Group; Gordon Agency, Charlotte; Graham Literary Agency; Hawkins & Assoc., John; Heacock Literary Agency, Inc.; Hegler Literary Agency, Gary L.; Henshaw Group, Richard;

Herner Rights Agency, Susan; Hulburt Literary Agency, Helane; Img-Julian Bach Literary Agency; JABberwocky Literary Agency; Kellock Company; Kouts, Literary Agent, Barbara S.; Larsen/Elizabeth Pomada Literary Agents, Michael; Lasher Agency, Maureen; Levant & Wales, Literary Agency; Levine Communications, James; Lieberman Assoc., Robert; Lincoln Literary Agency, Ray; Literary Group; Love Literary Agency, Nancy; Lowenstein Associates; Lyceum Creative Properties; Macbride McBride Literary Agency, Margret; Mainhardt Agency, Ricia; Manus & Associates Literary Agency; Markowitz Literary Agency, Barbara; Metropolitan Talent Agency; Michaels Literary Agency; Multimedia Product Development; Mura Enterprises, Dee; Nazor Literary Agency, Karen; New England Publishing Associates; Norma-Lewis Agency; Palmer & Dodge Agency; Parks Agency, Richard; Paton Literary Agency, Kathi J.; Pryor, Roberta; Quicksilver Books-Literary Agents; Raymond, Literary Agent, Charlotte Cecil; Robbins Literary Agency, BJ; Rose Literary Agency; Rowland Agency, Damaris; Rubenstein Literary Agency, Pesha; Schmidt Literary Agency, Harold; Schulman, Susan; Seligman, Literary Agent, Lynn; Shepard Agency; Siegel Literary Agency, Bobbe; Sierra Literary Agency; Singer Literary Agency, Evelyn; Spitzer Literary Agency, Philip G.; Stauffer Assoc., Nancy; Steele & Co., Lyle; Stepping Stone; Taylor Literary Enterprises, Sandra; Toad Hall; Travis Literary Agency, Susan; Ubel Assoc., Robert; Urstadt Agency, Susan P.; Wald Assoc., Mary Jack; Ware Literary Agency, John A.; Waterside Productions; Watkins Loomis Agency; Wecksler-Incomco; Wieser & Wieser; Writers House; Ziegler Literary Agency, George

New Age/metaphysics. Acton, Leone, Hanson & Jaffe; Author's Agency; Becker Literary Agency, Wendy; Behar Literary Agency, Josh; Bernstein, Pam; Brown Associates Inc., Marie; Buck Agency, Howard; Cantrell-Colas, Literary Agency; Castiglia Literary Agency; Circle of Confusion; de la Haba Agency, Lois; DH Literary; Diamant, Anita; Doyen Literary Services; Dystel Literary Management, Jane; Ellenberg Literary Agency, Ethan; Ellison, Nicholas; Flaming Star Literary Enterprises; Fleury Agency, B.R.; Franklin Assoc., Lynn C.; Gibson Agency, Sebastian; Hardy Agency; Hawkins & Assoc., John; Heacock Literary Agency, Inc.; Henshaw Group, Richard; Herner Rights Agency, Susan; Hulburt Literary Agency, Helane; Ievleva Literary Agency; J de S Assoc.; Larsen/Elizabeth Pomada Literary Agents, Michael; Levant & Wales, Literary Agency; Levine Communications, James; Lewis & Co., Karen; Literary Group; Love Literary Agency, Nancy; Lowenstein Associates; Lyceum Creative Properties; Mainhardt Agency, Ricia; Miller Agency; Naggar Literary Agency, Jean V.; Palmer & Dodge Agency; Pevner, Stephen; Publishing Services; Quicksilver Books-Literary Agents; Rowland Agency, Damaris; Russell-Simenauer Literary Agency; Schmidt Literary Agency, Harold; Schulman, Susan; Steele & Co., Lyle; Stepping Stone; Toad Hall; Waterside Productions; Watt & Assoc., Sandra

Open to all nonfiction categories. Authors' Literary Agency; Barrett Books, Loretta; Brown, Curtis; Bykofsky Assoc., Sheree; Candace Lake Agency; Cohen Literary Agency, Hy; Congdon Associates, Don; Dragon Literary; Dupree/Miller and Assoc.; Fleming Agency, Peter; Goldfarb & Graybill, Attorneys at Law; Greenburger Assoc., Sanford J.; Gusay Literary Agency, Charlotte; Hamilburg Agency, Mitchell J.; Hoffman Literary Agency, Berenice; Int'l Publisher Associates Inc.; Lazear Agency; Madsen Agency, Robert; Martell Agency; Ober Assoc., Harold; Pelter, Rodney; Rock Literary Agency; Rogers Literary Representation, Irene; Samdum & Assoc.; Snell Literary Agency, Michael; Van Der Leun & Assoc.; Zahler Literary Agency, Karen Gantz

Popular culture. Acton, Leone, Hanson & Jaffe; Adler & Robin Books; Author's Agency; Becker Literary Agency, Wendy; Bernstein, Pam; Brown, Curtis; Brown Literary Agency, Andrea; Buck Agency, Howard; Bykofsky Assoc., Sheree; Charlton Assoc., James; Circle of Confusion; Collins Purvis, Ltd.; Cypher, Author's Representative, James R.; Daves Agency, Joan; DH Literary; DHS Literary; Doyen Literary Services; Dystel Literary Management, Jane; Elek Assoc., Peter; Elliott Agency; Elmo Agency, Ann; Emerald Literary Agency; Eth Literary Representation, Felicia; Flaherty, Literary Agent, Joyce A.; Fleury Agency, B.R.; Fogelman Literary Agency; Gibson Agency, Sebastian; Halsey Agency, Reece; Heacock Literary Agency, Inc.; Henderson Literary Representation; Henshaw Group, Richard; Herner Rights Agency, Susan; Ievleva Literary Agency; JABberwocky Literary Agency; James Peter Assoc.; Kellock Company; Kidde, Hoyt & Picard; Lampack Agency, Peter; Larsen/Elizabeth Pomada Literary Agents, Michael; Lasher Agency, Maureen; Levine Literary Agency, Ellen; Lindstrom Literary Group; Literary Group; Love Literary Agency, Nancy; Lowenstein Associates; McBride Literary Agency, Margret; Mainhardt Agency, Ricia; Manus & Associates Literary Agency; March Tenth; Markowitz Literary Agency, Barbara; Metropolitan Talent Agency; Multimedia Product Development; Nazor Literary Agency, Karen; New Brand Agency Group; Normalewis Agency, The Norma-Lewis Agency; Orr Agency, Alice; Palmer & Dodge Agency; Parks Agency, Richard; Perkins Assoc., L.; Pevner, Stephen; Pryor, Roberta; Publishing Services; Quicksilver Books-Literary Agents; Rinaldi Literary Agency, Angela; Robbins Literary Agency, BJ; Russell-Simenauer Literary Agency; Sanders Literary Agency, Victoria; Schulman, Susan; Seligman, Literary Agent, Lynn; Spitzer Literary Agency, Philip G.; Stauffer Assoc., Nancy; Toad Hall; Travis Literary Agency, Susan; Urstadt Agency, Susan P.; Vines Agency; Ware Literary Agency, John A.; Watkins Loomis Agency; Wreschner, Authors' Representative, Ruth

Photography. Author's Agency; Baldi Literary Agency, Malaga; Becker Literary Agency, Wendy; Brown Literary Agency, Andrea; Buck Agency, Howard; Collins Purvis, Ltd.; DH Literary; Doyen Literary Services; Ellison, Nicholas; Elmo Agency, Ann; Feiler Literary Agency, Florence; Fleury Agency, B.R.; Gibson Agency, Sebastian; Hawkins & Assoc., John; Henderson Literary Representation; Kellock Company; Larsen/Elizabeth Pomada Literary Agents, Michael; Nazor Literary Agency, Karen; Norma-Lewis Agency; Otitis Media; Pevner, Stephen; Pryor, Roberta; Seligman, Literary Agent, Lynn; Urstadt Agency, Susan P.; Wald Assoc., Mary Jack; Wecksler-Incomco

Psychology. Acton, Leone, Hanson & Jaffe; Agents Inc. for Medical and Mental Health Professionals; Altshuler Literary Agency, Miriam; Appleseeds Management; Author's Agency; Authors' Literary Agency; Baldi Literary Agency, Malaga; Becker Literary Agency, Wendy; Bernstein, Pam; Boates Literary Agency, Reid; Brandt & Brandt Literary Agents; Brown Associates Inc., Marie; Buck Agency, Howard; Bykofsky Assoc., Sheree; Cantrell-

Colas, Literary Agency; Carvainis Agency, Maria; Castiglia Literary Agency; Clausen Assoc., Connie; Collins Purvis, Ltd.; Coover Agency, Doe; Cypher, Author's Representative, James R.; DH Literary; Diamant, Anita; Diamond Literary Agency; Dijkstra Literary Agency, Sandra; Doyen Literary Services; Dystel Literary Management, Jane; Ellenberg Literary Agency, Ethan; Ellison, Nicholas; Elmo Agency, Ann; Emerald Literary Agency; Eth Literary Representation, Felicia; Farber Literary Agency; Feiler Literary Agency, Florence; Flaherty, Literary Agent, Joyce A.; Fleury Agency, B.R.; Franklin Assoc., Lynn C.; Garon-Brooke Assoc. Inc., Jay; Gartenberg, Literary Agent, Max; Gibson Agency, Sebastian; Goddard Book Group; Gordon Agency, Charlotte; Green, Literary Agent, Randall Elisha; Hawkins & Assoc., John; Heacock Literary Agency, Inc.; Hegler Literary Agency, Gary L.; Henderson Literary Representation; Henshaw Group, Richard; Herman Agency, Jeff; Herner Rights Agency, Susan; Hulburt Literary Agency, Helane; Ievleva Literary Agency; Img-Julian Bach Literary Agency; James Peter Assoc.; Kellock Company; Kidde, Hoyt & Picard; Klinger, Harvey; Kouts, Literary Agent, Barbara S.; Larsen/Elizabeth Pomada Literary Agents, Michael; Lasher Agency, Maureen; Levant & Wales, Literary Agency; Levine Communications, James; Levine Literary Agency, Ellen; Lieberman Assoc., Robert; Lincoln Literary Agency, Ray; Lindstrom Literary Group; Literary Group; Love Literary Agency, Nancy; Lowenstein Associates; Lyceum Creative Properties; McBride Literary Agency, Margret; McGrath, Helen; Mainhardt Agency, Ricia; Mann Agency, Carol; Manus & Associates Literary Agency; Miller Agency; Naggar Literary Agency, Jean V.; New England Publishing Associates; Nine Muses and Apollo; Palmer & Dodge Agency; Parks Agency, Richard; Paton Literary Agency, Kathi J.; Pine Assoc., Arthur; Potomac Literary Agency; Protter Literary Agent, Susan Ann; Quicksilver Books-Literary Agents; Raymond, Literary Agent, Charlotte Cecil; Rinaldi Literary Agency, Angela; Robbins Literary Agency, BJ; Rose Literary Agency; Russell-Simenauer Literary Agency; Sanders Literary Agency, Victoria; Schmidt Literary Agency, Harold; Schulman, Susan; Sebastian Literary Agency; Seligman, Literary Agent, Lynn; Shepard Agency; Siegel Literary Agency, Bobbe; Singer Literary Agency, Evelyn; Snell Literary Agency, Michael; Spitzer Literary Agency, Philip G.; Steele & Co., Lyle; Stepping Stone; Stern Literary Agency, Gloria (TX); Teal Literary Agency, Patricia; Travis Literary Agency, Susan; Ubel Assoc., Robert; Vines Agency; Ware Literary Agency, John A.; Waterside Productions; Weingel-Fidel Agency; Wieser & Wieser; Wreschner, Authors' Representative, Ruth; Writers House; Zeckendorf Assoc., Susan

Religious/inspirational. Acton, Leone, Hanson & Jaffe; Author's Agency; Bernstein, Pam; Brandenburgh & Assoc. Literary Agency; Brown Associates Inc., Marie; Buck Agency, Howard; Bykofsky Assoc., Sheree; Castiglia Literary Agency; Ciske & Dietz Literary Agency; Coover Agency, Doe; de la Haba Agency, Lois; DH Literary; Diamant, Anita; Dystel Literary Management, Jane; Ellenberg Literary Agency, Ethan; Ellison, Nicholas; Emerald Literary Agency; Feiler Literary Agency, Florence; Franklin Assoc., Lynn C.; Gibson Agency, Sebastian; Green, Literary Agent, Randall Elisha; Heacock Literary Agency, Inc.; Hegler Literary Agency, Gary L.; Henderson Literary Representation; Henshaw Group, Richard; Herner Rights Agency, Susan; Holub and Assoc.; Hulburt Literary Agency, Helane; Ievleva Literary Agency; Jordan Literary Agency, Lawrence; Kellock Company; Larsen/Elizabeth Pomada Literary Agents, Michael; Levine Communications, James; Literary Group; Lowenstein Associates; McBride Literary Agency, Margret; Multimedia Product Development; Naggar Literary Agency, Jean V.; New Brand Agency Group; Nine Muses and Apollo; Palmer & Dodge Agency; Pevner, Stephen; Printed Tree; Quicksilver Books-Literary Agents; Rose Agency; Rowland Agency, Damaris; Russell-Simenauer Literary Agency; Schulman, Susan; Seymour Agency; Shepard Agency; Singer Literary Agency, Evelyn; Stepping Stone; Toad Hall; Travis Literary Agency, Susan; Wreschner, Authors' Representative, Ruth; Ziegler Literary Agency, George

Science/technology. Acton, Leone, Hanson & Jaffe; Agents Inc. for Medical and Mental Health Professionals; Author's Agency; Author's Agency; Baldi Literary Agency, Malaga; Balkin Agency; Becker Literary Agency, Wendy; Bernstein, Pam; Boates Literary Agency, Reid; Bova Literary Agency, Barbara; Brandt & Brandt Literary Agents; Brown Literary Agency, Andrea; Buck Agency, Howard; Cantrell-Colas, Literary Agency; Carvainis Agency, Maria; Castiglia Literary Agency; Collins Purvis, Ltd.; Coover Agency, Doe; Curtis Associates, Richard; Cypher, Author's Representative, James R.; Darhansoff & Verrill Literary Agents; DH Literary; Diamant, Anita; Dijkstra Literary Agency, Sandra; Doyen Literary Services; Ducas, Robert; Dystel Literary Management, Jane; Educational Design Services; Elek Assoc., Peter; Ellenberg Literary Agency, Ethan; Elliott Agency; Ellison, Nicholas; Eth Literary Representation, Felicia; Flaming Star Literary Enterprises; Fleury Agency, B.R.; Gartenberg, Literary Agent, Max; Gibson Agency, Sebastian; Goddard Book Group; Graham Literary Agency; Hawkins & Assoc., John; Hegler Literary Agency, Gary L.; Henderson Literary Representation; Henshaw Group, Richard; Herner Rights Agency, Susan; Hulburt Literary Agency, Helane; Ievleva Literary Agency; JABberwocky Literary Agency; Jordan Literary Agency, Lawrence; Kellock Company; Ketz Agency, Louise B.; Klinger, Harvey; Larsen/Elizabeth Pomada Literary Agents, Michael; Lasher Agency, Maureen; Levant & Wales, Literary Agency; Levine Communications, James; Levine Literary Agency, Ellen; Lieberman Assoc., Robert; Lincoln Literary Agency, Ray; Lindstrom Literary Group; Lipkind Agency, Wendy; Literary Group; Love Literary Agency, Nancy; Lowenstein Associates; McBride Literary Agency, Margret; Madsen Agency, Robert; Mainhardt Agency, Ricia; Multimedia Product Development; Mura Enterprises, Dee; Nazor Literary Agency, Karen; New England Publishing Associates; Nine Muses and Apollo; Palmer & Dodge Agency; Parks Agency, Richard; Perkins Assoc., L.; Pevner, Stephen; Potomac Literary Agency; Protter Literary Agent, Susan Ann; Quicksilver Books-Literary Agents; Rose Literary Agency; Schmidt Literary Agency, Harold; Seligman, Literary Agent, Lynn; Singer Literary Agency, Evelyn; Snell Literary Agency, Michael; Steele & Co., Lyle; Stern Literary Agency, Gloria (TX); Ubel Assoc., Robert; Wallace Literary Agency; Ware Literary Agency, John A.; Weingel-Fidel Agency; Witherspoon & Associates, Inc.; Wreschner, Authors' Representative, Ruth; Writers House; Zeckendorf Assoc., Susan

Self-help/personal improvement. Acton, Leone, Hanson & Jaffe; Agents Inc. for Medical and Mental Health Professionals; Ajlouny Agency, Joseph S.; Appleseeds Management; Author's Agency; Authors' Literary Agency; Baldi Literary Agency, Malaga; Becker Literary Agency, Wendy; Behar Literary Agency, Josh;

Bernstein, Pam; Boates Literary Agency, Reid; Bova Literary Agency, Barbara; Brandt & Brandt Literary Agents; Brown Associates Inc., Marie; Buck Agency, Howard; Bykofsky Assoc., Sheree; Cantrell-Colas, Literary Agency; Castiglia Literary Agency; Charlton Assoc., James; Ciske & Dietz Literary Agency; Clausen Assoc., Connie; Collins Purvis, Ltd.; Columbia Literary Assoc., Inc.; Curtis Associates, Richard; Cypher, Author's Representative, James R.; de la Haba Agency, Lois; DH Literary; Diamant, Anita; Diamond Literary Agency; Dijkstra Literary Agency, Sandra; Doyen Literary Services; Ellenberg Literary Agency, Ethan; Elmo Agency, Ann; Emerald Literary Agency; Feiler Literary Agency, Florence; Flaherty, Literary Agent, Joyce A.; Flaming Star Literary Enterprises; Fleury Agency, B.R.; Fogelman Literary Agency; Franklin Assoc., Lynn C.; Garon-Brooke Assoc. Inc., Jay; Gartenberg, Literary Agent, Max; Gibson Agency, Sebastian; Goddard Book Group; Hawkins & Assoc., John; Hegler Literary Agency, Gary L.; Henderson Literary Representation; Henshaw Group, Richard; Herman Agency, Jeff; Herner Rights Agency, Susan; Holub and Assoc.; Hulburt Literary Agency, Helane; Ievleva Literary Agency; Img-Julian Bach Literary Agency; J de S Assoc.; James Peter Assoc.; Jordan Literary Agency, Lawrence; Kellock Company; Kidde, Hoyt & Picard; Klinger, Harvey; Kouts, Literary Agent, Barbara S.; Larsen/Elizabeth Pomada Literary Agents, Michael; Lasher Agency, Maureen; Levant & Wales, Literary Agency; Levine Communications, James; Lewis & Co., Karen; Lincoln Literary Agency, Ray; Lindstrom Literary Group; Literary and Creative Artists Agency; Literary Group; Love Literary Agency, Nancy; Lowenstein Associates; McBride Literary Agency, Margret; McGrath, Helen; Madsen Agency, Robert; Mainhardt Agency, Ricia; Mann Agency, Carol; Manus & Associates Literary Agency; Michaels Literary Agency; Miller Agency; Multimedia Product Development; Mura Enterprises, Dee; Naggar Literary Agency, Jean V.; New England Publishing Associates; Nine Muses and Apollo; Norma-Lewis Agency; Palmer & Dodge Agency; Parks Agency, Richard; Pine Assoc., Arthur; Potomac Literary Agency; Printed Tree; Publishing Services; Quicksilver Books-Literary Agents; Rinaldi Literary Agency, Angela; Robbins Literary Agency, BJ; Rogers Literary Representation, Irene; Rose Agency; Rose Literary Agency; Russell-Simenauer Literary Agency; Schmidt Literary Agency, Harold; Schulman, Susan; Sebastian Literary Agency; Seligman, Literary Agent, Lynn; Shepard Agency; Siegel Literary Agency, Bobbe; Sierra Literary Agency; Singer Literary Agency, Evelyn; Stauffer Assoc., Nancy; Steele & Co., Lyle; Stepping Stone; Stern Literary Agency, Gloria (TX); Targ Literary Agency, Inc., Roslyn; Teal Literary Agency, Patricia; Toad Hall Inc Toad Hall; Travis Literary Agency, Susan; 2M Comm.; Urstadt Agency, Susan P.; Watt & Assoc., Sandra; Weiner Literary Agency, Cherry; Witherspoon & Associates, Inc.; Wreschner, Authors' Representative, Ruth; Writers House; Ziegler Literary Agency, George

Sociology. Agents Inc. for Medical and Mental Health Professionals; Ajlouny Agency, Joseph S.; Author's Agency; Baldi Literary Agency, Malaga; Balkin Agency; Becker Literary Agency, Wendy; Bernstein, Pam; Brandt & Brandt Literary Agents; Brown Associates Inc., Marie; Brown Literary Agency, Andrea; Buck Agency, Howard; Cantrell-Colas, Literary Agency; Castiglia Literary Agency; Collins Purvis, Ltd.; Coover Agency, Doe; Cypher, Author's Representative, James R.; DH Literary; Dijkstra Literary Agency, Sandra; Doyen Literary Services; Educational Design Services; Ellison, Nicholas; Eth Literary Representation, Felicia; Flaherty, Literary Agent, Joyce A.; Fleury Agency, B.R.; Gibson Agency, Sebastian; Goddard Book Group; Gordon Agency, Charlotte; Hawkins & Assoc., John; Heacock Literary Agency, Inc.; Henderson Literary Representation; Henshaw Group, Richard; Herner Rights Agency, Susan; Hochmann Books, John L.; Hulburt Literary Agency, Helane; Hull House Literary Agency; J de S Assoc.; JABberwocky Literary Agency; Kellock Company; Kidde, Hoyt & Picard; Larsen/Elizabeth Pomada Literary Agents, Michael; Lasher Agency, Maureen; Levine Communications, James; Lieberman Assoc., Robert; Lincoln Literary Agency, Ray; Lipkind Agency, Wendy; Literary Group; Love Literary Agency, Nancy; Lowenstein Associates; Lyceum Creative Properties; McBride Literary Agency, Margret; Mainhardt Agency, Ricia; Mann Agency, Carol; Multimedia Product Development; Mura Enterprises, Dee; Naggar Literary Agency, Jean V.; Nazor Literary Agency, Karen; New England Publishing Associates; Palmer & Dodge Agency; Parks Agency, Richard; Paton Literary Agency, Kathi J.; Pevner, Stephen; Pryor, Roberta; Quicksilver Books-Literary Agents; Raymond, Literary Agent, Charlotte Cecil; Rinaldi Literary Agency, Angela; Robbins Literary Agency, BJ; Rose Literary Agency; Schmidt Literary Agency, Harold; Schulman, Susan; Sebastian Literary Agency; Seligman, Literary Agent, Lynn; Shepard Agency; Spieler, F. Joseph; Spitzer Literary Agency, Philip G.; Stauffer Assoc., Nancy; Steele & Co., Lyle; Stern Literary Agency, Gloria (TX); Valcourt Agency, Richard R.; Wald Assoc., Mary Jack; Waterside Productions; Weiner Literary Agency, Cherry; Weingel-Fidel Agency; Zeckendorf Assoc., Susan

Sports. Acton, Leone, Hanson & Jaffe; Agency Chicago; Agents Inc. for Medical and Mental Health Professionals; Allan Agency, Lee; Author's Agency; Becker Literary Agency, Wendy; Black Literary Agency, David; Boates Literary Agency, Reid; Brandt & Brandt Literary Agents; Brown Literary Agency, Andrea; Buck Agency, Howard; Circle of Confusion; Curtis Associates, Richard; Cypher, Author's Representative, James R.; DH Literary; DHS Literary; Diamant, Anita; Dijkstra Literary Agency, Sandra; Doyen Literary Services; Ducas, Robert; Esq. Literary Productions; Flaming Star Literary Enterprises; Fleury Agency, B.R.; Gartenberg, Literary Agent, Max; Gibson Agency, Sebastian; Greene, Arthur B.; Hawkins & Assoc., John; Heacock Literary Agency, Inc.; Henderson Literary Representation; Henshaw Group, Richard; Ievleva Literary Agency; Img-Julian Bach Literary Agency; J de S Assoc.; JABberwocky Literary Agency; Jordan Literary Agency, Lawrence; Kellock Company; Ketz Agency, Louise B.; Klinger, Harvey; Larsen/Elizabeth Pomada Literary Agents, Michael; Lasher Agency, Maureen; Levant & Wales, Literary Agency; Levine Communications, James; Lincoln Literary Agency, Ray; Literary Group; Lowenstein Associates; McBride Literary Agency, Margret; Macgrath, Helen McGrath, Helen; Mainhardt Agency, Ricia; Markowitz Literary Agency, Barbara; Michaels Literary Agency; Miller Agency; Mura Enterprises, Dee; Nazor Literary Agency, Karen; New Brand Agency Group; Pocono Literary Agency; Pom; Potomac Literary Agency; Quicksilver Books-Literary Agents; Robbins Literary Agency, BJ; Rose Literary Agency; Russell-Simenauer Literary Agency; Shepard Agency; Siegel Literary Agency, Bobbe; Spitzer Literary Agency, Philip G.; Steele & Co., Lyle; Stern Literary Agency, Gloria (TX); Urstadt Agency, Susan P.; Ware Literary Agency, John A.; Waterside Productions; Watt & Assoc., Sandra

Translations. Author's Agency; Balkin Agency; Buck Agency, Howard; Crown International Literature and Arts Agency, Bonnie R.; Daves Agency, Joan; Ellison, Nicholas; Gibson Agency, Sebastian; Ievleva Literary Agency; J de S Assoc.; Lyceum Creative Properties; Sanders Literary Agency, Victoria; Schmidt Literary Agency, Harold; Schulman, Susan; Seligman, Literary Agent, Lynn; Stauffer Assoc., Nancy; Wald Assoc., Mary Jack; Wieser & Wieser

True crime/investigative. Act I; Acton, Leone, Hanson & Jaffe; Adler & Robin Books; Agency Chicago; Allen, Literary Agency, James; Appleseeds Management; Author's Agency; Authors' Literary Agency; Baldi Literary Agency, Malaga; Balkin Agency; Bernstein, Pam; Boates Literary Agency, Reid; Bova Literary Agency, Barbara; Brandt & Brandt Literary Agents; Buck Agency, Howard; Bykofsky Assoc., Sheree; Cantrell-Colas, Literary Agency; Carvainis Agency, Maria; Charisma Communications; Circle of Confusion; Ciske & Dietz Literary Agency; Clausen Assoc., Connie; Cohen, Inc. Literary Agency, Ruth; Collin Literary Agent, Frances; Collins Purvis, Ltd.; Coover Agency, Doe; Crawford Literary Agency; Curtis Associates, Richard; Cypher, Author's Representative, James R.; DH Literary; DHS Literary; Diamant, Anita; Dijkstra Literary Agency, Sandra; Doyen Literary Services; Ducas, Robert; Dystel Literary Management, Jane; Elek Assoc., Peter; Ellenberg Literary Agency, Ethan; Elliott Agency; Ellison, Nicholas; Elmo Agency, Ann; Eth Literary Representation, Felicia; Feiler Literary Agency, Florence; Flaherty, Literary Agent, Joyce A.; Fleury Agency, B.R.; Fogelman Literary Agency; Garon-Brooke Assoc. Inc., Jay; Gartenberg, Literary Agent, Max; Goddard Book Group; Graham Literary Agency; Green, Literary Agent, Randall Elisha; Halsey Agency, Reece; Hawkins & Assoc., John; Heacock Literary Agency, Inc.; Hegler Literary Agency, Gary L.; Henderson Literary Representation; Henshaw Group, Richard; Herner Rights Agency, Susan; Hulburt Literary Agency, Helane; Hull House Literary Agency; Ievleva Literary Agency; Img-Julian Bach Literary Agency; JABberwocky Literary Agency; Ketz Agency, Louise B.; Klinger, Harvey; Lampack Agency, Peter; Larsen/ Elizabeth Pomada Literary Agents, Michael; Lasher Agency, Maureen; Literary Group; Love Literary Agency, Nancy; Lowenstein Associates; McBride Literary Agency, Margret; Madsen Agency, Robert; Mainhardt Agency, Ricia; Mann Agency, Carol; Manus & Associates Literary Agency; Metropolitan Talent Agency; Multimedia Product Development; Mura Enterprises, Dee; Naggar Literary Agency, Jean V.; Nathan, Ruth; New England Publishing Associates; Norma-Lewis Agency; Nugent Literary; Otitis Media; Parks Agency, Richard; Potomac Literary Agency; Pryor, Roberta; Quicksilver Books-Literary Agents; Renaissance—H.N. Swanson; Rinaldi Literary Agency, Angela; Robbins Literary Agency, BJ; Rose Literary Agency; Russell-Simenauer Literary Agency; Schmidt Literary Agency, Harold; Schulman, Susan; Sebastian Literary Agency; Seligman, Literary Agent, Lynn; Siegel Literary Agency, Bobbe; Spitzer Literary Agency, Philip G.; Steele & Co., Lyle; Stern Literary Agency, Gloria (TX); TCA; Teal Literary Agency, Patricia; Van Duren Agency, Annette; Vines Agency; Wald Assoc., Mary Jack; Wallace Literary Agency; Ware Literary Agency, John A.; Waterside Productions; Watkins Loomis Agency; Watt & Assoc., Sandra; Wieser & Wieser; Witherspoon & Associates, Inc.; Wreschner, Authors' Representative, Ruth; Wright Representatives, Ann; Writers House; Zeckendorf Assoc., Susan

Women's issues/women's studies. Act I; Acton, Leone, Hanson & Jaffe; Adler & Robin Books; Altshuler Literary Agency, Miriam; Author's Agency; Authors' Literary Agency; Baldi Literary Agency, Malaga; Becker Literary Agency, Wendy; Behar Literary Agency, Josh; Bernstein, Pam; Boates Literary Agency, Reid; Borchardt, Georges; Bova Literary Agency, Barbara; Brandt & Brandt Literary Agents; Brown Associates Inc., Marie; Buck Agency, Howard; Bykofsky Assoc., Sheree; Cantrell-Colas, Literary Agency; Carvainis Agency, Maria; Casselman Literary Agent, Martha; Castiglia Literary Agency; Circle of Confusion; Ciske & Dietz Literary Agency; Clausen Assoc., Connie; Cohen, Inc. Literary Agency, Ruth; Collins Purvis, Ltd.; Coover Agency, Doe; Crawford Literary Agency; Crown International Literature and Arts Agency, Bonnie R.; Cypher, Author's Representative, James R.; Daves Agency, Joan; de la Haba Agency, Lois; DH Literary; Diamant, Anita; Dijkstra Literary Agency, Sandra; Doyen Literary Services; Dystel Literary Management, Jane; Educational Design Services; Ellison, Nicholas; Elmo Agency, Ann; Emerald Literary Agency; Eth Literary Representation, Felicia; Feiler Literary Agency, Florence; Flaherty, Literary Agent, Joyce A.; Fogelman Literary Agency; Gartenberg, Literary Agent, Max; Gibson Agency, Sebastian; Goddard Book Group; Gordon Agency, Charlotte; Halsey Agency, Reece; Hass Literary Agency, Rose; Hawkins & Assoc., John; Heacock Literary Agency, Inc.; Henderson Literary Representation; Henshaw Group, Richard; Herner Rights Agency, Susan; Hill Associates, Frederick; Hulburt Literary Agency, Helane; Ievleva Literary Agency; Img-Julian Bach Literary Agency; JABberwocky Literary Agency; Kellock Company; Kidde, Hoyt And Picard Kidde, Hoyt & Picard; Klinger, Harvey; Kouts, Literary Agent, Barbara S.; Kroll Literary Agency, Edite; Lampack Agency, Peter; Larsen/Elizabeth Pomada Literary Agents, Michael; Lasher Agency, Maureen; Levant & Wales, Literary Agency; Levine Communications, James; Levine Literary Agency, Ellen; Lewis & Co., Karen; Lincoln Literary Agency, Ray; Lindstrom Literary Group; Literary Group; Love Literary Agency, Nancy; Lowenstein Associates; McBride Literary Agency, Margret; Maccoby Literary Agency, Gina; McGrath, Helen; Mainhardt Agency, Ricia; Mann Agency, Carol; Manus & Associates Literary Agency; Markowitz Literary Agency, Barbara; Michaels Literary Agency; Miller Agency; Multimedia Product Development; Mura Enterprises, Dee; Naggar Literary Agency, Jean V.; Nazor Literary Agency, Karen; New England Publishing Associates; Nine Muses and Apollo; Norma-Lewis Agency; Palmer & Dodge Agency; Parks Agency, Richard; Paton Literary Agency, Kathi J.; Pom; Printed Tree; Pryor, Roberta; Publishing Services; Quicksilver Books-Literary Agents; Raymond, Literary Agent, Charlotte Cecil; Rees Literary Agency, Helen; Rinaldi Literary Agency, Angela; Robbins Literary Agency, BJ; Rose Literary Agency; Rowland Agency, Damaris; Russell-Simenauer Literary Agency; Sanders Literary Agency, Victoria; Schmidt Literary Agency, Harold; Schulman, Susan; Sebastian Literary Agency; Seligman, Literary Agent, Lynn; Shepard Agency; Siegel Literary Agency, Bobbe; Sierra Literary Agency; Singer Literary Agency, Evelyn; Snell Literary Agency, Michael; Spieler, F. Joseph; Stepping Stone; Stern Literary Agency, Gloria (TX); TCA; Teal Literary Agency, Patricia; Travis Literary Agency, Susan; 2M Comm.; Urstadt Agency, Susan P.; Vines Agency; Waterside Productions; Watkins Loomis Agency; Watt & Assoc., Sandra; Weingel-Fidel Agency; Witherspoon & Associates, Inc.; Wreschner, Authors' Representative, Ruth; Writers House; Zeckendorf Assoc., Susan

Fee-charging literary agents/Fiction

Action/adventure. Acacia House; AEI/Atchity Editorial/Entertainment Int'l; Ahearn Agency; Authentic Creations Literary Agency; Author Aid Assoc.; Brinke Literary Agency; Brown, Literary Agent, Antoinette; Browne, Pema; Cambridge Literary Assoc.; Catalog Literary Agency; Chadd-Stevens Literary Agency; Collier Assoc.; Dorese Agency; Fishbein, Frieda; Flannery, White and Stone; ForthWrite Literary Agency; Fran Literary Agency; GEM Literary Services; Gladden Unlimited; Hamilton's Literary Agency, Andrew; Hilton Literary Agency, Alice; Hubbs Agency, Yvonne Trudeau; Independent Publishing Agency; Jenks Agency, Carolyn; Kaltman Literary Agency, Larry; Kellock & Assoc., J.; Kern Literary Agency, Natasha; Kirkland Literary Agency; Law Offices of Robert L. Fenton PC; Lee Literary Agency, L. Harry; Lighthouse Literary Agency; Literary Group West; McKinley, Literary Agency, Virginia C.; Marshall Agency, Evan; Montgomery Literary Agency; Nelson, BK; Northwest Literary Services; Pell Agency, William; Penmarin Books; PMA Literary & Film Management; Portman Organization; Puddingstone Literary Agency; QCorp Literary Agency; Southern Literary Agency; Steinberg Literary Agency, Michael; Stern Agency, Gloria (CA); Strong Literary Agency, Marianne; Wallerstein Agency, Gerry B.; West Coast Literary Assoc.; Westchester Literary Agency, Inc.; Writer's Consulting Group

Cartoon/comic. Chadd-Stevens Literary Agency; Colby: Literary Agency; Fran Literary Agency; Hamilton's Literary Agency, Andrew; Howard Agency, Eddy; Independent Publishing Agency; Montgomery Literary Agency; Nelson, BK; Northeast Literary Agency

Confessional. Author Aid Assoc.; Chadd-Stevens Literary Agency; Hamilton's Literary Agency, Andrew; Hilton Literary Agency, Alice; Independent Publishing Agency; Kaltman Literary Agency, Larry; Northwest Literary Services; QCorp Literary Agency; Visions Press

Contemporary issues. AEI/Atchity Editorial/Entertainment Int'l; Ahearn Agency; Author Aid Assoc.; Bartczak Assoc., Gene; Browne, Pema; Cambridge Literary Assoc.; Chester, Literary Agency, Linda; Connor Literary Agency; Dorese Agency; Fishbein, Frieda; Fran Literary Agency; Hamilton's Literary Agency, Andrew; Hilton Literary Agency, Alice; Hubbs Agency, Yvonne Trudeau; Independent Publishing Agency; Jenks Agency, Carolyn; Kaltman Literary Agency, Larry; Kellock & Assoc., J.; Kern Literary Agency, Natasha; Kirkland Literary Agency; Law Offices of Robert L. Fenton PC; Lighthouse Literary Agency; Lopopolo Literary Agency, Toni; McKinley, Literary Agency, Virginia C.; Marshall Agency, Evan; Montgomery Literary Agency; Nelson, BK; Northwest Literary Services; Novak III Literary Representation, Edward A.; Penmarin Books; PMA Literary & Film Management; QCorp Literary Agency; Steinberg Literary Agency, Michael; Stern Agency, Gloria (CA); Strong Literary Agency, Marianne; Tornetta Agency, Phyllis; Visions Press; Wallerstein Agency, Gerry B.; West Coast Literary Assoc.; Westchester Literary Agency, Inc.; Writer's Consulting Group

Detective/police/crime. Acacia House; Ahearn Agency; Allegra Literary Agency; Authentic Creations Literary Agency; Author Aid Assoc.; Brinke Literary Agency; Browne, Pema; Cambridge Literary Assoc.; Chadd-Stevens Literary Agency; Clark Literary Agency, SJ; Colby: Literary Agency; Collier Assoc.; Connor Literary Agency; Dorese Agency; Fishbein, Frieda; Fran Literary Agency; GEM Literary Services; Gladden Unlimited; Hamilton's Literary Agency, Andrew; Hilton Literary Agency, Alice; Independent Publishing Agency; Kaltman Literary Agency, Larry; Kellock & Assoc., J.; Kern Literary Agency, Natasha; Kirkland Literary Agency; Law Offices of Robert L. Fenton PC; Lee Literary Agency, L. Harry; Lighthouse Literary Agency; Literary Group West; Lopopolo Literary Agency, Toni; M.H. Int'l Literary Agency; McKinley, Literary Agency, Virginia C.; Marshall Agency, Evan; Montgomery Literary Agency; Nelson, BK; Northeast Literary Agency; Northwest Literary Services; Novak III Literary Representation, Edward A.; Pell Agency, William; Penmarin Books; PMA Literary & Film Management; Portman Organization; Puddingstone Literary Agency; QCorp Literary Agency; SLC Enterprises; Southern Literary Agency; Steinberg Literary Agency, Michael; Stern Agency, Gloria (CA); Strong Literary Agency, Marianne; Taylor Literary Agency, Dawson; Toomey, Assoc., Jeanne; Wallerstein Agency, Gerry B.; West Coast Literary Assoc.; Westchester Literary Agency, Inc.; Writer's Consulting Group

Erotica. AEI/Atchity Editorial/Entertainment Int'l; Authentic Creations Literary Agency; Author Aid Assoc.; Cambridge Literary Assoc.; Chadd-Stevens Literary Agency; Hamilton's Literary Agency, Andrew; Hilton Literary Agency, Alice; Howard Agency, Eddy; Independent Publishing Agency; Kaltman Literary Agency, Larry; Lee Literary Agency, L. Harry; Lopopolo Literary Agency, Toni; Marshall Agency, Evan; Northwest Literary Services; QCorp Literary Agency; Steinberg Literary Agency, Michael; Stern Agency, Gloria (CA); Visions Press

Ethnic. Ahearn Agency; Author Aid Assoc.; Backman, Elizabeth H.; Browne, Pema; Chadd-Stevens Literary Agency; Chester, Literary Agency, Linda; Connor Literary Agency; Dorese Agency; Flannery, White and Stone; Gladden Unlimited; Hamilton's Literary Agency, Andrew; Hilton Literary Agency, Alice; Independent Publishing Agency; Kaltman Literary Agency, Larry; Kellock & Assoc., J.; Kern Literary Agency, Natasha; Kirkland Literary Agency; Law Offices of Robert L. Fenton PC; Lopopolo Literary Agency, Toni; McKinley, Literary Agency, Virginia C.; Marshall Agency, Evan; Montgomery Literary Agency; Northwest Literary Services; Penmarin Books; QCorp Literary Agency; Visions Press

Experimental. Author Aid Assoc.; Chadd-Stevens Literary Agency; Connor Literary Agency; Howard Agency, Eddy; Independent Publishing Agency; Kellock & Assoc., J.; Montgomery Literary Agency; Northwest Literary Services; Penmarin Books; QCorp Literary Agency; West Coast Literary Associates

Family saga. Ahearn Agency; Authentic Creations Literary Agency; Author Aid Assoc.; Cambridge Literary Assoc.; Catalog Literary Agency; Chadd-Stevens Literary Agency; Connor Literary Agency; Dorese Agency; Fishbein, Frieda; Flannery, White and Stone; ForthWrite Literary Agency; GEM Literary Services; Hamilton's Literary Agency, Andrew; Hubbs Agency, Yvonne Trudeau; Kaltman Literary Agency, Larry; Kellock & Assoc., J.; Kern Literary Agency, Natasha; Kirkland Literary Agency; Lee Literary Agency, L. Harry; Lopopolo Literary Agency, Toni; McKinley, Literary Agency, Virginia C.; Marcil Literary Agency, Denise; Marshall Agency, Evan; Montgomery Literary Agency; Nelson, BK; Northwest Literary Services; Portman Organization; QCorp Literary Agency; Strong Literary Agency, Marianne; Wallerstein Agency, Gerry B.; Westchester Literary Agency, Inc.; Writer's Consulting Group

Fantasy. Ahearn Agency; Authentic Creations Literary Agency; Author Aid Assoc.; Backman, Elizabeth H.; Brinke Literary Agency; Cambridge Literary Assoc.; Chadd-Stevens Literary Agency; Collier Assoc.; Fishbein, Frieda; Fran Literary Agency; GEM Literary Services; Gislason Agency; Hilton Literary Agency, Alice; Howard Agency, Eddy; Hubbs Agency, Yvonne Trudeau; Independent Publishing Agency; Jenks Agency, Carolyn; Kellock & Assoc., J.; Kirkland Literary Agency; Lee Literary Agency, L. Harry; McKinley, Literary Agency, Virginia C.; Montgomery Literary Agency; Nelson, BK; Northwest Literary Services; QCorp Literary Agency; Stern Agency, Gloria (CA), Gloria

Feminist. Ahearn Agency; Bartczak Assoc., Gene; Browne, Pema; Chester, Literary Agency, Linda; Dorese Agency; Fishbein, Frieda; Flannery, White and Stone; GEM Literary Services; Gislason Agency; Hubbs Agency, Yvonne Trudeau; Independent Publishing Agency; Jenks Agency, Carolyn; Kaltman Literary Agency, Larry; Kellock & Assoc., J.; Kern Literary Agency, Natasha; Lopopolo Literary Agency, Toni; McKinley, Literary Agency, Virginia C.; Nelson, BK; Northwest Literary Services; QCorp Literary Agency; SLC Enterprises; Stern Agency, Gloria (CA); Writer's Consulting Group

Gay. Ahearn Agency; Browne, Pema; Chadd-Stevens Literary Agency; Dorese Agency; Flannery, White and Stone; Jenks Agency, Carolyn; Kaltman Literary Agency, Larry; QCorp Literary Agency; Visions Press; Westchester Literary Agency, Inc.

Glitz. Ahearn Agency; Author Aid Assoc.; Browne, Pema; Chadd-Stevens Literary Agency; Connor Literary Agency; Dorese Agency; Gladden Unlimited; Hubbs Agency, Yvonne Trudeau; Jenks Agency, Carolyn; JLM Literary Agents; Kaltman Literary Agency, Larry; Kellock & Assoc., J.; Kirkland Literary Agency; Law Offices of Robert L. Fenton PC; Lopopolo Literary Agency, Toni; Marshall Agency, Evan; Montgomery Literary Agency; Nelson, BK; QCorp Literary Agency; Stern Agency, Gloria (CA); Strong Literary Agency, Marianne; Wallerstein Agency, Gerry B.

Horror. AEI/Atchity Editorial/Entertainment Int'l; Ahearn Agency; Author Aid Assoc.; Cambridge Literary Assoc.; Catalog Literary Agency; Chadd-Stevens Literary Agency; Connor Literary Agency; Fran Literary Agency; GEM Literary Services; Gladden Unlimited; Hilton Literary Agency, Alice; Kellock & Assoc., J.; Kirkland Literary Agency; Lee Literary Agency, L. Harry; Marshall Agency, Evan; Montgomery Literary Agency; Nelson, BK; PMA Literary & Film Management; Puddingstone Literary Agency; Stern Agency, Gloria (CA); Writer's Consulting Group

Humor/satire. Ahearn Agency; Browne, Pema; Colby: Literary Agency; Collier Assoc.; Collier Assoc.; Connor Literary Agency; Fishbein, Frieda; Flannery, White and Stone; Fran Literary Agency; Hamilton's Literary Agency, Andrew; Hilton Literary Agency, Alice; Howard Agency, Eddy; Independent Publishing Agency; Kaltman Literary Agency, Larry; Kellock & Assoc., J.; Law Offices of Robert L. Fenton PC; Lee Literary Agency, L. Harry; Lopopolo Literary Agency, Toni; McKinley, Literary Agency, Virginia C.; Marshall Agency, Evan; Northeast Literary Agency; Northwest Literary Services; Pell Agency, William; QCorp Literary Agency; Southern Literary Agency; Wallerstein Agency, Gerry B.

Historical. Acacia House; AAEI/Atchity Editorial/Entertainment Int'l; Ahearn Agency; Authentic Creations Literary Agency; Author Aid Assoc.; Backman, Elizabeth H.; Brown, Literary Agent, Antoinette; Browne, Pema; Cambridge Literary Assoc.; Chadd-Stevens Literary Agency; Dorese Agency; Fishbein, Frieda; Flannery, White and Stone; ForthWrite Literary Agency; Fran Literary Agency; GEM Literary Services; Hilton Literary Agency, Alice; Hubbs Agency, Yvonne Trudeau; Independent Publishing Agency; Jenks Agency, Carolyn; Kaltman Literary Agency, Larry; Kellock & Assoc., J.; Kern Literary Agency, Natasha; Kirkland Literary Agency; Law Offices of Robert L. Fenton PC; Lee Literary Agency, L. Harry; Literary Group West; Lopopolo Literary Agency, Toni; M.H. Int'l Literary Agency; Marcil Literary Agency, Denise; Marshall Agency, Evan; Montgomery Literary Agency; Nelson, BK; Northwest Literary Services; Novak III Literary Representation, Edward A.; Penmarin Books; Portman Organization; QCorp Literary Agency; SLC Enterprises; Strong Literary Agency, Marianne; Wallerstein Agency, Gerry B.; West Coast Literary Assoc.; Westchester Literary Agency, Inc.

Juvenile. Ahearn Agency; Allegra Literary Agency; Alp Arts; Authentic Creations Literary Agency; Author Aid Assoc.; Bartczak Assoc., Gene; Browne, Pema; Cambridge Literary Assoc.; Catalog Literary Agency; Chadd-Stevens Literary Agency; Clark Literary Agency, SJ; Flannery, White and Stone; ForthWrite Literary Agency; Fran Literary Agency; GEM Literary Services; Hamilton's Literary Agency, Andrew; Hilton Literary Agency, Alice; Howard Agency, Eddy; Independent Publishing Agency; Kellock & Assoc., J.; Lighthouse Literary Agency; McKinley, Literary Agency, Virginia C.; Montgomery Literary Agency; Northwest Literary Services; QCorp Literary Agency; SLC Enterprises; Westchester Literary Agency, Inc.

Lesbian. Ahearn Agency; Author Aid Assoc.; Browne, Pema; Chadd-Stevens Literary Agency; Dorese Agency; Flannery, White and Stone; Hamilton's Literary Agency, Andrew; Jenks Agency, Carolyn; Kaltman Literary Agency, Larry; QCorp Literary Agency; Visions Press; Westchester Literary Agency, Inc.

Literary. Acacia House; AEI/Atchity Editorial/Entertainment Int'l; Ahearn Agency; Authentic Creations Literary Agency; Author Aid Assoc.; Browne, Pema; Cambridge Literary Assoc.; Chadd-Stevens Literary Agency; Chester, Literary Agency, Linda; Connor Literary Agency; Dorese Agency; Flannery, White and Stone; ForthWrite Literary Agency; GEM Literary Services; Hilton Literary Agency, Alice; Howard Agency, Eddy; Independent Publishing Agency; Jenks Agency, Carolyn; Kaltman Literary Agency, Larry; Kellock & Assoc., J.; Kirkland Literary Agency; Lee Literary Agency, L. Harry; Lighthouse Literary Agency; Lopopolo Literary Agency, Toni; McKinley, Literary Agency, Virginia C.; Marshall Agency, Evan; Montgomery Literary Agency; Nelson, BK; Northwest Literary Services; Novak III Literary Representation, Edward A.; Penmarin Books; PMA Literary & Film Management; QCorp Literary Agency; Rydal; SLC Enterprises; Stern Agency, Gloria (CA); Strong Literary Agency, Marianne; Wallerstein Agency, Gerry B.; West Coast Literary Assoc.; Westchester Literary Agency, Inc.

Mainstream. Acacia House; AEI/Atchity Editorial/Entertainment Int'l; Ahearn Agency; Allegra Literary Agency; Authentic Creations Literary Agency; Author Aid Assoc.; Bartczak Assoc., Gene; Browne, Pema; Cambridge Literary Assoc.; Catalog Literary Agency; Chadd-Stevens Literary Agency; Chester, Literary Agency, Linda; Collier Assoc.; Dorese Agency; Fishbein, Frieda; Flannery, White and Stone; ForthWrite Literary Agency; Fran Literary Agency; GEM Literary Services; Gladden Unlimited; Hilton Literary Agency, Alice; Howard Agency, Eddy; Hubbs Agency, Yvonne Trudeau; Independent Publishing Agency; Kaltman Literary Agency, Larry; Kern Literary Agency, Natasha; Kirkland Literary Agency; Law Offices of Robert L. Fenton PC; Lee Literary Agency, L. Harry; Lighthouse Literary Agency; Literary Group West; Lopopolo Literary Agency, Toni; Marshall Agency, Evan; Montgomery Literary Agency; Nelson, BK; Northwest Literary Services; Novak III Literary Representation, Edward A.; Penmarin Books; PMA Literary & Film Management; QCorp Literary Agency; Rydal; Southern Literary Agency; Steinberg Literary Agency, Michael; Stern Agency, Gloria (CA); Strong Literary Agency, Marianne; Visions Press; Wallerstein Agency, Gerry B.; West Coast Literary Assoc.; Westchester Literary Agency, Inc.; Writer's Consulting Group

Mystery/suspense. Acacia House; AEI/Atchity Editorial/Entertainment Int'l; Ahearn Agency; Allegra Literary Agency; Authentic Creations Literary Agency; Author Aid Assoc.; Backman, Elizabeth H.; Brinke Literary Agency; Brown, Literary Agent, Antoinette; Browne, Pema; Cambridge Literary Assoc.; Chadd-Stevens Literary Agency; Chester, Literary Agency, Linda; Clark Literary Agency, SJ; Colby: Literary Agency; Collier Assoc.; Connor Literary Agency; Dorese Agency; Fishbein, Frieda; Flannery, White and Stone; ForthWrite Literary Agency; Fran Literary Agency; GEM Literary Services; Gislason Agency; Hamilton's Literary Agency, Andrew; Hilton Literary Agency, Alice; Hubbs Agency, Yvonne Trudeau; Independent Publishing Agency; Jenks Agency, Carolyn; JLM Literary Agents; Kaltman Literary Agency, Larry; Kellock & Assoc., J.; Kern Literary Agency, Natasha; Kirkland Literary Agency; Law Offices of Robert L. Fenton PC; Lee Literary Agency, L. Harry; Lighthouse Literary Agency; Lopopolo Literary Agency, Toni; M.H. Int'l Literary Agency; McKinley, Literary Agency, Virginia C.; Marcil Literary Agency, Denise; Marshall Agency, Evan; Nelson, BK; Northeast Literary Agency; Northwest Literary Services; Novak III Literary Representation, Edward A.; Penmarin Books; PMA Literary & Film Management; Porcelain, Sidney E.; QCorp Literary Agency; Southern Literary Agency; Steinberg Literary Agency, Michael; Taylor Literary Agency, Dawson; Tornetta Agency, Phyllis; Wallerstein Agency, Gerry B.; West Coast Literary Assoc.; Westchester Literary Agency, Inc.; Writer's Consulting Group

Open to all fiction categories. Bernstein Literary Agency, Meredith; Brinke Literary Agency; Evans & Assoc.; Follendore & Ikeyama Literary Agency; Morgan Literary Agency, David H.; Northeast Literary Agency; Pacific Literary Services; Raintree Agency, Diane; Total Acting Experience

Picture book. Alp Arts; Authentic Creations Literary Agency; Author Aid Assoc.; Browne, Pema; Chadd-Stevens Literary Agency; Clark Literary Agency, SJ; Flannery, White and Stone; ForthWrite Literary Agency; Fran Literary Agency; GEM Literary Services; Hilton Literary Agency, Alice; Howard Agency, Eddy; Independent Publishing Agency; Kellock & Assoc., J.; Lighthouse Literary Agency; Montgomery Literary Agency; Northeast Literary Agency; Northwest Literary Services; QCorp Literary Agency; SLC Enterprises

Psychic/supernatural. Ahearn Agency; Author Aid Assoc.; Brinke Literary Agency; Browne, Pema; Chadd-Stevens Literary Agency; Clark Literary Agency, SJ; Dorese Agency; Flannery, White and Stone; GEM Literary Services; Hamilton's Literary Agency, Andrew; Hilton Literary Agency, Alice; Howard Agency, Eddy; Hubbs Agency, Yvonne Trudeau; Independent Publishing Agency; JLM Literary Agents; Kirkland Literary Agency; Lopopolo Literary Agency, Toni; Marshall Agency, Evan; Montgomery Literary Agency; Nelson, BK; Northwest Literary Services; QCorp Literary Agency; Toomey, Assoc., Jeanne

Regional. Ahearn Agency; Author Aid Assoc.; Backman, Elizabeth H.; Cambridge Literary Assoc.; Chadd-Stevens Literary Agency; Dorese Agency; Fran Literary Agency; Howard Agency, Eddy; Jenks Agency, Carolyn; Kaltman Literary Agency, Larry; Lighthouse Literary Agency; Montgomery Literary Agency; QCorp Literary Agency; Rydal; SLC Enterprises; West Coast Literary Assoc.; Westchester Literary Agency, Inc.

Religious/inspiration. Allegra Literary Agency; Authentic Creations Literary Agency; Author Aid Assoc.; Brinke Literary Agency; Browne, Pema; Cambridge Literary Assoc.; Chadd-Stevens Literary Agency; GEM Literary Services; Hamilton's Literary Agency, Andrew; McKinley, Literary Agency, Virginia C.; Marshall Agency, Evan; QCorp Literary Agency; Strong Literary Agency, Marianne; Westchester Literary Agency, Inc.

Romance. Acacia House; Ahearn Agency; Allegra Literary Agency; Authentic Creations Literary Agency; Author Aid Assoc.; Brown, Literary Agent, Antoinette; Browne, Pema; Cambridge Literary Assoc.; Catalog Literary Agency; Chadd-Stevens Literary Agency; Collier Assoc.; Fishbein, Frieda; Flannery, White and Stone; ForthWrite Literary Agency; GEM Literary Services; Gislason Agency; Hamilton's Literary Agency, Andrew; Hilton Literary Agency, Alice; Hubbs Agency, Yvonne Trudeau; Jenks Agency, Carolyn; JLM Literary Agents; Kaltman Literary Agency, Larry; Kellock & Assoc., J.; Kern Literary Agency, Natasha; Kirkland Literary Agency; Law Offices of

Robert L. Fenton PC; Lee Literary Agency, L. Harry; M.H. Int'l Literary Agency; McKinley, Literary Agency, Virginia C.; Marcil Literary Agency, Denise; Marshall Agency, Evan; Montgomery Literary Agency; Nelson, BK; Northwest Literary Services; Novak III Literary Representation, Edward A.; Portman Organization; QCorp Literary Agency; SLC Enterprises; Strong Literary Agency, Marianne; Tornetta Agency, Phyllis; Visions Press; Wallerstein Agency, Gerry B.; Warren Literary Agency, James; West Coast Literary Assoc.; Westchester Literary Agency, Inc.

Science fiction. AEI/Atchity Editorial/Entertainment Int'l; Ahearn Agency; Authentic Creations Literary Agency; Author Aid Assoc.; Backman, Elizabeth H.; Brinke Literary Agency; Browne, Pema; Cambridge Literary Assoc.; Catalog Literary Agency; Chadd-Stevens Literary Agency; Collier Assoc.; Fishbein, Frieda; Flannery, White and Stone; Fran Literary Agency; GEM Literary Services; Gislason Agency; Hilton Literary Agency, Alice; Hubbs Agency, Yvonne Trudeau; Kellock & Assoc., J.; Kirkland Literary Agency; Law Offices of Robert L. Fenton PC; Lee Literary Agency, L. Harry; Lighthouse Literary Agency; Marshall Agency, Evan; Montgomery Literary Agency; Nelson, BK; Northeast Literary Agency; Northwest Literary Services; Portman Organization; Puddingstone Literary Agency; QCorp Literary Agency; Steinberg Literary Agency, Michael; Stern Agency, Gloria (CA); West Coast Literary Associates

Sports. Authentic Creations Literary Agency; Author Aid Assoc.; Backman, Elizabeth H.; Cambridge Literary Assoc.; Chadd-Stevens Literary Agency; Colby: Literary Agency; Dorese Agency; Hamilton's Literary Agency, Andrew; Hilton Literary Agency, Alice; Kaltman Literary Agency, Larry; Kellock & Assoc., J.; Law Offices of Robert L. Fenton PC; Lee Literary Agency, L. Harry; Lighthouse Literary Agency; Montgomery Literary Agency; Nelson, BK; Northwest Literary Services; Novak III Literary Representation, Edward A.; Portman Organization; QCorp Literary Agency; SLC Enterprises

Thriller/espionage. Acacia House; AEI/Atchity Editorial/Entertainment Int'l; Ahearn Agency; Authentic Creations Literary Agency; Author Aid Assoc.; Backman, Elizabeth H.; Brinke Literary Agency; Brown, Literary Agent, Antoinette; Browne, Pema; Cambridge Literary Assoc.; Catalog Literary Agency; Chadd-Stevens Literary Agency; Clark Literary Agency, SJ; Colby: Literary Agency; Collier Assoc.; Connor Literary Agency; Fishbein, Frieda; Flannery, White and Stone; Fran Literary Agency; GEM Literary Services; Gladden Unlimited; Hamilton's Literary Agency, Andrew; Hilton Literary Agency, Alice; Hubbs Agency, Yvonne Trudeau; Independent Publishing Agency; Jenks Agency, Carolyn; Kaltman Literary Agency, Larry; Kellock & Assoc., J.; Kern Literary Agency, Natasha; Kirkland Literary Agency; Law Offices of Robert L. Fenton PC; Lee Literary Agency, L. Harry; Lighthouse Literary Agency; Literary Group West; M.H. Int'l Literary Agency; Marshall Agency, Evan; Montgomery Literary Agency; Nelson, BK; Northeast Literary Agency; Northwest Literary Services; Novak III Literary Representation, Edward A.; Pell Agency, William; Penmarin Books; PMA Literary & Film Management; Portman Organization; Puddingstone Literary Agency; QCorp Literary Agency; Southern Literary Agency; Steinberg Literary Agency, Michael; Stern Agency, Gloria (CA); Strong Literary Agency, Marianne; Taylor Literary Agency, Dawson; Toomey, Assoc., Jeanne; Wallerstein Agency, Gerry B.; West Coast Literary Assoc.; Westchester Literary Agency, Inc.; Writer's Consulting Group

Westerns/frontier. Ahearn Agency; Authentic Creations Literary Agency; Author Aid Assoc.; Browne, Pema; Cambridge Literary Assoc.; Chadd-Stevens Literary Agency; Colby: Literary Agency; Collier Assoc.; Flannery, White and Stone; Fran Literary Agency; GEM Literary Services; Hamilton's Literary Agency, Andrew; Hilton Literary Agency, Alice; Jenks Agency, Carolyn; Kaltman Literary Agency, Larry; Kellock & Assoc., J.; Kern Literary Agency, Natasha; Kirkland Literary Agency; Law Offices of Robert L. Fenton PC; Lee Literary Agency, L. Harry; Lighthouse Literary Agency; Lopopolo Literary Agency, Toni; McKinley, Literary Agency, Virginia C.; Marshall Agency, Evan; Montgomery Literary Agency; Nelson, BK; Northwest Literary Services; Portman Organization; QCorp Literary Agency; Rydal; Stern Agency, Gloria (CA); Strong Literary Agency, Marianne; Wallerstein Agency, Gerry B.; West Coast Literary Assoc.; Westchester Literary Agency, Inc.

Young adult. Ahearn Agency; Alp Arts; Authentic Creations Literary Agency; Author Aid Assoc.; Bartczak Assoc., Gene; Browne, Pema; Cambridge Literary Assoc.; Chadd-Stevens Literary Agency; Clark Literary Agency, SJ; Dorese Agency; Fishbein, Frieda; Flannery, White and Stone; ForthWrite Literary Agency; Fran Literary Agency; GEM Literary Services; Hamilton's Literary Agency, Andrew; Hilton Literary Agency, Alice; Howard Agency, Eddy; Independent Publishing Agency; Jenks Agency, Carolyn; Kellock & Assoc., J.; Kern Literary Agency, Natasha; Lee Literary Agency, L. Harry; Lighthouse Literary Agency; Montgomery Literary Agency; Northwest Literary Services; PMA Literary & Film Management; QCorp Literary Agency; SLC Enterprises; Visions Press; Wallerstein Agency, Gerry B.; Westchester Literary Agency, Inc.

Fee-charging literary agents/Nonfiction

Agriculture/horticulture. Authentic Creations Literary Agency; Catalog Literary Agency; Follendore & Ikeyama Literary Agency; ForthWrite Literary Agency; Fran Literary Agency; Howard Agency, Eddy; Kern Literary Agency, Natasha; Montgomery Literary Agency; Nelson, BK; Northwest Literary Services; Toomey, Assoc., Jeanne; Wallerstein Agency, Gerry B.

Animals. Acacia House; Ahearn Agency; Authentic Creations Literary Agency; Author Aid Assoc.; Bartczak Assoc., Gene; Brinke Literary Agency; Catalog Literary Agency; Fishbein, Frieda; Follendore & Ikeyama Literary Agency; ForthWrite Literary Agency; Fran Literary Agency; Hamilton's Literary Agency, Andrew; Howard Agency, Eddy; Jenks Agency, Carolyn; Kellock & Assoc., J.; Kern Literary Agency, Natasha; Lighthouse Literary Agency; Lopopolo Literary Agency, Toni; McKinley, Literary Agency, Virginia C.; Marshall Agency, Evan; Montgomery Literary Agency; Nelson, BK; Northwest Literary Services; Penmarin Books; Toomey, Assoc., Jeanne; Total Acting Experience; Wallerstein Agency, Gerry B.

Anthropology. AEI/Atchity Editorial/Entertainment Int'l; Authentic Creations Literary Agency; Author Aid Assoc.; Brinke Literary Agency; Browne, Pema; Catalog Literary Agency; ForthWrite Literary Agency; Howard Agency, Eddy; Independent Publishing Agency; Kellock & Assoc., J.; Kern Literary Agency, Natasha; Lighthouse Literary Agency; Lopopolo Literary Agency, Toni; Montgomery Literary Agency; Nelson, BK; Paraview; Penmarin Books; Rydal; Southern Literary Agency; Toomey, Assoc., Jeanne; Total Acting Experience; Wallerstein Agency, Gerry B.

Art/architecture/design. Browne, Pema; Chester, Literary Agency, Linda; Dorese Agency; Follendore & Ikeyama Literary Agency; ForthWrite Literary Agency; Independent Publishing Agency; Kellock & Assoc., J.; Kern Literary Agency, Natasha; Lighthouse Literary Agency; Lopopolo Literary Agency, Toni; Marshall Agency, Evan; Montgomery Literary Agency; Nelson, BK; Northwest Literary Services; Novak III Literary Representation, Edward A.; Paraview; Penmarin Books; Strong Literary Agency, Marianne; Toomey, Assoc., Jeanne; Total Acting Experience; Wallerstein Agency, Gerry B.

Biography/autobiography. Acacia House; AEI/Atchity Editorial/Entertainment Int'l; Ahearn Agency; Authentic Creations Literary Agency; Author Aid Assoc.; Backman, Elizabeth H.; Bartczak Assoc., Gene; Brinke Literary Agency; Browne, Pema; Cambridge Literary Assoc.; Chester, Literary Agency, Linda; Collier Assoc.; Dorese Agency; Fishbein, Frieda; Follendore & Ikeyama Literary Agency; ForthWrite Literary Agency; Fran Literary Agency; GEM Literary Services; Gladden Unlimited; Hamilton's Literary Agency, Andrew; Independent Publishing Agency; Jenks Agency, Carolyn; JLM Literary Agents; Kellock & Assoc., J.; Kern Literary Agency, Natasha; Law Offices of Robert L. Fenton PC; Lawyer's Literary Agency; Lighthouse Literary Agency; Lopopolo Literary Agency, Toni; McKinley, Literary Agency, Virginia C.; Marshall Agency, Evan; Montgomery Literary Agency; Nelson, BK; Northeast Literary Agency; Northwest Literary Services; Novak III Literary Representation, Edward A.; Paraview; Pell Agency, William; Penmarin Books; Portman Organization; SLC Enterprises; Southern Literary Agency; Steinberg Literary Agency, Michael; Stern Agency, Gloria (CA); Strong Literary Agency, Marianne; Toomey, Assoc., Jeanne; Total Acting Experience; Wallerstein Agency, Gerry B.; West Coast Literary Assoc.; Writer's Consulting Group

Business. AEI/Atchity Editorial/Entertainment Int'l; Ahearn Agency; Authentic Creations Literary Agency; Backman, Elizabeth H.; Brown, Literary Agent, Antoinette; Browne, Pema; Cambridge Literary Assoc.; Catalog Literary Agency; Chester, Literary Agency, Linda; Collier Assoc.; Connor Literary Agency; Dorese Agency; Executive Excellence; Flannery, White and Stone; Follendore & Ikeyama Literary Agency; ForthWrite Literary Agency; Fran Literary Agency; GEM Literary Services; Gladden Unlimited; Hamilton's Literary Agency, Andrew; Independent Publishing Agency; JLM Literary Agents; Kellock & Assoc., J.; Kern Literary Agency, Natasha; Law Offices of Robert L. Fenton PC; Lighthouse Literary Agency; Lopopolo Literary Agency, Toni; McKinley, Literary Agency, Virginia C.; Marcil Literary Agency, Denise; Marshall Agency, Evan; Montgomery Literary Agency; Nelson, BK; Northeast Literary Agency; Novak III Literary Representation, Edward A.; Paraview; Penmarin Books; PMA Literary & Film Management; Puddingstone Literary Agency; SLC Enterprises; Southern Literary Agency; Steinberg Literary Agency, Michael; Stern Agency, Gloria (CA); Strong Literary Agency, Marianne; Total Acting Experience; Wallerstein Agency, Gerry B.; Westchester Literary Agency, Inc.; Writer's Consulting Group

Child guidance/parenting. AEI/Atchity Editorial/Entertainment Int'l; Ahearn Agency; Authentic Creations Literary Agency; Backman, Elizabeth H.; Brinke Literary Agency; Browne, Pema; Catalog Literary Agency; Chester, Literary Agency, Linda; Connor Literary Agency; Dorese Agency; Flannery, White and Stone; Follendore & Ikeyama Literary Agency; ForthWrite Literary Agency; Fran Literary Agency; GEM Literary Services; Hamilton's Literary Agency, Andrew; Independent Publishing Agency; Kellock & Assoc., J.; Kern Literary Agency, Natasha; Law Offices of Robert L. Fenton PC; Lighthouse Literary Agency; Lopopolo Literary Agency, Toni; McKinley, Literary Agency, Virginia C.; Marcil Literary Agency, Denise; Marshall Agency, Evan; Montgomery Literary Agency; Nelson, BK; Northwest Literary Services; Novak III Literary Representation, Edward A.; Penmarin Books; Southern Literary Agency; Stern Agency, Gloria (CA); Strong Literary Agency, Marianne; Total Acting Experience; Wallerstein Agency, Gerry B.; Westchester Literary Agency, Inc.

Computers/electronics. AEI/Atchity Editorial/Entertainment Int'l; Catalog Literary Agency; Collier Assoc.; GEM Literary Services; Jenks Agency, Carolyn; Law Offices of Robert L. Fenton PC; Lighthouse Literary Agency; Montgomery Literary Agency; Nelson, BK; Steinberg Literary Agency, Michael; Stern Agency, Gloria (CA); Total Acting Experience

Cooking/food/nutrition. Acacia House; Authentic Creations Literary Agency; Backman, Elizabeth H.; Browne, Pema; Catalog Literary Agency; Collier Assoc.; Connor Literary Agency; Dorese Agency; Fishbein, Frieda; ForthWrite Literary Agency; Fran Literary Agency; GEM Literary Services; Hamilton's Literary Agency, Andrew; Howard Agency, Eddy; Independent Publishing Agency; Jenks Agency, Carolyn; Kellock & Assoc., J.; Kern Literary Agency, Natasha; Lighthouse Literary Agency; Lopopolo Literary Agency, Toni; Marcil Literary Agency, Denise; Marshall Agency, Evan; Montgomery Literary Agency; Nelson, BK; Northwest Literary Services; Penmarin Books; SLC Enterprises; Stern Agency, Gloria (CA); Strong Literary Agency, Marianne; Total Acting Experience; Wallerstein Agency, Gerry B.

Crafts/hobbies. Acacia House; Authentic Creations Literary Agency; Catalog Literary Agency; Collier Assoc.; Connor Literary Agency; Dorese Agency; Follendore & Ikeyama Literary Agency; ForthWrite Literary Agency; Fran Literary Agency; Howard Agency, Eddy; Independent Publishing Agency; Lighthouse Literary Agency; Marshall Agency, Evan; Montgomery Literary Agency; Nelson, BK; Northwest Literary Services; Penmarin Books; Total Acting Experience; Wallerstein Agency, Gerry B.

Current affairs. Acacia House; Ahearn Agency; Authentic Creations Literary Agency; Author Aid Assoc.;

Backman, Elizabeth H.; Browne, Pema; Cambridge Literary Assoc.; Catalog Literary Agency; Chester, Literary Agency, Linda; Connor Literary Agency; Dorese Agency; Fishbein, Frieda; Flannery, White and Stone; Follendore & Ikeyama Literary Agency; GEM Literary Services; Hamilton's Literary Agency, Andrew; Hubbs Agency, Yvonne Trudeau; Independent Publishing Agency; JLM Literary Agents; Kellock & Assoc., J.; Kern Literary Agency, Natasha; Kirkland Literary Agency; Law Offices of Robert L. Fenton PC; Lighthouse Literary Agency; Literary Group West; Marshall Agency, Evan; Montgomery Literary Agency; Nelson, BK; Novak III Literary Representation, Edward A.; Paraview; Penmarin Books; Portman Organization; SLC Enterprises; Stern Agency, Gloria (CA); Strong Literary Agency, Marianne; Total Acting Experience; Wallerstein Agency, Gerry B.; West Coast Literary Assoc.; Westchester Literary Agency, Inc.; Writer's Consulting Group

Education. Authentic Creations Literary Agency; Browne, Pema; Catalog Literary Agency; Follendore & Ikeyama Literary Agency; Howard Agency, Eddy; Kern Literary Agency, Natasha; Montgomery Literary Agency; Nelson, BK; Stern Agency, Gloria (CA); Strong Literary Agency, Marianne; Total Acting Experience; Wallerstein Agency, Gerry B.; Westchester Literary Agency, Inc.; Writer's Consulting Group

Ethnic/cultural interests. Ahearn Agency; Author Aid Assoc.; Backman, Elizabeth H.; Brown, Literary Agent, Antoinette; Browne, Pema; Catalog Literary Agency; Connor Literary Agency; Flannery, White and Stone; Follendore & Ikeyama Literary Agency; Fran Literary Agency; Hamilton's Literary Agency, Andrew; Independent Publishing Agency; Kern Literary Agency, Natasha; Literary Group West; Lopopolo Literary Agency, Toni; McKinley, Literary Agency, Virginia C.; Montgomery Literary Agency; Nelson, BK; Northwest Literary Services; Novak III Literary Representation, Edward A.; Rydal; Stern Agency, Gloria (CA); Total Acting Experience; Visions Press; Wallerstein Agency, Gerry B.; West Coast Literary Associates

Gay/Lesbian issues. Ahearn Agency; Browne, Pema; Dorese Agency; Flannery, White and Stone; GEM Literary Services; Jenks Agency, Carolyn; Kern Literary Agency, Natasha; Northwest Literary Services; Novak III Literary Representation, Edward A.; Stern Agency, Gloria (CA); Visions Press; Wallerstein Agency, Gerry B.; Westchester Literary Agency, Inc.

Government/politics/law. AEI/Atchity Editorial/Entertainment Int'l; Authentic Creations Literary Agency; Backman, Elizabeth H.; Browne, Pema; Cambridge Literary Assoc.; Catalog Literary Agency; Connor Literary Agency; Dorese Agency; Flannery, White and Stone; Follendore & Ikeyama Literary Agency; GEM Literary Services; Gislason Agency; Hamilton's Literary Agency, Andrew; Independent Publishing Agency; Law Offices of Robert L. Fenton PC; Lawyer's Literary Agency; Marshall Agency, Evan; Montgomery Literary Agency; Nelson, BK; Novak III Literary Representation, Edward A.; Penmarin Books; Toomey, Assoc., Jeanne; Total Acting Experience; Wallerstein Agency, Gerry B.; West Coast Literary Assoc.; Westchester Literary Agency, Inc.

Health/medicine. Acacia House; AEI/Atchity Editorial/Entertainment Int'l; Ahearn Agency; Authentic Creations Literary Agency; Author Aid Assoc.; Backman, Elizabeth H.; Brown, Literary Agent, Antoinette; Browne, Pema; Catalog Literary Agency; Chester, Literary Agency, Linda; Connor Literary Agency; Dorese Agency; Flannery, White and Stone; Follendore & Ikeyama Literary Agency; ForthWrite Literary Agency; Fran Literary Agency; Hamilton's Literary Agency, Andrew; Howard Agency, Eddy; Independent Publishing Agency; Jenks Agency, Carolyn; Kellock & Assoc., J.; Kern Literary Agency, Natasha; Law Offices of Robert L. Fenton PC; Lighthouse Literary Agency; Lopopolo Literary Agency, Toni; McKinley, Literary Agency, Virginia C.; Marcil Literary Agency, Denise; Marshall Agency, Evan; Montgomery Literary Agency; Nelson, BK; Northwest Literary Services; Novak III Literary Representation, Edward A.; Paraview; Penmarin Books; Raintree Agency, Diane; Southern Literary Agency; Stern Agency, Gloria (CA); Strong Literary Agency, Marianne; Total Acting Experience; Wallerstein Agency, Gerry B.; Westchester Literary Agency, Inc.; Writer's Consulting Group

History. Ahearn Agency; Authentic Creations Literary Agency; Author Aid Assoc.; Backman, Elizabeth H.; Brinke Literary Agency; Brown, Literary Agent, Antoinette; Cambridge Literary Assoc.; Chester, Literary Agency, Linda; Collier Assoc.; Dorese Agency; Follendore & Ikeyama Literary Agency; ForthWrite Literary Agency; Fran Literary Agency; Hamilton's Literary Agency, Andrew; Hubbs Agency, Yvonne Trudeau; Independent Publishing Agency; Jenks Agency, Carolyn; Kellock & Assoc., J.; Lee Literary Agency, L. Harry; Lighthouse Literary Agency; Lopopolo Literary Agency, Toni; Marshall Agency, Evan; Montgomery Literary Agency; Nelson, BK; Northeast Literary Agency; Northwest Literary Services; Novak III Literary Representation, Edward A.; Paraview; Penmarin Books; Portman Organization; SLC Enterprises; Southern Literary Agency; Steinberg Literary Agency, Michael; Strong Literary Agency, Marianne; Toomey, Assoc., Jeanne; Total Acting Experience; Wallerstein Agency, Gerry B.; West Coast Literary Assoc.; Westchester Literary Agency, Inc.

How to. AEI/Atchity Editorial/Entertainment Int'l; Authentic Creations Literary Agency; Author Aid Assoc.; Bartczak Assoc., Gene; Brinke Literary Agency; Browne, Pema; Cambridge Literary Assoc.; Catalog Literary Agency; Collier Assoc.; Connor Literary Agency; Follendore & Ikeyama Literary Agency; Fran Literary Agency; GEM Literary Services; Gislason Agency; Kern Literary Agency, Natasha; Lopopolo Literary Agency, Toni; Marcil Literary Agency, Denise; Marshall Agency, Evan; Montgomery Literary Agency; Nelson, BK; Northeast Literary Agency; Northwest Literary Services; Paraview; Penmarin Books; Puddingstone Literary Agency; Steinberg Literary Agency, Michael; Stern Agency, Gloria (CA); Strong Literary Agency, Marianne; Total Acting Experience; Wallerstein Agency, Gerry B.; Westchester Literary Agency, Inc.

Humor. AEI/Atchity Editorial/Entertainment Int'l; Authentic Creations Literary Agency; Author Aid Assoc.; Cambridge Literary Assoc.; Coast To Coast Talent and Literary; Connor Literary Agency; Follendore & Ikeyama Literary Agency; Fran Literary Agency; GEM Literary Services; Howard Agency, Eddy; Kirkland Literary Agency; Marshall Agency, Evan; Montgomery Literary Agency; Northeast Literary Agency; Northwest Literary Services; Total Acting Experience; Wallerstein Agency, Gerry B.; Westchester Literary Agency, Inc.

Interior design/decorating. Authentic Creations Literary Agency; Connor Literary Agency; Dorese Agency; Follendore & Ikeyama Literary Agency; ForthWrite Literary Agency; Fran Literary Agency; Lighthouse Literary Agency; Marshall Agency, Evan; Strong Literary Agency, Marianne; Toomey, Assoc., Jeanne; Total Acting Experience; Wallerstein Agency, Gerry B.

Juvenile nonfiction. Ahearn Agency; Alp Arts; Authentic Creations Literary Agency; Author Aid Assoc.; Bartczak Assoc., Gene; Browne, Pema; Cambridge Literary Assoc.; Catalog Literary Agency; Fishbein, Frieda; Flannery, White and Stone; Follendore & Ikeyama Literary Agency; ForthWrite Literary Agency; Fran Literary Agency; GEM Literary Services; Hamilton's Literary Agency, Andrew; Howard Agency, Eddy; Independent Publishing Agency; Kellock & Assoc., J.; Lighthouse Literary Agency; McKinley, Literary Agency, Virginia C.; Montgomery Literary Agency; Northwest Literary Services; Strong Literary Agency, Marianne; Total Acting Experience; Westchester Literary Agency, Inc.

Language/literature/criticism. Acacia House; AEI/Atchity Editorial/Entertainment Int'l; Author Aid Assoc.; Connor Literary Agency; Dorese Agency; Follendore & Ikeyama Literary Agency; Independent Publishing Agency; Kellock & Assoc., J.; Kern Literary Agency, Natasha; Lopopolo Literary Agency, Toni; Marshall Agency, Evan; Montgomery Literary Agency; Nelson, BK; Northwest Literary Services; Puddingstone Literary Agency; Stern Agency, Gloria (CA); Total Acting Experience; Wallerstein Agency, Gerry B.; West Coast Literary Assoc.; Westchester Literary Agency, Inc.

Military/war. Acacia House; Authentic Creations Literary Agency; Author Aid Assoc.; Browne, Pema; Cambridge Literary Assoc.; Catalog Literary Agency; Dorese Agency; Fishbein, Frieda; Follendore & Ikeyama Literary Agency; Fran Literary Agency; Independent Publishing Agency; Law Offices of Robert L. Fenton PC; Lee Literary Agency, L. Harry; Literary Group West; McKinley, Literary Agency, Virginia C.; Marshall Agency, Evan; Montgomery Literary Agency; Nelson, BK; Novak III Literary Representation, Edward A.; Paraview; Portman Organization; Puddingstone Literary Agency; Strong Literary Agency, Marianne; Taylor Literary Agency, Dawson; Total Acting Experience; Wallerstein Agency, Gerry B.

Money/finance/economics. AEI/Atchity Editorial/Entertainment Int'l; Authentic Creations Literary Agency; Browne, Pema; Catalog Literary Agency; Chester, Literary Agency, Linda; Connor Literary Agency; Dorese Agency; Flannery, White and Stone; Follendore & Ikeyama Literary Agency; ForthWrite Literary Agency; Gem GEM Literary Services; Hamilton's Literary Agency, Andrew; Independent Publishing Agency; JLM Literary Agents; Kern Literary Agency, Natasha; Law Offices of Robert L. Fenton PC; Lighthouse Literary Agency; Lopopolo Literary Agency, Toni; McKinley, Literary Agency, Virginia C.; Marcil Literary Agency, Denise; Marshall Agency, Evan; Montgomery Literary Agency; Nelson, BK; Novak III Literary Representation, Edward A.; Penmarin Books; Southern Literary Agency; Steinberg Literary Agency, Michael; Stern Agency, Gloria (CA); Strong Literary Agency, Marianne; Toomey, Assoc., Jeanne; Total Acting Experience; Wallerstein Agency, Gerry B.; Writer's Consulting Group

Music/dance/theater/film. Acacia House; AAEI/Atchity Editorial/Entertainment Int'l; Ahearn Agency; Author Aid Assoc.; Backman, Elizabeth H.; Chester, Literary Agency, Linda; Coast To Coast Talent and Literary; Dorese Agency; ForthWrite Literary Agency; GEM Literary Services; Hamilton's Literary Agency, Andrew; Howard Agency, Eddy; Independent Publishing Agency; Jenks Agency, Carolyn; JLM Literary Agents; Kellock & Assoc., J.; Law Offices of Robert L. Fenton PC; Lighthouse Literary Agency; McKinley, Literary Agency, Virginia C.; Marcil Literary Agency, Denise; Marshall Agency, Evan; Montgomery Literary Agency; Nelson, BK; Northeast Literary Agency; Northwest Literary Services; Novak III Literary Representation, Edward A.; Paraview; Portman Organization; Stern Agency, Gloria (CA); Total Acting Experience; Wallerstein Agency, Gerry B.; West Coast Literary Assoc.; Writer's Consulting Group

Nature/environment. Acacia House; AEI/Atchity Editorial/Entertainment Int'l; Authentic Creations Literary Agency; Author Aid Assoc.; Browne, Pema; Catalog Literary Agency; Chester, Literary Agency, Linda; Fishbein, Frieda; Flannery, White and Stone; Follendore & Ikeyama Literary Agency; ForthWrite Literary Agency; Fran Literary Agency; Howard Agency, Eddy; Independent Publishing Agency; Jenks Agency, Carolyn; JLM Literary Agents; Kellock & Assoc., J.; Kern Literary Agency, Natasha; Lighthouse Literary Agency; Lopopolo Literary Agency, Toni; McKinley, Literary Agency, Virginia C.; Marshall Agency, Evan; Montgomery Literary Agency; Nelson, BK; Northwest Literary Services; Novak III Literary Representation, Edward A.; Penmarin Books; Raintree Agency, Diane; Rydal; Toomey, Assoc., Jeanne; Total Acting Experience; Wallerstein Agency, Gerry B.; West Coast Literary Assoc.; Westchester Literary Agency, Inc.

New Age/metaphysics. AEI/Atchity Editorial/Entertainment Int'l; Author Aid Assoc.; Brinke Literary Agency; Browne, Pema; Clark Literary Agency, SJ; Coast To Coast Talent and Literary; Dorese Agency; Flannery, White and Stone; Follendore & Ikeyama Literary Agency; GEM Literary Services; Howard Agency, Eddy; Jenks Agency, Carolyn; Kellock & Assoc., J.; Kern Literary Agency, Natasha; Lopopolo Literary Agency, Toni; Marcil Literary Agency, Denise; Marshall Agency, Evan; Montgomery Literary Agency; Northwest Literary Services; Paraview; Total Acting Experience

Open to all nonfiction categories. Authors Resource Center/Tarc Literary Agency; Bernstein Literary Agency, Meredith; Chadd-Stevens Literary Agency; Evans & Assoc.; Morgan Literary Agency, David H.; Northeast Literary Agency; Pacific Literary Services; QCorp Literary Agency; Wallerstein Agency, Gerry B.

Popular culture. Acacia House; AEI/Atchity Editorial/Entertainment Int'l; Ahearn Agency; Authentic Creations Literary Agency; Author Aid Assoc.; Browne, Pema; Cambridge Literary Assoc.; Catalog Literary Agency; Connor Literary Agency; Follendore & Ikeyama Literary Agency; Independent Publishing Agency; JLM Literary

Agents; Kern Literary Agency, Natasha; Lopopolo Literary Agency, Toni; Montgomery Literary Agency; Nelson, BK; Northwest Literary Services; Penmarin Books; PMA Literary & Film Management; Stern Agency, Gloria (CA); Total Acting Experience; Wallerstein Agency, Gerry B.; Westchester Literary Agency, Inc.; Writer's Consulting Group

Photography. Backman, Elizabeth H.; Catalog Literary Agency; Connor Literary Agency; Dorese Agency; ForthWrite Literary Agency; Howard Agency, Eddy; Independent Publishing Agency; Lighthouse Literary Agency; Montgomery Literary Agency; Northwest Literary Services; Pell Agency, William; Rydal; Total Acting Experience; Wallerstein Agency, Gerry B.

Psychology. Acacia House; AEI/Atchity Editorial/Entertainment Int'l; Authentic Creations Literary Agency; Author Aid Assoc.; Backman, Elizabeth H.; Browne, Pema; Catalog Literary Agency; Chester, Literary Agency, Linda; Dorese Agency; Flannery, White and Stone; Follendore & Ikeyama Literary Agency; ForthWrite Literary Agency; Hamilton's Literary Agency, Andrew; Howard Agency, Eddy; Independent Publishing Agency; Jenks Agency, Carolyn; JLM Literary Agents; Kern Literary Agency, Natasha; Lighthouse Literary Agency; Lopopolo Literary Agency, Toni; McKinley, Literary Agency, Virginia C.; Marcil Literary Agency, Denise; Marshall Agency, Evan; Montgomery Literary Agency; Nelson, BK; Paraview; Penmarin Books; Southern Literary Agency; Steinberg Literary Agency, Michael; Stern Agency, Gloria (CA); Total Acting Experience; Wallerstein Agency, Gerry B.; West Coast Literary Assoc.; Westchester Literary Agency, Inc.; Writer's Consulting Group

Religious/inspirational. Allegra Literary Agency; Authentic Creations Literary Agency; Author Aid Assoc.; Backman, Elizabeth H.; Brown, Literary Agent, Antoinette; Browne, Pema; Cambridge Literary Assoc.; Executive Excellence; Flannery, White and Stone; Follendore & Ikeyama Literary Agency; ForthWrite Literary Agency; Fran Literary Agency; GEM Literary Services; Hamilton's Literary Agency, Andrew; Independent Publishing Agency; Jenks Agency, Carolyn; JLM Literary Agents; Law Offices of Robert L. Fenton PC; McKinley, Literary Agency, Virginia C.; Marcil Literary Agency, Denise; Marshall Agency, Evan; Nelson, BK; Northwest Literary Services; Paraview; Strong Literary Agency, Marianne; Total Acting Experience; Visions Press; Westchester Literary Agency, Inc.

Science/technology. AAEI/Atchity Editorial/Entertainment Int'l; Authentic Creations Literary Agency; Author Aid Assoc.; Backman, Elizabeth H.; Browne, Pema; Catalog Literary Agency; Follendore & Ikeyama Literary Agency; ForthWrite Literary Agency; GEM Literary Services; Howard Agency, Eddy; Independent Publishing Agency; Jenks Agency, Carolyn; Kern Literary Agency, Natasha; Law Offices of Robert L. Fenton PC; Marshall Agency, Evan; Montgomery Literary Agency; Nelson, BK; Northeast Literary Agency; Novak III Literary Representation, Edward A.; Penmarin Books; Total Acting Experience; Wallerstein Agency, Gerry B.; Writer's Consulting Group

Self-help/personal improvement. AEI/Atchity Editorial/Entertainment Int'l; Ahearn Agency; Authentic Creations Literary Agency; Author Aid Assoc.; Backman, Elizabeth H.; Brinke Literary Agency; Brown, Literary Agent, Antoinette; Browne, Pema; Catalog Literary Agency; Coast To Coast Talent and Literary; Collier Assoc.; Connor Literary Agency; Dorese Agency; Executive Excellence; Fishbein, Frieda; Flannery, White and Stone; Follendore & Ikeyama Literary Agency; ForthWrite Literary Agency; Fran Literary Agency; GEM Literary Services; Gislason Agency; Gladden Unlimited; Hamilton's Literary Agency, Andrew; Howard Agency, Eddy; Independent Publishing Agency; JLM Literary Agents; Kellock & Assoc., J.; Kern Literary Agency, Natasha; Kirkland Literary Agency; Law Offices of Robert L. Fenton PC; Lighthouse Literary Agency; Lopopolo Literary Agency, Toni; McKinley, Literary Agency, Virginia C.; Marcil Literary Agency, Denise; Marshall Agency, Evan; Montgomery Literary Agency; Nelson, BK; Northwest Literary Services; Novak III Literary Representation, Edward A.; Paraview; Penmarin Books; Southern Literary Agency; Steinberg Literary Agency, Michael; Stern Agency, Gloria (CA); Strong Literary Agency, Marianne; Total Acting Experience; Visions Press; Wallerstein Agency, Gerry B.; Westchester Literary Agency, Inc.; Writer's Consulting Group

Sociology. Author Aid Assoc.; Brinke Literary Agency; Catalog Literary Agency; Dorese Agency; Flannery, White and Stone; Follendore & Ikeyama Literary Agency; ForthWrite Literary Agency; Hamilton's Literary Agency, Andrew; Independent Publishing Agency; JLM Literary Agents; McKinley, Literary Agency, Virginia C.; Montgomery Literary Agency; Nelson, BK; Penmarin Books; Raintree Agency, Diane; Stern Agency, Gloria (CA); Total Acting Experience; Wallerstein Agency, Gerry B.; Westchester Literary Agency, Inc.

Sports. Authentic Creations Literary Agency; Author Aid Assoc.; Backman, Elizabeth H.; Browne, Pema; Cambridge Literary Assoc.; Catalog Literary Agency; Connor Literary Agency; Dorese Agency; Flannery, White and Stone; Hamilton's Literary Agency, Andrew; Howard Agency, Eddy; Independent Publishing Agency; Kellock & Assoc., J.; Law Offices of Robert L. Fenton PC; Lighthouse Literary Agency; McKinley, Literary Agency, Virginia C.; Montgomery Literary Agency; Nelson, BK; Northwest Literary Services; Novak III Literary Representation, Edward A.; Penmarin Books; Portman Organization; SLC Enterprises; Taylor Literary Agency, Dawson; Total Acting Experience; Wallerstein Agency, Gerry B.; Westchester Literary Agency, Inc.

Translations. AEI/Atchity Editorial/Entertainment Int'l; Author Aid Assoc.; Howard Agency, Eddy; M.H. Int'l Literary Agency; Northwest Literary Services; Total Acting Experience; Westchester Literary Agency, Inc.

True crime/investigative. AEI/Atchity Editorial/Entertainment Int'l; Ahearn Agency; Authentic Creations Literary Agency; Author Aid Assoc.; Browne, Pema; Cambridge Literary Assoc.; Chester, Literary Agency, Linda; Clark Literary Agency, SJ; Coast To Coast Talent and Literary; Collier Assoc.; Connor Literary Agency; Dorese Agency; Fishbein, Frieda; Follendore & Ikeyama Literary Agency; GEM Literary Services; Gislason Agency; Gladden Unlimited; Hamilton's Literary Agency, Andrew; Independent Publishing Agency; JLM Literary Agents;

Kellock & Assoc., J.; Kern Literary Agency, Natasha; Law Offices of Robert L. Fenton PC; Lawyer's Literary Agency; Literary Group West; Lopopolo Literary Agency, Toni; Marcil Literary Agency, Denise; Marshall Agency, Evan; Montgomery Literary Agency; Nelson, BK; Northeast Literary Agency; Northwest Literary Services; Novak III Literary Representation, Edward A.; Penmarin Books; PMA Literary & Film Management; Portman Organization; Puddingstone Literary Agency; Stern Agency, Gloria (CA); Strong Literary Agency, Marianne; Toomey, Assoc., Jeanne; Total Acting Experience; Wallerstein Agency, Gerry B.; West Coast Literary Assoc.; Writer's Consulting Group

Women's issues/women's studies. AEI/Atchity Editorial/Entertainment Int'l; Ahearn Agency; Authentic Creations Literary Agency; Author Aid Assoc.; Backman, Elizabeth H.; Bartczak Assoc., Gene; Brown, Literary Agency, Antoinette; Browne, Pema; Catalog Literary Agency; Chester, Literary Agency, Linda; Coast To Coast Talent and Literary; Collier Assoc.; Connor Literary Agency; Dorese Agency; Fishbein, Frieda; Flannery, White and Stone; Follendore & Ikeyama Literary Agency; ForthWrite Literary Agency; GEM Literary Services; Hamilton's Literary Agency, Andrew; Howard Agency, Eddy; Hubbs Agency, Yvonne Trudeau; Independent Publishing Agency; Jenks Agency, Carolyn; JLM Literary Agents; Kellock & Assoc., J.; Kern Literary Agency, Natasha; Law Offices of Robert L. Fenton PC; Lighthouse Literary Agency; Lopopolo Literary Agency, Toni; McKinley, Literary Agency, Virginia C.; Marcil Literary Agency, Denise; Marshall Agency, Evan; Nelson, BK; Northwest Literary Services; Novak III Literary Representation, Edward A.; Paraview; PMA Literary & Film Management; Portman Organization; Raintree Agency, Diane; SLC Enterprises; Stern Agency, Gloria (CA); Strong Literary Agency, Marianne; Total Acting Experience; Visions Press; Wallerstein Agency, Gerry B.; West Coast Literary Assoc.; Westchester Literary Agency, Inc.

Script agents/Fiction and Nonfiction

Action/adventure. Act I; AEI/Atchity Editorial/Entertainment Int'l; Agapé Prod.; Agency, The; Allan Agency, Lee; All-Star Talent Agency; Amato Agency, Michael; Apollo Entertainment; Artists Agency; Brown Ltd., Curtis; Bulger And Associates, Kelvin C.; Cameron Agency, Marshall; Circle of Confusion; Client First—A/K/A Leo P. Haffey Agency; Coast to Coast Talent and Literary; Douroux & Co.; Durkin Artists Agency; Dykeman Assoc.; Earth Tracks Agency; Epstein-Wyckoff & Assoc.; F.L.A.I.R. or First Literary Artists Int'l Representatives; Fleury Agency, B.R.; Fran Literary Agency; Gardner Agency; Gold/Marshak & Assoc.; Greene, Arthur B.; Heacock Literary Agency; Hodges Agency, Carolyn; Howard Agency, Eddy; Hudson Agency; International Leonards Corp.; Jenks Agency, Carolyn; Kay Agency, Charlene; Ketay Agency, Joyce; Kjar Agency, Tyler; Kohner, Paul; Lake Agency, Candace; Lee Literary Agency, L. Harry; Lenhoff/Robinson Talent & Literary Agency; Lindstrom Literary Group; Metropolitan Talent Agency; Monteiro Rose Agency; Montgomery Literary Agency; Montgomery-West Literary Agency; Mura Enterprises, Dee; Otitis Media; Panda Talent; Partos Co.; Part-Time Prod.; Pevner, Stephen; Picture Of You, A; PMA Literary & Film Management; Producers & Creatives Group; Renaissance—H.N. Swanson Inc.; Rogers and Assoc., Stephanie; Sanders Literary Agency, Victoria; Scagnetti Talent & Literary Agency, Jack; Silver Screen Placements; Sister Mania Prod.; Star Literary Service; Tauro Brothers Management; Total Acting Experience; Acting Experience; Van Duren Agency, Annette; Wright Concept; Wright Representatives, Ann; Writer's Consulting Group

Biography/autobiography. Agapé Prod.; Bethel Agency; Dykeman Assoc.; Gordon & Assoc., Michelle; Hogenson Agency, Barbara; Star Literary Service

Cartoon/comic. Agapé Prod.; Agency, The; Bethel Agency; Bulger And Associates, Kelvin C.; Circle of Confusion; Client First—A/K/A Leo P. Haffey Agency; Fran Literary Agency; Howard Agency, Eddy; International Leonards Corp.; Lake Agency, Candace; Lenhoff/Robinson Talent & Literary Agency; Metropolitan Talent Agency; Monteiro Rose Agency; Mura Enterprises, Dee; Renaissance—H.N. Swanson Inc.; Tauro Brothers Management; Total Acting Experience; Van Duren Agency, Annette; Wright Concept

Comedy. AEI/Atchity Editorial/Entertainment Int'l; Agapé Prod. Agency, The; Allan Agency, Lee; All-Star Talent Agency; Artists Agency; Bennett Agency; Bethel Agency; Brown Ltd., Curtis; Bulger and Assoc., Kelvin C.; Camden; Cameron Agency, Marshall; Circle of Confusion; Client First—A/K/A Leo P. Haffey Agency; Coast to Coast Talent and Literary; Douroux & Co.; Durkin Artists Agency; Earth Tracks Agency; Epstein-Wyckoff & Assoc.; F.L.A.I.R. or First Literary Artists Int'l Representatives; Fleury Agency, B.R.; Fran Literary Agency; French, Inc., Samuel; Gardner Agency; Gold/Marshak & Assoc.; Heacock Literary Agency; Hogenson Agency, Barbara; Howard Agency, Eddy; Hudson Agency; International Leonards Corp.; Jenks Agency, Carolyn; Ketay Agency, Joyce; Kick Entertainment; Kohner, Paul; Lake Agency, Candace; Lee Literary Agency, L. Harry; Lenhoff/Robinson Talent & Literary Agency; Lindstrom Literary Group; Metropolitan Talent Agency; Monteiro Rose Agency; Montgomery Literary Agency; Montgomery-West Literary Agency; Mura Enterprises, Dee; Otitis Media; Palmer, Dorothy; Panda Talent; Partos Co.; Pevner, Stephen; Picture Of You, A; PMA Literary & Film Management; Producers & Creatives Group; Redwood Empire Agency; Renaissance—H.N. Swanson Inc.; Sanders Literary Agency, Victoria; Scagnetti Talent & Literary Agency, Jack; Schulman, Susan; Silver Screen Placements; Sister Mania Prod.; Tauro Brothers Management; Total Acting Experience; Van Duren Agency, Annette; Wright Concept; Wright Representatives, Ann; Writer's Consulting Group

Contemporary issues. AEI/Atchity Editorial/Entertainment Int'l; Agency, The; Allan Agency, Lee; Apollo Entertainment; Artists Agency; Bethel Agency; Bulger And Associates, Kelvin C.; Camden; Cameron Agency, Marshall; Circle of Confusion; Client First—A/K/A Leo P. Haffey Agency; Durkin Artists Agency; Dykeman Assoc.; Earth Tracks Agency; Epstein-Wyckoff & Assoc.; F.L.A.I.R. or First Literary Artists Int'l Representatives; Fran Literary Agency; French, Inc., Samuel; Gardner Agency; Gold/Marshak & Assoc.; Gordon & Assoc., Michelle; Heacock Literary Agency; Hodges Agency, Carolyn; Hudson Agency; International Leonards Corp.; Jenks Agency, Carolyn; Ketay Agency, Joyce; Lake Agency, Candace; Lee Literary Agency, L. Harry; Legacies; Lenhoff/Robinson Talent & Literary Agency; Manus & Assoc. Literary Agency; Metropolitan Talent Agency; Monteiro Rose Agency; Montgomery Literary Agency; Mura Enterprises, Dee; Partos Co.; Part-Time Prod.; Pevner, Stephen; PMA Literary & Film Management; Producers & Creatives Group; Redwood Empire Agency; Renaissance—H.N. Swanson Inc.; Rogers and Assoc., Stephanie; Sanders Literary Agency, Victoria; Schulman, Susan; Silver Screen Placements; Tauro Brothers Management; Total Acting Experience; Van Duren Agency, Annette; Watt & Assoc., Sandra; Writer's Consulting Group

Detective/police/crime. Act I; AEI/Atchity Editorial/Entertainment Int'l; Agency, The; Allan Agency, Lee; All-Star Talent Agency; Apollo Entertainment; Artists Agency; Bethel Agency; Brown Ltd., Curtis; Camden; Cameron Agency, Marshall; Circle of Confusion; Client First—A/K/A Leo P. Haffey Agency; Coast to Coast Talent and Literary; Douroux & Co.; Dykeman Assoc.; Earth Tracks Agency; Epstein-Wyckoff & Assoc.; F.L.A.I.R. or First Literary Artists Int'l Representatives; Feiler Literary Agency, Florence; Fleury Agency, B.R.; Fran Literary Agency; French, Inc., Samuel; Gardner Agency; Gold/Marshak & Assoc.; Gordon & Assoc., Michelle; Greene, Arthur B.; Heacock Literary Agency; Hodges Agency, Carolyn; Hudson Agency; International Leonards Corp.; Ketay Agency, Joyce; Kohner, Paul; Lake Agency, Candace; Lee Literary Agency, L. Harry; Lenhoff/Robinson Talent & Literary Agency; Lindstrom Literary Group; Major Clients Agency; Manus & Assoc. Literary Agency; Metropolitan Talent Agency; Monteiro Rose Agency; Montgomery Literary Agency; Montgomery-West Literary Agency; Mura Enterprises, Dee; Palmer, Dorothy; Panda Talent; Partos Co.; Part-Time Prod.; Pevner, Stephen; Picture Of You, A; Producers & Creatives Group; Renaissance—H.N. Swanson Inc.; Scagnetti Talent & Literary Agency, Jack; Schulman, Susan; Silver Screen Placements; Sister Mania Prod.; Star Literary Service; Tauro Brothers Management; Total Acting Experience; Acting Experience; Watt & Assoc., Sandra; Wright Concept; Wright Representatives, Ann; Writer's Consulting Group

Erotica. Act I; AEI/Atchity Editorial/Entertainment Int'l; Circle of Confusion; Coast to Coast Talent and Literary; Earth Tracks Agency; Epstein-Wyckoff & Assoc.; F.L.A.I.R. or First Literary Artists Int'l Representatives; Gardner Agency; Gold/Marshak & Assoc.; Howard Agency, Eddy; Lake Agency, Candace; Lenhoff/Robinson Talent & Literary Agency; Major Clients Agency; Metropolitan Talent Agency; Part-Time Prod.; Picture Of You, A; PMA Literary & Film Management; Producers & Creatives Group; Redwood Empire Agency; Renaissance—H.N. Swanson Inc.; Tauro Brothers Management; Total Acting Experience; Acting Experience

Ethnic. Agency, The; Bethel Agency; Brown Ltd., Curtis; Bulger & Assoc., Kelvin C.; Circle of Confusion; Durkin Artists Agency; Earth Tracks Agency; Fleury Agency, B.R.; French, Inc., Samuel; Gold/Marshak & Assoc.; Hodges Agency, Carolyn; Hudson Agency; Ketay Agency, Joyce; Kohner, Paul; Lake Agency, Candace; Legacies; Lenhoff/Robinson Talent & Literary Agency; Lindstrom Literary Group; Monteiro Rose Agency; Panda Talent; Partos Co.; PMA Literary & Film Management; Producers & Creatives Group; Renaissance—H.N. Swanson Inc.; Tauro Brothers Management; Total Acting Experience; Wright Concept

Experimental. Circle of Confusion; Earth Tracks Agency; French, Inc., Samuel; Gardner Agency; Hodges Agency, Carolyn; Howard Agency, Eddy; Ketay Agency, Joyce; Lenhoff/Robinson Talent & Literary Agency; Partos Co.; Renaissance—H.N. Swanson Inc.; Sister Mania Prod.; Total Acting Experience

Family Saga. Agapé Prod.; Agency, The; Apollo Entertainment; Bennett Agency; Bethel Agency; Bulger & Assoc., Kelvin C.; Camden; Circle of Confusion; Client First—A/K/A Leo P. Haffey Agency; Douroux & Co.; Durkin Artists Agency; Epstein-Wyckoff & Assoc.; F.L.A.I.R. or First Literary Artists Int'l Representatives; Feiler Literary Agency, Florence; Fleury Agency, B.R.; Fran Literary Agency; Gold/Marshak & Assoc.; Heacock Literary Agency; Howard Agency, Eddy; Hudson Agency; Jenks Agency, Carolyn; Kay Agency, Charlene; Ketay Agency, Joyce; Kjar Agency, Tyler; Kohner, Paul; Lake Agency, Candace; Lee Literary Agency, L. Harry; Legacies; Lenhoff/Robinson Talent & Literary Agency; Lindstrom Literary Group; Major Clients Agency; Manus & Assoc. Literary Agency; Metropolitan Talent Agency; Monteiro Rose Agency; Montgomery-West Literary Agency; Mura Enterprises, Dee; Palmer, Dorothy; Panda Talent; Partos Co.; Picture Of You, A; Producers & Creatives Group; Redwood Empire Agency; Renaissance—H.N. Swanson Inc.; Sanders Literary Agency, Victoria; Scagnetti Talent & Literary Agency, Jack; Silver Screen Placements; Sister Mania Prod.; Total Acting Experience; Acting Experience; Watt & Assoc., Sandra; Writer's Consulting Group

Fantasy. Agency, The; All-Star Talent Agency; Apollo Entertainment; Bethel Agency; Camden; Circle of Confusion; Douroux & Co.; Dykeman Assoc.; F.L.A.I.R. or First Literary Artists Int'l Representatives; Fleury Agency, B.R.; French, Inc., Samuel; Gardner Agency; Hodges Agency, Carolyn; Howard Agency, Eddy; Ketay Agency, Joyce; Lake Agency, Candace; Lee Literary Agency, L. Harry; Lenhoff/Robinson Talent & Literary Agency; Metropolitan Talent Agency; Monteiro Rose Agency; Mura Enterprises, Dee; Partos Co.; Part-Time Prod.; Picture Of You, A; Producers & Creatives Group; Redwood Empire Agency; Renaissance—H.N. Swanson Inc.; Silver Screen Placements; Total Acting Experience; Acting Experience; Wright Concept

Feminist. Apollo Entertainment; Bethel Agency; Brown Ltd., Curtis; Circle of Confusion; Epstein-Wyckoff & Assoc.; Gardner Agency; Gold/Marshak & Assoc.; Gordon & Assoc., Michelle; Heacock Literary Agency; Hodges Agency, Carolyn; Hudson Agency; Ketay Agency, Joyce; Kohner, Paul; Lake Agency, Candace; Legacies; Manus & Assoc. Literary Agency; Montgomery-West Literary Agency; Mura Enterprises, Dee; Partos Co.; Part-Time Prod.; PMA Literary & Film Management; Producers & Creatives Group; Redwood Empire Agency; Schulman, Susan; Writer's Consulting Group

Gay. Apollo Entertainment; Bethel Agency; Brown Ltd., Curtis; Camden; Circle of Confusion; Epstein-Wyckoff

& Assoc.; Feiler Literary Agency, Florence; Gold/Marshak & Assoc.; Hodges Agency, Carolyn; Ketay Agency, Joyce; Lake Agency, Candace; Mura Enterprises, Dee; Partos Co.; Part-Time Prod.; Pevner, Stephen; Picture Of You, A; Redwood Empire Agency; Renaissance—H.N. Swanson Inc.; Tauro Brothers Management; Wright Representatives, Ann

Glitz. Apollo Entertainment; Bethel Agency; Circle of Confusion; Epstein-Wyckoff & Assoc.; Gardner Agency; Hodges Agency, Carolyn; Ketay Agency, Joyce; Lake Agency, Candace; Metropolitan Talent Agency; Montgomery-West Literary Agency; Mura Enterprises, Dee; Pevner, Stephen

Historical. Agency, The; All-Star Talent Agency; Apollo Entertainment; Bethel Agency; Brown Ltd., Curtis; Bulger & Assoc., Kelvin C.; Circle of Confusion; Client First—A/K/A Leo P. Haffey Agency; Douroux & Co.; Epstein-Wyckoff & Assoc.; Feiler Literary Agency, Florence; Fleury Agency, B.R.; Fran Literary Agency; Gardner Agency; Hodges Agency, Carolyn; Howard Agency, Eddy; Hudson Agency; Jenks Agency, Carolyn; Ketay Agency, Joyce; Kohner, Paul; Lake Agency, Candace; Lee Literary Agency, L. Harry; Legacies; Lindstrom Literary Group; Monteiro Rose Agency; Mura Enterprises, Dee; Otitis Media; Part-Time Prod.; PMA Literary & Film Management; Redwood Empire Agency; Renaissance—H.N. Swanson Inc.; Scagnetti Talent & Literary Agency, Jack; Schulman, Susan; Silver Screen Placements; Tauro Brothers Management; Total Acting Experience; Acting Experience; Wright Representatives, Ann

Horror. AEI/Atchity Editorial/Entertainment Int'l; Agency, The; Allan Agency, Lee; All-Star Talent Agency; Apollo Entertainment; Brown Ltd., Curtis; Camden; Circle of Confusion; Durkin Artists Agency; Earth Tracks Agency; Fleury Agency, B.R.; Fran Literary Agency; French, Inc., Samuel; Gardner Agency; Greene, Arthur B.; Heacock Literary Agency; International Leonards Corp.; Kick Entertainment; Kjar Agency, Tyler; Lake Agency, Candace; Lindstrom Literary Group; Major Clients Agency; Metropolitan Talent Agency; Mura Enterprises, Dee; Partos Co.; Part-Time Prod.; Pevner, Stephen; Picture Of You, A; PMA Literary & Film Management; Producers & Creatives Group; Renaissance—H.N. Swanson Inc.; Scagnetti Talent & Literary Agency, Jack; Sister Mania Prod.; Tauro Brothers Management; Total Acting Experience; Wright Representatives, Ann; Writer's Consulting Group

Juvenile. Agency, The; All-Star Talent Agency; Bethel Agency; Cameron Agency, Marshall; Circle of Confusion; Durkin Artists Agency; Epstein-Wyckoff & Assoc.; F.L.A.I.R. or First Literary Artists Int'l Representatives; Feiler Literary Agency, Florence; Fleury Agency, B.R.; Fran Literary Agency; Howard Agency, Eddy; Hudson Agency; Jenks Agency, Carolyn; Ketay Agency, Joyce; Lake Agency, Candace; Metropolitan Talent Agency; Monteiro Rose Agency; Montgomery-West Literary Agency; Mura Enterprises, Dee; Partos Co.; PMA Literary & Film Management; Producers & Creatives Group; Redwood Empire Agency; Renaissance—H.N. Swanson Inc.; Silver Screen Placements; Tauro Brothers Management; Total Acting Experience; Van Duren Agency, Annette; Wright Concept

Lesbian. Apollo Entertainment; Bethel Agency; Brown Ltd., Curtis; Circle of Confusion; Epstein-Wyckoff & Assoc.; Feiler Literary Agency, Florence; Gold/Marshak & Assoc.; Hodges Agency, Carolyn; Ketay Agency, Joyce; Lake Agency, Candace; Partos Co.; Part-Time Prod.; Pevner, Stephen; Redwood Empire Agency; Renaissance—H.N. Swanson Inc.; Tauro Brothers Management; Wright Representatives, Ann

Mainstream. AEI/Atchity Editorial/Entertainment Int'l; Agency, The; All-Star Talent Agency; Apollo Entertainment; Bennett Agency; Bethel Agency; Brown Ltd., Curtis; Camden; Cameron Agency, Marshall; Circle of Confusion; Douroux & Co.; Earth Tracks Agency; Epstein-Wyckoff & Assoc.; F.L.A.I.R. or First Literary Artists Int'l Representatives; Fleury Agency, B.R.; Fran Literary Agency; Gardner Agency; Gold/Marshak & Assoc.; Heacock Literary Agency; Hodges Agency, Carolyn; Howard Agency, Eddy; Jenks Agency, Carolyn; Ketay Agency, Joyce; Kick Entertainment; Kohner, Paul; Lake Agency, Candace; Lee Literary Agency, L. Harry; Lenhoff/Robinson Talent & Literary Agency; Lindstrom Literary Group; Major Clients Agency; Manus & Assoc. Literary Agency; Metropolitan Talent Agency; Monteiro Rose Agency; Montgomery-West Literary Agency; Mura Enterprises, Dee; Palmer, Dorothy; Partos Co.; Part-Time Prod.; Pevner, Stephen; Picture Of You, A; PMA Literary & Film Management; Producers & Creatives Group; Renaissance—H.N. Swanson Inc.; Scagnetti Talent & Literary Agency, Jack; Schulman, Susan; Silver Screen Placements; Total Acting Experience; Acting Experience; Van Duren Agency, Annette; Wright Representatives, Ann; Writer's Consulting Group

Military/War. Agency, The; Bethel Agency; Kohner, Paul; Panda Talent; Tauro Brothers Management

Multimedia. Agency, The; Circle of Confusion; Howard Agency, Eddy; International Leonards Corp.; Jenks Agency, Carolyn; Lenhoff/Robinson Talent & Literary Agency; Montgomery Literary Agency; Total Acting Experience; Acting Experience

Mystery/suspense. Act I; AEI/Atchity Editorial/Entertainment Int'l; Agency, The; Allan Agency, Lee; All-Star Talent Agency; Artists Agency; Bethel Agency; Brown Ltd., Curtis; Cameron Agency, Marshall; Circle of Confusion; Client First—A/K/A Leo P. Haffey Agency; Coast to Coast Talent and Literary; Douroux & Co.; Durkin Artists Agency; Dykeman Assoc.; Epstein-Wyckoff & Assoc.; F.L.A.I.R. or First Literary Artists Int'l Representatives; Feiler Literary Agency, Florence; Fleury Agency, B.R.; Fran Literary Agency; French, Inc., Samuel; Gardner Agency; Gold/Marshak & Assoc.; Greene, Arthur B.; Heacock Literary Agency; Hodges Agency, Carolyn; Howard Agency, Eddy; Hudson Agency; International Leonards Corp.; Jenks Agency, Carolyn; Ketay Agency, Joyce; Kohner, Paul; Lake Agency, Candace; Lee Literary Agency, L. Harry; Lenhoff/Robinson Talent & Literary Agency; Lindstrom Literary Group; Major Clients Agency; Manus & Assoc. Literary Agency; Metropolitan Talent Agency; Monteiro Rose Agency; Montgomery Literary Agency; Montgomery-West Literary Agency; Mura Enterprises, Dee; Otitis Media; Palmer, Dorothy; Panda Talent; Partos Co.; Pevner, Stephen; Picture Of You, A; PMA Literary &

Film Management; Producers & Creatives Group; Renaissance—H.N. Swanson Inc.; Scagnetti Talent & Literary Agency, Jack; Schulman, Susan; Silver Screen Placements; Star Literary Service; Total Acting Experience; Acting Experience; Wright Concept; Wright Representatives, Ann; Writer's Consulting Group

Open to all fiction. Agency for the Performing Arts; American Play Co.; Circle of Confusion; Coppage Company; Gary-Paul Agency; Gersh Agency; Hilton Literary Agency, Alice; Hogenson Agency, Barbara; Keron Assoc., Charles; Marbea Agency; Media Artists Group; Sherman & Assoc., Ken; Wright, Marc; Writers & Artists

Open to all nonfiction. Agency for the Performing Arts; American Play Co.; Sherman & Assoc., Ken

Packaging agents. Ketay Agency, Joyce; Lee Literary Agency, L. Harry; Palmer, Dorothy; Panda Talent

Psychic/supernatural. AEI/Atchity Editorial/Entertainment Int'l; Agapé Prod.; Agency, The; Allan Agency, Lee; All-Star Talent Agency; Apollo Entertainment; Bethel Agency; Brown Ltd., Curtis; Circle of Confusion; Coast to Coast Talent and Literary; F.L.A.I.R. or First Literary Artists Int'l Representatives; Fleury Agency, B.R.; Gardner Agency; Gold/Marshak & Assoc.; Gordon & Assoc., Michelle; Heacock Literary Agency; Hodges Agency, Carolyn; Howard Agency, Eddy; Ketay Agency, Joyce; Lake Agency, Candace; Lee Literary Agency, L. Harry; Lenhoff/Robinson Talent & Literary Agency; Metropolitan Talent Agency; Monteiro Rose Agency; Mura Enterprises, Dee; Partos Co.; Part-Time Prod.; Picture Of You, A; PMA Literary & Film Management; Producers & Creatives Group; Renaissance—H.N. Swanson Inc.; Total Acting Experience; Acting Experience; Watt & Assoc., Sandra; Wright Representatives, Ann; Writer's Consulting Group

Religious/inspirational. Agency, The; Bethel Agency; Dykeman Assoc.; French, Inc., Samuel; Howard Agency, Eddy; Lake Agency, Candace; Lenhoff/Robinson Talent & Literary Agency; Metropolitan Talent Agency; Mura Enterprises, Dee; Picture Of You, A; Renaissance—H.N. Swanson Inc.; Tauro Brothers Management; Total Acting Experience; Watt & Assoc., Sandra

Regional. Bethel Agency; Bulger & Assoc., Kelvin C.; Circle of Confusion; Hodges Agency, Carolyn

Romance. Act I; Apollo Entertainment; Bethel Agency; Camden; Client First—A/K/A Leo P. Haffey Agency; Coast to Coast Talent and Literary; Hodges Agency, Carolyn; Kay Agency, Charlene; Lee Literary Agency, L. Harry; Montgomery-West Literary Agency; Palmer, Dorothy; Redwood Empire Agency; Renaissance—H.N. Swanson Inc.; Sister Mania Prod.; Tauro Brothers Management; Acting Experience

Romantic comedy. AEI/Atchity Editorial/Entertainment Int'l; Agency, The; Allan Agency, Lee; All-Star Talent Agency; Artists Agency; Brown Ltd., Curtis; Cameron Agency, Marshall; Circle of Confusion; Douroux & Co.; Durkin Artists Agency; Epstein-Wyckoff & Assoc.; F.L.A.I.R. or First Literary Artists Int'l Representatives; Feiler Literary Agency, Florence; Fleury Agency, B.R.; Fran Literary Agency; Gardner Agency; Gold/Marshak & Assoc.; Howard Agency, Eddy; Hudson Agency; International Leonards Corp.; Jenks Agency, Carolyn; Ketay Agency, Joyce; Kick Entertainment; Kjar Agency, Tyler; Kohner, Paul; Lake Agency, Candace; Lenhoff/Robinson Talent & Literary Agency; Lindstrom Literary Group; Manus & Assoc. Literary Agency; Monteiro Rose Agency; Monteiro Rose Agency; Montgomery Literary Agency; Montgomery-West Literary Agency; Mura Enterprises, Dee; Otitis Media; Palmer, Dorothy; Panda Talent; Partos Co.; Pevner, Stephen; PMA Literary & Film Management; Producers & Creatives Group; Rogers and Assoc., Stephanie; Sanders Literary Agency, Victoria; Scagnetti Talent & Literary Agency, Jack; Total Acting Experience; Van Duren Agency, Annette; Watt & Assoc., Sandra; Watt & Assoc., Sandra; Wright Concept; Wright Representatives, Ann; Writer's Consulting Group

Romantic drama. AEI/Atchity Editorial/Entertainment Int'l; Agency, The; Allan Agency, Lee; All-Star Talent Agency; Artists Agency; Brown Ltd., Curtis; Cameron Agency, Marshall; Circle of Confusion; Douroux & Co.; Epstein-Wyckoff & Assoc.; F.L.A.I.R. or First Literary Artists Int'l Representatives; Feiler Literary Agency, Florence; Fleury Agency, B.R.; Fran Literary Agency; Gardner Agency; Gold/Marshak & Assoc.; Hudson Agency; Jenks Agency, Carolyn; Ketay Agency, Joyce; Kick Entertainment; Kjar Agency, Tyler; Kohner, Paul; Lake Agency, Candace; Lee Literary Agency, L. Harry; Lenhoff/Robinson Talent & Literary Agency; Lindstrom Literary Group; Metropolitan Talent Agency; Metropolitan Talent Agency; Montgomery-West Literary Agency; Mura Enterprises, Dee; Otitis Media; Palmer, Dorothy; Panda Talent; Partos Co.; Pevner, Stephen; Picture Of You, A; PMA Literary & Film Management; Producers & Creatives Group; Sanders Literary Agency, Victoria; Scagnetti Talent & Literary Agency, Jack; Total Acting Experience; Van Duren Agency, Annette; Watt & Assoc., Sandra; Wright Concept; Wright Representatives, Ann; Writer's Consulting Group

Science Fiction. Act I; AEI/Atchity Editorial/Entertainment Int'l; Agapé Prod.; Agency, The; Allan Agency, Lee; All-Star Talent Agency; Apollo Entertainment; Camden; Circle of Confusion; Client First—A/K/A Leo P. Haffey Agency; Douroux & Co.; Durkin Artists Agency; Fleury Agency, B.R.; Fran Literary Agency; Gardner Agency; Gold/Marshak & Assoc.; Hodges Agency, Carolyn; Howard Agency, Eddy; Hudson Agency; International Leonards Corp.; Kjar Agency, Tyler; Lake Agency, Candace; Lee Literary Agency, L. Harry; Lenhoff/Robinson Talent & Literary Agency; Metropolitan Talent Agency; Monteiro Rose Agency; Montgomery Literary Agency; Montgomery-West Literary Agency; Mura Enterprises, Dee; Panda Talent; Partos Co.; Part-Time Prod.; Pevner, Stephen; PMA Literary & Film Management; Producers & Creatives Group; Renaissance—H.N. Swanson Inc.; Silver Screen Placements; Acting Experience; Van Duren Agency, Annette

Sports. All-Star Talent Agency; Bethel Agency; Circle of Confusion; Client First—A/K/A Leo P. Haffey Agency; Fleury Agency, B.R.; Gold/Marshak & Assoc.; Heacock Literary Agency; Howard Agency, Eddy; Hudson Agency; International Leonards Corp.; Lake Agency, Candace; Lee Literary Agency, L. Harry; Lenhoff/Robinson Talent & Literary Agency; Major Clients Agency; Mura Enterprises, Dee; Renaissance—H.N. Swanson Inc.; Scagnetti Talent & Literary Agency, Jack; Total Acting Experience; Wright Representatives, Ann

Teen. AEI/Atchity Editorial/Entertainment Int'l; Agency, The; Apollo Entertainment; Bethel Agency; Circle of Confusion; Earth Tracks Agency; Epstein-Wyckoff & Assoc.; F.L.A.I.R. or First Literary Artists Int'l Representatives; Fleury Agency, B.R.; Gardner Agency; Howard Agency, Eddy; Hudson Agency; Kjar Agency, Tyler; Lake Agency, Candace; Lenhoff/Robinson Talent & Literary Agency; Metropolitan Talent Agency; Monteiro Rose Agency; Montgomery-West Literary Agency; Mura Enterprises, Dee; Partos Co.; Pevner, Stephen; PMA Literary & Film Management; Producers & Creatives Group; Renaissance—H.N. Swanson Inc.; Total Acting Experience

Thriller/espionage. AEI/Atchity Editorial/Entertainment Int'l; Agapé Prod.; Agency, The; Allan Agency, Lee; All-Star Talent Agency; Apollo Entertainment; Artists Agency; Bethel Agency; Brown Ltd., Curtis; Camden; Cameron Agency, Marshall; Circle of Confusion; Client First—A/K/A Leo P. Haffey Agency; Coast to Coast Talent and Literary; Douroux & Co.; Durkin Artists Agency; Dykeman Assoc.; Earth Tracks Agency; Epstein-Wyckoff & Assoc.; F.L.A.I.R. or First Literary Artists Int'l Representatives; Feiler Literary Agency, Florence; Fleury Agency, B.R.; Fran Literary Agency; French, Inc., Samuel; Gardner Agency; Gold/Marshak & Assoc.; Heacock Literary Agency; Hodges Agency, Carolyn; Howard Agency, Eddy; Hudson Agency; International Leonards Corp.; Jenks Agency, Carolyn; Kay Agency, Charlene; Ketay Agency, Joyce; Lake Agency, Candace; Lee Literary Agency, L. Harry; Lenhoff/Robinson Talent & Literary Agency; Lindstrom Literary Group; Major Clients Agency; Manus & Assoc. Literary Agency; Metropolitan Talent Agency; Monteiro Rose Agency; Montgomery-West Literary Agency; Mura Enterprises, Dee; Otitis Media; Palmer, Dorothy; Partos Co.; Part-Time Prod.; Pevner, Stephen; Picture Of You, A; PMA Literary & Film Management; Producers & Creatives Group; Renaissance—H.N. Swanson Inc.; Rogers and Assoc., Stephanie; Sanders Literary Agency, Victoria; Scagnetti Talent & Literary Agency, Jack; Silver Screen Placements; Sister Mania Prod.; Star Literary Service; Tauro Brothers Management; Total Acting Experience; Acting Experience; Van Duren Agency, Annette; Wright Concept; Wright Representatives, Ann; Writer's Consulting Group

True crime/investigative. Agapé Prod.; Bethel Agency; F.L.A.I.R. or First Literary Artists Int'l Representatives; Gordon & Assoc., Michelle; Hogenson Agency, Barbara; Kohner, Paul; Manus & Assoc. Literary Agency; Palmer, Dorothy; Panda Talent; Sister Mania Prod.; Tauro Brothers Management

Western/frontier. Agapé Prod.; Agency, The; Allan Agency, Lee; All-Star Talent Agency; Bethel Agency; Brown Ltd., Curtis; Camden; Cameron Agency, Marshall; Circle of Confusion; Client First—A/K/A Leo P. Haffey Agency; Douroux & Co.; Fleury Agency, B.R.; Fran Literary Agency; Gardner Agency; Howard Agency, Eddy; Hudson Agency; Jenks Agency, Carolyn; Ketay Agency, Joyce; Lake Agency, Candace; Lee Literary Agency, L. Harry; Lenhoff/Robinson Talent & Literary Agency; Metropolitan Talent Agency; Monteiro Rose Agency; Montgomery Literary Agency; Mura Enterprises, Dee; Panda Talent; Picture Of You, A; PMA Literary & Film Management; Renaissance—H.N. Swanson Inc.; Scagnetti Talent & Literary Agency, Jack; Total Acting Experience; Acting Experience; Wright Concept; Wright Representatives, Ann

Women's issues/women's studies. Agency, The; Bethel Agency; F.L.A.I.R. or First Literary Artists Int'l Representatives; Gold/Marshak & Assoc.; Gordon & Assoc., Michelle; Palmer, Dorothy

Script agents/Format Index

Animation. Above The Line Agency; Agency, The; Amato Agency, Michael; American Play Co.; Buchwald Agency, Don; Coast to Coast Talent and Literary; Douroux & Co.; Epstein-Wyckoff & Assoc.; Fran Literary Agency; Gersh Agency; Heacock Literary Agency; Howard Agency, Eddy; International Leonards Corp.; Kohner, Paul; Lenhoff/Robinson Talent & Literary Agency; Media Artists Group; Metropolitan Talent Agency; Metropolitan Talent Agency; Monteiro Rose Agency; Mura Enterprises, Dee; Renaissance—H.N. Swanson Inc.; Total Acting Experience; Van Duren Agency, Annette; Wright Concept; Wright Concept; Wright, Marc; Wright, Marc

Documentary. Amato Agency, Michael; American Play Co.; Buchwald Agency, Don; Bulger & Assoc., Kelvin C.; Coast to Coast Talent and Literary; Fleury Agency, B.R.; Fran Literary Agency; Gardner Agency; Heacock Literary Agency; Hilton Literary Agency, Alice; Howard Agency, Eddy; Hudson Agency; Jenks Agency, Carolyn; Kohner, Paul; Media Artists Group; Metropolitan Talent Agency; Mura Enterprises, Dee; Total Acting Experience; Wright, Marc

Episodic drama. Agency, The; Allan Agency, Lee; All-Star Talent Agency; Alpern Group; Amato Agency, Michael; Buchwald Agency, Don; Camden; Coast to Coast Talent and Literary; Coppage Company; Douroux & Co.; Epstein-Wyckoff & Assoc.; Feiler Literary Agency, Florence; Fleury Agency, B.R.; Fran Literary Agency; Gardner Agency; Gold/Marshak & Assoc.; Howard Agency, Eddy; Jenks Agency, Carolyn; Keron Assoc., Charles; Ketay Agency, Joyce; Kohner, Paul; Lake Agency, Candace; Lee Literary Agency, L. Harry; Lenhoff/Robinson Talent & Literary Agency; Media Artists Group; Monteiro Rose Agency; Mura Enterprises, Dee; Palmer, Dorothy; Panda Talent; Picture Of You, A; Producers & Creatives Group; Renaissance—H.N. Swanson Inc.; Scagnetti Talent & Literary Agency, Jack; Total Acting Experience; Acting Experience; Wright Concept; Wright, Marc; Wright Representatives, Ann; Writers & Artists

Feature film. Above The Line Agency; Act I; AEI/Atchity Editorial/Entertainment Int'l; Agapé Prod.; Agency, The; Agency for the Performing Arts; Allan Agency, Lee; All-Star Talent Agency; Alpern Group; Amato Agency, Michael; American Play Co.; Apollo Entertainment; Artists Agency; BDP & Associates Talent Agency ; Buchwald Agency, Don; Bulger & Assoc., Kelvin C.; Camden; Cameron Agency, Marshall; Circle of Confusion; Coast to Coast Talent and Literary; Coppage Company; Douroux & Co.; Durkin Artists Agency; Earth Tracks Agency; Epstein-Wyckoff & Assoc.; Feiler Literary Agency, Florence; Fishbein, Frieda; Fleury Agency, B.R.; Fran Literary Agency; Gardner Agency; Geddes Agency; Gelff Agency, Laya; Gersh Agency; Gold/Marshak & Assoc.; Gordon & Assoc., Michelle; Graham Agency; Greene, Arthur B.; Gurman Agency, Susan; Halsey Agency, Reece; Heacock Literary Agency; Hilton Literary Agency, Alice; Hodges Agency, Carolyn; Howard Agency, Eddy; Hudson Agency; International Leonards Corp.; Jenks Agency, Carolyn; Kallen Agency, Leslie; Kay Agency, Charlene; Keron Assoc., Charles; Ketay Agency, Joyce; Kick Entertainment; Kjar Agency, Tyler; Kohner, Paul; Lake Agency, Candace; Lee Literary Agency, L. Harry; Legacies; Lenhoff/Robinson Talent & Literary Agency; Lindstrom Literary Group; Major Clients Agency; Manus & Assoc. Literary Agency; Marbea Agency; Media Artists Group; Metropolitan Talent Agency; Monteiro Rose Agency; Montgomery Literary Agency; Montgomery-West Literary Agency; Mura Enterprises, Dee; Otitis Media; Palmer, Dorothy; Panda Talent; Partos Co.; Pevner, Stephen; Picture Of You, A; PMA Literary & Film Management; Producers & Creatives Group; Redwood Empire Agency; Renaissance—H.N. Swanson Inc.; Rogers and Assoc., Stephanie; Sanders Literary Agency, Victoria; Scagnetti Talent & Literary Agency, Jack; Sister Mania Prod.; Stanton & Assoc. Literary Agency; Star Talent Service; Talent Source; Tauro Brothers Management; Total Acting Experience; Acting Experience; Van Duren Agency, Annette; Warden, White & Kane; Watt & Assoc., Sandra; Whittlesey Agency, Peregrine; Wright Concept; Wright, Marc; Wright Representatives, Ann; Writers & Artists; Writer's Consulting Group

Miniseries. Act I; Agency, The; Alpern Group; Amato Agency, Michael; Buchwald Agency, Don; Camden; Coast to Coast Talent and Literary; Epstein-Wyckoff & Assoc.; Gardner Agency; Gersh Agency; Gold/Marshak & Assoc.; Howard Agency, Eddy; Hudson Agency; Keron Assoc., Charles; Kjar Agency, Tyler; Kohner, Paul; Lenhoff/Robinson Talent & Literary Agency; Lindstrom Literary Group; Media Artists Group; Metropolitan Talent Agency; Mura Enterprises, Dee; Picture Of You, A; PMA Literary & Film Management; Producers & Creatives Group; Sanders Literary Agency, Victoria; Wright, Marc; Writers & Artists

Movie of the week. Above The Line Agency; Act I; AEI/Atchity Editorial/Entertainment Int'l; Agency, The; Allan Agency, Lee; All-Star Talent Agency; Alpern Group; Amato Agency, Michael; American Play Co.; Artists Agency; BDP & Associates Talent Agency ; Buchwald Agency, Don; Bulger & Assoc., Kelvin C.; Camden; Cameron Agency, Marshall; Coast to Coast Talent and Literary; Douroux & Co.; Earth Tracks Agency; Epstein-Wyckoff & Assoc.; Feiler Literary Agency, Florence; Fishbein, Frieda; Fran Literary Agency; Gardner Agency; Gersh Agency; Gold/Marshak & Assoc.; Greene, Arthur B.; Heacock Literary Agency; Hilton Literary Agency, Alice; Hodges Agency, Carolyn; Howard Agency, Eddy; Hudson Agency; International Leonards Corp.; Jenks Agency, Carolyn; Kallen Agency, Leslie; Kay Agency, Charlene; Keron Assoc., Charles; Ketay Agency, Joyce; Kjar Agency, Tyler; Kohner, Paul; Lake Agency, Candace; Lee Literary Agency, L. Harry; Legacies; Lenhoff/Robinson Talent & Literary Agency; Lindstrom Literary Group; Major Clients Agency; Manus & Assoc. Literary Agency;

Media Artists Group; Metropolitan Talent Agency; Monteiro Rose Agency; Montgomery-West Literary Agency; Mura Enterprises, Dee; Otitis Media; Palmer, Dorothy; Panda Talent; Partos Co.; Pevner, Stephen; PMA Literary & Film Management; Producers & Creatives Group; Redwood Empire Agency; Renaissance—H.N. Swanson Inc.; Rogers and Assoc., Stephanie; Sanders Literary Agency, Victoria; Scagnetti Talent & Literary Agency, Jack; Stanton & Assoc. Literary Agency; Star Literary Service; Total Acting Experience; Acting Experience; Van Duren Agency, Annette; Watt & Assoc., Sandra; Wright Concept; Wright, Marc; Wright Representatives, Ann; Writers & Artists; Writer's Consulting Group

Sitcom. Act I; Agency, The; Agency for the Performing Arts; All-Star Talent Agency; Buchwald Agency, Don; Camden; Coast to Coast Talent and Literary; Coppage Company; Douroux & Co.; Earth Tracks Agency; Epstein-Wyckoff & Assoc.; Gersh Agency; Gold/Marshak & Assoc.; Hilton Literary Agency, Alice; Howard Agency, Eddy; International Leonards Corp.; Keron Assoc., Charles; Ketay Agency, Joyce; Kjar Agency, Tyler; Kohner, Paul; Lake Agency, Candace; Lee Literary Agency, L. Harry; Legacies; Major Clients Agency; Media Artists Group; Metropolitan Talent Agency; Mura Enterprises, Dee; Palmer, Dorothy; Panda Talent; Pevner, Stephen; Producers & Creatives Group; Renaissance—H.N. Swanson Inc.; Total Acting Experience; Acting Experience; Van Duren Agency, Annette; Wright Concept; Wright, Marc; Wright Representatives, Ann

Soap opera. Buchwald Agency, Don; Coast to Coast Talent and Literary; Epstein-Wyckoff & Assoc.; Gold/Marshak & Assoc.; Howard Agency, Eddy; Kohner, Paul; Media Artists Group; Mura Enterprises, Dee; Palmer, Dorothy; Picture Of You, A; Producers & Creatives Group; Total Acting Experience; Wright, Marc

Stage play. Agapé Prod.; American Play Co.; BDP & Associates Talent Agency ; Buchwald Agency, Don; Dramatic Publishing; Epstein-Wyckoff & Assoc.; Feiler Literary Agency, Florence; Fishbein, Frieda; French, Inc., Samuel; Gold/Marshak & Assoc.; Graham Agency; Greene, Arthur B.; Gurman Agency, Susan; Howard Agency, Eddy; Jenks Agency, Carolyn; Keron Assoc., Charles; Ketay Agency, Joyce; Kjar Agency, Tyler; Kohner, Paul; Lee Literary Agency, L. Harry; Legacies; Lenhoff/Robinson Talent & Literary Agency; Media Artists Group; Metropolitan Talent Agency; Montgomery Literary Agency; Otitis Media; Pevner, Stephen; Total Acting Experience; Whittlesey Agency, Peregrine; Wright, Marc; Writers & Artists

Variety show. Act I; Buchwald Agency, Don; Coast to Coast Talent and Literary; French, Inc., Samuel; Howard Agency, Eddy; International Leonards Corp.; Keron Assoc., Charles; Kohner, Paul; Lenhoff/Robinson Talent & Literary Agency; Media Artists Group; Mura Enterprises, Dee; Total Acting Experience; Wright Concept; Wright, Marc

Geographic Index

Nonfee-charging literary agents

California
Agents Inc. for Medical and Mental Health Professionals
Allen Literary Agency, Linda
Andrews & Associates Inc., Bart
Appleseeds Management
Brandenburgh & Associates Literary Agency
Brown Literary Agency, Andrea
Candace Lake Agency, The
Casselman, Martha
Castiglia Literary Agency
Cohen, Inc. Literary Agency, Ruth
Dijkstra Literary Agency, Sandra
Emerald Literary Agency
Esq. Literary Productions
Eth Literary Rep., Felicia
Feiler Literary Agency, Florence
Fleming Agency, Peter
Gibson Agency, The Sebastian
Gusay Literary Agency, The Charlotte
Halsey Agency, Reece
Hamilburg Agency, The Mitchell
Hardy Agency, The
Heacock Literary Agency, Inc.
Hill Associates, Frederick
Ievleva Literary Agency, The
Larsen/Elizabeth Pomada Literary Agents, Michael
Lasher Agency, The Maureen
McBride Literary Agency, Margret
Macgrath, Helen †McGrath, Helen
Madsen Agency, Robert
Manus & Associates Literary Agency, Inc.
Markowitz Literary Agency, Barbara
Metropolitan Talent Agency
Nazor Literary Agency, Karen
Popkin, Julie
Renaissance—H.N. Swanson
Rinaldi Literary Agency, Angela
Robbins Literary Agency, BJ
Sebastian Literary Agency
Sierra Literary Agency
Teal Literary Agency, Patricia
Travis Literary Agency, Susan
Van Duren Agency, Annette
Waterside Productions, Inc.

Watt & Associates, Sandra

Colorado
Diamond Literary Agency, Inc.
Pelham Literary Agency

Connecticut
Holub & Associates
J de S Associates Inc.
New England Publishing Associates, Inc.
Urstadt Inc. Agency, Susan P.
Van Der Leun & Associates

District of Columbia
Adler & Robin Books Inc.
Goldfarb & Graybill, Attorneys at Law
Literary and Creative Artists Agency Inc.

Florida
Act I
Bova Literary Agency, The Barbara
Elmo Agency Inc., Ann
Fleury Agency, B.R.
Hass Literary Agency, Rose
International Publisher Associates Inc.
Nugent Literary

Georgia
Baldi Literary Agency, Malaga
Brandt Agency, The Joan
Graham Literary Agency, Inc.
Pelter, Rodney
Schmidt Literary Agency, Harold

Hawaii
Schmidt Literary Agency, Harold

Idaho
Author's Agency, The

Illinois
Agency Chicago
Apollo Entertainment
First Books, Inc.
Goddard Book Group
Hulburt Literary Agency, Helane
Multimedia Product Development, Inc.

Indiana
Printed Tree Inc.

Rose Agency

Iowa
Doyen Literary Services, Inc.

Kentucky
Green, Literary Agent, Randall Elisha

Louisiana
Gautreaux—a literary agency, Richard
Rogers Literary Representation, Irene

Maine
Kroll Literary Agency, Edite

Maryland
Columbia Literary Associates
Potomac Literary Agency, The

Massachusetts
Axelrod Agency, The
Balkin Agency, Inc.
Coover Agency, The Doe
McDonough, Literary Agent, Richard P.
Moore Literary Agency
Palmer & Dodge Agency, The
Raymond, Literary Agent, Charlotte Cecil
Rees Literary Agency, Helen
Riverside Literary Agency
Snell Literary Agency, Michael
Stauffer Associates, Nancy

Michigan
Ajlouny Agency, The Joseph S.

Minnesota
Lazear Agency Incorporated
Otitis Media

Missouri
Flaherty, Literary Agent, Joyce A.
Siegel Literary Agency, Bobbe

New Hampshire
Crawford Literary Agency
Taylor Literary Enterprises, Sandra

New Jersey
Boates Literary Agency, Reid

Henderson Literary Representation
James Peter Associates, Inc.
March Tenth, Inc.
Paul Agency, The Richard
Russell-Simenauer Literary Agency Inc.
Seligman, Literary Agent, Lynn
Siegel, International Literary Agency, Inc., Rosalie
Weiner Literary Agency, Cherry

New York

Acton, Leone, Hanson & Jaffe
Altshuler Literary Agency, Miriam
Amsterdam Agency, Marcia
Baldi Literary Agency, Malaga
Barber Literary Agency, Inc., Virginia
Barrett Books Inc., Loretta
Becker Literary Agency, The Wendy
Behar Literary Agency, Josh
Black Literary Agency, David
Blassingame Spectrum Corp.
Borchardt Inc., Georges
Brandt & Brandt Literary Agents
Brown Associates Inc., Marie
Brown Limited, Curtis
Buck Agency, Howard
Bykofsky Associates, Sheree
Cantrell-Colas Inc., Literary Agency
Carvainis Agency, Inc., Maria
Charisma Communications, Ltd.
Charlton Associates, James
Circle of Confusion Ltd.
Clausen Associates, Connie
Cohen Literary Agency Ltd., Hy
Collins Purvis, Ltd.
Congdon Associates, Inc., Don
Cornfield Literary Agency, Robert
Crown International Literature and Arts Agency, Bonnie R.
Curtis Associates, Inc., Richard
Cypher, Author's Representative, James R.
Darhansoff & Verrill Literary Agents
Daves Agency, Joan
de la Haba Agency Inc., The Lois
Diamant, The Writer's Workshop, Inc., Anita
Dolger Agency, The Jonathan
Donadio and Ashworth, Inc.
Ducas, Robert
Dystel Literary Management, Jane
Educational Design Services, Inc.
Elek Associates, Peter
Ellenberg Literary Agency, Ethan
Elliott Agency
Ellison Inc., Nicholas
Elmo Agency Inc., Ann
Farber Literary Agency Inc.
Flaming Star Literary Enterprises
Flannery Literary

Foley Literary Agency, The
Franklin Associates, Ltd., Lynn
Garon-Brooke Assoc. Inc., Jay
Gartenberg, Literary Agent, Max
Gordon Agency, Charlotte
Greenburger Associates, Inc., Sanford J.
Greene, Arthur B.
Gregory Associates, Maia
Grimes Literary Agency, Lew
Hampton Agency, The
Hawkins & Associates, Inc., John
Henshaw Group, Richard
Herman Agency, Inc., The Jeff
Herner Rights Agency, Susan
Hochmann Books, John L.
Hoffman Literary Agency, Berenice
Hogenson Agency, Barbara
Hull House Literary Agency
Img-Julian Bach Literary Agency
International Creative Management
JABberwocky Literary Agency
Jordan Literary Agency, Lawrence
Kellock Company, Inc., The
Ketz Agency, Louise B.
Kidde, Hoyt & Picard
Kirchoff/Wohlberg, Authors' Representation Division
Klinger, Inc., Harvey
Kouts, Literary Agent, Barbara
Lampack Agency, Inc., Peter
Lantz-Joy Harris Literary Agency Inc., The Robert
Lescher & Lescher Ltd.
Levine Communications, James
Levine Literary Agency, Ellen
Lieberman Associates, Robert
Lipkind Agency, Wendy
Literary Group, The
Lord Literistic, Inc., Sterling
Love Literary Agency, Nancy
Lowenstein Associates, Inc.
Maass Literary Agency, Donald
Maccampbell Inc., Donald
Maccoby Literary Agency, Gina
Mainhardt Agency, Ricia
Mann Agency, Carol
Manus & Associates Literary Agency, Inc.
Markson Literary Agency, Elaine
Martell Agency, The
Michaels Literary Agency, Inc., Doris S.
Miller Agency, The
Miller Associates, Roberta
Morris Agency, William
Morrison, Inc., Henry
Mura Enterprises, Inc. Dee
Naggar Literary Agency, Jean V.
Nathan, Ruth
Nine Muses and Apollo
Nolan Literary Agency, Betsy
Norma-Lewis Agency, The
Ober Associates, Harold
Orr Agency, Inc., Alice
Oscard Agency, Inc., Fifi

Parks Agency, The Richard
Paton Literary Agency, Kathi J.
Pelter, Rodney
Perkins Associates, L.
Pevner, Inc., Stephen
Pine Associates, Inc, Arthur
Pom Inc.
Priest Literary Agency, Aaron M.
Protter Literary Agent, Susan Ann
Pryor, Inc., Roberta
Publishing Services
Quicksilver Books-Literary Agents
Robbins Office, Inc., The
Rose Literary Agency
Rotrosen Agency, Jane
Rubenstein Literary Agency, Inc., Pesha
Sanders Literary Agency, Victoria
Sandum & Associates
Schmidt Literary Agency, Harold
Schulman, A Literary Agency, Susan
Schwartz Agency, Laurens R.
Seymour Agency, The
Shepard Agency, The
Shukat Company Ltd., The
Siegel Literary Agency, Bobbe
Singer Literary Agency Inc., Evelyn
Smith, Literary Agent, Valerie
Sommer, Inc., Elyse
Spieler, F. Joseph
Spitzer Literary Agency, Philip G.
Steele & Co., Ltd., Lyle
Stepping Stone
Targ Literary Agency, Roslyn
TCA
2M Communications Ltd.
Ubell Associates, Robert
Valcourt Agency, The Richard R.
Vines Agency, Inc., The
Wald Associates, Inc., Mary Jack
Wallace Literary Agency, Inc.
Ware Literary Agency, John A.
Wasserman Literary Agency, Inc., Harriet
Watkins Loomis Agency, Inc.
Wecksler-Incomco
Weingel-Fidel Agency, The
Weyr Agency, Rhoda
Wieser & Wieser, Inc.
Witherspoon & Associates, Inc.
Wreschner, Authors' Representative, Ruth
Wright Representatives, Ann
Writers House
Writers' Representatives, Inc.
Zahler Literary Agency, Karen Gantz
Zeckendorf Assoc. Inc., Susan
Ziegler Literary Agency, George Bernstein, Pam

Pennsylvania

Allen, Literary Agency, James
Butler, Art and Literary Agent, Jane
Collin Literary Agent, Frances

Kidd, Literary Agent, Virginia
Lincoln Literary Agency, Ray
Pocono Literary Agency, Inc.

Tennessee
New Brand Agency Group

Texas
Authors' Literary Agency
DHS Literary, Inc.
Dupree/Miller and Associates
Inc. Literary

Fogelman Literary Agency
Hegler Literary Agency, Gary L.
Lewis & Company, Karen
Lyceum Creative Properties, Inc.
Stern Literary Agency, Gloria

Utah
Dragon Literary, Inc.

Vermont
Rowland Agency, The Damaris

Virginia
Lindstrom Literary Group
St. Clair Literary Agency

Washington
Levant & Wales, Literary Agency

Wisconsin
Allan Agency, Lee
Ciske & Dietz Literary Agency

Fee-charging literary agents

Arizona
Authors Resource Center/Tarc
Literary Agency, The

California
AEI/Atchity Editorial/Entertain-
ment International
Brinke Literary Agency, The
Catalog Literary Agency, The
Clark Literary Agency, SJ
Coast To Coast Talent & Literary
Colby: Literary Agency
Dorese Agency Ltd.
Follendore & Ikeyama Literary
Agency
ForthWrite Literary Agency
Gladden Unlimited
Hilton Literary Agency, Alice
Hubbs Agency, Yvonne Trudeau
JLM Literary Agents
Literary Group West
Lopopolo Literary Agency, Toni
Pacific Literary Services
Penmarin Books
Stern Agency, Gloria
Total Acting Experience, A
Visions Press
Warren Literary Agency, James
West Coast Literary Associates
Writer's Consulting Group

Colorado
Alp Arts Co.
Flannery, White and Stone

Connecticut
Independent Publishing Agency
Mews Books Ltd.
Toomey Associates, Jeanne

Florida
Collier Associates
Lawyer's Literary Agency, Inc.
Taylor Literary Agency, Dawson
Westchester Literary Agency, Inc.

Georgia
Allegra Literary Agency

Authentic Creations Literary
Agency

Illinois
Portman Organization, The
SLC Enterprises
Steinberg Literary Agency, Mi-
chael

Louisiana
Ahearn Agency, Inc., The

Massachusetts
Cambridge Literary Associates
Jenks Agency, Carolyn

Michigan
Law Offices of Robert L. Fenton
M.H. International Literary
Agency

Minnesota
Gislason Agency, The
Collier Associates
Connor Literary Agency
Dorese Agency Ltd.
Executive Excellence
Flannery, White and Stone

North Carolina
Lighthouse Literary Agency

New Hampshire
Northeast Literary Agency

New Jersey
Howard Agency, The Eddy
Marshall Agency, The Evan
Puddingstone Literary Agency

New Mexico
Rydal

New York
Author Aid Associates
Backman, Elizabeth H.
Bartczak Associates Inc., Gene
Bernstein Literary Agency,
Meredith

Brod Literary Agency, Ruth Hagy
Browne Ltd., Pema
Chester, Literary Agency, Linda
Connor Literary Agency
Fishbein Ltd., Frieda
Gelles-Cole Literary Enterprises
Goldberg Literary Agents, Inc.,
Lucianne S.
Lee Literary Agency, L. Harry
Marcil Literary Agency, Inc., The
Denise
Nelson Literary Agency & Lec-
ture Bureau, BK
Paraview, Inc.
Pell Agency, William
PMA Literary and Film Manage-
ment, Inc.
Raintree Agency, Diane
Strong Literary Agency, Mari-
anne
Tornetta Agency, Phyllis
Wright Authors' Representative,
Stephen

Ohio
Evans And Associates †Evans &
Associates
GEM Literary Services
Hamilton's Literary Agency, An-
drew

Oregon
Kern Literary Agency, Natasha
QCorp Literary Agency

Pennsylvania
Novak III Literary Representa-
tion, Edward A.
Porcelain, Sidney E.
Wallerstein Agency, The Gerry B.

Texas
Blake Group Literary Agency
Chadd-Stevens Literary Agency
Fran Literary Agency
Kirkland Literary Agency, The
Southern Literary Agency

Utah
Executive Excellence

Virginia
Brown, Literary Agent,
  Antoinette
Kaltman Literary Agency, Larry
Morgan Literary Agency, Inc.,
  David H.

Washington
Catalog Literary Agency, The

Wisconsin
McKinley, Literary Agency,
  Virginia C.

Canada
Acacia House Publishing
  Services Ltd.

Kellock & Associates Ltd., J.
Northwest Literary Services

Script agents

Arizona
Star Literary Service

California
Above The Line Agency
AEI/Atchity Editorial/Entertain-
  ment International
Agency, The
Agency for the Performing Arts
All-Star Talent Agency
Alpern Group, The
Artists Agency, The
BDP & Associates Talent
  Agency
Bennett Agency, The
Camden
Cinema Talent International
Coast to Coast Talent and Literary
Coppage Company, The
Douroux & Co.
Durkin Artists Agency
Epstein-Wyckoff and Associates
Feiler Literary Agency, Florence
Geddes Agency
Gelff Agency, The Laya
Gersh Agency, The
Gibson Agency, The Sebastian
Gold/Marshak & Associates
Gordon & Associates, Michelle
Halsey Agency, Reece
Heacock Literary Agency, Inc.
Hilton Literary Agency, Alice
International Creative Manage-
  ment
Kallen Agency, Leslie
Kjar Agency, Tyler
Kohner, Inc., Paul
Lake Agency, The Candace
Lenhoff/Robinson Talent and Lit-
  erary Agency, Inc.
Major Clients Agency
Manus & Associates Literary
  Agency, Inc.
Media Artists Group
Metropolitan Talent Agency
Monteiro Rose Agency
Panda Talent
Partos Company, The
Producers & Creatives Group
Redwood Empire Agency
Renaissance—H.N. Swanson Inc.
Rogers and Associates, Stephanie
Scagnetti Talent & Literary
  Agency, Jack

Sherman & Associates, Ken
Tauro Brothers Management
Total Acting Experience, A
Turtle Agency, The
Van Duren Agency, Annette
Warden, White & Kane, Inc.
Watt & Associates, Sandra
Whittlesey Agency, Peregrine
Wright Concept, The
Wright, Marc
Writer's Consulting Group

Colorado
Hodges Agency, Carolyn
Pelham Literary Agency

Connecticut
Gary-Paul Agency, The

Florida
Act I
Cameron Agency, The Marshall
Fleury Agency, B.R.
Legacies
Marbea Agency

Georgia
Talent Source

Illinois
Apollo Entertainment
Bulger And Associates, Kelvin C.
Dramatic Publishing
Part-Time Productions
Silver Screen Placements

Indiana
Agape Productions
International Leonards Corp.

Louisiana
Gauthreaux A Literary Agency,
  Richard

Maryland
Montgomery Literary Agency

Massachusetts
Jenks Agency, Carolyn

Minnesota
Otitis Media

New Jersey
Howard Agency, The Eddy

New York
Amato Agency, Michael
American Play Co., Inc.
Amsterdam Agency, Marcia
Berman, Boals and Flynn
Bethel Agency
Brown Ltd., Curtis
Buchwald Agency, Don
Circle of Confusion Ltd.
Earth Tracks Agency
F.L.A.I.R. or First Literary Artists
  International Representatives
Fishbein Ltd., Frieda
Freedman Dramatic Agency, Inc.,
  Robert A.
French, Inc., Samuel
Graham Agency
Greene, Arthur B.
Gurman Agency, The Susan
Hogenson Agency, Barbara
Hudson Agency
Kerin Associates, Charles
Ketay Agency, The Joyce
Lee Literary Agency, L. Harry
Manus & Associates Literary
  Agency, Inc.
Mura Enterprises, Inc., Dee
Palmer, Dorothy
Pevner, Inc., Stephen
PMA Literary and Film Manage-
  ment, Inc.
Sanders Literary Agency, Victoria
Schulman, A Literary Agency,
  Susan
Tantleff Office, The
Vines Agency, Inc., The
Wright Representatives, Ann
Writers & Artists

Ohio
Kick Entertainment
Picture Of You, A

Pennsylvania
Sister Mania Productions, Inc.

Tennessee
Client First—A/K/A Leo P. Haffey Agency

Texas
Dykeman Associates Inc.
Fran Literary Agency
Lyceum Creative Properties
Stanton & Associates Literary
  Agency

Utah
Dragon Literary, Inc.
Montgomery-West Literary
  Agency

Virginia
Communications and Entertain-
  ment, Inc.
Gardner Agency, The
Lindstrom Literary Group

Wisconsin
Allan Agency, Lee

Canada
Kay Agency, Charlene

Agents Index

This index of agent names was created to help you locate agents you may have read or heard about even when you do not know which agency they work for. Agent names are listed with their agencies' names. Check the Listing Index for the page number of the agency.

A

Abel, Dominick (Dominick Abel Literary Agency, Inc.)

Abend, Sheldon (American Play Co.)

Abrahams, John (Writers House)

Acton, Edward J. (Acton, Leone, Hanson & Jaffe)

Adams, Deborah (The Jeff Herman Agency Inc.)

Adler, Jr., Bill (Adler & Robin Books Inc.)

Agarwal, Rajeev K. (Circle of Confusion Ltd.)

Agyeman, Janell Walden (Marie Brown Associates Inc.)

Ahearn, Pamela G. (The Ahearn Agency, Inc.)

Ajlouny, Joseph (The Joseph S. Ajlouny Agency)

Alexander, Barbara (Media Artists Group)

Alexander, Masha (Lynn C. Franklin Associates, Ltd.)

Ali, Geisel (BK Nelson Literary Agency & Lecture Bureau)

Allen, James (James Allen, Literary Agency)

Allen, Linda (Linda Allen Literary Agency)

Allred, Robert (All-Star Talent Agency)

Aloia, Jr., Richard (The Richard Paul Agency)

Alperen, Julie (Kirchoff/Wohlberg, Inc., Authors' Representation Division)

Alpern, Jeff (The Alpern Group)

Alterman, Eric (New Brand Agency Group)

Altshuler, Miriam (Miriam Altshuler Literary Agency)

Amato, Mary Ann (Legacies)

Amato, Michael (Michael Amato Agency)

Amparan, Joann (Wecksler-Incomco)

Amsterdam, Marcia (Marcia Amsterdam Agency)

Anderson, Jeff (M.H. International Literary Agency)

Andiman, Lori (Arthur Pine Associates)

Andrews, Bart (Bart Andrews & Associates Inc.)

Aragi, Nicole (Watkins Loomis Agency, Inc.)

Armenta, Judith (Martha Casselman, Literary Agent)

Arnovitz, Scott (Int'l Creative Management—CA)

Atchity, Kenneth (AEI/Atchity Editorial/Entertainment Int'l)

Athans, Nicholas (Cinema Talent Int'l)

Axelrod, Steven (The Axelrod Agency)

B

Bach, Julian (IMG-Julian Bach Literary Agency)

Backman, Elizabeth H. (Elizabeth H. Backman)

Bailey, George (Producers & Creatives Group)

Baldi, Malaga (Malaga Baldi Literary Agency)

Balkin, Richard (Balkin Agency, Inc.)

Ballard, Nicole (Toni Lopopolo Literary Agency)

Bankoff, Lisa (Int'l Creative Management-NY)

Barber, Virginia (Virginia Barber Literary Agency, Inc.)

Barmeier, Jim (Writer's Consulting Group)

Barquette, Jim (The Partos Company)

Barr, Hollister (L. Harry Lee Literary Agency)

Barr, Mary (Sierra Literary Agency)

Barrett, Loretta A. (Loretta Barrett Books Inc.)

Barrett, Robin (Flannery, White and Stone)

Bartczak, Gene (Gene Bartczak Associates Inc.)

Bartczak, Sue (Gene Bartczak Associates Inc.)

Bartlett, Bruce (Above The Line Agency)

Barvin, Jude (The Brinke Literary Agency)

Bearden, James L. (Communications and Entertainment)

Becker, Wendy (The Wendy Becker Literary Agency)

Behar, Josh (Josh Behar Literary Agency)

Bellacicco, Dan A. (A Total Acting Experience)

Belzer, Leonard (Paraview, Inc.—The Sandra Martin Literary Agency)

Bennett, Carole (The Bennett Agency)

Benson, Jeffrey A. (Major Clients Agency)

Benson, John (BK Nelson Literary Agency & Lecture Bureau)

Benson, JW (BK Nelson Literary Agency & Lecture Bureau)

Berger, Mel (William Morris Agency-NY)

Berkman, Edwina (L. Harry Lee Literary Agency)

Berkower, Amy (Writers House)

Berman, Lois (Berman, Boals and Flynn)

Bernard, Alec (Puddingstone Literary Agency)

Bernstein, Meredith (Meredith Bernstein Literary Agency)

Bernstein, Pam (Pam Bernstein)

Bernstein, Ron (The Gersh Agency)

Berry, Henry (Independent Publishing Agency)

Bialer, Matthew (William Morris Agency-NY)

Biggis, Charis (L. Harry Lee Literary Agency)

Bilmes, Joshua (JABberwocky Literary Agency)

Bitterman, Annette (Author Aid Associates)

Black, David (David Black Literary Agency, Inc.)

Blake, Laura J. (Curtis Brown Ltd.)

Blankson, Joanna (Marie Brown Associates Inc.)

Blanton, Sandra (Peter Lampack Agency, Inc.)

Blick, Carolyn Hopwood (Pocono Literary Agency)

Bloom, Leonard (Jack Scagnetti Talent & Literary Agency)

Diamant, Anita (Anita Diamant, The Writer's Workshop)

Dickensheid, Diane (Victoria Sanders Literary Agency)

Diehl Kruger, Linda (Fogelman Literary Agency)

Dietz, Patricia (Ciske & Dietz Literary Agency)

Dijkstra, Sandra (Sandra Dijkstra Literary Agency)

DiLeonardo, Ingrid (Otitis Media)

Dintsman, Lee (Agency for the Performing Arts)

Diver, Lucienne (Blassingame Spectrum Corp.)

Dixon, Sherrie (Esq. Literary Productions)

Dolger, Jonathan (The Jonathan Dolger Agency)

Donadio, Candida (Donadio and Ashworth, Inc.)

Donnelly, Dave (BK Nelson Literary Agency & Lecture Bureau)

Doran, Michael (Southern Literary Agency)

Dorese, Alyss Barlow (Dorese Agency Ltd.)

Douglas, Mitch (Int'l Creative Management-NY)

Douglass, Bill (Int'l Creative Management—CA)

Douroux, Michael E. (Douroux & Co.)

Doyen, B.J. (Doyen Literary Services, Inc.)

Dreyfus, Barbara (Int'l Creative Management—CA)

Duane, Dick (Jay Garon-Brooke Associates Inc.)

Dubuisson, Anne (Ellen Levine Literary Agency, Inc.)

Ducas, Robert (Robert Ducas)

Dudin, Ludmilla (The Portman Organization)

Dunow, Henry (Harold Ober Associates)

Durkin, Debbie E. (Durkin Artists Agency)

Dykeman, Alice (Dykeman Associates Inc.)

Dystel, Jane (Jane Dystel Literary Management)

E

Eagle, Theodora (John L. Hochmann Books)

Eckstut, Arielle (James Levine Communications, Inc.)

Egan-Miller, Danielle (Multimedia Product Development, Inc.)

Elek, Peter (Peter Elek Associates)

Ellenberg, Ethan (Ethan Ellenberg Literary Agent)

Elliott, Elaine (Elliott Agency)

Ellison, Nicholas (Nicholas Ellison, Inc.)

Elmo, Ann (Ann Elmo Agency Inc.)

Elsell, Jake (Wieser & Weiser, Inc.)

Emer, Phyllis (The Portman Organization)

Emmons, Don (Northeast Literary Agency)

Engel, Anne (Jean V. Naggar Literary Agency)

Epley, Thomas F. (The Potomac Literary Agency)

Esersky, Garth (Carol Mann Agency)

Eth, Felicia (Felicia Eth Literary Representation)

Ettling, H. Allen (Lawyer's Literary Agency, Inc.)

Evans, Bryan (Evans & Associates)

Evans, Clyde (Evans & Associates)

Evereaux, Anastassia (L. Harry Lee Literary Agency)

F

Farber, Ann (Farber Literary Agency)

Faria, Judith (L. Harry Lee Literary Agency)

Feder, Josh (Peter Elek Associates)

Feldman, Leigh (Darhansoff & Verrill Literary Agents)

Feldman, Richard (Int'l Creative Management—CA)

Fenton, Robert L. (Law Offices of Robert L. Fenton PC)

Ferenczi, Charmaine (The Tantleff Office)

Fernandez, Justin (Paraview, Inc.—The Sandra Martin Literary Agency)

Fidel, Loretta (The Weingel-Fidel Agency)

Finch, Diana (Ellen Levine Literary Agency, Inc.)

Fineman, Ross (Major Clients Agency)

Fishbein, Janice (Frieda Fishbein Ltd.)

Fisher, Stephen (Renaissance—H.N. Swanson, Inc.)

FitzGerald Robert (Flannery, White and Stone)

Flaherty, John (Joyce A. Flaherty, Literary Agent)

Flaherty, Joyce (Joyce A. Flaherty, Literary Agent)

Fleming, Peter (Peter FLeming Agency)

Fogelman, Evan (Fogelman Literary Agency)

Foiles, S. James (Appleseeds Management)

Foley, Joan (The Foley Literary Agency)

Foley, Joseph (The Foley Literary Agency)

Follendore, Joan (Follendore & Ikeyama Literary Agency)

Fontino, Donna Williams (Major Clients Agency)

Forbes, Jamie (The Jeff Herman Agency Inc.)

Foss, Gwen (The Joseph S. Ajlouny Agency)

Fox, Laurie (Linda Chester Literary Agency)

Franklin, Lynn C. (Lynn C. Franklin Associates, Ltd.)

Franklin, Peter (William Morris Agency-NY)

Fraser, Dianne (Major Clients Agency)

Free, Jean (Jay Garon-Brooke Associates Inc.)

Freedman, Robert (Robert A. Freedman Dramatic Agency)

Freymann, Sarah Jane (Stepping Stone)

Friedman, Lisa (James Charlton Associates)

Friedman, Sharon (John Hawkins & Associates)

Friedrich, Molly (Aaron M. Priest Literary Agency)

Frisk, Mark (Howard Buck Agency)

Frohbieter-Mueller, Jo (Printed Tree Inc.)

Fugate, David (Waterside Productions)

Fuller, Sandy Ferguson (Alp Arts Co.)

G

Gail, Francine (The Eddy Howard Agency)

Gardner, Anthony (The Tantleff Office)

Gartenberg, Max (Max Gartenberg, Literary Agent)

Gault, Louise (Elizabeth H. Backman)

Gauthreaux, Richard (Richard Gauthreaux—A Literary Agency)

Gaylor, Mary Lee (L. Harry Lee Literary Agency)

Geddes, Ann (Geddes Agency)

Geiger, Ellen (Curtis Brown Ltd.)

Gelff, Laya (The Laya Gelff Agency)

Gelles-Cole, Sandi (Gelles-Cole Literary Enterprises)

Geminder, Michele (Witherspoon & Associates)

Gibson, Sebastian (The Sebastian Gibson Agency)

Ginsberg, Debra (Sandra Dijkstra Literary Agency)

Ginsberg, Peter L. (Curtis Brown Ltd.)

Ginsberg, Susan (Writers House)

Giordano, Pat (Hudson Agency)

Giordano, Susan (Hudson Agency)

Gislason, Barbara J. (The Gislason Agency)

Gladden, Carolan (Gladden Unlimited)

Gladstone, Bill (Waterside Productions)

Glasser, Carla (The Betsy Nolan Literary Agency)

Gluck, Suzanne (Int'l Creative Management-NY)

Goddard, Connie (Goddard Book Group)

Goderich, Miriam (Jane Dystel Literary Management)

Goldberg, Jonah (Lucianne S. Goldberg Literary Agents, Inc.)

Goldberger, Amy (Publishing Services)

Golden, Winifred (Margret McBride Literary Agency)

Goldfarb, Ronald (Goldfarb & Graybill, Attorneys at Law)

Golin, Carole (SLC Enterprises)

Gordon, Charlotte (Charlotte Gordon Agency)

Gordon, Michelle (Michelle Gordon & Associates)

Gores, Martha R. (The Authors Resource Center)

Gotler, Joel (Renaissance—H.N. Swanson, Inc.)

Gottlieb, Robert (William Morris Agency-NY)

Grace, Audrey (Panda Talent)

Graham, Earl (Graham Agency)

Graham, Susan L. (Graham Literary Agency)

Grau, James W. (Charisma Communications, Ltd.)

Graybill, Nina (Goldfarb & Graybill, Attorneys at Law)

Greco, Gerardo (Peter Elek Associates)

Green, Dan (POM Inc.)

Green, Simon (POM Inc.)

Green, Sue (Agape Productions)

Greenblatt, Ken (Media Artists Group)

Greenburger, Francis (Sanford J. Greenburger Associates, Inc.)

Greene, Arthur B. (Arthur B. Greene)

Greene, Randall Elisha (Randall Elisha Greene, Literary Agent)

Greensberg, Daniel (James Levine Communications, Inc.)

Greer, Rima Bauer (Above The Line Agency)

Gregory, Maia (Maia Gregory Associates)

Griffith, Valerie (Levant & Wales, Literary Agency, Inc.)

Grimes, Lew (Lew Grimes Literary Agency)

Grossman, Elizabeth (Sterling Lord Literistic)

Grosvenor, Deborah (Literary and Creative Artists Agency Inc.

Guber, Cynthia (The Partos Company)

Gurman, Susan (The Susan Gurman Agency)

Gusay, Charlotte (The Charlotte Gusay Literary Agency)

H

Haas, Paul (Int'l Creative Management—CA)

Haffey Jr., Leo P. Haffey (Client First—A/K/A Leo P. Haffey Agency)

Hagen, Peter (Writers & Artists)

Halff, Albert H. (The Blake Group Literary Agency)

Halsey, Dorris (Reece Halsey Agency)

Hamilburg, Michael (The Mitchell J. Hamilburg Agency)

Hamilton, Andrew (Andrew Hamilton's Literary Agency)

Hamlin, Faith (Sanford J. Greenburger Associates, Inc.)

Handaris, Marisa (M.H. Int'l Literary Agency)

Hanke, Mellie (M.H. Int'l Literary Agency)

Hanna, Frances (Acacia House Publishing Services Ltd.)

Hanson, Ingrid (Acton, Leone, Hanson & Jaffe)

Harbison, Lawrence (Samuel French, Inc.)

Harcar, Christina (Nicholas Ellison, Inc.)

Harper, Laurie (Sebastian Literary Agency)

Harriet, Dr. Sydney J. (Agents Inc. for Medical and Mental Health Professionals)

Harrington, Bruce (Apollo Entertainment)

Harrington, Dale (Northeast Literary Agency)

Harris, Hannibal (Otitis Media)

Harris, Joy (The Robert Lantz-Joy Harris Literary Agency)

Harris, Sloan (Int'l Creative Management-NY)

Hartley, Glen (Writers' Representatives, Inc.)

Hass, Rose (Rose Hass Literary Agency)

Hasseler, Jeffrey (Marbea Agency)

Hawkins, John (John Hawkins & Associates)

Hayes, Linda (Columbia Literary Associates, Inc.)

Heacock, Rosalie (Heacock Literary Agency Inc.)

Heckler, Marie (Cinema Talent Int'l)

Hegler, Gary L. (Gary L. Hegler Literary Agency)

Heifetz, Merrillee (Writers House)

Henderson, Rita Elizabeth (Henderson Literary Representation)

Hendin, David (DH Literary)

Hengen, Jennifer (Sterling Lord Literistic)

Henshaw, Richard (Richard Henshaw Group)

Herman, Jeff (The Jeff Herman Agency Inc.)

Herner, Susan (Susan Herner Rights Agency)

Herr, Tania (The Bennett Agency)

Hibbert, Edward (Donadio and Ashworth, Inc.)

Hiltebrand, Cyril (Lucianne S. Goldberg Literary Agents, Inc.)

Hilton, Alice (Alice Hilton Literary Agency)

Hochman, Gail (Brandt & Brandt Literary Agents, Inc.)

Hochmann, John L. (John L. Hochmann Books)

Hodges, Carolyn (Carolyn Hodges Agency)

Hoffman, Berenice (Berenice Hoffman Literary Agency)

Hogenson, Barbara (Barbara Hogenson Agency)

Holman, Sheri (Aaron M. Priest Literary Agency)

Holtje, Bert (James Peter Associates, Inc.)

Holub, William (Holub & Associates)

Horn, Clare (Margret McBride Literary Agency)

Hotchkiss, Joseph (Sterling Lord Literistic)

Howart, Phil (Charisma Communications, Ltd.)

Hubbs, Thomas D. (Yvonne Trudeau Hubbs Agency)

Hubbs, Yvonne (Yvonne Trudeau Hubbs Agency)

Hudson, Scott (Writers & Artists)

Hulburt, Helane (Helane Hulburt Literary Agency)

Hull, David Stewart (Hull House Literary Agency)

I

Ievleva, Julie (The Ievleva Literary Agency)

Ikeyama, Carolyn (Follendore & Ikeyama Literary Agency)

J

Jackson, Jennifer (Donald Maass Literary Agency)

Jacobson, Emilie (Curtis Brown Ltd.)

Jaffe, Mark (Acton, Leone, Hanson & Jaffe)

Jarvis, Sharon (Toad Hall, Inc.)

Jeff Ordway (Camden)

Jenks, Carolyn (Carolyn Jenks Agency)

Jennemann, Leslie (The Hampton Agency)

Jennings, Phillip (Marbea Agency)

Jensen, Kathryn (Columbia Literary Associates, Inc.)

Jenson, Jennette (Gold/Marshak & Associates)

Johnson, B.J. (Literary Group West)

Johnson, Doris (Helen McGrath)

Johnson, Ray (Literary Group West)

Jordan Browne, Jane (Multimedia Product Development, Inc.)

Jordan, Lawrence (Lawrence Jordan Literary Agency)

Jordan, Lee F. (Chadd-Stevens Literary Agency)

Josephson, Nancy (Int'l Creative Management—CA)

K

Kallen, Leslie (Leslie Kallen Agency)

Kaltman, Larry (Larry Kaltman Literary Agency)

Kamins, Ken (Int'l Creative Management—CA)

Kane, Jay (The Tantleff Office)

Kane, Merrily (The Artists Agency)

Kane, Michael (Warden, White & Kane)

Kangas, Sandra (Lighthouse Literary Agency)

Kaplan, Elizabeth (Ellen Levine Literary Agency, Inc.)

Kato, Gordon (Int'l Creative Management-NY)

Katz, Clarissa (William Pell Agency)

Kay, Charlene (Charlene Kay Agency)

Kellock, Alan C. (The Kellock Company Inc.)

Kellock, Joanne (J. Kellock & Associates, Ltd.)

Kellock, Loren (The Kellock Company Inc.)

Kelly, Martha (M.H. Int'l Literary Agency)

Kelly, Susan (William Pell Agency)

Kelmenson, Paul (Metropolitan Talent Agency)

Kepler, Jim (Lyle Steele & Co. Ltd.)

Kerin, Charles (Charles Kerin Associates)

Kern, Natasha (Natasha Kern Literary Agency)

Ketay, Joyce (The Joyce Ketay Agency)

Ketz, Louise B. (Louise B. Ketz Agency)

Kidd, Virginia (Virginia Kidd Literary Agent)

Kidde, Katharine (Kidde, Hoyt & Picard)

Killeen, Frank (L. Harry Lee Literary Agency)

Kimball, Clark (Rydal)

Kinzie, Davie (Alice Hilton Literary Agency)

Kiwitt, Sidney (AEI/Atchity Editorial/Entertainment Int'l)

Kjar, Tyler (Tyler Kjar Agency)

Klein, Cindy (Georges Borchardt Inc.)

Klein, Sam (Kick Entertainment)

Klinger, Harvey (Harvey Klinger, Inc.)

Knappman, Edward W. (New England Publishing Associates Inc.)

Knappman, Elizabeth Frost (New England Publishing Associates Inc.)

Kneerim, Jill (The Palmer & Dodge Agency)

Knowlton, Perry (Curtis Brown Ltd.)

Knowlton, Timothy (Curtis Brown Ltd.)

Knowlton, Virginia (Curtis Brown Ltd.)

Kossow, Amy (Linda Allen Literary Agency)

Kouts, Barbara (Barbara S. Kouts, Literary Agent)

Kraas, Ashley (Anita Diamant, The Writer's Workshop)

Kramer, Sidney B. (Mews Books Ltd.)

Krinsky, David (Earth Tracks Agency)

Kriton, George (Cinema Talent Int'l)

Kroll, Edite (Edite Kroll Literary Agency)

Krupp, Carolyn (IMG-Julian Bach Literary Agency)

Kuffel, Frances (Jean V. Naggar Literary Agency)

L

Lada, D.S. (Esq. Literary Productions)

Laitsch, Jason (Authentic Creations Literary Agency)

Laitsch, Mary Lee (Authentic Creations Literary Agency)

Laitsch, Ronald E. (Authentic Creations Literary Agency)

Lake, Candace (The Candace Lake Agency)

Lambert, Cynthia (Allegra Literary Agency)

Lampack, Peter (Peter Lampack Agency, Inc.)

Landsman, Liza (Writers House)

Lange, Heide (Sanford J. Greenburger Associates, Inc.)

Langlie, Laura (Kidde, Hoyt & Picard)

Larsen, Michael (Michael Larsen/Elizabeth Pomada Literary Agents)

Lasher, Maureen (The Maureen Lasher Agency)

Laster, Owen (William Morris Agency-NY)

Laughren, Brent (Northwest Literary Services)

Lazear, Jonathon (Lazear Agency Incorporated)

Lebowitz, Fran (Writers House)

Lee, L. Harry (L. Harry Lee Literary Agency)

Lee, Lettie (Ann Elmo Agency Inc.)

Lee, Tom (Part-Time Productions)

Lehr, Donald (The Betsy Nolan Literary Agency)

Lenhoff, Charles (Lenhoff/Robinson Talent and Literary Agency, Inc.)

Leonards, Davie (Int'l Leonards Corp.)

Leone, Adele (Acton, Leone, Hanson & Jaffe)

Lescher, Robert (Lescher & Lescher Ltd.)

Lescher, Susan (Lescher & Lescher Ltd.)

Levin, William (Silver Screen Placements)

Levine, Ellen (Ellen Levine Literary Agency, Inc.)

Levine, James (James Levine Communications, Inc.)

Levine, Victor A. (Northeast Literary Agency)

Lewis, Karen (Karen Lewis & Company)

Lieberman, Robert (Robert Lieberman Associates)

Liebert, Norma (The Norma-Lewis Agency)

Liff, Samuel (William Morris Agency-NY)

Lincoln, (Mrs.) Ray (Ray Lincoln Literary Agency)

Lincoln, Jerome (Ray Lincoln Literary Agency)

Linder, Bertram L. (Educational Design Services)

Lindstrom, Kristin (Lindstrom Literary Group)

Lipkind, Wendy (Wendy Lipkind Agency)

Lipson, Brian (Renaissance—H.N. Swanson, Inc.)

Liss, Laurie (Harvey Klinger, Inc.)

Lloyd, Lem (Mary Jack Wald Associates, Inc.)

Lockwood, Hal (Penmarin Books)

Lopopolo, Toni (Toni Lopopolo Literary Agency)

Lord, Sterling (Sterling Lord Literistic)

Love, Nancy (Nancy Love Literary Agency)

Lowenstein, Barbara (Lowenstein Associates, Inc.)

Lucas, Ling (Nine Muses and Apollo, Inc.)

Luttinger, Selma (Robert A. Freedman Dramatic Agency)

Lynch, John (Connor Literary Agency)

Lyons, Jenifer (Joan Daves Agency)

M

Maass, Donald (Donald Maass Literary Agency)

Maccoby, Gina (Gina Maccoby Literary Agency)

Mackey, Elizabeth (The Robbins Office, Inc.)

Madsen, Robert (Robert Madsen Agency)

Maggiore, Chris (Tauro Brothers Management)

Mainhardt, Ricia (Ricia Mainhardt Agency)

Maley, Margot (Waterside Productions)

Mann, Carol (Carol Mann Agency)

Manus, Janet Wilkens (Manus & Associates Literary Agency, Inc.)

Manus, Jillian (Manus & Associates Literary Agency, Inc.)

Marcil, Denise (The Denise Marcil Literary Agency, Inc.)

Markowitz, Barbara (Barbara Markowitz Literary Agency)

Marks, Stephen E. (Major Clients Agency)

Markson, Elaine (Elaine Markson Literary Agency)

Marlow, Marilyn (Curtis Brown Ltd.)

Marshall, Evan (The Evan Marshall Agency)

Martell, Alice Fried (The Martell Agency)

Martin, Sandra (Paraview, Inc.—The Sandra Martin Literary Agency)

Massie, Maria (Witherspoon & Associates)

Matson, Peter (Sterling Lord Literistic)

Matthias, Lee (Lee Allan Agency)

Mattis, Lawrence (Circle of Confusion Ltd.)

Maynard, Gary (The Gary-Paul Agency)

Mazmanian, Joan (Helen Rees Literary Agency)

McBride, Margret (Margret McBride Literary Agency)

McCartan, Ed (Author Aid Associates)

McCarthy, Andrew (Leslie Kallen Agency)

McCleary, Carol (Harvey Klinger, Inc.)

McClendon, Carole (Waterside Productions)

McCormick, Janet (Printed Tree Inc.)

McDonough, Richard P. (Richard P. McDonough, Literary Agent)

McGrath, Helen (Helen McGrath)

McGuigan, Harrison (PMA Literary and Film Management, Inc.)

McKenna, Rosemary (AEI/Atchity Editorial/Entertainment Int'l)

McKeown, Andrea (AEI/Atchity Editorial/Entertainment Int'l)

McKinley, Peggi (Act I)

McKinley, Virginia C. (Virginia C. McKinley, Literary Agency)

Melnick, Jeff (Gold/Marshak & Associates)

Meo, Amy Victoria (Richard Curtis Associates, Inc.)

Merola, Marianne (Brandt & Brandt Literary Agents, Inc.)

Merrilat, Jim (Samuel French, Inc.)

Meth, David L. (Writers' Productions)

Meyers, Louise (Charlene Kay Agency)

Meyst, Charles G. (The Gardner Agency)

Michael, Douglas (Frieda Fishbein Ltd.)

Michaels, Doris S. (Doris S. Michaels Literary Agency)

Miller, Jan (Dupree/Miller and Associates Inc. Literary)

Miller, Peter (PMA Literary and Film Management, Inc.)

Miller, Roberta (Roberta Miller Associates)

Miller, Stuart M. (Agency for the Performing Arts)

Miller-Jones, Bill (Heacock Literary Agency Inc.)

Minelli, Lenny (A Picture of You)

Mohyde, Colleen (The Doe Coover Agency)

Moncur, Susie (Lazear Agency Incorporated)

Monteiro, Candace (Monteiro Rose Agency)

Moore, Claudette (Moore Literary Agency)

Moran, Maureen (Donald MacCampbell Inc.)

Morel, Madeleine (2M Communications Ltd.)

Morgan, David H. (David H. Morgan Literary Agency)

Morgan, Walter (The Agency)

Morgart, Erin Jones (M.H. Int'l Literary Agency)

Morrison, Henry (Henry Morrison, Inc.)

Mortimer, Lydia (Hull House Literary Agency)

Moseley, Jane (Lucianne S. Goldberg Literary Agents, Inc.)

Moskowitz, Dara (The Gislason Agency)

Mulert, Carl (The Joyce Ketay Agency)

Mura, Dee (Dee Mura Enterprises)

Murphy, Patricia (Annette Van Duren Agency)

N

Nadell, Bonnie (Frederick Hill Associates)

Naggar, Jean V. (Jean V. Naggar Literary Agency)

Nathan, Ruth (Ruth Nathan)

Nazor, Karen (Karen Nazor Literary Agency)

Negretti, Annmarie (Circle of Confusion Ltd.)

Nellis, Muriel (Literary and Creative Artists Agency Inc.

Nelson, Bonita (BK Nelson Literary Agency & Lecture Bureau)

Nevins, Allan (Renaissance—H.N. Swanson, Inc.)

Newberg, Esther (Int'l Creative Management-NY)

Newton, Pam (Samuel French, Inc.)

Nolan, Betsy (The Betsy Nolan Literary Agency)

Novak, Ed (Edward A. Novak III Literary Representation)

Nugent, Ray (Nugent Literary)

O

Oei, Lilu (Watkins Loomis Agency, Inc.)

Oertle, Noelle (Executive Excellence)

Olsen, M.E. (Montgomery Literary Agency)

Olson, Neil (Donadio and Ashworth, Inc.)

Orr, Alice (Alice Orr Agency, Inc.)

Orrmont, Arthur (Author Aid Associates)

Osborne, Geoff (Lyceum Creative Properties, Inc.)

P

Pace, Dee (The Kirkland Literary Agency)

Palmer, Dorothy (Dorothy Palmer)

Pantel, Elena (The Joseph S. Ajlouny Agency)

Papadopoulos, Costas (M.H. Int'l Literary Agency)

Park, Theresa (Sanford J. Greenburger Associates, Inc.)

Parker, Gilbert (William Morris Agency-NY)

Parker, Stacy (L. Harry Lee Literary Agency)

Parkes, Walter (The Partos Company)

Parks, Richard (The Richard Parks Agency)

Pasquale, Victoria (The Martell Agency)

Pasternack, Dan (Lenhoff/Robinson Talent and Literary Agency, Inc.)

Paton, Kathi (Kathi J. Paton Literary Agency)

Patrick, Jean (Diamond Literary Agency, Inc.)

Pelham, Howard (Pelham Literary Agency)

Pell, William (William Pell Agency)

Pelter, Rodney (Rodney Pelter)

Perkins, Lori (L. Perkins Associates)

Perkins, M. (Acton, Leone, Hanson & Jaffe)

Pevner, Stephen (Stephen Pevner, Inc.)

Pevovar, Eddy Howard (The Eddy Howard Agency)

Pfenninger, Darla (Gem Literary Services)

Piel, Sarah (Arthur Pine Associates)

Pine, Arthur (Arthur Pine Associates)

Pine, Richard (Arthur Pine Associates)

Pinzow, Anne (Toad Hall, Inc.)

Polk, Katie (L. Harry Lee Literary Agency)

Pollock, Jack (Producers & Creatives Group)

Pomada, Elizabeth (Michael Larsen/Elizabeth Pomada Literary Agents)

Popkin, Julie (Julie Popkin)

Porcelain, Sidney (Sidney E. Porcelain)

Portman, Julien John (The Portman Organization)

Posner, Marcy (William Morris Agency-NY)

Prentis, Linn (Virginia Kidd Literary Agent)

Prescott, Ashton (The Marshall Cameron Agency)

Prescott, Margo (The Marshall Cameron Agency)

Preston, Harry (Stanton & Associates Literary Agency)

Price, Jean (The Kirkland Literary Agency)

Price, Trent (Executive Excellence)

Priest, Aaron (Aaron M. Priest Literary Agency)

Protter, Susan (Susan Ann Protter Literary Agent)

Pryor, Roberta (Roberta Pryor, Inc.)

Pulitzer-Voges, Elizabeth (Kirchoff/Wohlberg, Inc., Authors' Representation Division)

Purvis, Michael C. (Collins Purvis, Ltd.)

R

Rabineau, Steve (Int'l Creative Management—CA)

Raintree, Diane (Diane Raintree Agency)

Ramer, Susan (Don Congdon Associates Inc.)

Rathmann, Fran (Fran Literary Agency)

Ray, Roslyn (Communications and Entertainment)

Raymond, Charlotte Cecil (Charlotte Cecil Raymond, Literary Agent)

Rees, Helen (Helen Rees Literary Agency)

Regnis, Lynn (Evelyn Singer Literary Agency Inc.)

Reiss, William (John Hawkins & Associates)

Rejaunier, Jean (BK Nelson Literary Agency & Lecture Bureau)

Ricci, Cathie (Van der Leun & Associates)

Richards, Jay (Richard Gauthreaux—A Literary Agency)

Richardson, Bruce D. (Dragon Literary, Inc.)

Riley, John (Anita Diamant, The Writer's Workshop)

Rinaldi, Angela (Angela Rinaldi Literary Agency)

Robbins, B.J. (BJ Robbins Literary Agency)

Robbins, Kathy P. (The Robbins Office, Inc.)

Roberts, Jane (Literary and Creative Artists Agency Inc.

Robinov, Jeff (Int'l Creative Management—CA)

Robinson, Jennifer (PMA Literary and Film Management, Inc.)

Robinson, Lloyd (Lenhoff/Robinson Talent and Literary Agency, Inc.)

Rock, Andrew T. (Rock Literary Agency)

Rodman, Debra (Emerald Literary Agency)

Roenbeck, Patti (L. Harry Lee Literary Agency)

Rogers, Elaine (The Palmer & Dodge Agency)

Rogers, Irene (Irene Rogers Literary Representation)

Rogers, Stephanie (Stephanie Rogers & Associates)

Rose, Fredda (Monteiro Rose Agency)

Rose, Mitchell (Rose Literary Agency)

Rose, Stephen L. (Major Clients Agency)

Rosen, Jim (Int'l Creative Management—CA)

Rosenfeld, Erv (BK Nelson Literary Agency & Lecture Bureau)

Rosenstiel, Leonie (Author Aid Associates)

Rosenthal, Judith (Barbara Markowitz Literary Agency)

Ross, Lisa (F. Joseph Spieler)

Rothery, Charles (L. Harry Lee Literary Agency)

Rotrosen, Jane (Jane Rotrosen Agency)

Rowland, Damaris (The Damaris Rowland Agency)

Roy, Dave (Lyceum Creative Properties, Inc.)

Rubenstein, Pesha (Pesha Rubenstein Literary Agency, Inc.)

Rubie, Peter (L. Perkins Associates)

Rubin, Michele (Writers House)

Rue, Robin (Anita Diamant, The Writer's Workshop)

Rumanes, George N. (Cinema Talent Int'l)

Russell, Margaret (Russell-Simenauer Literary Agency Inc.)

S

St. Clair, Kelly (St. Clair Literary Agency)

Salt, Gary (Paul Kohner, Inc.)

Sanders, Victoria (Victoria Sanders Literary Agency)

Sandum, Howard E. (Sandum & Associates)

Sanford, Steve (Int'l Creative Management—CA)

Santoianni, John (The Tantleff Office)

Santucci, Ernest (Agency Chicago)

Scagnetti, Jack (Jack Scagnetti Talent & Literary Agency)

Schiano, Ralph (The Hampton Agency)

Schmalz, Wendy (Harold Ober Associates)

Schmidt, Harold (Harold Schmidt Literary Agency)

Schroder, Heather (Int'l Creative Management-NY)

Schulman, Ruth (F.L.A.I.R.)

Schulman, Susan (Susan Schulman, A Literary Agency)

Listing Index

More Great Books
for Writers

1996 Writer's Market—Celebrating 75 years of helping writers realize their dreams, this newest edition contains information on 4,000 writing opportunities. You'll find all the facts vital to the success of your writing career, including an up-to-date listing of buyers of books, articles and stories, plus articles and interviews with top professionals. *#10432/$27.99/1008 pages*

How to Write Fast (While Writing Well)—Discover what makes a story and what it takes to research and write one. Then, learn step-by-step how to cut wasted time and effort by planning interviews for maximum results, beating writer's block with effective plotting and getting the most information from traditional library research and on-line computer databases. *#10473/$15.99/208 pages/paperback*

1996 Novel & Short Story Writer's Market—Get the information you need to get your short stories and novels published. You'll discover listings of fiction publishers, plus original articles on fiction writing techniques; detailed subject categories to help you target appropriate publishers; and interviews with writers, publishers and editors! *#10441/$22.99/624 pages*

The Writer's Ultimate Research Guide—Save research time and frustration with the help of this guide. Three hundred fifty-two information-packed pages will point you straight to the information you need to create better, more accurate fiction and nonfiction. Hundreds of books and database listings reveal how current the information is, the content, organization and much more! *#10447/$19.99/352 pages*

Freeing Your Creativity—Discover how to escape the traps that stifle your creativity. You'll tackle techniques for banishing fears and nourishing ideas so you can get your juices flowing again. *#10430/$14.99/176 pages/paperback*

1996 Children's Writer's & Illustrator's Market—This directory brings together the two key aspects of children's publishing—writing and illustrating. In one handy volume you'll find helpful articles on how to make it in this lucrative field, followed by detailed listings of book publishers, magazines, audiovisual, audiotape and scriptwriting markets. *#10442/$22.99/384 pages.*

The Writer's Digest Guide to Manuscript Formats—No matter how good your ideas, an unprofessional format will land your manuscript on the slush pile! You need this easy-to-follow guide on manuscript preparation and presentation—for everything from books and articles to poems and plays. *#10025/$19.99/200 pages*

Mystery Writer's Sourcebook: Where to Sell Your Manuscripts—Part market guide, part writing guide, this is an invaluable companion for all mystery, suspense and crime writers. You'll discover in-depth market reports on 120 mystery book and magazine publishers, techniques from top writers and editors and 125 agents who represent mystery writers. *#10455/$19.99/475 pages*

How to Write a Book Proposal—Don't sabotage your great ideas with a so-so proposal. This guide includes a complete sample proposal, a nine-point Idea Test to check the salability of your book ideas, plus hot tips to make your proposal a success! *#10173/$12.99/136 pages/paperback*

Writing for Money—Discover where to look for writing opportunities—and how to make them pay off. You'll learn how to write for magazines, newspapers, radio and TV, newsletters, greeting cards and a dozen other hungry markets! *#10425/$17.99/256 pages*

How to Write Like an Expert About Anything—Find out how to use new technology and traditional research methods to get the information you need, envision new markets and write proposals that sell, find and interview experts on any topic and much more. *#10449/$17.99/224 pages*

Beginning Writer's Answer Book—This book answers 900 of the most often asked questions about the writing process. You'll find business advice, tax tips, plus information about online networks, databases and more. *#10394/$17.99/336 pages*

How to Fire Your Agent, Gracefully _____

If you are having a problem with your agent, it is usually best to discuss the problem honestly. If this does not work, or if the agent simply isn't selling your work or is doing a poor job, follow these guidelines:

1. If you have a written agreement with your agent, read it over carefully. Follow its provisions for ending your relationship to the letter. If you have no written agreement, skip to the next step.

2. Write a brief, polite, firm, businesslike letter to your agent. In it state the following:
    a. You no longer think that your relationship is beneficial to you.
    b. You wish to cease to be the agent's (and, if appropriate, the agency's) client.
    c. The agent shall make no more submissions of any of your work.
    d. The agent shall remain your representative on any submissions that are still live, for a period of 60 days.
    e. You wish to receive a list of all organizations (publishers and/or production companies) and people (editors, producers, and/or directors) who have rejected any of your unsold works. Also ask for a list of people and organizations that are still considering